Advanced Mac OS X Programming

THE BIG NERD RANCH GUIDE

MARK DALRYMPLE

BiG
nerd
ranch

Advanced Mac OS X Programming: The Big Nerd Ranch Guide

by Mark Dalrymple

ISBN 10 0321706250
ISBN 13 978-0321706256

Library of Congress Control Number 2011931708

First printing, August 2011

Dedication

For Zoe. May she grow up to be as geeky as her Weird Uncle Bork.

Acknowledgments

This book is based upon the experiences teaching a five-day class at The Big Nerd Ranch called *Advanced Mac OS X Bootcamp*. The patience and curiousity of my students has made this a more complete and comprehensible introduction to the plumbing that makes Mac OS X a reliable, flexible, and high-performance system.

Special thanks go to Jeremy Sherman. Jeremy stepped up and taught one of the Advanced Bootcamps when I was unable to so. Along the way he made numerous improvements to this book and associated course materials, helping to modernize and robusticize the code. Jeremy is also responsible for the excellent under-the-hoods look at Blocks.

Incredible thanks go to Aaron Hillegass, my co-author on the first two editions of this book. Many moons ago Aaron took a chance on this random guy sitting in the back of a Cocoa class in Asheville. Over the years I've learned from Aaron more than I imagined possible about writing, teaching, and treating others well.

Susan Loper, the tireless editor, performed acts of magic on the purple prose she was given.

In preparing this book, many people reviewed the drafts and brought errors to our attention. The most astonishing quantity of corrections over the years came from Bill Monk. It would be difficult to overstate Bill's contributions. Other technical reviewers who submitted errors or offered suggestions: John Vink, Juan Pablo Claude, Carl-Johan Kihlborn, Mike Morton, Ajeya Vempati, Eric Peyton, Chris Ridd, Michael Simmons, David Southwick, Jeremy Wyld, Richard Wolf, Tom Van Lenten, Dave Zarzycki, James Spencer, Greg Miller, Anne Halsall, Roy Lovejoy, Jonathan Saggau, Jim Magee, and Rob Rix. They made this book better with their useful corrections and suggestions. Any errors that remain in this book are completely my fault.

I would also like to thank my wife, my "Spousal Overunit" Sharlotte DeVere, for her support, patience and understanding.

Table of Contents

Foreword

In 1989, the band Living Colour released the song *Glamour Boy* which explained that the world was filled with glamour boys who valued appearance over other, deeper properties. And the song proclaims "I ain't no glamour boy."

Many programmers are glamour boys. They lack a deep understanding of what is happening under the surface, so they are pleased simply to ship an application that the client doesn't hate. If they had a better comprehension of how the operating system does its work, their code would be faster, more reliable, and more secure.

If you are a Mac OS X or iOS programmer, the knowledge that separates really good coders from glamour boys is in this book. It demystifies the plumbing of Mac OS X. It helps you interpret mysterious messages from the compiler and debugger. When you finish reading this book, you will be a better programmer than when you started.

I met Mark Dalrymple shortly after Mac OS X shipped. I was astonished by his deep knowledge of Mac OS X's Unix core and how Apple had extended and enhanced it. I begged him to write the first edition of this book. The result was even better than I had hoped for.

If you read this third edition, you will master:

- Blocks
- Grand Central Dispatch
- Multithreading
- Operation queues
- Network programming
- Bonjour
- The run loop

- File I/O and metadata
- Forking off tasks
- File system events
- Keychain access
- Performance tuning
- Instruments and DTrace
- Memory and the garbage collector

Don't be a glamour boy.

Aaron Hillegass
Big Nerd Ranch
July 1, 2011

Introduction

Mac OS X: Built to Evolve

Complex systems come into existence in only two ways: through careful planning or through evolution. An airport is an example of something that is planned carefully beforehand, built, and then undergoes only minor changes for the rest of its existence. Complex organisms (like humans) are an example of something that has evolved continually from something simple. In the end, organisms that are well suited to evolution will always win out over organisms that are less suited to evolve.

An operating system evolves. Of course, the programmer who creates a new operating system designs it carefully, but in the end, an operating system that is well suited to evolution will replace an operating system that is not. It is, then, an interesting exercise to think about what traits make an operating system capable of evolution.

The first version of Unix was developed by Ken Thompson at Bell Laboratories in 1969. It was written in assembly language to run on a PDP-7. Dennis Ritchie, also at Bell Labs, invented the C programming language. Among computer languages, C is pretty low level, but it is still much more portable than assembly language. Together, Thompson and Ritchie completely rewrote Unix in C. By 1978, Unix was running on several different architectures. Portability, then, was the first indication that Unix is well suited to evolution.

In 1976, Bell Labs began giving the source code for Unix to research facilities. The Computer Systems Research Group at UC Berkeley got a copy and began tinkering with it. The design of Unix was exceedingly elegant and a perfect platform upon which to build two important technologies: virtual memory and TCP/IP networking. By freely distributing the source code, Bell Labs was inviting people to extend Unix. Extensibility was the second indication that Unix is well suited to evolution.

4.4BSD was the last release of Unix produced by Berkeley. It was used as the basis for FreeBSD, OpenBSD, NetBSD, and Mac OS X. Today, Unix is used as an operating system for cellular phones and supercomputers. It is the most popular operating system for web servers, mail servers, and engineering workstations. The manner in which it has found a home in so many niches is yet another indication that Unix is capable of evolving.

Mac OS X is based upon a hybrid of Mach and 4.4BSD, but notice that this new niche, a desktop operating system that your grandmother will love as well as a mobile device operating system that your kids will love, is very different from Unix's previous purposes. To reach this goal, Apple has made several important additions to its Unix core.

The Unix part of Mac OS X is called *Darwin*. The large additions to Darwin that Apple has made are known as the *core technologies*. Apple, recognizing that Unix must continue to evolve, has released the source code to Darwin and most of the core technologies.

This Book

My thought is that things shouldn't be "magic" in your field of expertise. I don't expect someone to implement a compiler or operating system, but they shouldn't be mystical black boxes.

—Paul Kim, Chief Noodler, Noodlesoft

I didn't realize until after my friend Paul uttered the above statement on IRC one day that one of the goals of this book, and the Big Nerd Ranch Advanced Mac OS X Bootcamp in general, is to help demystify the fundamental Mac OS X technologies. A programmer can live a long time solely in the Cocoa Layer, only to be faced with inscrutable bugs when dealing with NSTask or network communication. I believe that knowledge of the lower levels of the OS will help you use the higher levels more effectively. That's what I hope to accomplish here by showing you how the lower-level Unix APIs work and then showing you how the higher-level technology uses them.

This book intends to bridge the gap between higher-level books dedicated to the graphical aspects of Mac and iOS programming and the low-level kernel internal tomes. Some of the Unix API you may have seen in a college-level operating systems course, but I've stripped away some of the historical and no longer relevant details. For instance, you won't see anything about managing pseudo-ttys.

When you finish this book, you will be able to:

- Create applications that leverage the full power of the Unix APIs.

- Use advanced ideas like multithreading and task queues to increase the performance of your applications.

- Add networking capabilities to event-driven applications.

- Make networked applications Bonjour-aware.

- Use the keychain and authorization capabilities of the security framework.

- Understand and use **gcc**, the linker, the debugger, Instruments, and the occasional Xcode dark corner.

- Use performance tools to evaluate and improve the responsiveness of your existing applications.

The ideas in this book can be broken into three basic groups:

Unix APIs	There is a set of standard Unix APIs that every programmer should know how to use. Even if higher-level abstractions alleviate the need to ever call them directly, understanding these functions and structures will give you a much deeper knowledge of how your system works. Much of what is said here will also be true for Linux.
Framework APIs	Apple has added a whole set of daemons and frameworks to its version of Unix. These frameworks are exceedingly powerful, and sometimes Apple has been slow to document how they work and how they are to be used.
Tools	The Mac OS X developer tools suite, in addition to the system's built-in utilities, provides a veritable toy store for developers. This book covers lower-lever Unix-heritage tools such as **gcc**, **gdb**, the linker, and DTrace, as well as higher-level tools such as Instruments.

The majority of the code in this book is ANSI C. Occasionally some C99 features will be used. Some of the chapters use the Cocoa APIs, so you should have a basic understanding of Cocoa and Objective-C. You can gain the necessary expertise by reading the first nine chapters of Aaron

Hillegass' *Cocoa Programming for Mac OS X*. iOS developers can take advantage of many OS features as well. I have sought to point out differences between Mac OS X and iOS where they exist.

Typographical Conventions

To make the book easier to comprehend, we have used several typographical conventions.

Function names will appear in a bold, fixed-width font. All standard Unix functions are completely lowercase. Functions developed by Apple are often mixed case. To make it clear that it is a function, the name will be followed by a set of parentheses. For example, you might see, "Use **NSLog()** or **printf()** to display the computed value."

In Objective-C, class names are always capitalized. In this book, they will also appear in a bold, fixed-width font. In Objective-C, method names start with a lowercase letter. Method names will also appear in a bold, fixed-width font. So, for example, you might see, "The class **NSObject** has the method **-dealloc**."

Other literals that you would see in code will appear in a regular fixed-width font. Filenames will appear in this same font. Thus, you might see, "In SomeCode.c, set the variable foo to nil."

Command-line tools and other commands will appear in a slightly-smaller bold font. For instance, "Join the two files with **lipo** and use the **file** command to verify the result."

Occasionally, there will be an excerpt from a terminal window. What you should type will appear in a bold, fixed-width font. The computer's response will appear in a regular, fixed-width font. Example:

```
$ ls /var
at       cron    empty   mail    named    root   tmp     yp
backups  db      log     msgs    netboot  run    spool   vm
```

Online Materials

The code in this book can be downloaded from http://www.borkware.com/corebook/.

1

C and Objective-C

The Macintosh and iPhone are general-purpose computing platforms. You can program them in any number of languages from Fortran to Tcl, Ruby to Nu, C to Java. However, the primary application programming interfaces (APIs) from Apple are designed to work in plain C and Objective-C. The Unix API is C-based, while Cocoa and Cocoa Touch are Objective-C based.

A solid grounding in C and Objective-C, though, is very important. Basic C and Objective-C will not be covered here since there are a number of very good introductory texts available online and at the bookstore. This chapter covers aspects of C and Objective-C that are not ordinarily covered in introductory texts or are recent additions to the language.

C

The Compiler pipeline

C is a compiled language, unlike scripting languages, which are usually interpreted. This means that there is no REPL (Read, Evaluate, Print Loop) for interactive exploration. When you build your program, you need to run your source code through the C compiler which then emits a binary object file. After each of your source files have been compiled into object files, the linker combines your object files, along with system libraries and frameworks (and your own libraries and frameworks), to create the final executable program. And to make things more complicated, your C source files are manipulated by the C preprocessor, which subjects your source code to textual manipulations before the compiler sees it. This whole pipeline is shown in Figure 1.1.

Figure 1.1   The compiler pipeline

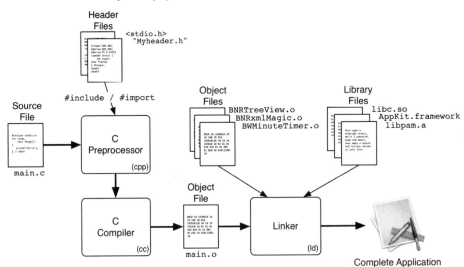

The C preprocessor

The C preprocessor is a simple tool that performs textual manipulations, such as replacing specific text with other text, expanding macros with arguments, including text from other files, and conditionally including or excluding text.

The C preprocessor only does textual manipulations. It has no knowledge of the C language, so you can happily use the preprocessor to create a real mess or to come up with some cool hacks. (Sometimes the two are indistinguishable.)

Preprocessor symbols

You define symbols in the preprocessor with #define. The leading # indicates a directive to the preprocessor. All preprocessor directives are processed and removed before the compiler sees the text.

```
#define SOME_SYMBOL 23
#define ANOTHER_SYMBOL
#define MACRO(x) doSomethingCoolWith(x)
```

The first #define tells the preprocessor to substitute the text 23 whenever it encounters SOME_SYMBOL in your source file. The second #define tells the preprocessor that "ANOTHER_SYMBOL exists, but it has no value." If the preprocessor sees ANOTHER_SYMBOL in the source file, it will take out the text.

The third defines a macro expansion. Whenever the preprocessor sees MACRO with an argument, it expands to the text on the right-hand side of the #define, substituting the argument for x. For instance, MACRO(bork) will end up doSomethingCoolWith(bork) after the preprocessor finishes its work. Example 1.1 shows preprocessor macros in action.

Example 1.1   expansion.m

```
// expansion.m -- look at macro expansion
```

```
// gcc -g -Wall -o expansion expansion.m

#include <stdio.h>  // for printf()

int main (void) {

#define FNORD hello
    int FNORD = 23;
    printf ("hello, your number today is %d\n", hello);

#define NOBODY_HOME
    static unsigned NOBODY_HOME int thing = 42;
    printf ("thing, your number today is %d\n", thing);

// This is actually a dangerous way to do this.  See
// the section about macro hygiene.
#define SUM(x, y)  x + y
    int value = SUM(23, 42);
    printf ("value, your number today is %d\n", value);

    return 0;

} // main
```

When you compile and run this program, you should see this output:

```
$ ./expansion
hello, your number today is 23
thing, your number today is 42
value, your number today is 65
```

The symbol FNORD expanded into the string "hello," which made the first assignment look like

```
int hello = 23;
```

The symbol NOBODY_HOME just vanishes because it was never given a replacement value. This leaves thing's declaration looking like

```
static unsigned int thing = 42;
```

Lastly, the SUM macro makes the value assignment look like

```
int value = 23 + 42;
```

You can define symbols on the command line using the -D flag:

```
gcc ... -DTHING_1  -DTHING_2=123
```

The preprocessor will behave as if you had these lines at the top of your source file:

```
#define THING_1
#define THING_2 123
```

You can also define macros in Xcode projects by including a space-separated list of definitions in the Preprocessor Macros build setting.

Be careful what you decide to #define, especially if you define commonly used tokens like if. You might run into situations where a structure field was #defined to another name, presumably to hack around an error in an API or to change a name but preserve backwards compatibility. This macro could end up clobbering a variable name used in another context.

Stringization and concatenation

The # character can be used in a macro definition to turn an argument into a literal string rather than having it evaluated. ## can be used to textually paste two tokens together. Example 1.2 shows some simple uses.

Example 1.2   stringization.m

```
// stringization.m -- show token stringization and concatenaton

#import <stdio.h>  // for printf()
#import <math.h>   // for sqrt()

//gcc -g -Wall -o stringization stringization.m

#define FIVE 5

int main (void) {
#define PRINT_EXPR(x) printf("%s = %d\n", #x, (x))
    PRINT_EXPR (5);
    PRINT_EXPR (5 * 10);
    PRINT_EXPR ((int)sqrt(FIVE*FIVE) + (int)log(25 / 5));

#define SPLIT_FUNC(x,y)  x##y
    SPLIT_FUNC (prin, tf) ("hello\n");

    return 0;

} // main
```

which when run looks like this:

```
$ ./stringization
5 = 5
5 * 10 = 50
(int)sqrt(FIVE*FIVE) + (int)log(25 / 5) = 6
hello
```

You can see the x argument in PRINT_EXPR is printed out and also evaluated. Notice that the stringization happens before any other symbols are expanded. The concatenating example pieces "prin" and "tf" into "printf."

Conditional compilation

The preprocessor can be used to conditionally include or exclude text based on the value (or existence) of a particular symbol.

#ifdef some_symbol tells the preprocessor to test for the existence of some_symbol, whether or not it actually has a value. If some_symbol does not exist, the preprocessor omits all the text until it sees an #endif or an #else directive. Use #ifndef if you are interested in knowing if a symbol is not defined.

#if some_symbol works like #ifdef except that it uses the value of the symbol when deciding whether to include the following text. If the symbol has a non-zero numeric value, the text following the #if is allowed to pass through to the compiler. Any other symbol, whether alphanumeric or a macro, will cause the text following the #if to be omitted until the preprocessor sees an #endif or #else directive. #if statements can also contain expressions based on the numeric value of the symbol. Example 1.3 shows conditional compilation.

Example 1.3   conditional-compilation.m

```
// conditional-compilation.m -- look at macro expansion

// gcc -g -Wall -o conditional-compilation conditional-compilation.m

#include <stdio.h>  // for printf()

#define DEFINED_NO_VALUE
#define VERSION 10
#define ZED 0

int main (void) {

#ifdef DEFINED_NO_VALUE
    printf ("defined_no_value is defined\n");
#else
    i can has syntax error;
#endif

#ifdef ZED
    printf ("zed is defined\n");
#endif

#if ZED
    printf ("zed evaluates to true\n");
#else
    printf ("zed evaluates to false\n");
#endif

#if VERSION > 5 && VERSION < 20
    printf ("version is in the correct range.\n");
#endif

    return 0;

} // main
```

You should see this output when you compile and run this program.

```
% ./conditional-compilation
defined_no_value is defined
zed is defined
zed evaluates to false
version is in the correct range.
```

Conditional compilation is useful when you have multi-platform code and you need to be able to turn compatibility features on or off. A library call may have different arguments on OS X than on a Linux system. It also can be used for turning features on or off with just a compiler flag, such as including or excluding encryption from a web server communications driver, or removing the ability to print from a trial version of a text editing application. You could include some computationally expensive sanity checking for a debug-only build.

Predefined symbols

The compiler comes with a lot of preprocessor symbols predefined, many of which vary based on OS version, compiler version, or processor architecture. You can see them all with this command:

```
% gcc -E -dM - < /dev/null
```

```
#define __DBL_MIN_EXP__ (-1021)
#define __FLT_MIN__ 1.17549435e-38F
#define __CHAR_BIT__ 8
#define __WCHAR_MAX__ 2147483647
#define __DBL_DENORM_MIN__ 4.9406564584124654e-324
#define __LITTLE_ENDIAN__ 1
...
#define __APPLE__ 1
#define __GNUC__ 4
#define __MMX__ 1
#define OBJC_NEW_PROPERTIES 1
#define __GXX_ABI_VERSION 1002
```

The -E flag tells **gcc** to display preprocessor output, -dM is a **gcc** debugging flag that dumps out symbols at some point during the compilation process, and - < /dev/null tells **gcc** to expect its program text from standard in and feeds it /dev/null to indicate there is actually no text coming in. You can feed the same arguments to **clang** to see what symbols Apple's new compiler defines automatically.

Some of the symbols are pretty esoteric, and some can be very useful. Some of the more useful ones include:

__APPLE__	Defined for an Apple platform, such as OS X.
__APPLE_CC__	This is an integer value representing the version of the compiler.
__OBJC__	Defined if the compiler is compiling in Objective-C mode.
__cplusplus	Defined if the compiler is compiling in C++ mode.
__MACH__	Defined if the Mach system calls are available.
__LITTLE_ENDIAN__	Defined if you are compiling for a little endian processor, like Intel or ARM.
__BIG_ENDIAN__	Defined if you are compiling for a big endian processor, like PowerPC.
__LP64__	Defined if you are compiling in 64-bit mode.

There are also some built-in preprocessor symbols that have varying values:

__DATE__	The current date, as a char *.
__TIME__	The current time, as a char *.
__FILE__	The name of the file currently being compiled, as a char *.
__LINE__	The line number of the file before preprocessing, as an int.
__func__	The name of the function or Objective-C method being compiled, as a char *. This is not actually a preprocessor feature but something that comes from the compiler. Remember that the preprocessor does not know anything about the languages of the files it processes.
__FUNCTION__	Equivalent to __func__ and available in older versions of **gcc** where __func__ is not. With modern Mac or iOS programming, they are interchangeable.

__PRETTY_FUNCTION__   The name of the function as a char *, as with __func__, but it includes type information.

These do not appear when you ask the compiler to display all of the built-in macros because they are being expanded by the compiler, not the preprocessor. Example 1.4 shows some of the predefined macros.

Example 1.4   predef.m

```
// predef.mm -- play with predefined macros

// g++ -g -Wall -o predef -framework Foundation predef.mm

#import <Foundation/Foundation.h>
#import <stdio.h>  // for printf()

void someFunc (void) {
    printf ("file %s, line %d\n", __FILE__, __LINE__);
    printf ("  function: %s\n", __FUNCTION__);
    printf ("  pretty function: %s\n", __PRETTY_FUNCTION__);
} // someFunc

@interface SomeClass : NSObject
+ (void) someMethod;
+ (void) someMethod: (int) num  withArguments: (NSString *) arg;
@end

@implementation SomeClass
+ (void) someMethod {
    printf ("file %s, line %d\n", __FILE__, __LINE__);
    printf ("  function: %s\n", __FUNCTION__);
    printf ("  pretty function: %s\n", __PRETTY_FUNCTION__);
} // someMethod

+ (void) someMethod: (int) num  withArguments: (NSString *) arg {
    printf ("file %s, line %d\n", __FILE__, __LINE__);
    printf ("  function: %s\n", __FUNCTION__);
    printf ("  pretty function: %s\n", __PRETTY_FUNCTION__);
} // someMethod:withArguments

@end

class SomeOtherClass {
public:
    void SomeMemberFunction (int arg1, const char *arg2) {
        printf ("file %s, line %d\n", __FILE__, __LINE__);
        printf ("  function: %s\n", __FUNCTION__);
        printf ("  pretty function: %s\n", __PRETTY_FUNCTION__);
    }
};

int main (int argc, char *argv[]) {
    printf ("__APPLE__: %d\n", __APPLE__);
    printf ("today is %s, the time is %s\n",
            __DATE__, __TIME__);

    printf ("file %s, line %d\n", __FILE__, __LINE__);
    printf ("  function: %s\n", __FUNCTION__);
    printf ("  pretty function: %s\n", __PRETTY_FUNCTION__);
```

```
    someFunc ();

    [SomeClass someMethod];
    [SomeClass someMethod: 23  withArguments: @"snork"];

    SomeOtherClass something;
    something.SomeMemberFunction (23, "hi");
#if __LITTLE_ENDIAN__
    printf ("I'm (most likely) running on intel! woo!\n");
#endif
#if __BIG_ENDIAN__
    printf ("I'm (most likely) running on powerPC! woo!\n");
#endif
    return 0;
} // main
```

And a sample run would look like this:

```
$ ./predef
__APPLE__: 1
today is Jan 17 2011, the time is 14:23:33
file predef.mm, line 48
  function: main
  pretty function: int main(int, char**)
file predef.mm, line 9
  function: someFunc
  pretty function: void someFunc()
file predef.mm, line 21
  function: +[SomeClass someMethod]
  pretty function: void +[SomeClass someMethod](objc_object*, objc_selector*)
file predef.mm, line 27
  function: +[SomeClass someMethod:withArguments:]
  pretty function: void +[SomeClass someMethod:withArguments:] \
      (objc_object*, objc_selector*, int, NSString*)
file predef.mm, line 37
  function: SomeMemberFunction
  pretty function: void SomeOtherClass::SomeMemberFunction(int, const char*)
I'm (most likely) running on intel! woo!
```

File inclusion

The preprocessor #include directive takes the contents of one file and inserts it into the stream of text that it feeds to the compiler. You can specify the file name in angle brackets to indicate the file being included is a "system" header:

```
#include <stdio.h>
```

The preprocessor looks in some well-known locations, such as /usr/include, to find the file named stdio.h. You specify the file name in quotes to indicate that the file being included is one that belongs to your project:

```
#include "ATMMachine.h"
```

Files that are #included can also #include other files. It's possible that a file can be included more than once. This can cause problems for C header files: the compiler doesn't like it when you declare a structure twice, for instance. Consider this program:

```
#include <fcntl.h>    // for open()
#include <ulimit.h>   // for ulimit()
#include <pthread.h>  // for pthread_create()
#include <dirent.h>   // for opendir()

int main (void) {
    // nobody home
    return 0;
} // main
```

This is a pretty typical set of #includes for a Unix program. Sometimes you can have a dozen or more includes to pull in different sets of library types and function prototypes. Each of those #includes includes other files, ending up with something that looks like Figure 1.2

Figure 1.2   Nested #includes

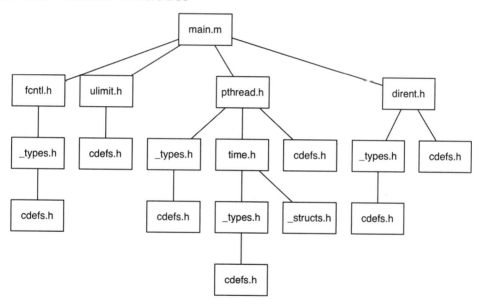

Notice that many headers are included multiple times, such as <sys/cdefs.h>, which gets included seven times. There is a standard trick you can use to prevent multiple inclusions of a file from causing errors: an *include guard*, shown in Example 1.5:

Example 1.5   include-guard.h

```
// include-guard.h -- making sure the contents of the header
//                    are included only once.
#ifndef INCLUDE_GUARD_H
#define INCLUDE_GUARD_H

// Put the real header contents here.

#endif // INCLUDE_GUARD_H
```

So how does this work? The first time include-guard.h is #included, the symbol INCLUDE_GUARD_H is undefined, so #ifndef INCLUDE_GUARD_H will evaluate to true, and the text after that is included, including the #define of INCLUDE_GUARD_H. If include-guard.h is included again while preprocessing this source file, `INCLUDE_GUARD_H` has been defined, so the `#ifndef` test fails, and the file is skipped down through the `#endif`.

There are two drawbacks to this technique. The first is that the guard symbol has to be unique across all header files that might be included together; otherwise one header's contents won't be included when they need to be. The other drawback is that the preprocessor has to scan through the entire header file, even if all of it is going to be thrown out. For a situation like Figure 1.2, `<sys/cdefs.h>` will still be opened and read 7 times even though the file's contents will be used only the first time through.

Luckily, the compiler includes optimizations to avoid doing all of this extra work when include guards are in place. It also supports the `#pragma once` directive, which tells the compiler to only include the file containing the pragma a single time. In Objective-C, life is even simpler. Instead of `#include`, Objective-C uses the `#import` directive, which directs the compiler to include the file only once.

Macro hygiene

Earlier you read about the preprocessor being stupid. It really is. It has no clue about the context of your code, so it cannot do what you mean, just what you say. So be careful how you say things.

You might have a preprocessor macro that looks like this:

```
#define SQUARE(x)    x*x
```

Pretty simple. `SQUARE(5)` turns into 5*5, which yields the desired result. If someone uses `SQUARE(2+3)`, the text expansion will get fed to the compiler as 2+3*2+3, which due to C precedence rules is actually calculated as 2 + (3*2) + 3, which is 11, not 25. Oops. If you parenthesize the arguments instead:

```
#define SQUARE(x)   (x)*(x)
```

Then `SQUARE(2+3)` will turn into (2+3)*(2+3), the correct expression. It is generally a good idea to surround the whole macro result in parentheses, such as:

```
#define SQUARE(x)    ((x)*(x))
```

which prevents problems if the macro expands into an expression with operators of higher precedence.

Beware of side effects in macros. Preprocessor macro expansion is strictly textual substitution. The code `SQUARE(i++)` will expand to `((i++) * (i++))`, which actually is undefined in the C standard. It might cause `i` to be incremented twice. Then again, it might not. Similarly, using functions with side effects, or that are computationally expensive, in a macro like this one could be bad news.

Multiline macros

Sometimes you want a macro to be more than one line of code, such as this one that increases a global error count and then displays an error for the user. The backslashes are necessary to let a single macro span multiple source lines.

```
#define FOUND_AN_ERROR(desc)    \
        error_count++;    \
        fprintf(stderr, "Found an error '%s' at file %s, line %d\n",    \
            desc, __FILE__, __LINE__)
```

The macro can be used like this:

```
if (argc == 2) {
    FOUND_AN_ERROR ("something really bad happened");
}
```

Example 1.6 uses the macro:

Example 1.6 multilineMacro.m

```
#import <stdio.h>

// gcc -g -Wall -o multilineMacro multilineMacro.m

#define FOUND_AN_ERROR(desc)    \
        error_count++;    \
        fprintf(stderr, "Found an error '%s' at file %s, line %d\n",  \
                desc, __FILE__, __LINE__)

int error_count;

int main (int argc, char *argv[]) {
    if (argc == 2) {
        FOUND_AN_ERROR ("something really bad happened");
    }
    printf ("done\n");
    return 0;

} // main
```

If you compile and run it, you see the "success" case:

```
$ ./multilineMacro
done
```

Now run it with an argument, which is the "error" case:

```
$ ./multilineMacro bork
Found an error 'something bad happened' at file multilineMacro.m, line 13
done
```

Looks like it works fine. Ship it!

There is one lurking problem, though: What happens if a programmer on your team does not fully brace their single-line if statements? The code looks innocent enough if you take out the braces:

```
if (argc == 2)
    FOUND_AN_ERROR ("something bad happened");
```

But, if you run the program now without an argument (the "success" case), you get an error:

```
$ ./multilineMacro
Found an error 'something bad happened' at file multilineMacro.m, line 13
done
```

That's not good. Previously correct code is now considered an error. Take a look at what is happening as the preprocessor mutates your code from:

```
if (argc == 2)
    FOUND_AN_ERROR ("something bad happened");
```

to

```
if (argc == 2)
    error_count++;
    fprintf (stderr, "Found an error '%s' at file %s, line %d\n",
            "something bad happened", "multilineMacro.m", 13);
```

This is what it looks like indented the way that it is actually being executed:

```
if (argc == 2)
    error_count++;
fprintf(stderr, "Found an error '%s' at file %s, line %d\n",
        "something bad happened", "multilineMacro.m", 13);
```

You need to wrap these multiline macros in curly braces so that they are essentially one statement. It will then become one statement as far as the compiler is concerned.

If you change the macro to read:

```
#define FOUND_AN_ERROR(desc)    \
    do {   \
        error_count++;   \
        fprintf(stderr, "Found an error '%s' at file %s, line %d\n",  \
                desc, __FILE__, __LINE__); \
    } while (0)
```

and rerun it, the program works properly. As you can see, the macro is wrapped with a `do {} while (0)` statement, which means that the code inside of the loop will be executed only once. This idiom has the side-effect of turning the multi-line operation into a single statement, which makes the unbraced `if` behave as expected. This is a technique known as "eating the semicolon." Using braces alone does not work because you end up with stray semicolons that confuse the compiler if there is an `else` clause.

This solution hides one last problem. What happens if there is a `break` in the macro or something included in the expansion? Granted, hiding a `break` or `continue` in a macro is not a terribly good idea, but sometimes you need to do it. The `while` loop will consume the `break` and not let it affect the loop that contains the macro.

```
#define FOUND_AN_ERROR(desc)  \
    do {   \
        error_count++;   \
        fprintf(stderr, "Found an error '%s' at file %s, line %d\n",  \
                desc, __FILE__, __LINE__);  \
        break;  \
    } while (0)

while (no_error) {
    if (x > 10) FOUND_AN_ERROR ("x too large");
    /* do something with x */
}
```

The `while` loop continues as long as x is not greater than 10. If it is, the macro logs an error and then performs a `break`. But it only breaks out of the loop used in the macro's implementation.

Here is one solution to this `break`-capturing problem:

```
#define FOUND_AN_ERROR(desc)  \
    if (1) {   \
        error_count++;   \
        fprintf(stderr, "Found an error '%s' at file %s, line %d\n",  \
                desc, __FILE__, __LINE__); \
        break;  \
    } else do {} while (0)
```

The `if (1)` gives you a new scope for your macro and also turns the macro into a single expression. The empty `do {} while` at the end eats the semicolon. For the most part, just wrapping your macro in do/while will address multi-line macro issues, with the if (1) technical there if you need to play games with loop control.

Const and volatile variables

const is a C keyword that tells the compiler that a variable will not be modified. The compiler is allowed to make assumptions about the variable that can help in optimization and also flag as errors any attempts to modify the variable after its declaration. const used with a scalar variable makes that variable a constant:

```
const int i = 23;
i = 24; // error: assignment of read-only variable 'i'
```

When dealing with pointers, const can apply to the pointer, to what the pointer points to, or both.

Listing const first causes the data being pointed to be considered read-only:

```
// pointer to const char
const char *string = "bork"; // The data pointed to by string is const.
string = "greeble"; // Pointer reassignment is ok.
string[0] = 'f';     // error: assignment of read-only location
```

Putting const after the * causes the pointer itself to be considered read-only without affecting the mutability of what it points to:

```
// const pointer to char
char *const string2 = "bork";  // The pointer itself is const.
string2 = "greeble"; // error: assignment of read-only variable 'string2'
string2[0] = 'f';    // This is ok.
```

Putting const in both places causes both the pointer and data to be considered read-only:

```
// const pointer to const char
const char * const string3 = "bork"; // Pointer and pointee are const
string3 = "greeble"; // error: assignment of read-only variable 'string3'
string3[0] = 'f';    // error: assignment of read-only location
```

Keeping these separate in your brain is easy – look at what the const is next to. If it is next to a data type, then the data is what is considered constant. If const immediately follows the *, then the pointer itself is considered constant.

const does not affect the underlying data – only what you can and cannot do with data accessible through a const-qualified variable. While you can play games with pointers and addresses and casts to alter any variable's "constant" data, please don't do this.

volatile is the opposite of const. A variable that is volatile may be changed at any time, independent of what the program is currently doing. The instigator of this change might be an interrupt handler, a signal handler, another thread, or a **longjmp()** (discussed in Chapter 5: *Exceptions, Error Handling, and Signals*). Declaring a variable volatile means the value of the variable is reloaded from memory every time it is used. This guarantees that you will have the correct value when you need it, but it also negates some possible compiler optimizations, like caching the value in a register in addition to its location in memory.

Variable argument lists

Variadic function is a fancy name for a function that takes a variable number of arguments. These can provide a flexible and powerful programming interface. The functions belonging to the **printf** family are variadic functions, which combine one function, a small, expressive command language, and a variable number of arguments leading to an incredibly powerful tool. The stdarg manpage contains the full details on using variable argument lists.

To handle variable arguments in your own functions, you first declare a variable of type va_list, which acts like a pointer to argument values, as shown in Figure 1.3. Initialize it with **va_start()** giving it the name of the last declared function argument. The va_list now points to the first of the additional arguments.

To get the actual argument values, you call **va_arg()** with the type of data you expect that argument to be. It will return the correct number of bytes for type and advance the va_list to point to the next argument. Keep on calling **va_arg()**, giving it the expected types, until you are done processing the arguments. Call **va_end()** to clean up any internal state.

Example 1.7 shows a function that adds up the integers that are passed to it, using zero as a sentinel value to stop processing:

Example 1.7   vararg.m

```
// vararg.m -- use varargs to sum a list of numbers

// gcc -g -Wall -o vararg vararg.m

#import <stdio.h>
#import <stdarg.h>

// sum all the integers passed in.  Stopping if it's zero
int addemUp (int firstNum, ...) {
    va_list args;

    int sum = firstNum;
    int number;

    va_start (args, firstNum);
    while (1) {
        number = va_arg (args, int);
        sum += number;
        if (number == 0) {
            break;
        }
    }
    va_end (args);

    return sum;

} // addemUp

int main (int argc, char *argv[]) {
    int sumbody;

    sumbody = addemUp (1, 2, 3, 4, 5, 6, 7, 8, 9, 0);
    printf ("sum of 1..9 is %d\n", sumbody);

    sumbody = addemUp (1, 3, 5, 7, 9, 11, 0);
    printf ("sum of odds from 1..11 is %d\n", sumbody);

    return 0;
} // main
```

Build and run it:

```
$ ./vararg
sum of 1..9 is 45
sum of odds from 1..11 is 36
```

When you call **va_start()**, an internal pointer is initialized to point into the call stack at the end of the supplied argument, as illustrated in Figure 1.3. Each time you call **va_arg()**, it returns the amount of data making up the supplied type and advances the internal pointer to the end of that data. **va_arg()** uses the supplied data type to determine how far it needs to advance its pointer.

Figure 1.3   Variadic function stack usage

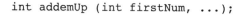

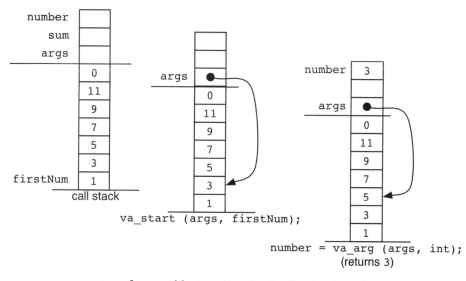

That sounds dangerous – what if the actual argument's type is a different size than the type you expected? If there are fewer arguments than you expect, how does **va_arg()** know when to stop? It has no idea. There is no magic that automatically plants a flag at the end of a function's parameters or communicates the total number and types of arguments that are passed in. Your code will need to know when to stop. You can do this by having some kind of pre-supplied description like the format string passed to **printf()**. You can use a sentinel value like zero or NULL. [NSArray arrayWithObjects:] uses nil (a zero pointer value) to signal the end of the list of objects to populate the array with.

While this helps with the number of arguments problem, there is unfortunately nothing you can do about the wrong argument type problem. As you can imagine, this can be a major source of run-time errors. If you supply a bad format string to **printf()** or do not include the terminating sentinel value, the function processing the call stack could wander off into random data, causing a crash or data corruption.

To help make calling variable argument functions safer, **gcc** lets you tag a function or a method declaration with __attribute__((sentinel)). Then, when your **gcc** command line includes the

-Wformat flag, **gcc** will emit a warning if you fail to terminate the argument list with a zero pointer value like NULL or nil. This flag also causes **gcc** to warn of bad calls to **printf()**. Cocoa programmers can use the symbol NS_REQUIRES_NIL_TERMINATION instead of using the (somewhat confusing) attribute syntax. Example 1.8 shows a string printing function that uses NULL for its sentinel value.

Example 1.8   sentinel.m

```
// sentinel.m -- Show __attribute__((sentinel)) in action

#import <stdio.h>  // for printf()
#import <stdarg.h> // for va_start() and friends

// gcc -g -Wall -o sentinel sentinel.m

void printStrings(char *first, ...) __attribute__((sentinel));

void printStrings(char *first, ...) {
    va_list args;
    va_start (args, first);
    char *string = first;

    while (string != NULL) {
        printf ("%s", string);
        string = va_arg (args, char *);
    }
    va_end (args);
    printf ("\n");
} // printStrings


int main (void) {
    printStrings ("spicy", "pony", "head", NULL);
    printStrings ("machine", "tool"); // should warn

    return 0;
} // main
```

The compiler warns you about the second **printStrings()** call:

```
$ gcc -g -Wall -o sentinel sentinel.m
sentinel.m: In function 'main':
sentinel.m:31: warning: missing sentinel in function call
```

A run of this program on a PowerPC machine or 64-bit Intel machine prints the first string okay, but it crashes with the second call. When run with 32-bit Intel, it kind of works:

```
$ gcc -arch i386 -g -Wall -o sentinel sentinel.m
$ ./sentinel
spicyponyhead
machinetoolhead
```

In this case, the second **printStrings()** call is using stale data left on the stack after the first call.

gcc also provides an __attribute__((format_arg)) tag you can use for functions that take a printf-style format string.

Some families of variadic functions make it easy for you to add an extra value to them. You might want a version of **printf()** that takes a debug severity level and only prints out text if the level exceeds some globally set value. To do this, you can write a function to accept the debug level, the format string, and the arguments. You can then examine the debug level, and if it is in the right range, call **vprintf()**, a version of **printf()** that takes a va_list rather than a format string and arguments. A leading or trailing "v" is sometimes used for the name of a function or method that takes a va_list, such as **vsnprintf()** or **NSLogv()**. Example 1.9 shows a way of performing conditional logging.

Example 1.9   debuglog.m

```
// debuglog.m -- a function for conditional logging

// gcc -g -Wall -o debuglog debuglog.m

#import <stdio.h>
#import <stdarg.h>

int globalLevel = 50;

void debugLog (int logLevel, const char *format, ...)
{
    if (logLevel > globalLevel) {
        va_list args;
        va_start (args, format);
        vprintf (format, args);
        va_end (args);
    }

} // debugLog

int main (int argc, char *argv[])
{
    debugLog (10, "this will not be seen: %d, %s, %d\n",
              10, "hello", 23);
    debugLog (87, "this should be seen: %s, %d\n",
              "bork", 42);
    return 0;
} // main
```

Compile and then run it:

```
$ ./debuglog
this should be seen: bork, 42
```

You can create variable argument methods in Objective-C the same way as in C, so there is no new syntax to learn. Be aware you cannot create **NSInvocation**s that reference variable argument methods.

Example 1.10 has a **SomeClass** object that has a weird little method that takes an arbitrary number of objects (terminated by nil) and prints out their descriptions.

Example 1.10   describeObjects.m

```
// describeObjects.m -- varargs with Objective-C

// gcc -g -Wall -o describeObjects -framework Foundation describeObjects.m

#import <Foundation/Foundation.h>

@interface Describer : NSObject
```

```
- (void) describeObjects: (id) firstObject, ...
    __attribute__((sentinel));

@end // Describer

@implementation Describer

- (void) describeObjects: (id) firstObject, ... {
    va_list args;
    id obj = firstObject;

    va_start (args, firstObject);

    while (obj) {
        NSString *string = [obj description];
        NSLog (@"the description is:\n    %@", string);
        obj = va_arg (args, id);
    }

    va_end (args);

} // describeObjects

@end // Describer

int main (int argc, char *argv[]) {
    NSAutoreleasePool *pool = [[NSAutoreleasePool alloc] init];

    Describer *obj = [[Describer alloc] init];

    NSString *someString = @"someString";
    NSNumber *num = [NSNumber numberWithInt: 23];
    NSDate *date = [NSCalendarDate calendarDate];

    [obj describeObjects:someString, num, date, nil];

    [pool drain];

    return (0);

} // main
```

Compile and run it:

```
$ ./describeObjects
2011-01-17 15:08:11.678 describeObjects[2830:903] the description is:
    someString
2011-01-17 15:08:11.680 describeObjects[2830:903] the description is:
    23
2011-01-17 15:08:11.680 describeObjects[2830:903] the description is:
    2011-01-17 15:08:11 -0500
```

There are other Foundation methods that accept va_lists much like **vprintf()** does, such as **NSString**'s **-initWithFormat:arguments:** and **NSPredicate**'s **+predicateWithFormat:arguments:**.

Varargs gotchas

Making assumptions about the sizes of data passed to functions that take a variable number of arguments is a common error. For example:

```
size_t mysize = somevalue;
printf ("mysize is %d\n", mysize);
```

This code assumes sizeof(size_t) == sizeof(int), which is correct for 32-bit programming (both are four bytes) but not for 64-bit programming where size_t is eight bytes and int is four bytes. The compiler pushes 8 bytes of data onto the call stack, but **printf()** has been told to expect an int, so it only pulls four bytes off the stack. You will either crash or get bad data if there are subsequent arguments.

One way to fix this is to cast your size_t argument to the type specified in the format string:

```
printf ("mysize is %d\n", (int)mysize);
```

This can be necessary when dealing with types whose size might vary from platform to platform. A better way is to ensure your format specifiers use the right types:

```
printf ("mysize is %zu\n", mysize);
```

Here, z is a length modifier that alters the unsigned conversion specifier u to match the size of the platform-dependent type size_t. Only a few such types have corresponding length modifiers; you can find the list in the **printf(3)** manpage.

QuietLog

QuietLog() is a function like **NSLog()** except that it does not prepend the extra information such as process ID and the current time to the subsecond level, greatly reducing the volume of output. What makes the implementation a little more interesting is that we cannot use **vprintf()** because **vprintf()** does not understand the Cocoa's %@ conversion specifier for printing an object's description. A temporary **NSString** is created, and then printed, as shown in Example 1.11.

Example 1.11   quietlog.m

```
// quietlog.m -- NSLog, but quieter

// gcc -g -Wall -framework Foundation -o quietlog quietlog.m

#import <Foundation/Foundation.h>

void QuietLog (NSString *format, ...) {
    va_list argList;
    va_start (argList, format);

    // NSString luckily provides us with this handy method which
    // will do all the work for us, including handling %@
    NSString *string;
    string = [[NSString alloc] initWithFormat: format
                               arguments: argList];
    va_end (argList);

    printf ("%s\n", [string UTF8String]);

    [string release];
} // QuietLog

int main (void) {
    NSAutoreleasePool *pool = [[NSAutoreleasePool alloc] init];
```

```
    NSLog (@"NSLog is %@", [NSNumber numberWithInt: 23]);
    QuietLog (@"QuietLog is %@", [NSNumber numberWithInt: 42]);

    [pool drain];
    return (0);
} // main
```

And after compiling and running it, you would see something like this:

```
$ ./quietlog
2011-01-17 15:15:19.001 quietlog[2868:903] NSLog is 23
QuietLog is 42
```

Variadic macros

gcc has supported variadic macros for a long time as a **gcc**-specific extension. C99, the version of the C language specified by an ISO standard released in 1999, has adopted variadic macros into the mainstream language.

As you can tell by the name, these are macros that accept a variable number of arguments. You cannot address individual arguments in your macros, but you can use the symbol __VA_ARGS__ to reference the remaining arguments. Remember this is still textual manipulation; a va_list is not created in the process.

Unfortunately, there is one problem with __VA_ARGS__ when you are writing macros that take an optional number of arguments. You might have a macro that looks like this:

```
#define THING(string, ...) printf (string, __VA_ARGS__)
```

If you invoke the THING macro with more than one argument, things work out okay.

```
THING ("hello %s %s\n", "there", "george");
```

turns into

```
printf ("hello %s %s\n", "there", "george");
```

If you do not supply any additional arguments, you get a leftover comma and an accompanying syntax error:

```
THING ("hi\n");
```

turns into

```
printf ("hi\n", );
```

If you foresee this being a problem with your macro, use ##__VA_ARGS__, prepending two pound signs, which causes the preprocessor to eat the preceding comma. With THING defined as

```
#define THING(string, ...) printf (string,## __VA_ARGS__)
```

the failing example

```
THING ("hi\n");
```

now expands to

```
printf ("hi\n");
```

Example 1.12 is functionally the same as Example 1.9 but uses a macro rather than a function for checking the debug level.

Example 1.12   debuglog-macro.m

```
// debuglog-macro.m -- a macro for conditional logging

// gcc -g -Wall -o debuglog-macro debuglog-macro.m

#import <stdio.h>
#import <stdarg.h>

int globalLevel = 50;

#define DEBUG_LOG(logLevel, format, ...) \
do { \
    if ((logLevel) > globalLevel) printf((format), ##__VA_ARGS__); \
} while (0)

int main (int argc, char *argv[]) {
    DEBUG_LOG (10, "this will not be seen: %d, %s, %d\n", 10, "hello", 23);
    DEBUG_LOG (87, "this should be seen: %s, %d\n", "bork", 42);
    DEBUG_LOG (87, "and this should be seen\n");

    return 0;
} // main
```

A sample run is exactly the same as it was before.

```
$ ./debuglog-macro
this should be seen: bork, 42
and this should be seen
```

Bitwise operations

C lets you manipulate the individual bits in a piece of memory. If you use higher-level toolkits and languages, you can ignore the bitwise operators most of the time. However, the Cocoa API occasionally needs you to assemble and test bit flags, and the Unix API requires it more often. So it is good to be familiar with these operations.

A bit can contain the value of zero or one. A byte is a collection of eight bits, also referred to as "octets." The examples that follow use the two numbers shown in Figure 1.4. The bit pattern is listed first, then the value in hex, and then in decimal.

Figure 1.4   Two bytes

A: | 1 | 1 | 0 | 0 | 1 | 1 | 0 | 0 | = 0xCC = 204

B: | 1 | 1 | 1 | 1 | 0 | 0 | 0 | 0 | = 0xF0 = 240

Bitwise operators

There are four different operations you can perform on bits: AND, OR, XOR, and NOT. You can also shift the bits around in an integral value.

When you AND two bits, the resulting bit is *set* (one) only if both bits are set. The resulting bit is *clear* (zero) in all other cases.

Values larger than a single bit are ANDed bit-by-bit; this is the *bitwise* element of the bitwise AND operator. You can imagine stacking the values' bit representations and then ANDing the columns, as shown in Figure 1.5.

Figure 1.5   Bitwise AND

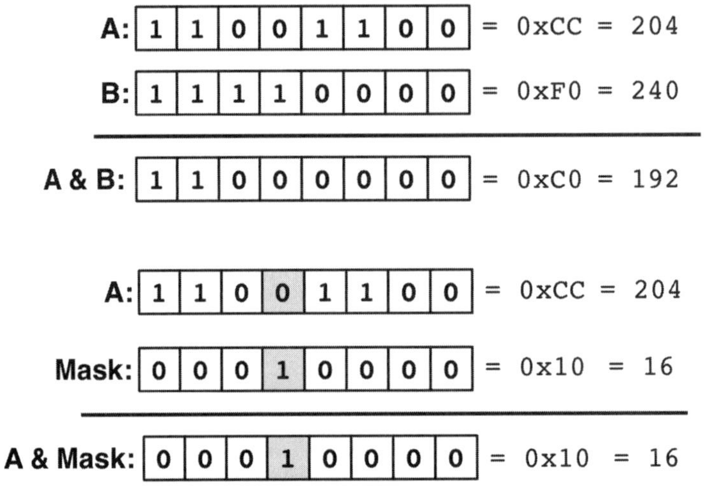

A: | 1 | 1 | 0 | 0 | 1 | 1 | 0 | 0 | = 0xCC = 204

B: | 1 | 1 | 1 | 1 | 0 | 0 | 0 | 0 | = 0xF0 = 240

A & B: | 1 | 1 | 0 | 0 | 0 | 0 | 0 | 0 | = 0xC0 = 192

A: | 1 | 1 | 0 | 0 | 1 | 1 | 0 | 0 | = 0xCC = 204

Mask: | 0 | 0 | 0 | 1 | 0 | 0 | 0 | 0 | = 0x10 = 16

A & Mask: | 0 | 0 | 0 | 1 | 0 | 0 | 0 | 0 | = 0x10 = 16

When you OR two values, the bits in the result are set wherever either of the original two values has a bit set or where both bits are set. Conversely, the resulting bits are clear only if both bits are zero.

Figure 1.6   Bitwise OR

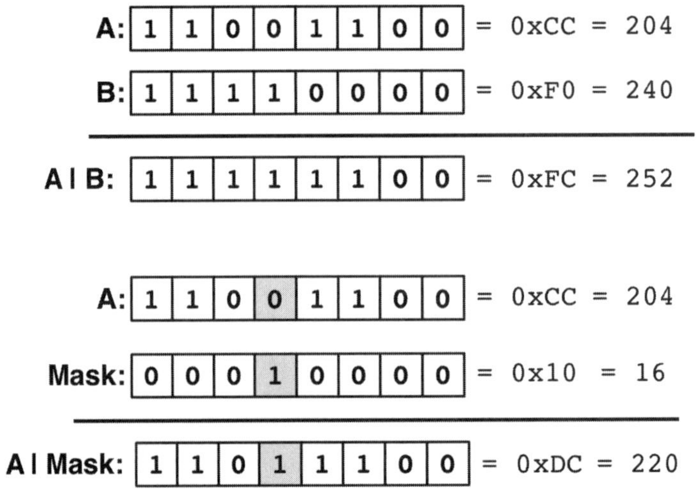

A: | 1 | 1 | 0 | 0 | 1 | 1 | 0 | 0 | = 0xCC = 204

B: | 1 | 1 | 1 | 1 | 0 | 0 | 0 | 0 | = 0xF0 = 240

A | B: | 1 | 1 | 1 | 1 | 1 | 1 | 0 | 0 | = 0xFC = 252

A: | 1 | 1 | 0 | 0 | 1 | 1 | 0 | 0 | = 0xCC = 204

Mask: | 0 | 0 | 0 | 1 | 0 | 0 | 0 | 0 | = 0x10 = 16

A | Mask: | 1 | 1 | 0 | 1 | 1 | 1 | 0 | 0 | = 0xDC = 220

XOR, "exclusive or," uses the ^ (hat or caret) operator. When you XOR two values, the bit is set in the result only if the corresponding bit is set in one value or the other value but not both. The resulting bit is clear if both bits are set or if both bits are clear. You can think of XOR like the question "Would you like soup or salad with that?" at a restaurant. You can have one or the other, but not both (unless you pay extra).

Figure 1.7   Bitwise XOR

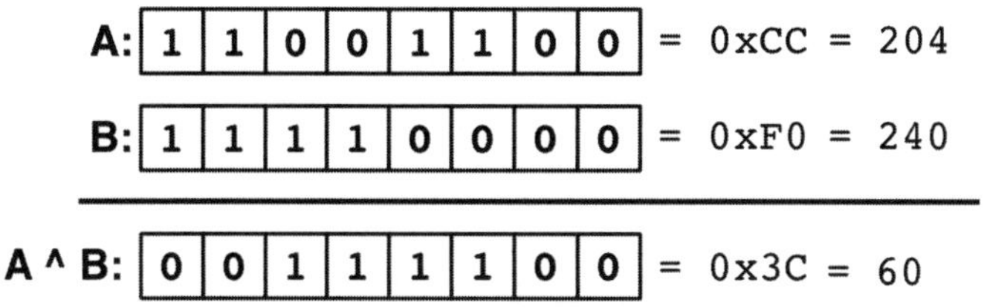

| A: | 1 | 1 | 0 | 0 | 1 | 1 | 0 | 0 | = 0xCC = 204 |

| B: | 1 | 1 | 1 | 1 | 0 | 0 | 0 | 0 | = 0xF0 = 240 |

A ^ B: | 0 | 0 | 1 | 1 | 1 | 1 | 0 | 0 | = 0x3C = 60

NOT complements (flips) the value of each of the bits using the ~ (tilde, twiddle) operator. What was zero becomes one, what was one becomes zero.

Figure 1.8   Bitwise NOT

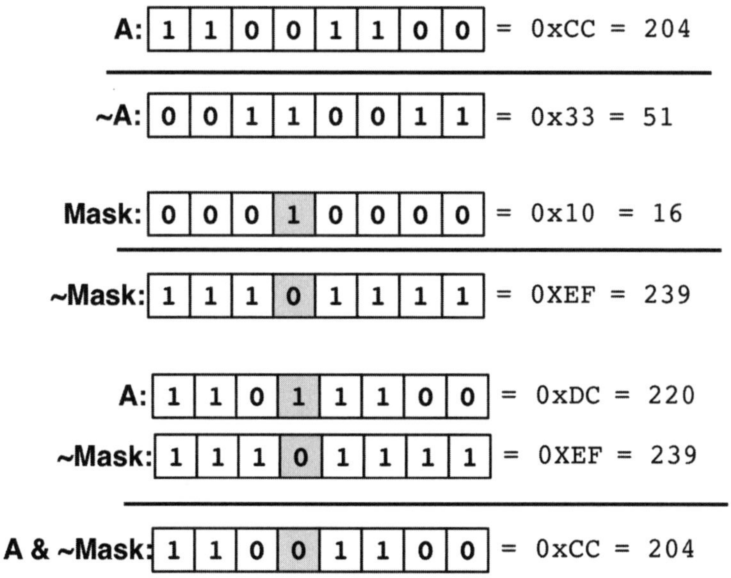

A: | 1 | 1 | 0 | 0 | 1 | 1 | 0 | 0 | = 0xCC = 204

~A: | 0 | 0 | 1 | 1 | 0 | 0 | 1 | 1 | = 0x33 = 51

Mask: | 0 | 0 | 0 | 1 | 0 | 0 | 0 | 0 | = 0x10 = 16

~Mask: | 1 | 1 | 1 | 0 | 1 | 1 | 1 | 1 | = 0XEF = 239

A: | 1 | 1 | 0 | 1 | 1 | 1 | 0 | 0 | = 0xDC = 220

~Mask: | 1 | 1 | 1 | 0 | 1 | 1 | 1 | 1 | = 0XEF = 239

A & ~Mask: | 1 | 1 | 0 | 0 | 1 | 1 | 0 | 0 | = 0xCC = 204

There are two shifting operators in C. << shifts the bits of an integral value to the left a specified number of places, filling in the low bits with zeros and dropping the high bits on the floor. The >> operator shifts the bits a specified number of places to the right. The behavior of what gets shifted-in for the higher bits is implementation defined.

Back in the old days, shifts were used as optimizations for multiplication and division by two, but there are a number of corner cases with signed values that can make them dangerous to use. These days, the most common use for bit shifting is using the left shift to position a one-bit at a particular location, as shown in Figure 1.9. You can see the one-bit being shifted four positions to the left, having a final value of 16.

Figure 1.9   Bitwise shift

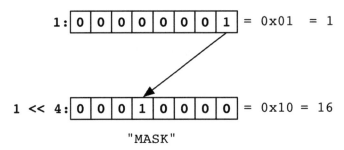

Setting and clearing bits

You can use AND, OR, NOT, and shifting to compactly store information in integers by attaching meaning to specific bit positions. For example, the NSEnumerationOptions specifies two bit flags:

```
enum {
    NSEnumerationConcurrent = (1UL << 0),    // binary 0001
    NSEnumerationReverse = (1UL << 1),       // binary 0010
};
typedef NSUInteger NSEnumerationOptions;
```

When presenting enumeration options to a call such as **-enumerateObjectsWithOptions:usingBlock:**, you set the zeroth bit to one to indicate you want a concurrent enumeration and set the first bit to one to indicate you want the enumeration to happen in reverse. There are four combinations: all clear (non-concurrent, forward), either one set, or both set (concurrently backwards).

This is commonly called "bitmasking" – a constant such as NSEnumerationConcurrent is used as a mask on a collection of bits, hiding the bits we are not interested in.

The usual way to use bitmasks is by defining constants for each bit (or set of bits) with a specific meaning. You can also use a numeric value that you know sets the right bit. The bit to set is defined using either the appropriate integer value:

```
#define BIT_POSITION 8    // 00001000
```

or using a bit shifting expression:

```
#define BIT_POSITION (1 << 3)    // 00001000
```

You set a bitmask's bits using bitwise OR:

```
flags |= BIT_POSITION;
```

Figure 1.10   Setting a bit

| flags: | 0 | 1 | 1 | 0 | **0** | 0 | 0 | 1 | = 0x61 = 97 |

| BIT_POSITION: | 0 | 0 | 0 | 0 | **1** | 0 | 0 | 0 | = 0x08 = 8 |

| flags \| BIT_POSITION: | 0 | 1 | 1 | 0 | **1** | 0 | 0 | 1 | = 0x69 = 105 |

You test whether a bitmasks bits are set using bitwise AND:

```
if (flags & BIT_POSITION) {
    // do something appropriate
}
```

Figure 1.11   Testing a bit

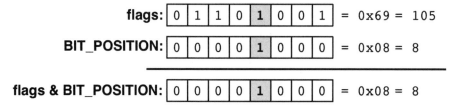

You clear a bitmask's bits by ANDing the value with the bitmask's complement:

```
flags &= ~BIT_POSITION;
```

This one is a bit trickier. What you need is a new mask that will let through all the original values of the bits of the variable you are masking, *except* the masked bit.

Figure 1.12   Clearing a bit

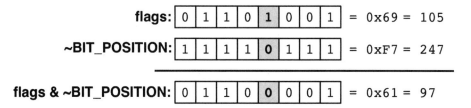

When you are using a mask with multiple bits set, it is safer to compare against the mask rather than doing a simple logical test:

```
#define MULTI_BITS  0xF0  // 11110000
```

And assuming that `flags` is `0x61` (`01100001`), the statement

```
if (flags & MULTI_BITS) {
    // do something if all bits are set
}
```

may be bad code. The result of the bitwise AND is:

Figure 1.13

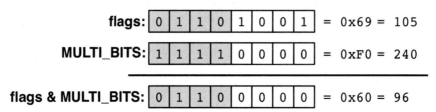

The result is `0x60`. This will be treated by the `if` as a true value, even if only a couple of the bits in `MULTI_BITS` is set. Correct code would be:

```
if ((flags & MULTI_BITS) == MULTI_BITS) {
    // do something if all bits are set
}
```

Example 1.13 shows a number of bitwise operations.

Example 1.13   bitmask.m

```
// bitmask.m -- play with bitmasks

// gcc -g -Wall -o bitmask bitmask.m

#include <stdio.h>         // for printf

#define THING_1_MASK    1        // 00000001
#define THING_2_MASK    2        // 00000010
#define THING_3_MASK    4        // 00000100
#define ALL_THINGS      (THING_1_MASK | THING_2_MASK | THING_3_MASK) // 00000111

#define ANOTHER_MASK    (1 << 5)  // 00100000
#define ANOTHER_MASK_2  (1 << 6)  // 01000000

#define ALL_ANOTHERS    (ANOTHER_MASK | ANOTHER_MASK_2)    // 01100000
#define ALL_USEFUL_BITS (ALL_THINGS | ALL_ANOTHERS)        // 01100111

static void showMaskValue (int value) {
    printf ("\n"); // space out the output
    printf ("value %x:\n", value);

    if (value & THING_1_MASK) printf ("  THING_1\n");
    if (value & THING_2_MASK) printf ("  THING_2\n");
    if (value & THING_3_MASK) printf ("  THING_3\n");

    if (value & ANOTHER_MASK) printf ("  ANOTHER_MASK\n");
```

```
    if (value & ANOTHER_MASK_2) printf ("  ANOTHER_MASK_2\n");

    if ((value & ALL_ANOTHERS) == ALL_ANOTHERS) printf ("  ALL ANOTHERS\n");
} // showMaskValue

static int setBits (int value, int maskValue) {
    // Set a bit by just OR-ing in a value.
    value |= maskValue;
    return value;
} // setBits

static int clearBits (int value, int maskValue) {
    // To clear a bit, AND it with the complement of the mask.

    value &= ~maskValue;
    return value;
} // clearBits

int main (void) {
    int intval = 0;

    intval = setBits (intval, THING_1_MASK);    // 00000001 = 0x01
    intval = setBits (intval, THING_3_MASK);    // 00000101 = 0x05
    showMaskValue (intval);

    intval = setBits (intval, ALL_ANOTHERS);    // 01100101 = 0x65
    intval = clearBits (intval, THING_2_MASK);  // 01100101 = 0x65
    intval = clearBits (intval, THING_3_MASK);  // 01100001 = 0x61
    showMaskValue (intval);

    return 0;
} // main
```

When you compile and run, you get this output:

```
% ./bitmask
value 5:
  THING_1
  THING_3

value 61:
  THING_1
  ANOTHER_MASK
  ANOTHER_MASK
  ALL ANOTHERS
```

Objective-C

Objective-C is the language used to program the Cocoa toolkit. It is a thin layer on top of C with a little additional syntax, a runtime component, and a big pile of metadata to support the dynamic nature of the language. But fundamentally, Objective-C is still C. Many programmers forget Objective-C's C heritage and fail to take advantage of C's language features and libraries.

C callbacks in Objective-C

A question that comes up fairly frequently in online forums is, "How do I put a method into a function pointer?" Nine times out of ten, the poster actually wants to use Cocoa with an existing C API that uses callbacks. A much better question is, "I'm using a C API that uses callbacks with Cocoa, how do I make it work?"

Even though Objective-C methods are fundamentally C functions, you cannot use Objective-C methods as callbacks for a C API. When you send a message to an object, the compiler replaces your square-bracket method call with a function call to **objc_msgSend()** or one of its variants. **objc_msgSend()** is prototyped like this:

```
id objc_msgSend(id self, SEL op, ...);
```

When you make a call like

```
[box drawInRect: someRect]
```

it gets turned by the compiler into

```
objc_msgSend (box, @selector(drawInRect:), someRect);
```

It passes the receiver of the message as the first argument. This becomes the self pointer inside of the method. It passes the selector as the second argument, which is accessible with _cmd. The existence of these two hidden arguments is what prevents you from using methods for callbacks.

Using objects in callbacks requires using a C function as a trampoline to bounce off of. Most C callback APIs allow you to specify some kind of pointer-sized rock to hide some data under, whether it's called userData, info, refcon, or context.

For example, the Core Foundation framework provides an XML parser that is based on using C callbacks. Programmers build their own data structures using information the callbacks supply about the XML file's content. Suppose we have a **Watcher** object that wants its **-watchCreateStructure:** method to be triggered whenever CFXML invokes the callback.

You would set up your context to include your Objective-C object:

```
Watcher *watcher = [[Watcher alloc] init];
CFXMLParserContext context = { 0, watcher, NULL, NULL, NULL };
```

Set up your callbacks to include the C functions:

```
CFXMLParserCallBacks callbacks = { 0, createStructure, addChild,
                                   endStructure, resolveEntity,
                                   handleError };
```

And then create your parser (notice the passing of the context for the last parameter):

```
parser = CFXMLParserCreate (kCFAllocatorDefault, (CFDataRef)xmlData, NULL,
                            kCFXMLParserAllOptions,
                            kCFXMLNodeCurrentVersion,
                            &callbacks, &context);
```

The CFXMLParser will grovel through the XML and call the callbacks as needed. From there, you can cast the info pointer into an object pointer and call a method. For instance,

```
void *createStructure (CFXMLParserRef parser,
                       CFXMLNodeRef node, void *info) {
    Watcher *watcher = (Watcher *) info;
    [watcher watchCreateStructure: node];
```

```
    // ... do some work ...
    return newXMLStructureDealie;
} // createStructure
```

Alternatively, you could create an `NSInvocation` or a block and use that for your context pointer. Then you can have a generic callback that just casts the incoming context pointer to an invocation or a block and then executes it.

Objective-C 2.0

Mac OS X 10.5 included a 2.0 update to the Objective-C language. While relatively minor, the additional features improve programmer efficiency and program reliability by eliminating a lot of boilerplate code and by moving common Cocoa idioms into the compiler where they can be sanity-checked and optimized. The new features include additions to protocols, class extensions, a new enumeration syntax, enhancements to the runtime, garbage collection, and properties. You cannot use these new features if you have to support 10.4. You have to use the 10.5 SDK or later to get Objective-C 2.0.

Protocols

An Objective-C protocol is similar to a Java interface: a list of methods that a class adopting the protocol must implement. The compiler will complain if any methods are left unimplemented. This can be inconvenient if you want to require some methods and have others be optional. For example, the `NSInputServiceProvider` protocol has 15 methods. If you adopt this protocol, you have to implement all 15 methods, even if you only need one or two to get your work done.

Informal protocols can be used to work around this annoyance. An informal protocol is a category on **NSObject** that lists the methods that might (or might not) be implemented. This solves the "thou shalt implement everything" problem, but it causes problems when there are methods that really do need to be implemented. The **NSTableDataSource** category includes two methods you must implement: **-numberOfRowsInTableView:** and **-tableView:objectValueForTableColumn:row:**. Informal protocols do not require you to implement these, so **NSTableView** relies on runtime checks on its data sources to make sure these are implemented.

Objective-C 2.0 introduces a better solution with two new directives for use within protocols: `@required` and `@optional`. `@required` precedes the declaration of methods that must be implemented. Protocol methods default to being `@required`. `@optional` flags methods that do not have to be implemented. If you were implementing something like the table view data source, you would create something like Example 1.14:

Example 1.14   datasource.m

```
// datasource.m -- look at ObjC2 protocol additions.

// gcc -g -Wall -framework Foundation -o datasource datasource.m

#import <Foundation/Foundation.h>

// -------------------------------------------------
// Datasource for the new table view
```

```
@protocol NewTableViewDataSource
- (NSUInteger) rowCount; // defaults to being required

@optional
- (BOOL) shouldEncheferizeStrings;
- (NSIndexSet *) emptyRows;

@required
- (id) dataValueAtRow: (NSUInteger) row;
@end // NewTableViewDataSource protocol

// -------------------------------------------------
// a datasource class

@interface DataSource : NSObject <NewTableViewDataSource>
@end // DataSource

@implementation DataSource

- (NSUInteger) rowCount {
    return 23;
} // rowCount

- (id) dataValueAtRow: (NSUInteger) row {
    return [NSNumber numberWithInt: row * 7];
} // dataValueAtRow

- (BOOL) shouldEncheferizeStrings {
    return YES; // bork bork bork
} // should EncheferizeStrings

@end // DataSource

// -------------------------------------------------
// the new table view

@interface NewTableView : NSObject {
    id datasource;
}

- (void) setDataSource: (id <NewTableViewDataSource>) ds;
- (void) doStuff;

@end // NewTableView

@implementation NewTableView

- (void) setDataSource: (id <NewTableViewDataSource>) ds {
    datasource = ds;
} // setDataSource

- (void) doStuff {
    // Don't need to check for respondsToSelector - the compiler does
    // some sanity checking for us.
    NSLog (@"rowCount: %u", [datasource rowCount]);
    NSLog (@"value at row 5: %@", [datasource dataValueAtRow: 5]);

    // These are optional, so check that the datasource responds to
    // them.
```

```
    if ([datasource respondsToSelector: @selector(shouldEncheferizeStrings)]) {
        NSLog (@"bork bork bork? %@",
               [datasource shouldEncheferizeStrings] ? @"YES" : @"NO");
    }
    if ([datasource respondsToSelector: @selector(emptyRows)]) {
        NSLog (@"the empty rows: %@", [datasource emptyRows]);
    }

} // doStuff

@end // NewTableView

// -------------------------------------------------
// Use everything.

int main (void) {
    NSAutoreleasePool *pool = [[NSAutoreleasePool alloc] init];

    NewTableView *tableview = [[NewTableView alloc] init];

    DataSource *ds = [[DataSource alloc] init];

    [tableview setDataSource: [NSNull null]]; // should warn
    [tableview setDataSource: ds];
    [tableview doStuff];

    [pool drain];
    return 0;
} // main
```

Example 1.14 starts out by declaring the NewTableViewDataSource protocol with
two required methods (**-rowCount** and **-dataValueAtRow:**) and two optional methods
(**-shouldEncheferizeStrings** and **-emptyRows**). Following that is the **DataSource** class that adopts
the new protocol. The compiler will warn if you do not implement either of the required methods. Only
one of the optional methods is implemented.

The next class is the **NewTableView** class with the datasource instance variable, whose setter requires
that the object given to **-setDataSource:** adopt the datasource protocol. The compiler will warn you
if you try to pass in an object that does not adopt this protocol. This guarantees (assuming you don't
ignore the warnings) that your data source implements what it has to and that you do not give the new
table view something that will not handle the required messages. That simplifies the implementation
of the **-doStuff** method, which can assume its datasource implements the required methods. You still
need to check at runtime for the presence of the optional methods.

When you compile the program, you should get this warning for the line trying to feed a bad data
source to the tableview:

```
datasource.m: In function 'main':
datasource.m:92: warning: class 'NSNull' does not implement
    the 'NewTableViewDataSource' protocol
```

And running it should give you output like this:

```
$ ./datasource
2011-01-18 12:39:43.211 datasource[4488:903] rowCount: 23
2011-01-18 12:39:43.213 datasource[4488:903] value at row 5: 35
2011-01-18 12:39:43.214 datasource[4488:903] bork bork bork? YES
```

Class extensions

Another Objective-C convention is using categories to declare methods outside of a class @interface. The two main reasons programmers do this are 1) to split up a long method list into smaller, easier to understand chunks, such as **NSWindow**'s NSKeyboardUI, NSToolbarSupport, and NSDrag categories, and 2) to declare "private" methods, in either a different header file or at the top of a class implementation file. The problem with using a category is that the compiler cannot check to make sure you actually implement what you say you will. For example, you could have a category like this in your class header file:

```
@interface BigShow(SlideManipulation)
- (void) moveToNextSlide;
- (int) currentSlideIndex;
@end
```

But your implementation might have a typo:

```
- (int) currentSlideINdex {
    return index;
} // currentSlideIndex
```

This error will only be caught at runtime and might not be caught until you have shipped your application to customers.

Objective-C 2.0 added *class extensions* to address this. A class extension is declared as a nameless category:

```
@interface BigShow ()
- (void) moveToNextSlide;
- (int) currentSlideIndex;
@end
```

This tells the compiler that these methods are part of the class, even though they are specified in a different place. The compiler will issue a warning if you do not provide an implementation for these methods in the class @implementation block.

Some programmers refer to class extensions as "class continuations." Continuation, though, is the name of another (more interesting) computer science concept, so it is best to refer to class extensions by their proper name.

In addition to forward-declaring methods in a class extension, you can also adopt protocols in them. Snow Leopard and iOS have moved many informal protocols into protocols and require your class to adopt those protocols before you can use your object as a delegate or a datasource. You can either list the protocol adoption in your header file:

```
@interface GroovyController : UIViewController <UITableViewDataSourceProtocol>
```

or in a class extension in your implementation:

```
@interface GroovyController () <UITableViewDataSourceProtocol>
```

By using the class extension, you move implementation details out of your header. This can also reduce compile time if your own classes make heavy use of protocols, where the adoption is just an implementation detail and not really part of the public interface. If you adopt a protocol (such as the NewTableViewDataSource protocol seen earlier) in your header file, you must include the data source header that defines the protocol, leading to longer compile times for every file that includes the original object's header.

Fast enumeration

One of the most common Cocoa idioms is iterating through a collection. Typical enumeration code looks like this:

```
NSEnumerator *enumerator = [array objectEnumerator];
NSString *string;
while ((string = [enumerator nextObject])) {
    NSLog (@"%@", string);
}
```

This is rather verbose, requires memory allocation for the enumerator, and might involve a copy of the collection in some circumstances. Iterating through an array with **-objectAtIndex:** is somewhat faster, but it ties your loop to **NSArray**, making future maintenance more difficult if you change collection classes.

Objective-C 2.0 adopts the "for-in" syntax found in many scripting languages for iterating through a collection, which is equivalent to the previous code.

```
for (NSString *string in array) {
    NSLog (@"%@", string);
}
```

The string variable is scoped to the loop. If you declared string outside of the loop, its value would be visible outside of the loop. If the iteration went through the whole collection, string would be nil when the loop exits. You can also supply an **NSEnumerator** instead of a collection:

```
NSEnumerator *enumerator = [array objectEnumerator];
for (NSString *string in enumerator) {
    NSLog (@"%@", string);
}
```

The for-in syntax is not only more compact; it is also significantly faster than other collection iteration methods. It takes advantage of the new NSFastEnumeration protocol, which lets the collection being iterated leverage its implementation details to provide the best performance possible. In addition, for-in will raise an exception if you mutate the collection while iterating through it, which has long been a Cocoa invariant, though one previously not always enforced.

To implement your own fast enumerable collection, you need to adopt the NSFastEnumeration protocol. It has only one method:

```
- (NSUInteger) countByEnumeratingWithState: (NSFastEnumerationState *) state
                                   objects: (id *) stackbuf
                                     count: (NSUInteger) len;
```

stackbuf is a pointer to an array of len object pointers on the stack, which the method can fill in but is not required to. The method returns the number of items supplied for this round of iteration or zero if iteration is finished.

The state parameter is a pointer to a structure that describes the current state of the enumeration:

```
typedef struct {
    unsigned long state;
```

```
    id *itemsPtr;
    unsigned long *mutationsPtr;
    unsigned long extra[5];
} NSFastEnumerationState;
```

The state field is zero the first time `-countByEnumeratingWithState:objects:count:` is called. You should set this to a non-zero value during the first call so you can tell when you are in a second (or subsequent) call.

You return objects for iteration in the array pointed to by `itemsPtr`. You can point this into the collection's data structures if the collection stores object pointers linearly in memory. Otherwise, you can put as many as `len` object pointers into the `stackbuf` parameter and point `itemsPtr` there. The `mutationsPtr` should be set to a valid address that functions as some kind of change counter for the object to catch the case of iterating over a mutating collection; immutable collections can just use `self`. The `extra` values are scratch space available for your `-countByEnumeratingWithState:objects:count:` implementation's use.

Here is a class that stores a C array of **NSString**s. The full text of this program can be found in `fastenum.m` in the sample code download, which includes the implementation of the variadic method and the code that maintains the mutations value.

```
@interface CArray : NSObject <NSFastEnumeration> {
    NSString **_strings;
    int _stringCount;
    unsigned long _mutations;
}

- (void) setStrings: (NSString *)string, ... NS_REQUIRES_NIL_TERMINATION;

@end // CArray
```

It has a C array of **NSString** pointers, a `stringCount` holding the length of the array, and a mutation count instance variable that gets incremented any time the set of strings is manipulated. A variadic method is provided to set the strings. Because **CArray** adopts NSFastEnumeration, it needs to implement `-countByEnumeratingWithState:objects:count:`:

```
- (NSUInteger) countByEnumeratingWithState: (NSFastEnumerationState *) state
                                    objects: (id *) stackbuf
                                      count: (NSUInteger) len {
    if (state->state == 0) {
        // First call, do initializations.
        state->state = 1;
        state->mutationsPtr = &_mutations;
        state->itemsPtr = _strings;

        return (_stringCount);

    } else {
        // We returned everything the first time through, so we're done.
        return 0;
    }

} // countByEnumeratingWithState
```

The first call to this method finds the state's `state` value to be zero, so it does first time initialization. It changes the state to a non-zero value so we know not to do the initialization work again. Then it sets the state's `mutationsPtr` to point to the `mutations` instance variable and points the `itemsPtr` to the C array instance variable. **CArray** stores all of its string pointers sequentially in memory, so we can tell the caller the total collection count. The for-in loop will then iterate over all of them. When this method is called a second time, it returns zero signifying that all iteration has been completed, and the for-in loop terminates. No matter how big our collection is, this **-countByEnumeratingWithState:objects:count:** method is only called twice.

This code populates and iterates a **CArray**:

```
CArray *carray = [[CArray alloc] init];
[carray setStrings: @"I", @"seem", @"to", @"be", @"a", @"verb", nil];

for (NSString *string in carray) {
    NSLog (@"%@", string);
}
```

And a sample run:

```
2011-01-18 15:47:15.531 fastenum[4688:903] I
2011-01-18 15:47:15.534 fastenum[4688:903] seem
2011-01-18 15:47:15.534 fastenum[4688:903] to
2011-01-18 15:47:15.534 fastenum[4688:903] be
2011-01-18 15:47:15.535 fastenum[4688:903] a
2011-01-18 15:47:15.535 fastenum[4688:903] verb
```

You do not actually have to iterate over a real collection. You can use fast enumeration for number generators. Whether this is actually a good idea is open to debate, but it is possible.

One number sequence popular with technical interviewers and book authors is the Fibonacci sequence, which is a recursive definition that says to start a sequence of numbers with two 1 values, then the next value is the sum of the previous two: 1, 1, 2, 3, 5, 8, 13, and so on. There are iterative and recursive solutions to this problem.

The fast enumeration solution takes advantage of two facts: **-countByEnumeratingWithState:** is given a chunk of space that can hold a number of pointers. Empirically, it looks like Cocoa provides 16 pointers worth of space. There is also some scratch space in the `state` structure for us to play with. The generator uses the stack space for pointers to **NSNumber**s for the sequence of numbers and uses the scratch space to hold the N-1 and N-2 values of the sequence.

The **FibonacciSequence** object does not have any state of its own, so any number of independent sequences can be generated from the same object. Here is the class interface:

```
@interface FibonacciSequence : NSObject <NSFastEnumeration>
@end // FibonacciSequence
```

And the lone method of this class does all of the dirty work:

```
- (NSUInteger) countByEnumeratingWithState: (NSFastEnumerationState *) state
                                   objects: (id *) stackbuf
                                     count: (NSUInteger) len {
    assert(len >= 2); // because we pre-populate two values on first-call
    id *scan, *stop;

    if (state->state == 0) {
        // first call, do initializations
        state->state = 1;
        state->mutationsPtr = (unsigned long *)self; // not applicable
        state->itemsPtr = stackbuf;
```

```
        // extra[0] has the N - 2 value, extra[1] has the N - 1 value
        // seed with correct values
        state->extra[0] = 1;
        state->extra[1] = 1;

        // fill in the first two values
        state->itemsPtr[0] = [NSNumber numberWithInt: state->extra[0]];
        state->itemsPtr[1] = [NSNumber numberWithInt: state->extra[1]];

        // tweak the scanning pointers because we've already filled
        // in the first two slots.
        scan = &state->itemsPtr[2];
        stop = &state->itemsPtr[0] + len;

    } else {
        // Otherwise we're in the Pink, and do normal processing for
        // all of the itemPtrs.
        scan = &state->itemsPtr[0];
        stop = &state->itemsPtr[0] + len;
    }

    while (scan < stop) {
        // Do the Fibonacci algorithm.
        int value = state->extra[0] + state->extra[1];
        state->extra[0] = state->extra[1];
        state->extra[1] = value;

        // populate the fast enum item pointer
        *scan = [NSNumber numberWithUnsignedLong: value];

        // and then scoot over to the next value
        scan++;
    }

    // Always fill up their stack buffer.
    return len;
} // countByEnumeratingWithState
```

This loop spins through a portion of the sequence:

```
FibonacciSequence *fibby = [[FibonacciSequence alloc] init];

int boredom = 0;
for (NSNumber *number in fibby) {
    NSLog (@"%@", number);
    if (boredom++ > 40) {
        break;
    }
}
```

And when run, looks like this:

```
2011-01-18 15:47:15.536 fastenum[4688:903] 1
2011-01-18 15:47:15.536 fastenum[4688:903] 1
2011-01-18 15:47:15.536 fastenum[4688:903] 2
...
2011-01-18 15:47:15.580 fastenum[4688:903] 102334155
2011-01-18 15:47:15.581 fastenum[4688:903] 165580141
2011-01-18 15:47:15.581 fastenum[4688:903] 267914296
```

Runtime enhancements and garbage collection

Objective-C 2.0 also enhances the language's runtime component. The runtime has been rewritten for 64-bit programming, which includes things like compatibility with C++ exceptions, discussed in Chapter 5: *Exceptions, Error Handling, and Signals*, and solving the fragile base class problem, discussed in Chapter 2: *The Compiler*.

Objective-C 2.0 has an optional garbage collector, which can be used instead of manual reference counting with retain, release, and autorelease. The garbage collector is general purpose enough to be used outside of Objective-C and is discussed in Chapter 7: *Memory*.

Properties

Another common Cocoa idiom is setters and getters, pairs of methods that affect instance variables. Suppose you have a botanical simulation and you model plants with a name, a color, and a size. You will want to have methods for users of a plant to have a way to change its attributes:

```
@interface LotusBlossom : NSObject {
    NSString *_name;
    NSColor *_color;
    int _size;
}

- (void) setName: (NSString *) name;
- (NSString *) name;

- (void) setColor: (NSColor *) color;
- (NSColor *) color;

- (void) setSize: (int) size;
- (int) size;

@end // LotusBlossom
```

The data that comes into each **-setWhatever:** method is treated in different ways: a string should be copied, a color should be retained, and no memory management is necessary for an int. Plus you need to maintain memory management hygiene, along with making checks to make sure you are not releasing an object unnecessarily:

```
- (void) setName: (NSString *) name {
    if (_name != name) {
        [_name release];
        _name = [name copy];
    }
} // setName
- (NSString *) name {
    return _name;
} // name

- (void) setColor: (NSColor *) color {
    if (_color != color) {
        [_color release];
        _color = [color retain];
    }
}
- (NSColor *) color {
    return _color;
```

```
} // color

- (void) setSize: (int) size {
    _size = size;
} // setSize
- (int) size {
    return _size;
} // size
```

This code sidesteps issues relating to atomicity or exception handling. Still, that is a lot of boilerplate code. There are utilities that will take a class definition and generate the setters and getters for you, but these are still lines of code that have to be maintained. Properties push the work of creating this repetitive code into the compiler. The equivalent code with Objective-C 2.0 properties looks like this:

```
@interface LotusBlossom : NSObject {
    NSString *_name;
    NSColor *_color;
    int _size;
}
@property (copy) NSString *name;
@property (retain) NSColor *color;
@property (assign) int size;

@end // LotusBlossom (properties)

@implementation LotusBlossom
@synthesize name = _name;
@synthesize color = _color;
@synthesize size = _size;

- (void) dealloc {
    [_name release];
    [_color release];

    [super dealloc];
} // dealloc

- (NSString *) description {
    return [NSString stringWithFormat: @"blossom %@ : %@ / %d",
                        _name, _color, _size];
} // description

@end // LotusBlossom(properties)
```

Notice the use of underscores in instance variable names and the "assignment" in the @synthesize directive. This is not a required style, but a common one chosen to remove a source of errors. If the instance variable is the same as the property, it is very easy to use the instance variable, say name directly rather than referencing the property, say self.name, leading to inconsistent use of accessors. By prepending underscores to instance variables, there is no name, making it obvious when an instance variable is being accessed via _name and a property, via self.name.

Properties also add a new syntactic element to Objective-C 2.0: the dot operator. When used with an object pointer, the dot operator is the equivalent of using setters and getters:

```
LotusBlossom *blossom = [[LotusBlossom alloc] init];
blossom.name = @"Hoff";
blossom.color = [NSColor whiteColor];
blossom.size = 23;
```

```
NSLog (@"%@ of color %@ has size %d",
       blossom.name, blossom.color, blossom.size);
```

The dot notation can be used independently of properties. You can even use the above code with the first **LotusBlossom** class declaration that explicitly listed declarations for the setters and getters.

The use of the dot operator does not cause ambiguity with the language. You cannot use it with a pointer, so stealing it for properties lets Objective-C 2.0 clean up the general syntax.

Properties introduce three new directives: @property, which declares the contract the property declares: its name, its type, and how it behaves with respect to memory management. @synthesize is an optional way of telling the compiler to automatically create the accessor implementation at compile-time. The compiler requires implementation of the methods, whether through your explicit implementation, @synthesize, or some combination. Use @dynamic to tell the compiler to trust you that the accessor methods will be there at runtime, perhaps through some toolkit magic or loaded from a shared library.

There are four classes of parameters that @property provides:

Mutability: whether the property is immutable (readonly) or mutable (readwrite, the default)

Memory management: whether setting the property is a simple assignment (assign, the default), requires a retain (retain), or requires a copy (copy). For objects like delegates, you would use assign; for other object references, you would use retain or copy. You should copy strings unless there is a good reason not to. It is very easy for a mutable string to find its way into a graph of objects, especially if you are getting strings from user interface classes. The copy operation is a no-op for immutable strings, so you will not be paying a copy penalty for immutable strings. In a garbage collected world, assign and retain are both strong references.

Concurrency: In a garbage collected (GC) world, assignments to properties are atomic for free. There is no chance that another thread will see your assignment in-progress, even for complex types like C structs. In a non-GC world, assignments via properties are atomic, but it comes at a price of using an implicit lock when accessing the property. If you are in a non-GC program, noticing performance problems with properties, and accessing the properties in a single thread, then you can use nonatomic to suppress the use of these locks. Plain structure value assignments via the = operator are never atomic. If you assign a struct in an accessor and you want the operation to be atomic, you will need to provide explicit locking. For performance reasons on iOS, you should make all of your properties nonatomic unless you have a reason not to.

API control: By default, a property will use the property name as the name of the getter, and the name of the property prepended by "set" as the name of the setter. For example, for the property duration, the accessor names would be **-duration** and **-setDuration:**. You can override these with setter= and getter=. The methods you supply have to have the proper types for argument and return values.

Some examples:

```
@property (readonly) NSString *name;
```

name is an **NSString**, and it can only be read, not written.

```
@property (assign) id delegate;
```

delegate can be read and changed. It is a simple pointer assignment and not retained in a non-GC world.

```
@property (nonatomic, copy) NSString *foobage;
```

foobage can be read and changed, and when the property is changed, the string will be copied. It is non-atomic, so only set/get it in a single thread.

A subclass or a class extension can change a property from readonly to readwrite. This allows for mutable subclasses and private testing methods to change a property.

@synthesize is used to generate accessors. You can optionally tell @synthesize to use a particular instance variable to read or write; otherwise it will use an instance variable named after the property. The 32-bit (classic Objective-C) runtime requires that you declare the instance variables in the class @interface declaration. The 64-bit runtime does not require this. It will add the instance variable to the class at run-time.

Some examples:

```
@synthesize name;
```

This creates a **-name** method. Because name was declared readonly, no **-setName:** is created.

```
@synthesize delegate = hoobiedoo;
```

This creates **-delegate** and **-setDelegate:** methods, and the instance variable that holds the delegate value is called hoobiedoo. hoobiedoo is assigned the value of the new delegate, and it is not retained.

There was no @synthesize for foobage, so you are responsible for writing the **-foobage** and **-setFoobage:** methods and making sure that foobage has copy semantics. There is no compiler verification of this. It assumes we are upholding our end of the contract.

Lastly, there is @dynamic, which just takes the name of the property:

```
@dynamic someProperty;
```

@dynamic tells the compiler not to look for or generate setters or getters for the property. Instead, you will provide them at runtime somehow. You might load a dynamic library that contains the implementation. In addition to the **-forwardInvocation:** method, **NSObject** also has added two new methods, **+resolveInstanceMethod** and **+resolveClassMethod**. Each takes a SEL and returns a BOOL. A class gets a chance to resolve a missing method and add it dynamically to the class at run-time before the forwarding machinery takes over. One of the **+resolve** calls will be invoked, and it has the chance of using the Objective-C runtime functions to add a method to a class. The **+resolve** are much faster than using **-forwardInvocation:**. Core Data also takes advantage of this mechanism to map properties to Core Data attributes.

Exercises

1. Use @dynamic, **+resolveInstanceMethod**, and the **class_addMethod()** function to add a property implementation method at runtime. Manipulating the Objective-C runtime is not covered here, but you can find out about this in Apple's Objective-C 2.0 Runtime Reference.

2. Measure the performance of atomic and nonatomic properties in garbage collected and non-garbage collected environments. Are there real performance differences?

3. The requirement that collections not mutate while you are iterating over them can be inconvenient at times, especially if you are doing a "scan the collection and pull out stuff that shouldn't be there"

operation. What would it take to make a classic array enumerator support having the collection mutated during iteration? What impact would this have on fast enumeration?

4. C99, the current version of C, as well as Objective-C, have the `restrict` keyword. What does it do?

5. **FibonacciSequence** rapidly exceeds the range of values an `unsigned long` can hold, which is why the code here cheats and stops after 40 iterations. One way to fix this (or at least allow us to get farther into the sequence) would be to use more of the extra values in the NSFastEnumerationState structure. `long longs` may get you farther, as might the **NSDecimal** functions or the **NSDecimalNumber** class. There are also "BigNum" libraries out on the Internet that provide numbers of arbitrary size.

2

The Compiler

The compiler is the fundamental tool in your programming arsenal. No matter what editor you use for source code and no matter if you build your programs with Xcode or **make**, the compiler is involved. Apple ships the *GNU Compiler Collection* with the developer tools. You can invoke the compiler with the **gcc** command, but you can also use the **cc** command.

The Mac OS X 10.4 and 10.5 development tools include **gcc** versions 3.3 and 4.0. You can use the older compiler if you have code that will not compile with the newer compiler or if you need to support versions of Mac OS X prior to version 10.3.9. **gcc** 4.2 is the default for 10.6 and is incompatible with the 10.4 (and earlier) SDKs. Also, **gcc** 4.2 is the minimum compiler you can use with Xcode 4, so you can't use the latest Xcode to build applications for 10.4.

Apple has been working on its own compiler technology for some time through the LLVM (Low-Level Virtual Machine) project. LLVM technology has been used behind the OpenGL Shader Language and OpenCL on the Mac. **clang** is a front-end to LLVM that parses C code. You can use **clang** to parse the code and use the LLVM or **gcc** back-ends to generate the object code. The **clang** front-end generates much better errors and warnings than **gcc** does. The Xcode static analyzer is based on **clang**. For maximal compatibility, you would use **gcc** for everything. To get the better errors and warnings, plus faster compile times, you can use "LLVM **gcc**," which uses the **clang** parser and the **gcc** code generation. Use the "LLVM compiler" to get all of the new goodies.

gcc supports a number of languages. The C-dialect languages are the ones that are used for typical Mac OS X development. The extension of the source file tells the compiler what dialect to use:

.c	Regular C
.m	Objective-C
.C	C++ (but do not use on HFS+ file systems since it is not case sensitive)
.cpp, .cc	C++
.mm	Objective-C++, a blend of C++ and Objective-C

Handy Flags

The documentation for **gcc** is included with Xcode. Beware that **gcc** is huge and comes with lots of options, lots of features, lots of flags, and lots of extensions to the languages it compiles. It also has lots of cool stuff. Here are some command-line flags that you might find useful. You can control a number of these settings in Xcode, but not all of **gcc**'s flags are exposed via the GUI. You would need to add them in the Other C Flags or Other C++ Flags configuration.

-g	Add debugging symbols. Turn this on using the Level of Debug Symbols in Xcode's Build tab in the Project or Target info panel.
-E	See preprocessor output. You can tell Xcode to preprocess a file by using the Preprocess menu item in the contextual menu in the Xcode 3 code editor. This menu item also lives in the Build menu. As of this writing, Xcode 4 has moved it to the Generated Output portion of the assistant.
-S	See generated assembly code.
-save-temps	Keep temporary files around.
-Wall, -Wmost	Show more warnings.
-Werror	Treat warnings as errors. Turn this on by checking Treat Warnings as Errors in Xcode's Build tab in the Project or Target info panel.
-DSYMBOL	#define from the command line.
-DSYMBOL=value	#define with a value from the command line. You can tweak the macro settings by editing Preprocessor Macros in Xcode's Build tab in the Project or Target info panel.
-O#	Set optimization levels (described below). Use the Optimization Level setting in the Project or Target info panel's Build tab to control this in Xcode.
-std	Choose a standard, or non-standard, C dialect. Supplying -std=c99 will give you C99, which adds several **gcc** extensions and C++ features to the language but disallows any additional **gcc** extensions. You can also use -std=gnu99 to get both C99 and **gcc**'s extensions.

Debugging

The -g flag enables debugging symbols, which are chunks of extra data that allow debugging tools to map an arbitrary address in your executable code back to the source that generated it. It also contains information about your types, variable names, and data structures. Enabling debugging symbols can make your program bigger and may also expose some implementation details that you might prefer to be hidden. The **strip** command will remove these symbols, and Xcode provides a number of options for controlling symbol stripping.

The downside of stripping your executables, or not building your application with -g in the first place, means that you will not have symbolic stack traces when debugging in the field and you will not be able to easily analyze crash reporter stack traces that people email you.

If you held on to a version of your application prior to stripping, you can use the **atos** command to map addresses back to program symbols. You can also hang on to the external dSYM and feed it to **atos**. It is always a good idea to use -g during development because -g only adds debugging symbols and does not affect the code generation.

The Apple development tools support two different debug symbol information formats: Stabs and DWARF. Stabs was the default for older Xcodes, and DWARF is the default for Xcode 3 and beyond.

Warnings

Compiler warnings are a good thing. If the compiler is complaining about something you wrote, most likely your code has something questionable that could lead to errors somewhere down the line. A good goal to strive for is to have your code always compile cleanly without warnings. -Wall will show a lot of warnings for most everything the **gcc** developers consider questionable. -Wmost is a good middle ground when using the Cocoa frameworks.

Specific warnings can be independently turned on and off based on your specific coding style. Say you are using a library that uses macros that leave unused variables lying around. Messy, but pretty much harmless since the compiler won't allocate space for them. Example 2.1 shows some warnings when compiling.

Example 2.1   warning.m

```
// warning.m -- show generation of compiler warnings

// gcc -Wall -o warning warning.m

int main (int argc, char *argv) {
    int i;
} // main
```

Then if you build it:

```
$ gcc -Wall -o warning warning.m
warning.m:5: warning: second argument of 'main' should be 'char **'
warning.m: In function 'main':
warning.m:6: warning: unused variable 'i'
warning.m:7: warning: control reaches end of non-void function
```

Two of those warnings are really interesting since they are actually errors: The parameters to **main()** are messed up, and nothing is being returned from **main()**. But (in this case) the unused variable is not a show-stopper. Fix the code otherwise:

```
int main (int argc, char *argv[]) {
    int i;
    return 0;
} // main
```

```
$ gcc -Wall warning.m
warning.m: In function `main':
warning.m:6: warning: unused variable 'i'
```

You can turn that warning off with

```
$ gcc -Wall -Wno-unused warning.m
(no complaints)
```

You will still get other warnings if you make mistakes. If you wanted to only see warnings for unused variables and no others, use -Wunused (drop the no-):

```
$ gcc -Wunused warning.m
warning.m: In function `main':
warning.m:9: warning: unused variable `i'
```

The **gcc** documentation has the full set of warnings described in detail.

If you have a file that has warnings that you want to ignore, but you do not want to turn them off project-wide, you can add per-file compiler flags in Xcode. For Xcode 3, select the source file in the Compile Sources phase of the target section of your Xcode project, choose Get Info, and then add your compiler flags to the build tab of the info window. The important thing to remember is that you set this deep in your target, not on your source file up in your source file Xcode groups.

Xcode 4 has moved this feature to the Build Phases tab for your target. Expand Compile Sources and enter the compiler flags for the source file.

It is worth your time to reduce your warning count. If you have a lot of warnings that you "just ignore all the time," useful warnings will get lost in the noise. It is best to either fix them or suppress the ones you consider useless. Treating warnings as errors is an excellent way to enforce good warning discipline.

And lastly, for a quick syntax check and no code generation, give **gcc** the -fsyntax-only flag.

Seeing Preprocessor Output

Sometimes you get an inscrutable error and have no idea why the compiler is complaining. Or you may have code that looks reasonable and compiles OK, but it behaves in a way that defies sanity even when you take the phase of the moon into account. This is a good time to examine the preprocessor's output so you can see *exactly* what the compiler is seeing. The -E flag tells **gcc** to send the preprocessed source code to standard out. You can use Xcode 3's Preprocess command as well, or Xcode 4's generated output.

Example 2.2 looks simple enough. It will read a line from standard in and print it back out.

Example 2.2   preprocTest.m

```
// preprocTest.m -- a program to show preprocessor output

// cc -g -Wall -o preprocTest preprocTest.m
// or
// cc -g -Wall -E preprocTest.m > junk.i
// (and then look at junk.i)

#import <stdio.h>

#define BUFFER_SIZE 2048

int main (int argc, char *argv[]) {
    char buffer[BUFFER_SIZE];   /* this is my buffer, there are many like it */
    char *thing;

    thing = fgets (buffer, BUFFER_SIZE, stdin);
```

```
    printf ("%s", thing);

    /* happiness and light */
    return 0;

} // main
```

Compile it and run it:

```
$ gcc -g -Wall -o preprocTest preprocTest.m
$ ./preprocTest
hello[return]
hello
$
```

Now dig into its preprocessed output. Compile your program like this now:

```
$ gcc -Wall -E preprocTest.m > junk.i
```

This command tells **gcc** to preprocess the source file and write the results to `junk.i`, where the `.i` extension is for preprocessed output. `junk.i` will be a couple of hundred lines long due to the size and complexity of the header files it includes. Open it up in your favorite text editor and scroll to the end. You will see something like this:

```
int main (int argc, char *argv[]) {
    char buffer[2048];
    char *thing;

    thing = fgets (buffer, 2048, __stdinp);
    printf ("%s", thing);


    return 0;

}
```

It is somewhat recognizable as the original program. Notice that all the comments are gone. `#define BUFFER_SIZE 2048` is gone also, but you can see where 2048 has been substituted into the text stream. Notice that `stdin` has been expanded into `__stdinp`. What is that? Search in `junk.i` for it and find

```
extern FILE *__stdinp;
```

which is a `FILE` pointer. Because you are seeing exactly what the compiler is seeing, you can look at the guts of the `FILE` structure: all sorts of goodies like function pointers, buffers, and block size variables are in there. This is not the kind of information you would want your code to depend on, but it can be a big help when debugging. Plus, it's fun to dig into things, see how they work, and see how things change over time.

It is useful to view the preprocessed output when you are debugging macros. Write your macro, run it through the preprocessor, and see if it has the effect you want.

Seeing the Generated Assembly Code

The real hard-core hackers can look at the assembly code generated by the compiler. Sometimes you need this to track down compiler problems or OS problems. Or you can browse around just for general amusement and education. To get the assembly code, compile with the -S flag, and the results will be put into an .s file based on the name of your source file. For instance, running

```
$ gcc -g -Wall -S preprocTest.m
```

will create a preprocTest.s. If you want to assemble the resulting file, feed it to the compiler like this:

```
$ gcc -o preprocTest preprocTest.s
```

Xcode 3 provides a Show Assembly Code item in the editor's contextual menu so you can see what your code will assemble into. Xcode 4 has removed this feature, as of this writing.

You can also use **otool** to disassemble existing programs if you do not want to muck around with compiler flags or finding an installer for Xcode 3. This command will disassemble **preprocTest**:

```
$ otool -t -V preprocTest
...
_main:
0000000100000e94        pushq   %rbp
0000000100000e95        movq    %rsp,%rbp
0000000100000e98        subq    $0x00000830,%rsp
0000000100000e9f        movl    %edi,0xfffff7dc(%rbp)
0000000100000ea5        movq    %rsi,0xfffff7d0(%rbp)
0000000100000eac        movq    0x00000185(%rip),%rax
0000000100000eb3        movq    (%rax),%rdx
0000000100000eb6        movq    %rdx,0xf8(%rbp)
0000000100000eba        xorl    %edx,%edx
0000000100000ebc        movq    0x0000017d(%rip),%rax
0000000100000ec3        movq    (%rax),%rdx
0000000100000ec6        leaq    0xfffff7f0(%rbp),%rdi
0000000100000ecd        movl    $0x00000800,%esi
0000000100000ed2        callq   0x100000f1e    ; symbol stub for: _fgets
...
```

If you want to save all the intermediate elements, including some not covered here, you can use the -save-temps flag.

Compiler Optimization

There are two classes of argument flags for controlling optimization, which controls how the compiler generates machine code from your C code, as well as how it rewrites your code to behave more optimally. You can use -O with a number or letter to control the optimization level.

-O0   Do no optimizations.

-O1   Do some optimization (also what's used if you use -O without a number).

-O2 and -O3   Use yet more aggressive optimization.

-Os   Optimize for size. It does the same optimizations as -O2 but doesn't do function inlining.

Higher optimization levels can make code unstable as more and more mechanical operations happen to it, so be sure to test when changing levels. Sometimes failures that happen at higher optimization levels can actually be indications of programming errors, so if you have the time, it may be worthwhile to pursue any failures that happen at higher optimization levels.

If you know of specific optimizations that you want to enable or disable, like strength reduction or common subexpression evaluation, you can turn them on or off individually. For example:

`-fstrength-reduce`	Enables strength reduction.
`-fno-strength-reduce`	Turns off strength reduction, even if the `-O#` setting would have it enabled otherwise.

The **gcc** documentation describes all the available control flags, and there are a lot of them.

Having an optimization level set to `-O2` or higher will issue a warning (when `-Wall` is engaged) if a variable is used before initialization. The compiler needs to do flow analysis to determine if this happens, and that analysis only happens with `-O` levels of 2 or higher.

gcc supports both `-g` (debugging) and `-O` (optimization) at the same time. This combination has historically been unsupported in C compilers. This means you can use **gdb** on an optimized program, but there may be unexpected behavior because code can be re-ordered and variables may be eliminated. For example, single-stepping through some code in the debugger can make your "current line" indicator bounce all over the place when you are dealing with code that has been run through the optimizer.

Apple recommends using `-Os` to optimize for size, even on fast new machines. It might not produce the best optimization for a specific program, but it gives the best overall system performance since the system working set seems to be a big constraint on performance, as well letting more code live in the processor caches.

GCC Extensions

One of the constants of GNU products is a huge number of features. **gcc** has an incredible number of extensions available. They can help improve your code, but they can also destroy portability if you target a platform that does not have **gcc** or you are not using **gcc** on Mac OS X.

Here are a handful of interesting extensions:

* `long long` and `unsigned long long`: quadword (i.e., 64-bit) integers are treated as first class citizens. You can perform basic math (+,-,*,/), modular arithmetic, and bitwise operations with them.

* Complex numbers: in C++ you can create complex numbers as a first class type, but **gcc** C has them built in.

* Variable length automatic arrays: like you can use in C++, declaring the size of a stack-based array at runtime:

```
int size = some_function();
char buffer[size];
```

The array also gets deallocated when the brace level the array was declared in is exited.

* Inline functions (like in C++).

- Macros with variable number of arguments, very handy for wrappers around **printf** and friends.

- Packed structures, which remove any alignment padding the compiler might otherwise include. Add `__attribute((packed))` at the end of your structure definition.

A number of these extensions have made their way into C99, the most recent version of the ISO C standard, such as variable automatic arrays and complex numbers. Also, Objective-C with the **gcc** compiler lets you declare variables anywhere, just like in C++.

Name Mangling

C++ uses name mangling for doing typesafe linking. The compiler encodes type information in a function's name, which can lead to unreadable error messages or indecipherable output from Unix tools like **nm** You might be poking around an object file and see something like this:

```
$ nm slidemaster.o
...
00000030 s EH_frame1
         U __ZN12BigNerdRanch7BigShow5Slide13DisplayInViewEP7BigView
         U ___gxx_personality_v0
...
```

That "__ZN12BigNerdRanch..." symbol looks interesting. Here it is made human readable:

```
$ c++filt __ZN12BigNerdRanch7BigShow5Slide13DisplayInViewEP7BigView
BigNerdRanch::BigShow::Slide::DisplayInView(BigView*)
```

Testing the compiler version

gcc supplies a number of preprocessor macros that you can use in your code to test what version of the compiler you are using and enable or disable code based on it. For instance, you could use long doubles if the code is being compiled with **gcc** 4 but fall back and use regular doubles on **gcc** 3. The version macros are:

__GNUC__	The major revision number. For gcc 4.0.1, __GNUC__ would be 4.
__GNUC_MINOR__	The minor revision number. For gcc 4.0.1, __GNUC_MINOR__ would be 0.
__GNUC_PATCHLEVEL__	The patch level number. For gcc 4.0.1, __GNUC_PATCHLEVEL__ would be 1.

The Optimizer

The optimizer gets changed and improved with every **gcc** version, as well as with new versions of **clang**/LLVM. Many of the same optimizer flags work as they did before, and new flags are added. It is entirely possible there are compiler bugs related to aggressive optimization of correct code. As with any change to the toolchain for building a program, it pays to do appropriate testing to make sure new problems are not introduced when upgrading your compiler.

-O0 is for no optimization and a maximally debuggable application. -O is a tradeoff of compile speed and execution speed. -O2 performs the optimizations that do not involve a space-for-time tradeoff, but it does attempt function inlining when specified. -O3 is best for code that makes heavy use of loops and lots of computation. It considers all functions in the current compilation unit (source file) for inlining, even those not declared inline. -Os optimizes for code size rather than speed. There is no loop unrolling, but performance should still be about -O2 levels. Apple still recommends using -Os, which will lead to smaller executables, so there will be less paging from disk for large programs, plus more code will fit in the processor's caches.

-fast is an optimization flag that changes the overall optimization strategy for **gcc**. The optimizations happen at the expense of code size. -fast sets the optimization level to -O3, enables a number of optimization flags, and ignores all other flags, except for those that specify the target architecture.

-fastcp, doesn't do anything different than -fast in **gcc** 4.0 and is for C++ users only. It may change in the future to add optimizations to C++ code. -fastf is for C code made from fortran-to-C translators or if your code has fortran semantics.

The -fast family of flags can break IEEE-754 conformance for floating point math. Round-off errors can grow if you are doing lots of calculations, so you will need to decide if your floating point calculations need IEEE-754's guarantees of accuracy. It also changes the alignment mode of data types, which affects the layout of members of a struct. This can create binary compatibility issues. Code compiled with -fast cannot always be linked against code compiled without it.

Vectorization

gcc 4.0 also includes an autovectorizer. The compiler attempts to convert code, such as loops or sequences of similar operations over chunks of data, into code for the vector processor, such as PowerPC's Altivec, or Intel's SSE2/SSE3. To use the vectorizer, you need to supply the -ftree-vectorize compiler flag. This only works at optimization levels -O2 or higher because **gcc** only computes a probable data flow graph using -O2 and higher.

-ftree-vectorize also enables the -fstrict-aliasing which lets the compiler make some assumptions based on the type of expressions it sees. In particular, an object of one type is assumed never to reside at the same address as an object of a different type unless they are "almost the same." An unsigned int can alias an int, but not a pointer or a double. Doing something like taking the address of an int and storing a double there breaks this strict-aliasing assumption. The -Wstrict-aliasing flag will cause the compiler to emit warnings about most places that might break the strict aliasing rules.

Even More Compiler Flags

gcc has always had a lot of command-line flags that can control many aspects of the compiler, such as the dialect of the language being compiled, the manipulations performed on the resulting object code, and controlling what warnings are emitted.

In Xcode, you can pass these flags to the compiler by setting the Other C Flags (for optimization and other general flags) and Other Warning Flags (for flags related to warnings) in the target inspector. The warning flags are placed before the other C flags in case there is an order dependency between a set of flags.

Here are some flags that might be of interest to you:

-Wno-protocol

This flag makes Objective-C's @protocol feature more useful in some circumstances. The default behavior of @protocol is to issue a warning for every method declared in the protocol that is not defined in the class that is adopting the protocol, even if the methods are implemented by a superclass. By giving **gcc** this flag, methods from the superclass will be considered to be implemented, and no warning will be issued.

-fobjc-call-cxx-cdtors

Objective-C++ has had a limitation regarding C++ objects that are embedded in Objective-C objects: constructors for the C++ objects never get called when the Objective-C object was allocated and initialized. The whole block of memory for the Objective-C object was zeroed as usual by the **alloc** method, and so the C++ object also was cleared out to all zeros. But its constructor is not called. This means the C++ object might be in a broken state having not been constructed properly. Likewise, destructors were never invoked on the embedded C++ object when the Objective-C object is deallocated, so the C++ object could leak memory. You could work around this by using a pointer to a C++ object and allocating it with **new**.

By adding this flag, the compiler will create a pair of Objective-C methods (called **.cxx_construct** and **.cxx_destruct**) that are called by the Objective-C runtime to construct and destruct the C++ objects.

-Wundeclared-selector

This flag tells the compiler to warn you if you use a @selector() that it has not seen yet. You might have an **NSTimer** callback method called **-moveMonsterTowardsPlayer:**, and you accidentally use @selector(moveMonsterToPlayer:). The compiler will issue a warning if you use this flag. Needless to say, this can save you some headaches by catching typos at compile time rather than runtime.

-Q

This last one is purely for geeky fun. It tells the compiler to display the name of functions and methods as they are compiled, along with random statistics about the compilation:

```
-[BWCrossStitchList addStitch:atRow:column:]
-[BWCrossStitchList markRemovedAtRow:column:]
-[BWCrossStitchList changeEnumerator]
-[BWCrossStitchList isChangeAtRow:column:]
-[BWCrossStitchList count]

Execution times (seconds)
  preprocessing      :    0.02 ( 1%) wall
  lexical analysis   :    0.01 ( 0%) wall
  parser             :    0.98 (61%) wall
  tree gimplify      :    0.01 ( 1%) wall
  expand             :    0.01 ( 1%) wall
  global alloc       :    0.02 ( 1%) wall
  final              :    0.01 ( 0%) wall
```

```
symout              :   0.05 ( 3%) wall
TOTAL               :             1.61
```

64-Bit Computing

Mac OS X 10.4 introduced 64-bit computing to the Mac platform. 64-bit computing means that a process can directly address more than the 4 gig address space that 32-bit computing allows. The process might not actually *get* more than 4 gigs of memory to play with, but it will have the extra address space. That depends on what the user has installed in the machine, per-process limits, different operating system settings, and so on.

How much bigger is the 64-bit address space compared to the 32-bit one? A common analogy is this: if a byte is a dot the size of the period at the end of this sentence, then a 32-bit address space would cover the surface of the Golden Gate Bridge. A 64-bit address space would cover the entire land surface of the Earth.

Mac OS X supports 64-bit programming while using a 32-bit kernel. The kernel itself does not need to address huge chunks of memory directly, so it can easily run in a 32-bit address space. The data structures it manipulates can be 64-bit, so it can support a 64-bit program. This means that there is just one version of Mac OS X that users will be running, and no need for them to install a special 64-bit version of the OS to take advantage of 64-bit applications.

There is a 64-bit Mac OS X kernel available, which is 64-bit top to bottom. It can still run 32-bit applications fine. The main reason to run the 64-bit kernel is when you have a large amount of physical RAM, exceeding 32 gigabytes. The in-memory tables for managing the memory start consuming more and more of the 32-bit kernel's address space, leaving less room for things like the file system cache. Note that all kernel extensions will need to be rebuilt for a 64-bit kernel. Some tools, such as the Shark profiler, do not work at all with the 64-bit kernel.

The 64-bit programming model

The 64-bit programming model used by Mac OS X is called LP64. This means that longs and pointers are 64 bits, while ints remain 32 bits. long long is still 64 bits. Unix systems, including Linux, use an LP64 model. In comparison, Windows is LLP64. In LLP64, long long is 64 bits, as are pointers, but ints and longs remain 32 bits. This is something to keep in mind if you have a cross-platform code base.

Code compiled with the 32-bit model is not compatible with code compiled with the 64-bit model. There are changes to the Mach-O ABI to support 64-bit computing. bools are still one byte in size, and the alignment in structs is "natural," so fields will be padded so that the pointers are 8-byte aligned. Calling conventions in code differs between 32-bit and 64-bit. 64-bit code on Intel has access to many more registers, so more kinds of structs are passed by value in registers.

This also means that 64-bit programs can only use 64-bit frameworks. Mac OS X 10.4 only supplied 64-bit versions of the System and Accelerate frameworks. None of the user interface frameworks were supplied in a 64-bit version. Also, only C and C++ were supported in Tiger 64-bit code, not Objective-C. Supplying a user interface to your 64-bit programs required you to split the program into 32-bit client part and a 64-bit server part and then have them communicate via shared memory, sockets, pipes, or some other IPC mechanism.

OS X 10.5 and beyond have 64-bit versions of the system frameworks, meaning that you can have a 64-bit Cocoa application. There are some things that are 32-bit only, such as parts of QuickTime and the user interface portions of Carbon, and there are API differences with some deprecated calls and classes being unavailable in 64-bit mode.

Because you cannot mix 32-bit and 64-bit code, you cannot use 32-bit plugins in a 64-bit program. There is also a code impact from the change in the sizes of the primitive data types.

When using interprocess communication, networking, and binary data files, you should be careful when you choose your data types. Explicitly sized data types, like uint32_t, will stay the same size in both 32-bit and 64-bit worlds and are more predictable than generic types, like long, which can change sizes

Alignment of data also changes between the two worlds. Pointers and longs will need to have 64-bit rather than 32-bit alignment which can make structures larger. The general rule of thumb is putting larger elements early on in the structure. That should give you good use of space vs. padding caused by data alignment.

64-bit cleanliness

Be careful of mixing 64-bit (long) and 32-bit (int) values. You can get unexpected results like truncation of values. If you assign a pointer to a 64-bit long, pass it as a 32-bit int function argument, and convert the function result back into a pointer, then the upper 4 bytes will be stripped off due to the smaller int argument.

If you are seeing problems with data truncation, try using the -Wconversion compiler flag. This flag will cause the compiler to warn you about any data conversions it thinks are suspect. This will generate warnings for some legitimate conversions, but it will be a place to start looking for the problem.

There are also some pre-defined types to hold values that might overflow an int:

uintptr_t	Use this as the destination when casting between 64-bit pointers and integer types.
ptrdiff_t	An integer sufficiently large to hold the result of pointer arithmetic.
size_t	The type that sizeof returns. This has become a 64-bit value.
fpos_t	An integer sufficiently large to hold a file position. This type is primarily used with the standard C library, such as with **fgetpos()**.
off_t	An integer sufficiently large to hold a file offset. This type is used by system calls, such as **lseek()**.

Also, never assume you know the size of any type or structure. Always use sizeof.

The OS helps you catch some pointer truncation errors by making the first four gigabytes of a 64-bit process' address space to be one huge zero page. Any attempt to read, write, or execute from this address range will result in a program crash. This forces all of your 64-bit pointers to have significant bits in the upper four bytes, causing any pointer truncation to end up with a value of zero there, at least when using Intel processors.

Bitmasks of type long have some gotchas. By default, masks expressed in code as constants are treated as an unsigned int, meaning that any significant digits implicitly added by the compiler will be zeros.

That is fine if you want zeros in the upper bits of your mask. If you want ones in the upper part of your mask, you'll want to write the mask as the bitwise inverse of the mask's inverse. If you're wanting the mask 0xfffc to be sign-extended through all 64 bits, you'll want to do something like the second line. The first line shows you what bitmask would result without using this inversion trick:

```
0xfffffffc // 0x00000000fffffffc (64 bits)
~0x3       // 0xfffffffc (32 bits) or 0xfffffffffffffffc (64 bits)
```

Be careful of making assumptions about how many bits are in a `long` if you are shifting through its bits. Use the `LONG_BIT` constant to figure out the number of bits involved.

Cocoa on Leopard introduces the `NSInteger` and `NSUInteger` types. These are primitive types that are 32 bits wide in 32-bit code and 64 bits wide in 64-bit code. Most of the integral types used as Cocoa method and function parameters have been changed to be `NS[U]Integer`s. Even though it is called "NSInteger," these are not classes like **NSNumber**.

So why introduce these new types? Prior to 64-bit support, Cocoa methods took and returned integer values using native C types. `-[NSArray count]` returns an unsigned int, for instance. This return value would be 32 bits in LP64. It would be nice to be able to accept and return larger values. The Cocoa team could either change all `int`s to `long`s, but that would break 32-bit binary compatibility. By introducing a layer of abstraction with the `NS[U]Integer` types, Apple can build Cocoa with 32-bit integer types for 32-bit land and maintain binary compatibility, and at the same time build Cocoa with 64-bit integers.

The `CGFloat` is the floating-point equivalent to `NSInteger`. It is a float (32 bits) in 32-bit code and a double (64 bits) in 64-bit code. Graphical quantities such as `NSRect` and `NSPoint` use `CGFloat`s now. In 64-bit code, `CGRect` and `NSRect` are identical, so there's no need to play typecast games when converting between `CGRect` and `NSRect`. You can define the preprocessor token `NS_BUILD_32_LIKE_64` to have your 32-bit code use these types.

Should you go 64-bit?

So, should you immediately go for 64 bits? Sure, if you need it now. For some developers, 64-bit computing will not have much of an immediate impact.

You truly *need* a 64-bit address space when you need random access to huge data objects (greater than 2 GiB) or you need concurrent access to a quantity of data that will not fit into a 32-bit address space, like multi-gig data modeling, data mining, web caches, large-scale 3D rendering, very large databases, etc.

If your app uses a streaming data access model, or just uses 64-bit integer math, you do not absolutely need 64-bit computing. You also don't need 64-bit computing when dealing with very large files. The file system API is capable of handling 64-bit offsets.

You may see some performance improvement going to 64 bits on Intel processors. The 64-bit ABI has more registers available to it (16 vs. 8), and the registers are wider (64 vs. 32 bits). The 64-bit calling conventions are also register-based rather than stack-based.

You will not see much, if any, performance improvement with 64-bit PowerPC, since the PowerPC family was designed from the outset for 64-bitness. If anything, you could see a performance decrease: 64-bit code is larger, and it deals with larger data, so cache misses will happen more often. Larger apps and larger data can require more memory and may end up paging if there is not enough physical RAM on the machine.

Instruction sequences to get an address or a constant into a register are longer in 64-bit code. And some situations, such as using a 32-bit signed integer as an array index, will require the value to be sign-extended on every access if it is not stored in a register.

On the other hand, most of the applications shipped by Apple are 64-bit native, with iTunes being the main holdout. If your app is 32-bits, and no other 32-bit applications are running, the system will need to load all of the 32-bit frameworks it uses, which will increase overall system memory usage and delay your launch time.

New Objective-C runtime

Apple has upgraded the Objective-C runtime for 64-bit programming. This new runtime is also used on iOS.

The new runtime solves the *fragile base class problem* for Objective-C. When you access instance variables in Objective-C, the compiler turns the reference into a pointer+offset operation. Each instance variable lives at a fixed offset from the beginning of the object. Subclasses can add instance variables, which just get stuck at the end of the object structure. This makes it impossible for the base class to add or remove any instance variables or change the size of any of them (say, to move from 32-bit to 64-bit pointers). The new runtime solves this problem by waiting until runtime to calculate the instance variable offsets.

This means you can't think of an Objective-C object as a fixed-size struct. If, for whatever reason, you were using **sizeof()** against an object, you would need to make another call such as **class_getInstanceSize()**. Similarly, **offsetof()**, which gives you the offset from the base pointer for an instance variable, must be replaced by a runtime call like **ivar_getOffset()**. Also, the @defs operator, which gives you the instance variable layout for a class, is no longer useful.

The new runtime adds stricter instance variable access control. Before, you could access @private instance variables. With the modern runtime, you can get a link error if you try directly accessing an instance variable of an object in a different framework.

Universally Fat Binaries

Mach-O supports "fat" files, officially called "universal" files by Apple. These let you have PowerPC, Intel, and the 32-bit and 64-bit flavors of each kind of code in the same file. This allows for a single application or a single framework to service all the computing worlds.

Fat binaries from the command line

You can use **gcc** on the command-line, or in makefiles, to generate object code for any of the supported architectures. You can also build the final fat binaries using these command-line tools.

gcc's -arch flag controls which architecture(s) it should build. For Mac OS X, you can give -arch the ppc, i386, ppc64, and x86_64 flags. iOS is an ARM architecture, so you would use armv6 or armv7 if you were constructing your own **gcc** commands. armv7-capable processors appeared in the iPhone 3GS and later.

Example 2.3 sizeprinter.c

```
#include <stdio.h>  // for printf()

int main (void) {
    printf ("sizeof(int*) is %zu\n", sizeof(int*));

    return 0;

} // main
```

Compiling this code in 64-bit mode and running it on a 32-bit machine, such as a first-generation MacBook, will get you rejected:

```
macbook$ gcc -arch x86_64 -g -Wall -o sizeprinter sizeprinter.c
macbook$ ./sizeprinter
./sizeprinter: Bad CPU type in executable.
```

The program works fine when run on a 64-bit capable machine like a MacBookPro:

```
macpro$ ./sizeprinter
sizeof(int*) is 8
```

You will still get rejected if you try running it on the wrong architecture. In this case, an x86_64 executable on a G4:

```
g4$ ./sizeprinter
./sizeprinter: Bad CPU type in executable.
```

It is legal to run a PowerPC executable on Intel on Leopard, thanks to the Rosetta emulation technology. Snow Leopard has moved Rosetta to an optional install, so it might not be available on all user's machines.

```
macbook$ gcc -arch ppc -g -Wall -o sizeprinter sizeprinter.c
macbook$ ./sizeprinter
sizeof(int*) is 4
```

Rosetta does not support 64-bit PowerPC, just 32-bit.

An easy way to create a fat binary is to give **gcc** all of the architectures on the command line at once. Here is how to make a fat binary using the code from Example 2.3.

```
g4$ gcc -arch ppc -arch ppc64 -arch i386 -arch x86_64 \
    -g -Wall -o sizeprinter sizeprinter.c

g4$ ./sizeprinter
sizeof(int*) is 4
```

and the same executable run on a G5:

```
g5$ ./sizeprinter
sizeof(int*) is 8
```

and the same executable run on a 32-bit MacBook:

```
386$ ./sizeprinter
sizeof(int*) is 4
```

The **file** command will tell you about the fatness of a program:

```
$ file sizeprinter
sizeprinter: Mach-O universal binary with 4 architectures
sizeprinter (for architecture ppc7400): Mach-O executable ppc
sizeprinter (for architecture ppc64):   Mach-O 64-bit executable ppc64
sizeprinter (for architecture i386):     Mach-O executable i386
sizeprinter (for architecture x86_64):   Mach-O 64-bit executable x86_64
```

Your file actually gets compiled multiple times when you specify multiple architectures, and the resulting set of object code is merged into the output file. Example 2.4 uses some preprocessor macros to figure what mode the compiler is currently in. __ppc__ is defined when compiling in 32-bit PowerPC mode, __ppc64__ when compiling in PPC 64-bit mode, __i386__ when compiling for Intel 32-bit, and __x86_64__ when compiling for Intel 64-bit.

__LP64__ is defined when using the LP64 model, so it will be defined when __ppc64__ or __x86_64__ is defined. If you are mainly interested in whether you are compiling for 64 bits, use __LP64__ rather than one of the specific chip architecture symbols.

Example 2.4 uses the #warning preprocessor directive to tell us what chunks of code are being compiled at any particular point in time.

Example 2.4   fat-macro-warn.c

```
/* compile with
gcc -o fat-macro-warn fat-macro-warn.c
or
gcc -arch ppc64 -o fat-macro-warn fat-macro-warn.c
or
gcc -arch ppc64 -arch ppc -arch x86_64 \
    -arch i386 -o fat-macro-warn fat-macro-warn.c
*/

int main(void) {
#warning compiling the file

#ifdef __LP64__
#warning in LP64
#endif

#ifdef __ppc64__
#warning in __ppc64__
#endif

#ifdef __ppc__
#warning in __ppc__
#endif

#ifdef __i386__
#warning in __i386__
#endif

#ifdef __x86_64__
#warning in __x86_64__
#endif
    return 0;
} // main
```

Compiling it without extra flags on a G4 or G5 tells us the __ppc__ section gets compiled. On an Intel system, it will be compiling with __i386__ defined.

```
g4$ gcc -o fat-macro-warn fat-macro-warn.c
fat-macro-warn.c:12:2: warning: #warning compiling the file
fat-macro-warn.c:23:2: warning: #warning in __ppc__
```

Compiling it with -arch ppc64 tells us it finds the __ppc64__ and __LP64__ sections:

```
g4$ gcc -arch ppc64 -o fat-macro-warn fat-macro-warn.c
fat-macro-warn.c:12:2: warning: #warning compiling the file
fat-macro-warn.c:15:2: warning: #warning in LP64
fat-macro-warn.c:19:2: warning: #warning in __ppc64__
```

And, finally, here is compiling for all four architectures at once:

```
% gcc -arch ppc64 -arch ppc -arch x86_64 -arch i386 -o fat-macro-warn fat-macro-warn.c
fat-macro-warn.c:12:2: warning: #warning compiling the file
fat-macro-warn.c:23:2: warning: #warning in __ppc__
fat-macro-warn.c:12:2: warning: #warning compiling the file
fat-macro-warn.c:15:2: warning: #warning in LP64
fat-macro-warn.c:19:2: warning: #warning in __ppc64__
fat-macro-warn.c:12:2: warning: #warning compiling the file
fat-macro-warn.c:27:2: warning: #warning in __i386__
fat-macro-warn.c:12:2: warning: #warning compiling the file
fat-macro-warn.c:15:2: warning: #warning in LP64
fat-macro-warn.c:31:2: warning: #warning in __x86_64__
```

Notice the order, or lack thereof; it changes on each invocation of the command. **gcc** is parallelizing the compilation. If you watch Xcode's build log, you can see that it actually compiles each architecture with its own command. This keeps the warnings and errors from becoming confusingly intermixed and also allows Xcode to apply per-architecture build settings. You do not have to compile multiple architectures at the same time. Instead, you can compile them separately and then use the **lipo** command to assemble them together into fat versions. "Lipo" comes from the Greek word for "fat," which is why "fat" has been used in this chapter.

Be aware that the term "Universal" means different things on Mac OS X and iOS. On Mac OS X, universal binaries have different independent chip binaries packaged together. Different code is run whether it is run on a G4 or a 64-bit Intel machine. On iOS, a universal app is one that runs both on the iPhone and the iPad, but it's same executable running on both devices. You make runtime checks to decide whether to enable iPad functionality and to choose whether to load iPhone or iPad nib files.

Continuing on with Example 2.3, here are steps that will create four object files and one fat binary. Here are the PowerPC versions:

```
$ gcc -arch ppc -g -o sizeprinter-32 sizeprinter.c
$ gcc -arch ppc64 -g -o sizeprinter-64 sizeprinter.c
```

And the Intel versions:

```
$ gcc -arch i386 -g -o sizeprinter-i32 sizeprinter.c
$ gcc -arch x86_64 -g -o sizeprinter-i64 sizeprinter.c
```

Join them with **lipo** and use the **file** command to verify the result is indeed a fat binary:

```
$ lipo -create -output sizeprinter-fat \
  sizeprinter-32 sizeprinter-64   sizeprinter-i32 sizeprinter-i64
$ file sizeprinter-fat
sizeprinter: Mach-O universal binary with 4 architectures
sizeprinter (for architecture ppc7400): Mach-O executable ppc
sizeprinter (for architecture ppc64):   Mach-O 64-bit executable ppc64
```

```
sizeprinter (for architecture i386):    Mach-0 executable i386
sizeprinter (for architecture x86_64):  Mach-0 64-bit executable x86_64
```

You can use the **posix_spawn()** function to control which architecture is run if you are launching your own process.

Fat binaries in Xcode

Xcode will of course let you create fat binaries in any permutation you want. The user interface for choosing which architectures to use seems to change with every Xcode version. Searching for "arch" in the Build Settings will get you to the place where you can make the settings.

Fat binary considerations

Even though Xcode makes it very easy to make *N*-way executables, the decision whether to go to a 2-way or 4-way fat binary is not one to take lightly because your testing matrix gets larger. A fat 32-bit executable requires testing both the Intel and PowerPC versions. You can do much of your 32-bit PowerPC testing in Rosetta on an Intel machine. Performance will be different, and it is good to test on a real live PowerPC machine to cover any unknown corner cases. Adding both 64-bit versions doubles the testing and verification burden.

Back during the Mac's first architecture transition (from the Motorola 68000 to PowerPC), there was a clever mixed mode system where a single executable could execute either kind of code. There is no "mixed mode" in OS X between the Intel and PowerPC worlds and the 32-bit and 64-bit worlds.

As mentioned before, this means that there are Intel and PowerPC, 32-bit and 64-bit versions of the system frameworks. If you have a have a bunch of 32-bit applications running and then you run a 64-bit program, all of the 64-bit frameworks will need to be brought into memory, which can take a noticeable amount of time on first launch, not to mention the additional memory consumption. Eventually all applications will be 64-bit, and 32-bit applications will become the bad guys, dragging in system frameworks that only they are using.

Also, you can run into issues if your program supports plug-ins. The plug-ins need to match the host application's architecture. If you ship a 4-way executable, then your plug-ins will need to be 4-way also. This may have an impact on any third parties that supply plug-ins.

Blocks

One shortcoming of C and Objective-C is code that performs a particular task becomes scattered around the code base. Say you are performing an operation on a C array of People structs and you need to sort the list by last name. Luckily, there is the library function **qsort()** to sort the array. **qsort()** is well-optimized and does its job well, but it needs some help. It does not know how items are compared to each other so that they end up in the proper sorted order.

```
...
qsort (peopleArray, count, sizeof(Person), personNameCompare);
...

int personNameCompare (const void *thing1, const void *thing2) {
    Person *p1 = (Person *) thing1;
    Person *p2 = (Person *) thing2;
    return strcmp(p1->lastName, p2->lastName);
} // compare
```

The compare function is not close to the invocation of **qsort()**. If you want to know exactly what the comparison is doing while you are reading or maintaining the code, you will need to find **personNameCompare()**, perhaps look at surrounding code, and then return to your original place.

Similarly, in Cocoa you frequently initiate some process that is handled in a place distant from the initial call, kicking asynchronous work that is completed in callbacks. Say the user pushes a button to load an image, and an **NSOpenPanel** is displayed:

```
- (IBAction) startImageLoad: (id) sender {
    NSOpenPanel *panel = [NSOpenPanel openPanel];
    ...
    [panel beginSheetForDirectory: nil
        ...
        modalDelegate: self
        didEndSelector: @selector(openPanelDidEnd:returnCode:contextInfo:)
        contextInfo: nil];
} // startImageLoad
```

The callback method is somewhere else in the source file:

```
- (void) openPanelDidEnd: (NSOpenPanel *) sheet
            returnCode: (int) code
            contextInfo: (void *) context {
    if (code == NSOKButton) {
        NSArray *filenames = [sheet filenames];
        // Do stuff with filenames.
    }
} // openPanelDidEnd
```

The initiation of the open panel is separated both in time and space from the handling of the open panel's results. You need to find a place to hide any data that needs to be communicated from one place to another, such as in a context parameter, instance variable, or global variable.

Wouldn't it be nice to have these auxiliary chunks of code near where they are being invoked? That way you can take in the entirety of an operation in a single screenful of code without having to hop around your codebase.

Blocks are a new feature added by Apple to the C family of languages, available in Mac OS X 10.6 and later and iOS 4.0 and later. Blocks allow you to put code that does work on behalf of other code in one place.

The **qsort()** function call would look this when expressed with blocks:

```
qsort_b (elements, count, sizeof(element),
        ^(const void *thing1, const void *thing2) {
            Person *p1 = (Person *) thing1;
            Person *p2 = (Person *) thing2;
            return strcmp(p1->lastName, p2->lastName);
        } );
```

The open panel code would look something like this:

```
[panel beginSheetModalForWindow: window
        // ...
        completionHandler: ^(NSInteger result) {
            if (result == NSOKButton) {
                NSArray *fileNames = [sheet filenames];
                // do stuff with fileNames
            }
        } ];
```

Block Syntax

A block is simply a piece of inline code. Here is an **NSBlockOperation** that logs a line of text when the operation is scheduled to run.

```
NSBlockOperation *blockop;
blockop = [NSBlockOperation blockOperationWithBlock: ^{
        NSLog (@"The operation block was invoked");
    }];
```

The block is introduced by the caret with the code of the block surrounded by braces. Bill Bumgarner from Apple said that the caret was chosen because "it is the only unary operator that cannot be overloaded in C++, and the snowman ☃ is out because we can't use unicode."

The code inside of the block is not executed at the same time as the function or method call that contains the block. The **NSLog** above will not be executed when the **NSBlockOperation** has been created; instead, it will be called at a later time when the operation is finally run.

Blocks can take arguments. **NSArray**'s **-enumerateObjectsUsingBlock:** will enumerate all objects in the array, invoking the block for each one. The block takes three parameters: the object to look at, the index of the object in the array, and a stop pointer to a BOOL. Setting *stop to YES will cause the iteration to cease before the array has been exhausted:

```
NSArray *array = [NSArray arrayWithObjects:
```

```
                    @"hi", @"bork",
                    @"badger", @"greeble",
                    @"badgerific", nil];

[array enumerateObjectsUsingBlock:
        ^(id object, NSUInteger index, BOOL *stop) {
      NSLog (@"object at index %d is %@", index, object);
    }];
```

will print:

```
  object at index 0 is hi
  object at index 1 is bork
  object at index 2 is badger
  object at index 3 is greeble
  object at index 4 is badgerific
```

Return Values

Blocks can also return values. The return type of the block can be specified after the caret, but if you omit it, the compiler will try to infer as much information about the return value as it can, allowing you to write more succinct code. This is a fully qualified block literal for **NSArray**'s **-indexesOfObjectsPassingTest:** method:

```
^BOOL (id object, NSUInteger index, BOOL *stop) { return YES; }
```

But you can reduce it a bit because the return type will be inferred:

```
^(id object, NSUInteger index, BOOL *stop) { return YES; }
```

A block that takes no arguments and returns no value can be drastically reduced:

```
^void (void) { ... }
^(void) { ... }
^{ ... };
```

All three are equivalent: a block that takes no arguments and returns no values.

Rather than printing out each element of the array, say you want to know which elements contain the word "badger." **-indexesOfObjectsPassingTest:** will invoke a block for each object in the array. It uses a return value of YES or NO to control whether that object's index is added to the index set that is ultimately returned.

```
NSIndexSet *indices =
    [array indexesOfObjectsPassingTest:
            ^(id object, NSUInteger index, BOOL *stop) {
          NSRange match = [object rangeOfString: @"badger"];
          if (match.location != NSNotFound) {
              return YES;
          } else {
              return NO;
          }
        }];

NSLog (@"%@", indices);
```

This prints:

```
<NSIndexSet> [number of indexes: 2 (in 2 ranges), indexes: (2 4)]
```

which corresponds to "badger" and "badgerific."

Accessing Enclosing Scope

Blocks can also access their enclosing scope. Say you wanted to print out each of the words that contains "badger." You can use a variation of the previous code, using **-enumerateObjectsUsingBlock:**

```
[array enumerateObjectsUsingBlock:
        ^(id object, NSUInteger index, BOOL *stop) {
      NSRange match = [object rangeOfString: @"badger"];
      if (match.location != NSNotFound) {
          NSLog (@"found a '%@' : %@", @"badger", object);
      }
   }];
```

Which would print out

```
found a 'badger' : badger
found a 'badger' : badgerific
```

It would be nice to be able to generalize this code so "badger" is not hard-coded. Blocks can capture the values of variables defined in the scope that contains the block. Here is a more general version:

```
NSString *subString = @"badger";

[array enumerateObjectsUsingBlock:
        ^(id object, NSUInteger index, BOOL *stop) {
      NSRange match = [object rangeOfString: subString];
      if (match.location != NSNotFound) {
          NSLog (@"found a '%@' : %@", subString, object);
      }
   }];
```

As you would expect, this also prints out

```
found a 'badger' : badger
found a 'badger' : badgerific
```

The subString variable does not have to be a hard-coded assignment either. It could be a value retrieved from an **NSTextField** or **UITextField**.

So, what is happening here? The compiler emits code that captures the value of any variables in the outer scope that are used inside of the block. The block, in essence, takes a snapshot of the world at this point in time. Captured local variables are treated as constant. You cannot assign to subString inside of the block; if you do, you will get an error.

Captured Objective-C objects are retained. subString therefore has been retained. It will automatically be released when the block goes away.

Changing Enclosing Scope

Blocks can also change their enclosing scope. Say you want to count the number of badgers found inside of the list of words. You want the flexibility of providing subString to the block, but you also want a way for multiple invocations of the block to calculate a value and let the enclosing scope know about that value. A return value from the block will not work here because the badger count is calculated across an arbitrary number of block invocations. You cannot use a captured variable because they are const.

__block, with two leading underscores, is a new compiler keyword introduced to indicate that an enclosing scope variable can be modified from inside of the block.

Here is an enumeration that counts the number of badgers:

```
NSString *subString = @"badger";

__block int count = 0;

[array enumerateObjectsUsingBlock:
        ^(id object, NSUInteger index, BOOL *stop) {
    NSRange match = [object rangeOfString: subString];
    if (match.location != NSNotFound) {
        count++;
    }
    }];

NSLog (@"found %d %@s", count, subString);
```

prints

```
  found 2 badgers
```

The block will be invoked once for each object in the array executing the code from top to bottom. count is incremented if object contains subString. Because count is __block scoped, a common piece of memory is having its value changed. __block says "Hey, this variable can be changed inside of a block." Of course, global variables and function-scoped static variables can be changed inside of a block without needing the __block qualifier.

Captured objects are not retained with __block. There are no thread safety guarantees with __block variables, so if your block could be executed on multiple threads simultaneously, you will need to take proper thread safety precautions.

Programmers familiar with other languages may recognize these block features under different names: Lambdas, closures, anonymous functions, as well as "blocks" in languages like Ruby and Smalltalk.

Block Variables

Blocks are not limited to living in-line in method or function calls. You can have variables, whether local, global, or instance, that point to blocks. The syntax is like standard C function pointer syntax but using a caret instead of a star:

```
void (^blockPtrVar) (NSString *arg) = ^(NSString *arg) { NSLog (@"%@", arg); };
```

The name of the variable is blockPtrVar. The block returns nothing (void) and takes a single **NSString** argument.

Invoke it like a function pointer:

```
blockPtrVar (@"hello");
```

which prints "hello."

Things become more readable when you use a `typedef`:

```
typedef void (^BlockType) (NSString *arg);

BlockType blockPtrVar = ^(NSString *arg) { NSLog (@"%@", arg); };

blockPtrVar (@"there");
```

which prints out "there" as you would expect.

Variable Capture Redux

Let's revisit variable capture. Each of the blocks here is the same code, but they are "created" at different times – each after the value of `val` has changed.

```
typedef void (^BoringBlock) (void);

int val = 23;
BoringBlock block1 = ^{ NSLog (@"%d", val); };

val = 42;
BoringBlock block2 = ^{ NSLog (@"%d", val); };

val = 17;
BoringBlock block3 = ^{ NSLog (@"%d", val); };
```

`block1` points to a block that has captured `val` when it had a value of 23. `block2` points to a block that has captured `val` when it had a value of 42, and likewise `block3`'s `val` captured the value of 17. Invoking the blocks prints out the captured values of `val`:

```
block1 ();
block2 ();
block3 ();
```

prints

```
    23
    42
    17
```

Now, make a single change to the code, making `val` a `__block`-scoped variable:

```
typedef void (^BoringBlock) (void);

__block int val = 23;
BoringBlock block1 = ^{ NSLog (@"%d", val); };

val = 42;
BoringBlock block2 = ^{ NSLog (@"%d", val); };

val = 17;
BoringBlock block3 = ^{ NSLog (@"%d", val); };
```

Invoking the blocks as above will print:

```
    17
```

```
17
17
```

The same value is printed because all blocks are sharing the same storage for `val` rather than making copies.

Blocks as Objects

Interestingly enough, blocks are also objects and can be stored in collections. Blocks start out life on the call stack, making them the only stack-based Objective-C objects. The block's executable code does not actually live on the stack, but all of the data the block uses, such as local variables and captured variables, lives there.

Because these blocks live on the stack, you need to make a copy of the block into the heap if it is to live beyond the current scope. When you copy a block, any captured variables are copied into the heap as well. Figure 3.1 shows the block data on the stack for this block:

```
int stride = 10;

__block int summation = 0;

BoringBlock blockPtr = ^{
    summation += stride;
};
```

Because `summation` is `__block`-scoped, the code inside and outside of the block refers to the same location in memory. `stride`, on the other hand, is a simple const-captured variable. Its value, at the time the block is defined, is duplicated and placed in another location in memory, so any changes made to `stride` will not corrupt the value that has been captured.

Figure 3.1   Block storage starts on the stack

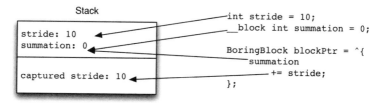

You can make a copy of a block using the **-copy** method, or with the **Block_copy()** function:

```
void *Block_copy (const void *block);
```

You can **-release** the copied block or use **Block_release()**:

```
void Block_release (const void *block);
```

After the copy, memory looks like Figure 3.2. The captured values for `summation` and the captured `stride` have been moved to the heap, and a pointer has been put into place for summation so that the value can be found in the heap. This means that the address of a `__block`-scoped variable can change, so do not rely on it being constant.

Figure 3.2   Copies get moved to the heap

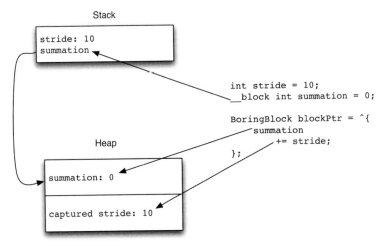

The first copy of a block can be expensive because it requires dynamic allocation. Subsequent copies of the block just turn into retains, and so are fast.

In general, **-copy** and **Block_copy()** are interchangeable, except when you are running under garbage collection. If you use **-copy**, you need to keep a strong reference to the block to prevent it from getting collected. **Block_copy** under GC behaves more like **CFRetain**, preventing the block from being collected even if there are no strong references to it.

Sending **-retain** to a block is a no-op until the block has been copied.

When To Copy

So when do you need to copy a block? Make a copy whenever a block will outlive the scope it is defined in. In particular, these snippets are broken:

```
if (rand() % 1 == 0) {
    blockPtr = ^{ NSLog (@"You are a winner!"); };
} else {
    blockPtr = ^{ NSLog (@"Please try again!"); };
}
```

The braces for the branches of the `if` statement introduce a new scope, so the blocks are invalid afterwards.

```
blockPtr = ^{ NSLog (@"Help me"); };
return blockPtr;
```

Like returning the address of a local variable, returning a block that is still on the stack will cause problems later on, especially if you capture any local variables whose storage vanishes when the function ends.

```
BoringBlock blocks[10];
for (int i = 0; i < 10; i++) {
```

```
    blocks[i] = ^{
        NSLog (@"captured %d", i);
    };
}
```

Similar to the `if` branches, the body of the `for` loop is a different scope, so the blocks are invalid once the loop ends.

Blocks in Collections

You need to copy a block before you add it to a Cocoa collection class. Consider this erroneous code:

```
NSMutableArray *blockArray = [NSMutableArray array];
[blockArray addObject: ^{
        NSLog (@"Jen makes great cupcakes!");
    }];
```

The stack-based block object has its address passed to **-addObject:**. **-addObject:** retains the passed-in object. Because the block is still on the stack, **-retain** is a no-op. The block becomes invalid when the calling function exits, waiting to blow up when you use it in the future. You fix this by copying it before putting it into the collection. Do not forget to offset the implicit retain from **-copy**.

```
[array addObject: [[^{
        NSLog (@"Jen makes great cupcakes!");
    } copy] autorelease]];
```

Yes. It looks weird, but it's necessary.

Block Retain Cycles

Blocks have retain counts. If you have retain counts, you can get retain cycles. Here is a `typedef` for a simple block, and a class that references the block, along with a string instance variable.

```
typedef void (^BoringBlock)(void);

// The leaky object.
@interface Leakzor : NSObject {
    NSString *_string;
    BoringBlock _blockhead;
}

// Print |string|.
- (void) funk;

@end // Leakzor
```

And here are -init and -dealloc.

```
- (id) init {
    if ((self = [super init])) {
        _string = @"snork";

        // |string| is same as self->string, so |self| is retained.
        _blockhead = Block_copy(^{
                NSLog (@"string is %@", _string);
            });
```

```
    }
    return self;
} // init

- (void) dealloc {
    [_string release];
    [_blockhead release];
    [super dealloc];
} // dealloc
```

The _string instance variable is used in the block. Instance variable references like this are actually a pointer dereference off of self, so

```
NSLog (@"string is %@", _string);
```

is the same as

```
NSLog (@"string is %@", self->_string);
```

Because self is a variable in the outside scope that is being captured, it is retained. self will not be released until the block is released in **-dealloc**, but **-dealloc** will not be called until self has been released. This is the cause of the retain cycle.

You can break the retain cycle by using a __block-scoped local variable that points to self. __block-scoped objects are not retained automatically, so the retain cycle is not created:

```
- (id) init {
    if ((self = [super init])) {
        _string = @"snork";

        // blockSelf is __block scope, so won't be auto-retained
        __block Leakzor *blockSelf = self;
        _blockhead = Block_copy(^{
                NSLog (@"string is %@", blockSelf->_string);
            });
    }
    return self;
} // init
```

You do not have to jump through this hoop for every block you make because most blocks have a very short lifespan. Just be aware that if you have a block that has the same lifetime as its owning object and you are freeing the block at **-dealloc** time, you can get a retain cycle.

New API Using Blocks

Several new C library calls have been introduced using blocks. They have _b appended to their names to indicate they are block calls, similar to the way some library functions have _r appended to indicate re-entrant calls. Some of the more useful ones are:

qsort_b()	quicksort using a block for a comparator
bsearch_b()	binary search using a block for a comparator
psort_b()	parallel sort using a block for a comparator
glob_b()	generate pathnames matching a pattern, using a block for an error callback

`scandir_b()`   collect pathnames, using blocks for a path selection and comparison

Cocoa has introduced a large number of block-oriented methods. An easy way to find them all is to search through the framework headers looking for the caret. The caret operator is rarely used in Cocoa header files, so it is a good way to find block methods. Here are some interesting new Cocoa methods:

```
[array enumerateObjectsUsingBlock:
    ^(id obj, NSUInteger index, BOOL *stop) { ... }];
```

You have seen this before. It iterates through the array, invoking a block for each object.

```
[array enumerateObjectsWithOptions:
        NSEnumerationReverse | NSEnumerationConcurrent
    usingBlock:
        ^(id obj, NSUInteger index, BOOL *stop) { ... }];
```

You can include some extra options when enumerating an array. Interesting options are NSEnumerationReverse, which iterates through the array backwards, and NSEnumerationConcurrent, which will automatically parallelize the iteration.

```
[dictionary enumerateKeysAndObjectsUsingBlock:
    ^(id key, id object, BOOL *stop) { ... }];
```

This is the fastest way to iterate the keys and values in a dictionary. Fast enumeration over a dictionary only gives you the keys, so getting the corresponding value requires an **-objectForKey:** call.

```
NSPredicate *p = [NSPredicate predicateWithBlock:
    ^BOOL (id obj, NSDictionary *bindings) { ... }];
```

This creates an **NSPredicate** that is backed by arbitrary code, which allows you to express more sophisticated predicates than can be constructed using the predicate format language.

Grand Central Dispatch is also heavily block-based and will be covered in Chapter 22: *Grand Central Dispatch*).

For the More Curious: Blocks Internals

Blocks and __block variables are implemented by a combination of structures and functions. These are generated by the compiler and maintained by a runtime environment. Knowing how things work under the hood is useful for understanding the details of memory management and debugging.

Implementation

The compiler interprets the new, block-specific syntax and generates data to interface with the runtime and code that relies on functions provided by the runtime. The blocks runtime enables the use of blocks while the application is actually running.

The specific compiler is irrelevant to our discussion. The most visible difference between **gcc** and **clang** is in the names generated for the private structures and functions created by the compiler to support blocks and __block variables.

Those private structures and functions make up the heart of the blocks implementation.

Block literals

Each block literal definition triggers the compiler to generate two structures and at least one function. The two structures describe the block and its runtime information. The function contains the executable code of the block.

The two structures are the *block literal* (also known as the "block holder") and the *block descriptor*.

A block descriptor looks like:

```
static const struct block_descriptor_NAME {
    unsigned long reserved;
    unsigned long literal_size;

    /* helper functions - present only if needed */
    void (*copy_helper)(void *dst, void *src);
    void (*dispose_helper)(void *src);
};
```

The `reserved` field is currently unused. The `literal_size` field is set to the size of the corresponding block literal. The two helper function pointers are only present if needed. They are needed when the block references an Objective-C or C++ object or a `__block` variable. When helper functions are necessary, the compiler generates them in addition to the function implementing the body of the block literal.

A block literal looks like:

```
struct block_literal_NAME {
    void *isa;
    int flags;
    int reserved;
    void (*invoke)(void *literal, ...);
    struct block_descriptor_NAME *descriptor;
    /* referenced captured variables follow */
};
```

The `isa` pointer is what makes a block into an Objective-C object. Even when not using Objective-C, the `isa` pointer is still used by the blocks runtime to indicate what kind of block it is dealing with.

The `isa` field will point to:

_NSConcreteStackBlock	when the block is on the stack.
_NSConcreteGlobalBlock	when the block is in global storage.
_NSConcreteMallocBlock	when the block is on the heap.
_NSConcreteAutoBlock	when the block is in collectable memory. This class is used when running under the garbage collector and a stack block not referencing a C++ object is copied to the heap.
_NSConcreteFinalizingBlock	when the block is in collectable memory and must have a finalizer run when it is collected. This class is used when running under the garbage collector and a stack block referencing a C++ object is copied to the heap, because the

runtime must ensure that the C++ object's destructor is called when the block is collected.

All of these block classes are subclasses of **_NSAbstractBlock**. The abstract class provides implementations for the memory-related methods used by blocks. The various concrete subclasses exist solely to indicate information about where the block is stored.

The `flags` field provides further information about the block:

```
enum {
    BLOCK_REFCOUNT_MASK     = (0xFFFF),
    BLOCK_NEEDS_FREE        = (1 << 24),
    BLOCK_HAS_COPY_DISPOSE  = (1 << 25),
    BLOCK_HAS_CXX_OBJ       = (1 << 26),
    BLOCK_IS_GC             = (1 << 27),
    BLOCK_IS_GLOBAL         = (1 << 28),
    BLOCK_HAS_DESCRIPTOR    = (1 << 29),
};
```

`BLOCK_REFCOUNT_MASK`, `BLOCK_NEEDS_FREE`, and `BLOCK_IS_GC` are set as appropriate by the runtime when a block is copied.

`BLOCK_IS_GLOBAL` is set at compile time for blocks in global storage. Copying and releasing such a block has no effect, as the block is always present in the application's memory. The compiler might opt to hoist a stack-local block into static memory and set the `BLOCK_IS_GLOBAL` flag if it has no references to any stack-local (which includes `__block`) variables.

`BLOCK_HAS_DESCRIPTOR` is always set. It was added to distinguish the version of the blocks implementation that was eventually released with Snow Leopard from an earlier implementation.

Every block invoke function takes a pointer to the calling block literal as its first argument. This provides the function with access to the block's captured variables. This is functionally identical to the `this` pointer passed as the first argument to C++ member functions, which the member function uses to access the member variables, and the `self` pointer supplied as the first argument to Objective-C instance methods, which the method uses to access the instance variables. As in C++, the return value and remaining arguments of the block invoke function are those declared by the programmer. (Objective-C adds one more implicit argument between `self` and the programmer-declared arguments, `_cmd`, which is set to the method's selector.)

Aside from the obvious referenced captured variables, blocks also are considered to have referenced all variables referenced by any blocks nested within them. Consider this brief example:

```
int x = 0;
int y = 1;
int (^b)(void) = ^{
    int (^c)(void) = ^{
        return y;
    };
    return x + c();
}
```

Here, the block assigned to b is considered to have referenced both x and y.

To see how block literals, block descriptors, and block invoke functions come together, consider this code:

```
void f(void) {
    int x = 0;
    int (^b)(void) = ^{ return x + 1; };
    int y = b();
}
```

The compiler would turn that code into something like this:

```
typedef void (*generic_invoke_funcptr)(void *, ...);
struct __block_literal {
    void *isa;
    int flags;
    int reserved;
    generic_invoke_funcptr invoke;
    struct __block_descriptor_tmp *descriptor;
    const int captured_x;
};

static const struct __block_descriptor_tmp {
    unsigned long reserved;
    unsigned long literal_size;
    /* no copy/dispose helpers needed */
} __block_descriptor_tmp = {
    0UL, sizeof(struct __block_literal)
};

// ^int (void) { return x + 1; }
int __f_block_invoke_(struct __block_literal *bp) {
    return bp->captured_x + 1;
}
typedef int (*iv_funcptr)(struct __block_literal *);

void f(void) {
    int x = 0;
    // int (^b)(void) = ^{ return x + 1 };
    struct __block_literal __b = {
        .isa = &_NSConcreteStackBlock,
        .flags = BLOCK_HAS_DESCRIPTOR,
        .reserved = 0,
        .invoke = (generic_invoke_funcptr)__f_block_invoke_,
        .descriptor = &__block_descriptor_tmp,
        .captured_x = x
    };
    struct __block_literal *b = &__b;
    int y = (*(iv_funcptr)(b->invoke))(b);
}
```

Notice that the block variable is really a pointer to a structure created on the stack. It can be helpful to keep this in mind when thinking about when a block literal must be copied or not.

__block variables

Like block literals, __block variables can move from the stack to the heap and their variable data can require memory management, such as when it is an Objective-C object. Consequently, __block variables are also compiled into a struct and, if necessary, ancillary functions.

In order that all manipulations of the __block variable deal with the current location of the variable, all access is mediated by a forwarding pointer. When a __block variable is copied from the stack to the heap, the forwarding pointers of both the on-stack and in-heap structures are updated to point to the in-heap structure.

Because all __block variable access is by reference, the names of the structure and functions associated with __block variables embed "byref."

The byref structure looks like:

```
struct Block_byref {
    void *isa;
    struct Block_byref *forwarding;
    int flags;
    int size;

    /* helper functions - present only if needed */
    void (*byref_keep)(struct Block_byref *dst, struct Block_byref *src);
    void (*byref_destroy)(struct Block_byref *);

    /* actual variable data follows */
}
```

The isa field is always NULL to start with. When a __weak-qualified __block variable is copied, the field is set to &NSConcreteWeakBlockVariable.

The forwarding pointer always points to the start of the authoritative byref header. To begin with, this will always be the address of the containing byref structure itself.

The flags field is used to indicate whether copy and dispose helper functions are present. If they are not, it will be initialized to 0; otherwise, it will be initialized to BLOCK_HAS_COPY_DISPOSE. As with block literals, when the structure is copied at runtime, the flags field will be updated with memory management information. If it is copied into scanned memory, BLOCK_IS_GC will be set. Otherwise, BLOCK_NEEDS_FREE will be set and the bottom two bytes used to store a reference count.

The size is set to the size of the particular Block_byref structure.

Helper functions will be synthesized by the compiler if the byref variable is a block reference, an Objective-C object, or a C++ object. If they are present, flags will include BLOCK_HAS_COPY_DISPOSE. They will be invoked when copying and when releasing a block that references a __block variable.

When a block captures a __block variable, it holds onto the byref structure's forwarding pointer and uses that to interact with the variable. The block will then need copy and dispose helpers to handle copying and disposing of the captured __block variable.

As an example, we will return to the function **f**. We will change it slightly by moving the referenced variable x from auto storage to __block storage:

```
void f(void) {
    __block int x = 0;
    int (^b)(void) = ^{ return x + 1; };
    int y = b();
}
```

In response, the compiler will generate something like the following code (the changes wrought by adding __block have been emphasized):

```
// __block int x
struct __byref_x {
```

```
    /* header */
    void *isa;
    struct __byref_x *forwarding;
    int flags;
    int size;

    /* no helpers needed */

    int x;
};


typedef void (*generic_invoke_funcptr)(void *, ...);
struct __block_literal {
    void *isa;
    int flags;
    int reserved;
    generic_invoke_funcptr invoke;
    struct __block_descriptor_tmp *descriptor;

    struct __byref_x *captured_x;

};


void __copy_helper_block_(struct __block_literal *dst,
                          struct __block_literal *src);
void __destroy_helper_block_(struct __block_literal *bp);


typedef void (*generic_copy_funcptr)(void *, void *);
typedef void (*generic_dispose_funcptr)(void *);
static const struct __block_descriptor_tmp {
    unsigned long reserved;
    unsigned long literal_size;

    /* helpers to copy __block reference captured_x */
    generic_copy_funcptr copy;
    generic_dispose_funcptr dispose;

} __block_descriptor_tmp = {
    0UL, sizeof(struct __block_literal),

    (generic_copy_funcptr)__copy_helper_block_,
    (generic_dispose_funcptr)__destroy_helper_block_

};

// ^int (void) { return x + 1; }
int __f_block_invoke_(struct __block_literal *bp) {
    return bp->captured_x->forwarding->x + 1;
}
typedef int (*iv_funcptr)(struct __block_literal *);


void f(void) {

    // __block int x = 0;
    struct __byref_x x = {
        .isa = NULL,
```

```
        .forwarding = &x,
        .flags = 0,
        .size = sizeof(x),
        .x = 0
    };

    // int (^b)(void) = ^{ return x + 1 };
    struct __block_literal __b = {
        .isa = &_NSConcreteStackBlock,
        .flags = BLOCK_HAS_DESCRIPTOR,
        .reserved = 0,
        .invoke = (generic_invoke_funcptr)__f_block_invoke_,
        .descriptor = &__block_descriptor_tmp,

        .captured_x = x.forwarding

    };
    struct __block_literal *b = &__b;
    int y = (*(iv_funcptr)(b->invoke))(b);


    // Clean up before leaving scope of x.
    _Block_object_dispose(x.forwarding, BLOCK_FIELD_IS_BYREF);
}


void __copy_helper_block_(struct __block_literal *dst,
                          struct __block_literal *src) {
  _Block_object_assign(&dst->captured_x, src->captured_x,
                       BLOCK_FIELD_IS_BYREF);
}

void __destroy_helper_block_(struct __block_literal *bp) {
  _Block_object_dispose(bp->captured_x, BLOCK_FIELD_IS_BYREF);
}
```

Of particular note here is the call to **_Block_object_dispose()** at the end of **f()**. This is because, when garbage collection is not being used, the runtime must adjust the reference count of the __block variable whenever it goes out of scope. When all references have been eliminated, the runtime releases any allocated storage.

The functions used by the helper functions, **_Block_object_assign()** and **_Block_object_dispose()**, are provided by the blocks runtime for use by the compiler. Their behavior is heavily determined by the final argument, *const int flags*, which provides information on the type of the object being assigned or disposed of. The possible values of this field are:

```
enum {
    BLOCK_FIELD_IS_OBJECT   =   3,
    BLOCK_FIELD_IS_BLOCK    =   7,
    BLOCK_FIELD_IS_BYREF    =   8,
    BLOCK_FIELD_IS_WEAK     =  16,
    BLOCK_BYREF_CALLER      = 128
};
```

The BLOCK_BYREF_CALLER flag is used to signal to the functions that they are being called by a byref structure's byref_keep or byref_destroy function. It is only ever set by such functions.

The other flags are set as appropriate for the type of the object being assigned or disposed. Notice that a block field is also an object, since BLOCK_FIELD_IS_BLOCK & BLOCK_FIELD_IS_OBJECT results in BLOCK_FIELD_IS_OBJECT. Where distinguishing between an object and a block object is important, the runtime functions are careful to test whether the block flag is set before testing whether the object flag is set.

Debugging

Debugging blocks can be tricky as the debugging environment straddles the line between the abstraction and the implementation. **gcc** provides far better debugging information than **clang**, but this might change in the future.

gdb comes with only one block-specific command: **invoke-block**, which you can unambiguously abbreviate to **inv**. Its arguments are a block reference or the address of a block literal structure followed by the declared arguments to the block function. The arguments are separated by spaces, so arguments with spaces must be enclosed in double quotation marks. Double quotation marks within quoted arguments must be escaped with a backslash. The only time you are likely to encounter this is in passing a string argument to a block; the resulting command would look like:

```
inv string_block "\"string argument\""
```

gcc and **clang** differ significantly in the debugging information they supply for blocks.

gcc's debugging information

gcc embeds a goodly amount of debugging information about blocks. The **print** command (**p** for short) picks up that block references are pointers, and you can use **ptype** to print the compiler-generated type of a block:

```
(gdb) p local_block
$1 = (struct __block_literal_2 *) 0xbfffff854
(gdb) ptype local_block
type = struct __block_literal_2 {
    void *__isa;
    int __flags;
    int __reserved;
    void *__FuncPtr;
    struct __block_descriptor_withcopydispose *__descriptor;
    const char *enc_vbv;
    struct __Block_byref_1_i *i;
} *
(gdb) ptype local_block->__descriptor
type = struct __block_descriptor_withcopydispose {
    long unsigned int reserved;
    long unsigned int Size;
    void *CopyFuncPtr;
    void *DestroyFuncPtr;
} *
```

You can also use the Objective-C command **print-object** (**po** for short) to get a different view on the block:

```
(gdb) po local_block
<__NSStackBlock__: 0xbfffff854>
```

Getting information on local variables within a block will show that **gcc** adds the __func__ variable, which is set to the name of the function. If you get information on the function arguments, you will see the implicit block literal pointer argument:

```
(gdb) i args
.block_descriptor = (struct __block_literal_2 *) 0xbffff854
```

The debugging information generated by **gcc** pretends that __block variables are identical to their auto counterparts, so that if you have a variable __block int i, you will find that printing the i and its size will behave the same as printing a variable int i.

clang's debugging information

clang, unfortunately, provides no debugging information for block references. The debugger finds no type information for block references. It also has no way to look up the block implementation function for a block so that **invoke-block** always fails.

You can still set breakpoints in blocks by setting them at a line in a file or at the invocation function, if you can determine its name, but you will find that **clang** pretends that block implementation functions have the same arguments as the block literal, so you cannot readily gain access to the implicit block literal pointer argument. Interestingly, **clang** does not report any __func__ local variable; it generates a warning if you use it from a block literal, but you will find that the variable is in fact present, regardless of what the debugging information says.

clang also emits no debugging information for __block variables. They do not appear in the list of local variables, and any attempt to reference them results in a message like:

```
No symbol "i" in current context.
```

While you could make headway by using what you know of the blocks implementation to cadge the desired information out of a program compiled using **clang**, until these issues are fixed, you would do well to use **gcc** when compiling an application using blocks where you plan to rely on the debugging information in future.

Dumping runtime information

Apple's blocks runtime includes a couple functions for dumping information about a block reference and a __block variable.

These functions are:

```
const char *_Block_dump(const void *block);
const char *_Block_byref_dump(struct Block_byref *src);
```

You can call these from **gdb** to dump information about a block or __block variable. If you have the following declarations:

```
__block int i = 23;
void (^local_block)(void) = ^{ /*...*/ };
```

then you can dump information about them as follows:

```
(gdb) call (void)printf((const char *)_Block_dump(local_block))
^0xbffff854 (new layout) =
isa: stack Block
```

```
flags: HASDESCRIPTOR HASHELP
refcount: 0
invoke: 0x1e50
descriptor: 0x20bc
descriptor->reserved: 0
descriptor->size: 28
descriptor->copy helper: 0x1e28
descriptor->dispose helper: 0x1e0a

(gdb) set $addr = (char *)&i - 2*sizeof(int) - 2*sizeof(void *)
(gdb) call (void)printf((const char *)_Block_byref_dump($addr))
byref data block 0xbffff870 contents:
   forwarding: 0xbffff870
   flags: 0x0
   size: 20
```

Note that, though the debugging information supplied by **gcc** pretends that the __block variable i is simply an int variable, the address of the variable is in fact its address within the byref structure. Since we know the layout of the structure, we can calculate the address of the start of the structure and pass that to **_Block_byref_dump()**.

You can wrap these calls in user-defined commands. Adding the following definitions to your .gdbinit file will make them available whenever you run **gdb**:

```
define dump-block-literal
    printf "%s", (const char *)_Block_dump($arg0)
end

document dump-block-literal
    Dumps runtime information about the supplied block reference.
    Argument is the name or address of a block reference.
end



define dump-block-byref
    set $_dbb_addr = (char *)&$arg0 - 2*sizeof(int) - 2*sizeof(void *)
    printf "%s", (const char *)_Block_byref_dump($_dbb_addr)
end

document dump-block-byref
    Dumps runtime information about the supplied __block variable.
    Argument is a pointer to the variable embedded in a block byref structure.
end
```

With these commands defined, dumping that information is as simple as:

```
(gdb) dump-block-literal local_block
^0xbffff854 (new layout) =
isa: stack Block
flags: HASDESCRIPTOR HASHELP
refcount: 0
invoke: 0x1e50
descriptor: 0x20bc
descriptor->reserved: 0
descriptor->size: 28
descriptor->copy helper: 0x1e28
descriptor->dispose helper: 0x1e0a
(gdb) dump-block-byref i
```

```
byref data block 0xbffff870 contents:
  forwarding: 0xbffff870
  flags: 0x0
  size: 20
```

Evolving the implementation

This chapter has described the blocks runtime as released with Mac OS X 10.6 (Snow Leopard). The blocks runtime is unlikely to make any changes that would break code compiled to that interface, but it will not stop evolving.

There are several extension points built into the current runtime. The various `flags` fields can be carefully extended; `reserved` fields can be repurposed; and new fields can be tacked on at the ends of the various structures.

One minor extension that might see release is the addition of a `signature` field at the end of the block descriptor structure. This field would contain a pointer to the Objective-C type encoding of the block invoke function.

(For those curious, blocks themselves are encoded by the `@encode` directive as `@?`; this parallels the function pointer encoding of `^?`, which literally reads as "pointer to unknown type.")

To indicate that this field is present, the `BLOCK_HAS_DESCRIPTOR` flag would no longer be set, and a new flag, `BLOCK_HAS_SIGNATURE = (1 << 30)`, would be set in all blocks compiled for the new runtime.

With the ability to test for `BLOCK_HAS_SIGNATURE` to check for a block compiled against a newer version of the runtime, the way is opened for other changes, including repurposing `BLOCK_HAS_DESCRIPTOR` to signal that a block returns a structure large enough to require special handling on some architectures. The flag could be renamed `BLOCK_USE_STRET`. This is similar to the way that **objc_msgSend_stret()** is used by the Objective-C runtime instead of **objc_msgSend()** in the same situation.

A more significant change would be to add the signature of the variables captured by a block. This would allow the runtime to eliminate helper functions in favor of using the type information now encoded along with the block to itself do the right thing for all captured variables when a block is copied or disposed.

Compiler-generated names

Both **gcc** and **clang** automatically generate names for the structures and functions that make up blocks and __block variables. Sometimes during debugging, it would be useful to be able to guess the names generated in implementing a given block or __block variable.

Unfortunately, outside of toy examples, this is generally not possible without reference to a disassembly of the code. Both compilers disambiguate the names of the structures and helper functions they generate by appending numbers to the end of the same string. Thus, you can judge the type of support structure or helper you are looking at, but you cannot readily trace it back to the block or __block variable that caused its generation.

Fortunately, the outlook is not so bleak when it comes to block invoke functions. Block invoke functions not defined at global scope embed the name of the outermost enclosing function. The first block in a function **f()** will be named __f_block_invoke_1 if generated by **gcc** and __f_block_invoke_ if generated by **clang**. The numeric suffix is incremented prior to generating the name of the block invoke function of each subsequent block encountered within the function. (**clang** starts by appending the number 1 and increments it like **gcc** thereafter.) Objective-C method names will be embedded just as C function names, leading to block invoke function names like __-[Foo init]_block_invoke_1. C++ member functions are neither qualified nor mangled for embedding, so a block defined within the member function **Foo::Bar()** will cause the compiler to generate a block invoke function named __Bar_block_invoke_ (append a 1 if the compiler is **gcc**).

The block invoke functions of blocks defined at global scope are harder to track down, since they have no enclosing function to anchor them. **gcc** names such functions starting with __block_global_1. **clang** uses the same name scheme as for blocks defined within a function, only it substitutes global as the function name. Consequently, the first block defined at global scope that **clang** encounters is named __global_block_invoke_, and the second, __global_block_invoke_1.

One surprising result of the naming conventions for blocks at global scope is that when several source files are compiled into a single executable, each one can have its own __global_block_invoke_ function. The resulting executable will have several functions with the identical name distinguished by their being at different addresses.

Whenever possible, specify breakpoints in block functions using the file and line number rather than the name. The name generation scheme could change in future and does not guarantee uniqueness within a linked executable, only within a compilation unit.

Exercises

1. Rewrite this function as a block:

```
int k(void) {
    return 1;
}
```

2. Write a function **create_k** that accepts a single integer argument *i* and returns a block. The returned block accepts no arguments and always returns the value of *i* passed to **create_k()**. Use this function in a test program. (Be careful with the block memory management!)

3. Define two blocks called **add_one** and **add_two** that accept no arguments and return nothing. These should both increment the same integer by one or two. (You will need the __block storage specifier.)

4. Use typedefs to simplify the following block reference declaration:

```
int (^(*(^get_block_factory_funcptr)(void))(int))(void);
```

4

Command-Line Programs

Much of the power that Unix brings to the user is in the command-line tools, where the user can set up pipelines of independent programs that manipulate data. It's time to take a peek under the hood of a typical command-line tool and see how it works, as many of the command-line concepts (processing arguments, checking the environment) apply to any Unix program. Here you are going to write a program that filters its input by changing any letters it finds to upper or lower case.

Figure 4.1 shows a typical command-line program along with its three communication streams. The standard-in stream (also called "stdin") supplies data to the program. The data you are to process comes from standard-in. You are done once the stream dries up. While you process the data, you write new data to the standard-out stream (also called "stdout"). If you need to report any errors or output any information other than the processed data, you can write that information to the standard-error stream (also called "stderr").

When you type a pipeline command in a shell, like cat words.txt | wc -l, the shell creates new processes, one for each command. For this command, there are two new processes, one for **cat** and one for **wc**. The shell then hooks the standard-out of **cat** to the standard-in of **wc**, and also hooks the standard-out of **wc** back to the shell so that the shell can read its output. By using the stream redirection features of your shell, you can pour a file's contents into the standard-in of a program or save the standard-out output to a file.

Figure 4.1 The standard file streams

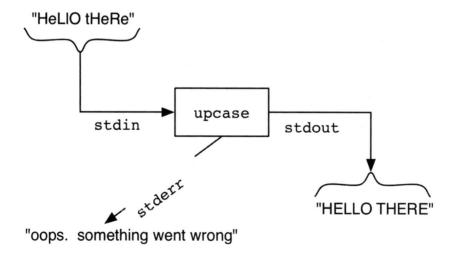

The Basic Program

The `stdio.h` header file (among other stuff) defines global symbols that represent the three file streams: `stdin`, `stdout`, and `stderr`, which represent standard-in, standard-out, and standard-error respectively.

Here's a source file called `upcase.m`. First import the header files. You will always need some kind of header files:

```
#import <Foundation/Foundation.h>    // for BOOL
#import <stdlib.h>                    // for EXIT_FAILURE/SUCCESS
#import <stdio.h>                     // for standard I/O stuff
```

Importing `Foundation.h` pulls in the headers for the Cocoa Foundation Kit. For now, you're just going to be using the BOOL type.

`stdlib.h` brings in much of the C standard library. Here we will be using the `EXIT_FAILURE` and `EXIT_SUCCESS` constants.

`stdio.h` provides the declarations for the standard input/output types and functions.

Next is a function to change the case of all the characters in a buffer:

```
void changecaseBuffer (char buffer[], size_t length, BOOL upcase) {
    char *scan = buffer;
    char *const stop = buffer + length;

    while (scan < stop) {
        *scan = upcase? toupper(*scan) : tolower(*scan);
        scan++;
    }
} // changecaseBuffer
```

changecaseBuffer() scans over every byte in the buffer calling the **toupper()** or **tolower()** function on each one. The functions change a character's case appropriately if it is a letter, and they leave it alone if not. This code assumes an ASCII-style character encoding. A string in a multi-byte encoding like UTF-8 will get trashed.

You will need a chunk of memory to hold the incoming data while it is being processed. The program will process things in 2-KiB chunks.

```
#define BUFFER_SIZE (2048)
```

Last is the **main()** function, which is where program control flow starts when the program is run. **main()** reads and processes the input:

```
int main(int argc, char *argv[]) {
    char buffer[BUFFER_SIZE];
    const BOOL upcase = YES;

    while (!feof(stdin)) {
        const size_t length = fread(buffer, 1, BUFFER_SIZE, stdin);
        changecaseBuffer(buffer, length, upcase);
        fwrite(buffer, 1, length, stdout);
    }
    return EXIT_SUCCESS;
} // main
```

You can build this program in Xcode using the Command Line Tool template as a starting point. (In Xcode 3, look for the Foundation Tool template.) Or you can compile it on the command line:

```
$ gcc -o upcase upcase.m
```

This command runs the C compiler on upcase.m, which generates an executable program with the name **upcase**. If you do not include **-o upcase**, the compiler will, for historical reasons, use the name a.out.

Invoke your new program with **./upcase**. The program will just sit there doing nothing. You need to type some stuff, then press return followed by Control-D, the end-of-file key sequence:

```
$ ./upcase
HooVeR Ni BOrK
^D
HOOVER NI BORK
```

This program also works in simple pipelines:

```
$ echo "HooVeR" | ./upcase
HOOVER
```

It works for more complex pipelines as well:

```
$ cat /usr/share/dict/words | ./upcase | grep BADGER
BADGER
BADGERBRUSH
BADGERER
BADGERINGLY
...
(and a couple more BADGER-like words)
```

Inside the Central Loop

Take a look at the central loop in **main**:

```
    while (!feof(stdin)) {
```

Loop over the body of the while statement until the standard-in stream indicates that it has reached EOF (end of file). End of file happens when you explicitly type Control-D on a new line if you are typing text into the program. When in a pipeline, the standard-in stream will be closed when the program writing to it exits or otherwise closes the outgoing pipe on its end.

```
        const size_t length = fread (buffer, 1, BUFFER_SIZE, stdin);
```

Read in no more than BUFFER_SIZE bytes. The **fread()** function is a record-oriented function that you'll see more of in Chapter 11: *Files, Part 1: I/O and Permissions*. This function reads x items composed of n bytes. Here you are interested in the number of bytes read, so we tell **fread()** to read up to BUFFER_SIZE records of one byte each.

```
        changecaseBuffer (buffer, length, upcase);
```

Call **changecaseBuffer** to process the buffer. Note that the length is passed as an argument. **fread** will not append a null terminating character ('\0', hex 0x00) to the string, so the receiving function will not know where to stop processing unless you tell it where to stop.

Finally, use the same idea of "writing length records of 1 byte each" to write to the standard-out stream:

```
fwrite (buffer, 1, length, stdout);
```

Changing Behavior By Name

Now it's time to let the user control the program behavior. One easy way is to look at the name the user used to invoke the program. There is a Linux utility called BusyBox that implements many of the standard Unix command-line programs in one small executable, changing its behavior based on the name. On your system you probably have a /usr/bin/ranlib which is a symbolic link to the **libtool** program. In this case, **libtool** works like **ranlib** when invoked using the **ranlib** name.

Example 4.1 changes the program's behavior depending on if it is run as "upcase" or "downcase." To do this, look at the argv array that is passed to **main**. argv is a contraction of the phrase "argument vector." You could call that parameter anything you wanted to, but typically it will just be argv.

The argv array has all of the command-line arguments passed to the program. The shell breaks the command the user typed into arguments (usually at whitespace characters, but that can be overridden by quotes). The program invocation is in the first element of the array at argv[0]: this is the command as entered by the user. If the program was run with **./upcase**, argv[0] would be "./upcase." If the program was started with **/Users/bork/projects/book/chapter2/upcase**, argv[0] would have this value too, so you cannot really depend on finding a specific string value there. Luckily, there is a little convenience function called **fnmatch** that does shell-style filename matching. By seeing if the string in argv[0] matches "*upcase" or "*downcase," you can decide how the program will operate.

Example 4.1   upcase.m

```
// upcase.m -- convert text to upper case

// gcc -g -Wall -o upcase upcase.m

#import <Foundation/Foundation.h>    // for BOOL
#import <stdlib.h>                    // for EXIT_FAILURE
#import <stdio.h>                     // for standard I/O stuff
#import <fnmatch.h>                   // for fnmatch()

#define BUFFER_SIZE (2048)

// changecaseBuffer is unchanged

int main(int argc, char *argv[]) {
    char buffer[BUFFER_SIZE];

    BOOL upcase = YES;

    if (fnmatch("*upcase", argv[0], 0) == 0) {
        fprintf ("upcase!\n", stderr);
        upcase = YES;
    } else if (fnmatch("*downcase", argv[0], 0) == 0) {
        fprintf ("downcase!\n", stderr);
        upcase = NO;
    }


    while (!feof(stdin)) {
        const size_t length = fread(buffer, 1, BUFFER_SIZE, stdin);
        changecaseBuffer(buffer, length, upcase);
        fwrite(buffer, 1, length, stdout);
```

```
    }
    return EXIT_SUCCESS;
}   // main
```

Compile your program as before with:

```
$ gcc -g -Wall -o upcase upcase.m
```

Here is a sample run:

```
$ echo "bLaRg" | ./upcase
upcase!
BLARG
```

Now make a symbolic link that points to **upcase**:

```
$ ln -s upcase downcase
```

and run the program like this:

```
$ echo "bLaRg" | ./downcase
downcase!
blarg
```

Looking at the Environment

Another way to influence program behavior is through *environment variables*. Environment variables, such as those in Figure 4.2, are key-value pairs that are under user control via the shell. The **getenv()** function is used to read the variables the user has set (directly or indirectly) in the environment from which your program has been run.

Figure 4.2   Environment variables

SHELL	/bin/csh
HOME	/Users/markd
USER	markd
LANG	en_US
MACHTYPE	i386
HOST	borkbook.local.

getenv ("HOME"); ⟶ "/Users/markd"

Supply **getenv()** with the name of the environment variable you want. If the variable does not exist in the environment, you get NULL back. If it does exist, you will get back a string with the value. The system owns the memory for the string returned by **getenv()**, so you do not need to free it.

The next version of the program uses the CASE_CONV environment variable to control the case conversion program A value of LOWER will have it massage strings to lower case, and UPPER, to upper case. The default behavior is to upper case.

Remove

```
#import <fnmatch.h>
```

because you won't be using **fnmatch()**. The declarations for **getenv()** and family live in stdlib.h, which has already been included.

Also remove the two if blocks that use **fnmatch()** and replace them with:

```
const char *envSetting = getenv ("CASE_CONV");
if (envSetting != NULL) {
    if (strcmp(envSetting, "UPPER") == 0) {
        fprintf (stderr, "upper!\n");
        upcase = YES;
    } else if (strcmp(envSetting, "LOWER") == 0) {
        fprintf (stderr, "lower!\n");
        upcase = NO;
    }
}
```

Recompile it with:

```
$ gcc -o upcase upcase.m
```

and give it a whirl:

```
$ export CASE_CONV=LOWER
$ ./upcase
lower!
GrEEblE
greeble
```

Check out the other case:

```
$ export CASE_CONV=UPPER
$ ./upcase
upper!
GrEEblE
GREEBLE
```

Parsing the Command Line

Aside from reading some configuration file, the last way to influence program behavior is through command-line arguments. This is also the most common way to control program behavior for command-line programs.

Recall earlier that the "choose behavior based on program name" version of **upcase** looked at the first element of argv to get the program name. The argv array in fact has all of the program's arguments, living at argv indexes greater than zero. Recall that argc is the number of arguments on the command line, including the program name.

Example 4.2 is a quick little program that prints out command-line arguments:

Example 4.2   dumpargs.m

```
// dumpargs.m -- show program arguments
```

```
gcc -g -std=c99 -Wall -o dumpargs dumpargs.m

#include <stdio.h>    // for printf()
#include <stdlib.h>   // for EXIT_SUCCESS

int main(int argc, char *argv[]) {
    for (int i = 0; i < argc; i++) {
        printf("%d: %s\n", i, argv[i]);
    }
    return EXIT_SUCCESS;
} // main
```

Now feed this program various arguments:

```
$ ./dumpargs
0: ./dumpargs
```

As expected, the name of the program lives in the 0th element of the argv array.

```
$ ./dumpargs -oop -ack -blarg
0: ./dumpargs
1: -oop
2: -ack
3: -blarg
```

You can also see the effect of shell file name globbing and quotation marks:

```
$ ./dumpargs "dump*" dump*
0: ./dumpargs
1: dump*
2: dumpargs
3: dumpargs.m
```

The first argument, because it is in quotes, is given to you explicitly as dump*. The second dump* was intercepted by the shell and expanded to list all of the files whose names start with dump. In this case, it matches the name of the program and the name of the .m file.

Now back to upcase.m. We'll use the -u flag for uppercase and -l (ell) for lowercase.

Remove the code you added for handling the environment variables and add this:

```
    if (argc >= 2) {
        if (strcmp(argv[1], "-u") == 0) {
            fprintf (stderr, "upper!\n");
            upcase = YES;
        } else if (strcmp(argv[1], "-l") == 0) {
            fprintf (stderr, "lower!\n");
            upcase = NO;
        }
    }
```

Recompile and try it out:

```
$ ./upcase -u
upper!
GrEEbLe
GREEBLE

$ ./upcase -l
lower!
```

GrEEbLe
greeble

One thing some experienced programmers will notice is the distinct lack of error checking in these programs. Much of the work of programming Unix is catching and handling errors, whether they are user errors (typing invalid or conflicting command arguments) or system errors (a disk fills up).

You may have noticed the return EXIT_SUCCESS; at the end of each of the **main()** functions throughout this book. EXIT_SUCCESS is a macro that expands to zero, which when returned, tells the shell that the command succeeded. Any non-zero return value tells the shell that the command failed. The shell uses this return value to decide whether to continue with the work it is doing, whether running a shell script or just a command pipeline. For **upcase**, you should do a little checking of arguments, such as whether the user entered too many or entered one that is invalid.

Return EXIT_FAILURE, a macro that expands to the value 1, to tell the shell that something went wrong. You can use any number less than 256 for the return value, but using the symbolic constant makes it obvious that you're indicating an error condition. An attempt has been made to categorize some error return values. Check out /usr/include/sysexits.h, which has an email-subsystem flavor.

Here is **upcase** with some error checking (replace the argv code you entered above with this):

```
if (argc > 2) {
    fprintf(stderr,
            "%s: Too many arguments - supply at most one.\n",
            argv[0]);
    return EXIT_FAILURE;
} else if (argc == 2) {
    BOOL found = NO;
    if (strcmp(argv[1], "-u") == 0) {
        upcase = YES;
        found = YES;
    } else if (strcmp(argv[1], "-l") == 0) {
        upcase = NO;
        found = YES;
    }
    if (!found) {
        fprintf (stderr,
                "%s: unexpected command-line argument: '%s'\n",
                argv[0], argv[1]);
        fprintf (stderr, "%s: expected: -u or -l\n", argv[0]);
        return EXIT_FAILURE;
    }
}
```

When you discover that something is wrong, print out a complaint message to the standard error stream and bail out with an error code.

In real life programs, there is usually some cleanup work that would need to be done, like closing files or freeing memory before returning from a function that detected errors. The operating system will clean up any open files or allocated memory for your program when it terminates, but it's a good idea to be tidy so that resource monitoring tools won't accuse you of leaking resources. You might want to do this cleanup in debug versions, so you can have maximal tool support, but also have the fastest possible shutdown in release versions.

Throughout this book, you will see one way of handling errors: keeping all of the cleanup code at the end of the function and using a goto to jump to a label at the end and bypass any additional work in the function. Unfortunately, too many in the programming industry have been trained to have a knee-jerk reaction to goto, when in many cases it can lead to much more readable cleanup than the alternatives.

For example, in pseudo-code:

```
int someFunction (void) {
    ...
    result = failure;
    blah = allocate_some_memory();
    if (do_something(blah) == failure) {
        goto bailout;
    }
    ack = open_a_file();
    if (process_file(blah, ack) == failure) {
        goto bailout;
    }
    hoover = do_something_else();
    if (have_fun(blah, hoover) == failure) {
        goto bailout;
    }
    // we survived! yay
    result = success;

  bailout:
    if (blah) free_the_memory (blah);
    if (ack) close_the_file (ack);
    if (hoover) clean_this_up (hoover);

    return result;
}
```

If you are using C++, you can use exception handling (a fancy form of goto) and stack-based cleanup objects to simplify cleanup. Objective-C users can use a @finally block to accomplish something similar. In plain C, you must either nest ifs, introduce an auxiliary success variable, or employ goto.

Here is the final **main** function, including error checking of the command-line arguments and a single exit point:

```
int main(int argc, char *argv[]) {
    int exitReturn = EXIT_FAILURE;
    char buffer[BUFFER_SIZE];
    BOOL upcase = YES;

    if (argc > 2) {
        fprintf (stderr, "%s: Too many arguments - supply at most one.\n", argv[0]);
        goto bailout;
    } else if (argc == 2) {
        BOOL found = NO;
        if (strcmp(argv[1], "-u") == 0) {
            upcase = YES;
            found = YES;
        } else if (strcmp(argv[1], "-l") == 0) {
            upcase = NO;
            found = YES;
        }
        if (!found) {
            fprintf (stderr, "%s: unexpected command-line argument: '%s'\n",
                    argv[0], argv[1]);
            fprintf (stderr, "%s: expected: -u or -l\n", argv[0]);
```

```
            goto bailout;
        }
    }

    while (!feof(stdin)) {
        const size_t length = fread (buffer, 1, BUFFER_SIZE, stdin);
        changecaseBuffer (buffer, length, upcase);
        fwrite (buffer, 1, length, stdout);
    }
    exitReturn = EXIT_SUCCESS;

bailout:
    return exitReturn;
}   // main
```

getopt_long()

Parsing Unix command lines correctly is actually a very tricky proposition. You can have individual arguments:

$ **someprogram -a -b -c**

By convention, you can glom all of the single-character arguments together:

$ **someprogram -abc**

Some arguments can take additional values:

$ **someprogram -dTwitter -f filename**

and there are also more verbose (called "long") arguments, introduced by two dashes:

$ **someprogram --kthx --cheezburger**

There is a convention where `--` will terminate processing of command-line arguments and use the remaining contents of the command line as-is, even if they look suspiciously like more command-line arguments.

$ **someprogram --hoover -- -not --really --arguments -now**

That's an awful lot of complexity. Luckily, you do not have to implement all of this logic yourself. The standard library supplies **getopt_long()** to handle this drudge-work. There is an older function called **getopt()** that performs similar duties, but it does not handle long argument processing. **getopt_long()** takes a number of parameters:

```
    int getopt_long (int argc, char * const *argv,
                     const char *optstring,
                     const struct option *longopts,
                     int *longindex);
```

argc and argv are the command-line parameters passed to **main()**. optstring is a character string that describes the short, single-character options, while longopts describes the longer, more verbose options. longindex, if supplied, returns the index into longopts when it processes an argument. Usually you will just pass NULL here.

Call **getopt_long()** repeatedly in a loop until it indicates that it has processed all of the arguments by returning -1. It will return ' : ' if there was a missing argument to an option that requires an argument, or '?' if the user supplied an unknown or ambiguous option. Otherwise, it returns a value, controlled by optstring and longopts, that you can then use for argument processing.

optstring is a string that has all of the single character arguments you wish to support. Use a colon after arguments that take a required additional argument and two colons after arguments that take an optional additional argument. So, if we had a program that took arguments of -c, -o and -f, where -f took an argument (say a filename), the optstring argument would look like "cof:". **getopt_long()** will let you use the command-line syntax -fBlah as well as -f Blah for indicating the argument. **getopt_long()** returns the appropriate character when it sees any of these arguments as it runs through the command line.

longopts is a bit more complicated. You provide **getopt_long()** an array of option structures, terminated by a sentinel that has zero/NULL values in all fields. This array is almost always statically created in your source file. The option structure looks like this:

```
struct option {
    char *name;
    int   has_arg;
    int  *flag;
    int   val;
};
```

name is the verbose name of the option. has_arg is one of the constants no_argument, optional_argument, and required_argument that describe whether this particular command-line option requires an additional argument.

flag and val work together. If flag is NULL, val will be the return value from **getopt_long()** if it sees the long option indicated by name. You typically use a single-character return value that matches one of the options described in your optstring. This lets you process single-character and verbose commands that are the same.

Non-NULL flag values should be a pointer to an integer value. When **getopt_long()** processes the verbose option described by name, it puts val's value into the integer where flag points. When **getopt_long()** processes one of these options, it returns zero to indicate that it just set a variable for you. This mechanism only works for verbose arguments.

To phrase it another way, if you have a verbose option that also has a single-character equivalent, you want flag to be NULL and val to be that character. Otherwise, if you have a verbose option that does not take an argument, you can have **getopt_long()** automatically set an arbitrary integer variable to a given value.

Example 4.3 shows **getopt_long()** in-action.

Example 4.3   argparse.m

```
// argparse.m -- using getopt_long to parse arguments

// gcc -Wall -std=c99 -g -o argparse argparse.m

#import <getopt.h>  // for getopt_long()
#import <stdio.h>   // for printf()
#import <stdlib.h>  // for EXIT_SUCCESS

static const char *optstring = "gf:c::o";
```

```
static int thing1, thing2, thing3;

static struct option longopts[] = {
    { "filename",  required_argument,  NULL,    'f' },
    { "cattoy",    optional_argument,  NULL,    'c' },
    { "oop",       no_argument,        NULL,    'o' },
    { "thing1",    no_argument,        &thing1,  1 },
    { "thing2",    no_argument,        &thing2,  2 },
    { "thing3",    no_argument,        &thing3,  3 },
    { NULL,        0,                  NULL,     0 }
};

int main(int argc, char *argv[]) {
    int ch;

    while ((ch = getopt_long(argc, argv, optstring, longopts, NULL)) != -1) {
        switch (ch) {
        case 'g':
            puts ("  greeble!");
            break;
        case 'f':
            printf ("  file name is %s\n", optarg);
            break;
        case 'c':
            printf ("  cat toy is %s\n", (optarg == NULL) ? "string" : optarg);
            break;
        case 'o':
            puts ("  oop!");
            break;
        case 0:
            puts ("  getopt_long set a variable");
            break;
        case ':':
            puts ("  missing required argument");
            break;
        case '?':
            puts ("  oops, unknown option");
            break;
        }
    }

    // See if the thing variables got manipulated.
    printf ("thing1: %d  thing2: %d  thing3: %d\n", thing1, thing3, thing3);

    // Mop up any remaining arguments.
    argc -= optind;
    argv += optind;

    if (argc > 0) {
        puts ("additional trailing arguments:");
        for (int i = 0; i < argc; i++) {
            printf ("  %s\n", argv[i]);
        }
    }
    return EXIT_SUCCESS;
} // main
```

The first thing of interest is the `optstring`:

```
static const char *optstring = "gf:c::o";
```

This says that there are four single-character command-line options, -g, -f, -c, and -o. -f requires an argument, while -c takes an optional argument.

After that is the array describing the longopts:

```
static struct option longopts[] = {
    { "filename",  required_argument,  NULL,     'f' },
    { "cattoy",    optional_argument,  NULL,     'c' },
    { "oop",       no_argument,        NULL,     'o' },
    { "thing1",    no_argument,        &thing1,   1 },
    { "thing2",    no_argument,        &thing2,   2 },
    { "thing3",    no_argument,        &thing3,   3 },
    { NULL,        0,                  NULL,      0 }
};
```

There is no direct connection between the two argument descriptions. In a real program, you'd want to generate the option string from your longopts table so you wouldn't have two places to modify if you added more arguments at a later time.

There are three long arguments that correspond to three of our short arguments. There is one short argument, -g, that has no verbose equivalent. This is perfectly OK. You can see that --cattoy takes an optional argument.

The three "--thing" arguments have no single-character equivalent. If --thing1 is seen on the command line, the thing1 variable will be set to the value 1. If --thing3 is seen, then thing3 will have the value of 3.

The body of **main()** then calls **getopt_long()** repeatedly. As described earlier, the return value is the character for the argument, for single-character arguments.

One of the cases is interesting:

```
        case 'c':
            printf ("  cat toy is %s\n", (optarg == NULL) ? "string" : optarg);
            break;
```

This case will be hit if the argument -c (or --cattoy) was provided. optarg is a global variable that is set to the argument provided by the user. If no argument is provided, which is possible for this case since --cattoy's argument has been flagged as optional both in the optstring by the two colons following 'c' and in the longopts, then optarg will be NULL. That's your cue to supply whatever default value is appropriate.

The loop terminates when **getopt_long()** returns -1. After that, the values of the three thing variables are printed. These values are set if the user provides arguments like --thing1, and the only hint this happens is when zero is returned during the loop.

There is another global variable manipulated by **getopt_long()** used here – optind. This is how far it processed into argv. Arguments after this have not been processed and are yours to do with as you please. A program might use them as file names to process. **getopt_long()** automatically handles using -- as an indicator to stop processing arguments.

Here are some runs of this program:

Lack of arguments is not terribly interesting:

```
$ ./argparse
thing1: 0  thing2: 0  thing3: 0
```

Single-character arguments are handled as well:

```
$ ./argparse -og
  oop!
  greeble!
thing1: 0  thing2: 0  thing3: 0
```

The optional argument is handled as well:

```
$ ./argparse --cattoy
  cat toy is string
thing1: 0  thing2: 0  thing3: 0
```

As are things that accept arguments:

```
$ ./argparse --filename=somefile -f file
  file name is somefile
  file name is file
thing1: 0  thing2: 0  thing3: 0
```

As well as trailing arguments:

```
$ ./argparse --filename=somefile -- -f file
  file name is somefile
thing1: 0  thing2: 0  thing3: 0
additional trailing arguments:
  -f
  file
```

getopt_long() also does some rudimentary error checking:

```
$ ./argparse -f
argparse: option requires an argument -- f
oops, unknown option
thing1: 0  thing2: 0  thing3: 0
```

The first line is emitted by **getopt_long()** itself, while the "oops" line is generated by the program. Note that **getopt_long()** has returned '?' even though we've encountered a missing argument, not an unknown option. You can disable **getopt_long()**'s error messages by setting opterr to 0. To get it to return ':' for a missing argument, you must begin optstring with a colon; this also disables its error messages. You cannot configure it both to return ':' and supply error messages.

User Defaults

Cocoa's **NSUserDefaults** class can also be used as a crude form of command-line processing. **NSUserDefaults** automatically takes parameters of the form -parameter value and adds them to the defaults domain NSArgumentDomain. Every parameter must take a single argument. You cannot have optional arguments or parameters with no arguments when using this technique.

This is a volatile domain, so its values will not be saved to the user preferences. You probably do not want to use **NSUserDefaults** as the main configuration interface for command-line programs because it is inflexible, but it can be useful when you want to supply some optional command-line options. This is handy for supplying debugging or testing flags to a GUI program.

Example 4.4 shows a program that looks for file names and cat toys on the command line and prints out the values it sees.

Example 4.4   defargs.m

```
// defargs.m -- Get command-line arguments from user defaults.

#import <Foundation/Foundation.h>
#import <stdlib.h<

// gcc -g -Wall -framework Foundation -o defargs defargs.m

int main(int argc, const char *argv[]) {
    NSAutoreleasePool *const pool = [[NSAutoreleasePool alloc] init];
    NSUserDefaults *const defs = [NSUserDefaults standardUserDefaults];

    NSLog(@"cat toy: %@", [defs stringForKey:@"cattoy"]);
    NSLog(@"file name: %@", [defs stringForKey:@"filename"]);

    [pool drain];
    return EXIT_SUCCESS;
} // main
```

Just running the program shows that there are no values:

```
$ ./defargs
2010-09-20 19:34:59.549 defaults[5405:807] cat toy: (null)
2010-09-20 19:34:59.551 defaults[5405:807] file name: (null)
```

But you can provide arguments:

```
$ ./defargs -cattoy flamingo
2010-09-20 19:35:15.765 defaults[5406:807] cat toy: flamingo
2010-09-20 19:35:15.767 defaults[5406:807] file name: (null)

$ ./defargs -filename bork -cattoy flamingo
2010-09-20 19:53:49.226 defargs[5501:807] cat toy: flamingo
2010-09-20 19:53:49.227 defargs[5501:807] file name: bork
```

One nice thing about using **NSUserDefaults** for settings like these is that you can use the **defaults** command-line tool to set them persistently. Because this program has no bundle identifier, you must use the program name. Set a default like this:

```
$ defaults write defargs filename -string "bork"
```

And then run the program:

```
$ ./defargs
2010-09-20 19:55:29.038 defargs[5504:807] cat toy: (null)
2010-09-20 19:55:29.039 defargs[5504:807] file name: bork
```

5

Exceptions, Error Handling, and Signals

One of the grisly facts of programming life is that errors can happen, and program code must react to those errors and deal with them appropriately. With the Unix APIs, there are two primary ways that exceptional conditions are communicated to programs. One is through return codes from function calls plus a global variable that describes the error in more detail. The other is through signals sent to the program from the OS. The Objective-C compiler and Cocoa framework in Mac OS X also provide an exception-handling architecture that programs can take advantage of.

errno

Most of the library functions and system calls provided by Unix systems have a return value that signifies that an error happened during the execution of the call. The global integer variable `errno` will be set to a value to indicate what went wrong. If nothing went wrong, `errno` is meaningless; it should only be consulted when the function returns a value that indicates failure (generally, -1) and is documented to set `errno` on failure.

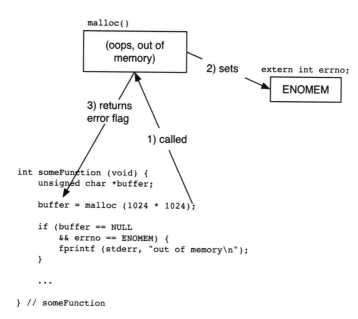

You can use the function **strerror()** to get a human description of the error. The prototype for **strerror()** lives in <string.h>. It is necessary to #include <errno.h> to get the definition of errno. You can look in /usr/include/sys/errno.h for the complete set of errno values. It is important to include errno.h rather than providing your own extern int errno, since errno is implemented in a thread-safe manner that is more than just a simple global int.

The manpages for Unix calls spell out in detail what the error code is and what specific errno values are set. For example, from the open(2) manpage:

```
OPEN(2)                    System Calls Manual                    OPEN(2)

NAME
     open - open or create a file for reading or writing

SYNOPSIS
     #include <fcntl.h>

     int
     open (char *path, int flags, mode_t mode);

DESCRIPTION
     The file name specified by path is opened for reading and/or writing, as
     specified by the argument oflag; the file descriptor is returned to the
     calling process.
     ....

RETURN VALUES
     If successful, open() returns a non-negative integer, termed a file
     descriptor.  It returns -1 on failure, and sets errno to indicate the
     error.

ERRORS
     The named file is opened unless:

        [ENOSPC]            O_CREAT is specified, the file does not exist, and
                            there are no free inodes on the file system on which
                            the file is being created.

        [ENOTDIR]           A component of the path prefix is not a directory.

        [ENAMETOOLONG]      A component of a pathname exceeded
                            {NAME_MAX} characters, or an entire path
                            name exceeded {PATH_MAX} characters.

        [ENOENT]            O_CREAT is not set and the named file does not exist.

        [ENOENT]            A component of the path name that must exist does not exist.

        ...

        [EFAULT]            Path points outside the process' allocated address space.

        [EEXIST]            O_CREAT and O_EXCL were specified and the file exists.

        [EOPNOTSUPP]        An attempt was made to open a socket (not currently
                            implemented.
```

The symbols in square brackets are the errno values that **open()** can set when it returns -1.
Example 5.1 has code that looks for specific errors. A real life program would handle these errors in an appropriate manner.

Example 5.1   open.m

```
// open.m -- Try opening files and getting different errors.

// gcc -g -Wmost -o open open.m

#import <errno.h>        // for errno
#import <fcntl.h>        // for open()
#import <stdio.h>        // for printf() and friends
#import <stdlib.h>       // for EXIT_SUCCESS, etc
#import <string.h>       // for strerror()
#import <sys/stat.h>     // for permission flags
#import <unistd.h>       // for close()

// Given a path and access flags, try to open the file.  If an error
// happens, write it out to standard error.

void tryOpen (const char *path, int flags) {
    // Attempt to open read/write for user/group.
    int result = open (path, flags, S_IRUSR | S_IWUSR | S_IRGRP  | S_IWGRP);

    if (result == -1) {
        fprintf (stderr, "an error happened opening %s\n", path);

        switch (errno) {
          case ENOTDIR:
            fprintf (stderr, "    part of the path is not a directory\n");
            break;

          case ENOENT:
            fprintf (stderr, "    something doesn't exist, like part of a path, or\n"
                     "    O_CREAT is not set and the file doesn't exist\n");
            break;

          case EISDIR:
            fprintf (stderr, "    tried to open a directory for writing\n");
            break;

          default:
            fprintf (stderr, "    another error happened:  errno %d, strerror: %s\n",
                     errno, strerror(errno));
        }

    } else {
        close (result);
    }

    fprintf (stderr, "\n");

} // tryOpen

int main (void) {
    // trigger ENOTDIR
    tryOpen ("/mach.sym/blah/blah", O_RDONLY);
```

```
// trigger ENOENT, part of the path doesn't exist
tryOpen ("/System/Frameworks/bork/my-file", O_RDONLY);

// trigger ENOENT, O_CREAT not set and file doesn't exist
tryOpen ("/tmp/my-file", O_RDONLY);

// trigger EISDIR
tryOpen ("/dev", O_WRONLY);

// trigger EEXIST
tryOpen ("/private/var/log/system.log", O_CREAT | O_EXCL);

return EXIT_SUCCESS;

} // main
```

In most cases it is not possible to handle *every* possible error condition (like ENFILE: System file table is full). In general, try to handle whichever errors makes sense and have a catch-all case that will log the error.

The main downside with this return code/errno reporting technique is that it is necessary to check the result code of *every* library function call, which can get tedious pretty quickly. Plus, all of the error-handling code obscures the flow of control. Some programmers write error-handling wrappers around library functions so that return codes do not pollute the mainline code; others instead use goto to jump to error-handling code at the end of the function.

With that caveat in mind, you are free to use this convention for your own code, which can be nice when you are supplying a library to programmers familiar with the Unix conventions. There is no standard way to add your own error strings to **strerror()**, unfortunately.

setjmp, longjmp

Languages like C++ and Java have exception-handling features built in. This is where code can happily go about its business, ignoring anything that might go wrong with the functions it is calling. But if something does go wrong, an exception can be thrown which will terminate the current flow of execution. Control resumes execution at a previously registered exception handler, which can then decide how best to recover from the problem and resume the work.

C has a primitive form of exception handling that can be used in a similar manner. The **setjmp** and **longjmp** functions are used like a super-goto:

```
int setjmp (jmp_buf env);

void longjmp (jmp_buf env, int value);
```

jmp_buf is a data structure that holds the current execution context (the current program counter, stack pointer, etc). You **setjmp** where you want execution to return (equivalent to your exception handler) and call **longjmp()** when you want to branch back to that point (equivalent to throwing an exception).

Example 5.2 shows how to use **longjmp()**.

Example 5.2   longjmp.m

```
// longjmp.m -- use setjmp, longjmp

// gcc -g -Wall -o longjmp longjmp.m
```

```
#import <setjmp.h>      // for setjmp / longjmp
#import <stdio.h>       // for printf
#import <stdlib.h>      // for EXIT_SUCCESS

static jmp_buf handler;

void doEvenMoreStuff () {
    printf ("        entering doEvenMoreStuff\n");
    printf ("        done with doEvenMoreStuff\n");
} // doEvenMoreStuff

void doMoreStuff () {
    printf ("    entering doMoreStuff\n");
    doEvenMoreStuff ();
    longjmp (handler, 23);
    printf ("    done with doMoreStuff\n");
} // doMoreStuff

void doStuff () {
    printf ("entering doStuff\n");
    doMoreStuff ();
    printf ("done with doStuff\n");
} // doStuff

int main (void) {
    int result;

    if ( (result = setjmp(handler)) ) {
        printf ("longjump called, setjmp returned again: %d\n", result);
    } else {
        doStuff ();
    }

    return (EXIT_SUCCESS);
} // main
```

A sample run:

```
$ ./longjmp
entering doStuff
    entering doMoreStuff
        entering doEvenMoreStuff
        done with doEvenMoreStuff
longjump called, setjmp returned again: 23
```

Two of the functions never get to print out their "done with" statements. They just get jumped over.

The interesting piece here is the if statement. When **setjmp()** is called, it returns zero, so the second branch of the if is taken. When **longjmp()** is called, that if statement is essentially evaluated again, and execution begins again at that point. The value argument to **longjmp()** is what is returned from **setjmp()** the second time it returns.

Any number of **setjmp()** calls can be active at any point in time as long as they use different memory locations for their jmp_bufs. You can maintain a stack of jmp_bufs so that **longjmp** knows to jump to the closest **setjmp()**. This is what Cocoa uses for its "classic" exception handling mechanism (discussed after Signals).

There is one rule to remember when using **setjmp()** and **longjmp()**: any local variables in the function that calls **setjmp()** that might be used after a **longjmp()** must be declared volatile. That will force the compiler to read the variables from memory each time rather than using processor registers. **setjmp()** saves some processor state, but it does not save every register. When **longjmp()** branches back to its matching **setjmp()**, any garbage in the registers can give you wrong values in variables.

Signals

Signals are like software interrupts: they can be delivered to your program at any time due to a number of well-defined conditions, like when you write outside of your mapped memory pages, you will get sent a SIGBUS (bus error) or a SIGSEGV (segmentation violation) signal. If a subprocess of yours terminates, you will get a SIGCHLD (child stopped) signal. If your controlling terminal goes away, there is SIGHUP (terminal hung up), and if you use the **alarm()** function, you will get sent SIGALRM when the time expires. The system defines about 31 different signals, many of which deal with job control or specific hardware issues.

A signal is delivered to your program asynchronously whenever it enters the operating system, whether it be via a system call or just regular process scheduling. This means that your code can be interrupted by a signal at pretty much any time.

As you saw above, signals are named with SIG plus an abbreviation of what the signal does. These are defined in <sys/signal.h> if you are curious. The signal manpage has the complete list of signals. The **signal** function (a simplified form of sigaction() that we will discuss shortly) is used to provide a handler for a signal.

Handling a signal

Use the **signal** function to register a signal handler.

```
typedef void (*sig_t) (int);

sig_t signal (int sig, sig_t func);
```

where sig is the signal number (e.g., SIGHUP) and **func** is the handler function. If you do not call **signal()** for a particular signal, the system default handler is used. Depending on the signal, the default handler will either ignore the signal or terminate the process. Check the signal(2) manpage for details on which is which.

Example 5.3 shows a program that registers signal handlers for three signals. The program will catch the signals and either print out that the signal that was caught (SIGHUP and SIGUSR1) or exit (SIGUSR2). By the way, SIGUSR1 and SIGUSR2 are signals that your program can use for its own purposes. The OS will not send you those signals unless explicitly told to.

Example 5.3   catch.m

```
// catch.m -- catch some signals

// gcc -g -std=c99 -Wall -o catch catch.m

#import <signal.h>      // for signal functions and types
#import <stdio.h>       // printf and friends
#import <stdlib.h>      // for EXIT_SUCCESS
#import <string.h>      // for strlen
#import <unistd.h>      // for sleep

static void writeString (const char *string) {
    int length = strlen (string);
```

```
        write (STDOUT_FILENO, string, length);
    } // writeString

    void handleHUP (int signo) {
        writeString ("got a HUP!\n");
    } // handleHUP

    void handleUsr1Usr2 (int signo) {
        if (signo == SIGUSR1) {
            writeString ("got a SIGUSR1\n");

        } else if (signo == SIGUSR2) {
            writeString ("got a SIGUSR2. exiting\n");
            exit (EXIT_SUCCESS);
        }
    } // handleUsr1Usr2

    int main (void) {
        // Register the signal handlers

        (void) signal (SIGHUP, handleHUP);
        (void) signal (SIGUSR1, handleUsr1Usr2);
        (void) signal (SIGUSR2, handleUsr1Usr2);

        // Now for our "real work"
        for (int i = 0; i < 500000; i++) {
            printf ("i is %d\n", i);
            sleep (1);
        }

        return EXIT_SUCCESS;
    } // main
```

Here is a sample run. It can be done with two terminals: one to see the output and the other to run the **kill** command, which sends signals to programs. Or it can be performed in one terminal because **catch** is put into the background for easy access to its process ID.

```
Terminal 1                      Terminal 2
$ ./catch &
[1] 7429  (this is the process ID)
1
2
3
4
5
6
7                               kill -HUP 7429
got a HUP!
8
9
10
11
12                              kill -USR1 7429
got a SIGUSR1
13
14
15
16
17
```

```
18                              kill -USR2 7429
got a SIGUSR2, exiting
[1]  Done  ./catch
```

A signal handler can handle more than one signal. Also, the return value of **signal()** is the previously registered function. If you are adding a signal handler to a library, or know that more than one handler will be registered for a signal, you should hang on to that return value and call that when your handler is invoked. If you want to register the same function for a bunch of signals, you will need to call **signal()** a bunch of times.

To ignore a signal, use the constant SIG_IGN instead of a function address. To restore the default behavior, use SIG_DFL. You cannot ignore or block SIGKILL or SIGSTOP. These give system administrators the ability to stop or kill any process that has run amok.

Use the **raise()** system call to send yourself a signal.

```
int raise (int sig);
```

sig is the number of the signal to raise. Your program can terminate itself by raising SIGKILL.

Blocking signals

Sometimes it is inconvenient to have a signal handler called during a critical piece of code. You may want to use a signal to interrupt a long-running process, but you do not want to stop in the middle of a complex data structure change and leave your program's environment in an inconsistent state. The signal mask can help you protect these critical sections.

Every running program has a signal mask associated with it. This is a bitmask that specifies which signals are blocked from delivery, as shown in Figure 5.1. The kernel tracks which blocked signals have been sent to the application so it can deliver them when they become unblocked, but it does not track the number of times a signal has been sent. A blocked signal will only be delivered to a process after it has been unblocked.

Figure 5.1   Blocking signals

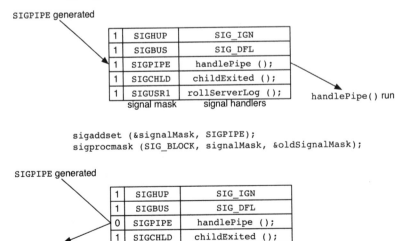

You use **sigprocmask()** to control the signal mask:

```
int sigprocmask (int how, const sigset_t *set, sigset_t *oset);
```

how is one of

SIG_BLOCK   Add the given signals to the program's signal mask (union).

SIG_UNBLOCK   Remove the signals from the program's signal mask (intersection).

SIG_SETMASK   Replace the program's signal mask with the new one.

sigset_t is an abstract type that represents the signal mask. set is the set of signals you want to add or remove, and oset is the original set (which is handy for feeding back into **sigprocmask** with SIG_SETMASK). You manipulate sigset_t with these functions (defined in man sigsetops(3)):

```
int sigemptyset (sigset_t *set);
```
Clears a set to all zeros (no signals).

```
int sigfillset (sigset_t *set);
```
Fill it with all ones (all signals).

```
int sigaddset (sigset_t *set, int signo);
```
Add a specific signal to the set.

```
int sigdelset (sigset_t *set, int signo);
```
Remove a specific signal from the set.

```
int sigismember (const sigset_t *set, int signo);
```
Test a signal's membership in the set.

Example 5.4 is a variation of the catch program above, but instances in which i is not a multiple of five are considered a critical section.

Example 5.4   catchblock.m

```
// catchblock.m -- Catch and block some signals

// gcc -g -std=c99 -Wall -o catchblock catchblock.m

#import <signal.h>      // for signal functions and types
#import <stdio.h>       // printf and friends
#import <stdlib.h>      // for EXIT_SUCCESS
#import <string.h>      // for strlen
#import <unistd.h>      // for sleep

static void writeString (const char *string) {
    int length = strlen (string);
    write (STDOUT_FILENO, string, length);
} // writeString

void handleHUP (int signo) {
    writeString ("got a HUP!\n");
} // handleHUP

void handleUsr1Usr2 (int signo) {
    if (signo == SIGUSR1) {
        writeString ("got a SIGUSR1\n");

    } else if (signo == SIGUSR2) {
```

```
            writeString ("got a SIGUSR2. exiting\n");
            exit (EXIT_SUCCESS);
        }
    } // handleUsr1Usr2

int main (void) {
        // Register our signal handlers
        (void) signal (SIGHUP, handleHUP);
        (void) signal (SIGUSR1, handleUsr1Usr2);
        (void) signal (SIGUSR2, handleUsr1Usr2);

        // construct our signal mask.  We don't want to be bothered
        // by SIGUSR1 or SIGUSR2 in our critical section.
        // but we'll leave SIGHUP out of the mask so that it will get
        // delivered

        sigset_t signalMask;
        sigemptyset (&signalMask);
        sigaddset (&signalMask, SIGUSR1);
        sigaddset (&signalMask, SIGUSR2);

        // now do our Real Work

        sigset_t oldSignalMask;

        for (int i = 0; i < 500000; i++) {
            printf ("i is %d\n", i);

            if ( (i % 5) == 0) {
                printf ("blocking at %i\n", i);
                sigprocmask (SIG_BLOCK, &signalMask, &oldSignalMask);
            }

            if ( (i % 5) == 4) {
                printf ("unblocking at %i\n", i);
                sigprocmask(SIG_SETMASK, &oldSignalMask, NULL);
            }

            sleep (1);
        }

        return EXIT_SUCCESS;
    } // main
```

A sample run:

Terminal 1	Terminal 2
./catchblock &	
[1] 7533	
i is 0	
blocking at 0	
i is 1	
i is 2	
i is 3	
i is 4	
unblocking at 4	
i is 5	
blocking at 5	
i is 6	**kill -HUP 7533**
got a HUP!	

```
i is 7
i is 8                              kill -HUP 7533
got a HUP!
i is 9
unblocking at 9
i is 10
blocking at 10
i is 11                             kill -USR1 7533
i is 12
i is 13
i is 14
unblocking at 14
got a SIGUSR1
i is 15
blocking at 15
i is 16                             kill -USR1 7533
i is 17                             kill -USR1 7533
i is 18                             kill -USR1 7533
i is 19
unblocking at 19
got a SIGUSR1
i is 20
blocking at 20
i is 21
i is 22                             kill -USR2 7533
i is 23
i is 24
unblocking at 24
got a SIGUSR2. exiting
```

It works as expected: HUPs make it through immediately, and USR1 and USR2 are only handled once at the unblocking no matter how many times they have been sent.

You can use **sigpending()** to see if a signal of interest is pending:

```
int sigpending (sigset_t *set);
```

This returns by reference a mask of the pending signals.

Handling signals with sigaction()

sigaction() is the full-featured way to handle signals:

```
struct sigaction {
    void    (*sa_handler)();
    sigset_t sa_mask;
    int      sa_flags;
};

int sigaction (int sig, const struct sigaction *act,
               struct sigaction *oact);
```

Instead of just passing in a handler function, you pass in a structure containing the handler function, the set of signals that should be added to the process signal mask, and some flags. Usually you just set them to zero. The **sigaction()** manpage describes them, mainly used for some SIGCHLD signals or for controlling which stack is used when signals are handled.

Like **signal()**, the previous setting is returned, this time in the oact parameter if it is non-NULL.

Signal issues

Reentrancy

There are a number of difficult programming issues involved with signals which sometimes makes them more difficult to deal with than they're worth. The first is reentrancy, and the second concerns race conditions.

A reentrant function is one that will work if there are two execution streams active in it at one time. This can happen even without threads. For example, consider this code:

```
...
ptr = malloc (50);
...
```

The program is in the middle of calling `malloc()`, and `malloc()` is messing with its internal data structures and is in an inconsistent state. Then a signal happens. Because signals happen asynchronously, your program is interrupted, and the signal handler runs:

```
...
tempPtr = malloc (20);
...
```

Because `malloc()` is in the middle of its previous work, the program will most likely crash.

In your signal handlers, you should only use reentrant functions. The `sigaction()` manpage has a list of functions that are either reentrant or are not interruptable by signals.

In general, these are safe:

- `longjmp()`

- Reentrant versions of functions, like `strtok_r()`

- Program terminators like `abort()` and `exit()`

- Unbuffered I/O (`read()`, `write()`, `open()`, etc.)

- Interrogative functions (`getgid()`, `getpid()`, `getuid()`)

- Signal functions (`sigaction()`, `sigprocmask()`)

- Any of your own reentrant functions

These are unsafe:

- Buffered I/O (`printf()` and friends). That's why a custom `writeString` function was used earlier.

- `malloc()` and `free()`

- Anything using static buffer space, like `strtok()`

- Any of your own non reentrant functions

You do not need to make your signal handler reentrant. When a signal handler is entered, the signal that triggered the handler is automatically added to the process signal mask. The handler will not get triggered again until it returns. Note that if a handler is registered for more than one signal using **signal()** or **sigaction()**, you will need to make it reentrant unless the other signals are blocked by the sa_mask member of the structure supplied to **sigaction()**.

You may notice that **longjmp()** is on the set of safe functions. You are free to **longjmp()** out of a signal handler to wherever the matching **setjmp()** was placed. This is a way of handling the interruption of a long-running process.

You may wonder about the process signal mask. If you **longjmp()** out of a handler, is the signal still blocked? In Mac OS X, **longjmp()** automatically restores the signal mask when jumping out of a signal handler. If you do not want this behavior (like what exists on some other Unixes), you can use the **_setjmp()** and **_longjmp()** functions.

If you'd rather not rely on this behavior, for example you plan to use the code under another Unix-alike, you can use the **sigsetjmp()**/**siglongjmp()** pair of functions, which are guaranteed to save or not save and restore the signal mask at your choice:

```
int sigsetjmp (sigjmp_buf env, int savemask);

void siglongjmp (sigjmp_buf env, int val);
```

If savemask is non-zero, the signal mask will be saved and restored; if zero, the signal mask will be unaffected by use of **siglongjmp()**.

Example 5.5 is an example of breaking out of a long-running process.

Example 5.5   interrupt.m

```
// interrupt.m -- show interruption of a long-running process

// cc -g -std=c99 -Wall -o interrupt interrupt.m

#import <errno.h>        // for errno
#import <setjmp.h>       // for setjmp / longjmp
#import <signal.h>       // for signal functions and types
#import <stdbool.h>      // for bool type
#import <stdio.h>        // for printf
#import <stdlib.h>       // for EXIT_SUCCESS
#import <string.h>       // for strerror
#import <unistd.h>       // for sleep

static jmp_buf handler;

void handleSignal (int signo) {
    longjmp (handler, 1);
} // handleSignal


void doLotsOfWork () {
    for (int i = 0; i < 50000; i++) {
        printf ("i is %d\n", i);
        sleep (1);
    }
} // doLotsOfWork
```

```
int main (void) {
    struct sigaction action;
    sigemptyset (&action.sa_mask);
    sigaddset (&action.sa_mask, SIGTERM);

    action.sa_handler = handleSignal;
    action.sa_flags = 0;

    if (sigaction (SIGUSR1, &action, NULL) == -1) {
        fprintf (stderr, "error in sigaction: %d / %s\n",  errno, strerror(errno));
        return EXIT_FAILURE;
    }

    volatile bool handlerSet = 0;
    while (1) {
        if (!handlerSet) {
            if (setjmp (handler)) {
                // We longjmp'd to here.  Reset the handler next time around.
                handlerSet = 0;
                continue;
            } else {
                handlerSet = 1;
            }
        }

        printf("starting lots of work\n");
        doLotsOfWork ();
    }

    return EXIT_SUCCESS;

} // main
```

A sample run:

```
Terminal 1                              Terminal 2
$ ./interrupt &
[1] 7625
starting lots of work
i is 0
i is 1
i is 2
i is 3
i is 4
i is 5
i is 6                                  kill -USR1 7625
starting lots of work
i is 0
i is 1
i is 2                                  kill -USR1 7625
starting lots of work
i is 0
i is 1
i is 2
i is 3
i is 4                                  kill 7625

[1]    Terminated                       ./interrupt
```

The last kill sends a SIGTERM, which terminates the process if not handled.

Race conditions

The other bugaboo with signals is race conditions (a subject revisited, along with the entire signal model, in Chapter 20: *Multithreading*). A race condition happens when two different streams of execution hit an ambiguous area of code and the code's behavior changes depending on the order in which the two streams execute.

A piece of code as simple as

```
i = 5;
i = i + 7;
```

can be subject to race conditions. Depending on order of operations, you can get different results:

```
thread 1                thread 2
  i = 5
  copy i to register
  add 7 to 5
  store 12 into i
                        i = 12
                        copy i to register
                        add 7 to 12
                        store 19 into i

Final value: 19


thread 1                thread 2
  i = 5
  copy i to register
                        i = 5
                        copy i to register
                        add 7 to 5
                        store 12 into i
  add 7 to 5
  store 12 into i

Final value: 12
```

The interrupt.m program has a couple of race conditions in it. The first happens after you register the signal handler but before the call to **sigsetjmp()** on the sigjmp_buf. If a SIGUSR1 signal happens any time after the **sigaction()** and before the **sigsetjmp()**, you will crash by trying to **siglongjmp()** with an invalid jump buffer.

Likewise, if a SIGUSR1 signal happens between the time that the code returns from **sigsetjmp()** and you call **sigsetjmp()** again, you will crash from using an out-of-date sigjmp_buf. You can use **sigprocmask()** to block the signal during these vulnerable times.

Race conditions are not limited to interleaving C statements. Delivery of a signal could leave a variable half-set, in some otherwise impossible and entirely inconsistent state. This can happen when a type requires more than one machine instruction to update, such as might be the case with long long, double, or a struct.

Aside from calling explicitly async-safe functions, the only guaranteed-safe ways a signal handler can interact with global, static state are to write to a variable of type volatile sig_atomic_t and to read from errno. The volatile sig_atomic_t variable is typically a "signal happened" flag read by a function executing normally. You might find you can get away with ignoring these severe restrictions, but if you ignore them and things go wrong, that could very well be why.

Signal handling is a dangerous and ugly task. The kqueue interface (discussed in Chapter 16: *kqueue and FSEvents*) provides an easy-to-use and safe way of handling signals. Grand Central Dispatch Chapter 22: *Grand Central Dispatch* also has a signal-handling mechanism.

Exception Handling in Cocoa

Cocoa provides two exception-handling mechanisms similar to what C++ and Java offer. The older, "classic" way to handle exceptions is to wrap a body of code with a set of macros. The newer way, the "native" way, was introduced in Mac OS X 10.3 and adds language support for exceptions.

Classic exception handling

To handle exceptions, wrap your code in an NS_DURING clause. Any exceptional conditions will raise an exception, which can then be caught by an NS_HANDLER clause.

The way you work it is:

```
NS_DURING
    ... code that might throw an exception
NS_HANDLER
    ... code to examine the exception and possibly handle it
NS_ENDHANDLER
```

If any code between NS_DURING and NS_HANDLER raises an exception, execution immediately resumes with the first instruction after NS_HANDLER, as shown in Figure 5.2

Figure 5.2   Exception flow of control

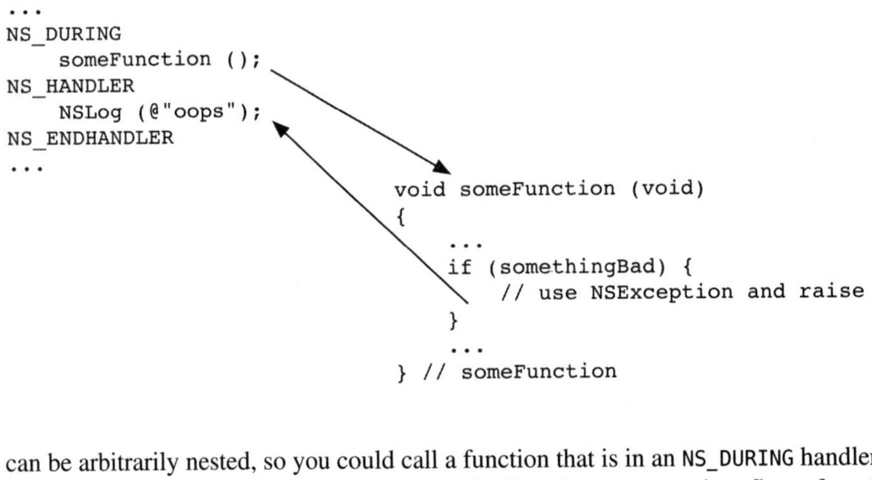

Handlers can be arbitrarily nested, so you could call a function that is in an NS_DURING handler, and it can set up its own NS_DURING handler. When someone finally raises an exception, flow of control will jump to the closest NS_HANDLER.

The macro for NS_HANDLER declares a local variable called localException that you can query for details about the exception – specifically, its name and the reason it happened. You can also use localException to "rethrow" the exception using [localException raise].

Example 5.6 is a little command-line tool to show exception handling in action. -[NSString characterAtIndex:] will raise an exception if you try to get a character that is beyond the length of the string.

Example 5.6   exception.m

```
// exception.m -- Show simple exception handling in Cocoa

// gcc -g -Wall -o exception -framework Foundation exception.m

#import <Foundation/Foundation.h>
#import <stdlib.h>                    // for EXIT_SUCCESS

int main (void) {
    NSAutoreleasePool *pool = [[NSAutoreleasePool alloc] init];
    NSString *string = @"hello";

    NS_DURING
        NSLog (@"character at index 0: %c", [string characterAtIndex: 0]);
        NSLog (@"character at index 1: %c", [string characterAtIndex: 1]);
        NSLog (@"character at index 2000: %c", [string characterAtIndex: 2000]);
        NSLog (@"character at index 2: %c", [string characterAtIndex: 2]);

    NS_HANDLER
        NSLog (@"inside of exception handler.");
        NSLog (@"name is : %@", [localException name]);
        NSLog (@"reason is : %@", [localException reason]);
        NSLog (@"userInfo dict: %@", [localException userInfo]);

    NS_ENDHANDLER

    [pool drain];

    return EXIT_SUCCESS;
} // main
```

A sample run:

```
$ ./exception
2011-05-20 13:18:37.449 exception[89626:903] character at index 0: h
2011-05-20 13:18:37.453 exception[89626:903] character at index 1: e
2011-05-20 13:18:37.459 exception[89626:903] inside of exception handler.
2011-05-20 13:18:37.460 exception[89626:903] name is : NSRangeException
2011-05-20 13:18:37.460 exception[89626:903] reason is :
        *** -[NSCFString characterAtIndex:]: Range or index out of bounds
2011-05-20 13:18:37.460 exception[89626:903] userInfo dict: (null)
```

The first two **characterAtIndex:** method calls succeed, and the third raised an exception, terminating the code in the NS_DURING section of code.

Specific Cocoa methods document whether they raise exceptions. Unfortunately there is not a centralized list of all methods that can raise exceptions.

Cocoa classic exception handling is based on **setjmp()/longjmp()**, so you must use volatile variables if they might be accessed after the **longjmp()** to your NS_HANDLER. There is no automatic cleanup of allocated objects when exceptions happen (like with stack objects in C++). Also, there are some restrictions in what you can do during the NS_HANDLER portion. Specifically, you should not **goto** or **return** out of an exception-handling domain (anywhere between NS_DURING and NS_HANDLER); if you do, the exception handler stack will be left in a bad state. If you want to return from an exception-handling domain, you must use the macros NS_VOIDRETURN and NS_VALUERETURN(value, value_type). Further, **setjmp()** and **longjmp()** should not be used if it crosses an NS_DURING statement. (In general, if you are using Cocoa exception handling, you will not need to use **setjmp()** and **longjmp()**, but be careful of library code.)

Cocoa exception handling is a heavy-weight operation, so do not use it for normal flow of control. It is better test a string's length when processing characters rather than falling off the string's end and depending on an exception to terminate your processing.

Cocoa provides the **NSException** object. You can allocate your own instances of this object and use them to raise your own exceptions. You can supply your own name and reason strings or use built-in ones.

Example 5.7 is a command-line tool that raises a custom exception:

Example 5.7   raise-classic.m

```
// raise-classic.m -- raise an exception in old-school Cocoa

// gcc -g -Wall -framework Foundation -o raise-classic raise-classic.m

#import <Foundation/Foundation.h>
#import <stdlib.h>                      // for EXIT_SUCCESS

void doSomethingElse () {
    NSDictionary *userInfo = [NSDictionary dictionaryWithObjectsAndKeys:
                                    @"hello", @"thing1",
                                    @"bork", @"thing2", nil];
    NSException *exception =
        [NSException exceptionWithName: @"GroovyException"
                    reason: @"doSomethingElse raised a GroovyException"
                    userInfo: userInfo];
    [exception raise];

    NSLog (@"after the raise.  This won't be printed.");

} // doSomethingElse


void doSomething () {
    doSomethingElse ();
} // doSomething


int main (void) {
    NSAutoreleasePool *pool = [[NSAutoreleasePool alloc] init];

    NS_DURING
        doSomething ();

    NS_HANDLER
        NSLog (@"inside of exception handler.");
        NSLog (@"name is : %@", [localException name]);
```

```
        NSLog (@"reason is : %@", [localException reason]);
        NSLog (@"userInfo dict: %@", [localException userInfo]);

    NS_ENDHANDLER

    [pool drain];

    return EXIT_SUCCESS;
} // main
```

A sample run:

```
$ ./raise-classic
... inside of exception handler.
... name is: GroovyException
... reason is: doSomethingElse raised a GroovyException
... userInfo dict:  {thing1 = hello; thing2 = bork; }
```

The Cocoa classic exception-handling mechanism is fundamentally string-based. There is no hierarchy of exception classes as there is in Java and C++. When code throws a built-in exception (like **NSGenericException**), the exception is actually just an **NSString** that gets put into an **NSException** object.

You can use **gdb** to halt execution when exceptions are thrown, just put a breakpoint on `-[NSException raise]` or `objc_exception_throw()`. The latter will be triggered with classic and native exceptions, and the former only with classic exceptions.

Native exception handling

Starting with Mac OS X 10.3, native exception handling was added to the Objective-C language. You need to turn it on before you can use it. You can provide **gcc** the `-fobjc-exceptions` flag when compiling on the command line or with makefiles. You can turn on native exception handling in Xcode's build configuration. Enabling native exceptions also enables some native thread-safety tools that will be discussed in Chapter 20: *Multithreading*.

Example 5.8 shows the syntax for native Objective-C exceptions.

Example 5.8   Objective-C Exception Syntax

```
@try {
    ...
    @throw expr;
}
@catch (SomeClass *exception) {
    ...
    @throw expr;
    ...
    @throw
}
@catch (AnotherClass *exception) {
    ...
}
@catch (id allOthers) {
    ...
}
@finally {
    ...
```

```
    @throw expr;
}
```

You wrap the code that might throw an exception inside of an @try block. If any exceptions are thrown from inside of that block, one of the @catch handlers might be entered. Unlike the classic exceptions, the native exceptions are object-based, so you can catch different classes of exceptions. If you @catch a particular class, any objects that are subclasses of that class will be caught by that block, too. Use id to designate the "catch-all" handler. Any exception that does not match any of the other classes will be caught here. Classes are matched in the order they are listed, so be sure to have any id @catch blocks at the end. Finally, the @finally section is run whether or not an exception was thrown or the @try block completed successfully.

To throw an exception, you @throw an object. Only Objective-C objects can be thrown and caught, so you cannot throw C++ objects or primitive C types. You can @throw an exception at any time. The code inside of an @catch section can throw a brand new exception if it wants, or it can use @throw; (without an object) to rethrow the current exception.

The native Objective-C exception mechanism is binary compatible with the NS_HANDLER idiom, but you can only use the new syntax on Mac OS X 10.3 or later because of support added to the Objective-C runtime.

If you want the debugger to break when an exception is @thrown, put a breakpoint on **objc_exception_throw()**. You can also have Xcode catch exceptions for you. In Xcode 3, use the Stop on Objective-C Exceptions menu command. In Xcode 4, add an exception breakpoint and choose whether you want to break on Objective-C or C++ exceptions and whether to break on throw or on catch.

Example 5.9 is the **raise-classic** program ported to use the native exception syntax. It throws an NSException object because it conveniently wraps some useful data, but you could throw any kind of object.

Example 5.9   raise-native.m

```objc
// raise-native.m -- Raise an exception using native Objective-C mechanisms

// gcc -g -Wall -framework Foundation -fobjc-exceptions -o raise-native
//    raise-native.m

#import <Foundation/Foundation.h>
#import <stdlib.h>                        // for EXIT_SUCCESS

void doSomethingElse () {
    NSDictionary *userInfo = [NSDictionary dictionaryWithObjectsAndKeys:
                                        @"hello", @"thing1",
                                        @"bork", @"thing2", nil];
    NSException *exception =
        [NSException exceptionWithName: @"GroovyException"
                    reason: @"doSomethingElse raised a GroovyException"
                    userInfo: userInfo];
    @throw exception;

    NSLog (@"after the throw.  This won't be printed.");

} // doSomethingElse
```

```
void doSomething () {
    doSomethingElse ();
} // doSomething


int main (void) {
    NSAutoreleasePool *pool = [[NSAutoreleasePool alloc] init];

    @try {
        doSomething ();
    }
    @catch (NSException *exception) {
        NSLog (@"inside of exception handler.");
        NSLog (@"name is : %@", [exception name]);
        NSLog (@"reason is : %@", [exception reason]);
        NSLog (@"userInfo dict: %@", [exception userInfo]);
    }
    @finally {
        [pool drain];
    }

    return EXIT_SUCCESS;

} // main
```

And the results are the same as **raise-classic**:

```
$ ./raise-native
... [21540] inside of exception handler.
... [21540] name is: GroovyException
... [21540] reason is: doSomethingElse raised a GroovyException
... [21540] userInfo dict: {thing1 = hello; thing2 = bork; }
```

In both native and classic exception handling, you must be careful not to deallocate the autoreleased exception object by draining a local autorelease pool prior to rethrowing the exception. Be particularly careful of draining pools in @finally blocks, because these execute before the next exception handler catches the rethrown exception.

Subclassing NSApplication to catch exceptions

In some applications (Xcode, for example), when an exception falls through the stack all the way to the run loop, the user is shown the exception in a panel. (Often, the panel just says something like "Something has gone wrong. You may want to save what you are working on and restart this application.") They accomplish this by using a custom subclass of **NSApplication**.

When an exception falls through the stack all the way to the run loop, the instance of **NSApplication** gets sent the following message:

```
- (void)reportException: (NSException *) theException
```

This method simply logs the exception using **NSLog()**, and the run loop begins again. If you would like to alter this behavior, you must subclass **NSApplication** and override **-reportException:**.

If you do this, make sure that you also alter the Info.plist for your application so that it uses your subclass instead of **NSApplication**:

```
<key>NSPrincipalClass</key>
```

```
<string>GroovyExceptionReportingApplication</string>
```

Note that this only works if your Objective-C code is in a Cocoa application. If you have written a Command Line Tool, you will call **NSSetUncaughtExceptionHandler()** and supply it with a pointer to a function with this signature:

```
volatile void Handler (NSException *e);
```

The Exception Handling framework's **NSExceptionHandler** class provides some default uncaught exception handling that can be helpful during debugging; you should check it out before rolling your own.

You might wonder at the `volatile void` return type. This is a GNU extension to standard C that indicates that the function does not return, similar to the `noreturn` attribute you could use to qualify wrappers around **exit()** and **abort()**.

64-bit Objective-C runtime

The new runtime introduced with Leopard's 64-bit support and now used on iOS, changes the way exceptions are implemented in Objective-C. Under the classic runtime, exceptions are **setjmp/longjmp** based. Recall that **setjmp** saves processor registers and other bits of state. This means that you pay a price for every @try, while the @throw is a very cheap operation.

The C++ exception model instead makes `try` operations very cheap, while incurring the computationally expensive portion when an exception is actually `thrown`. Entering and exiting `try` blocks is a much more common operation than actually throwing an exception, so this is a design win. The new Objective-C runtime adopts the C++ model and actually unifies the two exception mechanisms. You can now throw and catch C++ and Objective-C exceptions with each other's handling mechanism.

iOS development has its own considerations. iOS devices use the new runtime, including the unified exception model. In general, all exception work is relatively expensive, so you should measure the performance impact of any heavy exception work you might be doing.

NSError

Apple introduced **NSError** in Mac OS X 10.3 as a way of returning richer error results from methods. Consider reading the contents of a file into an **NSData** object:

```
+ (id) dataWithContentsOfFile: (NSString *) path;
```

If something goes wrong, you get `nil` back, and there's not much you can do to figure out what went wrong. The updated version of this method looks like this:

```
+ (id) dataWithContentsOfFile: (NSString *) path
                      options: (NSDataReadingOptions) readOptionsMask
                        error: (NSError **) errorPtr;
```

Notice the **NSError** that is passed in. The method wants a pointer to a pointer. The method will fill in this pointer if the method failed. The return value of `errorPtr` is undefined if the method succeeded. Therefore, you should *never* use the value (`nil` or non-nil) of an **NSError** pointer to decide if an error happened.

This is the usual usage pattern:

```
NSError *error;
NSData *data = [NSData dataWithContentsOfFile: pathname
                            options: 0
                            error: &error];
if (data == nil) {
    // Use error to figure out what went wrong.
}
```

Logging

In our development careers at one time or another we have all done "caveman debugging," putting in lots of print statements to see program flow and to see what values our variables have. Using stuff in Chapter 11: *Files, Part 1: I/O and Permissions*, you can even redirect those print statements to log files.

But there are times when you are logging and it is not debugging related, like server programs keeping an audit trail of connections or printing information that may be of interest to administrators (such as the disk is filling up). Most Unix systems have a daemon running called **syslogd**, the system logging daemon. System administrators can configure **syslogd** to log to a file or to send the log information from many machines to a central location (very useful if you have a lot of machines to keep an eye on).

syslog()

One programmatic interface to syslogd, the **syslog()** function, is:

```
void syslog (int priority, const char *message, ...);
```

The message is a **printf()**-style string. You can use any **printf()** token in there you want. There is also an added format string, "%m", to insert the current error message from **strerror()**. **syslog()** also adds a trailing newline if one is not already specified in the message string.

The priority argument controls whether the logging will be seen or not. Here are the priority levels from highest to lowest:

LOG_EMERG   A panic condition. This is normally broadcast to all users.

LOG_ALERT   A condition that should be corrected immediately, such as a corrupted system database.

LOG_CRIT   Critical conditions, e.g., hard device errors.

LOG_ERR   Errors.

LOG_WARNING   Warning messages.

LOG_NOTICE   Conditions that are not error conditions, but should possibly be handled specially.

LOG_INFO   Informational messages.

LOG_DEBUG   Messages that contain information normally of use only when debugging a program.

The configuration file for **syslogd**, /etc/syslogd.conf, contains the controls for setting the threshold where logging will occur. By default, LOG_DEBUG messages are not shown, but everything else is.

You can control some of the syslog behavior of the logging output by using **openlog()**:

```
void openlog (const char *ident, int logopt, int facility);
```

ident is the name to use for the program in the log. By default, the executable name is used. logopt is any one of these flags bitwise-OR'd together:

LOG_CONS   If **syslog()** cannot pass the message to **syslogd**, it will attempt to write the message to the console (/dev/console).

LOG_NDELAY   Open the connection to **syslogd(8)** immediately. Normally the open is delayed until the first message is logged. This is useful for programs that need to manage the order in which file descriptors are allocated.

LOG_PERROR   Write the message to standard error output as well as to the system log.

LOG_PID   Log the process ID with each message; this is useful for identifying instantiations of daemons.

The facility parameter tells **syslogd** that the program is a member of a standard system facility, like being a daemon, or that it is part of the security subsystem. For example, if you were writing a daemon that was part of the mail system, you would call **openlog()** with a facility of LOG_MAIL. These constants are listed in the man page.

Example 5.10 is a sample that logs to syslog, which by default gets written locally to /var/log/ system.log. This is the one of the logs that Console.app looks at.

Example 5.10   syslog.m

```
// syslog.m -- use the syslog functions

// gcc -g -Wall -o syslog syslog.m

#import <syslog.h>       // for syslog and friends
#import <stdlib.h>       // for EXIT_SUCCESS
#import <errno.h>        // for errno

int main (int argc, char *argv[]) {
    syslog (LOG_WARNING, "This is a warning message.");
    errno = EINVAL;
    syslog (LOG_ERR, "This is an error, %m");
    syslog (LOG_EMERG, "WHOOP!! WHOOP!!");

    openlog ("BNRsyslogTest", LOG_PID | LOG_NDELAY | LOG_CONS, LOG_DAEMON);

    syslog (LOG_DEBUG, "Debug message");
    syslog (LOG_NOTICE, "Notice message");

    return EXIT_SUCCESS;
} // main
```

A run of this produces in the log:

```
$ tail -f /private/var/log/system.log
(and run ./syslog in another terminal)

(beep) Broadcast Message from root@pheasantbook.local
        (no tty) at 13:39 EDT...
```

```
WHOOP!! WHOOP!!

May 20 13:39:18 pheasantbook ./syslog[89697]: This is a warning message.
May 20 13:39:18 pheasantbook ./syslog[89697]: This is an error, Invalid argument
May 20 13:39:18 pheasantbook ./syslog[89697]: WHOOP!! WHOOP!!
May 20 13:39:18 pheasantbook BNRsyslogTest[89697]: Notice message
```

Here you can see the LOG_EMERG getting broadcast to all the open terminals and then the various syslog messages. You can call **openlog()** at anytime. You can see how the LOG_PID option and "BNRSyslogTest" identifier appear.

ASL

The **syslog()** function is very portable and works on all modern Unix-flavored systems. Apple has introduced its own API that adds some value on top of **syslogd**. ASL, the Apple System Log facility, provides an alternate API for sending messages to **syslogd**, as well as a capability for querying **syslogd** for information about previously logged items.

ASL messages

ASL is based on messages, and these messages are an opaque type called aslmsg. A message is a container for key-value pairs with a number of pre-defined keys that have meaning for **launchd**. You create a new message using **asl_new()**:

```
aslmsg asl_new (uint32_t type);
```

asl_new() creates a new aslmsg and returns it to you. The type parameter can either be ASL_TYPE_MSG to create a new message or ASL_TYPE_QUERY to create a new search query.

When you are done with an aslmsg, release its resources using **asl_free()**, which takes an aslmsg as its only argument.

Use **asl_set()** to add keys and values to a message:

```
int asl_set (aslmsg message, const char *key, const char *value);
```

message is the aslmsg you are filling out. key and value are null-terminated strings (ASCII or UTF-8). The function returns zero on success, non-zero for failure. There are a number of pre-defined keys that have defaults set, and you are also allowed to add your own keys. The predefined keys are: ASL_KEY_TIME, ASL_KEY_HOST, ASL_KEY_SENDER (defaults to the process name), ASL_KEY_PID, ASL_KEY_UID, ASL_KEY_GID, ASL_KEY_LEVEL, and ASL_KEY_MSG (the text to actually log).

You can get a value out of a message for a specific key with **asl_get()** and iterate through a message's keys with **asl_key()**:

```
const char *asl_get (aslmsg message, const char *key);
```

Given a message and a key, this returns the value or NULL if there is no value under that key.

```
const char *asl_key (aslmsg message, uint32_t index);
```

Given a message, this returns the key at the position indicated by index. The function returns NULL if index falls off the end of the list of keys. You can spin through the keys by starting at 0 and incrementing an index. When the function returns NULL, you have reached the end. You can pass the returned key to **asl_get()** to retrieve the value.

Once you have constructed a message, you can send it off to **syslogd** using **asl_send()**:

```
int asl_send (aslclient client, aslmsg message);
```

The second argument, message, is the message that has already been constructed. The first argument, client, is an aslclient. If you pass NULL, a default client will be used. Access to a client is single-threaded, so if you want multiple threads to be able to log at the exact same time, you must create additional clients using **asl_open()**. **asl_open()** is not described further here; see the asl manpage for more information.

If nothing appears in the log, you may need to set the message level, such as

```
asl_set (message, ASL_KEY_LEVEL, "5");
```

The argument takes a string, not an ASL_LEVEL_* constant.

ASL supplies two convenience functions, **asl_log()** and **asl_vlog()**, so that you don't have to create a new aslmsg every time you want to log something:

```
int asl_log (aslclient client, aslmsg message, int level,
             const char *format, ...);
```

```
int asl_vlog (aslclient client, aslmsg message, int level,
              const char *format, va_list args);
```

You can pass NULL for the first argument, client. You only need additional clients in multi-threaded applications. The message argument is a template message that has some key-value pairs already added to it. The template will be merged with default values for the message. You can pass NULL if you don't have a template message you want to use. **asl_log()** handles its format string the same way as **syslog()**, so it includes support for the %m "current error string" format specifier. If you have a va_list handy, you can pass that to **asl_vlog()**.

ASL queries

Using ASL messages seems like a lot of work when you can just use **syslog()**. But unlike the syslog API, ASL provides a way to query **syslogd** for information about previously logged entries, turning **syslogd** into a mini-database of sorts. To query the database, you make a new message of type ASL_TYPE_QUERY and then use the **asl_set_query()** function to add predicates. You can set multiple predicates, which will be joined using logical ANDs.

```
int asl_set_query (alsmsg query, const char *key, const char *value,
                   uint32_t operation);
```

The query parameter is an aslmsg that was created with the ASL_TYPE_QUERY type. key is the key you want to search for, value is the value you want to search for, and operation is the way to search, along with some optional flags.

Here are the different query operations:

ASL_QUERY_OP_EQUAL	Compare values for equality. If the value for key in a logged message is equal to the value parameter, that message will be returned from the query.

ASL_QUERY_OP_GREATER	If the value for key in a logged message is strictly greater than the value parameter, that message will be returned from the query.
ASL_QUERY_OP_GREATER_EQUAL	If the value for key in a logged message is greater than or equal to the value parameter, that message will be returned from the query.
ASL_QUERY_OP_LESS	If the value for key in a logged message is strictly less than the value parameter, that message will be returned from the query.
ASL_QUERY_OP_LESS_EQUAL	If the value for key in a logged message is less than or equal to the value parameter, that message will be returned from the query.
ASL_QUERY_OP_NOT_EQUAL	If the value for key in a logged message is not equal to the value parameter, that message will be returned from the query.
ASL_QUERY_OP_REGEX	If the value for key in a logged message matches the regular expression specified by value parameter, that message will be returned from the query. Regular expression searches use the regex function; see the regex(3) manpage for details. Patterns are compiled using the REG_EXTENDED (use "modern" regular expressions) and REG_NOSUB (compile the regular expression for matching that only reports success or failure, not what was matched) options.
ASL_QUERY_OP_TRUE	Always true. Use this to test for the existence of a key.

There are also a number of modifiers you can bitwise-OR into **asl_set_query()**'s operation parameter:

ASL_QUERY_OP_CASEFOLD	Compare strings in a case-insensitive manner. This is the only modifier that is checked for the ASL_QUERY_OP_REGEX operation.
ASL_QUERY_OP_PREFIX	Match a leading substring.
ASL_QUERY_OP_SUFFIX	Match a trailing substring
ASL_QUERY_OP_SUBSTRING	Match any substring.
ASL_QUERY_OP_NUMERIC	Convert values to integers using **atoi()**. By adding this option to one of the relative operations (greater, greater_equal, etc.), you can do numeric comparisons instead of string comparisons. This is very handy when you want a specific range of message levels.

A common error is to forget to include a query operation like ASL_QUERY_OP_EQUAL along with ASL_QUERY_OP_SUBSTRING

After you have constructed the query message, you send it off to **syslogd** using **asl_search()**:

aslresponse **asl_search** (aslclient client, aslmsg query);

The client can be NULL unless you are calling this from multiple threads. query is the query message you built up with **asl_set_query**. The return value, an aslresponse, is an opaque iterator type that you feed to **aslresponse_next()** until it returns NULL. Release the query's resources with **aslresponse_free()** when you're done with it. Both of these aslresponse functions take an aslresponse returned by **asl_search()**

Example 5.11 will list all messages that **syslogd** has recently displayed. It uses a query with ASL_QUERY_OP_TRUE to match everything.

Example 5.11   asl-list.m

```
// asl-list.m -- show what asl messages have been logged so far

// gcc -g -Wall -o asl-list asl-list.m

#import <asl.h>         // for ASL API
#import <stdlib.h>      // for EXIT_SUCCESS
#import <stdio.h>       // for printf()
void dumpAslMsg (aslmsg message) {
    // walk the keys and values in each message
    const char *key, *value;

    uint32_t i = 0;
    while ((key = asl_key (message, i))) {
        value = asl_get (message, key);
        printf ("%u: %s -> %s\n", i, key, value);
        i++;
    }
} // dumpAslMsg


int main (void) {
    // Construct a query for all senders using a regular expression
    // that matches everything.
    aslmsg query;
    query = asl_new (ASL_TYPE_QUERY);
    asl_set_query (query, ASL_KEY_SENDER, "", ASL_QUERY_OP_TRUE);

    // Perform the search.
    aslresponse results = asl_search (NULL, query);

    // walk the returned messages
    aslmsg message;
    while ((message = aslresponse_next(results))) {
        dumpAslMsg (message);
        printf ("----------------------------------------\n");
    }

    aslresponse_free (results);
    asl_free (query);

    return EXIT_SUCCESS;
} // main
```

And here is a sample run:

```
$ ./asl-list

0: Time -> 1280870970
1: Host -> Pheasantbook
2: Sender -> kernel
3: PID -> 0
4: UID -> 0
5: GID -> 0
6: Level -> 3
7: Message -> (null)
8: ASLMessageID -> 65297
9: TimeNanoSec -> 0
10: ReadUID -> 0
11: ReadGID -> 80
12: Facility -> com.apple.system.fs
13: ErrType -> IO
14: ErrNo -> 5
15: IOType -> Read
16: PBlkNum -> 911281
17: LBlkNum -> 12995
18: FSLogMsgID -> 1438271333
19: FSLogMsgOrder -> First
20: ASLExpireTime -> 1312493370
----------------------------------------
0: Time -> 1280870970
1: Host -> Pheasantbook
2: Sender -> kernel
3: PID -> 0
4: UID -> 0
5: GID -> 0
6: Level -> 3
7: Message -> (null)
8: ASLMessageID -> 65299
9: TimeNanoSec -> 0
10: ReadUID -> 0
11: ReadGID -> 80
12: Facility -> com.apple.system.fs
13: DevNode -> /dev/disk2s2
14: MountPt -> /Volumes/Time Machine Backups
15: FSLogMsgID -> 1438271333
16: FSLogMsgOrder -> Last
17: ASLExpireTime -> 1312493370
```

There actually was a *lot* more output. This is just a representative sample.

Example 5.12 logs a simple message with **asl_log()**, and then it builds a template message and uses that for a couple of logs. The template has a custom key in it, "Suit" – presumably because the organization running this program wants to log when someone enters the research lab while wearing a specific kind of protective suit. Two people are logged as having been suited up. After the logs, a query is made to get the log messages for when Alex wears his suit.

Example 5.12   asl-log-n-query.m

```
// asl-log-n-query.m -- do some logs and some queries

#import <asl.h>       // for ASL function
#import <stdio.h>     // for printf()
#import <stdlib.h>    // for EXIT_SUCCESS
```

```
#import <syslog.h>   // for LOG_ constants
#import <inttypes.h> // for printf constant PRIu32

// gcc -g -std=c99 -Wall -o asl-log-n-query asl-log-n-query.m

void dumpAslMsg(aslmsg message) {
    // walk the keys and values in each message
    const char *key, *value;
    uint32_t i = 0;
    while ((key = asl_key(message, i))) {
        value = asl_get (message, key);
        printf ("%u: %s => %s\n", i, key, value);
        i++;
    }
} // dumpAslMsg


int main(void) {
    // Perform a simple log.
    asl_log (NULL, NULL, LOG_NOTICE, "Hello how are %s today?", "you");

    // Make a template message with our custom tags
    aslmsg template = asl_new (ASL_TYPE_MSG);
    asl_set (template, "Suit", "(4A)CGS");

    // Log some messages.
    asl_log (NULL, template, LOG_NOTICE, "Laurel has suited up");
    asl_log (NULL, template, LOG_NOTICE, "Alex has suited up");

    // Do a query to see how many times Alex has worn his (4A)CGS suit

    aslmsg query = asl_new (ASL_TYPE_QUERY);

    asl_set_query (query, "Suit", "(4A)CGS", ASL_QUERY_OP_EQUAL);
    asl_set_query (query, ASL_KEY_MSG, "Alex",
                   ASL_QUERY_OP_EQUAL | ASL_QUERY_OP_PREFIX);

    // Perform the search.
    aslresponse results = asl_search(NULL, query);

    // Walk the returned messages.
    aslmsg message = NULL;
    while ((message = aslresponse_next(results))) {
        dumpAslMsg(message);
        printf ("----------------------------------------\n");
    }

    // Cleanup.
    aslresponse_free (results);
    asl_free (query);
    asl_free( template);

    return EXIT_SUCCESS;
} // main
```

When you run the program, have a **tail -f** pointed at /var/system.log so you can see the three log messages:

```
$ tail -f /var/system.log
```

```
May 20 14:15:08 pheasantbook asl-log-n-query[90248]: Hello how are you today?
May 20 14:15:08 pheasantbook asl-log-n-query[90248]: Laurel has suited up
May 20 14:15:08 pheasantbook asl-log-n-query[90248]: Alex has suited up
```

Then the program displays the results from its query. It shows an earlier notice from 17:45:45 and the one from 19:20:57. The discrepancy in time stamps between the program's output and **syslogd**'s output is due to time zones: the time returned from the query is in UTC (coordinated universal time), while the log file uses the current time zone (Eastern Daylight Time in this case).

```
$ ./asl-log-n-query

0: Time => 1305914413
1: Host => pheasantbook
2: Sender => asl-log-n-query
3: PID => 89953
4: UID => 501
5: GID => 20
6: Level => 5
7: Message => Alex has suited up
8: ASLMessageID => 869458
9: TimeNanoSec => 360885000
10: Facility => user
11: Suit => 4ACGS
----------------------------------------
0: Time => 1305914522
1: Host => pheasantbook
2: Sender => asl-log-n-query
3: PID => 89979
4: UID => 501
5: GID => 20
6: Level => 5
7: Message => Alex has suited up
...
```

ASL also has some features that allow you to change the logging level of applications remotely, allowing you as a user or an administrator to crank up or down the volume of logging from an application. Check out the asl(3) and syslog(1) manpages.

For the More Curious: Assertions

Assertions are a programming technique where tests are added for conditions that cannot happen. The program kills itself when it enters such an impossible state, dumping a core file if it can.

The assert macro

assert (expression)

evaluates the expression. If the expression is zero (false), the process is terminated, a diagnostic message is written to the standard error stream, and the **abort()** function is called, which terminates the program by raising the signal SIGABRT. Because most programmers use asserts for debugging purposes, you can compile them out of a production program by using the preprocessor flag -DNDEBUG. Be aware of side effects due to code called in the **assert()** macro. This could cause your program to fail in a non-debug build.

Should you always leave assertions and debugging statements in your code? There are two schools of thought. One idea, usually held by programmers that primarily work on server software, is that programs should terminate immediately if something bad is detected. A server program will be restarted if it exits, and the faster you exit the less chance you have of corrupting the user's data and sending that corrupted data to permanent storage.

On the other hand, one of the worst things a GUI application can do is suddenly exit, wiping out any work the user has done. In that case, you would not want to immediately terminate the program, but instead put up some kind of "help help i am dying" alert and give the user an opportunity to save any data.

Cocoa also has an assertion mechanism, **NSAssertionHandler**. There you use macros like **NSAssert(test, msg)** (when in a method) and **NSCAssert(test, msg)** (when in a regular old C function) to evaluate a condition. If it evaluates to false, the message is passed to an **NSAssertionHandler** (one is associated with each thread). When invoked, this object prints an error message and raises an NSInternalInconsitencyException, which can be caught using @catch().

Static assertions

A neat trick is crafting an assertion so that it prevents the file from compiling if the assertion fails. This notifies you of the failed test without having to run the executable! The easiest way to make such a static assertion is to exploit the guarantee that arrays must have a non-negative size. For example, suppose you wanted to assert that sizeof(int) == sizeof(long). You can use a typedef to avoid any cost in space or speed to the program while still checking this predicate statically:

```
typedef char AssertIntAndLongHaveSameSize[(sizeof(int) == sizeof(long)) ? 0 : -1];
```

There's no problem compiling for i386 because both int and long are four bytes. But compiling it for x86_64 yields an error:

```
$ gcc -arch i386 isILP32.m
$ gcc -arch x86_64 isILP32.m
isILP32.m:4: error: size of array 'AssertIntAndLongHaveSameSize' is negative
```

AssertMacros.h

/usr/include/AssertMacros.h has a collection of useful debugging macros that can be used to control program flow in the face of error conditions. For example, require_noerr takes an error code and a label. In debug builds, if the label is not zero, otherwise known as noErr, it will invoke the DEBUG_ASSERT_MESSAGE macro, which will log the error value, file, line, etc and then jump to the indicated label. You can replace that macro with one that does other work, such as breaking into the debugger, for helping to catch "that can't possibly happen" circumstances. In production builds, it simply jumps to the label.

Exercises

1. Fix the race conditions in interrupt.m by using **sigprocmask()**. Should **sigsetjmp()** be saving the signal mask or not?

2. Tweak /etc/syslogd.conf to display the debug message from syslog.m in the system.log file.

6

Libraries

A library is a packaged collection of object files that programs can link against to make use of the features it provides. Traditional Unix has two kinds of libraries: static libraries, where the linker packages the object code into the application, and shared libraries, where the linker just stores a reference to a library and the symbols the application needs. Mac OS X also brings frameworks to the table. Frameworks package shared libraries with other resources, like header files, documentation, and subframeworks.

Static Libraries

Static libraries are the simplest libraries to work with. Many open source projects that you can download will frequently build static libraries, whether for your programs to link against or for internal use to simplify the build system where each major module is put into its own static library. All of these libraries are then linked together to make the final executable program. Figure 6.1 shows that the object code that lives in the shared libraries is physically copied into the final executable.

Figure 6.1   Static libraries

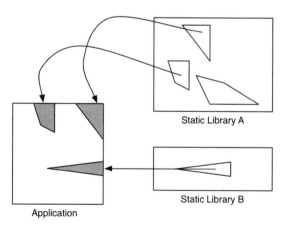

The **ar** program is what is used to create libraries, or in **ar**'s terminology, archives. **ar** can create an archive, add new files to it, and existing files can be extracted, deleted, or replaced. Files are named in the archive by their file name (any files specified with a path just use the file name).

In the online materials for this book, you will find five source files that look like Example 6.1:

Example 6.1   src0.c

```
// src0.c : a simple source file so we can fill a library

// gcc -g -Wall -c src0.c

int add_0 (int number) {
    return number + 0;
} // add_0
```

These are little functions that do not actually do anything useful. You can compile them all into object files by this command:

$ gcc -g -c src?.c

Recall that the shell will use ? as a one-character wildcard. You can see the source files:

$ ls src?.c
```
src0.c  src1.c  src2.c  src3.c  src4.c
```

and the associated object files:

$ ls src?.o
```
src0.o  src1.o  src2.o  src3.o  src4.o
```

Create the archive:

$ ar crl libaddum.a src?.o

with the final result looking like Figure 6.2. A static library is basically a collection of object files.

Figure 6.2   Inside a library

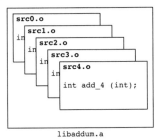

The flags are:

c   Create if the archive does not exist.

r   Replace or add the specified files to the archive.

l   The next argument is the name of the library file.

After you create or modify an archive, you may need to run the **ranlib** command, which builds the table of contents for the archive. The linker needs this table of contents to locate the object files it actually needs to link in. Frequently, **ranlib** can be used to "fix" broken libraries. If you get strange linker errors (particularly if you're not using Apple's development tools) when using a static library, run **ranlib** on it and see if it that helps things.

$ ranlib libaddum.a

To actually use a static library in your program, you need to use two compiler flags. -L tells the linker what directory to look in. -l (lowercase ell) tells the linker what files to look for. By convention, library file names are of the form libfoo.a, where foo is some descriptive name for the features the library provides. If you specify -lfoo, the linker knows to look for libfoo.a.

Example 6.2 uses some of the functions from the libaddum.a.

Example 6.2   useadd.m

```
// useadd.m -- use functions from a library

// gcc -g -Wall -o useadd useadd.m -L. -laddum

#import <stdlib.h>      // for EXIT_SUCCESS
#import <stdio.h>       // for printf

int main (int argc, char *argv[]) {
    int i;

    i = 5;
    printf ("i is %d\n", i);

    i = add_1 (i);
    printf ("i after add_1: %d\n", i);

    i = add_4 (i);
    printf ("i after add_4: %d\n", i);

    return EXIT_SUCCESS;
} // main
```

If you just try to compile like other programs, you will understandably get a complaint about the missing functions:

```
$ gcc -g -o useadd useadd.m
Undefined symbols for architecture x86_64:
  "_add_1", referenced from:
      _main in ccg3lIOO.o
  "_add_4", referenced from:
      _main in ccg3lIOO.o
ld: symbol(s) not found for architecture x86_64
collect2: ld returned 1 exit status
```

BSD systems frequently prepend an underscore to symbols during linking, and Mac OS X is no different. The missing symbol names are actually "add_1" and "add_4." Now add the flags to tell the linker where to look and what library to use:

```
$ gcc -g -o useadd useadd.m -L. -laddum
```

A sample run:

```
$ ./useadd
i is 5
i after add_1: 6
i after add_4: 10
```

Note that the library stuff is specified after the source file name. If it were the other way around:

```
$ gcc -g -o useadd -L. -laddum useadd.m
/usr/bin/ld: Undefined symbols:
```

```
_add_1
_add_4
```

you would still get the errors because the linker scans files left to right. It looks at the library, sees that nobody so far needs those symbols to link, and so discards the file. It then goes on to resolve the symbols for the useadd program itself. Since it already discarded the library, the linker complains about the missing symbols. Depending on the complexity of your libraries (e.g., circular references), you may need to specify a library more than once.

When you get one of these undefined symbol errors when using libraries provided by other parties, it can be a real hassle figuring out where a symbol lives. The **nm** command can come in handy, since it shows you information about the symbols that live in applications, libraries, and object files.

Compile the program but generate an object file instead of a program (the -c flag):

```
$ gcc -g -c useadd.m
$ ls -l useadd.o
-rw-r--r--  1 markd   staff   4108 May 18 15:09 useadd.o
```

And now **nm** it:

```
$ nm useadd.o
0000000000000450 s EH_frame1
0000000000000415 s LC0
000000000000041e s LC1
0000000000000431 s LC2
                 U _add_1
                 U _add_4
                 U _exit
0000000000000000 T _main
0000000000000468 S _main.eh
                 U _printf
```

The U is for "undefined," and the T stands for a defined text section symbol. Chapter 7: *Memory* discusses the text section, which is the area of the program file that contains the actual code that will be executed. You can see the two **add** functions that were used, **printf**, plus a little housekeeping.

You can **nm** libraries too:

```
$ nm libaddum.a
libaddum.a(src0.o):
0000000000000290 s EH_frame1
0000000000000000 T _add_0
00000000000002a8 S _add_0.eh

libaddum.a(src1.o):
0000000000000290 s EH_frame1
0000000000000000 T _add_1
00000000000002a8 S _add_1.eh

libaddum.a(src2.o):
0000000000000290 s EH_frame1
0000000000000000 T _add_2
00000000000002a8 S _add_2.eh

libaddum.a(src3.o):
0000000000000290 s EH_frame1
0000000000000000 T _add_3
00000000000002a8 S _add_3.eh
```

```
libaddum.a(src4.o):
0000000000000290 s EH_frame1
0000000000000000 T _add_4
00000000000002a8 S _add_4.eh
```

This shows each object file that has been put into the archive, as well as what symbols are present.

Using static libraries in Xcode is really easy. Just drag the libfoo.a file into your project. Xcode will automatically link it in.

Shared Libraries

When you use static libraries, the code is linked physically into your executable program. If you have a big library, say 10 megabytes, which is linked into a dozen programs, you will have 120 megabytes of disk space consumed. With today's huge hard drives, that's not too big of a deal, but you also have the libraries taking up those megabytes of space in each program's memory. This is a much bigger problem. Memory is a scarce shared resource, so having duplicate copies of library code each occupying its own pages in memory can put stress on the memory system and cause paging.

Shared libraries were created to address this problem. Instead of copying the code into the programs, just a reference is included. When the program needs a feature out of a shared library, the linker just includes the name of the symbol and a pointer to the library, as shown in Figure 6.3.

Figure 6.3   Shared libraries

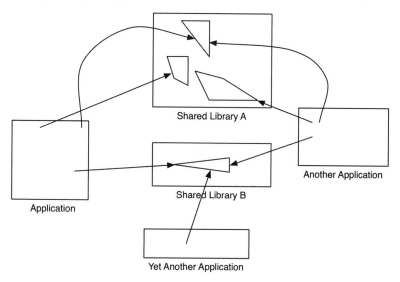

When the program is executed, the loader finds the shared libraries, loads them into memory and fixes up the references (resolves the symbols) so that they point to the now-loaded shared library. The shared library code can be loaded into shared pages of memory and shared among many different processes. In the example above, the dozen programs linking to a 10-megabyte shared library will not take up any extra space on disk – plus the library will only appear once in physical RAM and will be shared amongst the dozen processes. Of course, any space for variable data the shared library uses will be duplicated in each process.

Libraries on OS X support *two-level namespaces*. This means that the name of the library is stored along with the symbol. In the "flat namespace" model, just the symbol was stored, and the loader would search amongst various libraries for the symbol. That caused problems, for instance, if the **log()** function was defined in a math library and someone else defined a **log()** function to output text to a logfile. The math library function user might get the file logging function instead. The two-level namespaces handle this case for you so that the two **log()** functions can coexist. You can sometimes run into difficulty when building code from other Unix platforms. Adding the flag -flat_namespace to the link lines can fix many problems.

To build a shared library, use **ld**, the linker, rather than **ar**. To build the adder functions shared library, use the command

```
$ ld -dylib -o libaddum.dylib *.o
```

And link it into your program:

```
$ gcc -g -o useadd useadd.m libaddum.dylib
```

As an aside, you can specify a static library:

```
$ gcc -g -o useadd useadd.m libaddum.a
```

and you can use linker search paths with shared libraries:

```
$ gcc -g -o useadd useadd.m -L. -laddum
```

The linker, when given a choice between a shared library and a static library, will choose the shared library. There are no pure static programs on Mac OS X because everything links to libSystem, which is only available in dynamic form.

When you run the program, the loader searches for the shared libraries to load. It looks in a number of default places (like /usr/lib), and it also looks at the environment variable DYLD_LIBRARY_PATH. Any paths specified there (multiple paths can be separated by colons) are searched in order, looking for the library.

By convention on Mac OS X, shared libraries have an extension of .dylib, for Dynamic Library. On most other Unix systems, the extension is .so, for Shared Object.

nm can also be used to see what dynamic libraries an application links against by using -mg flags. In this case, **nm** is being run against a Cocoa application:

```
$ nm -mg BigShow
00000000 (absolute) external .objc_class_name_AppController
         (undefined [lazy bound]) external .objc_class_name_BigElement
             (from BigShowBase)
         (undefined [lazy bound]) external .objc_class_name_NSArray
             (from Cocoa)
         (undefined [lazy bound]) external .objc_class_name_NSBezierPath
             (from Cocoa)
         (undefined [lazy bound]) external .objc_class_name_NSBundle
             (from Cocoa)
         (undefined [lazy bound]) external .objc_class_name_NSColor
             (from Cocoa)
...
         (undefined) external __objcInit (from Cocoa)
         (undefined [lazy bound]) external _abort (from libSystem)
         (undefined [lazy bound]) external _atexit (from libSystem)
         (undefined [lazy bound]) external _calloc (from libSystem)
```

```
...
00007008 (__DATA,__data) [referenced dynamically] external _environ
         (undefined) external _errno (from libSystem)
         (undefined [lazy bound]) external _exit (from libSystem)
         (undefined [lazy bound]) external _free (from libSystem)
         (undefined) external _mach_init_routine (from libSystem)
```

This shows the symbols from Cocoa that are being used (**NSArray**, **NSBezierPath**), some of the standard C library symbols (**abort()**, **calloc()**), and some housekeeping calls (_objcInit).

Shared libraries can be loaded on demand after your program has started and are the standard Unix way for building a plug-in architecture to your program.

If you want to see all the shared libraries a program pulls in, run the program from the command line and set the DYLD_PRINT_LIBRARIES environment variable to 1. You can use this to peek into a program and see how it does some stuff. For instance:

```
$ DYLD_PRINT_LIBRARIES=1
$ /Applications/iTunes.app/Contents/MacOS/iTunes
loading libraries for image: /Applications/iTunes.app/
Contents/MacOS/iTunes
loading library: /usr/lib/libz.1.1.3.dylib
loading library: /usr/lib/libSystem.B.dylib
loading library: /System/Library/Frameworks/Carbon.framework/Versions/A/Carbon
loading library: /System/Library/Frameworks/IOKit.framework/Versions/A/IOKit
...
loading library: /System/Library/QuickTime/\
  QuickTimeFirewireDV.component/Contents/MacOS/QuickTimeFirewireDV
loading libraries for image: /System/Library/QuickTime/\
  QuickTimeFirewireDV.component/Contents/MacOS/QuickTimeFirewireDV
loading libraries for image: /System/Library/Extensions/\
  IOUSBFamily.kext/Contents/PlugIns/IOUSBLib.bundle/Contents/MacOS/\
  IOUSBLib
loading library:/System/Library/Frameworks/\
  ApplicationServices.framework/Versions/A/Frameworks/\
  CoreGraphics.framework/Resources/libCGATS.A.dylib
```

In all, over 130 libraries. It's pretty interesting to see some of the stuff in there, like Speech Synthesis, a cryptography library, and some of the private frameworks, like iPod framework and DesktopServicesPriv.

But I included the header!

A common error programmers coming from non-Unix, non-C systems make is assuming that including a header file is sufficient to use a particular library's features. Instead of a compiler error, you will get a link error. The header file just tells the compiler information like what data structures look like and signatures of functions and methods. Once the compiler is done generating an object file, it forgets about the header file. The linker never hears about the header, so it tries to link your program but doesn't find the necessary symbols to link against. This is why you also need to specify the library even though you have already included the header in your source.

Frameworks

Shared libraries are nice from a system implementation point of view, but straight shared libraries are a pretty inconvenient way to package and ship a complete product. When you are providing some kind of software library, like a database access API, you will want to provide not only the shared library that has the executable code, but also the header files that describe the API provided, the documentation, and any additional resources like images or sounds. With plain old shared libraries (on plain old Unix), you'll need to cook up your own packaging format or use whatever platform-specific delivery mechanisms (like RPMs on Red Hat Linux or the Ubuntu packaging system). Even then, the pieces of your product will probably get split up: libraries into /usr/lib, header files into /usr/include, and sound files and images go into who knows where.

NeXT came up with the framework idea to address these issues. Figure 6.4 shows a framework, a bundle that contains the shared library as well as subdirectories for headers and other resources.

Figure 6.4   A framework

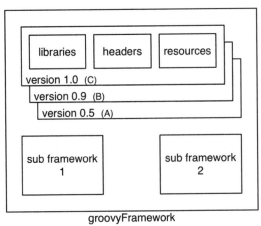

groovyFramework

Because the framework has a somewhat complex internal structure, including a directory hierarchy for versions and a set of symbolic links to indicate which version is current, it's best to just let Xcode do the work.

Figure 6.4 shows a maximally complex framework, including multiple versions. Most frameworks you will use or create will be simpler, having just one version and no subframeworks. But this explains why you will see a directory in the framework bundle called "Versions" with a subdirectory "A" with a symbolic link called "Current" pointing to it.

Here's how to make a shared library for the adder program in Xcode:

1. Launch Xcode.

2. File > New > New Project

3. Framework & Library > Cocoa Framework

4. Name the framework. In this case, called it Adder.

5. Drag in your source files: src0.c, etc.

6. If you wish, you can remove the Cocoa, Foundation, Core Data, and AppKit frameworks from the External Frameworks and Libraries folder, since this program will not link against them.

Now make a header file for the adder functions:

Example 6.3   adder.h

```
// adder.h -- header file for the little adder functions we have

int add_0 (int number);
int add_1 (int number);
int add_2 (int number);
int add_3 (int number);
int add_4 (int number);
```

Because it is a public header file, you need to tell Xcode that this header is public so that it will be added to the Headers directory of the framework.

1. Drag in the header file. You can drag it in from the Finder, or you can create it in place in Xcode. Your files should look like Figure 6.5

2. Make the header public by setting the Target Membership to Public in the File Inspector, as shown in Figure 6.6

3. And then build the framework.

When you are done, the project window should look like Figure 6.5

Figure 6.5   Framework source files

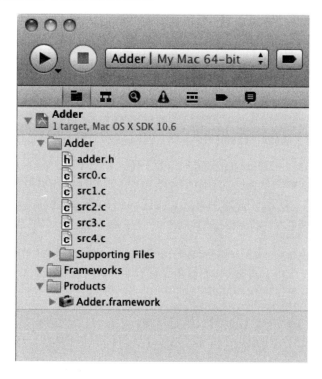

Figure 6.6   Setting the header's public target membership

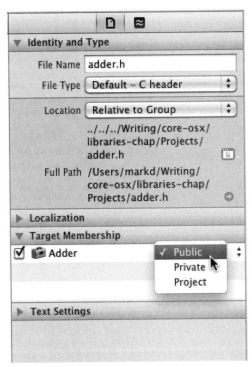

By default, Xcode 4 places build artifacts into ~/Library/Developer/Xcode/DerivedData/....
You can find the exact location of your framework by popping up the contextual menu on the
Adder.framework product, shown at the bottom of Figure 6.5 and choose Show in Finder.

Now that there is a shared library, build the useadd program:

```
$ ADDER_FRAMEWORK_PATH=/Users/markd/Library/Developer/Xcode/DerivedData/.../Debug
$ gcc -g -o useadd -F${ADDER_FRAMEWORK_PATH} -framework Adder useadd.m
```

Use -F to specify where the linker should search for the framework when linking. It works just like the
-L flag for static and shared libraries. If you run it now, you will get an error, though:

```
dyld: Library not loaded: /Library/Frameworks/Adder.framework/Versions/A/Adder
   Referenced from: /Users/markd/Writing/core-osx/libraries-chap/Projects/./useadd
   Reason: image not found
Trace/BPT trap
```

This is because the -F flag only affects compile-time behavior, finding the framework so the linker can
make sure all the symbols are there. At runtime, if the framework is not embedded in the program's
bundle, the system looks in these directories in this order:

1. ~/Library/Frameworks

2. /Library/Frameworks

3. /Network/Library/Frameworks

4. /System/Library/Frameworks

So copy the `Adder.framework` into your ~/Library/Frameworks (which you may need to manually create) and re-run the program:

```
$ ./useadd
i is 5
i after add_1: 6
i after add_4: 10
```

If you will be iterating, building this framework fairly often, you might want to make a symbolic link to the library. That way your **useadd** will always pick up the latest version as you rebuild the framework.

You can see the program using the new framework if you turn on `DYLD_PRINT_LIBRARIES`:

```
$ export DYLD_PRINT_LIBRARIES=1
$ ./useadd
dyld: loaded: /Users/markd/Writing/core-osx/libraries-chap/Projects/./useadd
dyld: loaded: /Users/markd/Library/Frameworks/Adder.framework/Versions/A/Adder
dyld: loaded: /usr/lib/libSystem.B.dylib
dyld: loaded: /usr/lib/system/libmathCommon.A.dylib
i is 5
i after add_1: 6
i after add_4: 10
```

You can see the Adder framework being loaded in the beginning.

Libraries or Frameworks?

So, should you be turning all of your common code into frameworks? In general, no. Frameworks are great if you are supplying libraries to third parties for them to be used as-is. Your users can include the frameworks in their application bundles and happily use your stuff.

Where you get into trouble is following along the line of thought "I have a suite of apps, so I'll make a bunch of shared frameworks that all of them can use and put them up in /Library/Frameworks." Along this path lies madness. You need administrator privileges to install and update the frameworks. You will need to use an install package, or else escalate privilege, to install your frameworks.

Once you have your shared frameworks installed, you need to worry about versioning issues. Even though frameworks have some versioning abilities, tool support for creating versioned frameworks and linking to particular versions just isn't there. So you will end up releasing your suite of apps in lock-step, perhaps releasing some apps before they're fully baked, and delaying releases of other apps until the rest of the suite catches up.

You will avoid the worst of these problems if you always include your frameworks into your application's bundle. That does mean that common code and resources will not be shared amongst multiple applications, but in today's age of huge disks and huge tracts of RAM this is less of an issue. Many shops either use static libraries or just include the necessary source files into their projects. The code will find its resources relative to the main bundle.

Also be aware that you cannot use your own frameworks on iOS. You can only statically link in code, whether via static libraries or including the source directly into your application project.

Writing Plug-ins

Shared libraries can be loaded on demand after the program has started running. They are the mechanism used to add plug-in features: build a shared library and have the program load it. Generic Unix applications can use the `dyld` functions to load shared libraries and get the addresses of symbols (including function pointers to executable code). Higher-level applications can load bundles at runtime. Cocoa can use the **NSBundle** class.

Bundles in Cocoa

A bundle is a directory containing some executable code, whether it's a shared library or an executable program, and the various resources that support the code. Cocoa applications are bundles, as are frameworks, screensavers, iPhoto export plug-ins, and a lot of other stuff. Bundles are how Cocoa handles plug-ins that are loaded after the program has launched. Some programs, like QuickSilver, have a tiny main program, and all of the functionality is implemented via plug-ins.

There are two sides to making an application accept plug-ins: the application doing the loading and the plug-in itself. You need to make each of them agree to some kind of protocol to communicate with each other. There is not any pre-defined protocol for doing this, so you are free to use whatever mechanism you care to. Here is a little command-line tool example that will load plug-ins that return a string, which the main program will print out. Once all the plug-ins have had a chance to print out their stuff, the program exits.

Create three projects in Xcode. First, create a Command Line Tool (or Foundation Tool in Xcode 3) called `BundlePrinter`. Then create a Cocoa Bundle called `SimpleMessage`, and another Cocoa Bundle called `ComplexMessage`.

Add a header file to `BundlePrinter` that looks like this:

Example 6.4   BundlePrinter.h

```
// BundlePrinter.h -- protocol for BundlePrinter plugins to use

@protocol BundlePrinterProtocol

+ (BOOL)activate;
+ (void)deactivate;

- (NSString *)message;

@end // BundlePrinterProtocol
```

This is very simple protocol. The class is given an opportunity to do stuff when activated and deactivated. Perhaps the plug-in needs to create and destroy a big image or load an mp3 file. Then there is an instance method for getting a string message to print.

Add this header file to the two bundle projects. Now go ahead and implement the plug-ins to conform to this protocol. Add a `SimpleMessage.m` file to the `SimpleMessage` project. Also set the `Principal Class` for the project to `SimpleMessage`. Go to the Targets pane, select `SimpleMessage` target, select the `Info` tab, and add a `Principal Class` with the string value `SimpleMessage`.

Here is what `SimpleMessage.m` looks like:

Example 6.5   SimpleMessage.m

```
// SimpleMessage.m -- a simple plug-in that returns a simple, hard-coded message

#import <Foundation/Foundation.h>
#import "BundlePrinter.h"

@interface SimpleMessage : NSObject <BundlePrinterProtocol>
@end // SimpleMessage

@implementation SimpleMessage

+ (BOOL) activate {
    NSLog (@"SimpleMessage plug-in activated");
    return YES;
} // activate

+ (void) deactivate {
    NSLog (@"SimpleMessage plug-in deactivated");
} // deactivate

- (NSString *) message {
    return (@"This is a Simple Message");
} // message

@end // SimpleMessage
```

Build it and fix any errors.

Do the same thing for `ComplexMessage` (set the `ComplexMessage` Principal class, and add the `ComplexMessage.m` source file).

Example 6.6   ComplexMessage.m

```
// ComplexMessage -- a plug-in that returns a message using some stored state

#import <Foundation/Foundation.h>

#import "BundlePrinter.h"

#import <stdlib.h>      // for random number routines
#import <time.h>        // for time() to seed the random generator

@interface ComplexMessage : NSObject <BundlePrinterProtocol> {
    NSUInteger _randomValue;
}
@end // ComplexMessage

@implementation ComplexMessage

+ (BOOL) activate {
    NSLog (@"ComplexMessage plug-in activated");
    return YES;
} // activate

+ (void) deactivate {
    NSLog (@"ComplexMessage plug-in deactivated");
} // deactivate
```

```
- (id) init {
    if ((self = [super init])) {
        srandom ((unsigned)time(NULL));
        _randomValue = random () % 500;
    }
    return self;

} // init

- (NSString *) message {
    return [NSString stringWithFormat: @"Here is a random number: %d",
                     _randomValue];
} // messagee

@end // ComplexMessage
```

This is more "complex" because it stores some state at initialization time and uses it later.

Build this and fix any errors.

Now, in the BundlePrinter project, edit main.m so that it looks like this:

Example 6.7   main.m

```
// main.m -- the main BundlePrinter program

#import <Foundation/Foundation.h>
#import "BundlePrinter.h"

NSString *processPlugin (NSString *path) {
    NSString *message = nil;

    NSLog (@"processing plug-in: %@", path);

    // Load the bundle
    NSBundle *plugin = [NSBundle bundleWithPath: path];

    if (plugin == nil) {
        NSLog (@"could not load plug-in at path %@", path);
        goto bailout;
    }

    // Get the class the bundle declares as its Principal one.
    // If there are multiple classes defined in the bundle, we
    // wouldn't know which one to talk to first
    Class principalClass = [plugin principalClass];

    if (principalClass == nil) {
        NSLog (@"could not load principal class for plug-in at path %@", path);
        NSLog (@"make sure the PrincipalClass target setting is correct");
        goto bailout;
    }

    // Do a little sanity checking
    if (![principalClass conformsToProtocol: @protocol(BundlePrinterProtocol)]) {
        NSLog (@"plug-in principal class must conform to the BundlePrinterProtocol");
        goto bailout;
    }
```

```
        // tell the plug-in that it's being activated
        if (![principalClass activate]) {
            NSLog (@"could not activate class for plug-in at path %@", path);
            goto bailout;
        }

        // make an instance of the plug-in and ask it for a message
        id pluginInstance = [[principalClass alloc] init];

        // get the message and dispose with the instance
        message = [pluginInstance message];
        [pluginInstance release];

        // ok, we're done with it
        [principalClass deactivate];

 bailout:
        return message;

} // processPlugin

int main (int argc, const char *argv[]) {
    NSAutoreleasePool *pool = [[NSAutoreleasePool alloc] init];

    // Walk the current directory looking for bundles.
    // An application would look in its bundle, or maybe a plugin
    // directory in ~/Library.
    NSFileManager *manager = [NSFileManager defaultManager];

    for (NSString *path in [manager enumeratorAtPath: @"."]) {

        // Only look for stuff that has a .bundle extension
        if ([[path pathExtension] isEqualToString: @"bundle"]) {

            // Invoke the plugin.
            NSString *message = processPlugin (path);

            if (message != nil) { // plugin succeeded
                printf ("\nmessage is: '%s'\n\n", [message UTF8String]);
            }
        }
    }

    [pool drain];
    return EXIT_SUCCESS;

} // main
```

main() looks in the directory you invoke the program from and searches for entries that end in .bundle. If it finds one, it attempts to load it and invoke methods on the class it finds there.

Here is a sample run after copying (or symlinking) the SimpleMessage and ComplexMessage bundles into a directory and running the program. In this case, copy them to the BundlePrinter project directory.

```
$ build/Debug/BundlePrinter
... BundlePrinter[4458] processing plug-in: ComplexMessage.bundle
... BundlePrinter[4458] ComplexMessage plug-in activated
... BundlePrinter[4458] ComplexMessage plug-in deactivated
```

```
message is: 'Here is a random number: 2342'

... BundlePrinter[4458] processing plug-in: SimpleMessage.bundle
... BundlePrinter[4458] SimpleMessage plug-in loaded
... BundlePrinter[4458] SimpleMessage plug-in unloaded

message is: 'This is a Simple Message'
```

There are a couple of limitations that are glossed over here. One is that you cannot load the same bundle twice. You will get a message from the Objective-C runtime about duplicate classes. The other is you cannot unload an Objective-C bundle. The Objective-C runtime gets its claws into the shared library and refuses to let go.

Shared Libraries and dlopen

If you don't want to use (or can't use) **NSBundle** for loading plug-ins, you can load a shared library instead. Loading a shared library does not give you ready access to resources like **NSBundle** does.

Mac OS X has a choice of API for manually loading bundles and shared libraries. There is the **NSModule** API, which includes functions such as **NSCreateObjectFileImageFromFile()**. Prior editions of this book described this mechanism. It has been deprecated in Mac OS X 10.5, and the documentation manpages have been removed. You can find information in the header located at /usr/include/mach-o/dyld.h.

dlopen()

dlopen() is used to open a shared library or a bundle at a given path:

```
void* dlopen (const char* path, int mode);
```

dlopen() opens the library and resolves any symbols it contains. It returns a module handle (an opaque pointer) to the library, which can be used in subsequent calls, or it returns NULL if the library could not be opened. The function **dlerror()** returns a string describing the error.

The path can be a full path or a relative path. If the path is just a leaf name (having no slash in the path, just a library name), **dlopen()** uses this algorithm to find the library:

1. The LD_LIBRARY_PATH environment variable (a colon-separated list of directories) is consulted, and the directories are searched (in order) to find the library.

2. If the DYLD_LIBRARY_PATH environment variable is set, those directories are searched for the leaf.

3. If the DYLD_FALLBACK_LIBRARY_PATH environment variable is set, those directories are searched. If this environment variable is not set, $HOME/lib, /usr/local/lib, and then /usr/lib are searched.

4. Finally, the path is treated like a regular path.

Because Mac OS X has fat binary files, there are no separate 32-bit and 64-bit search paths.

The mode parameter can take one of two options that control the binding of external functions, along with two optional flags. Here, "external" refers to functions not defined in the shared library that was just loaded:

RTLD_NOW	Each external function is bound immediately. You can use this flag to make sure that any undefined symbols are discovered at load-time.
RTLD_LAZY	Each external function is bound the first time it is called. You will usually use this form. It is more efficient because it doesn't bind functions that might never be called.
RTLD_GLOBAL	This is an optional bitwise-OR-in flag. Symbols exported from the loaded library will be available to any other libraries that are loaded, in addition to being available through calls to **dlsym()**. This is the default behavior.
RTLD_LOCAL	This is also an optional bitwise-OR-in flag. Symbols exported from the loaded library are generally hidden and only available to **dlsym()** when using the module handle for this library.

dlsym()

Once you have a module handle from **dlopen()**, you can use **dlsym()** to get the address of code or data at the location specified by a given symbol.

```
void* dlsym (void *module, const char *symbol);
```

module is a module handle returned by **dlopen()**. Unlike the dyld family of calls, you do not prepend the symbol with an underscore. If the symbol cannot be found, **dlsym()** returns NULL, and you can query **dlerror()** to see what the problem was.

There are two constants you can give to **dlsym()** instead of a module handle: RTLD_DEFAULT to search through every Mach-O image in the process in the order they were loaded. This can be an expensive operation since it will have to slog through all of the system frameworks. You can also use RTLD_NEXT to search for the symbol in any Mach-O images that were loaded after the one calling **dlsym()**. So, if you call **dlsym()** in your main program using RTLD_NEXT, it will look in any libraries loaded after your program started running.

BundlePrinter

bundleprinter uses bundle plug-ins similar to the Cocoa-based BundlePrinter. You can compile a shared library like

```
$ gcc -g -o simplemessage.msg -bundle simplemessage.m
```

You can also build it as a shared library:

```
$ gcc -g -o simplemessage.msg -dylib simplemessage.m
```

So what's the difference between a bundle and a shared library on Mac OS X? Practically, not a huge difference. **dlopen()** can load both of them and dig around the symbols inside. Bundles can be unloaded, while shared libraries cannot. Bundles that use Objective-C have to be unloaded in strict first-in, last-out order, which effectively makes them unloadable. Bundles can also be linked against executables to satisfy missing symbols. This allows a host application to provide an API that the plug-in can use.

.msg is the file extension used for these "message" plug-ins. Example 6.8 is the driver program, while Example 6.9 and Example 6.10 are the plug-in implementations.

Example 6.8   bundleprinter.m

```
// bundleprinter.m -- dynamically load plugins and invoke functions on them, using
//                    the dlopen() family of calls.

// gcc -g -o bundleprinter bundleprinter.m

#import <sys/dirent.h>  // for struct dirent
#import <dirent.h>      // for opendir and friends
#import <dlfcn.h>       // for dlopen() and friends
#import <errno.h>       // for errno/strerror
#import <stdio.h>       // for printf
#import <stdlib.h>      // for EXIT_SUCCESS
#import <string.h>      // for strdup

// We need a type to coerce a void pointer to the function pointer we
// need to jump through.  Having a type makes things a bit easier
// to read rather than doing this inline.

typedef int (*BNRMessageActivateFP) (void);
typedef void (*BNRMessageDeactivateFP) (void);
typedef char * (*BNRMessageMessageFP) (void);

char *processPlugin (const char *path) {
    char *message = NULL;

    void *module = dlopen (path, RTLD_LAZY);

    if (module == NULL) {
        fprintf (stderr,
                "couldn't load plugin at path %s.  error is %s\n",
                path, dlerror());
        goto bailout;
    }

    BNRMessageActivateFP activator = dlsym (module, "BNRMessageActivate");
    BNRMessageDeactivateFP deactivator = dlsym (module, "BNRMessageDeactivate");
    BNRMessageMessageFP messagator = dlsym (module, "BNRMessageMessage");

    if (activator == NULL || deactivator == NULL || messagator == NULL) {
        fprintf (stderr,
                "could not find BNRMessage* symbol (%p %p %p)\n",
                activator, deactivator, messagator);
        goto bailout;
    }

    int result = (activator)();
    if (!result) { // the module didn't consider itself loaded
        goto bailout;
    }

    message = (messagator)();

    (deactivator)();

  bailout:
```

```
        if (module != NULL) {
            result = (dlclose (module));
            if (result != 0) {
                fprintf (stderr, "could not dlclose %s.  Error is %s\n",
                        path, dlerror());
            }
        }

        return message;

} // processPlugin

int main (int argc, char *argv[]) {
    // walk through the current directory

    DIR *directory = opendir (".");

    if (directory == NULL) {
        fprintf (stderr,
                "could not open current directory to look for plugins\n");
        fprintf (stderr, "error: %d (%s)\n", errno, strerror(errno));
        exit (EXIT_FAILURE);
    }

    struct dirent *entry;
    while ((entry = readdir(directory)) != NULL) {
        // If this is a file of type .msg (an extension made up for this
        // sample), process it like a plug-in.

        if (fnmatch("*.msg", entry->d_name, 0) == 0) {
            char *message = processPlugin (entry->d_name);

            printf ("\nmessage is: '%s'\n\n", message);
            free (message);
        }
    }

    closedir (directory);

    return EXIT_SUCCESS;

} // main
```

Example 6.9   simplemessage.m

```
// simplemessage.m -- return a malloc'd block of memory to a simple message

// gcc -g -o simplemessage.msg -bundle simplemessage.m

#import <string.h>      // for strdup
#import <stdio.h>       // for printf

int BNRMessageActivate (void) {
    printf ("simple message activate\n");
    return 1;
} // BNRMessageActivate


void BNRMessageDeactivate (void) {
    printf ("simple message deactivate\n");
```

```
} // BNRMessageDeactivate


char *BNRMessageMessage (void) {
    return (strdup("This is a simple message"));
} // BNRMessageMessage
```

Example 6.10   simplemessage.m

```
// complexmessage.m -- return a malloc'd block of memory to a complex message

// gcc -g -o complexmessage.msg -bundle complexmessage.m

#import <stdio.h>       // for printf
#import <stdlib.h>      // for random number routines
#import <string.h>      // for strdup, and snprintf
#import <time.h>        // for time() to seed the random generator

static unsigned g_randomValue;

int BNRMessageActivate (void) {
    printf ("complex message activate\n");

    srandom ((unsigned)time(NULL));
    g_randomValue = random () % 500;

    return 1;

} // BNRMessageActivate


void BNRMessageDeactivate (void) {
    printf ("complex message deactivate\n");
} // BNRMessageDeactivate


char *BNRMessageMessage (void) {
    char *message;
    asprintf (&message, "Here is a random number: %d", g_randomValue);
    return message;
} // BNRMessageMessage
```

And here is a run:

```
$ ./bundleprinter
complex message activate
complex message deactivate

message is: 'Here is a random number: 230'

simple message activate
simple message deactivate

message is: 'This is a simple message'
```

For the More Curious: libtool

Earlier in the chapter, the class Unix tools **ar** and **ranlib** were used to build static libraries, and **gcc** was used to build a dynamic library. Mac OS X has a tool, **libtool**, which is peculiar to the platform, but provides a superset of features over **ar** and friends. The GNU project also has a **libtool**, but it is unrelated to the one in Mac OS X.

Make a static library like this and use it:

```
$ libtool -static -o libaddum.a src?.o
$ gcc -g -o useadd useadd.m -L. -laddum
```

And dynamic libraries (but not bundles) can be created thusly:

```
$ libtool -dynamic -macosx_version_min 10.5 -o libaddum.dylib src?.o
$ gcc -g -o useadd useadd.m -L. -laddum
```

For the More Curious: otool

otool is another library-oriented tool. Even though it shares the last four letters with **libtool**, **otool** will output a lot of information about an object file, library, or executable. **otool** has a ton of options, so check out the manpage for the whole suite. Here are a couple of interesting commands.

List the names and version numbers of the shared libs an object file or executable uses:

```
$ otool -L /Applications/Safari.app/Contents/MacOS/Safari
/Applications/Safari.app/Contents/MacOS/Safari:
    /usr/lib/libsqlite3.dylib (compatibility version 9.0.0, current version 9.6.0)
    /System/Library/Frameworks/PubSub.framework/Versions/A/PubSub \
        (compatibility version 1.0.0, current version 1.0.0)
    /System/Library/PrivateFrameworks/CrashReporterSupport.framework/Versions/A/ \
        CrashReporterSupport (compatibility version 1.0.0, current version 1.0.0)
    /usr/lib/libxar.1.dylib (compatibility version 1.0.0, current version 1.0.0)
    /System/Library/Frameworks/CoreLocation.framework/Versions/A/CoreLocation \
        (compatibility version 1.0.0, current version 11.0.0)
...
```

Disassemble the contents of the text section. The -V indicates a symbolic disassembly.

```
$ otool -V -t useadd
...
0000000100000e82        movl    0xfc(%rbp),%esi
0000000100000e85        leaq    0x000000ac(%rip),%rdi
0000000100000e8c        movl    $0x00000000,%eax
0000000100000e91        callq   0x100000efa     ; symbol stub for: _printf
0000000100000e96        movl    0xfc(%rbp),%edi
0000000100000e99        movl    $0x00000000,%eax
0000000100000e9e        callq   0x100000ee8     ; symbol stub for: _add_1
0000000100000ea3        movl    %eax,0xfc(%rbp)
...
```

Print out some Objective-C stuff:

```
$ otool -ov BundlePrinter
Contents of (__DATA,__objc_classrefs) section
0000000100002178 0x0
0000000100002180 0x0
0000000100002188 0x0
Contents of (__DATA,__objc_protolist) section
0000000100002060 0x1000021b0
Contents of (__DATA,__objc_msgrefs) section
  imp 0x0
  sel 0x100001e80 alloc
```

```
  imp 0x0
  sel 0x100001e8b release
  imp 0x0
  sel 0x100001eb6 countByEnumeratingWithState:objects:count:
  imp 0x0
  sel 0x100001ef6 isEqualToString:
Contents of (__DATA,__objc_imageinfo) section
  version 0
    flags 0x0
```

Point it to something big like /Applications/Safari/Contents/MacOS/Safari to see a huge amount of output.

For the More Curious: Runtime Environment Variables

Earlier you saw several environment variables that could be set to achieve different results. There are a number of environment variables you can set. Here's an interesting subset, and check out the dyld manpage for the complete list. When a list of things is mentioned, it is a colon-separated list of those objects.

The first set of environment variables control where the dynamic linker finds libraries and frameworks when a process is first loaded.

DYLD_FRAMEWORK_PATH	A list of directories that contain frameworks. The dynamic linker searches these directories first.
DYLD_FALLBACK_FRAMEWORK_PATH	A list of directories that contain frameworks. This is used as the default location for frameworks. By default, it includes the Frameworks directory in /Library, /Network, and /System/Library.
DYLD_LIBRARY_PATH	A list of directories that contain libraries. The dynamic linker searches these directories before it looks at the default location for the libraries. Handy for testing new versions of libraries.
DYLD_FALLBACK_LIBRARY_PATH	A list of directories that contain libraries. These are the default locations for libraries. By default, it is set to $(HOME)/lib:/usr/local/bin:/lib:/usr/lib

The second set causes the dynamic linker to emit output when interesting things happen. Some are good nerdy fun, and some can be useful when debugging or tracking down performance problems that happen before **main()** is called. The environment variables do not have to be set to any particular value, just so long as they are set.

DYLD_PRINT_STATISTICS	Prints out where the dynamic linker spent its time before **main()** is called.
DYLD_PRINT_INITIALIZERS	Prints when running each initializer in every image.
DYLD_PRINT_APIS	Prints when dynamic linker API is called, such as **dlsym()**.

DYLD_PRINT_SEGMENTS	Print out a line with the name and address range of each Mach-O segment the dynamic linker maps in.

Here is a sample run, showing statistics and API calls with **bundleprinter**:

```
$ export DYLD_PRINT_APIS=""
$ export DYLD_PRINT_STATISTICS=""
$ ./bundleprinter
_dyld_register_func_for_remove_image(0x7fff82fc6b76)
total time: 0.53 milliseconds (100.0%)
total images loaded:  3 (2 from dyld shared cache, 0 needed no fixups)
total segments mapped: 0, into 0 pages with 0 pages pre-fetched
total images loading time: 0.03 milliseconds (6.0%)
total dtrace DOF registration time: 0.02 milliseconds (5.5%)
total rebase fixups:  0
total rebase fixups time: 0.00 milliseconds (0.7%)
total binding fixups: 2
total binding fixups time: 0.02 milliseconds (5.1%)
total weak binding fixups time: 0.00 milliseconds (0.1%)
total bindings lazily fixed up: 0 of 0
total initializer time: 0.43 milliseconds (82.3%)
total symbol trie searches:    2
total symbol table binary searches:    0
total images defining/using weak symbols:  0/0

dlopen(complexmessage.msg, 0x00000001)
dlsym(0x100100260, BNRMessageActivate)
dlsym(0x100100260, BNRMessageDeactivate)
dlsym(0x100100260, BNRMessageMessage)

complex message activate
complex message deactivate

dlclose(0x100100260)

message is: 'Here is a random number: 99'

dlopen(simplemessage.msg, 0x00000001)

dlsym(0x100100260, BNRMessageActivate)
dlsym(0x100100260, BNRMessageDeactivate)
dlsym(0x100100260, BNRMessageMessage)

simple message activate
simple message deactivate

dlclose(0x100100260)

message is: 'This is a simple message'
```

153

Exercises

1. Take the Cocoa plug-in example and include it in a GUI program, putting the plug-in name and the message into an **NSTableView**. Write some additional plug-ins.

2. **otool** has a lot of options and additional flags. Write a Cocoa front-end so you can easily play with the options. You can use **NSTask**, covered in Chapter 19: *Using NSTask* to actually run **otool** from your application.

7

Memory

Virtual Memory

Virtual memory is a way for the computer to fake having more memory than it actually has. A machine might have four gigabytes of RAM, but you can write programs that manipulate data several times that amount. When you overflow the available amount of real memory, portions of the data are saved out to disk and read back in when the program needs it.

The operating system handles the grungy details of keeping data that is currently being worked on physically in memory and moving data that has not been touched in a while out to the disk. It also pulls the data back into memory from disk if the program wants to work with it again.

The operating system divides memory into *pages*, 4KB chunks of memory that the operating system addresses. Programs are given pages as they request memory. As pages are used, they are kept on a list of recently used pages. As programs request more and more memory from the system, the least recently used pages are written to disk, called "paging" or "swapping," and the chunk of physical memory is reused. iOS does not have this disk-based swapfile, so you will hit out-of-memory conditions sooner on that platform than with desktop Mac OS X.

Pages can be written out and then read back in at different physical addresses. A 4k page starting at address 0x5000 might be paged out and given to another program. The program that needs the data that was at 0x5000 now needs it again, so the OS reads the page from disk. The chunk of memory at 0x5000 may now be in use by the second program. Oops. To fix this, virtual addressing is used.

Figure 7.1 shows virtual memory in action. Virtual addresses are the memory addresses a program sees, and each program has its own address space. The virtual address gets mapped by the OS (and hardware in the CPU) to the physical address of a chunk of a page of RAM. Program A and program B each have a page of data at 0x8000. In physical memory, A's might live at physical address 0x15020, and B's might live at physical address 0x3150, but the address translation lets each program live with the fantasy of having their data at address 0x8000.

Figure 7.1   Virtual memory

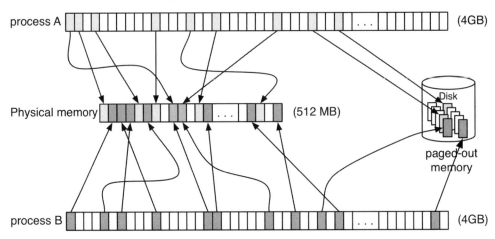

The total amount of memory that a program has allocated to it at a particular time is called its *virtual set*. The amount of memory that is actually located in RAM is called its *resident set*. The difference between the virtual set and the resident set is stored out on disk in a swap file, or in the files of read-only code segments such as the system frameworks. "Swap" derives its name from the pages that are swapped for each other when paging happens. You can also lock, or wire, memory down so it doesn't get swapped out. Some pages you absolutely don't want to be swapped out, such as pages containing decrypted passwords. These pages should be wired down with the `mlock()` function before decrypting the password.

Pages can have permissions, like read-only, read/write, and execute. This helps keep you from scribbling over your own code and helps prevent security exploits that try to execute code from a page that is not marked executable.

Program Memory Model

Mac OS X processes have a conceptual memory model, where memory is divided into space for the executable code, a stack, a heap, and other bits and pieces, as shown in Figure 7.2:

Figure 7.2   Unix program memory model

Text Segment	The executable program code lives here. At program launch time, the code is mapped into memory from the executable on disk as read-only pages. Since these pages are read-only, they can be easily shared among multiple processes, so the pages only have to appear in physical memory once and can still

be shared among multiple users. They can, of course, appear multiple times in the virtual memory of other processes. This is especially for shared libraries that are loaded into each program. Because the data is read-only, the kernel can recycle these pages without having to write them to the swapfile.

Initialized Data Segment

Initialized global and static variables live here – things like `float pi = 3.1415` outside of any functions or `static int blah = 25` inside of a function. The initialized data is stored in the data segment itself, which is just copied into memory into a read/write page that the program can then modify. Because the kernel is just reading in blocks of data from disk, it is very fast to load and initialize all of the globals. No real explicit initialization happens, just bulk data loads.

Uninitialized Data Segment

This is all the stuff that lives in global space but is not given an explicit initializer, like `int bork` outside of any functions or `static char buffer[5000]` inside of a function, and that all gets cleared to zero on program launch. These are not treated like the initialized data segment, which would mean lots of zero blocks in the executable. Only the size of this data segment is stored. On program load, the OS allocates that amount of space and zero-fills it.

This is also referred to as the "bss" segment in manpages and the historical literature. "bss" comes from an assembler instruction that means "block started by symbol."

Heap

The heap is the area where dynamic (runtime) allocations happen. If you **malloc()** 40K, that 40K will come from the heap.

Program Stack

The program call stack for the main thread. Local (automatic) variables are stored here, as well as the stack frame for each function call. When a function calls another function, the processor's registers and other assorted bookkeeping need to be stored before the new function is invoked. These values also need to be restored when the new function exits.

Memory "allocation" using the program stack is very fast. A processor register is used to indicate where the end of the stack is. Reserving space on the stack just involves adding a value to this address, whether it be four bytes or four thousand. You do not want to store *too* much stuff on the stack, such as big buffers, because there is a limit on how big the stack can be. Also, threads have limited stack space because each thread has its own chunk of memory to use for a stack. This is discussed in Chapter 20: *Multithreading*.

Example 7.1 is a program that has 8K of initialized data and a megabyte of uninitialized data:

Example 7.1   dataseg.m

```
// dataseg.m -- show size of data segments

#import <stdio.h>   // for printf()
#import <stdlib.h>  // for exit()

// gcc -arch x86_64 -g -o dataseg dataseg.m
// gcc -arch i386 -g -o dataseg-32 dataseg.m

// about 8K doubles. lives in the initialized data segment.
static double rdoubles[] = {
    0.0, 1.0, 2.0, 3.0, 4.0, 5.0, 6.0, 7.0, 8.0, 9.0,
    10.0, 11.0, 12.0, 13.0, 14.0, 15.0, 16.0, 17.0, 18.0, 19.0,
    ...
    1017.0, 1018.0, 1019.0, 1020.0, 1021.0,
    1022.0, 1023.0
};

// one meg, all zeros.  Lives in the uninitialzed data segment
static char buffer[1048576];

int main (void) {
    printf ("hi! %ld bytes of doubles, %ld bytes of buffer\n",
            sizeof(rdoubles), sizeof(buffer));
    return 0;
} // main
```

Here's a sample run:

```
$ ./dataseg
hi!  8192 bytes of doubles, 1048576 bytes of buffer
```

The **size** command will show the size of numerous segments of programs. Running **size** on this program yields:

```
$ size dataseg
__TEXT  __DATA   __OBJC  others      dec         hex
4096    1060864  0       4294971392  4296036352  100105000
```

Above is the **size** output for a 64-bit executable file. This is the **size** for a 32-bit version:

```
$ gcc -arch i386 -g -o dataseg-32 dataseg.m
$ size ./dataseg-32
__TEXT  __DATA   __OBJC  others  dec      hex
4096    1060864  4096    8192    1077248  107000
```

Here **size** combines the size of initialized and uninitialized data into the __DATA entry. 1060864 (the data segment size) minus 1048576 (the zero-filled uninitialized data) is 12288, which is 8192 (the 8K of double data) plus 4096 (4K of overhead and bookkeeping).

The 64-bit version, though, has a huge "others" section, weighing in at more than four gigabytes. Use the -m flag to get more details:

```
$ size -m dataseg
Segment __PAGEZERO: 4294967296
...
```

The __PAGEZERO segment is exactly four gigabytes large. The others segment was 4294971392, for a difference of 4096 bytes of bookkeeping. Remember that 64-bit processes have the bottom four gigabytes zeroed out to catch pointer truncation errors. The __PAGEZERO segment is how the loader is told to reserve that space.

Note finally that the application size is small even with those large chunks of zeros in the __PAGEZERO and empty buffer. The megabyte buffer of zeros comes from the uninitialized data segment:

```
$ ls -l dataseg
-rwxr-xr-x  1 markd  staff  17256 Jun 21 10:27 dataseg*
```

Memory Lifetime

Initialized and uninitialized data segment variables are around during the entire run time of the program. They will not go away. Memory on the heap is explicitly requested and explicitly released. Memory here can be deallocated, but it's under program control. Memory on the stack goes away, meaning that it can be reused by someone else as soon as it goes out of scope, even before a function exits, like within brace-delimited blocks within a function. The stack memory behavior can cause errors if you assume that memory will be valid longer than it actually is. A classic error is returning an address on the stack:

```
char *frobulate (void) {
    char buffer[5000];

    // work on buffer

    return buffer;

} // frobulate
```

buffer is allocated on the stack. There are five thousand bytes on the stack, and buffer contains the address of the first byte. Once buffer goes out of scope, this memory will be available for other functions to use. Anyone working with the return result of **borkulize()** is taking a chance that someone will clobber its contents, potentially much later in time after this function exits, leading to bugs that are hard to track down.

Dynamic Memory Allocation

"Dynamic memory" is memory that comes from the heap. The heap of the program starts off at an OS-defined default amount of space available for program consumption. As you allocate memory from the heap, it fills up, and then your program asks for more memory from the OS. Memory that you have released can be reused by your program. Memory allocated and subsequently freed is still charged to your program by the operating system. If you allocate 50 megabytes for temporary workspace and then free it all, your program will still have the 50 megabytes of memory allocated to it. This will eventually be swapped out to disk (on desktop systems) since you might not be using it. The total amount of memory can be considered a high water mark.

The primary functions for allocation and deallocating memory are:

```
void *malloc (size_t size);

void free (void *ptr);

void *realloc (void *ptr, size_t size);

void *reallocf (void *ptr, size_t size);
```

159

These functions give you memory from the heap.

malloc()

`malloc()` allocates a chunk of memory with the address of the block aligned to the strictest boundary required in the OS. That is, if an 8-byte `double` had the strictest alignment, `malloc()` would return addresses that were evenly divisible by 8. Example 7.2 allocates blocks of different sizes and shows the address of the returned memory.

Example 7.2   mallocalign.m

```
// mallocalign.m -- see how malloc aligns its pointers

// gcc -Wall -g -o mallocalign mallocalign.m

#import <stdio.h>   // for printf()
#import <stdlib.h>  // for malloc()

void allocprint (size_t size) {
    void *memory = malloc (size);
    printf ("malloc(%ld) == %p\n", size, memory);
    // Intentionally leaked so we get a new block of memory
} // allocprint

int main (void) {
    allocprint (1);
    allocprint (2);
    allocprint (sizeof(double));
    allocprint (1024 * 1024);
    allocprint (1);
    allocprint (1);

    return 0;
} // main
```

has a run of

```
$ ./mallocalign
malloc(1) == 0x100100080
malloc(2) == 0x100100090
malloc(8) == 0x1001000a0
malloc(1048576) == 0x100200000
malloc(1) == 0x1001000b0
malloc(1) == 0x1001000c0
```

These are all addresses evenly divisible by 16. Vector operations, such as Altivec or SSE, work best when aligned on 16-byte boundaries. You can see that the very large malloc starts at an address far away from the small allocations. The memory is being put on its own pages elsewhere in the address space.

You should always use the C `sizeof` operator to determine how much memory to allocate for specific data structures:

```
typedef struct Node {
    int blah; // 4 bytes
    int bork; // 4 bytes
```

```
} Node;

Node *mynode = malloc (sizeof(Node));  // 8 bytes
```

and for arrays

```
Node nodules[] = malloc (sizeof(Node) * 100);  // 800 bytes
```

malloc() is entitled to give you a block of memory that is larger than what you ask for, but you are only guaranteed to get as much memory as you ask for.

Example 7.3   mallocsize.m

```
// mallocsize.m -- see what kind of block sizes malloc is actually giving us

// gcc -g -Wall -o mallocsize mallocsize.m

#import <malloc/malloc.h>  // for malloc_size()
#import <stdio.h>          // for printf()
#import <stdlib.h>         // for malloc()

void allocprint (size_t size) {
    void *memory = malloc (size);
    printf ("malloc(%ld) has a block size of %ld\n",
            size, malloc_size(memory));
    // Intentionally leaked so we get a new block of memory

} // allocprint

int main (void) {
    allocprint (1);
    allocprint (sizeof(double));
    allocprint (14);
    allocprint (16);
    allocprint (32);
    allocprint (48);
    allocprint (64);
    allocprint (100);
    return 0;
} // main
```

Yields:

```
$ ./mallocsize
malloc(1) has a block size of 16
malloc(8) has a block size of 16
malloc(14) has a block size of 16
malloc(16) has a block size of 16
malloc(32) has a block size of 32
malloc(48) has a block size of 48
malloc(64) has a block size of 64
malloc(100) has a block size of 112
```

You can see that the actual block size is often larger than what was asked for. Memory allocation algorithms are an interesting area of computer science, and most any operating systems textbook will describe a number of different algorithms for managing dynamic memory. Apple has revved its memory allocation algorithms several times in the past.

Usually, your malloc arena has a bunch of buckets that each contain uniform-sized blocks of memory. The system chooses the smallest block size that will contain the requested amount of memory. Rather than have a whole bunch of 9-byte blocks and a whole bunch of 10-byte blocks and a whole bunch of 11-byte blocks (and so on), it will have larger increments. In the above case, it has 16 bytes, 32 bytes, 48 bytes, and 64 bytes. Powers of two or sums of powers of two.

Even though **malloc_size()** reports sizes (possibly) larger that what was initially allocated, you should not use it to see "how much memory is allocated to this pointer." For example, if a function is passed a pointer that had been allocated using malloc(8), but you use **malloc_size()** on the pointer and find its block size to be 16, don't subsequently treat the pointer like it had come from malloc(16). Doing that could cause problems. **malloc_size()** also won't work for pointers to stack memory. You will still need to pass around sizes of buffers.

In general, you cannot make any assumptions about memory placement with multiple calls to **malloc()**.

E.g., you cannot depend on this:

```
x = malloc (10);
y = malloc (10);
```

to look like Figure 7.3 in memory

Figure 7.3   Incorrect memory layout

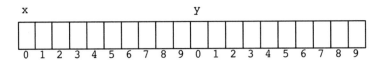

Depending on this **malloc()**, it most likely looks like: Figure 7.4

Figure 7.4   How blocks are actually laid out

There is no guarantee that blocks allocated one after the other are anywhere near each other in memory.

Dynamic memory allocation gives no guarantee of locality of reference. (Locality of reference means what is used together is placed near each other in memory, leading to fewer cache misses and less paging activity.) You could allocate two chunks of memory one after the other:

```
x = malloc (10);
y = malloc (10);
```

and it is perfectly legal for **malloc()** to give you a pointer to x from one end of your address space and a pointer to y from way on the other side. If you need locality of reference, you may be better off allocating one large chunk of memory and then doing suballocations yourself out of that buffer.

Finally, **malloc()** on Mac OS X is always thread safe. Some older Unix variants have a thread-safe **malloc()** if you link with special thread libraries.

free()

free() tells the system that you are done with a block of memory and that it can be reused by a subsequent call to **malloc()**. In earlier examples, especially mallocalign.m, the allocated memory was purposely never freed because the same block would keep getting returned, and it is hard to draw conclusions about memory alignment if you get the same starting address for a block of memory each time.

Not freeing allocated memory is termed a "memory leak," since the memory just kind of pours away and is not available for use any more. There is a discussion about memory leaks and memory leak detection tools later on.

Lastly, make sure you only feed **free()** addresses you get from **malloc()** or NULL. You will get unpredictable results (crash) if you give **free()** addresses of stack buffers or other memory not allocated by **malloc()**. Some functions call **malloc()** on your behalf, such as **strdup()**, and are documented that you need to **free()** their return values.

realloc()

realloc() resizes a chunk of memory that has been previously allocated. Essentially, **realloc()** does something like:

```
void *cheesyRealloc (void *ptr, size_t size) {
    void *newMem = malloc (size);
    memcpy (newMem, ptr, size);
    free (ptr);
    return newMem;
} // cheesyRealloc
```

realloc()'d blocks can therefore move in the heap, so if you have multiple pointers to the same starting address you may need to update them all after reallocating the block. You could have the pointer live in one place and wrap an API around it, or you could use two memory objects: a smaller one that will not move, like a tree node, and a larger one that the smaller one points to, like the user-editable label for the tree node. The larger object can be reallocated, but only the tree node needs to update the address change.

As you would expect, **realloc()** has optimizations so that it does not have to do the allocate/copy/free procedure every time a block is reallocated. As noted above, sometimes the block returned from **malloc()** is actually larger than what you asked for. **realloc()** can just say, "OK, you can now use the rest of the block." There are also games **realloc()** can play. There maybe be a free block in another bucket that is contiguous with the block of memory you want to reallocate. In this case, **realloc()** gloms that second block onto the first and lets you use the space without changing addresses on you.

But in any case, be sure to assign the return value of **realloc()** back to your pointer. Otherwise, you can have a lurking problem:

```
Node *blah = malloc (sizeof(Node) * 20);
...
realloc (blah, sizeof(Node) * 40); // this is bad!
...
```

Sometimes it will work, sometimes not. Always assign the return value of **realloc**.

```
blah = realloc (blah, sizeof(Node) * 40);
```

Even then, this code could cause problems. If there is not enough room for the new block, **realloc()** will return NULL, but otherwise it will leave the original memory block untouched. If you do not otherwise hang on to the original pointer, you would leak the block. The **reallocf()** function will free the memory block if it cannot successfully complete the reallocation.

calloc()

malloc() does not initialize the memory it returns to you, so you'll probably have a bunch of stale junk in the memory you get. A pretty common idiom is to allocate a chunk of memory and zero it out so that it is safer to use:

```
void *memory = malloc (sizeof(Node) * 50);
memset (memory, 0, sizeof(Node) * 50);
```

You can also use **calloc()** to do this in one operation:

```
void *calloc(size_t nelem, size_t elsize);
```

The arguments to **calloc()** assume that you are allocating an array. It's just doing a multiplication behind the scenes. So,

```
memory = calloc (sizeof(Node), 50);
```

gives identical results to the two-step sequence above. It is better to use **calloc()** because the OS can do some optimizations behind the scenes, like allowing the kernel to reserve the memory, but not actually allocate it. It can then give you zero-filled pages when it is actually accessed. When you **memset()** a block of memory, you are writing to every page, causing them all to be marked as dirty.

alloca()

```
void *alloca(size_t size);
```

alloca() (for alloc automatic) allocates memory for you on the call stack. This means that allocation is very fast, being just some pointer adjustments. You also do not need to perform an explicit **free()** on your memory to release it. When the function ends, the stack frame just goes away and with it the chunk of the frame that contains the allocated memory. As with stuff that appears too good to be true, there is always a catch. Don't go nuts and overflow your stack with lots of local storage, especially if you use recursion or if your code could be run in a threaded environment where stack sizes are much more limited. Also, using **alloca()** with runtime-calculated allocation sizes can confuse some performance tools.

Even though the manpage for **alloca()** says, "This is machine dependent, its use is discouraged," it is still a documented API you can use, and it can be useful at times. Also, C99 lets you declare local-variable arrays with a variable size, just like in C++, which works in a way very similar to **alloca()**.

Memory Ownership Issues

One of the difficulties involved when using dynamic memory is determining who is responsible for freeing a piece of allocated memory when nobody else is using it. This is known as memory ownership. There are many different solutions to this problem, each with their own tradeoffs and benefits, as witnessed by Java and Cocoa garbage collection, C++ RAII (resource acquisition is initialization), and Cocoa's reference counting.

There are no uniform rules for memory ownership for Unix and C library calls, so you pretty much need to check the manpage for the calls in question (which is usually a good idea anyway). For instance:

- `getenv()` returns a `char *`, but you do not need to free it since the environment variables are all stored in a global array and `getenv()` just returns a string contained in that array.

- `strdup()` returns a `char *`, which you do need to free since it allocates memory on your behalf.

- Some calls take buffers, which you can `malloc` or create on the stack and you are responsible for `free`ing the memory when you are done. A subset of these calls can be given `NULL` for the buffer argument, and they will allocate memory on your behalf. `getcwd()` behaves like this.

- Some other calls will give you a reference to memory that they own (usually some kind of global buffer), such as `ctime()` for converting a Unix time into a character constant.

- Finally, there are some APIs that wrap dynamic memory allocation in an API and depend on you to use that API to create and destroy objects, such as `opendir()` and `closedir()` for iterating through the contents of directories.

Nodepools

And, of course, you can use any of these techniques for modules and APIs that you create, choosing the one that is most appropriate. It is perfectly fine for you to do your own memory allocation out of a big block, if that gives you better behavior. Example 7.4 shows a common suballocation technique using a memory pool. A memory pool is an allocator for vending identically-sized objects, very handy for things like tree or list nodes.

Example 7.4   nodepool.m

```
// nodepool.m -- A simple memory pool for vending like-size pieces of
//               memory.  An example of custom memory management.

// gcc -Wall -std=c99 -g -Os -framework Foundation -o nodepool nodepool.m

#import <Foundation/Foundation.h>

#import <stdio.h>
#import <stdlib.h>

// The free list that runs through all the blocks
typedef struct BWPoolElement {
    struct BWPoolElement *next;
```

```
} BWPoolElement;

@interface BWNodePool : NSObject {
    unsigned char  *memblock; // A big blob of bytes.
    BWPoolElement  *freelist; // Pointer to the head of the freelist.
    size_t          nodeSize;
    size_t          count;
}

- (id) initWithNodeSize: (size_t) nodeSize  count: (size_t) count;
- (void *) allocNode;
- (void) freeNode: (void *) nodePtr;

@end // BWNodePool


@implementation BWNodePool

- (void) weaveFreeListFrom: (unsigned char *) startAddress
                   forCount: (size_t) theCount {
    unsigned char *scan = startAddress;
    for (int i = 0; i < theCount; i++) {
        if (freelist == NULL) {
            freelist = (BWPoolElement *) scan;
            freelist->next = NULL;
        } else {
            BWPoolElement *temp = (BWPoolElement*) scan;
            temp->next = freelist;
            freelist = temp;
        }
        scan += nodeSize;
    }
} // weaveFreeListFrom


- (id) initWithNodeSize: (size_t) theNodeSize  count: (size_t) theCount {
    if ((self = [super init])) {
        nodeSize = theNodeSize;
        count = theCount;

        // Make sure there's enough space to store the pointers for the freelist.
        if (nodeSize < sizeof(BWPoolElement)) {
            nodeSize = sizeof(BWPoolElement);
        }

        // Allocate memory for the block.
        memblock = malloc (nodeSize * count);

        // Walk through the block building the freelist.
        [self weaveFreeListFrom: memblock  forCount: theCount];
    }

    return self;

} // initWithNodeSize


- (void) dealloc {
    free (memblock);
    [super dealloc];
```

```
} // dealloc


- (void *) allocNode {
    if (freelist == NULL) {
        // We're out of space, so just throw our hands up and
        // surrender for now.  You can grow the pool by keeping an
        // array of memblocks and creating a new one when the previous
        // block fills up.
        fprintf (stderr, "out of space in node pool.  Giving up\n");
        abort ();
    }

    // take a new node off of the freelist
    void *newNode = freelist;
    freelist = freelist->next;

    return newNode;

} // allocNode


- (void) freeNode: (void *) nodePtr {
    // Stick the freed node at the head of the freelist.
    ((BWPoolElement *)nodePtr)->next = freelist;
    freelist = nodePtr;
} // freeNode

@end // BWNodePool


// The node we're using the nodepool for.

#define NODE_BUF_SIZE 137

typedef struct ListNode {
    int                 someData;
    struct ListNode     *next;
} ListNode;


void haveFunWithPool (int nodeCount) {
    NSLog (@"Creating nodes with the node pool");

    BWNodePool *nodePool =
        [[BWNodePool alloc] initWithNodeSize: sizeof(ListNode)
                                count: nodeCount];
    ListNode *node = NULL, *prev = NULL;

    for (int i = 0; i < nodeCount; i++) {
        node = [nodePool allocNode];
        node->someData = i;
        // If you wish, you can do some extra work.

        // Construct a linked list through the nodes
        node->next = prev;
        prev = node;
    }

    NSLog (@"Cleaning up");
```

```
    // Destroy all the nodes at once.  If each node has memory management
    // obligations, you would need to walk the list of nodes.
    [nodePool release];

    NSLog (@"Done");

} // haveFunWithPool


void haveFunWithMalloc (int nodeCount) {
    NSLog (@"Creating nodes with malloc");

    ListNode *node = NULL, *prev = NULL;
    for (int i = 0; i < nodeCount; i++) {
        node = malloc (sizeof(ListNode));
        node->someData = i;
        // If you wish, you can do some extra work.

        // Construct a linked list through the nodes
        node->next = prev;
        prev = node;
    }
    ListNode *head = node;

    NSLog (@"Cleaning up");

    while (head != NULL) {
        ListNode *node = head;
        head = head->next;
        free (node);
    }

    NSLog (@"Done");

} // haveFunWithMalloc


int main (int argc, char *argv[]) {
    int count;

    if (argc != 3) {
        fprintf (stderr, "usage: %s -p|-m #\n", argv[0]);
        fprintf (stderr, "        exercise memory allocation\n");
        fprintf (stderr, "        -p to use a memory pool\n");
        fprintf (stderr, "        -m to use malloc\n");
        fprintf (stderr, "        #  number of nodes to play with\n");
        return 1;
    }
    count = atoi (argv[2]);

    if (strcmp(argv[1], "-p") == 0) {
        haveFunWithPool (count);
    } else {
        haveFunWithMalloc (count);
    }

    return 0;

} // main
```

Once the pool is created, allocations and frees are constant time, being just a couple of pointer operations. `malloc()` usually takes longer due to the complexity of its internal data structures. If your pool nodes don't reference other objects, you can delete everything from the pool in one operation. Here are some timings (in seconds) of runs of the program on a 2010 model MacBook Pro. Timings come from the **time** command:

Count	Pool	`malloc()`
20,000,000	0.62	2.86
100,000,000	3.12	14.19

This shows there can be, under some circumstances, benefit to doing your own allocation. Generally, it is better to test first to find out what your bottlenecks are before implementing your own allocator, but it's nice to have the option when you need it.

You can override the new operator in C++ to use a pool for allocations. In one C++ project I worked on, I had a class that supported chained array subscripts for digging into a compacted data structure, with code performing access like `flavor['page']['sect']['styl'][5]`. This was very convenient coding-wise, but it caused a lot of temporary objects to be created and destroyed. A pool was put under this class' `operator new`, and performance improved by an order of magnitude.

One thing to note in the `nodepool.m` code is that it doesn't handle the pool growing case. You cannot just `realloc()` the memory block because it could move in memory, leaving the freelist pointers dangling, as well as any pointers the objects being allocated might have, such as the linked list pointers. This can be fixed by having an array of memory pointers; when you run out of memory, create a new block, add it to the array, and weave the freelist through the new block.

Operations on the nodepool are not thread-safe. There are exercises to make it thread safe in Chapter 20: *Multithreading* and Chapter 22: *Grand Central Dispatch*.

Debugging Memory Problems

Errors in memory management cause a huge number of problems when programming in C and can lead to difficult-to-track-down bugs since the manifestation of a problem can happen long after the actual program error happened.

Common API issues

When `malloc()` cannot allocate memory, it returns NULL. Many programmers tend to ignore NULL results from `malloc()`. The conventional wisdom was that if memory really is exhausted, then the system is in some pretty serious trouble and is swapping heavily. In that case, it is just easier to crash and restart. Plus, it can be tedious to check the return value of `malloc()` all the time. In these days of systems with many gigabytes of RAM, it's possible for an app to fill up its address space before physical memory is exhausted, so the system will not be swapping.

iOS will let you know when you are running short on memory by giving you low-memory warnings, such as calling the **UIApplication** delegate method **-applicationDidReceiveMemoryWarning:** as well as **UIViewController**'s **-viewDidUnload**.

The typical Cocoa idiom of allocation and initialization

```
NSArray *array = [[NSArray alloc] init];
[array addObject: myObject];
```

glosses over allocation problems. **alloc** may return a nil object, and since Objective-C messages to nil are legal, in the face of an allocation problem, this code will propagate this nil object without complaint.

If you are paranoid, and/or want to be robust in low memory conditions for your own allocations, you can put a wrapper around **malloc()** (say a **safeMalloc()** or use preprocessor tricks to rename **malloc()** itself) that on a NULL return from **malloc()** will attempt to free memory and try the allocation again, and perhaps call **abort()** when things are in complete dire straits.

You can get garbage collectors for C and C++ to do automatic cleanup of memory, and Objective-C 2.0 has introduced garbage collection for Cocoa.

Another common API issue is not assigning the return value of **realloc()**. Your program can work fine until the block of memory moves. Then you are pointing to old memory. If that old memory does not get reused right away, things will seem to work fine until the most inconvenient moment, when things will fall apart.

Only free allocated memory once: do not try to free the same pointer twice. That will usually lead to a crash as the **malloc()** data structures get confused. Also do not try to free memory you got from some other API, unless it explicitly says you can call **free()** on it. For instance, **opendir()** allocates a chunk of memory and returns it to you, but do not **free()** that memory, use **closedir()**.

Lastly, do not access memory you have just freed. The old (stale) data may still be there, but that is something you do not want to depend on, especially in a threaded environment.

Memory corruption

Memory corruption happens when a piece of code writes data into an unexpected location in memory. At best, you will try writing into memory you do not have access to and will crash. At worst, you will slightly corrupt some data structure, which will manifest itself in an error millions of instructions in the future or even on another run of your program. The most common kinds of memory errors in C are buffer overruns and dangling pointers.

Buffer overruns are when you think you have a certain amount of memory at your disposal, but you actually have less than that amount allocated. A classic example is forgetting to account for the trailing zero byte for C string termination.

For instance:

```
char *stringCopy = malloc (strlen(mystring));
strcpy (stringCopy, mystring);
```

You have just written one byte past the end of your allocated block of memory. To correct this, you need to account for that extra byte:

```
char *stringCopy = malloc (strlen(string) + 1);
strcpy (stringCopy, string);
```

Ideally, you should use a variant of the call that takes the buffer length:

```
char *stringCopy = malloc (strlen(string) + 1);
```

```
strncpy (stringCopy, string, strlen(string) + 1);
```

Even in the case where you have an insufficient buffer size, it will not write randomly off the end.

Off-by-one errors, also called "obiwans" or "fence-post errors," can also cause a buffer overrun. For example:

```
void doStuff () {
    ListNode nodes[20];
    char stringBuffer[1024];

    int i;
    for (i = 0; i <= 20; i++) {
        nodes[i].stuff = i;
        ...
    }
} // doStuff
```

The loop runs from 0 through 20, which will execute the body of the loop 21 times. The last time through, the loop is indexing past the end of the nodes array and (most likely) has just trashed the beginning of the stringBuffer array.

Another nasty side effect of buffer overruns is that malicious data could clobber the stack in such a way that program control will jump to an unexpected place when the function returns. Many cracker exploits work like this.

Dangling pointers are memory addresses stored in pointer variables that no longer have any correlation with the memory they should be pointing to. Uninitialized pointers can cause this, as can forgetting to assign the return value of **realloc()**. You can get dangling pointers if you do not propagate the address of something when it moves or is changed. For example:

```
char *g_username;

const char *getUserName () {
    return g_username;
}

void setUserName (const char *newName) {
    free (g_username);
    g_username = strdup (newName); // performs a malloc
}
```

Now consider this scenario:

```
name = getUserName(); // say it is address 0x1000, "markd"
setUserName ("bork"); // the memory at address 0x1000 has been freed
printf (name);        // using a dangling pointer now
```

This is fundamentally an error in memory ownership. Does someone own the memory after calling **getUserName()**? It could be part of **getUserName()**'s contract that changing the username invalidates previously vended pointers. But still, this is a programming error that will most likely lead to a crash.

The OS X **malloc()** libraries have built-in tools to help track down some of these conditions. You can control these tools by setting environment variables and then running your program. If you are debugging a GUI app, you can run it from the command line by doing open /path/to/your/ AppBundle.app. Xcode 4 will let you control these tools from the GUI.

```
$ export MallocHelp=1
```

will display help when your run your program. This is **bash** syntax. (C Shell users would use `setenv` `MallocHelp 1`). When you are done using MallocHelp, you can remove the environment variable by using the **unset** command. C Shell users would use **unsetenv**.

MallocGuardEdges

This puts a 4KB page with no permissions before and after large blocks. This will catch buffer overruns before and after the allocated block. The size of a "large block" is undefined, but experimentally, 12K and larger seem to be considered large blocks.

MallocStackLogging and MallocStackLoggingNoCompact

These turn on stack frame recording for memory management calls for later use by tools like **malloc_history**.The difference is that `MallocStackLoggingNoCompact` remembers the malloc history even after the block has been released.

MallocScribble

This writes over-freed blocks with a known value, (0x55), which will catch attempts to reuse memory blocks. This is a bad pointer value, an odd address, which will cause addressing errors if it gets dereferenced.

Example 7.5 shows MallocScribble in action.

Example 7.5   mallocscribble.m

```
// mallocscribble.m -- exercise MallocScribble
// Run this, then run after setting the MallocScribble environment
// variable to 1.

// gcc -o mallocscribble mallocscribble.m

#import <stdio.h>       // for printf()
#import <stdlib.h>      // for malloc()
#import <string.h>      // for strcpy()

typedef struct Thingie {
    char blah[16];
    char string[30];
} Thingie;


int main (void) {
    Thingie *thing = malloc (20);

    strcpy (thing->string, "hello there");
    printf ("before free: %s\n", thing->string);
    free (thing);
    printf ("after free: %s\n", thing->string);

    return 0;

} // main
```

Without anything set in the environment:

```
$ ./mallocscribble
before free: hello there
after free: hello there
```

And after:

```
$ export MallocScribble=1
$ ./mallocscribble
malloc[20701]: enabling scribbling to detect mods to free blocks
mallocscribble(5239) malloc: enabling scribbling to detect mods to free blocks
before free: hello there
after free: UUUUUUUUUUUUUUUUUUUUUUUUUUUUUUUUUUU
```

Guard Malloc

Xcode ships with libgmalloc (Guard Malloc), which is an aggressive debugging malloc library geared to catch memory overrun errors.

Each memory allocation is placed on its own virtual memory page when libgmalloc is enabled, with the end of the buffer placed at the end of the page's memory. The next page is kept unallocated. You will generate a signal if you try to access beyond the end of the buffer. This will immediately catch run-off-the-end errors.

When memory is freed, libgmalloc deallocates its virtual memory, causing subsequent reads or writes to cause a bus error. Because of the extra pressure put on the virtual memory system, your application can run ten to one hundred times slower, so you probably don't want to run this all of the time. But when you need help tracking down nasty memory corruption problems, this can be a life-saver.

To enable libgmalloc, set the environment variable DYLD_INSERT_LIBRARIES to have the value /usr/lib/libgmalloc.dylib. This will cause the libgmalloc library to be loaded and override the existing definitions of **malloc()** and **free()**. You can either set this in your environment before running the program:

```
$ export DYLD_INSERT_LIBRARIES=/usr/lib/libgmalloc.dylib
```

or set it in **gdb** before running your program:

```
(gdb) set env DYLD_INSERT_LIBRARIES /usr/lib/libgmalloc.dylib
```

lldb has a similar syntax:

```
(lldb) set env-vars DYLD_INSERT_LIBRARIES=/usr/lib/libgmalloc.dylib
```

The debugger will halt execution of your program when your program reads or writes off of the end of a dynamically allocated chunk of memory. You can then poke around and see what went wrong.

Memory leaks

Another common memory-related error is memory leaks. These are bits of memory that get allocated and never deallocated. Memory leaks frequently happen when you assign a pointer to a new value but do not free the old value:

```
char *somestring;
somestring = strdup ("hello"); // performs a malloc() and a string copy.
somestring = strdup ("there");
```

The first string, "hello," has been leaked. This memory can never be freed because the address was not preserved. On desktop systems, a little memory leaked here or there, aside from being a bit sloppy, is not all that bad when you have gobs of RAM coupled with unused memory getting paged back to disk. What are the real killers are leaks that happen often, like inside of a loop, or every time the user does a common operation. Leaking 100 bytes is not too bad. Leaking 100 bytes every time the user presses a key in a word processor can be deadly. Applications in Mac OS X tend to run for long periods of time, so the user may forget about an app, then click on it in the Dock to do something with it. A small memory leak can really add up when your program can be running for weeks between restarts. iOS devices have very constrained memory compared to desktop computers. Any memory leaks can quickly exhaust the available memory and will cause the operating system to kill your application outright.

One easy way to tell if your program is leaking is to run **top** or Activity Monitor, find your application in the list, and watch the VSIZE column. You probably have a memory leak if that number is continually increasing

OS X comes with the **leaks** command that will grovel around in your program's address space and find unreferenced memory. **leaks** is a good quick check to see if you have any leaks. It walks your program's address space like a garbage collector, looking for pointers into **malloc()** blocks. If it can't find one, **leaks** will report a leak, along with a dump of some of the bytes near the start of the block. If the leaked chunk of memory is an instance of an Objective-C object, **leaks** will show the name of the class:

```
$ leaks BorkGraph
Process 21669: 26306 nodes malloced for 2042 KB
Process 21669: 154 leaks for 5120 total leaked bytes.
Leak: 0x011f3c50  size=40
   0x77eb239b 0x00000020 0x011f3ca0 0x00000001    w.#.... ..X.....
   0x00000065 0x00000065 0x00000065 0x00000000    ...e...e...e....
   0x011b8de0 0x011b8e30 0x00000000 0x00000000    .......0........
Leak: 0x011f3ca0  size=48       string 'xrvt'
Leak: 0x02634eb0  size=32       instance of 'NSAffineTransform'
   0xa287e7ac 0x40ccb65b 0x80000000 0x80000000    ....@..[........
   0x40ccb65b 0xc226542a 0xc2f88fc7 0x00000000    @..[.xT*........
```

Memory leaks in Cocoa

In addition to **malloc()**-related memory leaks, you can also leak memory in Cocoa programs by not being careful with your retain and release calls. Example 7.6 intentionally leaks some objects.

For instance:

Example 7.6   objectleak.m

```
// objectleak.m -- Leak some Cocoa objects

//gcc -Wall -std=c99 -g -framework Foundation -o objectleak objectleak.m

#import <Foundation/Foundation.h>

int main (void) {
    NSAutoreleasePool *pool = [[NSAutoreleasePool alloc] init];

    NSMutableArray *array = [[NSMutableArray alloc] init];
    for (int i = 0; i < 20; i++) {
```

```
        NSNumber *number = [[NSNumber alloc] initWithInt: i]; // retain count of 1
        [number retain];
        [array addObject: number]; // number has retain count of 2
    }

    [array release]; // Each of the numbers have retain counts of 1.
    // Therefore we've leaked each of the numbers

    [pool drain];
    sleep (5000);
    // Now would be a good time to run leaks.
    exit 0;

} // main
```

Each of the NSNumber objects still has a retain count of one after the array is released, so they have been leaked. The leaks tool can show you these leaks:

```
$ leaks objectleak
...
Process 5409: 924 nodes malloced for 208 KB
Process 5409: 6 leaks for 192 total leaked bytes.
Leak: 0x10010d770  size=32  zone: DefaultMallocZone_0x100004000
    instance of 'NSCFNumber', type ObjC, implemented in Foundation
        0x70bbe6e8 0x00007fff 0x00001683 0x00000002     ...p...........
        0x0000000e 0x00000000 0x00000000 0x00000000     ...............
...
```

Other Tools

ps

The **ps** command, short for "process status," has some features for keeping tabs on your program's memory use. Here is one use of **ps**:

```
$ ps auxw | grep something-interesting
```

where something-interesting is the PID or program name of interest. So, something like

```
$ ps auxw | grep Finder
```

will show some information about the Finder process:

```
markd   229   0.0  1.9    2912584  33136  ?? S   0:43.11 /System/ \
Library/CoreServices/Finder.app/Contents/MacOS/Finder -psn_0_2621
```

In order, the columns are:

1. Owner of the process (markd).

2. Process ID (229).

3. CPU currently taken (0.0%).

4. Real memory in use (1.9%).

5. Virtual size, the total footprint of the program. The virtual size for 64-bit processes is very large due to the large volume of zero pages.

6. Resident set size, how much is living in RAM right now. This is 33136K, or about 33 megs.

7. Controlling terminal (not important).

8. Process state (more about this in Chapter 18: *Multiprocessing*).

9. Total CPU time consumed by the process (43 seconds).

10. Command with arguments that started the process.

Relating to memory, the fifth and sixth columns are the most interesting. You can look at just those with the command

```
ps -ax -o user,pid,vsz,rss,command
```

which will show the owner, the PID, the virtual size,the resident size, and the command:

```
$ ps -ax -o user,pid,vsz,rss,command
USER       PID     VSZ    RSS COMMAND
root         1 2456676    588 /sbin/launchd
root        10 2459596   1688 /usr/libexec/kextd
root        11 2452680   3760 /usr/sbin/DirectoryService
root        12 2444544    352 /usr/sbin/notifyd
root        13 2446808    808 /usr/sbin/diskarbitrationd
root        14 2474544   2440 /usr/libexec/configd
root        15 2457096    420 /usr/sbin/syslogd
```

ps can show a wealth of information about what is running on your system. You can run this repeatedly to see if your program (or any other) seems to be growing without bounds. Check out the manpage for more.

Resource limits

Because Unix is a multi-user system, there are safeguards in the OS to keep processes from dominating, and possibly bringing down, the system by consuming too many resources. There are a number of different resources that are controlled:

RLIMIT_DATA	Maximum size (bytes) of the data segment for a process, that is, the maximum size of the heap plus initialized + uninitialized data segments.
RLIMIT_RSS	Maximum size (bytes) to which a process' resident set may grow. That is, maximum amount of physical RAM to be given.
RLIMIT_STACK	Maximum size (bytes) of the stack segment. How deep your program stack can get. This does not apply to the stacks that threads use.
RLIMIT_MEMLOCK	Maximum size (bytes) which a process can lock (wire) into memory with the **mlock()** function.

There are also resources not related to memory:

RLIMIT_FSIZE   Maximum size (bytes) of a file that may be created.

RLIMIT_NOFILE   Maximum number of simultaneously open files.

RLIMIT_NPROC   Maximum number of simultaneous processes for the current user.

RLIMIT_CPU   Maximum amount of CPU time (in seconds).

RLIMIT_CORE   Largest size (in bytes) of core files.

Resource limits are expressed as a soft limit and a hard limit. When the soft limit is exceeded, the program may receive a signal, which is like a software interrupt. (Signals are discussed in depth in Chapter 5: *Exceptions, Error Handling, and Signals*.) The soft limits are usually lower than hard limits, but you can raise them to the hard limit. You can lower the hard limit, but you can never raise the hard limit unless you are running with superuser privileges.

Example 7.7 shows you the hard and soft limits currently in force:

Example 7.7   limits.m

```
// limits.m -- See the current resource limits.

// gcc -g -Wall -o limits limits.m

#import <sys/resource.h> // for the RLMIT_* constants
#import <errno.h>        // for errno
#import <stdio.h>        // for printf() and friends
#import <string.h>       // for strerror()

typedef struct Limit {
    int resource;
    const char *name;
} Limit;

Limit limits[] = {
    { RLIMIT_DATA,    "data segment maximum (bytes)" },
    { RLIMIT_RSS,     "resident size maximum (bytes)" },
    { RLIMIT_STACK,   "stack size maximum (bytes)" },
    { RLIMIT_MEMLOCK, "wired memory maximum (bytes)" },
    { RLIMIT_FSIZE,   "file size maximum (bytes)" },
    { RLIMIT_NOFILE,  "max number of simultaneously open files" },
    { RLIMIT_NPROC,   "max number of simultaneous processes" },
    { RLIMIT_CPU,     "cpu time maximum (seconds)" },
    { RLIMIT_CORE,    "core file maximum (bytes)" }
};

// Turn the rlim_t value in to a string, also translating the magic
// "infinity" value to something human readable
void stringValue (rlim_t value, char *buffer, size_t buffersize) {
    if (value == RLIM_INFINITY) strcpy (buffer, "infinite");
    else snprintf (buffer, buffersize, "%lld", value);
} // stringValue

// Right-justify the first entry in a field width of 45, then display
// two more strings.
#define FORMAT_STRING "%45s: %-10s (%s)\n"
```

```
int main (void) {
    Limit *scan = limits;
    Limit *stop = scan + (sizeof(limits) / sizeof(*limits));

    printf (FORMAT_STRING, "limit name", "soft-limit", "hard-limit");

    while (scan < stop) {
        struct rlimit rl;
        if (getrlimit (scan->resource, &rl) == -1) {
            fprintf (stderr, "error in getrlimit for %s: %d/%s\n",
                     scan->name, errno, strerror(errno));
        } else {
            char softLimit[20];
            char hardLimit[20];

            stringValue (rl.rlim_cur, softLimit, 20);
            stringValue (rl.rlim_max, hardLimit, 20);

            printf (FORMAT_STRING, scan->name, softLimit, hardLimit);
        }
        scan++;
    }
    return 0;
} // main
```

Here is the output on a OS X 10.6, MacBook Pro system:

```
                            limit name: soft-limit (hard-limit)
         data segment maximum (bytes): infinite   (infinite)
        resident size maximum (bytes): infinite   (infinite)
            stack size maximum (bytes): 8720000   (67104768)
        wired memory maximum (bytes): infinite   (infinite)
            file size maximum (bytes): infinite   (infinite)
   max number of simultaneously open files: 256   (infinite)
      max number of simultaneous processes: 266   (532)
              cpu time maximum (seconds): infinite   (infinite)
              core file maximum (bytes): 0         (infinite)
```

All things considered, the system is pretty kind to us.

You can read the current resource limits by using **getrlimit()** as shown in the code above, and you can change the resource limits by using **setrlimit()** and passing it an appropriately filled in struct rlimit.

Example 7.8 is a program that will attempt to open the same file over and over. It is easier to show resource limits with files than trying to overflow the stack.

Example 7.8   openfiles.m

```
// openfiles.m -- Exhaust open-files resource limit.

// gcc -Wall -std=c99 -o openfiles openfiles.m

#import <errno.h>  // for errno
#import <fcntl.h>  // for O_RDONLY
#import <stdio.h>  // for fprintf()
#import <stdlib.h> // for exit, open
```

```
#import <string.h> // for strerror

int main (int argc, char *argv[]) {
    if (argc > 2) {
        fprintf (stderr, "usage:  %s [open-file-rlimit]\n", argv[0]);
        return 1;
    }

    if (argc == 2) {
        struct rlimit rl = { .rlim_cur = atoi (argv[1]),
                             .rlim_max = RLIM_INFINITY };

        if (setrlimit(RLIMIT_NOFILE, &rl) == -1) {
            fprintf (stderr, "error in setrlimit for RLIM_NOFILE: %d/%s\n",
                     errno, strerror(errno));
            exit (1);
        }
    }

    for (int i = 0; i < 260; i++) {
        int fd = open ("/usr/include/stdio.h", O_RDONLY);
        printf ("%d: fd is %d\n", i, fd);
        if (fd < 0) break;
    }

    return 0;

} // main
```

When run, this happens:

```
$ ./openfiles
0: fd is 3
1: fd is 4
...
251: fd is 254
252: fd is 255
253: fd is -1
```

Notice that fd starts becoming -1, the error code return value from **open()**, because it cannot open the file. fd maxes out at 255, which correlates with the result of limits.m (Example 7.7), which said that the maximum number of simultaneously open files was 256. There are already the 3 files opened for us, stdin, stdout, stderror, which count as open files against the resource limit.

When run with an argument, the program changes the soft limit. Here are some sample runs:

```
$ ./openfiles 10
0: fd is 3
1: fd is 4
2: fd is 5
3: fd is 6
4: fd is 7
5: fd is 8
6: fd is 9
7: fd is -1

$ ./openfiles 1000000
0: fd is 3
1: fd is 4
```

```
2: fd is 5
...
257: fd is 260
258: fd is 261
259: fd is 262
```

Setting lower resource limits can be useful when you are spawning off other programs, discussed in Chapter 18: *Multiprocessing*. If you do not trust the other programs, or want to constrain their limits, you can fork, call **setrlimit()** on yourself in the child process, and then exec the child process, which will run under the reduced limits.

Miscellaneous tools

The **heap** command lists all the **malloc()**-allocated buffers in the heap of a program. Give it the PID or name of the program to examine.

heap is interesting when pointed at a Cocoa program because it shows Objective-C classes. Here is stuff from objectleak.m (edited down):

```
Zone DefaultMallocZone_0x7000:
Zone DefaultMallocZone_0x100004000: Overall size: 9215KB;
    925 nodes malloced for 208KB (2% of capacity);
    largest unused: [0x100826800-8037KB]

Zone DefaultMallocZone_0x7000: 558 nodes -
32KB[4] 8KB[2] 4KB[2] ... 48[66] 32[258] 16[246]

Found 490 ObjC classes in process 5307
Found 40 CFTypes in process 5307


--------------------------------------------------------------
Zone DefaultMallocZone_0x7000: 558 nodes (92560 bytes)
```

COUNT	BYTES	AVG	CLASS_NAME	TYPE	BINARY
803	156992	195.5	non-object		
51	1936	38.0	NSCFString	ObjC	Foundation
20	640	32.0	NSCFNumber	ObjC	Foundation
10	640	64.0	NSCFDictionary	ObjC	Foundation
8	512	64.0	CFBasicHash	CFType	CoreFoundation
5	560	112.0	NSRecursiveLock	ObjC	Foundation

We can see that we have a number of strings and numbers allocated.

malloc_history will show you a history of memory activity. This requires that you set MallocStackLogging to 1 in your environment before running.

Example 7.9 is a program that does some memory manipulations and then sleeps:

Example 7.9   mallochistory.m

```
// mallochistory.m -- Do some memory allocation to show off malloc_history.
// Be sure to set the environment variable MallocStackLoggingNoCompact to 1.
// Then run this program, and while
// it sleeps at the end, run 'malloc_history pid -all_by_size' or
// 'malloc_history pid -all_by_count'
```

```
// gcc -g -std=c99 -Wall -o mallochistory mallochistory.m

#import <unistd.h>   // for getpid(), sleep()
#import <stdlib.h>   // for malloc()
#import <stdio.h>    // for printf

void func2 () {
    char *stuff;

    for (int i = 0; i < 3; i++) {
        stuff = malloc (50);
        free (stuff);
    }
    stuff = malloc (50);
    // so we can use the malloc_history address feature
    printf ("address of stuff is %p\n", stuff);
    // intentionally leak stuff
} // func2

void func1 () {
    int *numbers = malloc (sizeof(int) * 100);
    func2 ();
    // intentionally leak numbers
} // func1

int main (void) {
    printf ("my process id is %d\n", getpid());
    func1 ();

    sleep (600);
    return 0;
} // main
```

When run, this program prints:

```
$ export MallocStackLoggingNoCompact=1
$ ./mallochistory
mallochistory(5889) malloc: recording malloc stacks to disk using standard recorder
mallochistory(5889) malloc: stack logging compaction turned off;
   size of log files on disk can increase rapidly
address of stuff is 0x1001002e0
```

Then in another terminal, see who has manipulated the block:

```
$ malloc_history 5889 0x1001002e0

Call [2] [arg=50]: thread_a04cdfa0 |0x1 | start | main | func1
  | func2 | malloc | malloc_zone_malloc
```

You can also see what stuff is currently allocated and who did it. In this case, the stack entries are ordered by size. Stuff that is purely overhead has been removed.

```
$ malloc_history 5889 -all_by_size
```

Looks like **printf()** and friends use a 4K buffer to do their work:

```
1 calls for 4096 bytes: thread_a04cdfa0 |0x1 | start | main | printf
  | vfprintf_l | __vfprintf | __swsetup | __smakebuf | malloc
```

```
| malloc_zone_malloc
```

Here is the numbers array:

```
1 calls for 400 bytes: thread_a04cdfa0 | start | main | func1
  | malloc | malloc_zone_malloc
```

And the final **malloc()** from **func2()**.

```
1 calls for 50 bytes: thread_a04cdfa0 | start | main | func1
  | func2 | malloc | malloc_zone_malloc
```

You can get info about a block from inside of **gdb** with the info malloc command:

```
$ export MallocStackLoggingNoCompact=1
$ gdb ./mallochistory
(gdb) run
...
address of stuff is 0x1001002e0
^C
(gdb) info malloc 0x1001002e0
Alloc: Block address: 0x00000001001002e0 length: 50
Stack - pthread: 0x7fff70c8ec20 number of frames: 6
    0: 0x7fff85695f2e in malloc_zone_malloc
    1: 0x7fff85694208 in malloc
    2: 0x100000dc3 in func2 at mallochistory.m:19
    3: 0x100000e1e in func1 at mallochistory.m:39
    4: 0x100000e51 in main at mallochistory.m:46
    5: 0x100000da0 in start
Dealloc: Block address: 0x00000001001002e0
Stack - pthread: 0x7fff70c8ec20 number of frames: 5
    0: 0x7fff8569863e in free
    1: 0x100000dd0 in func2 at mallochistory.m:18
    2: 0x100000e1e in func1 at mallochistory.m:39
    3: 0x100000e51 in main at mallochistory.m:46
    4: 0x100000da0 in start
...
```

This shows the stack traces, with file and lines when debug information is known, for each malloc history occurrence.

Instruments also has extensive tools for monitoring and analyzing memory allocation.

vm_stat

vm_stat shows some Mach virtual memory statistics. Here it is for my system right now:

```
Mach Virtual Memory Statistics: (page size of 4096 bytes)
Mach Virtual Memory Statistics: (page size of 4096 bytes)
Pages free:                     43272.
Pages active:                  251918.
Pages inactive:                107189.
Pages speculative:             457165.
Pages wired down:              123854.
"Translation faults":       632401789.
Pages copy-on-write:          2381892.
Pages zero filled:           54419747.
Pages reactivated:             787236.
Pageins:                      1472149.
```

```
Pageouts:                        800691.
Object cache: 87 hits of 648951 lookups (0% hit rate)
```

You could run **vm_stat** at different points in time to see if your system is swapping (lots of pageins and pageouts). The manpage has information on each of the entries.

Objective-C Garbage Collection

Objective-C 2.0 adds garbage collection to the language as a replacement to the traditional retain / release reference counting scheme. Garbage collection is automatic object memory management. The garbage collector figures out what objects are being referred to by other objects, and the collector will destroy the object if nobody has any interest in it. This is familiar behavior to programmers who have used languages like Java or Python, where memory management "just happens."

Objective-C garbage collection is opt-in. You can choose to use GC or continue to use reference counting. iOS does not currently support GC, so you must use reference counting there. Apple recommends using GC for new apps, but you can retrofit older applications to use it. Xcode is an example of a large application that has been retrofitted to use GC. Adopting GC limits you to OS X 10.5 or later since it was first introduced in Leopard. It can also be difficult to adopt if your existing application uses a lot of non-Cocoa code, such as Carbon or C++ libraries.

Objective-C GC is designed for Objective-C code and Objective-C objects since that is where most of the code for the platform is being written and optimized. Because Objective-C is a superset of C, we still have pointers, and those can complicate some memory management scenarios.

Apple's GC is a conservative, generational, and concurrent garbage collector. A *conservative* garbage collector never copies or moves pointers. Once you allocate memory, it sticks to the address where it first lands. This means you can allocate a buffer and then pass it to C functions and not worry about the memory floating away unexpectedly.

A *generational* garbage collector assumes that new objects turn to garbage quickly. Objects tend to stick around as they get older. A generational collector concentrates on new objects when looking for garbage and only looks at older objects a fraction of the time rather than scanning every object on every garbage collection cycle. Apple claims that 90% of objects are recovered with 10% of the effort when using the generational model.

A *concurrent* garbage collector runs on its own thread. It can also be collecting objects while other objects are being allocated. Apple's collector doesn't stop all the threads at once when collecting, and it tries not to interrupt any thread for very long. Threads that don't use any Objective-C code won't be stopped at all by the collector. There is a thread-local collector for each thread, which also improves GC concurrency.

How to use it

Turning on GC is easy. Just turn on the Objective-C Garbage Collection setting in Xcode's build settings. Use the Required setting for new projects, which is equivalent to the **gcc** command-line flag -fobjc-gc-only. This means that all of your code will run in a GC environment, and all frameworks and plug-ins must support garbage collection. The Supported setting is for frameworks that can run in either GC mode or with reference counting. -fobjc-gc is the command-line flag to use for this case.

To verify that garbage collection is enabled, you can ask **NSGarbageCollector**:

```
if ([NSGarbageCollector defaultCollector] != nil) {
    NSLog (@"GC active");
} else {
    NSLog (@"GC not active");
}
```

Assignment of pointers becomes memory management once GC is enabled. Example 7.10 contains a class that has a string instance variable. An instance of the class is created and assigned to a stack-local variable. The collector is run, and nothing happens. There is still a valid reference to the object. The local variable is then set to a nil value, and the collector is run again. The collector realizes that there are no more references to the object, calls the **-finalize** method, which prints out that the object is dying, and then the memory is reclaimed.

Example 7.10   gc-sample.m

```
// gc-sample.m -- A simple GC app that shows it working.

// gcc -fobjc-gc-only -g -Wall -framework Foundation -o gc-sample gc-sample.m

#import <Foundation/Foundation.h>
#import <objc/objc-auto.h>  // for GC runtime API

@interface Snorgle : NSObject {
    int number;
}
- (id) initWithNumber: (int) num;
@end // Snorgle

@implementation Snorgle

- (id) initWithNumber: (int) num {
    if ((self = [super init])) {
        number = num;
    }
    return (self);
} // initWithNumber

- (void)finalize {
    NSLog (@"finalized %d", number);
    [super finalize];
} // finalize

@end // Snorgle

int main (void) {
    NSGarbageCollector *gc = [NSGarbageCollector defaultCollector];

    if (gc != nil) NSLog (@"GC active");

    objc_startCollectorThread ();

    Snorgle *sn1 = [[Snorgle alloc] initWithNumber: 1];

    NSLog (@"collect with snorgle object still live.");
    [gc collectExhaustively];
    sleep (2);

    sn1 = nil;
```

```
    NSLog (@"collect after removing reference");
    [gc collectExhaustively];
    sleep (2);

    return 0;

} // main
```

Most applications you will write won't need to explicitly invoke the collector or start the collector thread as is done here. **NSApplication** takes care of those details for you. There's a little more work required on the part of command-line tools that do not have a user interface.

Here is Example 7.10 when run:

```
$ ./gc-sample
2010-06-22 23:33:23.861 gc-sample[6023:903] GC active
2010-06-22 23:33:23.864 gc-sample[6023:903] collect with snorgle object still live.
2010-06-22 23:33:25.864 gc-sample[6023:903] collect after removing reference
2010-06-22 23:33:25.865 gc-sample[6023:903] finalized 1
```

The act of assigning an object to a pointer causes it to stay alive. Removing the reference to the object, whether by assigning the pointer to `nil` or by pointing it to another object, causes the object to be collected eventually.

Accessor methods become trivial to write in the GC world. Just assign the new value to your instance variable and return the value:

```
- (void) setBlah: (Blah *) newBlah {
    blah = newBlah;
} // setBlah

- (Blah *) blah {
    return blah;
} // blah
```

There is no need to check that you are re-setting a previous value. There is also no need to use @synchronized to get atomic assignments, as those are handled automatically by the GC machinery.

Retain cycles are a problem when using reference counting memory management. Object A retaining B retaining C retaining A forms a cycle that will never get released. This is why delegate objects are not retained and why child objects do not retain their parents. If you have cycles of objects in GC, with A pointing to B, B pointing to C, and C pointing back to A, the collector will notice when there are no external references to any of those objects and will collect the entire cycle.

Nib loading works differently between the GC and reference-counted worlds. When nib files are loaded in a reference-counted application, top-level objects in the nib file leak by default. They do not get released. These objects will get collected and will go away under GC. If you have a top-level nib object that you do not want to disappear, then you need to store `self` someplace the collector knows about, such as a global, to get it rooted. For **AppController** style classes created in MainMenu.nib files, you can make it a delegate of the File's Owner (**NSApplication**). This is sufficient to keep it from being collected.

There are some Cocoa subsystems that require explicit disconnection before an object is destroyed. GC can handle some of these, such as unregistering with an **NSNotificationCenter**.

NSNotificationCenter uses weak references to registered objects. Weak references are described below.

Other subsystems, such as timers and KVO, need to disassociate the object. You can do this in **-finalize**, but see below about problems with **-finalize**. You can also construct your class interface so that there is an explicit "termination of service," or shutdown call, which can then unhook from these subsystems.

How it works

Cocoa GC manages all Objective-C objects, can manage Core Foundation objects like CFString and CFArray, and can also manage some forms of non-object memory.

The GC memory model is divided into four areas:

- global variables in the static data segment

- local variables on thread stacks

- the GC heap, where all collectable memory lives

- the **malloc()** zone

The first three play a role in the GC's behavior, while the **malloc()** zone is never touched or looked at by the collector.

The collector scans memory to figure out what is alive. It starts with some well-known root locations, specifically globals and local variables, and then scans through memory looking for things. Things to make it go.

- instance variables and globals of Objective-C object types

- instance variables and globals marked as __strong (There is more on strong and weak references below.)

- some thread stacks, those that have an associated **NSThread**

- some heap blocks that have been explicitly allocated as collectable and that should be scanned

The collector scans all of these areas looking for things that look like pointers. It then builds a data structure of connected and unconnected objects. Objects that have a connection up to a root are good. Objects that do not have such a connection are considered garbage and put on a list. After the collector does its scan, it walks the garbage list. It zeroes out weak references to garbage, sends **-finalize** to every object in the garbage, and reclaims the memory.

The collector does not look at instance variables and globals of C pointer types nor heap blocks from **malloc()** or **vm_allocate()**. This can cause problems if you put addresses of collectable objects into malloc'd blocks. The collector will not see these references, so it might collect an object before it is actually garbage.

In OS X 10.6, the GC heap is limited to 32 gigabytes of memory in 64-bit applications. If you need to control more memory than that, perhaps you are loading a lot of graphics tiles or caching a lot of pages from a database. You will want to put the data that does not contain pointers to other objects into the malloc zone and reference the malloc'd memory from collected objects.

You can use **NSGarbageCollector** methods like **-collectIfNeeded** and **-collectExhaustively** to hint to the collector that now would be a good time to do some cleanup. Any place where you performed explicit autorelease pool manipulations would be a good place to tickle the collector. The collector is automatically triggered at the bottom of the application's event loop.

Strong and weak references

A pointer pointing to a chunk of collectable memory can be a strong or a weak reference. A strong reference tells the collector not to collect the object since someone is using it. The collector finds objects by following strong references. Once all strong reference to an object are removed, the object is collected.

A weak reference tells the collector that you have an interest in the object being pointed to – but not enough of an interest to force the object to stay around once all of its strong references are gone. The pointer to that object is set to nil when a weak-referenced object is collected.

Object pointers are strong by default. You annotate non-object pointers with __strong:

```
int * __strong footCountRef;
```

If you got some collectable memory and then assigned it to footCountRef, the collector will make sure the object is not collected. If the __strong were missing from that declaration, the collector would not consider this a reference to the memory. Unless this is a local variable, which is considered a strong reference.

The compiler generates *write barriers* to catch assignments to variables with strong reference. A write barrier is simply a function call, like **objc_assign_ivar()** or **objc_assign_global()**, which can be found in the objc-auto.h header. The write barriers update the collector's view of the world and then update the variable's value in memory. Stack-based variables do not cause write barriers to be generated for the sake of efficiency. Instead, the collector scans the entire stack looking for pointers rather than using write barriers.

Weak references are automatically zero-filled when the object it points to is deleted. When accessing a weak reference, you either see the object or you get nil. This means you will not get dangling references.

In addition to generating a write barrier when a weak reference variable is changed, the compiler generates a read barrier. The read barrier catches the case when the pointed-to object has been collected and then zeros out the reference for the case when the collector has not already gotten around to zeroing out the reference by the time you access it.

Weak references are restricted to instance and global variables only. You cannot have a weak local variable. There is nothing the compiler can do to tell the collector when it scans call stacks that a local variable is weak. Weak references are more expensive than strong references because of this read barrier. Strong references are normal memory reads, but weak reference reads go through the read barrier function. Also, threads can block on the read barrier while weak references are being cleared.

The compiler only generates read and write barriers for Objective-C compiled code. .m and .mm files get it for free, but not .c or .cpp files. You can use the barrier calls yourself if you need to.

Finalize methods

The **-dealloc** method is never called when using GC. Instead, when an object meets its ultimate demise, the collector calls the object's **-finalize** method to let the object do any final cleanup. Finalize methods are not nearly as convenient as they sound and should be avoided if at all possible.

After the collector makes its pass through objects to see what is garbage, it clears out the weak references to the objects. Then the **finalize** methods are called in an arbitrary order. Messaging objects in your finalizer might find you sending messages to an object that has already been finalized. The finalizers also have to be thread safe. They can be called on the collector thread or in some other thread. Also, your object might be messaged after it was finalized due to finalize methods being called in an arbitrary order. You also cannot depend on when the finalize method will be called.

These restrictions make using finalizers inconvenient for doing non-memory-related cleanup, such as closing files or terminating a network connection. Rather than combining resource management and memory management together, Apple recommends adding a specific "all done" call to your API, like a **-closeFile** or **-terminateNetworkConnection**. By doing this, you can get by without having any finalize method at all. If you have memory buffers that need to be collected, consider using an **NSMutableData** or **NSAllocateCollectable()**, which will get cleaned up automatically.

Unlike Java, you cannot resurrect an object in its finalize by assigning it somewhere to make the object alive. You will get a runtime error if you try this.

Non Objective-C objects

In addition to Objective-C objects, the collector can deal with Core Foundation objects, as well as arbitrary blocks of collectable memory. CF*Ref objects are collector-disabled GC objects and are not considered GC types, so a Core Foundation pointer is not considered a __strong pointer. If you do want to make a CF object collectable, you should **CFRelease()** it or call **CFMakeCollectable()**.

The **-retain**, **-release**, and **-autorelease** methods are turned into no-ops when GC is active, being short-circuited in the method dispatch machinery. Therefore, autoreleasing a CF object will not do anything, and the object will leak.

As mentioned earlier, pointers to collectable memory should not be stored in a block of memory received from **malloc()** because the collector will not scan those blocks to see if the memory reference is still there. You can get a block of collectable memory, though, by calling **NSAllocateCollectable()**:

```
void *__strong NSAllocateCollectable (NSUInteger size,
                                       NSUInteger options);
void *__strong NSReallocateCollectable (void *ptr, NSUInteger size,
                                        NSUInteger options);
```

options can be zero or the bitwise OR of these flags:

- NSScannedOption : This tells the collector that it should scan the block looking for pointers to other bits of collectable memory. By default, the collector does not scan blocks returned by these calls.

- NSCollectorDisabledOption : This tells the collector not to attempt to collect the block.

Do not use **memmove()** or **memcpy()** to move the contents of collected memory around. Instead use **objc_memmove_collectable()**:

```
void *objc_memmove_collectable (void *dst, const void *src,
                                 size_t size);
```

This makes sure that the collector will catch any strong reference changes.

External reference counts

Even though GC objects seem like they don't have a reference count, they actually do, but it defaults to zero. When this reference count is zero, the collector assumes that it is in control of the object and will clean it up when it thinks there are no more strong references to it. When this reference count is non-zero, the collector leaves it alone. You can use this to keep an object alive if you are storing it in a place where the collector will not look.

You increase this reference count by calling **CFRetain()** or using **NSGarbageCollector**'s **-disableCollectorForPointer**. Likewise, decrease the reference count by calling **CFRelease()** or using **NSGarbageCollector**'s **-enableCollectorForPointer**. **CFMakeCollectable()** is equivalent to **CFRelease()** but does not look nearly as weird in code as creating a CF object, immediately releasing it, and then proceeding to use the object. If you use the external reference counts, you still need to worry about retain cycles.

The "new" collection classes

Weak references are useful when you are caching data. When the cached data is removed for whatever reason, the weak references to it are zeroed out. It would be nice if the Cocoa collection classes (**NSArray**, **NSSet**, etc) supported automatic removal via weak references. Unfortunately, these collections cannot contain `nil` values.

Luckily, there were a couple of function pointer based quasi-objects that have been in Cocoa since the early NeXTSTep days, **NSMapTable** and **NSHashTable**. In comparison to the rest of Cocoa, the API was strongly C-flavored and not object-oriented at all. Apple has taken these classes, objectified them, and made them useful in the GC world.

NSMapTable is like a dictionary with keys and values, but you can have keys and/or values that are held weakly. Entries are removed when one of the associated objects is collected. **NSHashTable** is like a set, with entries that can be removed when the object is collected. A new class, **NSPointerArray**, has been introduced that behaves like an **NSArray**, but can hold `nil` values.

There are many, many ways to configure these collection classes, with over 30 for **NSMapTable**, to fine-tune their behavior between objects, C pointers, and weak and strong references, whether through the use of flags, or using an **NSPointerFunctions** object.

NSMapTable provides a set of conveniences for common scenarios:

```
+ (id) mapTableWithStrongToStrongObjects;
+ (id) mapTableWithWeakToStrongObjects;
+ (id) mapTableWithStrongToWeakObjects;
+ (id) mapTableWithWeakToWeakObjects;
```

GC and threads

Threads created via **NSThread** will have their stacks crawled by the collector looking for active references. Threads created by the pthread API will not be collected unless you make an **NSThread** call in that thread or create an autorelease pool. That will register the thread with the collector. Performance-critical threads, like audio or video playback, should not be collected. The collector can temporarily interrupt a thread to do its work.

Be aware of race conditions if you pass GC memory from one thread to another. The memory might get collected before the thread starts and can add its own reference. This is a good place to use the external reference counts: increase the external reference count before starting the thread and then decrement it inside of the new thread.

Debugging

The main problems that can come up with GC involve objects that are collected too soon, usually because of a missing write barrier, or objects that are never collected and therefore leak. This is usually because of an unexpected reference.

gdb has two GC-related commands: `info gc-references` and `info gc-roots`. Give these commands an object pointer, and they will either tell you what references it or tell you the shortest path from a GC root.

There are a couple of environment variables you can set to control GC behavior::

- `OBJC_PRINT_GC` : set to YES to see the GC status of the application and any loaded libraries.

- `AUTO_LOG_COLLECTIONS` : set to YES to see collections as they happen.

- `OBJC_USE_TLC` : set to NO to turn off the thread-local collector. Some instruments do not play well with the thread-local collector, so you'll want to turn off TLC if Instruments is behaving oddly.

- `OBJC_DISABLE_GENERATIONAL` : set to YES to turn off the generational algorithm and force the collector to do a full collection every time.

Exercises

1. Add pool growing to `nodepool.m`.

2. Profile nodepool with Shark or Instruments. What's the major bottleneck for **-allocNode**? What causes it? How would you fix it?

3. Find all the errors in Example 7.11, some of which are memory related. (I found nine.)

Example 7.11   memerror.m

```
// memerror.m -- try to find (and fix!) all the memory-related errors in
//               this program

// Take a string from the command line.  Make a linked-list out of it in
// reverse order.  Traverse it to construct a string in reverse.  Then clean
// up afterwards.

// gcc -w -g -o memerror memerror.m
```

```
#import <stdio.h>
#import <stdlib.h>
#import <string.h>

typedef struct CharNode {
    char theChar;
    struct CharNode *next;
} CharNode;

// Build a linked list backwards, then walk the list.
void reverseIt (char *stringbuffer) {
    CharNode *head, *node;
    char *scan, *stop;

    // Clear out local vars
    head = node = NULL;

    // Find the start and end of the string so we can walk it
    scan = stringbuffer;
    stop = stringbuffer + strlen(stringbuffer) + 1;  // trailing null

    // Walk the string
    while (scan < stop) {
        if (head == NULL) {
            head = malloc (sizeof(CharNode*));
            head->theChar = *scan;
            head->next = NULL;
        } else {
            node = malloc (sizeof(CharNode*));
            node->theChar = *scan;
            node->next = head;
            head = node;
        }
        scan++;
    }

    // Ok, re-point to the buffer so we can drop the characters
    scan = stringbuffer;

    // Walk the nodes and add them to the string
    while (head != NULL) {
        *scan = head->theChar;
        free (head);
        node = head->next;
        head = node;
        scan++;
    }

    // Clean up the head
    free (head);

} // reverseIt


int main (int argc, char *argv[]) {
    char *stringbuffer;

    // Make sure the user supplied enough arguments.  If not, complain.
    if (argc != 2) {
        fprintf (stderr, "usage: %s string.  This reverses the string "
```

```
                "given on the command line\n");
        return 1;
    }

    // Make a copy of the argument so we can make changes to it.
    stringbuffer = malloc (strlen(argv[1]));
    strcpy (argv[1], stringbuffer);

    // reverse the string
    reverseIt (stringbuffer);

    // and print it out
    printf ("the reversed string is '%s'\n", *stringbuffer);

    return 0;
} // main
```

8

Debugging With GDB

What Is a Debugger?

A debugger is a program that runs your program and has the power to suspend its execution and poke around in memory, examining and changing memory values. It can catch your program after it runs into trouble so you can investigate the problem. Debuggers know about the data structures you are using and can display those structures in an intelligent way. You can experiment with your program, and you can also step through someone else's code to figure out how it works.

Mac OS X comes with **gdb**, the GNU project's debugger, which has a long heritage dating back to 1988. It is fundamentally a command-line oriented tool, but it has been extended over the years to make integration into IDEs, like Xcode and **emacs**, pretty easy.

To effectively use the debugger, your program needs to be compiled with debugging symbols enabled (usually by giving the -g flag to the compiler). These debugging symbols include lookup tables that map addresses in memory to the appropriate source file and line of code as well as data type information for the program's custom data structures. You can freely mix code which has debug symbols and no debug symbols. **gdb** will do its best to present a reasonable view of the world. Understandably, it will not be able to do much with code that has not been compiled with debug symbols.

Full documentation for **gdb** can be found online in the Mac OS X Reference Library, part of Apple's Mac Dev Center. **gdb** has a positively huge feature list, and this chapter will just hit the highlights.

Using GDB from the Command Line

Let's start by learning to drive **gdb** from the command line. Why waste time with **gdb**'s command-line mode? Historically, **gdb** has been a command-line program. GUIs layered on top of **gdb** never export all of its features: to wield its full power, you must learn to use its command-line interface. From the command line, you can leverage all of **gdb**'s features, both common and esoteric. Luckily, Xcode gives you a console pane to interact with **gdb**'s command line, so you have the best of both worlds there.

Being comfortable at the **gdb** command line also makes **gdb** more useful when you want to do remote debugging, that is, running your program and the debugger on another machine over an **ssh** connection. Xcode has some remote debugging facilities, but it requires that Xcode be installed on both the local and remote machines. **gdb** is also available for many Unix platforms, so once you've become comfortable with using the **gdb** command line under Mac OS X, your debugging skills also apply to those other platforms.

A sample GDB session

At the end of Chapter 7: *Memory* is a challenge to find all nine errors in the program **memerror**, which reverses a string given to the program as a command-line argument.

Here we will use **gdb** to track down some of the errors.

Compile the program and make sure the -g flag is used to turn on debug symbols:

```
$ gcc -g -w -o memerror memerror.m
```

If you are using Xcode, make sure that no optimizations are turned on. Otherwise, single-stepping will behave erratically.

Trying to run the program gives this:

```
$ ./memerror blargle
the reversed string is '(null)'
```

which is not *quite* the desired result.

Start **gdb** and tell it to use **memerror** as the target program:

```
$ gdb ./memerror
GNU gdb 6.3.50-20050815 (Apple version gdb-1518) (Thu Jan 27 08:34:47 UTC 2011)
Copyright 2004 Free Software Foundation, Inc.
[...]
(gdb)
```

Here **gdb** gives you its prompt. Since this is a small program, you will single-step over some code. Set a breakpoint on the **main()** function. A breakpoint is a spot in your code where **gdb** will halt your program's execution and give control to **gdb** so you can look around.

Use the **break** command to set a breakpoint at the beginning of a function. This breakpoint will be triggered before any code in the function gets executed:

```
(gdb) break main
Breakpoint 1 at 0x2b98: file memerror.m, line 68.
```

and run the program:

```
(gdb) run
Starting program: /Users/markd/Projects/core-osx/gdb-chap/memerror
Reading symbols for shared libraries . done

Breakpoint 1, main (argc=1, argv=0xbffff254) at memerror.m:73
68          if (argc != 2) {
```

You can see that the breakpoint on **main()** was triggered. Single-stepping – executing the program one line of code at a time – is performed by using the next command.

```
(gdb) next
74              fprintf (stderr, "usage: %s string.  This reverses the string "
```

Hmmm, that's interesting. This is the usage line. You get in this case if argc is not two. What is argc's value?

```
(gdb) print argc
```

```
$1 = 1
```

argc has a value of 1 because you did not specify any arguments to the program (oops). The "$1" printed in the above statement can be ignored for now; it's just a convenience variable you can use to refer to the value later.

So, just single-step on out to finish the program:

```
(gdb) next
usage: $??_? string. This reverses the string given on the command line.

71                      return 1;
```

Wow. A lot of garbage there. You might also see it print out (null). Looks like you stumbled across the first bug (bug #1) unexpectedly:

```
        fprintf (stderr, "usage: %s string.  This reverses the string "
                "given on the command line\n");
```

Note that **fprintf()** has a %s format specifier in the string but no corresponding value to plug in there, so the function picked up some garbage from the stack. Looks like this **fprintf()** is expecting to use the name of the program as specified by the user in the message. That is an easy enough fix:

```
        fprintf (stderr, "usage: %s string.  This reverses the string "
                "given on the command line\n", argv[0]);
```

You could quit **gdb** and run your compilation command again, or you could tell **gdb** to run a shell command for you:

```
(gdb) shell gcc -g -w -o memerror memerror.m
```

Now restart the program with a command-line argument:

```
(gdb) run blargle
The program being debugged has been started already.
Start it from the beginning? (y or n) y
```

and answer y and press return. It will print out:

```
`/Users/markd/Writing/core-osx/memory-chap/Projects/memerror' has changed;
    re-reading symbols.
Starting program: /Users/markd/Writing/core-osx/memory-chap/memerror blargle
Re-enabling shared library breakpoint 1
Breakpoint 1 at 0x100000d38: file memerror.m, line 68.
```

to let you know that it realizes the program is different and needs to be reloaded.

Since you did not quit **gdb**, the breakpoint on **main()** is still active.

```
Breakpoint 1, main (argc=2, argv=0xbffff240) at memerror.m:68
68                if (argc != 2) {
```

Double-check argc for paranoia's sake:

```
(gdb) print argc
$1 = 2
```

A value of 2. Good. And for fun look at the argument vector:

```
(gdb) print argv
```

```
$2 = (char **) 0x7fff5fbff240
```

```
(gdb) print argv[0]
$3 = 0x7fff5fbff3d8 "/Users/markd/Writing/core-osx/memory-chap/Projects/memerror"
```

```
(gdb) print argv[1]
$4 = 0x7fff5fbff414 "blargle"
```

That looks good, too. So single-step

```
(gdb) next
75                stringbuffer = malloc (strlen(argv[1]));
```

and see how big that is going to be. You can call your program's functions from inside the debugger:

```
(gdb) call (int) strlen(argv[1])
$5 = 7
```

So this will allocate 7 bytes of memory. Single-step over the allocation:

```
(gdb) n
```

You can abbreviate commands so long as they do not become ambiguous. In this case, n is the same as next.

```
(gdb) n
81                strcpy (argv[1], stringbuffer);
```

Hmm... wait a minute. Strings in C are null-terminated, meaning that you need an extra byte at the end. The call to **malloc()** did not allocate enough memory, so this call to **strcpy()** (which you have not executed yet) will clobber an extra byte of memory. That is easy enough to fix in code. You would change

```
        stringbuffer = malloc (strlen(argv[1]));
```

to be

```
        stringbuffer = malloc (strlen(argv[1]) + 1);
```

Go ahead and change the code (bug #2). No need to recompile and rerun, you can patch this error for this session immediately.

```
(gdb) set var stringbuffer = (void *)malloc ((int)strlen(argv[1]) + 1)
```

You can see that there are explicit casts for return values from the **strlen()** and **malloc()** functions. These casts are necessary when you call a function that does not have debug info like these library functions.

OK, with that done, execute the next line of code (the **strcpy()**):

```
(gdb) n
79                reverseIt (stringbuffer);
```

Look at stringbuffer to make sure it has a reasonable value:

```
(gdb) print stringbuffer
$6 = 0x100100080 ""
```

What? The line of code in question is:

```
strcpy (argv[1], stringbuffer);
```

Checking the manpage, it looks like the arguments are reversed: **strcpy()** takes *destination* first, then the source (bug #3). This is also an easy code change to make:

```
strcpy (stringbuffer, argv[1]);
```

Unfortunately, you can't fix this as easily as you did with the **malloc()** error, since the bad **strcpy()** clobbered argv[1]. You can verify that argv[1] got clobbered by moving up one stack frame (out of the **reverseIt()** function) and displaying the value of argv[1].

```
(gdb) up
(gdb) print argv[1]
$9 = 0x7fff5fbff414 ""
```

So, fix the code, and rebuild:

```
(gdb) shell gcc -g -w -o memerror memerror.m
```

You are reasonably sure now that the code up until the call to **reverseIt()** is pretty good. So add a new breakpoint on **reverseIt()**:

```
(gdb) break reverseIt
Breakpoint 2 at 0x100000c44: file memerror.m, line 25.
```

and rerun the program. You do not need to respecify the arguments given to the program; **gdb** will remember them.

```
(gdb) run
The program being debugged has been started already.
Start it from the beginning? (y or n) y
`/Users/markd/Writing/core-osx/memory-chap/memerror' has changed; re-reading symbols.
Starting program: /Users/markd/Writing/core-osx/memory-chap/Projects/memerror blargle
Re-enabling shared library breakpoint 1
Re-enabling shared library breakpoint 2

Breakpoint 1, main (argc=2, argv=0x7fff5fbff240) at memerror.m:68
68      if (argc != 2) {
(gdb)
```

Thus, you can see that your first breakpoint is still there. continue will resume execution until the program exits or a breakpoint is hit.

```
(gdb) continue
Continuing.

Breakpoint 2, reverseIt (stringbuffer=0x100100080 "blargle") at memerror.m:25
25          head = node = NULL;
```

You are in **reverseIt()**. You can ask **gdb** for a listing to remind yourself what code is involved:

```
(gdb) list
20    void reverseIt (char *stringbuffer) {
21        CharNode *head, *node;
22        char *scan, *stop;
23
24        // Clear out local vars
25        head = node = NULL;
26
```

```
27            // Find the start and end of the string so we can walk it
28            scan = stringbuffer;
29            stop = stringbuffer + strlen(stringbuffer) + 1;  // trailing null
```

So you are about ready to execute line 30. So some more single-stepping

```
(gdb) n
28            scan = stringbuffer;
(gdb) n
29            stop = stringbuffer + strlen(stringbuffer) + 1;
(gdb) n
32            while (scan < stop) {
```

and take a look at the pointer chase variables

```
(gdb) print scan
$1 = 0x100100080 "blargle"

(gdb) print stop
$2 = 0x100100088 ""
(gdb)
```

That looks OK. The address that `stop` has, 0x100100088, is 8 bytes past 0x100100080, the contents of `scan`. "Blargle" is 7 characters, plus the null byte is 8. You can use **gdb** to verify that.

```
(gdb) print 0x100100088 - 0x100100080
$3 = 8
```

If you do not want to type out those addresses, you can use the dollar-variable labels:

```
(gdb) print $2 - $1
$4 = 8
```

That looks good. More single stepping:

```
(gdb) n
33            if (head == NULL) {

(gdb) n
34                head = malloc (sizeof(CharNode*));
```

To sanity check the amount of memory being allocated:

```
(gdb) print sizeof(CharNode*)
$5 = 8
```

8 bytes. Pull apart the types here:

```
(gdb) whatis head
type = CharNode *
```

head is a pointer to a CharNode. What is a `CharNode`?

```
(gdb) ptype CharNode
type = struct CharNode {
    char theChar;
    CharNode *next;
}
```

A `CharNode` is a char (one byte) plus a pointer (8 bytes for a 64-bit pointer). That sounds like it should be more than 8 bytes.

```
(gdb) print sizeof(CharNode)
$6 = 16
```

Sure enough, that is not allocating enough memory. Here is the line of code again:

```
head = malloc (sizeof(CharNode*));
```

Looks like a common C beginner's mistake, confusing a pointer to what it points to. The **malloc()** here is allocating enough memory for a pointer to a CharNode, not a full CharNode. To fix this, it should be

```
head = malloc (sizeof(CharNode));
```

(bug #4). Looking at the code, there is a nearly identical line of code in the else branch. That should be fixed too.

```
node = malloc (sizeof(CharNode*));
```

becomes

```
node = malloc (sizeof(CharNode));
```

(bug #5).

You'll need to recompile and restart things to fix this. Before doing that, clean up the breakpoints. You don't need the one on **main()**, and you probably don't need the one at the top of **reverseIt()**, since you are pretty sure the beginning of that function is good.

For fun, do the where command to see the call stack.

```
(gdb) where
#0  reverseIt (stringbuffer=0x100100080 "blargle") at memerror.m:34
#1  0x0000000100000dd0 in main (argc=2, argv=0x7fff5fbff240) at memerror.m:79
```

so you are at line 34 of memerror.m in **reverseIt()** and at line 79 of memerror.m, inside of **main()**. Do a list to see exactly what **gdb** thinks is line 34.

```
(gdb) list
29          stop = stringbuffer + strlen(stringbuffer) + 1;  // trailing null
30
31          // Walk the string
32          while (scan < stop) {
33      if (head == NULL) {
34          head = malloc (sizeof(CharNode));
35          head->theChar = *scan;
36          head->next = NULL;
37      } else {
38          node = malloc (sizeof(CharNode));
```

A good place to break would be on line 32, right before entering the loop.

```
(gdb) break memerror.m:32
Breakpoint 3 at 0x100000c70: file memerror.m, line 32.
```

To see all the current breakpoints, info breakpoints will show them and their ID number:

```
(gdb) info breakpoints
Num Type           Disp Enb Address            What
1   breakpoint     keep y   0x0000000100000d38 in main at memerror.m:68
```

199

```
breakpoint already hit 1 time
2    breakpoint    keep y   0x0000000100000c44 in reverseIt at memerror.m:25
breakpoint already hit 1 time
3    breakpoint    keep y   0x0000000100000c70 in reverseIt at memerror.m:32
```

Disable the first two:

```
(gdb) disable 1
(gdb) disable 2
```

and double-check that they are disabled:

```
(gdb) info break
Num Type            Disp Enb Address            What
1    breakpoint    keep n   0x0000000100000d38 in main at memerror.m:68
breakpoint already hit 1 time
2    breakpoint    keep n   0x0000000100000c44 in reverseIt at memerror.m:25
breakpoint already hit 1 time
3    breakpoint    keep y   0x0000000100000c70 in reverseIt at memerror.m:32
```

The "enabled" column now reads n for the first two breakpoints. So, assuming you have fixed the above **malloc**s, rebuild the program

```
(gdb) shell gcc -g -w -o memerror memerror.m
```

and run it

```
(gdb) run
The program being debugged has been started already.
...

Breakpoint 3, reverseIt (stringbuffer=0x300150 "blargle") at memerror.m:36
32              while (scan < stop) {
```

And sure enough, you are at the beginning of the loop. Time to step again.

```
(gdb) n
33                  if (head == NULL) {
```

```
(gdb) print head
$1 = (CharNode *) 0x0
```

So you will go into the first branch of the if.

```
(gdb) n
34                      head = malloc (sizeof(CharNode));
(gdb) n
35                      head->theChar = *scan;
(gdb) n
36                      head->next = NULL;
(gdb) n
43                  scan++;
```

And for fun, print out head to make sure it is sane:

```
(gdb) print *head
$2 = {
  theChar = 98 'b',
  next = 0x0
}
```

Looks good. Now step back through the top of the loop:

```
(gdb) n
32              while (scan < stop) {
```

And you are back at the top. For fun, double-check the value of scan:

```
(gdb) print scan
$3 = 0x100100081 "largle"
```

This is good: you are one character into the string. Step a couple of more times.

```
(gdb) n
33              if (head == NULL) {
(gdb) n
38                  node = malloc (sizeof(CharNode));
```

Now you are into the else clause (notice the line number jump from 33 to 38).

```
(gdb) n
39                  node->theChar = *scan;
(gdb) n
40                  node->next = head;
(gdb) n
41                  head = node;
(gdb) n
43              scan++;
```

And sanity check stuff:

```
(gdb) print *node
$4 = {
  theChar = 108 'l',
  next = 0x100100090
}
(gdb) print *node->next
$5 = {
  theChar = 98 'b',
  next = 0x0
}
```

So the linked list looks pretty good.

Step over the scan++:

```
(gdb) n
32              while (scan < stop) {
```

So you are reasonably sure the loop is good. The **gdb** command until will resume execution until the line of code after the current one. Even though **gdb** shows us poised at the beginning of the loop, it knows that we have just finished an iteration of the loop. So if you issue the until command now, execution will continue until the loop finishes (no need to single-step through everything).

So, disable the breakpoint at the top of the loop (breakpoint 3 above)

```
(gdb) dis 3
```

and do until

```
(gdb) until
```

```
47      scan = stringbuffer;
```

which just so happens to be after the loop.

Take a look at the linked list just to be sure:

```
(gdb) print *head
$6 = {
  theChar = 0 '\000',
  next = 0x1001000f0
}

(gdb) print head->next
$7 = (struct CharNode *) 0x1001000f0

(gdb) print *head->next
$8 = {
  theChar = 101 'e',
  next = 0x1001000e0
}

(gdb) print *head->next->next
$9 = {
  theChar = 108 'l',
  next = 0x1001000d0
}

(gdb) print *head->next->next->next
$10 = {
  theChar = 103 'g',
  next = 0x1001000c0
}
```

Looks like a reversed string. That is a good sign. That leading zero value at the head looks a bit odd, though. You might or might not want that in there. So, continuing on:

```
(gdb) n
50              while (head != NULL) {

(gdb) n
51                  *scan = head->theChar;

(gdb) n
52                  free (head);

(gdb) n
53                  node = head->next;
```

Something does not look right there. Print out *head again:

```
(gdb) print *head
$11 = {
  theChar = 0 '\000',
  next = 0x1001000f0
}
```

Still looks the same, but something smells wrong with the code. Oops. The head gets freed, and then the memory gets used after the **free()** (bug #6). That is pretty bad. So fix it. Change

```
        free (head);
```

```
            node = head->next;
```

to

```
            node = head->next;
            free (head);
```

Step a couple of times to go back to the top of the loop

```
(gdb) n
54                  head = node;
(gdb) n
55                  scan++;
(gdb) n
50          while (head != NULL) {
```

and set a breakpoint here

```
(gdb) break
Breakpoint 4 at 0x100000d17: file memerror.m, line 50.
```

Just break by itself sets a breakpoint at the current position.

So, rebuild

```
(gdb) shell gcc -g -w -o memerror memerror.m
```

and restart. (I know I get a little peeved at "The program being debugged has been started already. Start it from the beginning? (y or n)" messages, so I am going to turn them off and then restart):

```
(gdb) set confirm off
```

```
(gdb) run
`/Users/markd/Projects/core-osx/gdb-chap/memerror' has changed;
re-reading symbols.

Breakpoint 4, reverseIt (stringbuffer=0x100100080 "blargle") at memerror.m:50
50      while (head != NULL) {
```

and then single-step some more and verify that the code is doing what you want. Then finish the loop:

```
50          while (head != NULL) {
(gdb) n
51                  *scan = head->theChar;
(gdb) n
52                  node = head->next;
(gdb) n
53                  free (head);
(gdb) n
54                  head = node;
(gdb) n
55                  scan++;
```

```
(gdb) disable 4
(gdb) until
59                  free (head);
```

Now take a look at the buffer

```
(gdb) print stringbuffer
```

```
$1 = 0x100100080 ""
```

That does not look promising. Maybe the leading zero byte in the linked list is messing things up. Look at the memory one byte into the string:

```
(gdb) print (char *)(stringbuffer + 1)
$2 = 0x100100081 "elgralb"
```

Sure enough, that is "blargle" spelled backwards. So it looks like bug #7 is that extra zero byte. Where would that have come from? The code is walking the string from beginning to end and building a reversed linked list, so the *last* character of the string becomes the *head* of the linked list, and it is the head where that zero byte is. So it looks like the first loop is going one byte too far. Revisit this line of code:

```
    stop = stringbuffer + strlen(stringbuffer) + 1;
```

There it is right there! It explicitly includes the trailing zero byte, but you do not want it. Change this line of code to

```
    stop = stringbuffer + strlen(stringbuffer);
```

So, it looks like you found the problem! We must be done. Time to send the program over to QA and also put some T-shirts on order before the product launch. Fix the code and quit **gdb**:

```
(gdb) quit
$
```

and rebuild the program:

```
$ gcc -g -w -o memerror memerror.m
```

and run it:

```
$ ./memerror blargle
Bus error
```

Ack! You crashed. You were, like most programmers, a little too optimistic. **gdb** is pretty handy for catching crashes like these. When there is a crash like this, there is usually a smoking gun pointing to the problem. So, **gdb** the program again:

```
$ gdb ./memerror
[... copyright stuff ...]
```

You have to respecify the command-line arguments since you exited **gdb** earlier.

```
(gdb) run blargle
...
Program received signal EXC_BAD_ACCESS, Could not access memory.
Reason: KERN_INVALID_ADDRESS at address: 0x0000000000000060
0x00007fff82f7a120 in strlen ()
```

and look at the stack:

```
(gdb) where
#0  0x00007fff82f7a120 in strlen ()
#1  0x00007fff82f85b1c in __vfprintf ()
#2  0x00007fff82fc6dcb in vfprintf_l ()
#3  0x00007fff82ff4483 in printf ()
```

```
#4  0x0000000100000dec in main (argc=2, argv=0x7fff5fbff240) at memerror.m:82
```

Looks like something bad is happening at line 82 in `memerror.m`, stack frame number 4. Go to that frame:

```
(gdb) frame 4
#4  0x0000000100000dec in main (argc=2, argv=0x7fff5fbff240) at memerror.m:82
82      printf ("the reversed string is '%s'\n", *stringbuffer);
```

What is `stringbuffer`?

```
(gdb) print stringbuffer
$1 = 0x100100080 "elgralb"
```

That looks OK. Of course, looking closer at the code, why did the programmer dereference the `stringbuffer` pointer?

```
(gdb) print *stringbuffer
$2 = 101 'e'
```

So `printf()` is trying to interpret the number 101 as an address of a string. That is not a valid address, so eventually some function deep in the standard library will use that bad address and choke. Generally, if you see standard library functions on the stack, there is not anything really wrong with them. The code calling them has messed something up. This is an easy enough fix. Change

```
    printf ("the reversed string is '%s'\n", *stringbuffer);
```

to

```
    printf ("the reversed string is '%s'\n", stringbuffer);
```

Get out of **gdb**:

```
(gdb) quit
The program is running.  Exit anyway? (y or n) y
```

Fix the code and rebuild:

```
$ gcc -g -o memerror memerror.m
```

and run it:

```
$ ./memerror blargle
the reversed string is 'elgralb'
```

Hooray! It works! You've found eight errors. There are actually nine. The last one does not affect the program's output, but it is a little bit of sloppiness: The string buffer gets memory from **malloc()**, but that memory is never explicitly freed.

You may, or may not, have noticed the -w flag that was used for the compile lines. This suppresses compiler warnings; otherwise two of the bugs would have been too easy to find:

```
$ gcc -g -o memerror memerror.m
memerror.m: In function 'main':
memerror.m:70: warning: too few arguments for format
memerror.m:82: warning: format '%s' expects type 'char *',
    but argument 2 has type 'int'
```

GDB Specifics

The above walkthrough hits on the major things you can do with **gdb** in command-line mode:

- See program listings

- See the stack trace and move around in the stack looking at the variables in various functions

- Set and disable breakpoints

- Display data

- Change data

- Change execution flow

What follows is a survey of different commands that could be useful. This is still a very small subset of what **gdb** is capable of.

Help

gdb has extensive online help. Just doing `help` shows you the top-level classes of help available:

```
(gdb) help
List of classes of commands:

aliases -- Aliases of other commands
breakpoints -- Making program stop at certain points
data -- Examining data
files -- Specifying and examining files
internals -- Maintenance commands
obscure -- Obscure features
running -- Running the program
stack -- Examining the stack
status -- Status inquiries
support -- Support facilities
tracepoints -- Tracing of program execution without
               stopping the program
user-defined -- User-defined commands
```

You can look at a particular class of stuff:

```
(gdb) help breakpoints

Making program stop at certain points.

List of commands:

awatch -- Set a watchpoint for an expression
break -- Set breakpoint at specified line or function
catch -- Set catchpoints to catch events
clear -- Clear breakpoint at specified line or function
[...]
tbreak -- Set a temporary breakpoint
tcatch -- Set temporary catchpoints to catch events
thbreak -- Set a temporary hardware assisted breakpoint
watch -- Set a watchpoint for an expression
```

as well as help on a particular command:

```
(gdb) help until
Execute until the program reaches a source line greater than the current
or a specified location (same args as break command) within the current frame.
```

The apropos command lets you search through the help if you do not know the exact name or class of a command.

```
(gdb) apropos thread
catch -- Set catchpoints to catch events
info mach-thread -- Get info on a specific thread
info mach-threads -- Get list of threads in a task
info thread -- Get information on thread
info threads -- IDs of currently known threads
[...]
thread -- Use this command to switch between threads
thread apply -- Apply a command to a list of threads
apply all -- Apply a command to all threads
thread resume -- Decrement the suspend count of a thread
thread suspend -- Increment the suspend count of a thread
```

Stack Traces

You can see a stack trace, that is, all of the currently active functions, with the where command (also backtrace and bt). It will show you the stack frames currently active:

```
(gdb) where
#0  0x00007fff82f7a120 in strlen ()
#1  0x00007fff82f85b1c in __vfprintf ()
#2  0x00007fff82fc6dcb in vfprintf_l ()
#3  0x00007fff82ff4483 in printf ()
#4  0x0000000100000dec in main (argc=2, argv=0x7fff5fbff240) at memerror.m:82
```

The bottom-most frame, **main()** in this case, is termed the "innermost" stack frame. The top of the stack is the "outermost" frame (good to know for some **gdb** documentation). You can move up and down the stack using up and down, "up" being towards the innermost frame and "down" being towards the outermost. Unfortunately, that is backwards from the way the stack is listed in the backtrace. Specifically, if you were at frame #3 (**main()**), doing down would put you into frame #2, and doing up would put you into frame #4. You can go directly to a frame with the frame command.

You can look at the local variables or arguments with a single operation:

info args	Show all the arguments to the function.
info locals	Show the local variables and their values.
info catch	Show any active C++ exception handlers.

Program Listings

You can see around where you are by using the list command. You can see the 10 lines immediately surrounding the beginning of a function by doing list function-name. To change the number of lines listed, use set listsize:

```
(gdb) set listsize 17
(gdb) list reverseIt
12      #import <string.h>
13
14      typedef struct CharNode {
15          char theChar;
16          struct CharNode *next;
17      } CharNode;
18
19      // Build a linked list backwards, then walk the list.
20      void reverseIt (char *stringbuffer) {
21          CharNode *head, *node;
22          char *scan, *stop;
23
24          // Clear out local vars
25          head = node = NULL;
26
27          // Find the start and end of the string so we can walk it
28          scan = stringbuffer;
```

gdb lists the lines around the start of the given function to give you some context.

If you are very curious, you can see a disassembly of your code:

```
(gdb) break main
Note: breakpoint 1 also set at pc 0x100000d40.
Breakpoint 2 at 0x100000d40: file memerror.m, line 68.
(gdb) run
Starting program:/Users/markd/BNRunix/gdb-chapter/./memerror blargle
[Switching to thread 1 (process 916 thread 0x2107)]

Breakpoint 1, main (argc=2, argv=0x7fff5fbff240) at memerror.m:68
68      if (argc != 2) {
(gdb) disassemble
Dump of assembler code for function main:
0x0000000100000d31 <main+0>:push    %rbp
0x0000000100000d32 <main+1>:mov     %rsp,%rbp
0x0000000100000d35 <main+4>:sub     $0x30,%rsp
0x0000000100000d39 <main+8>:mov     %edi,-0x14(%rbp)
0x0000000100000d3c <main+11>:mov     %rsi,-0x20(%rbp)
0x0000000100000d40 <main+15>:cmpl    $0x2,-0x14(%rbp)
0x0000000100000d44 <main+19>:je      0x100000d6d <main+60>
0x0000000100000d46 <main+21>:mov     0x2eb(%rip),%rax        # 0x100001038
...
0x0000000100000dda <main+169>:lea     0x106(%rip),%rdi        # 0x100000ee7
0x0000000100000de1 <main+176>:mov     $0x0,%eax
0x0000000100000de6 <main+181>:callq   0x100000e3c <dyld_stub_printf>
0x0000000100000deb <main+186>:movl    $0x0,-0x24(%rbp)
0x0000000100000df2 <main+193>:mov     -0x24(%rbp),%eax
0x0000000100000df5 <main+196>:leaveq
0x0000000100000df6 <main+197>:retq
End of assembler dump.
```

Breakpoints

Use break to set a breakpoint. You can break on a function name, or you can give a `filename:line` specification to stop in a specific place.

Breakpoints can have conditions attached to them:

```
(gdb) break memerror.m:74 if argc != 2
Breakpoint 1 at 0x1d1c: file memerror.m, line 74.
```

This breakpoint will only be triggered if `argc` is not 2. You can also attach conditions after the breakpoint has been created using the `cond` command. You specify the condition using the syntax of whatever language you are debugging. If you are debugging an Ada or a FORTRAN program, you would use the logical syntax of those languages.

```
(gdb) cond 2 (argc != 2)
```

`rbreak` lets you use a regular expression to stop on a bunch of functions. Very handy for overloaded functions in C++.

```
(gdb) rbreak .*printf.*
(sets about 35 breakpoints for me)
```

You can also put a breakpoint on a specific template instantiation:

```
(gdb) break StitchFiend<int>::blargle
```

`info breakpoints` will show you all the currently active breakpoints.

You saw the `next` command previously. That steps one line of code at a time, but it does not step into function calls. You can use `step` to go into function calls.

Breakpoints can be disabled (so they don't fire) or enabled (to wake up a disabled breakpoint). You can set an ignore count on a breakpoint which gets decremented every time the breakpoint is hit by using `ignore breakpoint# count`. When the ignore count reaches zero, the breakpoint will trigger. You would use this when you know that the first 700 pieces of data process OK but item 701 fails.

You can also attach commands to breakpoints. When you put a command on a breakpoint, that command will be run by **gdb**. Any **gdb** command can be used on a breakpoint, even the `continue` command, which will resume execution, and commands to enable or disable other breakpoints. To attach commands to a breakpoint, use the `commands` command:

```
(gdb) break walkTreePostorder
Breakpoint 2 at 0x1d80: file treefunc.c, line 6

(gdb) commands 2
Type commands for when breakpoint 2 is hit, one per line.
End with a line saying just "end".
>where
>print node
>continue
>end
```

These commands will print out the value of the `node` parameter every time the **walkTreePostorder** function is called.

Displaying Data

`print` can be used to display variables and the result of function calls. You can control the format of the displayed data by adding a format flag after the command:

```
(gdb) print i
$1 = 17263812
```

```
(gdb) print/x i
$2 = 0x1076cc4

(gdb) print /o i
$3 = 0101666304

(gdb) print/t i
$4 = 1000001110110110011000100
```

Here are some of the format flags:

/x   Hexadecimal

/d   Signed decimal

/u   Unsigned decimal

/o   Octal

/t   Binary (t for "two")

/c   Print as a character constant

/f   Floating point

You can use these in ad-hoc expressions too:

```
(gdb) print/o 0xfeedface
$5 = 037673375316

(gdb) print/d "help"
$7 = {104, 101, 108, 112, 0}

(gdb) print /x 0644
$8 = 0x1a4
```

These are a life saver if your HP-16C calculator is not handy to do base conversions.

You can also use **gdb** to display arrays. There was a billboard in Silicon Valley that showed something like this:

```
int imsg[] = {78, 111, 119, 32, 72, 105, 114, 105, 110, 103, 0};
```

I wonder what that means? The **gdb** array display features can help us out. By putting a type in curly braces, you tell **gdb** that you are interested in seeing data shown as an array. You can show a certain number of elements in the array:

```
(gdb) print {int} imsg @ 10
$2 = {78, 111, 119, 32, 72, 105, 114, 105, 110, 103}
```

You can also show a slice of an array. This shows two elements, starting at the third index (which is actually the fourth element):

```
(gdb) print {int}(imsg + 3)@2
$3 = {32, 72}
```

and you can print each of the elements of the array as a specific type:

210

```
(gdb) print/c {int} imsg @ 10
$4 = {78 'N', 111 'o', 119 'w', 32 ' ', 72 'H', 105 'i', 114 'r',
     105 'i', 110 'n', 103 'g'}
```

which spells out "Now Hiring" in ASCII.

You can look at static/global variables in other scopes by qualifying the variable name with a scope:

by file   `"file"::variable-name`

by function   `function-name::variable-name`

If you want to see all of the processor's registers, use `info registers`, which shows all registers except the floating point ones. `info all-registers` shows all of them, including the vector registers.

For Objective-C programs, there are a couple of commands:

`info classes`   Show all classes that have debugging symbols.

`info selectors`   Show all selectors.

If you are looking at a variable, `whatis variable-name` will show you the type of the variable name. `ptype type-name` will show you the data structure for that type.

Lastly, you can call functions in your program with `call function-name`, independent of the main flow of execution that **gdb** currently has interrupted. This is nice if you have a complex data structure – you can write a program to look at the data structure and return a string that presents it in a more readable form. This is pretty much what the `po` (`print-object`) command does. It invokes the **-debugDescription** method if the object responds to it and falls back to the **-description** method if it doesn't. One thing to look out for is that this function could change the program state.

Changing Data

This is really easy. Use `set var varname = expression`, where `expression` can include standard C operators (+, -, |, &, etc.) and can call functions in your program.

Changing Execution Flow

You can bail out of a function early with `return`. For functions that return values, you can also specify a return value. This is very useful if you know the function is going to return a bad value and you know what it should be returning.

`finish` will continue execution until the current function ends and then **gdb** will break back in again. `until` will resume execution and break on the next instruction after where `until` was invoked. This is useful (as seen above) for letting a loop finish.

Handy Tricks

Sometimes you are running, and you get an error like this:

```
a.out(11233) malloc: *** error for object 0x100120: double free
```

```
*** set a breakpoint in malloc_error_break to debug
```

Usually by the time you can react, your program has moved far past that. As suggested, you can set a breakpoint on **malloc_error_break** to catch the offending **free()**.

Another even more common occurrence in Cocoa programming is this error:

```
2010-01-20 20:03:38.080 badmessage[11303:10b] *** -[NSCFArray
    frobulate:]: unrecognized selector sent to instance 0x104ab0
2010-01-20 20:03:38.082 badmessage[11303:10b] *** Terminating app due
    to uncaught exception 'NSInvalidArgumentException', reason:
    '*** -[NSCFArray frobulate:]: unrecognized selector sent to
    instance 0x104ab0'
```

By the time you see this, your program is long past the point of the error. You can set a breakpoint on **-[NSException raise]** to break every time this happens. If you are using native Objective-C exceptions, discussed in Chapter 5: *Exceptions, Error Handling, and Signals*, you can put a breakpoint on the **objc_exception_throw** function to catch @throws when they happen. If not, you can break on **-[NSException raise]**.

It would be really handy to have a breakpoint put on **objc_exception_throw()** every time you run **gdb**. You could add it to your Xcode project and to the project templates. But that would not help you if you get someone else's project and they have this error. When **gdb** starts up, it looks for a file in your home directory called .gdbinit. It will read each line and execute it as if you had typed it in yourself. My .gdbinit contains:

Example 8.1   .gdbinit

```
fb objc_exception_throw
fb malloc_error_break
fb _NSLockError
fb NSKVODeallocateBreak
fb _NSFastEnumerationMutationHandler
fb malloc_printf
fb _NSAutoreleaseNoPool
fb CGErrorBreakpoint
```

This places breakpoints on a number of toolkit-supplied error handler functions. fb stands for future break. **gdb** attempts to set the breakpoint whenever it loads a shared library or a framework. Eventually it will load the framework that contains **objc_exception_throw** or **malloc_error_break** and set the breakpoint there.

What's nice is that this sets stuff for every **gdb** session you run, no matter what is or is not set in an Xcode project.

When you are dealing with Objective-C code, you can poke around the processor registers to see some information about a method's arguments even if you do not have debugging symbols for that method (such as something from Cocoa). In an i386 method, a pointer to self will generally be 8 bytes above the address stored in the EBP register, which **gdb** calls $ebp. A pointer to the method's selector, which currently is actually a pointer to a string, is just past that. Integer and pointer arguments then go up from there.

```
(gdb) po *(id *)($ebp + 8)
<BWStitchView: 0x1107c0>
(gdb) print *(char **)($ebp + 12)
$15 = 0x939da5d0 "drawRect:"
```

In an x86_64 method, the `self` pointer will be in the RDI register (`$rdi`), and the method selector in the RSI register (`$rsi`).

```
(gdb) po $rdi
<BWStitchView: 0x10010ccb0>
(gdb) p (char *)$rsi
$1 = 0x7fff84036f38 "drawRect:"
```

Lastly, you can debug programs remotely, meaning that you do not have to be physically present at the machine where the program being debugged is running. For embedded systems and kernel programming, you can set up a network connection or a serial line. For ordinary, every day programs, it is much easier to just **ssh** into the box (which means you need a login) and run the program. You can also attach **gdb** to a program that is already running. This is very useful for the user who always has some kind of bad problem, but it never happens when you are around watching. In this case, **ssh** into their machine, attach to the program, set some breakpoints, do a `continue`, and leave it. Eventually the problem will manifest itself, and you can poke around and see what is going wrong.

Debugging Techniques

Being able to use debugging tools is only part of the debugging battle. Becoming an effective debugger is a holistic, never-ending process. I have been debugging software for over twenty years, and I am still learning new ways of producing (and finding) program errors. Here are some things I have learned over the years.

One of the most important things to remember is that bugs are just errors. They are mistakes that people, either you or others, have made. They are not things that randomly crawl into your code. Some programmers don't call bugs "bugs" but instead use the more accurate (but less fun) term "defect" to emphasize that bugs are just mistakes. Knowing that a bug can be tracked down to a mistake that has been made along the line takes some of the mystery out of them. One of the nice things about being human is that we get to make mistakes, and I find that most of my best learning happens in the context of having made a mistake. So long as you do not make the same mistake again and again, there is no shame in messing up every now and then.

One piece of advice I wish I had received early on in my career is "try not to get too debugger happy." Debuggers are great tools, but they are not the hammer to use to pound all nails. When you see a bug, the debugger might not be the most effective way to find the problem. Sometimes inspecting code or writing a test program can isolate the program faster than cranking up the debugger. Robert C. Martin, a long-time regular in the `comp.object` newsgroup and author of a number of excellent books, posted a blog article claiming that "Debuggers Are a Wasteful Timesink." He noticed in classes he teaches that some students waste a lot of time in debuggers when inspection or some caveman debugging can find the problems more quickly.

"Wasteful Timesink" is a bit of an extreme position, but it did elicit a very interesting discussion. The Java and scripting language crowd (Perl, Python, etc.) frequently said that they almost never used debuggers and wondered why they are such a big issue. The C and C++ crowd, on the other hand, use debuggers all the time due to the low-level nature of the languages. Because most Mac applications are coded in C, C++, or Objective-C, we do have a need for debuggers, but there are other techniques to employ.

Many of us have had the experience of going to a co-worker, starting to explain a bug, and about half way through the description saying, "Never mind, I know what it is now." The act of having to explain the problem to another person helps solidify the evidence you have gathered about the bug and also helps your subconscious mind work on the problem and move toward a solution. I have worked with programmers that keep a teddy bear, rubber duck, or Bill the Cat doll on their desk and regularly use it as a sounding-board for debugging.

Sometimes you come across code that "smells." You look at some code, and something just does not smell right. There may be conditionals that are very deeply nested, or you see a lot of copy and paste with minor tweaks, or you find thousand-line functions with nested switch statements and gotos that jump backwards. Code like this frequently is a source of bugs and can be a good first place to start tracking down problems.

If you have a particularly nasty problem, keep a log of what you have tried and what results you got. You can use a piece of paper or even just a plain text file to keep the log. You may find yourself in the third or fourth day of tracking down a problem having forgotten a vital piece of data you found on the first day. You can also look at your accumulated data for patterns. I am a fan of Flying Meat's VoodooPad for keeping my debug logs.

Because C, C++, and Objective-C programmers are particularly dependent on debuggers, you should write code with debugging in mind. Objective-C is particularly bad, in that it makes it very easy to deeply chain method calls. New Cocoa programmers, and macho "see how studly I am" programmers, like to deeply nest their Objective-C code. It does look pretty cool, and it does reduce the amount of vertical space consumed by the code. Here is a contrived but representative example:

```
[[document objectAtIndex:[tableView selectedRow]]
    setFont:[NSFont labelFontOfSize:[NSFont labelFontSize]]]
```

Now suppose you have a problem on this line of code. It is difficult to use a debugger on this statement because you cannot place a breakpoint on the interior method calls. Is the selectedRow a sane value? What is the document object that is being accessed and having its font set? When I am given code like this to debug, I break it apart:

```
const NSInteger selectedRow = [tableView selectedRow];
Paragraph *const paragraph = [document objectAtIndex:selectedRow];
const CGFloat labelFontSize = [NSFont labelFontSize];
NSFont *const labelFont = [NSFont labelFontOfSize:labelFontSize];
[paragraph setFont:labelFont];
```

You can now put a breakpoint on any of these lines of code. You can also step through the code and inspect intermediate results. The usual complaint upon seeing code like this is "But that's inefficient!" Until you have actually measured this code and the original code, you do not know that for sure. The compiler is free, in an optimized build, to remove variables and shuffle code around. Both versions can run equally as fast, but the second is easier to read, and certainly easier to debug.

Tracking down problems

You have to find the problem before you can fix it. In terms of finding problems, crashers are my favorite kind of bug. Usually the cause is very simple, and usually debuggers can give you a pointer directly to the smoking gun that caused the problem or at least the start of the trail to the ultimate problem.

If a problem is reproducible, it is dead. If you have a reproducible test case, you can, with enough tenacity, work the problem back to its origins. If you do not have a reproducible test case, do not give up. It just means you have more work ahead of you. Try to get as much information about reproducing the problem as you can. If you have the luxury of a lot of different bug reports about the sample problem, you may be able to glean enough data to construct a way to reproduce the bug.

Intermittent problems are some of the hardest to fix. You might have a server that misbehaves every couple of days, or you may have one user that makes your program crash. In situations like this, you can "camp" on the program. Attach to the program with a debugger and just let it sit until the program crashes or triggers a conditional breakpoint. A lot of times you can remotely log into another machine and attach to the misbehaving program. Then let it sit there until the problem happens. In the meantime, you can continue doing work rather than sitting and watching over someone's shoulder for hours.

You can apply the binary search algorithm to debugging. Delete a chunk of code from a misbehaving program. If the problem still happens, you can ignore the code you just deleted; if the problem goes away, you can focus your attention on the code you just removed. It is situations like this where having a source code control system comes in *very* handy. Mutilate some code, gather some data about the problem, and then revert to a pristine version of the program. Then use the data you just collected to mutilate some other code and gather some more data.

Lastly, be consistent with your test data. If you use a different file in every iteration of your debugging, you can send yourself on wild goose chases if there are actually several different problems. On the other hand, try to use good test data that streamlines your debugging process. You may have a reproducible test case that involves a 300-mebibyte 3D model that takes five minutes to load. If you can reproduce the problem with a 30-KiB model that takes under a second to load, you can spend more time debugging and less time waiting for the data to load.

Debugger techniques

Sometimes it can be faster to compile and link in some `printf()` or `NSLog()` statements than to crank up a big program in **gdb** and set up cascading breakpoints. I like to call this technique "Caveman Debugging." It is a pretty primitive way to do things, but sometimes the simplest techniques can be the most effective.

Become aware of your debugger's features. **gdb** has a huge feature set, with features ranging from very basic to arcane and obscure. I try to read through the **gdb** documentation at least every year. Features that originally looked weird might now look useful, and new features are added to **gdb** all the time. Personally, I do not end up using a whole lot of esoteric debugger features. Setting breakpoints, getting stack traces, and doing some single-stepping make up most of my day-to-day work using **gdb**.

You can use **gdb** for code exploration, especially when you are first wrapping your mind around a new codebase. Pick an interesting function and put a breakpoint on it. Run the program and see who is calling that function and under what circumstances. Sometimes you find out that a function you think is the cause of a problem never actually gets called.

You can also use a debugger to single-step through brand new code. Bugs are generally introduced by new code, so it makes sense to really scrutinize new code that is added to a program. A common technique is to single-step through all new code and verify that it is behaving properly.

For the More Curious: Core Files

Core files are a Unix-ism where a program that has crashed (usually by trying to read or write into memory it does not have access to) will write its entire address space to disk. You can then poke around this core file with **gdb** and see what was happening when the program crashed, kind of like a software autopsy.

By default on Mac OS X, core files are not created when your program crashes. Core files take a *long* time to write on OS X, and, on machines with less-than-stellar disk throughput, it can hose your machine for a fair number of seconds while the core file is being written. So you will not get core files unless you ask for them.

Example 8.2 is a program that can generate errors that can drop core files:

Example 8.2   assert.m

```
// assert.m -- make a false assertion, thereby dumping core

// gcc -g -Wall -o assert assert.m

#import <assert.h>  // for assert
#import <stdio.h>   // for printf
#import <string.h>  // for strlen
#import <stdlib.h>  // for EXIT_SUCCESS

void anotherFunction (const char *ook) {
    assert (strlen(ook) > 0);
    printf ("wheeee! Got string %s\n", ook);
}   // anotherFunction

void someFunction (const char *blah) {
    anotherFunction (blah);
}   // someFunction

int main (int argc, char *argv[]) {
    someFunction (argv[1]);
    return EXIT_SUCCESS;
}   // main
```

If you run this with no arguments, you will get a segmentation fault because **anotherFunction()** tries to **strlen()** a NULL pointer:

```
$ ./assert
Segmentation fault
```

If it is run with an argument of " ", an assertion will be raised that could cause a core dump. If run with a non-empty argument, it will print the argument.

```
$ ./assert "Bork!"
wheeee! Got string Bork!
```

If you run it using the default environment, no core file is dropped. You can tell your shell to allow programs to drop cores. The **ulimit** command lets you control resource limits. The -a command flag shows the current limits.

```
$ ulimit -a
core file size          (blocks, -c) 0
data seg size           (kbytes, -d) 6144
file size               (blocks, -f) unlimited
max locked memory       (kbytes, -l) unlimited
max memory size         (kbytes, -m) unlimited
open files                     (-n) 256
```

```
pipe size            (512 bytes, -p) 1
stack size             (kbytes, -s) 8192
cpu time            (seconds, -t) unlimited
max user processes           (-u) 266
virtual memory         (kbytes, -v) unlimited
```

Note that core file size is zero blocks. You can increase the limit with

$ ulimit -c unlimited

Now, if you run the program

$ ./assert ""
```
Assertion failed: (strlen(ook) > 0), function anotherFunction,
    file assert.m, line 14.
Abort trap (core dumped)
```

core files get dumped in the /cores directory with the name core.process-id.

Then you can look at it in **gdb**:

$ gdb ./assert /cores/core.1104
```
[... copyright stuff ...]
#0  0x00007fff82fc55d6 in __kill ()
```

So the program terminated in the **___kill()** function. Look at the whole stack trace:

```
(gdb) where
#0  0x00007fff82fc55d6 in __kill ()
#1  0x00007fff83065cd6 in abort ()
#2  0x00007fff83052c9c in __assert_rtn ()
#3  0x0000000100000e2f in anotherFunction (ook=0x7fff5fbff699 "") at assert.m:11
#4  0x0000000100000e5b in someFunction (blah=0x7fff5fbff699 "") at assert.m:16
#5  0x0000000100000e7c in main (argc=2, argv=0x7fff5fbff528) at assert.m:20
```

Move to the third stack frame:

```
(gdb) frame 4
#3  0x0000000100000e2f in anotherFunction (ook=0x7fff5fbff699 "") at assert.m:11
11    assert (strlen(ook) > 0);
```

This is the assert, the smoking gun, so you know exactly what happened.

You can turn off core dumps by doing

```
$ ulimit -c 0
```

One place where core files are very useful is for crashes that happen out in the field, where the user can send you the core file for later dissection. However, having them run a shell and set limits might not be practical. You can programmatically tell the system you want to drop a core file even if the shell limit is zero. Recall the discussion in Chapter 7: *Memory* of process resource limits. One of the resource limits is RLIMIT_CORE, the largest size (in bytes) of core files. You can use the resource limit calls to increase the coredump size. Example 8.3 is a modified assert.m:

Example 8.3   assert2.m

```
// assert2.m -- make a false assertion, thereby dumping core
```

```
// gcc -std=c99 -g -Wall -o assert2 assert2.m

#import <assert.h>         // for assert
#import <stdio.h>          // for printf
#import <string.h>         // for strlen
#import <stdlib.h>         // for EXIT_SUCCESS
#import <sys/resource.h>   // for setrlimit
#import <errno.h>          // for errno

void anotherFunction (const char *ook) {
    assert (strlen(ook) > 0);
    printf ("wheeee! Got string %s\n", ook);
} // anotherFunction

void someFunction (const char *blah) {
    anotherFunction (blah);
} // someFunction

void enableCoreDumps (void) {
    struct rlimit rl = {
        .rlim_cur = RLIM_INFINITY,
        .rlim_max = RLIM_INFINITY
    };

    if (setrlimit(RLIMIT_CORE, &rl) == -1) {
        fprintf(stderr, "error in setrlimit for RLIMIT_CORE: %d (%s)\n",
                errno, strerror(errno));
    }
} // enableCoreDumps


int main (int argc, const char *argv[]) {
    enableCoreDumps();
    someFunction(argv[1]);
    return EXIT_SUCCESS;
} // main
```

If you run it now, you get a core file:

```
$ ./assert2 ""
Assertion failed: (strlen(ook) > 0), function anotherFunction,
    file assert2.m, line 16.
Abort trap (core dumped)
```

To use this in a real program, you might want to put in some secret way that the user can execute that function to allow core dumping. Like, "Command-Shift-Option-click the About box OK button, and you will get a debug panel. Check the Core Dump check box and then do whatever it is that crashes the program."

For the More Curious: Stripping

Debugging symbols are pretty big and can bloat your executable. A simple Cocoa application of mine weighs in at 262K with debug symbols, whereas without the symbols it is about 30K. Depending on the application, keeping debug symbols around might not be a bad thing. For a high-traffic web server application, we kept the debug symbols to make diagnosing production problems easier (and it really came in handy sometimes). If your program has 500 megs of graphics and support files, a couple of hundred K of debug symbols probably is not too bad. On the other hand, if you are writing smaller downloadable applications, the extra hundred K or a meg could be a significant barrier to your program being used. Having debug symbols also makes it easier for people to reverse-engineer your code.

To strip the debug symbols, you can either rebuild your program using the Deployment target in Xcode, or you can just run the **strip** program against the executable. For instance:

```
$ ls -l BorkPad
-rwxr-xr-x  1 markd   staff   262780 Aug 19 21:10 BorkPad
$ strip BorkPad
$ ls -l BorkPad
-rwxr-xr-x  1 markd   staff   30608 Aug 20 21:37 BorkPad
```

So what happens if your program crashes out in the field? If you can get a core file, you can load the core file into a **gdb** session with an unstripped version of your executable and be able to debug symbolically. For example, use the **assert2** program, make a stripped copy, and generate a core file:

```
$ cp assert2 stripped
$ strip stripped
$ ./stripped ""
Assertion failed: (strlen(ook) > 0), function anotherFunction,
    file assert2.m, line 16.
Abort trap (core dumped)
```

If you **gdb** the stripped program, the stack traces are not very useful:

```
$ gdb ./stripped /cores/core.2342
...
(gdb) bt
#0  0x9001b52c in kill ()
#1  0x9005ceec in abort ()
#2  0x00001d18 in dyld_stub_exit ()
#3  0x00001c20 in ?? ()
#4  0x00001c64 in ?? ()
#5  0x00001ca4 in ?? ()
#6  0x00001978 in ?? ()
#7  0x000017f8 in ?? ()
```

But if you use the original, unstripped file, you have good stack traces:

```
$ gdb assert2 /cores/core.2342
...
(gdb) bt
#0  0x9001b52c in kill ()
#1  0x9005ceec in abort ()
#2  0x00001d18 in dyld_stub_exit ()
#3  0x00001c20 in anotherFunction (ook=0xbffffb87 "\000"...)
    at assert2.m:19
#4  0x00001c64 in someFunction (blah=0xbffffb87 "\000"...)
    at assert2.m:27
#5  0x00001ca4 in main (argc=2, argv=0xbffffadc) at assert2.m:37
#6  0x00001978 in _start (argc=2, argv=0xbffffadc, envp=0xbffffae8)
    at /SourceCache/Csu/Csu-45/crt.c:267
#7  0x000017f8 in start ()
```

If you do not want to mess with **gdb**, or the user emails you a stack trace from the crash reporter, you can use **atos** to map the address to a symbol to see what function and line caused the problem.

```
$ atos -o assert2 0x00001ca4
_main (assert2.m:38)

$ atos -o assert2 0x00001c20
_anotherFunction (assert2.m:21)
```

More Advanced GDB Commands

Threads

gdb supports debugging threaded programs. We have lots to say about threading issues in Chapter 20: *Multithreading*, but for now, here are some useful commands relating to threads.

info threads   Shows information about all the currently active threads. Here is something from a simple Cocoa program while the Page Setup dialog is active:

```
(gdb) info threads
 3 process 128 thread 0x213 0x70978 in mach_msg_overwrite_trap()
 2 process 128 thread 0x1f7 0x70978 in mach_msg_overwrite_trap()
*1 process 128 thread 0x163 0x70978 in mach_msg_overwrite_trap()
```

You can change between threads with the thread command and then poke around and see what it is doing:

```
(gdb) thread 3
[Switching to thread 3 (process 1208 thread 0x2123)]
#0  0x70000978 in mach_msg_overwrite_trap ()
```

```
(gdb) bt
#0  0x70000978 in mach_msg_overwrite_trap ()
#1  0x70005a04 in mach_msg ()
#2  0x7017bf84 in __CFRunLoopRun ()
#3  0x701b70ec in CFRunLoopRunSpecific ()
#4  0x7017b8cc in CFRunLoopRunInMode ()
#5  0x7061be08 in XIOAudioDeviceManager::NotificationThread ()
#6  0x706141c0 in CAPThread::Entry ()
#7  0x7002054c in _pthread_body ()
```

thread apply   Apply a command to a list of threads. You can use all to run the same command in all threads.

```
(gdb) thread apply all where

...

Thread 2 (process 1208 thread 0x1f07):
#0  0x70000978 in mach_msg_overwrite_trap ()
#1  0x70005a04 in mach_msg ()
#2  0x70026a2c in _pthread_become_available ()
#3  0x70026724 in pthread_exit ()
#4  0x70020550 in _pthread_body ()


Thread 1 (process 1208 thread 0x1603):
#0  0x70000978 in mach_msg_overwrite_trap ()
#1  0x70005a04 in mach_msg ()
```

```
#2  0x7017bf84 in __CFRunLoopRun ()
#3  0x701b70ec in CFRunLoopRunSpecific ()
#4  0x7017b8cc in CFRunLoopRunInMode ()
...
#23 0x7938bed0 in NSApplicationMain ()
#24 0x000036b4 in _start ()
#25 0x000034e4 in start ()
#0  0x70000978 in mach_msg_overwrite_trap ()
```

When debugging, one thread is always the focus of debugging, known as the current thread. You can break in particular threads if you wish, using thread apply thread# break .... When the program stops, all threads stop, and when the program starts (even just doing a step), all threads potentially start as well. Note that during the time of the single-step, the other threads can run full bore. The single-stepping only applies to the current thread.

You can change this behavior using the set scheduler-locking mode command. The default mode is off – threads run as just described. You can also set scheduler-locking on to run only the current thread during all **gdb** commands, or set scheduler-locking step to run only the current thread during step commands, but otherwise let the other threads run as normal. You can view the current mode using show scheduler-locking. When scheduler locking is in effect, you must be careful not to deadlock the application when calling functions from **gdb**.

9

DTrace

DTrace is a *dynamic tracing* facility developed by Sun Microsystems for the Solaris operating system. DTrace lets administrators and developers explore the system and understand how it works. It can help you track down program bugs and performance problems. DTrace was introduced with Mac OS X 10.5. Prior to 10.5, **ktrace** served a similar, but more limited, purpose.

Overview

The heart of DTrace is the *probe,* where a probe is a named point in executing code. There are probes corresponding to kernel events, function calls, Objective-C message sends, system calls, and many other interesting events, as shown in Figure 9.1. Mac OS X includes tens of thousands of probes, and the count grows with each new OS release. You can add probes to your own applications and libraries to help in profiling and debugging the actions of your own code.

Figure 9.1   DTrace probes

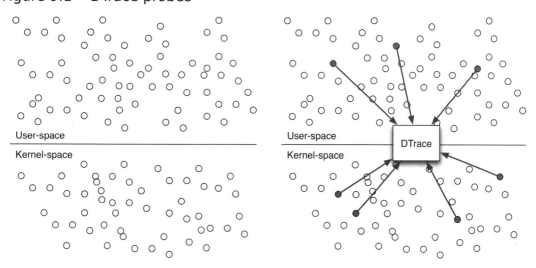

Probes are dynamically inserted as needed when you run an experiment. There is no impact on the system if probes are not engaged because the instrumentation is completely dynamic. This makes DTrace safe to use on a production system to diagnose runtime problems. Probes are implemented similarly to APE (Application Enhancer) or `mach_inject()`, where some slight of hand is performed to make a function branch to a different place by changing the first few instructions of the function. Therefore, there is no instrumentation code present for inactive probes and no performance degradation when not using DTrace. All probes are automatically disabled once your DTrace experiment ends. Probes are reference-counted, so you can run multiple experiments in parallel.

Providers are what provide the probes. For example, the syscall provider allows probes to be placed on system calls. The profile provider triggers probes at regular time intervals.

The command-line application **dtrace** is your gateway to all of DTrace's features. It can list the probes available to you, generate a header file for new probes you wish to add to your code, and trace system behavior. During tracing it engages probes and can aggregate and display data that it has gathered during the tracing.

You can use probes to trigger context-sensitive *actions* of your own design. The actions you associate with a probe can include getting a stack trace, looking at a time stamp, examining the argument to a function, or examining the return value from a function. Thus, another way to look at probes is as programmable sensors scattered throughout the system. You can attach code to each of the sensors to analyze system activity. The DTrace "workflow" is shown in Figure 9.2, with a script being fed to **dtrace**, being run in the kernel, accumulating data, and eventually reporting it back to the user.

Figure 9.2   DTrace workflow

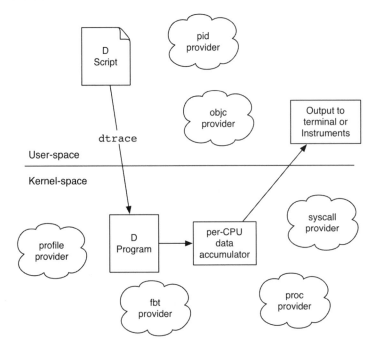

The D language

Actions are written using the "D" programming language. D is yet another scripting language, this time one which is heavily influenced by C. A large subset of C is supported along with a special set of functions specifically geared to analyzing system behavior. D programs actually run in kernel-land. Before being run, they are compiled into a safe intermediate form similar to Java bytecode and validated for safety. This is one reason why DTrace is safe to use in a production environment without danger of crashing or corrupting the system.

DTrace scripts conventionally use the filename extension .d. Apple supplies a number of sample scripts in the /usr/bin/ directory that are worth perusing.

Scripts

Example 9.1 is a sample DTrace script.

Example 9.1   keventwatch.d

```
/* Watch entry into kevent() */
syscall::kevent:entry
/execname == "dirwatcher" || execname == "DirectoryServic"/
{
    printf("%s called kevent()", execname);
}
```

You can see that D uses C-style /* comments */. Modern C / C++ style comments (//) are not supported.

Here is how you run it:

```
$ sudo dtrace -s keventwatch.d
dtrace: script 'keventwatch.d' matched 1 probe
CPU     ID   FUNCTION:NAME
  1   17238   kevent:entry DirectoryServic called kevent()
  0   17238   kevent:entry dirwatcher called kevent()
  0   17238   kevent:entry dirwatcher called kevent()
  1   17238   kevent:entry DirectoryServic called kevent()
  1   17238   kevent:entry DirectoryServic called kevent()
```

Use **sudo** because DTrace requires root privileges to run. This makes it less convenient than **ktrace**, which could run as an ordinary user (useful when diagnosing program problems in the field on someone else's machine). The -s flag tells **dtrace** to read a D program from a given file, similar to the -s flag you would give the shell or perl to execute the contents of a file. You can also use the Unix "shebang" technique and include #!/usr/sbin/dtrace -s at the top of a file and make the file executable to automatically invoke DTrace when the script is run.

This particular example watches all calls to **kevent()**, the primary kqueue interface, across the system. The script prints out the name of the program that called the function, provided it is either the program DirectoryServic[es], or the dirwatcher sample from Chapter 16: *kqueue and FSEvents*.

The DTrace output includes the CPU the particular **kevent()** was run on, the integer ID of the probe, the name of the probe, and then the output from our **printf()** statement. You can suppress the default output by giving **dtrace** the -q, for quiet, flag.

A D script is built from a collection of clauses. Example 9.1 has just one clause, but you can have arbitrarily many clauses. A clause is made up of three components:

• The probe description, which describes what it is you want to trace. In this case, we're tracing the entry into the **kevent()** system call.

- A set of actions enclosed by curly braces. If there are no actions supplied, just an empty set of braces, the name of the probe is printed out whenever it fires. In this case, we are printing out a line of text that includes a process name.

- An optional predicate, delimited by slashes. The actions are run only if the predicate evaluates to a true value. In this example, we are limiting the tracing to two programs. You can see all the programs across the system that call **kevent()** by removing the predicate.

Probes

A probe is a location or activity to which a set of actions can be bound. The syntax for specifying a probe is a colon specified list of up to four items:

- Provider - the instrumentation to be used. Some providers you will encounter are syscall to monitor system calls, io for disk io, and many others.

- Module - a specific program location. It could be the name of the module the probe is located in. It could also be the name of a kernel module or the name of a user library.

- Function - A specific function name.

- Name - An indication of the probe's semantic meaning. entry and return are common ones.

In keventwatch.d, the only probe was syscall::kevent:entry. The provider is syscall, there is no module, the function is kevent, and the name is entry. Missing probe components are interpreted as wildcards, matching everything they can. The probe description is evaluated from right to left in case there are fewer than four components are specified. You can use shell-style globbing characters for wildcarding: *, ?, [^...]

For example,

- syscall::open:entry will trace entries into the **open()** system call.

- syscall::open*:entry will trace any entries into functions that start with "open." This will match open, open_extended, and open_no_cancel.

- syscall:::entry will trace the entry into any system call.

- syscall::: will trace all probes published by syscall. There were 869 of these on an OS X 10.6.8 system.

There are a number of ways to explore the set of probes available on your system.

The command dtrace -l (dash ell) will print out every probe that is available in the kernel. On this system, there are a lot of them:

```
$ sudo dtrace -l | wc -l
   88632
```

This actually doesn't count all the available probes. Some are dynamically generated, such as the profiling probes discussed later. You can set probes on functions and Objective-C methods in user-space, so there is no real upper bound to the number of probable spots. There are also a number of probes that exist per running program. At the time the previous command was run, there were thirteen Cocoa applications being run as well. Quitting one application reduced the total probe count to 87576.

You can redirect dtrace -l out to a file and search through it with your favorite text editor. You can also see what probes match a given description with the -i flag. Here you can see what matches the examples listed earlier:

```
$ sudo dtrace -l -i syscall::open:entry
   ID   PROVIDER      MODULE              FUNCTION NAME
18649    syscall                          open entry

$ sudo dtrace -l -i "syscall::open*:entry"
   ID   PROVIDER      MODULE              FUNCTION NAME
18649    syscall                          open entry
19193    syscall                          open_extended entry
19435    syscall                          open_nocancel entry

$ sudo dtrace -l -i syscall:::entry | wc -l
   435

$ sudo dtrace -l -i syscall::: | wc -l
   869
```

syscall::open*:entry is quoted on the command line to prevent the shell from expanding the asterisk.

You can enable and manage thousands of probes. The more probes you enable, the longer it takes your script to start up because DTrace needs to enable each of the probes and some time to disable each of the probes when the experiment ends.

Providers

A provider is a facility that publishes the probes that you use in your D script. There are a number of built-in providers.

BEGIN and END providers

These are actually called dtrace:::BEGIN and dtrace:::END, but they are usually used as just BEGIN and END. The BEGIN probe fires when the D script begins execution, and the END probe fires when the script finishes. Example 9.2 shows using the BEGIN and END probes.

Example 9.2   begin-end.d

```
BEGIN
{
    trace("begin the beguine");
    exit(0);
}

END
{
    trace ("that's all, folks...");
}
```

Run it:

```
$ sudo dtrace -s begin-end.d
```

```
dtrace: script 'begin-end.d' matched 2 probes
CPU    ID        FUNCTION:NAME
  3     1             :BEGIN   begin the beguine
  0     2             :END     that's all, folks...
```

The **trace** function is like **printf**, but it does not take any formatting arguments. It also automatically generates a newline.

There is also a dtrace:::ERROR probe that fires when an error happens, such as attempting to dereference a NULL pointer.

pid provider

The pid provider lets you restrict a probe to a particular process ID. If you know that Safari is process ID 1313, you can get a list of all available probes with this command:

$ **sudo dtrace -l -i "pid1313:::" > safari.txt**

This might not actually work depending on how much RAM you have. You can try something similar on a smaller application like TextEdit.

DTrace allows you to access command-line arguments within the script. $1 is the first argument after all of arguments that **dtrace** will consume, $2 is the next one, and so on. Hard-coding a pid is unpleasant to do, so you will typically use $1 to pass a particular process ID on the command-line.

malloc-pid.d tells you when a particular application has called **malloc()** and how much memory was asked for.

Example 9.3   malloc-pid.d

```
pid$1:libSystem.B.dylib:malloc:entry
{
    printf ("malloc of %d bytes for %s\n", arg0, execname);
}
```

Run it like this:

```
$ sudo dtrace -q -s malloc-pid.d 1313
malloc of 32 bytes for Safari
malloc of 32 bytes for Safari
malloc of 512 bytes for Safari
malloc of 2048 bytes for Safari
malloc of 512 bytes for Safari
malloc of 620 bytes for Safari
^C
```

The -q flag is used to suppress the usual output from **dtrace**. The first non-dtrace argument is "1313," which is the value of $1 in the script. The probe actually becomes pid1313:libSystem.B.dylib:malloc:entry. Because **dtrace**'s default output has been suppressed, it was necessary to add a newline to Example 9.3's **printf** statement.

Notice that the script never ends. You need to interrupt it with Control-C in the terminal to make it stop.

syscall provider

The syscall provider supplies system call entry and return probes. For example:

- `syscall::read:entry` - probe whenever a process reads from a file descriptor

- `syscall::kill:entry` - run the action whenever a process calls **kill()**

profile provider

`profile` provides timed event probes. These are frequently used to display accumulated state at intervals. The `tick` name is used to specify the time, with a number to indicate the time and a suffix to specify the time unit to use. Example 9.4 shows the timer in action.

Example 9.4   lubdub.d

```
profile:::tick-5sec
{
  trace("five second timer");
}

profile:::tick-1min
{
  trace("one minute timer");
}

profile:::tick-800msec
{
  trace("800 millisecond timer");
}
```

This script prints out their messages after the indicated times. A sample run looks like this:

```
$ sudo dtrace -s lubdub.d
dtrace: script 'lubdub.d' matched 3 probes
CPU     ID             FUNCTION:NAME
  0   17370            :tick-800msec   800 millisecond timer
  0   17370            :tick-800msec   800 millisecond timer
  0   17370            :tick-800msec   800 millisecond timer
  0   17370            :tick-800msec   800 millisecond timer
  0   17370            :tick-800msec   800 millisecond timer
  0   17370            :tick-800msec   800 millisecond timer
  0   17368              :tick-5sec    five second timer
  0   17370            :tick-800msec   800 millisecond timer
  0   17370            :tick-800msec   800 millisecond timer
^C
```

Valid suffixes are `nsec`, `usec`, `msec`, for nano-, micro-, and milli- seconds. (`ns`, `us`, and `ms` are valid abbreviations.) `sec`, `min`, `hour`, and `day` are for longer values. (`s`, `m`, `h`, `d` are valid abbreviations.) There is also `hz` for hertz, frequency per second.

proc provider

The `proc` provider gives you process-level information, such as program launches and exits. Example 9.5 shows you when new processes have been created:

Example 9.5   execs.d

```
proc:::exec-success
{
```

```
    trace(execname);
}
```

A sample run looks like this:

```
$ sudo dtrace -s execs.d
dtrace: script 'execs.d' matched 2 probes
CPU     ID                    FUNCTION:NAME
  0   18488        __mac_execve:exec-success    ls
  0   18488        __mac_execve:exec-success    pwd
  0   18495        posix_spawn:exec-success    iChat
  0   18495        posix_spawn:exec-success    iChatAgent
^C
```

ls and **pwd** were performed in a Terminal window while iChat was launched in the Dock.

fbt provider

Another provider is the unpronounceable `fbt` provider, which stands for function boundary transition. These are probes inside of the kernel. An `fbt` probe is triggered when a function is entered or exited. Use the probe name `entry` or `return` to run an action when a function is entered or exited. On this Snow Leopard system, there are 18 thousand `fbt` probes:

```
$ sudo dtrace -l -i fbt::: | wc -l
   18531
```

You can look at some of the available probes:

```
$ sudo dtrace -l -i fbt::: | head -8
 ID   PROVIDER         MODULE          FUNCTION NAME
 41        fbt     mach_kernel     AllocateNode entry
 42        fbt     mach_kernel     AllocateNode return
 43        fbt     mach_kernel           Assert entry
 44        fbt     mach_kernel           Assert return
 45        fbt     mach_kernel        BF_decrypt entry
 46        fbt     mach_kernel        BF_decrypt return
 47        fbt     mach_kernel        BF_encrypt entry
```

Actions

Actions are the lines of code you write that execute whenever a probe is fired. You can assign values to variables, perform computations, and aggregate values over time.

D has no flow control, so there are no `if` statements and no loops. You can simulate `if` statements by using predicates, discussed below. The ternary operator (`?:`) is available, too.

The lack of loops is understandable. DTrace scripts, after they are compiled and verified, are run inside of the kernel. It would be a bad thing to have an unintentional infinite loop occur, locking up the system.

Variables

What is a programming language without variables? D has a number of kinds of variables. Simple (scalar) variables are familiar to those of us used to C, along with structures, associative arrays, aggregates, and even pointers.

Simple variables match C's standard types: char, int, short, long, long long, and all of their unsigned variants. You can perform the usual C-style casting between them. The size of these depend on the OS kernel's data model: a long on a 32 bit kernel would be 32 bits, and 64 bits on a 64 bit kernel. There are no floating point variables. You can display floating point values you get from probes, but you cannot perform floating point math. You cannot cast from a float to an integer value.

You don't need to declare a variable before you use it, just assign it, and the variable will use the type of the first assignment. You cannot declare a variable and assign it a value at the same time.

Variables are global by default. Typically you will declare the variable, if you choose to, outside of any clauses and then assign it an initial value inside of a BEGIN clause. Variables are zeroed initially.

The standard C operators (+, -, *, /, ++, etc) all work as expected, as do comparison operators (<, >, ! =, etc). && and || are available in logical statements, as is ^^, which is a logical XOR. XOR evaluates to true if exactly one operand is true. Logical OR and AND perform short-circuit evaluation, but XOR does not. Both expressions for an XOR are always evaluated.

Variables can have string values as well. Comparison operators with strings behave as if you had called strcmp() on the strings.

Example 9.6 sings a familiar song:

Example 9.6   beer.d

```
int bottles; /* optional */

BEGIN
{
  bottles = 99;
}

profile:::tick-1sec
{
  printf("%d bottles of beer on the wall\n", bottles);
  printf("%d bottles of beer.\n", bottles);
  printf("take one down, pass it around\n");
  printf("%d bottles of beer on the wall\n\n", bottles);

  bottles--;
}

END
{
  printf("that's all, folks...");
}
```

Run it like usual and interrupt it when you have had enough.

```
$ sudo dtrace -qs beer.d
99 bottles of beer on the wall
99 bottles of beer.
take one down, pass it around
99 bottles of beer on the wall

98 bottles of beer on the wall
98 bottles of beer.
take one down, pass it around
98 bottles of beer on the wall
```

```
^C
that's all, folks...
```

Scoped variables

There are two additional scopes for variables: per-thread, and per-clause. Thread-local variables are useful when you want to enable a probe and perform some work with individual thread. You prefix a thread-local variable with self->. A thread's identity is unique over the lifetime of a system, so you won't get any weird collisions that might happen if a kernel thread ID gets reused. A per-clause variable is like a static local variable in C. It is only in scope when a particular clause is being executed. Prefix clause-local variables with this->.

Built-in variables

D provides a number of built-in scalar variables. There are no built-in thread-local or clause-local variables.

int64_t arg0, arg1, ... arg9;	The first ten input arguments to a probe, as 64-bit integers. Undefined arguments are zero-filled.
args[]	Typed arguments to the current probe, using an integer index. For instance, the read system call is prototyped like ssize_t read(int fildes, void *buf, size_t nbyte); So args[0] will be an integer, the file descriptor; args[1] will be a pointer value, and args[2] is typed size_t, the size of the buffer.
cwd	Current working directory of the process that owns the thread that is triggering the probe.
errno	Error value returned by the last system call executed by the thread.
execname	Name of the executable that triggered the probe.
pid	Process id of the executable that triggered the probe.
stackdepth	Current thread's stackframe depth.
timestamp, vtimestamp	Current values of a nanosecond timestamp. The absolute value have no real meaning, but you use them to calculate delta values. timestamp is wall-clock time, and vtimestamp is per-CPU time, minus DTtrace overhead.
probeprov, probemod, probefunc, probename	Names of the four parts of the probe specification.

These last four are handy for knowing which particular probe is firing, especially if you have one probe specification that matches multiple probes. Example 9.7 traces all system calls made across the system.

Example 9.7   syscalls.d

```
syscall:::
/execname != "dtrace"/
{
    printf ("%s fired in %s\n", probefunc, execname);
}
```

This produces a *lot* of output:

```
$ sudo dtrace -qs syscalls.d
sigprocmask fired in WindowServer
__semwait_signal fired in fseventsd
lstat fired in fseventsd
getattrlist fired in backupd
__semwait_signal fired in mds
gettimeofday fired in Snak
gettimeofday fired in Snak
gettimeofday fired in Adium
gettimeofday fired in Adium
kevent fired in DirectoryServic
getrusage fired in Skype
getrusage fired in Skype
^C
```

The /execname != "dtrace"/ predicate is there to filter out system calls from **dtrace**, of which there are many. The clause will only be run if the name of the executable that triggered the probe was not **dtrace**.

You can access kernel and application data structures from your D script. You can reference a symbol external to DTrace, such as a kernel data structure, by prefixing the name with the backtick: `. Example 9.8 displays the system load average every five seconds. Remember that there are no floating point calculations available, so the integer and decimal components of the load average, stored in the avrunnable structure, must be calculated independently.

Example 9.8   loadaverage.d

```
profile:::tick-5sec
{
    this->fscale = `averunnable.fscale;
    this->loadInteger = `averunnable.ldavg[0] / this->fscale;
    this->loadDecimal = ((`averunnable.ldavg[0] % this->fscale) * 100)
                        / this->fscale;
    printf ("%d.%d\n", this->loadInteger, this->loadDecimal);
}
```

A sample run:

```
$ sudo dtrace -qs loadaverage.d
1.48
1.36
1.25
1.15
1.6
0.97
0.89
```

The machine had been used to perform an end-to-end build of a product which raised the load average. Here you can see the system "cooling off."

Functions

D provides a number of functions you can use in your action scripts. Here is a sampling.

printf	Standard C-style printf function
trace	Displays its argument, using a default format based on the type. Also appends a newline for you.
printa	Print aggregate values, described in more detail below.
ustack	Print the user level stack trace. If the process exits or is killed before the DTrace experiment has completed, DTrace might not be able to resolve the program counter, so you will get hex values rather than symbolic values.
exit	Terminate execution early. Otherwise, you have to type Control-C to quit.
copyin, copyinstr	DTrace scripts execute in kernel scope. Consider probing a system call like **write()**, which takes a pointer to a buffer with the data to be written. There is a problem if you want to use the contents of the buffer in your action. The pointer is to an address in user-space, and DTrace is running in kernel-space. Use one of these functions to get the data from user-space into kernel-space.

```
void *copyin (uintptr_t addr, size_t size)
```

Copies the specified size in bytes from the given user-space address into a DTrace scratch buffer and returns the address of the buffer. If there is insufficient scratch space available, or the given address is bad, an error is generated.

```
string copyinstr (uintptr_t addr)
```

Copies a zero-terminated C string from user-space into a scratch buffer and returns the buffer's address. You can use the returned address as a string.

Arrays

D provides associative arrays that are similar to hashtables and dictionaries in other languages. The index into the array can be a n-tuple of values, separated by commas. arrayname[pid, probefunc, "bork"] = 23; is a valid assignment. The types of the array index must match for every assignment, and the assigned values must be uniform. You cannot nest arrays.

Example 9.9 calculates the wall-clock time it takes to execute the **read()** system call:

Example 9.9   readtime.d

```
syscall::read:entry
```

```
{
    self->ts[pid, probefunc] = timestamp;
}

syscall::read:return
/self->ts[pid, probefunc] != 0/
{
    delta = timestamp - self->ts[pid, probefunc];
    printf ("read in %s took %d nsecs\n", execname, delta);
}
```

And a sample run:

```
$ sudo dtrace -qs ./readtime.d
read in Terminal took 18469 nsecs
read in emacs-i386 took 14714 nsecs
read in Terminal took 11391 nsecs
read in Terminal took 26777 nsecs
read in emacs-i386 took 23776797 nsecs
^C
```

The predicate is there to prevent the script from starting in the middle of a read and getting bad values in the timestamp calculation. If there was no corresponding start time, the time calculation code is skipped. The array is stored as a thead-local variable with self-> so that an application that is using **read()** in multiple threads won't get confused.

C arrays

Interestingly enough, D supports C-style arrays – address plus offset. D can access kernel and application data structures, which include pointers and arrays. You can dereference pointers and access arrays with the usual C syntax. D makes sure that all array and pointer access is safe, so you do not have to worry about triggering a SEGV in kernel-land. Your script may be terminated, and the dtrace:::ERROR probe triggered.

Predicates

Predicates are logical expressions that are enclosed by slashes. The action code is run if the expression evaluates to a true value when a probe fires. You can have the same probe used with different predicates and different action blocks. Clauses are executed in the order they appear in the source file.

Aggregates

Aggregates are DTrace's way of accumulating a lot of individual pieces of data into a more useful overall view. Seeing individual **read()** times can be useful, if a bit voluminous. Having a min / max / average of read times may be much more interesting.

The syntax for using a DTrace aggregate looks a bit like using array.

```
@name[key] = aggfunc();
```

The leading at-sign means that an aggregate is being used, and the assignment is a function rather than an expression. There are a number of aggregating functions:

count()   Keeps count of the number of times it is called.

`sum(expression)`	Accumulates the total value of the expression over time.
`avg(expression)`	Accumulates the arithmetic average of the expression over time.
`min(expression)`	Keeps the smallest expression that is seen over time.
`max(expression)`	Keeps the largest expression that is seen over time.
`quantize(expression)`	Keeps a power-of-two frequency distribution of the values of the given histogram. The value of the expression increments the value in a histogram bucket. When the program exits, **dtrace** prints an ASCII chart showing the bucket values.
`lquantize(expression, lower-bound, upper-bound, step-value)`	Similar to `quantize`, but uses a linear frequency distribution rather than a power-of-two distribution.

OK, so what does all that mean? Here are some examples. Example 9.10 counts the number of times the **read()** system call is made by any process.

Example 9.10   countread.d

```
syscall::read:entry
{
    @calls[execname] = count();
}
```

A sample run:

```
$ sudo dtrace -s ./countread.d
dtrace: script './countread.d' matched 1 probe
^C
  VoodooPad Pro        1
  socketfilterfw       1
  mds                 12
  DirectoryServic     21
  fseventsd           22
  Safari              62
  Terminal            86
  emacs-i386         141
```

dtrace helpfully displays aggregates for you when it exits. Unfortunately, this can make a mess if you have a couple of aggregates going. Example 9.11 counts the number of read calls and maintains the average calltime:

Example 9.11   avgread-1.d

```
syscall::read:entry
{
    @calls[execname] = count();
    self->ts = timestamp;
}

syscall::read:return
/self->ts/
```

```
{
    delta = timestamp - self->ts;
    @averagetime[execname] = avg(delta);
}
```

Some output from this script:

```
$ sudo dtrace -qs avgread-1.d
^C
  VoodooPad Pro         1
  csh                   1
  securityd             2
  open                 10
  Preview              40
  emacs-i386           55
  Terminal            122
  Terminal           7998
  emacs-i386        10062
  VoodooPad Pro     10232
  open              15512
  securityd         17807
  Preview           28280
```

There are counts and average times in there, but it is hard to tell where the counts stop and the average times begin. Example 9.12 controls the output by creating an END probe and using **printa()** to print out the aggregate.

Example 9.12   avgread-2.d

```
syscall::read:entry
{
    self->ts = timestamp;
}

syscall::read:return
/self->ts/
{
    delta = timestamp - self->ts;
    @averagetime[execname] = avg(delta);
    @callcount[execname] = count();
    @mintime[execname] = min(delta);
    @maxtime[execname] = max(delta);
    self->ts = 0;
}

END
{
    printf ("average time\n");
    printa ("%20s %@d\n", @averagetime);

    printf ("\ncall count\n");
    printa ("%20s %@d\n", @callcount);

    printf ("\nmintime\n");
    printa ("%20s %@d\n", @mintime);

    printf ("\nmaxtime\n");
    printa ("%20s %@d\n", @maxtime);
}
```

The script in action:

```
$ sudo dtrace -qs avgread-2.d
^C
average time
              Terminal 7941
           emacs-i386 9985
        mDNSResponder 17781
                Safari 24666
         VoodooPad Pro 55339
             fseventsd 527863979
                   mds 551164939

call count
        mDNSResponder 2
           emacs-i386 3
              Terminal 4
                   mds 6
             fseventsd 9
         VoodooPad Pro 270
                Safari 622
...
```

Charts are always fun. Example 9.13 aggregates read times, but this time, the times are represented as a histogram on process exit.

Example 9.13   avgquant.d

```
syscall::read:entry
{
    self->ts = timestamp;
}

syscall::read:return
/self->ts/
{
    delta = timestamp - self->ts;
    @quanttime[execname] = quantize(delta);
}
```

This is what a sample run looks like:

```
$ sudo dtrace -qs avgquant.d
Password:
^C

  securityd
           value  -------- Distribution -------- count
            4096 |                                0
            8192 |@@@@@@@@@@@@@@@@@@@@             1
           16384 |@@@@@@@@@@@@@@@@@@@@             1
           32768 |                                0

  open
           value  -------- Distribution -------- count
            2048 |                                0
            4096 |@@@@@@@@@@@@@@@@                 4
            8192 |@@@@@@@@@@@@                     3
           16384 |@@@@@@@@                         2
```

```
        32768  |@@@@                               1
        65536  |                                   0

Preview
        value  -------- Distribution -------- count
         2048  |                                   0
         4096  |@@@@@@@@@@@@@                       9
         8192  |@@@@@@@@@@@@@@@@@@@@@              13
        16384  |@@@@@                               3
        32768  |@@                                  1
        65536  |                                   0
```

Aggregate-related functions

There are several functions you can apply to an aggregate as a whole.

normalize, denormalize	Sometimes the values in an aggregate are not as useful as they could be. For example, you might have a **sum** of read times in an aggregate, but you may be more interested in read times over a period of time. The **normalize** function takes an aggregate and a scalar as arguments. The values of the aggregate are divided by the scalar value. The aggregate values are not permanently changed, so you can use **denormalize** to return to the original values.
clear	Removes all of the values but leaves the keys. Sometimes it may be interesting to know that a key has had a non-zero value in an aggregate.
trunc	Removes values as well as keys. **trunc** by itself will truncate the entire aggregate. **trunc** with a positive value will preserve the N largest values. **trunc** with a negative value will preserve the N smallest values.

Also, when a variable such as an array or an aggregate is assigned a zero value, DTrace will garbage collect the memory. When you are done with an array or an aggregate before the script ends, assign it to zero to conserve memory.

Random Leftovers

The C preprocessor

DTrace can run your script through the C preprocessor before the code is compiled. You can use all of the standard preprocessor features to make macros with common code and include C header files to include type definitions of library types. The D compiler automatically loads the set of C type descriptions for the kernel.

Pragmas

DTrace has a number of tunable parameters you can change via pragmas. Some useful ones:

#pragma D option quiet	same as passing -q on the command-line

239

`#pragma D option flowindent`   **dtrace** prints the name of the function if an action is empty. If you turn on this pragma, DTrace will indent function call names based on call depth, giving you a call trace.

Example 9.14 is a script that traces the flow of function calls in the kernel for the **open()** system call when invoked by the **ls** command-line tool:

Example 9.14   trace-ls.d

```
#pragma D option flowindent

BEGIN
{
    printf("waiting for 'ls'");
}

syscall::open:entry
/execname == "ls" && guard++ == 0/
{
    self->traceIt = 1;
}

fbt:::
/self->traceIt/
{
}

syscall:::return
/self->traceIt/
{
    self->traceIt = 0;
    exit (0);
}
```

Below is a sample run, truncated for brevity. This script uses an "ambush" technique to wait for a program to start running. Run **dtrace** in one terminal and perform an **ls** in another one.

```
$ sudo dtrace -s ./trace-ls.d
dtrace: script './trace-ls.d' matched 16834 probes
CPU FUNCTION
  1 | :BEGIN                                  waiting for 'ls'

  0   -> open
  0     -> __pthread_testcancel
  0       -> open_nocancel
  0         -> vfs_context_current
  0         <- vfs_context_current
  0         -> vfs_context_proc
  0           -> get_bsdthreadtask_info
  0           <- get_bsdthreadtask_info
  0           -> falloc
  0             -> lck_mtx_lock
  0             <- lck_mtx_lock
  0             -> falloc_locked
  0               -> fdalloc
  0               <- fdalloc
  0               -> proc_ucred
  0               <- proc_ucred
```

```
0                   -> mac_file_check_create
0                    -> mac_policy_list_conditional_busy
0                    <- mac_policy_list_conditional_busy
0                   <- mac_file_check_create
...
```

Here is a dissection of the clauses of the script:

```
#pragma D option flowindent
```

Indent the call graph

```
BEGIN
{
    printf("waiting for 'ls'");
}

syscall::open:entry
/execname == "ls" && guard++ == 0/
{
    self->traceIt = 1;
}
```

This clause is interested in the **open()** system call. When an **open()** call is made in a process called "ls," set the traceIt flag. The predicate makes us wait until we see **ls** before doing anything. The guard variable is to make sure we only trace one particular open call. This will protect the script from getting confused if there are multiple **ls** processes running, or if it uses **open()** in multiple threads.

```
fbt:::
/self->traceIt/
{
}
```

This action is invoked any time a kernel function is entered or exited. The kernel does a lot of stuff, and we are only interested in these function call transitions if the script is actively tracing. Because of the predicate of the previous action, we will only have one thread in one process tracing through the execution of **open()**..

```
syscall:::return
/self->traceIt/
{
    self->traceIt = 0;
    exit (0);
}
```

This probe is triggered on any system call exit. For the great majority of system call exits in the system, we just not interested. If the traceme thread-local variable is set, then that means this is an interesting thread – the one that is tracing the **open()** system call of our **ls** process. If traceIt is a true value, execute the code. Clear out the traceIt flag, so that any subsequent system call exits in **ls** are triggered. Then finally terminate the script.

Objective-C

Apple has extended **dtrace** to trace Objective-C method invocations, using a special objc provider. Some calls can be caught by the pid probe:

```
pid$1:AppKit:*:entry
```

traces the entry into any AppKit method.

```
pid$1:AppKit:*NSControl*:entry
```

traces the entry into any **NSControl** method.

The objc probe is like the pid probe, which requires a process ID. You can specify the pid explicitly, or by using the $1 built-in variable to take the first argument for the script. Trace an instance method:

```
objc$1:NSControl:-cell:return
```

Trace an instance method that takes an argument:

```
objc$1:NSControl:-setEnabled?:return
```

Both DTrace and Objective-C treat colons as important delimiters. Use the ?, match one character wildcard, to tell DTrace to match the Objective-C colons.

Trace an instance method that takes more than one argument:

```
objc$1:NSView:-convertRect?toView?:entry
```

You can trace class messages by using a leading + on the method name.

Exercises

1. Make beer.d actually stop when it runs out of bottles.

2. The stack trace returned by **ustack()** can be used as an index in an array or an aggregate. See how many unique stack traces in an application of your choice end up calling **malloc()**.

10

Performance Tuning

It has happened to all of us: you subject your program to real world data and discover that performance is sub-optimal, ranging from "could be faster" to "locks up instantly and CPU fans reach Mach 3." Finding out what the performance problem is can be a difficult task. Many times we think we *know* where the problem is, but we turn out to be wrong. Luckily, there are a number of tools available to give definite metrics of where the program spends its time and what kind of pressure it puts on the OS in general.

The End of Free Performance

Over the last several decades, computer performance has been doubling about every 18 months, a figure attributable to Moore's Law, which states that "The number of transistors in microchips will double about every 18 months." For a long time, this doubling of transistors translated into doubling of performance and was helped along by increases in the clock frequency of the processors, which went from megahertz to gigahertz.

As software developers, we have had the luxury of writing sub-optimal code while improvements in computer hardware have masked inefficiencies. This has allowed us to tackle larger, more interesting problems without having to obsess over every cycle; and let us use simpler algorithms with more expensive orders of complexity.

The major chip manufacturers have hit a hard barrier in the race to crank up clock speeds due to problems with the speed of light and heat dissipation. Moore's Law regarding those transistors is still in force, though. Manufacturers are still cramming more and more transistors into their processors, but these transistors are being used in other places. In particular, they are being used to increase parallelism.

CPUs have a great deal of internal parallelism, allowing multiple integer and floating point units to do calculations in parallel as well as vector units that operate on multiple pieces of data with a single instruction. In addition to separate processor units, CPUs these days are also multicore and hyperthreaded architectures. Multicore chips have several distinct CPUs on one physical chip. These processors operate in parallel to each other and have their own logic units. Hyperthread processors have two or more threads operating in parallel in a single CPU. Hyperthreads still share stuff like processor cache and math units, but it still allows the processor to chew through more instructions in a given time period. These can be combined, allowing an 8-core MacPro to appear to have 16 processors. Parallelism in GPUs, the graphical processing units found on graphics cards, is progressing even faster than with CPUs. It is not uncommon for a GPU to have 256 processors all running in parallel.

Parallel code is becoming more and more prevalent to take advantage of these multicore and hyperthreaded architectures. Parallel code usually is the domain of the more advanced programmers because of the difficulty in the writing correct concurrent programs. As you saw in Chapter 20: *Multithreading*, there are many issues that make parallel development difficult. More programmers will be needing to learn about this world and its problems so that we (as an industry) can continue developing software that behaves correctly and has the performance the users have come to expect. Tech such as Grand Central Dispatch helps alleviate some of the problems inherent in parallel programming, but it is still difficult to get right.

The design decisions occurring on the hardware side of the world have an impact on us living on the software side. Writing efficient code is coming back into style because we cannot count on processors "just getting faster" to help us.

The fact that users are dealing with ever-growing sets of data does not help the problem either. As computers get more powerful, users are using them to do more stuff to larger data sets. Consider iPhoto. People first used iPhoto to manage small libraries of relatively small photos. Now that we have terabyte hard drives, 16 core machines, and cheap high megapixel digital cameras, users are creating huge photo libraries of enormous images. Users will expect to be able to sling around ever larger sets of data as time goes on. They will not particularly care to hear any excuses about the gigahertz barrier.

Approaches To Performance

The key to keeping on top of your performance is to use profiling tools. Profile early, and profile often. Catch performance issues early in your development so you don't build a lot of code around an inefficient core. If you use Instruments, Shark, or other performance tools regularly, you can see possible performance issues on the horizon before they come close and bite you.

Be sure to profile with each new revision of the OS and on new hardware as it comes out. As Apple changes Mac OS X under the hood, things that were optimal may now be suboptimal and vice-versa. Hardware changes can change the game performance-wise. Consider look-up tables, which are a common way to avoid doing calculation. On PowerPC G4 and older processors, using a look-up table was often a big win, but the G5 could do a lot of calculation in the time it took to load data from memory. Having situations like this can be a real problem if you have to support older versions of the OS or if you want to optimally target vastly different hardware.

Be careful to not totally contort your design early on in a noble quest for Optimal Performance. You might be addressing performance issues that do not have a real impact on your final product. Reports from profilers are not gospel. A report may highlight a performance problem, but the problem may be something that doesn't need fixing. If a problem highlighted by a profiler will not affect the user experience of your program or if it is something that rarely happens, you can put your energies into optimizing something else.

Finally, do not just profile your development builds. If you use different compiler flags for deployment builds, especially with higher optimization levels, you will want to do some profiling on your final build so that you do not waste time fixing code paths that will change with compiler optimizations.

Major Causes of Performance Problems

Performance problems typically come from one or more of 5 major areas: algorithms, memory, CPU, disk, and graphics. Granted, that is pretty much everything your program interacts with in the machine. You can use performance tools to look at each aspect of computer performance in isolation to get a better handle on your overall performance issues, even if one problem is causing problems in several categories.

Memory

Even though modern machines have vast amounts of memory, RAM is still a scarce resource. Once your app or other apps on the system fill up memory, Mac OS X starts sending memory pages to disk, destroying performance. On iOS devices, your program may be killed outright in low-memory situations.

Typically if you optimize to reduce your memory usage (optimizing for space), you will often get reductions in execution time because the processor is not waiting for that extra data to arrive from memory. Also, because Mac OS X is a shared system with daemons running, with each user running lots of programs of their own, and potentially multiple users logged in, it is good to be conservative with your memory usage. This can be a tough discipline when each process has its own wide-open address space to play in, especially when using 64-bit addressing.

Locality of Reference

"Locality of reference" describes memory accesses that happen near each other. Reading a hundred bytes off one 4k page is faster than reading one byte off a hundred different pages scattered across the address space. When you ask for data from memory, the processor actually grabs a sequence of bytes, known as a cache line, under the assumption that you will be accessing memory in a contiguous manner. From the processor's point of view, it is just as fast to grab a 64-byte cache line as it is to grab a 4-byte integer. So, if you set up your loops to operate on memory sequentially, you can see a performance boost.

Example 10.1 creates a large two dimensional global array and accesses it in two different ways.

Example 10.1   locality.m

```
// locality.m -- time locality of reference

#include <stdio.h>      // for printf
#include <stdlib.h>     // for EXIT_SUCCESS
#include <time.h>       // for time_t, time()

// gcc -g -std=c99 -o locality locality.m

#define ARRAYSIZE 20000
int a[ARRAYSIZE][ARRAYSIZE]; // make a huge array

int main (int argc, char *argv[]) {
    // Walk the array in row-major order, so that once we're done
    // with a page we never bother with it again.

    time_t starttime = time(NULL);
    for (int i = 0; i < ARRAYSIZE; i++){
        for(int j = 0; j < ARRAYSIZE; j++){
            a[i][j] = 1;
        }
    }

    time_t endtime = time (NULL);

    printf("row-major: %d operations in %ld seconds.\n",
           ARRAYSIZE * ARRAYSIZE, endtime - starttime);
```

```
// Walk the array in column-major order.  It ends up touching a bunch of
// pages multiple times.

starttime = time(NULL);
for (int j = 0; j < ARRAYSIZE; j++){
    for(int i = 0; i < ARRAYSIZE; i++){
        a[i][j] = 1;
    }
}

endtime = time (NULL);

printf("column-major: %d operations in %ld seconds.\n",
       ARRAYSIZE * ARRAYSIZE, endtime - starttime);

return EXIT_SUCCESS;

} // main
```

Here is a sample run:

```
$ ./locality
row-major: 400000000 operations in 3 seconds.
column-major: 400000000 operations in 27 seconds.
```

A simple reversal of the for loops can result in a 9x performance penalty! The first loop follows the way that C has the array's memory organized, as shown in Figure 10.1. This loop accesses adjacent bytes, and as it works through the array, it has good locality of reference. Memory pages are accessed only once, and after the loop has stopped manipulating memory on a page, that page is no longer used.

Figure 10.1   Good memory access pattern

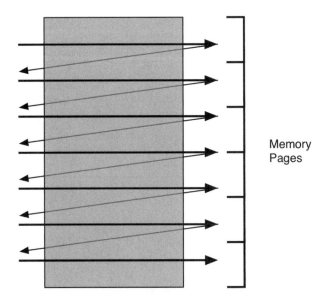

Memory
Pages

The second loop works "across the grain," as shown in Figure 10.2. It ends up hitting every page used by the array every time through the loop. This puts a lot of pressure on the virtual memory system because every page stays "warm," causing the kernel to keep shuffling its least-recently-used page lists. The first loop, because it does not touch a page once the work is done, is nicer to the kernel. Once the page ages out of the kernel's data structures, it is never seen again.

Figure 10.2   Bad memory access pattern

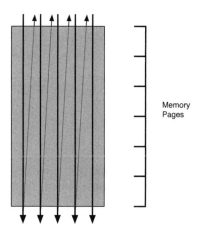

Memory
Pages

Caches

One common way to boost performance is caching, where you keep around some loaded or calculated data in memory. If you are not careful, this technique can have drawbacks in a system that employs virtual memory and paging. Recall that memory that hasn't been accessed recently can be paged out to disk and the space in RAM can be used by other processes. iOS devices do not page data to disk, so dirty pages are always resident.

If do you choose to cache information, it is best to split up your cache data and the metadata that describes the cached data. You don't want to use an architecture like Figure 10.3, which mixes the cache data and the metadata.

Figure 10.3   Bad locality of reference

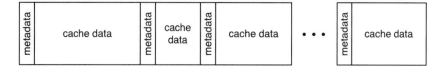

Instead, organize your data as shown in Figure 10.4. Keep your metadata together because you will have good locality of reference when walking through your cache looking for expired objects. You can even do your own form of virtual memory: if a cache entry has not been used in a while or if you get an iOS memory warning, you can remove your data blob from memory and then load it again when needed.

Figure 10.4   Good locality of reference

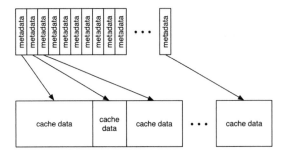

Memory is the New I/O

The motivation that drives programmers to cache data read from disk is that I/O from disk is hideously expensive. Waiting for one disk I/O can cost hundreds of thousands (or more) CPU cycles that could be put to better use.

With today's processors, memory subsystems, and bus architectures, RAM has become like I/O. Sometimes accessing memory can be extremely slow compared to CPU speed. For example, according to an Apple tech note, a G5 could do 16 to 50 vector adds in the time it takes to load a cache line from memory. And the situation can get even worse with modern processors.

The "precalculate and store in memory" technique can become a bottleneck compared to brute-force calculations. The CPU can grind through some calculations faster than the fetch from memory, and the look-up table can force more important data out of the CPU caches. The tech note goes on to say "In one example, vector code that converts unsigned char data to float and then applies a 9th order polynomial to it is still marginally faster than hand tuned scalar code that does a lookup into a 256 entry lookup table containing floats."

Level-1 Cache, the cache memory nearest the CPU logic units, has an area for instructions, but it is only 32 to 64 kilobytes large, per core. Optimizations that increase code length, like loop unrolling and 64-bit code in general, can blow out this cache, requiring code to be continually brought in from RAM. It becomes a balancing act between the size of code, what you calculate, and what you store and retrieve. Sometimes trial-and-error is the way to go to see what technique results in the best performance, especially if you have high-performance scientific modeling that will have long runtimes or if you are dealing with large volumes of data quickly, such as when processing video.

Semantics of the C language can get in the way, optimization-wise, especially with regards to memory. If the compiler knows how a particular chunk of memory is being accessed, it can cache the values in registers or even avoid loading data that has already been loaded. Because C has pointers, there can be aliasing problems. There may be a pointer elsewhere in the process that is pointing to (and could conceivably modify) a piece of memory that the compiler could otherwise optimize access to. This is why languages that do not have pointers, like FORTRAN, can perform much more aggressive optimizations.

When using a data structure through a pointer or a global variable in a loop, the compiler will emit code to reload that location in memory each time through the loop. It does this just in case the value was changed by someone else, either in another thread or by a function called inside the loop. Making a local variable to hold the global's value lets the compiler figure out that this data is not going to change and thus avoids the memory hit each time through the loop.

CPU

CPU usage is the metric that most programmers think about first when confronted with an optimization issue. "My app is pegging the CPU, and I need to speed it up." Typically when CPU usage becomes a dominant factor, the root cause is a slow algorithm. It might have a high level of complexity, or it might just be a poor implementation. In almost all cases, changing your algorithm will give you more speedups than most other kinds of code or system tweaking. The classic example is changing from a bubble-sort, an order $O(N^2)$ algorithm), to a quicksort or merge sort, which is $O(n \log n)$.

Sometimes a bad implementation of an algorithm can wreak havoc. For instance, a programming error turned **strstr()** in one version of SunOS 4.1.x from an O(N) operation to a worthless $O(N^2)$ one:

```
while (c < strlen(string)) {
    // do stuff with string[c]
}
```

Recall that C strings do not store their length. A string is just a sequence of bytes terminated by zero. **strlen()** has to traverse the entire string counting characters. There are tricks you can use to do the work in greater than one-byte chunks, but it's still an O(N) operation. In this particular case, the length of the string is not going to change, so there is no reason to take the length every time through the loop.

Luckily, high CPU usage can be easily discovered by noticing that the CPU meter is pegged in Activity Monitor, that **top** is showing your app consuming 99% of the available CPU power, or that your laptop case has started glowing. The sampling and profiling tools discussed later in this chapter are ideal for tracking down the cause of these problems.

Disk

Disk access is very slow – many orders of magnitude slower than accessing memory. In general, if you can avoid disk I/O, do so. If you are planning on caching data from disk, remember that the virtual memory system also uses the disk. If you cache a large amount of data, you could end up causing the VM system to do disk I/O. This is a very bad situation because you have now exchanged one disk read (from disk into memory) into a read and a write to page it out and then another read to page it back in from the disk into memory.

Locality of reference plays a part when optimizing disk access when VM paging involved. With bad locality of reference, you end up touching lots of pages. These pages cause other pages to "age out" of the VM cache and get sent to disk. Eventually you will touch them again which could cause disk I/O to retrieve the data on those pages.

You can avoid some of the expense of disk I/O by not doing the work at all. Putting windows into different .nib files and loading them on demand is a common technique. If you do not need to show the window, there is no reason to load it in memory.

Similarly, if you have a large database of information, accessing it piecemeal can yield significant speedups over loading the whole thing into memory. Using memory-mapped files can avoid disk activity because only the parts of the file being touched will make their way into memory.

Graphics

The Quartz graphics engine in Mac OS X puts a lot of pressure on the memory system. Quartz uses large graphic buffers, one for each window visible on the screen. There are also compositing operations to render the user's desktop. Quartz also uses the CPU to do some of its drawing effects, although many of these operations have been migrated to the graphics processing units on the graphics card. There are some operations that do not work well on the GPU, so these must be done on the CPU.

The key to optimizing graphics is to avoid drawing when you can. Use the Quartz Debug utility, shown in Figure 10.5, to see where you are doing unnecessary drawing. The most commonly used features are in the Drawing Information panel. Autoflush drawing causes drawing operations to appear on the screen as soon as they happen rather than being batched for the next update. Areas to the screen that are drawn to can be made to flash so you can see where you are drawing. Identical screen updates are highlighted in a different color so you can see where redundant work is happening.

Figure 10.5   Quartz Debug

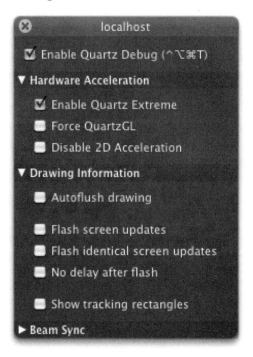

NSView has some features that let you decide which parts of the view need to be redrawn and which ones do not. You can hit-test the rectangle that is passed to NSView's drawRect: method and only perform drawing calls for items that live in that rectangle. This rectangle tends to be the union of all of the area that needs redrawing, so you can consult getRectsBeingDrawn: and needsToDrawRect: to hit-test against the areas that need to be redrawn.

One aspect of Quartz drawing that catches some programmers off guard is that overlapping lines in a single path can be very expensive. A lot of work happens at line crossings, such as anti-aliasing the intersections, as well as making sure that transparent colors do not get "painted" multiple times at the crossings and appear darker. If you need to draw lots of overlapping lines, especially if you are using opaque colors and do not care about antialiasing, you can get much better performance by drawing a bunch of small paths instead.

Before using any of the profiling tools

Forget any assumptions you may have about where the performance problems may be. Programmers are notoriously bad about predicting where performance problems are; otherwise, the problems would already be fixed. One programmer I worked with was convinced that file loading and disk I/O was the slow part of his program when loading files, and he was spending a lot of effort to optimize disk access. After a quick session with Shark, the problem actually turned out to be the marshaling of data into a tree so that `NSOutlineView` could use it. The time spent in actual file I/O was minimal.

Keep good notes on what you do and the measurements you make so that you can apply the optimizations to other situations. By keeping a record of execution times (for instance), you can tell if your optimization attempts are helping or are actually making the problem worse.

When tracking down performance problems, throw a large data set at your application. With the file-loading issue mentioned earlier, some of the test data were 5K files that took a second or two to load. That's too small a window in which to figure anything out. If your application is designed to edit 50-page research papers, then throw a 500- or 5000-page document at it. The larger data sets should make $O(N^2)$ algorithms stand out like the proverbial sore thumb. If your program is responsive when editing 5000-page documents, it should give the user a really nice experience when they are using it to edit 50-page documents. Do not bother with more than two or three orders of magnitude more data, since that much more data will probably require a redesign of your data structures and may become suboptimal for smaller data sets.

There is some debate over when you should optimize. One school of thought is "premature optimization is the root of all evil," and you should wait until the end of your development cycle to identify and fix performance problems. Unfortunately, that can require re-engineering large chunks of the product if there is a deeply-rooted bottleneck. Another school of thought is to act like you are on a diet and adopt a constant discipline about performance. The downside to that is that premature optimization can obscure the design and the code and make it harder to track down program errors before shipping.

As with most everything in life, the middle ground is a good place to live. Keep an eye out for algorithms that can be improved, but do not obfuscate code to trim every cycle you can too early in the development process. Throw large data sets at your program often. Do not wait until right before a trade show or a launch to subject your program to what the customer will throw at it. Keep an eye on your memory usage so that it does not grow too large too quickly. Also be sure to run the program in the user's environment. If you are writing a desktop app, be sure to have Safari and iTunes running, since the user will probably be using those apps, too. If your application is a memory pig and makes iTunes skip, you will definitely get some user complaints.

Command-Line Tools

Mac OS X comes with a number of command-line tools for tracking down particular types of performance problems. The nice thing about the command line is that you can remotely log into a machine and watch things as they happen. They also don't interfere with your application's user interface.

time

The simplest tool is **time**. It times command execution and shows you clock time, CPU time in userspace, and CPU time spent in the kernel. Here is a run of /usr/bin/time on TextEdit. The time measured was the time starting TextEdit up, loading /usr/share/dict/words, and then scrolling from the top to the bottom.

```
$ time /Applications/TextEdit.app/Contents/MacOS/TextEdit
real    0m14.619s
user    0m1.257s
sys     0m0.180s
```

This is 14 seconds of clock time, one second in user space, and less than a second in the kernel.

The C shell has its own version of time that gives more information:

```
% time /Applications/TextEdit.app/Contents/MacOS/TextEdit
2.515u 0.226s 0:15.01 18.1% 0+0k 22+43io 0pf+0w
```

This is 2.5 seconds in user space, 0.2 seconds in kernel space, and fifteen seconds clock time. The 18.1% is a utilization percentage: the ratio of user + system times to real time. Following the time information is memory information: shared + unshared memory usage, input + output operations, number of pagefaults and swaps. OS X seems not to report the shared + unshared memory usage.

time is very handy when comparing optimizations. Run a baseline or two with **time**, make the optimization, then try **time** again. If you are optimizing CPU usage and discover CPU time figures going up, you should reconsider that particular optimization.

dtruss

Many Unix systems have a utility that will show all of the system calls a program makes. On Solaris, it is called **truss**; on Linux, it's **strace**. Mac OS X 10.4 has **ktrace** (kernel tracing), and Mac OS X 10.5 and later have a similar utility, **dtruss**, based on DTrace.

dtruss requires root privileges to run because DTrace requires them. Run it like this:

```
$ sudo dtruss ls
```

This will generate a couple of hundred lines of output, like

```
SYSCALL(args)     = return
getpid(0x7FFF5FBFF600, 0x7FFFFFE00050, 0x0)    = 9234 0
open_nocancel("/dev/urandom\0", 0x0, 0x0)    = 3 0
read_nocancel(0x3, "...", 0x6C)    = 108 0
close_nocancel(0x3)    = 0 0
issetugid(0x100000000, 0x7FFF5FBFF8C8, 0x7FFF5FC40530)    = 0 0
geteuid(0x100000000, 0x7FFF5FBFF8C8, 0x0)    = 0 0
...
```

The output is not terribly easy to read, but there is a lot of information there. As **ls** started up, it called **getpid()**, which returned the value 9234, the process ID for **ls**. After the function exited, errno was zero. If there was an error, **dtruss** would print a result like this:

```
stat64("grausenstein\0", 0x7FFF5FBFEFB0, 0x1)    = -1 Err#2
```

with a return value of -1, and errno set to 2.

Being able to see the system call traffic can be a great debugging aid, especially if you have a program that will not start. You can see if the program is trying to load a missing shared library or if it needs some configuration file that is not supplied.

System call tracking can be a performance-tuning aid, too. You might discover a lot of one-byte writes that can be coalesced into a single operation, you may have given a bad timeout to **kevent()** so that it returns a lot sooner than you expect, or you can see why your program is blocking unexpectedly.

fs_usage and sc_usage

fs_usage and **sc_usage** are programs run as the root user that also show system call activity. **fs_usage** shows file system information, and **sc_usage** shows system call information.

Here is BigShow, the Big Nerd Ranch slide show application, about to start paging through slides:

```
$ sudo fs_usage
password:
18:38:06 open   /Preferences/com.apple.dock.plist 0.00005   BigShow
18:38:06 fstat                                     0.00000   BigShow
18:38:06 read                                      0.00029   BigShow
18:38:06 close                                     0.00002   BigShow
18:38:06 open   com.apple.dock.0003931024a6.plist 0.00015   BigShow
18:38:06 PAGE_IN                                   0.00070 W BigShow
18:38:06 open   /Library/Preferences/Network       0.00008   BigShow
18:38:06 open   com.apple.systempreferences.plist 0.00005   BigShow
```

Part of Cocoa is looking at the plist for the dock, presumably for getting size and location information so that it can properly place a window. You can see the open, a stat to get the size of the file, the file being read, and its close. Unlike **dtruss**, there is not an easy way to correlate specific calls like a **read()** with the file descriptor it is using, but **fs_usage** does show you how much time it took. **fs_usage** can be run on a system-wide basis, which can be handy if you have a problem that is slowing the entire machine down. **fs_usage** is also useful when you have a program that accesses the hard drive unexpectedly and you want to track down who is responsible.

One really snazzy feature of **fs_usage** can be seen when used on applications that make Carbon file-system calls. If you set the environment variable DYLD_IMAGE_SUFFIX to _debug, **fd_usage** will show the Carbon calls being made. Here is a peek at an old copy of Mozilla running:

```
18:34:38 GetCatInfo                            0.000174   LaunchCFMApp
18:34:38 PBMakeFSSpec  (0, 0x0, 0x0, 0x0)                 LaunchCFMApp
18:34:38 getattrlist   .vol/280763/Mozilla.app 0.000032   LaunchCFMApp
18:34:38 PBMakeFSSpec                           0.000064   LaunchCFMApp
18:34:38 GetCatInfo    (-100, 0x0, 0x0, 0x0)              LaunchCFMApp
18:34:38 getattrlist   .vol/280763/Mozilla.app 0.000046   LaunchCFMApp
```

sc_usage shows system calls for a program in a manner like **top**, with a continually updating display. Here is a snapshot from Safari:

```
Safari      12 preemptions  189 context switches   8 threads    16:05:42
             0 faults       706 system calls                     0:00:07
```

```
TYPE                          NUMBER      CPU_TIME   WAIT_TIME
----------------------------------------------------------------------
System        Idle                                   00:06.608(00:00.922)
System        Busy                                   00:00.368(00:00.065)
Safari        Usermode                  00:00.109

mach_msg_trap                 2004(382)   00:00.013  00:17.878(00:02.978) 3
kevent                        20(3)       00:00.000  00:05.531(00:01.005) W
semwait_signal                2(1)        00:00.000  00:05.496(00:01.003) W
select                        13          00:00.000  00:05.076(00:01.004) W

CURRENT_TYPE          LAST_PATHNAME_WAITED_FOR        CUR_WAIT_TIME THRD# PRI
----------------------------------------------------------------------
mach_msg_trap                                         00:00.016     0     46
mach_msg_trap                                         00:00.150     1     46
semwait_signal                                        00:00.496     2     47
kevent                                                00:00.481     3     49
workq_ops                                             00:00.478     4     47
select                                                00:01.391     5     46
mach_msg_trap                                         00:01.391     6     62
bsdthread_terminate                                   00:05.019     7     47
```

The `CPU_TIME` column is the amount of CPU time consumed, and `WAIT_TIME` is the absolute time the process waits.

If you think you have I/O performance problems, these two programs can help you track down the specific calls that could be causing problems.

top

Unix systems are complex beasts composed of multiple programs interacting. Sometimes performance problems manifest as overall system slowness while each program looks just fine in isolation. The **dtruss** and **sc_usage** utilities are useful for monitoring system calls in a particular program. **top**, on the other hand, can be used to monitor all the programs on the system. Running **top** without arguments will show the familiar OS information (memory distributions, load average). By default, it orders programs by launch order (most recent program listed first). This is useful if you are monitoring a recently launched program. The `-u` flag will sort the list by CPU usage.

top can also count and show system-wide events. top `-e` shows VM (virtual memory), network activity, disk activity, and messaging stats:

```
$ top -e

Processes: 70 total, 4 running, 66 sleeping, 260 threads        16:09:30
Load Avg: 0.19, 0.28, 0.24  CPU usage: 6.27% user, 5.51% sys, 88.20% idle
SharedLibs: 7424K resident, 7276K data, 0B linkedit.
MemRegions: 9361 total, 451M resident, 17M private, 290M shared.
PhysMem: 798M wired, 1062M active, 427M inactive, 2287M used, 1809M free.
VM: 168G vsize, 1041M framework vsize, 339589(0) pageins, 278055(0) pageouts.
Networks: packets: 2550949/3311M in, 1667316/160M out.
Disks: 561048/8214M read, 976911/21G written.

PID   COMMAND      %CPU TIME      #TH  #WQ #POR #MRE RPRVT RSHRD RSIZE  VPRVT
9317  top          3.8  00:00.63  1/1  0   24   33   920K  244K  1496K  17M
9316- WebKitPlug   0.3  00:03.47  6    2   110  245  9584K 30M   15M    49M
9306  Safari       0.2  00:12.02  11   2   167  533  97M   53M   153M   265M
9299  csh          0.0  00:00.04  1    0   15   26   612K  592K  1160K  17M
```

```
9268   mdworker     0.0   00:00.36 3    1   50    77   4388K   19M    12M     29M
9202   bash         0.0   00:00.03 1    0   17    25   320K    244K   976K    9576K
9198   csh          0.0   00:00.02 1    0   17    26   580K    592K   1164K   9648K
9197   login        0.0   00:00.02 1    0   22    54   472K    312K   1608K   10M
9180   ssh          0.0   00:00.04 1    0   22    25   508K    244K   1812K   9588K
8900   Preview      0.0   00:16.27 2    1   125   268  20M     73M    45M     28M
8886   WebKitPlug   0.0   00:00.01 2    2   28    51   544K    244K   988K    40M
8850   Activity M   0.0   00:35.63 2    1   106   243  5360K   75M    15M     25M
8700   VDCAssista   0.0   00:00.15 4    1   90    73   384K    19M    3104K   23M
8697-  Snak         1.5   07:03.51 5/1  1   192   232  3788K   43M    11M     40M
```

There is a lot of information here. 70 processes, 260 threads system-wide. Shared libraries take about 7 megabytes of memory, 1.8 gigs of physical memory free, 168 gigs of virtual memory allocated, network and disk I/Os. Each process has information such as the number of threads, work queues, mach ports, and memory regions. Resize your terminal window to see more columns, such as virtual size, process state, page faults, bsd system calls made, etc.

top -e shows cumulative output, while **top -d** will show things in a delta mode. The update interval is one second. That can be changed by using the -s flag to control the number of seconds between intervals.

Stochastic profiling

One useful low-tech tool is "stochastic profiling," where you run the program in the debugger and interrupt it occasionally to see what is on the call stack. If you see the same function(s) on the stack over and over again, you know where to start looking. This technique is handy if you are on a platform or in a situation where traditional performance tools are not available or do not work. Plus, it's fast and easy, especially if you are already running your program in a debugger.

sample

You can do some profiling from the command-line to answer quick-and-dirty "what is happening here?" kinds of questions. The **sample** program will sample a process at 10-millisecond intervals and then build a snapshot of what the program was doing. You can give sample a pid or give it the partial name of a program:

```
$ sample iTunes 5
Sampling process 216 each 10 msecs 500 times
Sample analysis of process 216 written file /tmp/iTunes_216.sample.txt
```

The resulting trace file shows a bunch of call stacks, one for each thread, along with the number of times it found those particular functions on a call stack. Here's an example of one thread that is waiting in a run loop.

```
434 Thread_1103
  434 _pthread_body
    434 dyld_stub_binding_helper
      434 CFRunLoopRun
        434 CFRunLoopRunSpecific
          434 __CFRunLoopRun
            434 mach_msg
              434 mach_msg_trap
                434 mach_msg_trap
```

This is the same output you get when sampling processes in Activity Monitor.

Precise Timing with mach_absolute_time()

Command-line tools are a great place to benchmark snippets of code, which is useful for those cases where you can isolate an algorithm or a programming technique out of your full application. A dozen-line or a couple-hundred-line command-line tool is a much more tractable problem than a million-line application. Not every problem can be put into a little benchmark, but enough of them can to make it a useful technique.

The nice thing about command-line programs is you can use the **time** command to get absolute figures of the running time of the program making it easy to compare and contrast changes you make to your target program.

But sometimes the **time** command does not have enough granularity. You might want more precise timing, or you may just be interested in timing a specific part of your program. You might not be interested in the time it takes to load the data to feed your algorithm. If loading the data takes 3 times as long as it takes the algorithm to run, you will want to do timing inside of the program yourself.

Mach, Mac OS X's kernel, provides some functions you can use for precise timing. **mach_absolute_time()** reads the CPU time base register and reports the value back to you. This time base register serves as the basis for other time measurements in the OS:

```
uint64_t mach_absolute_time (void);
```

mach_absolute_time() returns values based on the CPU time, so it is not directly usable for getting time values because you do not know what time span each increment of the counter represents.

To translate **mach_absolute_time()**'s results to nanoseconds, use **mach_timebase_info()** to get the scaling of **mach_absolute_time()**'s values:

```
kern_return_t mach_timebase_info (mach_timebase_info_t info);
```

Where mach_timebase_info_t is a pointer to this struct:

```
struct mach_timebase_info {
    uint32_t    numer;
    uint32_t    denom;
};
```

mach_timebase_info() fills in the struct with the fraction to multiply the result of **mach_absolute_time()** by to calculate nanoseconds. Multiply the result of **mach_absolute_time()** by numer and divide by denom.

Example 10.2 shows how to use these two functions. The code times how long it takes to call **mach_timebase_info()** and **printf()**. For real-life code, you would want to put something more interesting in there to time.

Example 10.2   machtime.m

```
// machtime.m -- exercise mach_absolute_time()

#import <mach/mach_time.h>  // for mach_absolute_time() and friends
```

```
#import <stdio.h>         // for printf()
#import <stdlib.h>        // for abort()

// gcc -g -Wall -o machtime machtime.m

int main (void) {
    uint64_t start = mach_absolute_time ();

    mach_timebase_info_data_t info;

    if (mach_timebase_info (&info) == KERN_SUCCESS) {
        printf ("scale factor : %u / %u\n", info.numer, info.denom);
    } else {
        printf ("mach_timebase_info failed\n");
        abort ();
    }

    uint64_t end = mach_absolute_time ();
    uint64_t elapsed = end - start;
    uint64_t nanos = elapsed * info.numer / info.denom;

    printf ("elapsed time was %lld nanoseconds\n", nanos);

    return 0;

} // main
```

And here it is in action:

```
$ ./machtime
scale factor : 1 / 1
elapsed time was 55055 nanoseconds
$ ./machtime
scale factor : 1 / 1
elapsed time was 95363 nanoseconds
$ ./machtime
scale factor : 1 / 1
elapsed time was 46839 nanoseconds
```

On this system, a 2010 Macbook Pro, the numerator and denominator of the conversion are both one. Some older machines, such as the original TiBook, had the numerator of the conversion at 1,000,000,000 and the denominator at 24,965,716, resulting in a scale value of 40.05. So there were about 40 nanoseconds for each increment of `mach_absolute_time()`.

Outside of the second run, it takes about 50,000 nanoseconds, or 50 microseconds to do the work between the two timings. So what's up with that middle run being twice as long as the others? When you are dealing with time values this short, *anything* can perturb them. Maybe some dynamic library lookup was necessary for that second run. Maybe iTunes was running and was loading a new track. Maybe Time Machine kicked in. For a real benchmark, you would run it for a longer period of time to hide those small one-time-only blips. And of course, you would run the benchmark a couple of times to get a good average and iron out the noise.

GUI Tools

Mac OS X comes with a number of GUI performance tools which are a good deal more powerful and easier to use than the command-line tools.

Activity Monitor

Each Mac OS X system includes the Activity Monitor application in the system's Utilities folder.

Figure 10.6   Activity Monitor

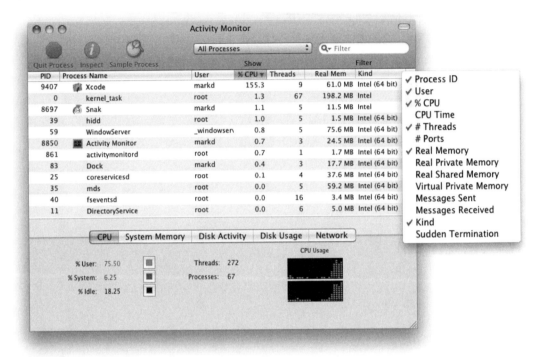

Activity Monitor shows basic information for each process in the table view, and you can pop up the contextual menu to dig into lower-level information. The pane at the bottom of the window lets you see colorful charts and graphs concerning the system as a whole. The Sample Process button runs the **sample** command and puts the output into a window. Sampling is handy for seeing what a locked-up process is blocked on.

Instruments

Instruments is Apple's suite of profiling tools. The Instruments application is itself a generic program allowing you to configure sets of individual tools, called instruments, to trace whatever information you specifically want to learn about your application. Many of Instruments' instruments can profile the system as a whole in addition to focusing on a single process.

You can run Instruments directly from the Finder, or you can choose to Profile in Xcode. You can edit the Profile scheme in Xcode to pick a default template to use when profiling, or you can have Instruments prompt you on launch. You can also run the **instruments** command-line tool to record a performance profile without running the GUI.

Window layout

The Instruments user interface was inspired by Garage Band but without the wood-grain window treatment (bummer). Figure 10.7 shows a blank template with the Leaks and Allocations instruments already dragged over from the Library window.

Figure 10.7 Instruments and Library windows

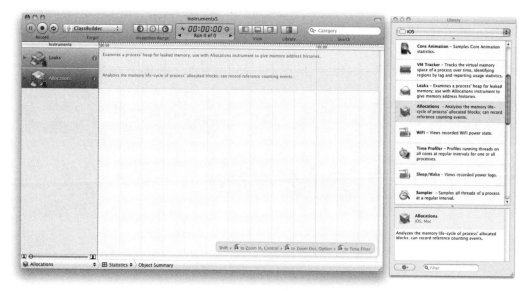

The left side of the Instruments window holds the different instruments that will be used to record profile activity. The track pane in the middle is where profile data will be displayed. The bottom part of the window shows more detailed information about a recorded trace, described a bit later.

The Toolbar

The toolbar at the top of the window has controls for recording a profile, controls for pausing it, and a loop control used when playing back user interface actions.

The Target menu selects the trace target for the document. The target tells Instruments which process or processes to gather information about. "All Processes" tells Instruments to collect system-wide information. Not all instruments support system-wide data collection.

The inspection range controls let you narrow your focus to a particular span of time. Perhaps you have to fiddle with your application a bit before you get to the part you really want to profile. You can adjust the inspection range to exclude the fiddly part. To set the inspection range, you move the playback head to the beginning of your interesting time range and click the left-hand Inspection Range button. Then move the playback head to the end of the range and click the right-hand button. Option-dragging in the trace area will also set the inspection range.

The LCD-style screen in the middle of the toolbar is the Time/Run control. It shows how much time has elapsed while recording or how long a completed trace is. The "Run X of Y" buttons let you navigate between multiple profiling runs done in the current session. The view buttons open and close various side panels, just like the similar-looking icons in Xcode do. From left to right, they control the instruments pane (left), the detail pane (bottom), and the extended detail pane (right).

Looking at memory leaks

Figure 10.8 shows the Instruments window after it has collected some data. The blank template was used with the Leaks and Allocations instruments dragged over from the library. The target application is Cycling Fusion's ClassBuilder™ app, which I was working on at the time this chapter was being written.

Figure 10.8   Instruments window after running the application

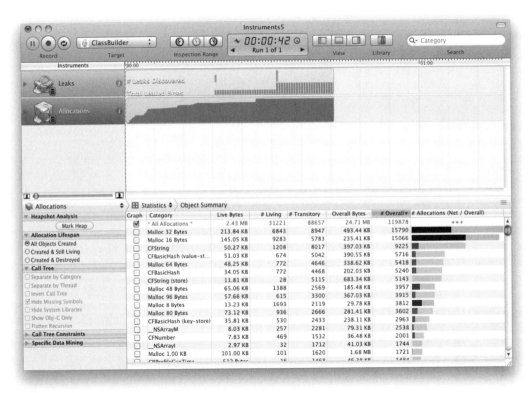

Notice that the track pane has some content now. The Leaks instrument has a stacked bar chart with the number of leaks discovered (top) and the count of leaked bytes (bottom). The Allocations instrument shows the amount of allocated memory. The Leaks instrument takes memory snapshots at relatively large intervals, defaulting to ten seconds, which explains why the leak markers do not correspond to growth in the allocation trace.

Scrubbing the playhead back and forth in the timeline shows little "inspection flags," tooltip windows that show data in the trace for that point in time. Figure 10.9 shows that the Leaks instrument found 29 individual leaks responsible for 4.62KB of leaked memory. The total application memory footprint due to memory allocation is about 2 megabytes.

Figure 10.9   Playhead detail popups.

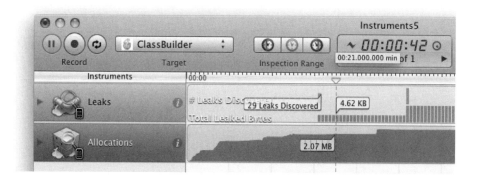

The detail panel is visible at the bottom of the window. The Allocations tool is currently selected in Figure 10.8, so the details panel is showing information about the allocations, including some colored bar graphs that show current and total allocations for different sizes of memory blocks and different kinds of objects.

Now let's figure out where the memory leaks actually happened. Figure 10.10 has the Leaks instrument selected. The details panel by default will show you everything it can, but you can narrow the timeline down with the Inspection Range to a particular span of time, and the details panel will update itself accordingly.

Figure 10.10   Detail panel showing leaked blocks

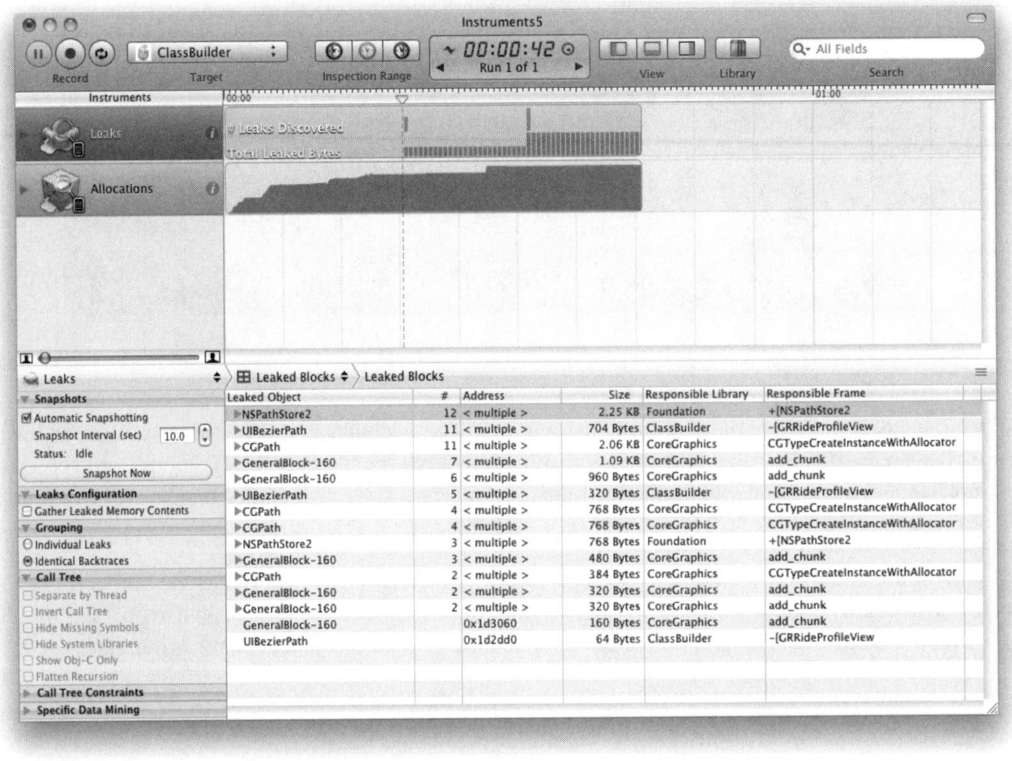

The bottom half of the window is broken up into two panes. The left pane holds various instrument-specific controls that can be used to modify the display in the details pane. They don't modify the data that has been collected, just how it is presented.

There are two Xcode-style jump bars in the window. The one in the instrument pane lets you choose which instrument you are looking at. It currently displays the Leaks instrument, but you can get a list of all the instruments in the document by clicking on it. You can also click the instrument trace directly to change the contents of the detail pane. The detail pane on the right has a jump bar that lets you change the view of the data. As you dig deeper into the data, the jump bar will let you back out to a higher-level view.

The detail area shows a lot of information: the kind of leaked memory, whether it's an Objective-C object or a chunk of memory, how many of those were leaked, how much memory was leaked, which library allocated the memory, and what the function or method actually caused the allocation.

Even though Foundation and CoreGraphics are listed as the responsible libraries, this does not mean the library itself is mishandling memory. It just means that Foundation or CoreGraphics allocated memory on behalf of the code that ultimately caused the leak. There are several graphics-related classes and libraries in the leak list: **UIBezierPath**, **CGPath**, and the CoreGraphics framework. The leak is probably graphics-related.

Figure 10.11 shows that the disclosure triangle next to **UIBezierPath** has been clicked, revealing a list of individually leaked objects. There are 11 objects for a total of 704 bytes. The arrow-in-a-circle button, properly called the focus button or the follow link button, replaces the contents of the detail pane with additional information about the object you are focusing on. Clicking on the focus button next to the first **UIBezierPath** takes you to Figure 10.12, which has the allocation history for memory located at address 0x1c3850. Over the course of time, some strings have lived here, an **NSThread** private class, a **CFData**, and some hash tables. The last allocation is most interesting one: a **malloc()** that was never freed. This is one of the leaks.

Figure 10.11   Individual leaked memory blocks

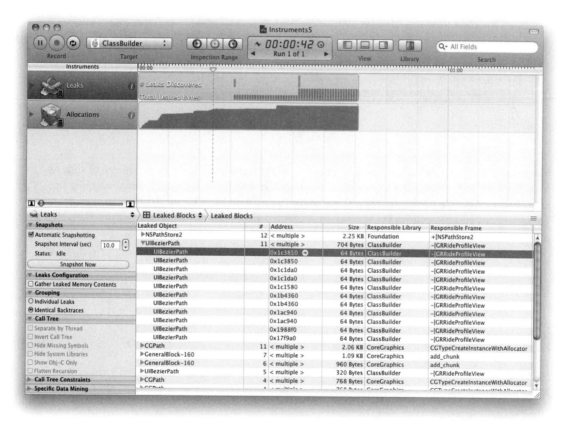

Figure 10.12   Memory allocation history

#	Category	Event Type	Timest...	RefCt	Address	Size	Responsible Lib...	Responsible Caller
6	CFString	Malloc	00:10.38...	1	0x1c3850	32	Foundation	-[NSPlaceholderString ini...
7	CFString	Free	00:10.38...	0	0x1c3850	-32	Foundation	-[NSPlaceholderString ini...
8	CFString	Malloc	00:10.38...	1	0x1c3850	32	Foundation	-[NSPlaceholderString ini...
9	CFString	Free	00:10.38...	0	0x1c3850	-32	Foundation	-[NSPlaceholderString ini...
10	CFString	Malloc	00:10.38...	1	0x1c3850	32	Foundation	-[NSPlaceholderString ini...
11	CFString	Free	00:10.38...	0	0x1c3850	-32	Foundation	-[NSPlaceholderString ini...
12	_NSThreadPerformInfo	Malloc	00:10.38...	1	0x1c3850	32	Foundation	-[NSObject(NSThreadPerf...
13	_NSThreadPerformInfo	Free	00:10.66...	0	0x1c3850	-32	Foundation	-[_NSThreadPerformInfo ...
14	CFData (store)	Realloc	00:10.68...	1	0x1c3850	64	liblockdown.dylib	lockconn_send_message
15	CFData (store)	Realloc	00:10.68...	1	0x1abc50	256	liblockdown.dylib	lockconn_send_message
16	CFData (store)	Realloc	00:10.68...	1	0xba7a00	1024	liblockdown.dylib	lockconn_send_message
17	CFData (store)	Free	00:10.68...	0	0xba7a00	-1024	liblockdown.dylib	lockconn_send_message
18	CFBasicHash (value-store)	Malloc	00:10.68...	1	0x1c3850	64	liblockdown.dylib	lockconn_receive_message
19	CFBasicHash (value-store)	Free	00:10.68...	0	0x1c3850	-64	liblockdown.dylib	send_get_value
20	CFBasicHash (key-store)	Malloc	00:10.68...	1	0x1c3850	64	liblockdown.dylib	lockconn_receive_message
21	CFBasicHash (key-store)	Free	00:10.68...	0	0x1c3850	-64	liblockdown.dylib	send_goodbye
22	CFString	Malloc	00:10.68...	1	0x1c3850	64	Foundation	-[NSPlaceholderString ini...
23	CFString	Free	00:10.68...	0	0x1c3850	-64	Foundation	-[NSAutoreleasePool release]
24	UIBezierPath	Malloc	00:10.69...	1	0x1c3850	64	ClassBuilder	-[GRRideProfileView upda...

The extended detail panel was opened by clicking on the right-hand View icon. The panel slides in from the right and shows a stack trace relating to what is selected in the detail view. Selecting the bottom entry from the allocation history will show the stack trace in Figure 10.13. The stack trace has library classes grayed out with the application's classes, or at least those classes and functions that have debug symbols, in black. It is pretty obvious who the culprit is.

Figure 10.13   Object leak stack trace

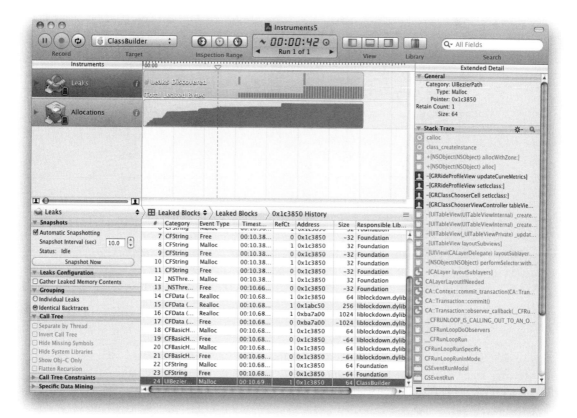

Most of the time you do not really care what toolbox classes are on the stack. They are often just implementation detail noise. You can use the slider at the bottom to pare down the stack to more interesting stack frames, typically those at the boundaries of libraries. Figure 10.14 shows the full stack trace on the left with the reduced stack trace on the right.

Figure 10.14   Full and reduced stack traces

-[GRRideProfileView updateCurveMetrics] is the source of the leak. To actually see the code, double-click its entry in the stack trace. The details panel will show you the code, as shown in Figure 10.15.

Figure 10.15   Leak with source code

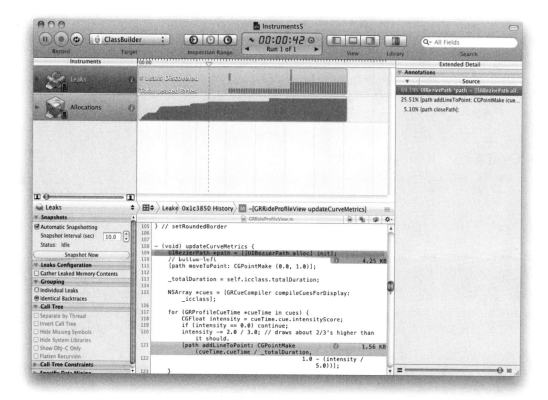

The code allocates and initializes a **UIBezierPath** and then never releases it. This is a classic Cocoa memory leak, which oddly enough did not get caught by the static analyzer. Notice that Instruments highlights two lines in the source code: the **alloc/init** leaked 4.25KB, while **-addLineToPoint:** leaked another 1.56KB of memory. You may be able to see a tiny dot in the trough of the scrollbar, just below the thumb. That shows there is another leak in the source file.

Earlier, Figure 10.11 indicated that **UIBezierPath** leaked 704 bytes in 11 objects, and now the source listing is saying it has leaked 4.25KB. Why the discrepancy? The 704 bytes was memory leaked just for **UIBezierPath** instances, not for any helper objects or additional blocks of memory they might have used. Objects tend to use lots of other objects, so the actual amount of leaked memory from this kind of error is actually much greater.

More Memory: Heapshots

Apple has a lot of memory-related instruments and features, mainly because memory issues are common when using C-based languages. Heapshots are another way of looking at and analyzing memory usage patterns.

The Leaks instrument is useful for finding memory and object leaks in your code, as you saw earlier. But sometimes your program's memory usage grows without objects being leaked in the classic sense: having a non-zero reference count and nobody pointing to them. Sometimes objects can still be retained and pointed to but are being held onto unnecessarily. Perhaps something is being cached too aggressively. Maybe an object was put into a collection and then forgotten. Apple calls these "abandoned" objects rather than "leaked" objects. In a way, they are worse than leaked objects because it is not obvious they are sitting around unused.

The Allocations instrument's Mark Heap button lets you take a snapshot of the current state of the dynamic allocation heap, shown in figure Figure 10.16. The first click tells Instruments to take a baseline reading of your memory usage. Subsequent clicks will add an entry into the details pane, which shows any new objects added to the heap.

Figure 10.16   Heapshot button

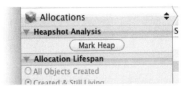

To use heap shots, warm up your application and take a baseline. Then perform an operation, ideally one which should leave the state of the world untouched, and then mark the heap again. There should be good reasons for any leftover objects. If not, you probably have memory being abandoned.

Instruments puts a little flag into the timeline when you take a heapshot, shown in Figure 10.17. Clicking a flag displays a pop-up window containing more details, although the heapshot flags do not have any additional information. Other instruments also add flags to indicate interesting events, and you can add your own by Option-clicking in the timeline.

Figure 10.17   Heapshot flags in the timeline

Another use for heapshots is to sanity-check your memory usage. Take a baseline, navigate to part of your app, and take another snapshot. Evaluate memory usage to make sure it is sane. For example, you might have a screen that displays 20 different objects that your app edits, like your stuffed animal collection. A heapshot showing 20 or 40 new strings makes sense, with a title for each object, and maybe some extra description. If you end up having 200 or 400 new strings, you might have a problem.

Figure 10.18 shows a ClassBuilder run that has had a baseline and two heapshots made. These correspond to the three flags shown in Figure 10.17. The baseline was made after the application had launched and was sitting idle, and then an operation was performed and another heapshot taken. This had 373KB of heap growth and 8000 new objects (yikes!). The operation was performed again, another heapshot taken, with a growth of 6KB and 100 new objects.

Figure 10.18   List of heapshots

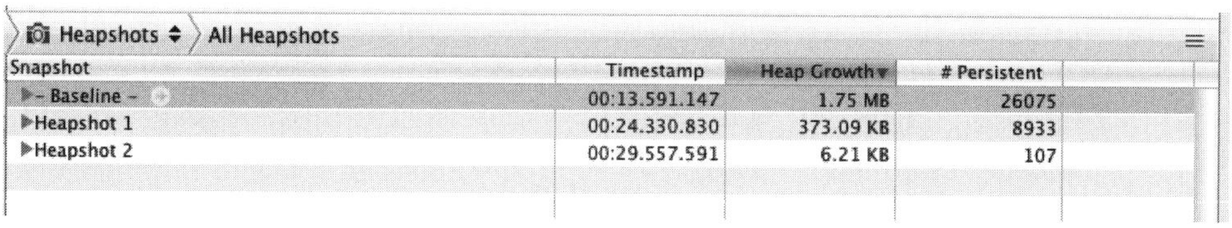

That is quite a disparity between the two operations.

Figure 10.19 shows the first heapshot expanded. 272 out of 373KB were allocated as "non-objects," which are chunks of memory obtained by `malloc()`. Expanding the disclosure triangle shows a list of the blocks of memory that are new.

Figure 10.19   Blocks left over after first run

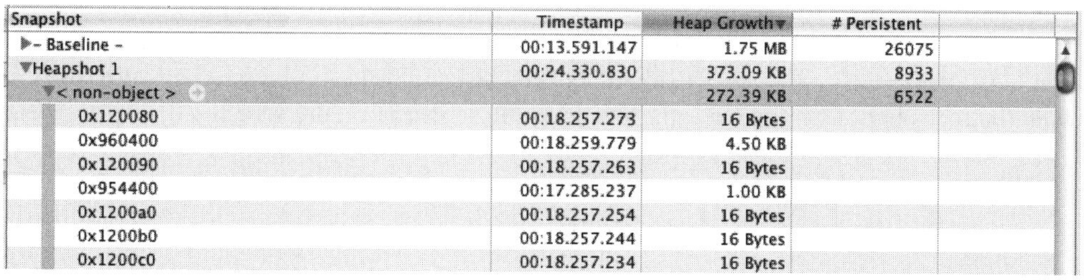

Clicking the focus button on the "<non-object>" line shows more detail, as shown in Figure 10.20. You can see that there are a lot of font-related calls. 12KB for some glyphs, 8KB for more glyphs, and so on. The bulk of the new memory being consumed looks like it is related to the fonts being used in the ClassBuilder feature that was being exercised. It's good to look at your code (and run the static analyzer again) to make sure you're not over-retaining font objects. In this case, it looks like that this memory growth is due to one-time font usage by the toolkit, so it is not an application problem.

Figure 10.20   List of leaked non-object blocks

#	Object Address	Category	Creation Time	Live	Size▼	Responsible Lib...	Responsible Caller
0	0x962400	Malloc 12.50 KB	00:18.161.890	•	12800	CoreGraphics	CGFontGetGlyphsForGlyph...
1	0x936800	Malloc 8.50 KB	00:18.259.845	•	8704	CoreGraphics	CGFontCreateGlyphPath
2	0x95c000	Malloc 8.00 KB	00:18.114.928	•	8192	CoreGraphics	CGFontGetGlyphsForGlyph...
3	0x957c00	Malloc 8.00 KB	00:17.660.689	•	8192	libsystem_c.dylib	tzsetwall_basic
4	0x95e800	Malloc 7.00 KB	00:18.161.653	•	7168	CoreGraphics	CGFontGetGlyphsForGlyph...
5	0x95ae00	Malloc 4.50 KB	00:18.114.772	•	4608	CoreGraphics	CGFontGetGlyphsForGlyph...
6	0x960400	Malloc 4.50 KB	00:18.259.779	•	4608	CoreGraphics	CGFontCreateGlyphPath
7	0x953a00	Malloc 2.50 KB	00:17.284.587	•	2560	CoreGraphics	CGFontCreateFontsWithPath
8	0x95e000	Malloc 2.00 KB	00:18.157.032	•	2048	CoreGraphics	CGFontCreateGlyphPath
9	0x955200	Malloc 2.00 KB	00:18.157.017	•	2048	CoreGraphics	CGFontCreateGlyphPath
10	0x953200	Malloc 2.00 KB	00:17.284.201	•	2048	CoreGraphics	CGFontCreateFontsWithPath
11	0x954c00	Malloc 1.50 KB	00:18.114.610	•	1536	CoreGraphics	CGFontStrikeCreate
12	0x412be00	Malloc 1.50 KB	00:17.357.061	•	1536	libsqlite3.dylib	sqlite3_extended_errcode
13	0x952800	Malloc 1.50 KB	00:17.917.917	•	1536	CoreGraphics	CGFontStrikeCreate
14	0x412a800	Malloc 1.50 KB	00:17.350.545	•	1536	libsqlite3.dylib	sqlite3_extended_errcode
15	0x951200	Malloc 1.50 KB	00:17.914.761	•	1536	CoreGraphics	CGFontStrikeCreate
16	0x957400	Malloc 1.50 KB	00:18.263.251	•	1536	CoreGraphics	CGFontStrikeCreate
17	0x956800	Malloc 1.50 KB	00:18.259.576	•	1536	CoreGraphics	CGFontGetGlyphBBoxesFor...

The second heap shot is more reasonable, weighing in at about 6 KB. The complete set of new objects is shown in Figure 10.21. There are 96 new non-objects for 5.76 KB, a **GSEvent** which is a low-level version of a **UIEvent**, a couple of event-related hash tables, and some core animation layer stuff. Following the focus button on the non-objects shows the screen in Figure 10.22

Figure 10.21   Leftover blocks from second heapshot

Snapshot	Timestamp	Heap Growth▼	# Persistent
▶ – Baseline – ⊙	00:13.591.147	1.75 MB	26075
▶Heapshot 1	00:24.330.830	373.09 KB	8933
▼Heapshot 2 ⊙	00:29.557.591	6.21 KB	107
▶< non-object >		5.76 KB	96
▶GSEvent		128 Bytes	1
▶__NSArrayM		64 Bytes	2
▶UIViewControllerWrapperView		48 Bytes	1
▶CFBasicHash		48 Bytes	1
▶CALayer		48 Bytes	1
▶UITouchData		48 Bytes	1
▶CALayerArray		32 Bytes	1
▶CFBasicHash (value-store)		32 Bytes	2
▶CFBasicHash (key-store)		16 Bytes	1

Figure 10.22   Leaking layers stack trace

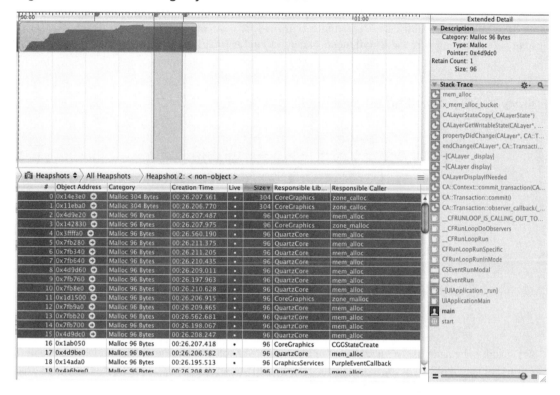

The top 16 objects come from the Quartz drawing frameworks, so they may be related. When you select multiple objects in a detail view, Instruments tries to determine a common stack trace, as shown on the right. Clicking each individual memory allocation shows a similar stack, with a lot of Core Animation calls lying around, and things that are called by a runloop timer function.

The particular feature exercised in the app does not directly use Core Animation, but there were animations happening as **UINavigationController** moved views around. So these new objects are considered to be leftover implementation details from the toolkit animations and not a sign of imminent doom. Perhaps the user took a heapshot before the animation had completed, or the toolkit is keeping layers around as an optimization for the next time an animation is made.

Time Profiler

The Time Profiler instrument measures CPU usage by your program and, optionally, across the entire system. The time profiler samples your program or the system on a regular basis, measured in milli- or micro- seconds, and records the stack traces it finds. Once you have accumulated enough of these stack traces, you can see what functions and methods appear on the stacks most often. This is the code that is taking the most time. If you are tracking down a performance bottleneck, this is a good place to start looking.

Launching Instruments from Xcode and choosing the Time Profiler template only profiles your application. A lot of times this is sufficient because performance problems, such as inefficient algorithms and just doing too much work, can be found. However, iOS, like Mac OS, is based on multiple cooperating processes, and many of Apple's frameworks are actually just thin communication layers that talk to background daemons. Sometimes work you do in your application can lead to extra work done by other processes, and sampling system-wide is necessary track down problems. You select system-wide profiling with the Target menu, shown in Figure 10.23.

Figure 10.23   Profiling all processes

ClassBuilder once again is the victim, this time to the Time Profiler instrument. One of the features of the program is to build an exercise class based on an iTunes playlist, and the instructor building a class needs to know how long each playlist is in order to pick an appropriate one. Unfortunately, as of iOS 4, the Media Player framework does not provide playlist duration as a built-in attribute, so ClassBuilder has to iterate over every song in a playlist, get the song duration, and sum them.

This takes a considerable amount of time in practice, blocking the main thread long enough for the watchdog timer to kill the app if the user has a lot of playlists. The time profiler helped show what was going wrong. Figure 10.24 shows a run with the trace showing some CPU activity at the beginning as the ClassBuilder UI was used to get to the screen where the playlist durations were calculated. You can see the CPU is pegged after the playlists start calculating.

Figure 10.24 Time Profiler instrument sample run

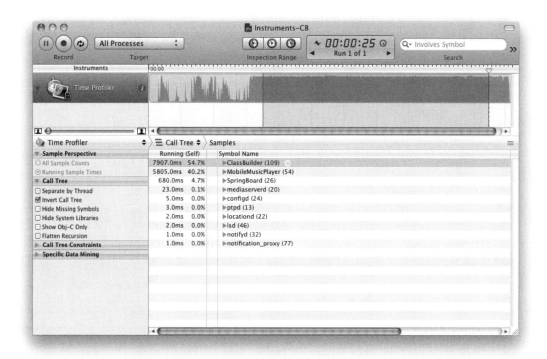

The detail view has some very interesting information in it even before you look at stack traces. ClassBuilder was responsible for about 55% of the sampled time, and the MobileMusicPlayer process accounted for 40%. That was unexpected. SpringBoard took some time as well, which is understandable because SpringBoard is responsible for compositing graphics on the screen. (The playlists, and the percentage of the playlist being calculated, were being displayed in a `UITableView` as their durations were calculated.)

It is interesting that MobileMusicPlayer is consuming so much processing power. One hypothesis is that the information for each song is stored in that process, and the Media Player framework uses interprocess communication to fetch the duration. There is no symbol information available for system processes so we can really only get detailed information from our own process. Expanding ClassBuilder's disclosure triangle shows the call tree as shown in Figure 10.25.

Figure 10.25 Time Profiler call tree

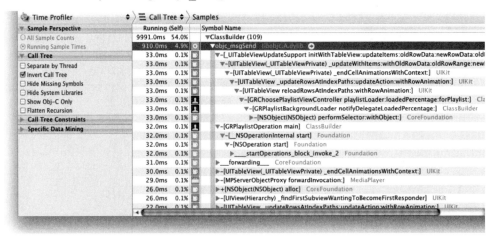

By default Instruments shows you the call tree "inverted." You see a method or function that has been "charged" with samples. Expanding the disclosure triangle for a particular call, say **objc_msgSend**, shows you the functions which make that call.

Figure 10.26 shows **objc_msgSend** expanded. You see a list of methods that have called **objc_msgSend()**, such as one from **UITableViewUpdateSupport** and another from **GRPlaylistOperation**, one of the ClassBuilder classes. You can then see what methods called them, and so on.

Figure 10.26 Expanding objc_msgSend to see its callers

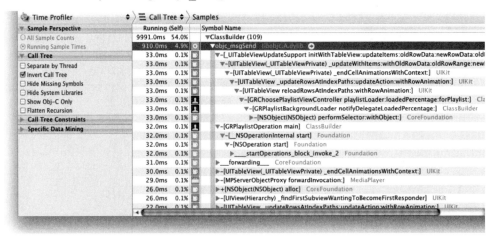

A regular, or "uninverted," call tree shows the top-level functions, such as **main**, and gives you the calling hierarchy, as shown in Figure 10.27. Here you can see **main()** called **UIApplicationMain**, which called **UIApplication**'s **_run**, and so on. Typically, the inverted call tree is more useful for sussing out performance issues.

Figure 10.27 Regular call tree

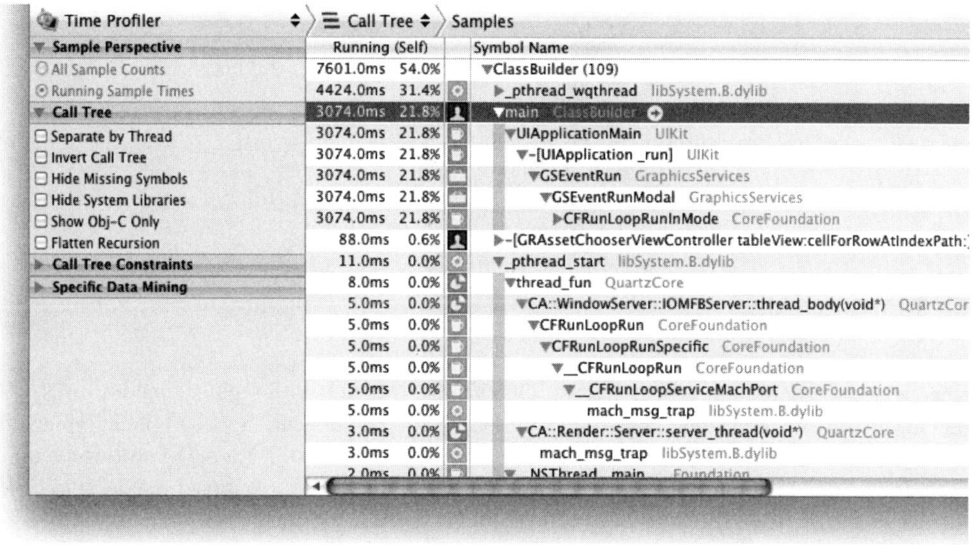

There is a lot of noise in this function list and too much low-level detail. To remove some of the noise, you can apply data mining, which "charges" time spent in a function to its callers. This removes lower-level details while giving you a better high-level overview. The two most useful forms of data mining are Hide System Libraries and Show Obj-C Only.

Hide System Libraries charges all code run in libraries to the functions that called into the libraries. If **-drawGroovyness** ended up spending four seconds in Core Graphics over the life of the trace, then after you click Hide System Libraries, **-drawGroovyness** will be shown as having consumed four more seconds, and all the Core Graphics calls will disappear. You might not be interested in the gory details of what Core Graphics spent its time on, but knowing that **-drawGroovyness** consumed a lot of processor time is information you can use to figure out how to optimize. Perhaps the method is just drawing too often or drawing a larger area than needed.

Figure 10.28 shows this trace with system libraries hidden. What's left is pretty much just application classes and functions. At the top is **GRMediaItem**'s **-duration** call. This jives with the hypothesis that fetching the song's durations is what is causing the performance problems.

Figure 10.28   Data mining by hiding system libraries

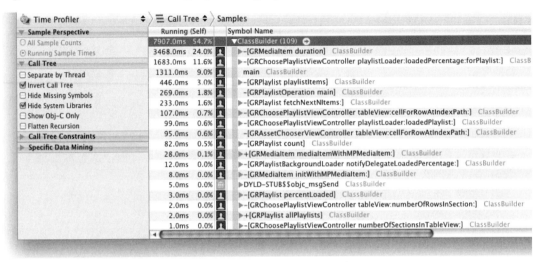

The other primary data mining setting is Show Obj-C Only. It removes all regular function calls, leaving Objective-C method calls. These calls will be from your application and Apple's frameworks. Figure 10.29 shows the call tree after turning on Show Obj-C Only, with a couple of entries having their disclosure triangles expanded. The top methods, the ones that take the most time, look to be IPC related: property list serialization called by a **CPDistributedMessagingCenter**. **NSArchiver** was called by **MPMediaPropertyPredicates** and **MPMediaQueries**, along with **CPDistributedMessagingCenter**. This last class is an Apple private class that deals with IPC, as indicated by the name.

Figure 10.29   Data mining by showing Objective-C only

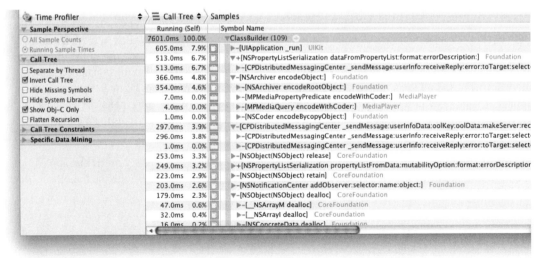

The original hypothesis of the time being consumed by IPC appears to be correct. Even though it seems like the application's hands are tied with regards to performance, further investigation showed that with real-life playlists created by instructors, there were a lot of repeated songs, e.g. favorite songs for warmup or cooldown. The durations of these songs were queried over and over again, triggering more IPC. The application already had a wrapper class around `MPMediaItems` to allow it to run in the simulator, so a cache was added for the song duration which reduced the amount of time calculating the playlists. Moving the calculations to a background thread using `NSOperation` made the user interface responsive again. As playlist durations were calculated, the main thread was informed, which then updated the UI.

Other Instruments

There are many more instruments that come with Instruments, and Apple is adding new ones regularly. Some instruments work on both iOS and Mac OS X, and some work on just one or the other. Instruments will complain if you try to use an instrument that is not appropriate for a given platform. Here is a sampling of some of the available instruments.

Memory

In addition to the Leaks and Allocations instruments you saw earlier, Instruments has a number of other memory-related instruments. These allow you to peek inside the garbage collector, see the virtual memory consumption of a process, track shared memory creation and destruction, and detect zombies, which are over-released objects that are subsequently messaged.

Automation

The Automation instrument is used to run test scripts against an application on a device. You write a JavaScript test script which drives the application, and then the Automation instrument uses the accessibility features of CocoaTouch to introspect and control the application. The scripts can test the running application and say "yes, the app passed this test" or "no, the app failed this test." The test results will show up in the Instruments trace.

Power

Power consumption is very important for iOS users. A user is cut off from the outside world if the device's battery dies in the middle of the day. Screen brightness, CPU usage, and the various radios (Cell, WiFi, BlueTooth, GPS) contribute to power drain on the device. The Energy Diagnostics template includes seven instruments, all of which are power-related. The Energy Usage instrument utilizes sensors close to the battery and shows the power drain. The CPU Usage instrument shows how much CPU is being used in four different classes of activity: graphics, audio processing, the foreground app, and the rest of the system. Graphics compositing happens in the Springboard process, and the media daemon handles audio.

The Display Brightness instrument shows how bright the screen is, based on user settings. You can use this to compare two different program runs and make sure the screen brightness is the same when comparing the power consumption. Sleep/Wake shows the transitions the device makes between sleeping and waking states.

Three radio-related instruments show the state of the Bluetooth, WiFi, and GPS radios. WiFi and Bluetooth show red when the user has configured them to be on, but these do not actually show when the radio is in use or not. GPS shows on/off state of the GPS receiver. If you run an app that uses Core Location and the framework decides to turn on the GPS, the GPS instrument will show red during those times. At this time, there is no instrument for the cellular network radio.

Important tip: you don't want to try to get an energy usage trace while the device is connected to a computer over USB. The battery will be charging causing your energy usage numbers to look absurdly low. You should turn on Power Logging in the Developer section of the Settings app and exercise the device. When you're done, hook up the device, open an Energy Diagnostics template, and choose Import Energy Diagnostics from Device from the File menu.

Figure 10.30 shows the various power-related instruments after running a trace. You can drag the playhead around to show the tooltip windows in the track area. You can see that the Bluetooth radio was turned off in the middle, the GPS was never on, and the display brightness was cranked all the way up.

Figure 10.30   The Power-oriented instruments

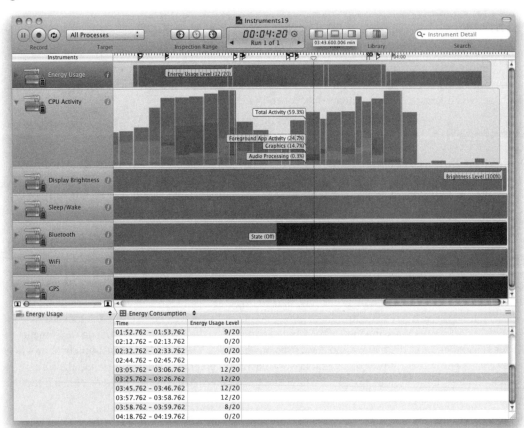

The Energy Usage instrument shows power consumption at the battery level, on a scale of 1 to 20. Apple states that the time to discharge a full battery at a power drain of 1 would be 20+ hours, a level of 10 would discharge a full battery in 10 hours, and a level of 20 would take less than one hour.

Finally the CPU Activity trace shows that where the playback head is positioned 0.3% of the CPU was spent on audio, 14.7% on graphics, the foreground app's processing is another 24.7%, for a total of 39.7% of the CPU. The total activity on the system was 59.3%, so other processes on the system account for 19.6% of the CPU usage. You could use the Time Profiler to see what the other parts of the system were doing.

Graphics

The Core Animation instrument shows you the current frames per second (FPS) that Core Animation is currently producing. In general, you want your FPS to be high, from 30 FPS up to the maximum of 60 FPS. The instrument reports the number of frames actually completed, not the total frame rate. For example, if your app produces 30 frames in half a second (60 FPS) and then stops, it will be reported as 30 FPS because only 30 frames were completed. Figure 10.31 shows a trace where the application had good animation performance, then a fairly low level. In this case, the application wasn't animating anything. Towards the end, you can see the app struggling at 15 FPS. The Core Animation template includes both the Core Animation and a Sampler instrument, allowing you to correlate CPU usage with animation speed issues.

Figure 10.31   Core Animation instrument

Core Animation also includes a Debug Options panel, as shown in Figure 10.32. The settings in this panel do not affect the data being collected but instead tell the device to do things to help you track down graphics performance issues. The first option, Color Blended Layers, is the option you will probably use most often. This puts a red overlay on layers that were drawn using blending, such as images with alpha and views that are marked as non-opaque. All other layers are drawn with a green overlay, as shown in Figure 10.33

Figure 10.32   Core Animation instrument debug options

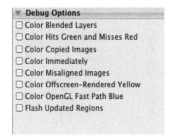

Figure 10.33   Core Animation instrument blended layer overlays

It may be difficult to tell in black and white printing, but the majority of the **UITableView** in the figure does not have any drawing issues, while the header of the screen has a number of views that are drawn non-opaquely. **UILabel**s are a pretty common source of blending warnings because they are non-opaque when dragged out of the Interface Builder library. You want to avoid non-opaque views in general on iOS. The system has to do extra compositing to draw them correctly. Opaque views can just be blasted straight to the screen without worrying about what is underneath them.

In addition to the Core Animation instrument, the OpenGL / OpenGLES Driver instruments give you a peek at your usage of OpenGL. Be sure to expand the extended detail panel on the right to get to all of the information the instruments are providing.

The OpenGLES Analyzer looks at your OpenGL usage, displays information in the track such as the number of GL calls, number of triangles rendered, and redundant state changes. The detail view has a set of warnings, telling you about things like redundant state calls, or if you are submitting vertices without using a VBO. The extended detail pane shows a textual recommendation, as well as the stack trace for the offending statement. This is shown in Figure 10.34.

Figure 10.34   The OpenGL Analyzer

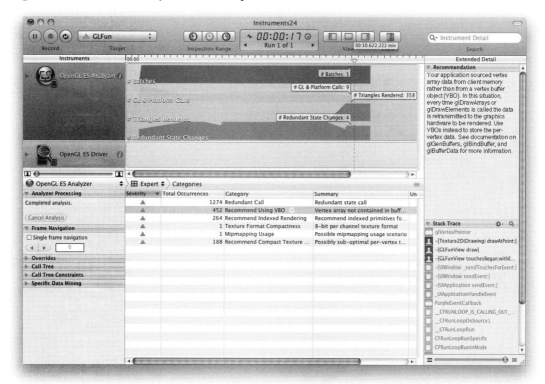

File System

The File Activity instrument traces when files are opened, closed, or statted, as well as when sockets and pipes are created. The Reads/Writes instrument tells you where all your reads and writes happen as well as how many bytes are actually read or written. It records the path (or socket) where the activity happened. File Attributes lets you know when any attributes of the file changed with the `chown()`, `chmod()` calls, and when they are changed indirectly, such as `open()` changing the last accessed time. Directory I/O tells you about directory activity, such as directory creation and unlinking, renaming, etc. Disk Monitor shows a trace of bytes read/written per second, as well as read/write operations per second.

System Details

There are also a couple of instruments that monitor low-level OS details. The Activity Monitor instrument records system activity, much like the Activity Monitor application. The Scheduling instrument records context switches for threads and processes and tells you the reason the thread was scheduled or unscheduled, such as pre-emption, trapping into the kernel, yielding the CPU due to blocking, etc. The System Calls instrument records system calls and how long they took (cpu and wait time) as well as process interruptions. VM Operations tracks low-level memory operations such as copy on write, page cache hit, zero fill, paging in from a file, and so on.

These instruments include a highlight view which shows aggregate data in bar and pie chart format, shown in Figure 10.35. This trace was recorded while some photos were being edited in Adobe's Lightroom and Photoshop CS5 applications. You can see information such as real memory usage by application, how many context switches and system calls were performed per application, the kinds of system calls, and so on. You can click on a larger chart to see the details for that particular instrument.

Figure 10.35   Highlight views

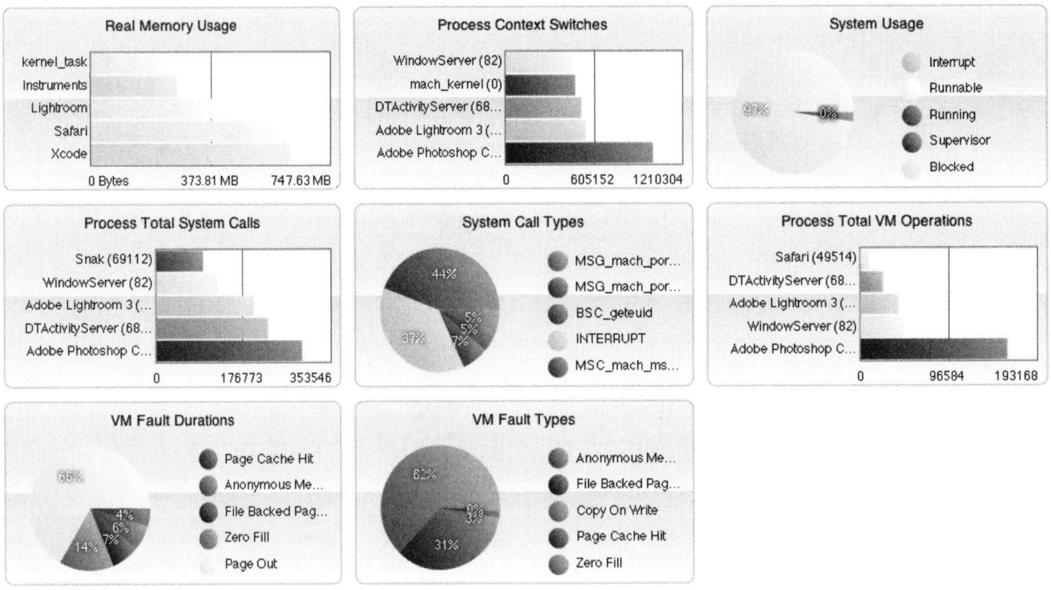

The Dispatch instrument tracks the lifetime of queues, as well as blocks dispatched on queues and how long they take to run. And finally, the Network Activity instrument shows how many bytes and packets the system is reading and writing.

Symbol Trace and DTrace

You can trace calls to an individual function or method as well. Choose Trace Symbol from the Instrument menu, and Instruments will ask you for a symbol to trace. Type a function or method name here. Then when you start recording a trace, Instruments will show the stack depth in the trace area every time that code is called.

Figure 10.36 shows a symbol trace for -[NSTableView drawRect:]. A vertical line was added to the trace as a table view was clicked in the program. You can see a call tree of when these were called, as well as seeing stack traces in the extended detail panel. Symbol traces are useful for answering questions like "is this function even getting called?" and "is this function getting called an insane number of times?", and they can be used to establish visible markers in the trace area. If you know a particular function or method is called right before a performance problem, a symbol trace will give you visible markers where you can start narrowing down your focus. You can click on an entry in the event list to set the playhead to the point in time when that call was made. You can then set the beginning or ending of the inspection range to exactly the time of that call, helping cut out extraneous information with precision.

Figure 10.36 Tracing table view drawing

Symbol Trace is a shortcut for creating a DTrace instrument. Double-clicking the tableview symbol trace instrument drops the sheet shown in Figure 10.37, or you could choose Build New Instrument from the Instrument menu. The panels and text fields there should look familiar if you have used DTrace before. Symbol Trace has created a DTrace probe for objc:NSTableView:-drawRect*:entry that will trigger when a table view draws. The action sets a timestamp and jots down the receiver of the message. There is also a :::return probe that will record the object and stack trace, as well as the duration of the call back to Instruments for display and analysis.

Figure 10.37 DTrace instrument configuration

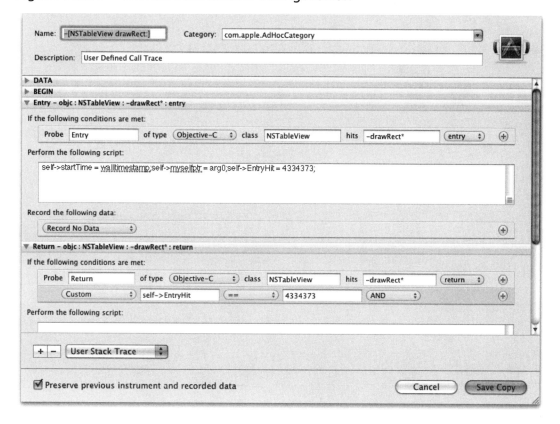

Much of what you can do in DTrace you can do in Instruments as well and have it appear in the same trace pane as Apple's instruments. Unfortunately, DTrace is not available on iOS devices as of iOS 4, so symbol traces and DTrace instruments are not available on that platform.

Summary

Performance is a never-ending game. The rules change constantly as new OS revisions and new hardware comes out. We are nearing the end of free performance gains from hardware, at least for applications that can only take advantage of one CPU. Efficiency in coding and in algorithms, as well as parallel processing, will become more and more important as time goes on. Luckily, we have a number of good tools to profile our code and highlight the areas where we should focus our attention.

Exercises

1. Profile your own program and find any unexpected hotspots.

2. Fix any unexpected hotspots

11

Files, Part 1: I/O and Permissions

Files are the permanent storage for the data that your programs generate. The verbs of handling files are similar to most every other common platform: open, read, write, seek to a particular location, close, with some added nuances that live in the details.

The idea of a file is a fundamental Unix concept. Pretty much everything is treated as a file. Ordinary "write the bits for a jpeg photo" go to files in the file system. Network connections are treated as files. Manipulating some physical devices is done with file operations. Interacting with the terminal is done the same way. Many forms of interprocess communication happen through logical files. This is pretty nice, being able to use the same API for reading and writing data to all of these disparate machine entities. The downside is that there is some additional complexity in the API to handle the different corner cases involved with accessing all of these OS features.

Unbuffered I/O

The unbuffered I/O APIs are the fundamental system calls upon which other interfaces, like the buffered I/O ones, can be built. A *system call* is a function that goes through the kernel to do its work. System calls are much more expensive than regular function calls because of the travel necessary through the application / kernel boundary.

Opening a file

open opens a file:

```
int open (const char *path, int flags, mode_t mode);
```

path specifies the path in the file system that locates the file to be opened, such as /Users/markd/ quotes.txt. There are a couple of limitations on the size of the path: the total length of the path cannot exceed the constant PATH_MAX (currently 1024 for Mac OS X 10.6 and earlier) and any individual component of the path cannot be longer than NAME_MAX (currently 255). If you exceed either of these limits, **open()** and any other system call that takes a path will return an error value and set errno to be ENAMETOOLONG.

The mode argument indicates the default permissions to use for newly created files, e.g., which person has authority to read and write to the file. The details will be discussed a little later. flags is a bitfield used to control the behavior when opening the file. Bitwise-OR in one of these flags:

O_RDONLY   Open the file read-only.

O_WRONLY   Open the file write-only.

O_RDWR   Open the file so you can read from it and write to it.

and any of these flags:

O_APPEND   Append on every write. This does an implicit seek to the end before writing, but it is atomic.

O_NONBLOCK   Do not block when opening and do not block when waiting for data.

O_CREAT   Create the file if it does not exist.

O_TRUNC   Truncate the file to zero bytes when it is opened.

O_EXCL   Return an error if the file already exists.

O_SHLOCK   Obtain a shared lock when opening the file.

O_EXLOCK   Obtain an exclusive lock (more on locks later).

On error, **open()** returns -1 and sets the errno global variable to the appropriate value. This "returning -1 and setting errno to an error" pattern is common to most of the file I/O functions but, unfortunately, not all.

A successful **open()** returns a non-negative integer called a *file descriptor*, frequently shortened to just fd. This integer value is the index into a per-process table that references open files. This file descriptor is used as a handle to the file for subsequent calls.

The three standard streams that shells establish for programs are located at file descriptor values zero (for standard in), one (for standard out), and two (for standard error). You can pass these numbers to the **read()** and **write()** functions, or you can use the symbolic constants STDIN_FILENO, STDOUT_FILENO, or STDERR_FILENO, as shown in Figure 11.1.

Figure 11.1   File descriptors

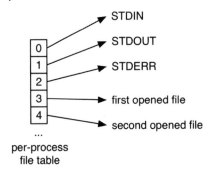

The file descriptor of newly-opened files is guaranteed to be the lowest numbered unused descriptor. This can be useful when you are reopening a file on one of the standard streams, although the **dup2()** call is better for that.

Example 11.1 closes stdout and reopens it to a logfile set in append-only mode. **printf()** writes to standard out, so it will log to this file.

Example 11.1   append.m

```
// append.m -- Show an opening of a logfile replacing a standard stream.

// gcc -g -Wall -o append append.m

#import <errno.h>        // for errno and strerror()
#import <fcntl.h>        // for open()
#import <stdio.h>        // for printf() and friends
#import <stdlib.h>       // for EXIT_SUCCESS
#import <string.h>       // for strerror()
#import <unistd.h>       // for STDOUT_FILENO

int main (void) {
    close (STDOUT_FILENO);

    // open a log file, write only, and to always automatically append.
    // oh, and create the file if it doesn't exist already
    int fd = open ("/tmp/logthingie.txt", O_WRONLY | O_CREAT | O_APPEND,
                   S_IRUSR | S_IWUSR);
    if (fd == -1) {
        fprintf (stderr, "can't open log file.  Error %d (%s)\n",
                 errno, strerror(errno));
        return EXIT_FAILURE;
    }
    printf ("wheee, we have a log file open\n");

    return EXIT_SUCCESS;

} // main
```

Here are some runs of the program:

```
$ ls -l /tmp/logthingie.txt
ls: /tmp/logthingie.txt: No such file or directory

$ ./append

$ ls -l /tmp/logthingie.txt
-rw-------  1 markd  wheel  31 Aug 10 11:55 /tmp/logthingie.txt*

$ cat /tmp/logthingie.txt
wheee, we have a log file open

$ ./append
$ ./append

$ cat /tmp/logthingie.txt
wheee, we have a log file open
wheee, we have a log file open
wheee, we have a log file open
```

That's a lot of header files to include for such a small program. Function prototypes and data types are pretty scattered around in the headers. Luckily, most of the manpages for functions tell you what headers to include to use particular features. For others, like finding where STDOUT_FILENO lives, you can resort to just grepping the files:

```
$ grep STDOUT_FILENO /usr/include/*.h
unistd.h:#define STDOUT_FILENO 1 /* standard output file */
```

If you don't find a value in /usr/include, look in /usr/include/sys. You can also Command-double-click most symbols in Xcode and see the corresponding definition.

Example 11.1 also writes directly to standard error. You could not use **printf()** to complain about the error opening the file because standard out has been redirected. After all, the file opening failed.

There are also some unpronounceable constants used to supply the initial file permissions to use for the newly created file. These will be discussed shortly.

Writing to a file

Use the **write()** system call to move bytes from memory to the disk:

```
ssize_t write (int fd, const void *buf, size_t nbytes);
```

Give it an address and a number of bytes to write, and the bytes will make it out to the file.

write() returns -1 in the case of an error, and it sets errno to whatever complaint the system is having. Otherwise, it returns the number of bytes written. The number of bytes written could be less than nbytes, such as writing a big block of data to a network connection or to a pipe, where you could be filling up limited-sized kernel buffers. The sample code in this chapter will just call **write()** without a loop since we will just be sending small chunks of data to files or to the terminal. Chapter 14: *Network Programming With Sockets* will demonstrate the paranoid way of calling **write()**.

Each open file has an offset associated with it. This offset is the location within the file where the next read or write operation will happen. You can think of it like the read/write head of a cassette player or a Turing machine. The offset is automatically updated on each read or write and can be explicitly set by **lseek()**. The O_APPEND flag overrides the offset for writes, forcing all writing to happen at the end of the file.

Example 11.2 uses **write()** to write a string provided on the command line out to a file. To add a little interest, it writes out the length of the string first. Example 11.3 will read the files generated by this program.

Example 11.2   writestring.m

```
// writestring.m -- take argv[1] and write it to a file, prepending the
//                  length of the string

// gcc -g -Wall -o writestring writestring.m

#import <errno.h>       // for errno
#import <fcntl.h>       // for open()
#import <stdint.h>      // for uint32_t
#import <stdio.h>       // for printf() and friends
#import <stdlib.h>      // for EXIT_SUCCESS et. al.
#import <string.h>      // for strerror()
#import <sys/stat.h>    // for permission flags
#import <unistd.h>      // for write() / close()

int main (int argc, char *argv[]) {
    if (argc != 2) {
        fprintf (stderr, "usage:  %s string-to-log\n", argv[0]);
        return EXIT_FAILURE;
    }
```

```
    int fd = open ("/tmp/stringfile.txt", O_WRONLY | O_CREAT | O_TRUNC,
                    S_IRUSR | S_IWUSR);

    if (fd == -1) {
        fprintf (stderr, "can't open file.  Error %d (%s)\n", errno, strerror(errno));
        return EXIT_FAILURE;
    }

    // Write the length of the string (four bytes).
    uint32_t stringLength = strlen (argv[1]);
    size_t result = write (fd, &stringLength, sizeof(stringLength));

    if (result == -1) {
        fprintf (stderr, "can't write to file.  Error %d (%s)\n",
                  errno, strerror(errno));
        return EXIT_FAILURE;
    }

    result = write (fd, argv[1], stringLength);

    if (result == -1) {
        fprintf (stderr, "can't write to file.  Error %d (%s)\n",
                  errno, strerror(errno));
        return EXIT_FAILURE;
    }

    result = close (fd);
    if (result == -1) {
        fprintf (stderr, "can't close the file.  Error %d (%s)\n",
                  errno, strerror(errno));
        return EXIT_FAILURE;
    }

    return EXIT_SUCCESS;

} // main
```

Here it is in action:

```
$ ./writestring "I seem to be a fish"
$
```

Looking at the size of the file:

```
$ ls -l /tmp/stringfile.txt
-rw-------  1 markd  wheel  23 Aug 10 12:24 /tmp/stringfile.txt
```

The file is 23 bytes, which is the exact size it should be: 4 bytes for the length, plus 19 for the text.

The **hexdump** program is useful for seeing inside of files:

```
$ hexdump -C /tmp/stringfile.txt
0000  13 00 00 00 49 20 73 65  65 6d 20 74 6f 20 62 65  |....I seem to be|
0010  20 61 20 66 69 73 68                              | a fish|
0017
```

Here's how you parse the output: the left-hand column is the number of bytes into the file that the particular line starts on. The bytes of hex are the contents of the file, 16 bytes per line. The right-hand columns show the ASCII interpretation, with unprintable characters replaced by periods.

This file is not portable between PowerPC and Intel machines due to differences in the way integers are represented for those processors. This issue is covered in more detail in Chapter 14: *Network Programming With Sockets*.

So, the first couple of bytes:

```
00000000   13 00 00 00
```

Starting at offset zero are four bytes of 13000000, which is hexadecimal 13, decimal 19, the length of the string. Following that are 19 bytes of the actual string data.

Reading from a file

Reading is the inverse of writing: it moves bytes from the file into memory. **read()** is nearly identical to **write()**:

```
ssize_t read (int d, void *buf, size_t nbytes);
```

buf is not a const void *, but just a void *, meaning that the function could change the contents of the buffer. Of course, that is the whole point of this function call.

Like **write**, **read()** returns -1 on an error, setting errno as appropriate. For a successful read, it returns the number of bytes actually read, returning zero on end of file (EOF). If you run a program from an interactive terminal and read from standard in, some magic happens under the hood causing **read()** to read entire lines. **read()** can return fewer bytes than what you asked for. This can happen when the end of file is reached or due to networking buffering, reading from the terminal, or when dealing with record-oriented devices like tape drives. **read()** also updates the current offset.

Example 11.3 is the counterpart to **writestring**. It takes the specially-formatted file and reads it back in.

Example 11.3   readstring.m

```
// readstring.m -- open /tmp/stringfile.txt and write out its contents

// gcc -g -Wall -o readstring readstring.m

#import <errno.h>        // for errno and strerror()
#import <fcntl.h>        // for open()
#import <stdint.h>       // for uint32_t
#import <stdio.h>        // for printf() and friends
#import <stdlib.h>       // for EXIT_SUCCESS et. al.
#import <string.h>       // for strerror()
#import <unistd.h>       // for read()

int main (int argc, char *argv[]) {
    int fd = open ("/tmp/stringfile.txt", O_RDONLY);

    if (fd == -1) {
        fprintf (stderr, "can't open file.  Error %d (%s)\n",
                errno, strerror(errno));
        return EXIT_FAILURE;
    }

    uint32_t stringLength;
    ssize_t result = read (fd, &stringLength, sizeof(stringLength));

    if (result == -1) {
        fprintf (stderr, "can't read file.  Error %d (%s)\n",
```

```
                errno, strerror(errno));
        return EXIT_FAILURE;
    }

    // +1 accounts for the trailing zero byte we'll be adding to terminate
    // the string.
    char *buffer = malloc (stringLength + 1);

    result = read (fd, buffer, stringLength);

    if (result == -1) {
        fprintf (stderr, "can't read file.  Error %d (%s)\n",
                errno, strerror(errno));
        return EXIT_FAILURE;
    }

    buffer[stringLength] = '\000';

    close (fd);

    printf ("the string is '%s'\n", buffer);

    free (buffer); // clean up our mess

    return EXIT_SUCCESS;

} // main
```

And the program in action:

```
$ ./readstring
the string is 'I seem to be a fish'
```

You may notice that **open()** is called with only two arguments. You do not need to supply permissions if you are not creating a file.

Closing files

To close a file, you use **close()**:

```
int close (int fd);
```

This removes the file descriptor from the per-process file table and frees up system resources associated with this open file. This has a return value of -1 to indicate error. Otherwise, it returns a zero on successful completion.

In the above samples, **readstring** did not check the return value from **close()** because the tool had already done everything it wanted to with the file and its contents. The file being closed successfully (or not) is uninteresting. **writestring** checks for success on the close because some file systems, especially networked file systems, might not flush the last of the file's data until the file is closed.

All open files are automatically closed when a process exits, and any data blocks waiting in kernel buffers are queued for writing.

Changing the read/write offset

The read/write offset is the number of bytes from the beginning of the file where the next read or write operation will take place. This offset is an attribute of the open file. Opening the same file twice will give you two file descriptors, each descriptor having an independent file offset. The initial offset is zero unless O_APPEND was used to open the file.

Use **lseek()** to change the offset:

```
off_t lseek (int fd, off_t offset, int whence);
```

offset, in combination with whence, is used to locate a particular byte in the file. whence can have one of three values:

SEEK_SET   offset is an absolute position.

SEEK_CUR   offset is a delta from the current location.

SEEK_END   offset is relative from the end of the file.

The offset can be negative for SEEK_CUR and SEEK_END. So, if you wanted to start writing five bytes from the end of the file, you would do:

```
blah = lseek (fd, -5, SEEK_END);
```

Note that the offset itself can never go negative; it is clamped to zero. You can see different seeking scenarios in Figure 11.2.

Figure 11.2   lseek()

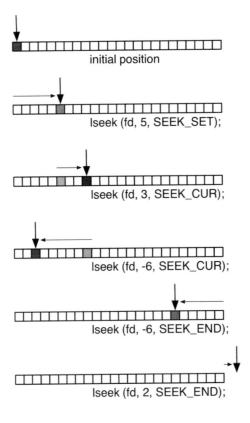

initial position

lseek (fd, 5, SEEK_SET);

lseek (fd, 3, SEEK_CUR);

lseek (fd, -6, SEEK_CUR);

lseek (fd, -6, SEEK_END);

lseek (fd, 2, SEEK_END);

The return value from **lseek()** is the resulting offset location in bytes from the beginning of the file. Otherwise, a -1 return value and errno are used to communicate back an error.

You are quite welcome to seek off the end of the file. Any bytes not explicitly written will default to zero. Note also that some devices are incapable of seeking, like a pipe or a network connection. **lseek()** is a not a physical operation. It's just updating a value in the kernel, so no actual I/O takes place until you perform a read or write.

Move a delta of zero from the current position to get the current offset:

```
off_t offset = lseek (fd, 0, SEEK_CUR);
```

This will also tell you if the device is capable of seeking. If you get an error, you know you cannot seek with this kind of file.

Why is it called **lseek()**? Back in the misty past, the function to perform this work was originally just called **seek**, but it took an int parameter, which could be 16 or 32 bit. When seek was extended to support larger files, a long argument was used, hence the "L."

Atomic operations

In manpages and around this chapter, you will see references to "atomic operations." These are operations that perform multiple actions, but they all happen within one system call, thereby preventing race condition errors with other programs.

For example, **open()** has the O_APPEND flag, which makes appending data to the file an atomic operation. You just **write()** to the file descriptor, and the output appears at the end.

Without O_APPEND, you'd have to make two calls:

```
lseek (fd, 0, SEEK_END); // seek to the end
write (fd, buffer, datasize);
```

The race condition happens if your program gets pre-empted by the kernel after the **lseek()** but before the **write()**, and some other process happens to be writing to the file as well.

Figure 11.3   Race condition start

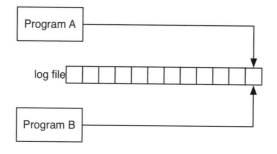

each performs lseek (fd, 0, SEEK_END);

Figure 11.4   Program A writes its data

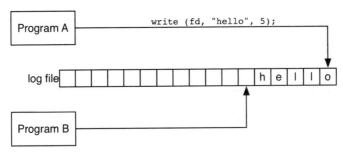

Figure 11.5   Program B clobbers it

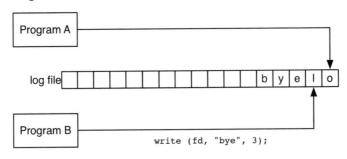

So say the end of log.txt looks like

```
finished frobulating the bork\nadded a hoover\n
```

and the last position is at offset 50,000.

- Program A does an **lseek()** to 50,000 and gets pre-empted.

- Program B does an **lseek()** to 50,000 and writes "removed the wikkit\n".

- Program A is scheduled again and writes "ack ack\n".

The file now looks like

```
finished frobulating the bork\nadded a hoover\nack ack\nhe wikkit\n
```

In short, it has been trashed. Atomic operations were introduced to prevent such errors.

Another example of an atomic operation is opening a file with O_CREAT and O_EXCL. The open will fail if the file exists. This is a handy way to check whether your program is already running, if you only want one copy to be active, like many internet server programs.

Scatter / Gather I/O

Frequently you will make multiple **write()** system calls for one logical piece of data. **writestring** in Example 11.2 calls **write()** twice: once for the size and once for the string. Web server software responds to a request with two distinct chunks of data: the reply headers and the actual data, which are usually kept in distinct data structures. In these cases, you can perform multiple writes, which have the overhead of multiple system calls, or you can copy all the data into a different buffer and then write it in one call. This has data copying overhead and possibly involves dynamic memory, which is another performance hit.

Or you can use the scatter/gather function **writev()** to gather up your data and have the kernel write it all in one operation. There is also the **readv()** that reads data scattered amongst different memory buffers.

```
ssize_t readv (int fd, const struct iovec *iov, int iovcnt);
```

```
ssize_t writev (int fd, const struct iovec *iov, int iovcnt);
```

Rather than taking a buffer, these two functions take an array of `struct iovec`

```
struct iovec {
    void *iov_base;
    size_t iov_len;
};
```

where `iov_base` is the buffer location and `iov_len` is how much data to read and write to that buffer (Figure 11.6).

Figure 11.6 Scatter / Gather I/O

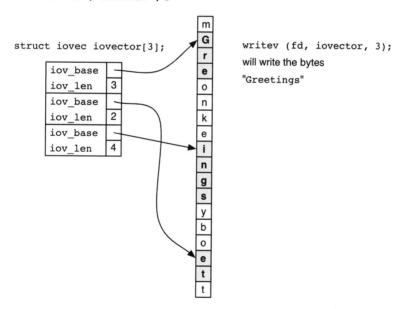

Example 11.4 and Example 11.5 are updated to use scatter/gather I/O:

Example 11.4   writevecstring.m

```
// writevecstring.m -- take argv[1] and write it to a file, prepending the
//                      length of the string.  and using scatter/gather I/O

// gcc -g -Wall -o writevecstring writevecstring.m

#import <errno.h>       // for errno
#import <fcntl.h>       // for open()
#import <stdint.h>      // for uint32_t
#import <stdio.h>       // for printf() and friends
#import <stdlib.h>      // for EXIT_SUCCESS et. al.
#import <string.h>      // for strerror()
#import <sys/stat.h>    // for permission flags
#import <sys/types.h>   // for ssize_t
#import <sys/uio.h>     // for writev() and struct iovec
#import <unistd.h>      // for close()

int main (int argc, char *argv[]) {
    if (argc != 2) {
        fprintf (stderr, "usage:  %s string-to-log\n", argv[0]);
        return EXIT_FAILURE;
    }

    int fd = open ("/tmp/stringfile.txt", O_WRONLY | O_CREAT | O_TRUNC,
                   S_IRUSR | S_IWUSR);

    if (fd == -1) {
        fprintf (stderr, "can't open file.  Error %d (%s)\n",
                 errno, strerror(errno));
        return EXIT_FAILURE;
    }

    uint32_t stringLength = strlen (argv[1]);

    struct iovec vector[2]; // one for size, one for string
    vector[0].iov_base =  &stringLength;
    vector[0].iov_len = sizeof (stringLength);
    vector[1].iov_base = argv[1];
    vector[1].iov_len = stringLength;

    size_t result = writev (fd, vector, 2);

    if (result == -1) {
        fprintf (stderr, "can't write to file.  Error %d (%s)\n",
                 errno, strerror(errno));
        return EXIT_FAILURE;
    }

    result = close (fd);
    if (result == -1) {
        fprintf (stderr, "can't write to file.  Error %d (%s)\n",
                 errno, strerror(errno));
        return EXIT_FAILURE;
    }

    return EXIT_SUCCESS;

} // main
```

Here is the corresponding reader:

Example 11.5   readvecstring.m

```
// readvecstring.m -- open /tmp/stringfile.txt and write out its contents
//                      using scatter/gather reads

// gcc -g -Wall -o readvecstring readvecstring.m

#import <errno.h>        // for errno and strerror()
#import <fcntl.h>        // for open()
#import <stdint.h>       // for uint32_t
#import <stdio.h>        // for printf() and friends
#import <stdlib.h>       // for EXIT_SUCCESS et. al.
#import <string.h>       // for strerror()
#import <sys/stat.h>     // for permission flags
#import <sys/types.h>    // for ssize_t
#import <sys/uio.h>      // for readv() and struct iovec
#import <unistd.h>       // for close()

int main (int argc, char *argv[]) {
    int fd = open ("/tmp/stringfile.txt", O_RDONLY);

    if (fd == -1) {
        fprintf (stderr, "can't open file.  Error %d (%s)\n",
                 errno, strerror(errno));
        return EXIT_FAILURE;
    }

    uint32_t stringLength;
    char buffer[4096];
    struct iovec vector[2];

    vector[0].iov_base = &stringLength;
    vector[0].iov_len = sizeof(stringLength);
    vector[1].iov_base = buffer;
    vector[1].iov_len = sizeof(buffer) - 1;

    ssize_t result = readv (fd, vector, 2);

    if (result == -1) {
        fprintf (stderr, "can't read file.  Error %d (%s)\n",
                 errno, strerror(errno));
        return EXIT_FAILURE;
    }

    buffer[stringLength] = '\000'; // need to zero-terminate it

    close (fd);

    printf ("our string is '%s'\n", buffer);

    return EXIT_SUCCESS;

} // main
```

Unfortunately, the reading side of things is not as pretty as the writing side. The size of the string is unknown, so a guess was made at the maximum size of the string. Hard-coded limits like this will be the source of errors in the future, as soon as someone writes a 4K+1 length string to one of these files.

In general, the `writev()` will be the most convenient way to write scattered data like this, but you will still do multiple reads to pull apart the data – either that or read a lot of stuff into a buffer and process the data in-place.

creat()

Just a historical note, there is also a `creat()` function, which you might see in your travels through other people's code:

```
int creat (const char *path, mode_t mode);
```

This creates empty files, but it has been superseded by `open()`. `creat`(path, mode) is equivalent to

```
open (path, O_CREAT | O_TRUNC | O_WRONLY, mode);
```

Ken Thompson, one of the inventors of Unix, was asked what he would do differently if he were redesigning the Unix system today. He said, "I'd spell `creat` with an e."

Blocking I/O

File I/O is blocking by default. This means the system call will not return until the I/O completes. If you open a file with the `O_NONBLOCK` flag, reads will return immediately with an error (`errno` of `EAGAIN`). You can also use the `select()` or `poll()` functions (discussed in detail in Chapter 14: *Network Programming With Sockets*) to see if I/O is possible for a particular file descriptor.

Buffered I/O

The system calls we have discussed here are generally called "unbuffered I/O." There is a little bit of buffering that happens in the kernel, probably no more than a couple of disk blocks, so that a physical I/O is not performed for every byte read or written. But for the most part, what you read and write is what you get in terms of physical I/O. If you want to read in large chunks of data and process the data out of that buffer, you will have to do the work yourself: refilling the buffer when it gets low, remembering your place in the buffer, handling reading and writing, and so on. Not hard work, just tedious.

The Standard C I/O functions are known as "buffered I/O." The library handles the details of buffer allocation I/O in optimally-sized chunks, only doing real physical I/O when the buffer is empty (for reading), is full (for writing), or is explicitly flushed to the disk.

Rather than passing file descriptors around, buffered I/O has an opaque type called FILE, also known as a stream, and you pass pointers to FILEs around. The file descriptor is wrapped in that FILE, along with the buffer and other pieces of housekeeping.

There are three kinds of buffering that you can use:

Fully Buffered	Actual I/O only happens when the buffer gets full. This is the default for files associated with non-interactive devices.
Line Buffered	I/O happens when a newline character is encountered on input or output. You can use a function to write one character at a time to a stream, but the actual I/O only happens on a newline or when the buffer is getting full.

Unbuffered   No buffering happens; calls just turn around and invoke **read()** or **write()**.
                    The standard error stream is usually unbuffered so that error messages appear
                    instantly. The other two standard streams are either fully or line buffered,
                    depending on whether they are attached to an interactive device like a terminal.

You can use **setbuf()** or **setvbuf()** to change the buffering behavior.

Opening files

The buffered I/O functions, with a few exceptions, begin with "f." So, opening files is done with
fopen():

```
FILE *fopen (char *path, char *mode);
```

fopen() returns a pointer to a newly-allocated FILE structure. You don't need to worry about allocating
it, but you are responsible for disposing of it with **fclose()**. It is an opaque type, but you can see
what's inside of it. You can look at the stdio.h header or print out a FILE structure in **gdb**.

fopen() takes a pathname to the file and a mode, which is a character string:

"r"   Open the file for reading.

"r+"   Open the file for reading and writing.

"w"   Truncate the file to zero length, or create it if it does not exist, and then open for writing.

"w+"   Truncate the file to zero length, or create it if it does not exist, and then open for reading and
         writing.

"a"   Create the file if it does not exist and then open it for writing in append mode.

"a+"   Create the file if it does not exist and then open it for reading and writing in append mode.

Or, put another way,

"r"   Open for reading; file must exist.

"w"   Truncate or create if necessary; file does not need to exist.

"a"   Create if necessary; file does not need to exist. Append mode.

And stick on a "+" to make both reading and writing possible.

There are some subtleties with "+" modes. Output cannot be followed by input without an explicit
fflush() or something that flushes the buffer, like an **fseek()**, **fsetpos()**, or a **rewind()**. Similarly,
input cannot be directly followed by output without calling of the above calls. This makes sense if you
remember that there is one buffer in the FILE, and it can't handle reading and writing at the same time.

There are buffered I/O versions of the three standard streams: stdin, stdout, stderr. You can pass any
of these to the buffered I/O functions.

Because buffered I/O comes from the portable standard C library, it has support for a distinction
between binary files and text files because some operating systems have that distinction. Unix makes
no such distinction, so any special binary flags (sticking a "b" onto a/a+/w/w+, etc.) passed for the
mode are ignored.

Text files are not automatically easy to deal with though. There are three different conventions for indicating the end of a line in a text file. Unix systems use the line feed character (LF / 0x0A) to terminate an end of line, Mac OS 9 used the carriage return (CR / 0x0D). Windows and MS-DOS uses both of them – a carriage return followed by a line feed (0x0D0A), commonly called "CRLF." If you need to support text files created by non-Unix platforms, you will need to do some extra processing to handle the different line-ending conventions.

Files created with **fopen()** have permissions rw-rw-rw-. You cannot change that directly with **fopen()**. Instead, use the **chmod()** or **fchmod()** system calls or control the creation permissions with **umask()**.

There are two companion calls to **fopen()**:

```
FILE *fdopen (int fd, char *mode);
```

```
FILE *freopen (char *path, char *mode, FILE *stream);
```

fdopen() takes an existing file descriptor (from **open()** or from a networking call) and wraps a FILE stream around it.

freopen() closes and reopens a given file pointer using the new path instead of what was used before. **freopen()** is very handy if you are redirecting the standard streams. You can do stdin = freopen ("/my/new/stdin.file", "w+", stdin); to redirect the standard in stream to stdin.file.

Closing files

```
int fclose (FILE *stream);
```

This dissociates the stream from its underlying file. Any buffered data is queued to the kernel using **fflush()**, and the enclosed file descriptor is closed. If the program terminates abnormally, any buffered data will not be flushed to the kernel and will be lost. **fclose()** returns zero on successful completion. Otherwise, EOF is returned, and it sets errno to the reason for the error.

Text I/O

The buffered I/O API has two concepts of I/O when it comes to reading and writing: one is text oriented, the other is binary oriented.

Text I/O can be done a character-at-a-time or a line-at-a-time. Here are the character-at-a-time functions:

```
int getc (FILE *stream);
```

```
int getchar ();
```

```
int fgetc (FILE *stream);
```

Each will try to get the next input character from the given stream or from stdin for **getchar()**. Notice that these functions return an int rather than a char. The return value is overloaded so that it returns either the function data or a status value. Since char's useful values cover its entire expressible range, some other bits are needed to hold unique result values. If end of file or a read error occurs, the return returns the constant EOF, usually -1. You need to use the routines **feof()** and **ferror()** to distinguish between end of file and an error. In the case of error, errno is set like in the unbuffered I/O functions. On a successful read, the return value is the character data. You can use the function **clearerr()** to clear the end of file and error indicators on the FILE stream.

The implementation of **getc()** and **fgetc()** are defined by the ANSI C standard: **getc()** is implemented by a macro and **fgetc()** is implemented as a function. The implications of this specification are that the argument to **getc()** should not have any side effects because the macro could evaluate its argument more than once. It also means that if you want to stash a character-getting function in a function pointer, you must use **fgetc()**. The actual time difference between **getc()** and **fgetc()** is negligible, so just use **fgetc()** unless you can measure that the function call overhead is a problem.

Example 11.6 is how to check for EOF and discriminate between error and end of file:

Example 11.6   buffread.m

```
// buffread.m -- show how to read using buffered I/O, including error / eof
//              handling

// gcc -g -Wall -o buffread buffread.m

#import <stdlib.h>      // for EXIT_SUCCES, etc
#import <stdio.h>       // all the buffered I/O API

int main (int argc, char *argv[]) {
    FILE *file = fopen ("buffread.m", "r");

    while (1) {
        int result = fgetc (file);
        if (result == EOF) {
            if (feof(file)) {
                printf ("EOF found\n");
            }
            if (ferror(file)) {
                printf ("error reading file\n");
            }
            break;
        } else {
            printf ("got a character: '%c'\n", (char) result);
        }
    }

    fclose (file);

    return EXIT_SUCCESS;

} // main
```

Not only can you read characters from the stream, you can push them back onto the stream with **ungetc()**:

```
int ungetc (int c, FILE *stream);
```

ANSI C only guarantees one character of pushback, but the OS X manpages say you can push back an arbitrary amount. Being able to push back characters is handy in some parsers. You can peek a character ahead to see if this particular chunk of text is interesting. If not, push that character back and let some other piece of code handle the parsing. **ungetc()** clears the EOF flag so you can unget a character on an EOF and then read it later. Note, however, that calls to a positioning function, like **fseek()**, **fsetpos()**, or **rewind()** will discard the pushed-back characters.

To write to a stream character-wise, use one of these:

```
int fputc (int c, FILE *stream);
```

```
int putchar(int c);
```

```
int putc (int c, FILE *stream);
```

These are exactly analogous to the reading functions. **fputc()** is a function, **putc()** is a macro, **putchar()** implicitly uses stdout.

For line-at-a-time I/O, use these functions:

```
char *fgets (char *str, int size, FILE *stream);
```

```
char *gets (char *str); // here be dragons
```

```
int fputs (const char *str, FILE *stream);
```

```
int puts (const char *str);
```

You give **fgets()** and **gets()** an already allocated character buffer. The functions will return when they see an end of line character or when they fill up the buffer. **gets()** does not accept a size, so there is no way to control how much data will be written into the buffer, making buffer overflows really easy; hence, you should avoid this call. **fgets()** stores the newline character in the buffer, while **gets()** does not. In both cases, a zero byte is appended to the end of the string. If an end of file or an error occurs, they return NULL, and you need to check **feof()** and **ferror()** to see what happened.

puts() writes to standard out. **fputs()** does not automatically put a newline to the stream, while **puts()** does.

Binary I/O

The problem with Text I/O is that zero-value bytes are significant, being the end-of-string indicator. Binary I/O treats all bytes the same. Binary I/O is not limited to just binary data: you can use it for blocks of text too. "Block I/O" would probably be a better name. These calls can be used to write arrays of structures to disk. Be aware of portability problems when blindly writing structures to disk. If any of the data types should change size or layout between platforms, you can end up breaking your file format.

```
size_t fread (void *ptr, size_t size, size_t nmemb, FILE *stream);
```

```
size_t fwrite (const void *ptr, size_t size, size_t nmemb, FILE *stream);
```

Each function has a pointer to memory, the size of the struct, and the number of elements in an array of these structs. The return value is the number of *elements* written, not the number of bytes written. Internally, it's just doing the multiplication and writing that number of bytes. These functions don't stop at zero bytes or newlines like the text I/O functions do. If the number of elements read or written is less than expected, check **ferror()** and **feof()**.

Example 11.7 shows binary reading:

Example 11.7   fbinaryio.m

```
// fbinaryio.m -- do some binary reading and writing using buffered i/o
```

```
// gcc -g -std=c99 -Wall -o fbinaryio fbinaryio.m
```

```
#import <errno.h>        // for errno
```

```
#import <stdint.h>      // for uint32_t
#import <stdio.h>       // for the buffered I/O API
#import <stdlib.h>      // for EXIT_SUCCES,p etc
#import <string.h>      // for strerror()

typedef struct Thing {
    uint32_t    thing1;
    float       thing2;
    char        thing3[8];
} Thing;

Thing things[] = {
    { 3, 3.14159, "hello" },
    { 4, 4.29301, "bye" },
    { 2, 2.14214, "bork" },
    { 5, 5.55556, "elf up" }
};

int main (int argc, char *argv[]) {
    size_t thingCount = sizeof(things) / sizeof(*things); // how many we have
    FILE *file = fopen ("/tmp/thingfile", "w");

    if (file == NULL) {
        fprintf (stderr, "error opening file: %d (%s)\n",
                 errno, strerror(errno));
        return EXIT_FAILURE;
    }

    size_t numWrote = fwrite (things, sizeof(Thing), thingCount, file);

    if (numWrote != thingCount) {
        fprintf (stderr, "incomplete write (%d out of %d).  Error %d (%s)\n",
                 (int)numWrote, (int)thingCount, errno, strerror(errno));
        return EXIT_FAILURE;
    }

    fclose (file);

    // now re-open and re-read and make sure everything is groovy
    file = fopen ("/tmp/thingfile", "r");

    if (file == NULL) {
        fprintf (stderr, "error opening file: %d (%s)\n",
                 errno, strerror(errno));
        return EXIT_FAILURE;
    }

    // we know we're reading in thingCount, so we can go ahead and
    // acquire that much space
    Thing readThings[sizeof(things) / sizeof(*things)];

    size_t numRead = fread (readThings, sizeof(Thing), thingCount, file);

    if (numRead != thingCount) {
        fprintf (stderr, "short read.  Got %d, expected %d\n",
                 (int)numRead, (int)thingCount);
        if (feof(file)) {
            fprintf (stderr, "we got an end of file\n");
        }
        if (ferror(file)) {
```

```
                    fprintf (stderr, "we got an error: %d (%s)\n",
                            errno, strerror(errno));
            }
        } else {
            // Just for fun, compare the newly read ones with the ones
            // we have statically declared
            for (int i = 0; i < thingCount; i++) {
                if ((things[i].thing1 != readThings[i].thing1)
                        || (things[i].thing2 != readThings[i].thing2)
                        || (strcmp(things[i].thing3, readThings[i].thing3) != 0)) {
                    fprintf (stderr, "mismatch with element %d\n", i);
                } else {
                    printf ("successfully compared element %d\n", i);
                }
            }
        }

        fclose (file);

        return EXIT_SUCCESS;

} // main
```

Here is a sample run:

```
$ ./fbinaryio
successfully compared element 0
successfully compared element 1
successfully compared element 2
successfully compared element 3
```

And just for fun, look at the file itself:

```
$ hexdump -C /tmp/thingfile
0000  03 00 00 00 d0 0f 49 40  68 65 6c 6c 6f 00 00 00  |......I@hello...|
0010  04 00 00 00 57 60 89 40  62 79 65 00 00 00 00 00  |....W`.@bye.....|
0020  02 00 00 00 d2 18 09 40  62 6f 72 6b 00 00 00 00  |.......@bork....|
0030  05 00 00 00 26 c7 b1 40  65 6c 66 20 75 70 00 00  |....&..@elf up..|
```

You can see that there are 4 bytes of integer, 4 bytes of float, and 8 bytes of character data. It just so happens to line up with the struct Thing definition. One word of warning: this code and data file are not portable between PowerPC and Intel Macintoshes. Here is the file from a PowerPC machine:

```
$ hexdump -C /tmp/thingfile
0000  00 00 00 03 40 49 0f d0  68 65 6c 6c 6f 00 00 00  |....@I..hello...|
0010  00 00 00 04 40 89 60 57  62 79 65 00 00 00 00 00  |....@.`Wbye.....|
0020  00 00 00 02 40 09 18 d2  62 6f 72 6b 00 00 00 00  |....@...bork....|
0030  00 00 00 05 40 b1 c7 26  65 6c 66 20 75 70 00 00  |....@..&elf up..|
```

See the section about network byte order in Chapter 14: *Network Programming With Sockets* for more details.

Positioning

Like unbuffered I/O, the buffered I/O FILE streams have a current position.

```
long ftell (FILE *stream);

int fseek (FILE *stream, long offset, int whence);
```

ftell() returns the current location in the file. **fseek()** is like **lseek()**. It has the same use of offset and whence (SEEK_SET, SEEK_CUR, SEEK_END). The return value of **fseek()** is zero on successful completion. Otherwise, -1 is returned and errno is set appropriately. Note that the offset type of these functions is long, which can limit file sizes. There are also versions that take off_t types, which could be larger than longs:

```
off_t ftello (FILE *stream);
```

```
int fseeko (FILE *stream, off_t offset, int whence);
```

An alternate interface is

```
int fgetpos (FILE *stream, fpos_t *pos);
```

```
int fsetpos (FILE *stream, const fpos_t *pos);
```

using the opaque fpos_t type. On some platforms, it's the same as an off_t. On other platforms, it's an 8-byte array.

```
void rewind (FILE *stream);
```

will reset the current location in the file to the very beginning, also clearing the error flag.

Formatted I/O

The **printf** family of calls lives under standard / buffered I/O because they write out to FILE streams, either explicitly or implicitly. **sprintf** and **snprintf** write to a buffer, but they have the same syntax as their I/O companions.

```
int printf (const char *format, ...);
```

```
int fprintf (FILE *stream, const char *format, ...);
```

```
int sprintf (char *str, const char *format, ...);
```

```
int snprintf (char *str, size_t size, const char *format, ...);
```

```
int asprintf (char **ret, const char *format, ...);
```

printf() writes to stdout. **fprintf()** writes to any FILE. **sprintf()** writes into a buffer, while **snprintf()** writes into a buffer but is given the amount of space it can write in. Always use **snprintf()** instead of **sprintf()**. There is no prevention of buffer overruns in **sprintf()**, especially if any user-entered data gets fed into the function. With **snprintf()**, buffer overruns will not happen. **asprintf()** takes **snprintf()** to the next level by automatically allocating a buffer for you that is the correct size. You will need to **free()** this buffer once you are done with it.

The specifics of the **printf**-style of formatting are covered in opaque detail in the manpage and in most every C 101 book out there.

You can do formatted input as well, using

```
int scanf (const char *format, ...);
```

```
int fscanf (FILE *stream, const char *format, ...);
```

```
int sscanf (const char *str, const char *format, ...);
```

These take format strings like **printf()**, but instead of just regular arguments in the ... section of the parameter list, you need to provide pointers to appropriate-sized areas of memory. The **scanf()**

functions will not allocate memory for you. There is not much in the way of error detection or recovery when using the functions. Outside of toy programs, you will probably want to write your own parsing code, use a regular expression library, or use lexer/parser generator tools.

Misc Functions

Here are some miscellaneous buffered I/O functions.

```
int fileno (FILE *stream);
```

This returns the file descriptor that the stream is wrapped around. This is handy if you need to use `fcntl()`, `fchmod()`, `fstat()`, or the `dup()` functions.

```
int getw (FILE *stream);
```

```
int putw (int w, FILE *stream);
```

These are like `getc()`/`putc()` but read or write an integer. The integers are not written in a canonical form (discussed in Chapter 14: *Network Programming With Sockets*), so if you want to be portable, you will need to put the bytes into a known byte order.

Buffered I/O vs. Unbuffered I/O

With buffered I/O, there is a lot of data copying happening:

program structures –> `FILE` buffer –> kernel buffer –> disk.

With unbuffered I/O, the copy to the `FILE` buffer is avoided, and with scatter/gather I/O, the kernel might be able to avoid a copy into its own buffers.

Since `read()` and `write()` are not buffered (except for a disk block or two in the kernel data structures), they can be slow when dealing with lots of smaller reads and writes. Buffered I/O would be a win here.

When doing big reads and writes, say dozens of K of image data, there is a win to using plain `read()` and `write()` calls to avoid the buffering step in between.

Fundamentally, everything boils down to the file descriptor. Even `FILE`s have a file descriptor at their heart. Be careful when mixing buffered and unbuffered I/O with the same file descriptor. The `FILE` part of the world does not get notified if you do I/O with the file descriptor, leading to some confusing synchronization errors.

There is some magic that happens in both the buffered and unbuffered I/O cases when input or output is going to a terminal device. `read()` takes on per-line semantics, and the buffered I/O calls take on line buffering behavior.

Lastly, when both buffered and unbuffered I/O perform a write operation, the data does not necessarily end up on disk immediately. The kernel will buffer the writing to reduce the number of physical I/O operations it has to do. This means that you can dutifully write your data, have the OS crash, and your data is lost. If you are truly paranoid about having data written to disk (like in a database system), you can use one of the sync calls:

```
void sync (void);
```

This forces the queuing of modified buffers in the block buffer for I/O. This call will return immediately, and the kernel will write the blocks at its leisure. This will force writing for all modified blocks system-wide.

```
int fsync (int fd);
```

This causes all modified data and metadata for a file to be flushed out to the physical disk. It applies to just one file. The call will block for all I/O to complete before returning.

Removing Files

Removing files is pretty easy. Use the **unlink()** system call:

```
int unlink (const char *path);
```

unlink() returns zero on successful completion or -1 if there was an error, with errno set to the error that actually happened. There can be multiple references to a file via hardlinks. **unlink()** removes a reference from a particular dictionary, but the file's contents are only removed when all references to it have been eliminated.

There is one subtlety when unlinking files that are currently open. The directory entry for the file is removed immediately. If you do an **ls** on the directory, you won't see the file. But the file's contents still exist on the disk, still consume space, and are still available to programs that have the file open. The actual space is reclaimed by the OS once all programs close the file. This is useful for temporary files, ones you do not want to hang around after the program goes away. By unlinking the temporary file immediately after opening it, you don't need to worry about deleting the file once your program is over. The space occupied by the file will be reclaimed even if your program crashes.

This behavior can occasionally lead to puzzling system administration issues. Imagine the scenario where a web server has a 500-meg log file open and the disk it is on is filling up. Someone deletes the file hoping to reclaim the space. Because the log file is still open, those 500 megs are still being used, but they will not show up using any command (like du).

Rather than deleting the file, you can truncate it with the command:

```
$ sudo cp /dev/null /the/log/file/name
```

The **sudo** command lets you run a command as the superuser.

If you have already deleted the file, you can use the command **lsof** to "ls Open Files" and see what is there. **lsof** is pretty handy anyway for peeking inside the system and seeing what is going on.

```
$ sudo lsof
(Huge amount of output.  Here are a couple lines.)

pbs   266 markd cwd   VDIR  14,9    1486     2 / (/dev/disk0s9)
pbs   266 markd  0u   VCHR   0,0  0t4015 262628 /dev/console
pbs   266 markd  1u   VCHR   0,0  0t4015 262628 /dev/console
pbs   266 markd  2u   VCHR   0,0  0t4015 262628 /dev/console
```

This is the pasteboard server, process ID 266, owned by user markd. It has three files open on fd 0, 1, 2, all open for read/write, and all going to /dev/console. It also has the directory / (the Unix root directory) open, as the current working directory.

```
Adium   1269 markd   7u  inet 0x0240d7bc    0t0    TCP
10.0.1.142:49249->toc-m04.blue.aol.com:9898 (ESTABLISHED)
```

Adium, an AIM client that is running with pid 1269, has fd 7 being an internet connection. On the local side, the IP address 10.0.1.142 port 49249 is connected to toc-m04.blue.aol.com, port 9898.

```
lsof   1361 markd   3r  VCHR    3,0          0t0 26234372 /dev/mem
lsof   1361 markd   4r  VCHR    3,1 0t26432612 26234244 /dev/kmem
lsof   1361 markd   5r  VREG   14,9     3169824    66862 /mach_kernel
```

Finally, this run of **lsof** has file descriptors 3, 4, 5 open, reading /dev/mem, /dev/kmem (kernel memory), and it also has the mach_kernel file open so it can resolve the data it finds in the memory devices.

Temporary Files

Temporary files, as the name implies, are files that are used by a program as it is running and then are not useful once the program goes away. Unix systems typically store temp files in a well known location so that people know where to clean out files that are left over accidentally. Some systems will clear out the directory that holds the temp files on startup.

A program needs a unique name when it wants to create temporary file so that it does not clash with another file already in the temp directory. If two programs ended up using the same temporary file, one or the other would probably fail in weird and wonderful ways.

Where is this temporary directory? There are a number of calls available for finding a temporary directory and for generating a file name inside of that directory. Most of them have security issues. You may have noticed that some examples in this book put things into /tmp. This is the "classic" Unix temporary directory. For simple one-offs test, or example code, it's ok because they will not be used as attack vectors.

Mac OS X provides temporary directories for each user, so you do not have to worry about another user snooping your temporary files. Use **NSTemporaryDirectory()** to get the directory, followed by **mkdtemp()** to make sure it exists. This second call will create any intervening directories with permissions that are only accessible by the current user. There are other functions you can use that will automatically open a temporary file for you in the temp directory.

```
NSString *NSTemporaryDirectory (void);
```

This is the path of the temporary directory for the current user. It is possible for this to return nil if the temporary directory cannot be determined for this user.

```
char *mktemp (char *template);
```

This takes the filename template and replaces part of it to create the filename you should use. This is guaranteed not to exist at the time of the function invocation, but it's entirely possible another application could create and open that file first. The template can be any path with some number of X's in it. The trailing X's are replaced with a unique alphanumeric combination. The more X's you have, the less chance of the file name being guessed or an accidental collision happening. It returns a pointer to the modified template on success and returns NULL on failure.

```
int mkstemp (char *template);
```

This makes the same replacement to the template as **mktemp()**, but it also creates and opens the file and returns a file descriptor. This is an atomic operation and avoids the race condition with **mktemp()**. It returns -1 on error and fills in errno.

```
int mkstemps (char *template, int suffixlen);
```

This works like **mkstemp()**, except it permits a suffix to exist in the template. The template should be of the form "/path/to/tmp/dir/blahXXXXXXsuffix". This allows you to use a file extension for your temporary file. It also returns -1 on error and fills in `errno`.

```
char *mkdtemp (char *template);
```

This makes the same replacement to the template as in **mktemp()** and creates the template directory with mode 0700 (read, write, execute only for the owner). It returns a pointer to the template on success and returns NULL on failure.

The temporary directories get cleared out at boot time, but if you store a lot of data in a temporary directory, you should somehow arrange for its cleanup before then because multi-week uptimes are not unheard of in Mac OS X. The automatically-opened files do not delete the temporary file. You may want to unlink the file after opening to reclaim the disk space when your program exits.

A common error that results in a crash is trying to pass a literal `"string"` for the template. These calls modify the template, which is not possible on a literal const string.

Example 11.8 shows **mkdtemp()** and **mkstemp()** in action. The other temp dir calls work similarly.

Example 11.8   tempfun.m

```
// tempfun.m -- see how different temp file names are generated

// gcc -g -Wall -framework Foundation -o tempfun tempfun.m

#import <Foundation/Foundation.h>
#import <stdio.h>        // for the temp name functions
#import <stdlib.h>       // for EXIT_SUCCESS, etc
#import <string.h>       // for strcpy()
#import <unistd.h>       // for mk[s]temp

int main (int argc, char *argv[]) {
    NSAutoreleasePool *pool = [[NSAutoreleasePool alloc] init];

    NSString *tempDir = NSTemporaryDirectory ();
    if (tempDir == nil) tempDir = @"/tmp";
    NSLog (@"tempDir is %@", tempDir);

    NSString *template = [tempDir stringByAppendingPathComponent: @"bork.XXXXXX"];
    NSLog (@"template is %@", template);

    char *mutableTemplate = strdup ([template fileSystemRepresentation]);
    char *path = mkdtemp (mutableTemplate);
    NSLog (@"after mkdtemp: %s", path);
    free (mutableTemplate);

    NSString *template2 =
        [tempDir stringByAppendingPathComponent: @"greebleXXXXXX.txt"];
    NSLog (@"template2 is %@", template2);

    mutableTemplate = strdup ([template2 fileSystemRepresentation]);
    int fd = mkstemps (mutableTemplate, 4);
    NSLog (@"after mkstemps: fd %d, path %s", fd, mutableTemplate);
    free (mutableTemplate);

    close (fd);
```

```
        [pool drain];
        sleep(5);
        return EXIT_SUCCESS;

} // main
```

And some output:

```
$ ./tempfun
tempDir is /var/folders/Su/Su23NV97E2Ctglsy3dnuEU+++TI/-Tmp-/
template is /var/folders/Su/Su23NV97E2Ctglsy3dnuEU+++TI/-Tmp-/bork.XXXXXX
after mkdtemp: /var/folders/Su/Su23NV97E2Ctglsy3dnuEU+++TI/-Tmp-/bork.0iQvXD
template2 is /var/folders/Su/Su23NV97E2Ctglsy3dnuEU+++TI/-Tmp-/greebleXXXXXX.txt
after mkstemps: fd 3,
    path /var/folders/Su/Su23NV97E2Ctglsy3dnuEU+++TI/-Tmp-/greebleCuSFWz.txt
```

In older versions of OS X, the temporary file name was related to the process ID of the running program. This made it easier for malicious programs to guess the name of the file, so a randomly generated string is used nowadays.

File Permissions

Because of OS X's Unix heritage, it has a multi-user permission model on the file system.

Users and groups

Every user on the system has an integer user ID. Each user belongs to one or more named groups, and each group has an ID. For instance:

```
$ ls -l chapter.txt
-rw-r--r--  1 markd  staff  48827 Aug 11 14:14 chapter.txt
```

The user is markd, the group is staff.

```
$ ls -l /bin/ls
-r-xr-xr-x  1 root  wheel  80688 Feb 11  2010 /bin/ls*
```

ls is owned by the user root, the group wheel.

You can see what users and groups are configured on your machine with the Directory Services tools **dscl** and **dscacheutil**. You can get a list of users and their user ID:

```
$ dscl . -list /Users UniqueID
_amavisd            83
_appowner           87
_appserver          79
...
bork                502
daemon              1
markd               501
nobody              -2
root                0
```

The accounts markd and bork are user accounts that were added to the machine.

You can see groups, and members of each group, with **dscacheutil**:

```
$ dscacheutil -q group
```

```
name: _amavisd
password: *
gid: 83

name: _appowner
password: *
gid: 87

name: _appserveradm
password: *
gid: 81
users: markd bork
...
name: admin
password: *
gid: 80
users: root markd bork
```

Groups are a way to aggregate users that should have similar access permissions on sets of files. You would want your developers to be able edit files on a shared documentation tree. Specifically, the user markd is in group admin, so that user can administer the computer. You can see what groups you are in by using the **id** command:

```
% id
uid=501(markd) gid=20(staff) groups=20(staff),
403(com.apple.sharepoint.group.2),204(_developer),100(_lpoperator),
98(_lpadmin),81(_appserveradm),80(admin),79(_appserverusr),
61(localaccounts),12(everyone),402(com.apple.sharepoint.group.1),
401(com.apple.access_screensharing)
```

On other systems that do not use Directory Services (which would be just about every other flavor of Unix out there), the files /etc/passwd and /etc/group contain user and group information.

You use the **chown** command to change the ownership of a file. You must have superuser privilege to give away one of your own files to another user. Otherwise, you could use that to defeat disk space quotas or trick another user into opening something malicious. For instance:

```
$ touch spoon

$ ls -l spoon
-rw-r--r--  1 markd   staff   0 Aug 11 14:40 spoon

$ chown bork spoon
chown: spoon: Operation not permitted

$ sudo chown bork spoon

$ ls -l spoon
-rw-r--r--  1 bork   staff   0 Aug 11 14:40 spoon
```

You can change groups with **chgrp**:

```
$ chgrp wheel spoon
chgrp: spoon: Operation not permitted

$ sudo chgrp wheel spoon

$ ls -l spoon
-rw-r--r--  1 bork   wheel   0 Aug 11 14:40 spoon
```

You can combine these two operations into one **chown** command if you wish:

```
$ sudo chown markd:staff spoon

$ ls -l spoon
-rw-r--r--  1 markd  staff  0 Aug 11 14:40 spoon
```

There are system calls for manually changing the owner and group of a file:

```
int chown (const char *path, uid_t owner, gid_t group);

int lchown (const char *path, uid_t owner, gid_t group);

int fchown(int fd, uid_t owner, gid_t group);
```

chown() changes the owner and group of a file, **lchown()** changes it for a symbolic link, and **fchown()** operates on a file that is already open.

If you need to look up the owner and group IDs:

```
struct passwd *getpwent (void);

struct passwd *getpwnam (const char *login);

struct passwd *getpwuid (uid_t uid);
```

There are equivalent operations (**getgrent()**, **getgrnam()**, **getgrgid()**) for group information.

If you are familiar with the /etc/password file format, `struct passwd` will look familiar:

```
struct passwd {
    char     *pw_name;              /* user name */
    char     *pw_passwd;           /* encrypted password */
    uid_t    pw_uid;               /* user uid */
    gid_t    pw_gid;               /* user gid */
    __darwin_time_t pw_change;     /* password change time */
    char     *pw_class;            /* user access class */
    char     *pw_gecos;            /* Honeywell login info */
    char     *pw_dir;              /* home directory */
    char     *pw_shell;            /* default shell */
    __darwin_time_t pw_expire;     /* account expiration */
};
```

getpwnam() will give you the information for one user, mapping a login name to the corresponding passwd entry. **getpwent()** can be used to iterate through the password list. **getpwuid()** maps a numeric userID to the appropriate passwd entry.

File permissions

There are a number of bits associated with each file and directory. The nine most important of those bits are the file permissions. When you **ls -l** a file, you will see them:

```
$ ls -l chapter.txt
-rw-r--r--  1 markd  staff  52655 Aug 11 15:11 chapter.txt
```

In particular, look at rw- r-- r-- three sets of three bits. The first set is permissions for the user who owns the file: markd, who can read from and write to the file. The second set is permissions for the group of the file: staff, who can read the file. Anyone who is a member of the staff group can read this file. The last set of bits is the permissions for all the others: anyone who is not markd and is not in the staff group.

Each of owner, group, and world can have these bits set:

r   Read

w   Write

x   Execute

The executable bit is the clue to the OS that a file is actually an executable program. There is not a magic file name suffix, like .EXE, that tells the OS that this file is executable.

Here are the permissions from some arbitrarily picked files from my file system:

```
$ ls -l /bin/ls
-r-xr-xr-x  1 root  wheel  80688 Jul 14  2009 /bin/ls*
```

The user (root), group (wheel), and others can all read and execute the file. Nobody can write to it. The wheel group is used to designate system administrators on BSD systems, coming from the term "Big Wheel."

```
$ ls -l /Developer/Documentation/Acknowledgements.rtf
-rw-rw-r--  1 root  admin  492494 May 11  2009 \
    /Developer/Documentation/Acknowledgements.rtf
```

The user (root) and group (admin) can each read and write the file. All others can only read it.

You will sometimes see file permissions expressed numerically. Each chunk of permissions is three bits, usually expressed in octal.

r   100

w   010

x   001

So a permission of rw is binary 110, which has an octal value of 6. A permission of rwx is binary 111, which has an octal value of 7.

rwx rw- r-- is the same as 111 110 100, which is 764 in octal. Figure 11.7 shows some permission values, their octal representation, and what ls -l would show you.

Figure 11.7   Permission bits

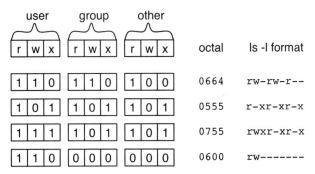

313

The **chmod** command lets you change these permission bits, either in octal or symbolically:

```
$ touch test
$ ls -l test
-rw-r--r--  1 markd   staff   0 Aug 11 15:23 test

$ chmod 775 test
$ ls -l test
-rwxr-xr-x  1 markd   staff   0 Aug 11 15:23 test

$ chmod 400 test
$ ls -l test
-r--------  1 markd   staff   0 Aug 11 15:23 test
```

There are symbols available for those folks who do not think in octal.

u   Modify user permissions.

g   Modify group permissions.

o   Modify other permissions.

+   Set the bits that follow.

-   Clear the bits that follow.

r   Read.

w   Write.

x   Execute.

```
$ chmod ugo+rw test
```

For user, group, and other, turn on the read and write bits.

```
$ ls -l test
-rw-rw-rw-  1 markd   staff   0 Aug 11 15:23 test
```

```
$ chmod +x test
```

This is shorthand for everything.

```
$ ls -l test
-rwxrwxrwx  1 markd   staff   0 Aug 11 15:23 test*
```

```
$ chmod g-wx test
```

Turn off write and execute for group.

```
$ ls -l test
-rwxr--rwx  1 markd   staff   0 Aug 11 15:23 test*
```

There is also an API for affecting the permission bits:

```
int chmod (const char *path, mode_t mode);

int fchmod (int fd, mode_t mode);
```

where **chmod()** affects a file in the file system and **fchmod()** changes the permissions on a file you already have open.

There's a whole slew of unpronounceable constants for specifying the mode:

```
#define S_IRWXU 0000700    /* RWX mask for owner */
#define S_IRUSR 0000400    /* R for owner */
#define S_IWUSR 0000200    /* W for owner */
#define S_IXUSR 0000100    /* X for owner */

#define S_IRWXG 0000070    /* RWX mask for group */
#define S_IRGRP 0000040    /* R for group */
#define S_IWGRP 0000020    /* W for group */
#define S_IXGRP 0000010    /* X for group */

#define S_IRWXO 0000007    /* RWX mask for other */
#define S_IROTH 0000004    /* R for other */
#define S_IWOTH 0000002    /* W for other */
#define S_IXOTH 0000001    /* X for other */
```

Notice that these are octal constants because they begin with zero.

So, to specify rwxrw-r--, you would assemble the permissions like this:

```
    user           group           other
    rwx             rw-             r--
     7               6               4
S_IRWXU |   (S_IRGRP | S_IWGRP)   | S_IROTH
```

There is one more complication that gets thrown into the mix – the umask set by the user. The user has control over what permissions are used when creating new files by using the **umask** command to specify a numeric (octal) value to specify the bits that should be left unset, as shown in Figure 11.8.

Figure 11.8   umask

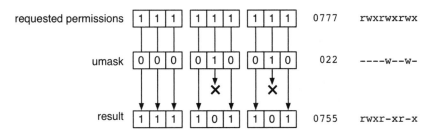

For example:

```
$ umask
22
$ touch test
$ ls -l test
-rw-r--r--  1 markd   staff   0 Aug 11 15:47 test
```

The umask "22" is binary 000 010 010. The middle bit is the "w" write bit. So a umask of 22 will remove the write bit for group and others. If you change the umask

```
$ umask 002
```

```
$ umask
2
$ rm test
$ touch test
$ ls -l test
-rw-rw-r--  1 markd  staff  0 Aug 11 15:48 test
```

now only the "other" group of permissions has the write bit stripped out. If you are truly paranoid, you can use a very restrictive umask:

```
$ umask 077
$ umask
77
$ rm test
$ touch test
$ ls -l test
-rw-------  1 markd  staff  0 Aug 11 15:49 test
```

077, which is all bits being set for group and other, causes all of those permission bits to be stripped out, so now only the owner has any access to the files.

A umask of 002 is most friendly if you are using groups to control permissions. You will not be creating files that cannot be written to by the group.

The **umask()** system call lets you change your processes' umask on the fly.

```
mode_t umask (mode_t numask);
```

The umask is inherited by child processes, which is useful if you want to make the umask more restrictive before spawning off a subprocess.

chmod does not change the modification date of the file. The file itself is not affected, just the metadata.

There is one last commonly used permission bit associated with files, the "set-uid" bit. There are some operations that can only be performed with the permission of root, the superuser, such as modifying the password file. But some of these operations (like changing a password) you want ordinary mortals to be able to do. The way traditional Unix works around this problem is having a bit that says, "when you run this program, run it as if the user were the same user as the file's owner, rather than running the program as the logged in user."

If you look at /usr/bin/passwd:

```
$ ls -l /usr/bin/passwd
-r-sr-xr-x  1 root  wheel  111968 Jun 23  2009 /usr/bin/passwd*
```

Notice the "s" in the user execute bit. That means when /usr/bin/passwd is run, it runs as root rather than as the logged-in user markd.

If you look at, say, one of the program files in the Oracle database:

```
$ cd $ORACLE_HOME/bin
$ ls -l oracle
-rwsr-s--x  1 oracle  oinstall 23389261 May 13 1997 oracle*
```

This is suid-oracle. When you run this program, it runs as if the logged in user were oracle. Also notice the second "s" in the group execute bit. That means the program will run as the group oinstall.

When a program runs, there are actually 6 (or more) IDs associated with it:

The real user ID and real group ID	This is who you really are, who you were when you logged in. These typically do not change during the life of a running program.
The effective user ID, effective group ID, supplementary group IDs	These are used for file permission checks. When you run an suid-root binary, your effective user ID is root.
The saved set-group-ID and saved set-user-ID	These are used by the exec functions, which will be discussed in Chapter 18: *Multiprocessing*.

Example 11.9   uid.m

```
// uid.m -- experiment with user and group ids.
//          run as normal, then change this to be suid, and run again

// gcc -g -Wall -o uid uid.m

#import <sys/types.h>    // for struct group/struct passwd
#import <grp.h>          // for getgrgid
#import <pwd.h>          // for getpwuid
#import <stdio.h>        // printf and friends
#import <stdlib.h>       // EXIT_SUCCESS
#import <unistd.h>       // for getuid(), etc

int main (int argc, char *argv[]) {
    uid_t user_id = getuid ();
    uid_t effective_user_id = geteuid ();

    gid_t group_id = getgid ();
    gid_t effective_group_id = getegid ();

    struct passwd *user = getpwuid (user_id);
    printf ("real user ID is '%s'\n", user->pw_name);

    user = getpwuid (effective_user_id);
    printf ("effective user ID is '%s'\n", user->pw_name);

    struct group *group = getgrgid (group_id);
    printf ("real group is '%s'\n", group->gr_name);

    group = getgrgid (effective_group_id);
    printf ("effective group is '%s'\n", group->gr_name);

    return EXIT_SUCCESS;

} // main
```

Here is a run just as markd:

```
$ ls -l uid
-rwxr-xr-x  1 markd  staff  9216 May 26 15:54 uid*
$ ./uid
real user ID is 'markd'
effective user ID is 'markd'
real group is 'staff'
```

```
effective group is 'staff'
```

Now run with **sudo**, so that it is actually run as root:

```
$ sudo ./uid
real user ID is 'root'
effective user ID is 'root'
real group is 'wheel'
effective group is 'wheel'
```

Now make it suid root:

```
$ sudo chown root:wheel uid
$ sudo chmod ug+s uid
$ ls -l uid
-rwsr-sr-x  1 root   wheel  9216 May 26 15:54 uid*
(note the s bits)
$ ./uid
real user ID is 'markd'
effective user ID is 'root'
real group is 'staff'
effective group is 'wheel'
```

So now this program is running with privileges of root when run by an ordinary user.

Finally, let's try it as another ordinary user:

```
$ sudo chown bork:admin uid
$ ls -l uid
-rwsr-sr-x  1 bork   admin  9216 May 26 15:54 uid*

$ ./uid
real user ID is 'markd'
effective user ID is 'bork'
real group is 'staff'
effective group is 'admin'
```

One thing to note is that the setuid bits get cleared if a non-privileged program writes to the setuid file.

```
$ ls -l uid
-rwsr-sr-x  1 markd  staff  9216 May 26 15:54 uid*
$ cat >> uid
1 [control-D for end of file]
$ ls -l uid
-rwxr-xr-x  1 markd  staff  9217 May 26 15:58 uid*
```

That is a security measure to keep some malicious program from replacing a setuid program and running hostile code with root privileges. Also, programs on disk images, such as FileValue volumes, will not be allowed to become setuid-root.

setuid-root is generally bad. Apple's sanctioned way of performing privileged operations is to have a launchd-controlled daemon that does the heavy lifting and use interprocess communication to tell the daemon to do the work.

Directory Permissions

Directories have the same permission bits as files, rwx for user, group, and other, but with slightly different interpretations. You cannot run directories as programs, so the execute bit takes on a different meaning: it acts like a search bit. When opening any type of file by path, the user must have execute permission on every directory mentioned in the path. The execute bit can match the user, group, or other. Read permission is different from the execute/search permission. Read permission lets you read the directory itself, like with the **ls** command, to obtain a list of all the file names in the directory. Execute just means that you can pass through, or execute programs in that directory. You do not need read permissions along the way.

As an example, you create a directory and copy a program into it

```
$ mkdir permtest
$ cp /bin/hostname permtest
$ chmod -rw permtest
$ ls -ld permtest
d--x--x--x  3 markd  staff  58 Aug 11 16:52 permtest/
```

Now you have turned off everything but the search bits.

```
$ ls permtest
ls: permtest: Permission denied
```

No read permission, so you get an error.

```
$ ./permtest/hostname
localhost
```

But you can still run programs in there.

Permission-Check Algorithms

Here is a quick overview of how permissions interact with the file operations discussed earlier:

- You must have read permission to open a file for reading with O_RDONLY or O_RDWR.

- You must have write permission to open a file for writing with O_WRONLY and O_RDWR.

- You must have write permission to O_TRUNC a file.

- You must have write and execute permission on a directory to create a new file. You need write permission so you can modify the directory entry, and you need execute permission so the directory can be searched.

- You must have write and execute permission on a directory to delete a file. You do not actually need read/write permissions on the file itself because the operation just manipulates the directory's data structures.

- You must have the execute bit set to run a file program as a program.

- For accessing a file:

  - If the effective user ID is zero, which is the superuser / root ID, access is allowed.

  - If the effective user ID is the same as the owner ID of the file, check the appropriate permission bit and allow access.

- If the effective group ID or supplementary group ID is the same as the group ID of the file, check the appropriate permission bit and allow access.

- If the appropriate access permission bit is set, allow access.

- Otherwise, do not allow access.

For the More Curious: Memory-Mapped Files

Memory-mapped files are a blend of the virtual memory system and the file system, where a file's contents are mapped onto a range of bytes in memory. When you get bytes from that range of memory, you are actually reading from the file. When you change bytes in that range of memory, you are writing to the file. In essence, you are doing I/O without using **read()** and **write()**. The virtual memory system gets to do the work of buffering, reading, and writing, only bringing in the blocks from disk that are actually used. To use memory-mapped files, you need to open the file, then call

```
caddr_t mmap (caddr_t addr, size_t len, int prot, int flags, int fd, off_t offset);
```

The return value is the address where the mapped file starts. Otherwise, -1 is returned, and errno is set.

Here are the arguments:

addr   A non-zero value hints to the OS where to start mapping the file in memory. **mmap()** is free to use or ignore this value. Usually, you just pass in zero.

len   The number of bytes to map from the file. If you have a huge file, you can map just a portion of it to make things faster.

prot   Protection on the mapped memory. Pass a bitwise OR of one or more of these values:

PROT_EXEC   Code may be executed on the mapped pages. This is available only on Mac OS X because iOS does not allow arbitrary execution.

PROT_READ   You can read from the pages.

PROT_WRITE   You can write to the pages.

These flags need to match the open mode of the file. For instance, you cannot PROT_WRITE a read-only file.

flags   Specifies various options. Here are the commonly used flags:

MAP_FIXED   Return value must equal addr. If that is not possible, an error is returned.

MAP_SHARED   Storing bytes in memory will modify the mapped file. Be sure to set this if you expect your memory writes to be reflected back in the file.

MAP_PRIVATE   Storing bytes in memory causes a copy of the mapped pages to be made, and all subsequent references reference the copy.

MAP_FILE   Map from a regular file or a character special device. This is the default and does not need to be specified.

MAP_INHERIT   Permit mapped regions to be mapped across **exec()** system calls so you can pass the mapped regions onto child processes.

fd   The file descriptor for the open file.

offset   The number of bytes into the file to start mapping. Usually, you just pass in zero.

To unmap pages, use

```
int munmap (caddr_t addr, size_t len);
```

This returns zero on success, -1/setting errno on error. You will generate invalid memory references if you try to access this memory after the **munmap()**. **close()** does not unmap pages, but pages will get unmapped when your program exits.

addr and offset should be multiples of the system's virtual memory page size. This should be 512 bytes, but use **sysconf()** to figure it out.

Use **msync()** to flush modified pages back to the file system:

```
int msync (void *addr, size_t len, int flags);
```

If len is zero, all modified pages will be flushed. Possible flag values are

MS_ASYNC   Return immediately and let the write happen at the kernel's convenience.

MS_SYNC   Perform synchronous writes.

MS_INVALIDATE   Invalidate all cached data (presumably to force a re-read from the file).

Some rules to remember:

- You can memory-map regular files but not networked file descriptors or device files.

- You need to be careful if the size of the underlying file could change after it gets mapped; otherwise, memory access errors might be triggered.

- You cannot use **mmap()** and memory writes to memory to extend files. You will need to seek and write to accomplish that.

Example 11.10 is a program that opens files, **mmap()**s them, and then walks the memory, performing the "rot-13" encryption on them. Rot-13 (short for "rotate 13") is a simple letter substitution cypher. It replaces letters with those that are 13 positions ahead of it in the alphabet. rot-13 is reversible. If you rot-13 text, you can rot-13 it again to get the original text back.

Example 11.10   mmap-rot13.m

```
// mmap-rot13.m -- use memory mapped I/O to apply the rot 13 'encryption'
//                 algorithm to a file.

// gcc -g -std=c99 -Wall -o mmap-rot13 mmap-rot13.m

#import <ctype.h>        // for isalpha(), etc
```

```
#import <errno.h>        // for errno
#import <stdio.h>        // for printf, etc
#import <stdlib.h>       // for EXIT_SUCCESS, etc
#import <string.h>       // for strerror()
#import <sys/fcntl.h>    // for O_RDWR and open()
#import <sys/mman.h>     // for mmap, etc
#import <sys/stat.h>     // for fstat() and struct stat
#import <sys/types.h>    // for caddr_t
#import <unistd.h>       // for close()

// walk the buffer shifting alphabetic characters 13 places
void rot13 (caddr_t base, size_t length) {
    char *scan = base;
    char *stop = scan + length;

    while (scan < stop) {
        // there are tons of implementations of rot13 out on the net
        // much more compact than this
        if (isalpha(*scan)) {
            if ((*scan >= 'A' && *scan <= 'M') || (*scan >= 'a' && *scan <= 'm')) {
                *scan += 13;
            } else if ((*scan >= 'N' && *scan <= 'Z')
                       || (*scan >= 'n' && *scan <= 'z')) {
                *scan -= 13;
            }
        }
        scan++;
    }

} // rot13

void processFile (const char *filename) {
    // open the file first
    int fd = open (filename, O_RDWR);
    if (fd == -1) {
        fprintf (stderr, "could not open %s: error %d (%s)\n",
                 filename, errno, strerror(errno));
        goto bailout;
    }

    // figure out how big it is
    struct stat statbuf;
    int result = fstat (fd, &statbuf);
    if (result == -1) {
        fprintf (stderr, "fstat of %s failed: error %d (%s)\n",
                 filename, errno, strerror(errno));
        goto bailout;
    }
    size_t length = statbuf.st_size;

    // mmap it
    caddr_t base = mmap (NULL, length, PROT_READ | PROT_WRITE, MAP_SHARED, fd, 0);
    if (base == (caddr_t) -1) {
        fprintf (stderr, "could not mmap %s: error %d (%s)\n",
                 filename, errno, strerror(errno));
        goto bailout;
    }

    // bitrot it.
    rot13 (base, length);
```

```
        // flush the results
        result = msync (base, length, MS_SYNC);
        if (result == -1) {
            fprintf (stderr, "msync failed for %s: error %d (%s)\n",
                    filename, errno, strerror(errno));
            goto bailout;
        }

bailout:
        // clean up any messes we've made
        if (base != (caddr_t) -1) munmap (base, length);
        if (fd != -1) close (fd);

} // processFile

int main (int argc, char *argv[]) {
    if (argc == 1) {
        fprintf (stderr, "usage: %s /path/to/file ... \n"
                "rot-13s files in-place using memory mapped i/o\n", argv[0]);
        exit (EXIT_FAILURE);
    }

    for (int i = 1; i < argc; i++) {
        processFile (argv[i]);
    }

    exit (EXIT_SUCCESS);

} // main
```

And of course, a sample run or two:

```
$ cat > blorf
Blorf is the name of a bunny rabbit.

$ ./mmap-rot13 blorf
$ cat blorf
Oybes vf gur anzr bs n ohaal enoovg.

$ ./mmap-rot13 blorf
$ cat blorf
Blorf is the name of a bunny rabbit.
```

12

Files, Part 2: Directories, File Systems, and Links

Directories are the counterparts to files. Files are containers of information, while directories are containers of files. Directories can be nested inside of other directories, giving the hierarchical structure to the file system. The file system itself is conceptually built upon data blocks which store information, and inodes that store metadata. Both files and directories make use of data blocks and inodes. Links (hard links and symbolic links) allow a file or directory to appear in more than one location.

Directories

Compared to files, there is very little that can be done to directories. You can create them, remove them, and iterate through their contents.

Creation and destruction

```
int mkdir (const char *path, mode_t mode);
```

`mkdir()` creates a new directory at the given `path`. The permissions on the directory are specified by mode using the `S_I*` constants discussed with `chmod()` on page 315. The umask is applied, clearing bits in the mode that are set in the umask, and do not forget to set the execution bits. `mkdir()` returns zero on success, -1 on error with `errno` set as appropriate. `mkdir()` does not create intervening directories if they do not exist, returning an error instead.

```
int rmdir (const char *path);
```

`rmdir()` removes the directory at `path`. The directory must be empty of any files or subdirectories; otherwise, an error will be returned. Like `mkdir()`, zero is returned on success and -1 will be returned on error with `errno` set.

Directory iteration

The opendir() Family

These are the functions you use to iterate through the contents of a directory:

```
DIR *opendir (const char *filename);

struct dirent *readdir(DIR *dirp);

long telldir (const DIR *dirp);

void seekdir (DIR *dirp, long loc);

void rewinddir (DIR *dirp);

int closedir (DIR *dirp);
```

The typical use of this API is to call **opendir()**, supplying the path you want a director listing for. **opendir()** returns an opaque DIR handle whose resources are released by **closedir()**. Call **readdir()** in a loop until it tells you it is done by returning NULL. **telldir()** lets you know where you are in a directory stream. **seekdir()** will move the position of the directory stream to the indicated location, and **rewinddir()** will reset the position to the beginning of the directory. The struct dirent returned from **readdir()** looks like:

```
struct dirent {
    ino_t       d_fileno;               /* file number (inode) of entry */
    uint16_t    d_reclen;               /* length of this record */
    uint8_t     d_type;                 /* the type of the file   */
    uint8_t     d_namlen;               /* length of string in d_name */
    char        d_name[MAXNAMLEN + 1];  /* name of the file */
};
```

The size of the integer fields is larger when building in 64-bit mode.

d_name, the name of the file, is the piece of information that is most interesting. On HFS+ file systems, file names are returned in alphabetical order, but this isn't a guarantee provided by the API.

Example 12.1 is a cheap version of **ls**, without any features:

Example 12.1   cheapls.m

```
// cheapls.m -- a featureless ls program using the directory iteration
//              functions

// gcc -g -Wall -Wextra -o cheapls cheapls.m

#import <dirent.h>      // for opendir and friends
#import <errno.h>       // for errno
#import <stdio.h>       // for printf
#import <stdlib.h>      // for EXIT_SUCCESS
#import <string.h>      // for strerror
#import <sys/dirent.h>  // for struct dirent
#import <sys/types.h>   // for random type definition

int main (int argc, char *argv[]) {
    if (argc != 2) {
        fprintf (stderr, "usage: %s /path/to/directory\n", argv[0]);
        return EXIT_FAILURE;
    }

    DIR *directory = opendir (argv[1]);
    if (directory == NULL) {
        fprintf (stderr, "could not open directory '%s'\n", argv[1]);
        fprintf (stderr, "error is is useful: %d (%s)\n", errno, strerror(errno));
```

```
        return EXIT_FAILURE;
    }

    struct dirent *entry;
    while ((entry = readdir(directory)) != NULL) {
        long position = telldir (directory);
        printf ("%3ld: %s\n", position, entry->d_name);
    }

    int result = closedir (directory);
    if (result == -1) {
        fprintf (stderr, "error closing directory: %d (%s)\n",
                 errno, strerror(errno));
        return EXIT_FAILURE;
    }
    return EXIT_SUCCESS;
} // main
```

And some sample runs (edited):

```
$ ./cheapls .
  1: .
  2: ..
  3: #uid.m#
  4: .#chapter.txt
  5: .#uid.m
  6: .DS_Store
  7: .gdb_history
  8: access
  9: access.m
 10: access.m~
 11: append
 12: append.m
    ...
 49: writestring.m
 50: writevecstring
 51: writevecstring.m

$ ./cheapls /Developer/Applications
  1: .
  2: ..
  3: .DS_Store
  4: Audio
  5: Dashcode.app
  6: Graphics Tools
  7: Instruments.app
  8: Performance Tools
  9: Quartz Composer.app
 10: Utilities
 11: Xcode.app
```

Current working directory

The current working directory is the default location used for file operations that don't specify a full path. If a partial path is supplied to a function, such as **open()**, the full path is constructed by appending the path to the current working directory. You use this concept all the time in the shell when you **cd** to a directory and perform operations without specifying a full path, that is, a path beginning with a slash character.

```
int chdir (const char *path);
```

```
int fchdir (int fd);
```

chdir() sets your current working directory to path, while **fchdir()** uses a file descriptor of an open directory. On success, it returns zero, and on error, it returns -1 with errno set appropriately.

getcwd() tells you what the current directory is:

```
char *getcwd (char *buf, size_t size);
```

Pass it a buffer and the buffer size. You should make sure that buf is MAXPATHLEN bytes or larger. You can also pass NULL and have the function allocate memory on your behalf. Make sure you **free()** it.

buf is returned after a successful call, with NULL returned in case of error and errno set. The **getcwd()** manpage warns not to use **getcwd()** to save a directory for the purpose of returning to it, like when using the **pushd** command in a shell. Instead, you should open the current directory ("."), stash away the file descriptor, and then use **fchdir()** to return to it.

The current working directory is a global value, so it is not a thread-safe concept. One thread could change the working directory and then get pre-empted by another thread, which then changes the working directory. When the first thread gets control, the current working directory will be wrong. If you are going to be dealing with multiple directories in a threaded app, use full path names.

Inside The File System

Figure 12.1 shows that the physical disk is divided up into partitions:

Figure 12.1   Partitions

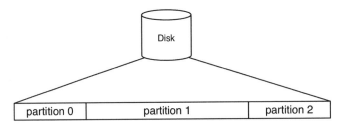

Figure 12.2 shows an idealized Unix file system on a particular partition. HFS+ is actually implemented differently, but this mental model will help you understand the upcoming system calls.

Figure 12.2   Filesystem

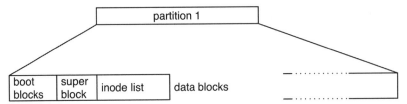

The superblock is a block in a known location that has pointers to the rest of the on-disk data structures. Frequently there are redundant copies of the superblock in case the primary superblock gets destroyed.

An inode, short for "indirect block," is the handle used to reference an individual file, as shown in Figure 12.3. Each file has an inode that contains the metadata for the file like the size, modification dates, etc., as well as a list of datablocks that compose the file. The inode has a link count, which is a reference count of the number of directory entries that point to the inode. The file is actually deleted, and its data blocks recycled, when this count goes to zero.

Figure 12.3   inodes

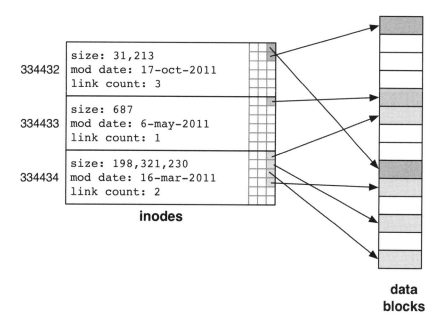

A data block can contain either file data or directory data, as shown in Figure 12.4. Directory blocks have a flag saying that this block represents a directory. A directory is just a list of file names and inode addresses. The directory does not actually store a copy of the inode itself. When you iterate through a directory, you are picking up the filename from the directory and then you can find the actual file by using the inode.

Figure 12.4   Directory structure

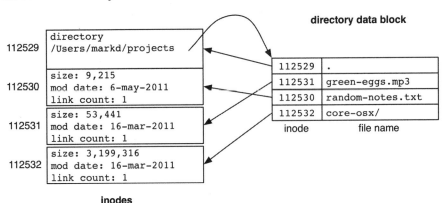

The special files in directories are just inode references. For instance, "." (the current directory) is the inode that references the directory, and ".." (the parent directory) references the enclosing directory. Since the inode points within a particular file system, you cannot have a directory with files that cross file system boundaries. This means that moving a file to a new place in the current filesystem happens because of a couple of directory block manipulations. No data is actually copied. If you move a file to a different filesystem, the data needs to be copied.

There are some points to be taken from this. Since files are referenced by their inode number, which you can see when you do an **ls -i**, a file can physically appear in more than one place. These are hard links, which are covered below. It also means that there is a finite pool of inodes available. You can use **df -i** to see the number of inodes in use and free. If you run out of inodes, you will not be able to create any more files on that file system even if there is plenty of space. When you create new file systems from scratch, you need to decide on the inode density. For a file system that will primarily be storing digital video, you do not need a whole lot of inodes since you will have relatively few individual files. If you are creating a file system to store a usenet newsfeed, you will want to have a much higher density of inodes, since newsfeeds tend to have a huge number of tiny files. For typical consumer use, the defaults strike a good balance between inode density and available disk space.

There are some hard-coded limits regarding the filesystem, particularly things like file names and path names. Path names are limited to the constant PATH_MAX, which is defined as 1024 bytes. This is an unfortunate choice, since languages like Korean have 3-byte characters in UTF-8. Likewise, the maximum size for a file name is 1024 bytes.

Standard Unix file systems are not journaled. Journaled filesystems always keep the metadata on the disk in a consistent state. Mac HFS+ has had journaling support since OS X 10.3.

Links

A "link" is a way reference a file from more than one place. You may have software that makes assumptions about where a file lives in the filesystem, but it might be more convenient for that file to actually live elsewhere, perhaps on another file system. You may also have a large file, say a video tutorial, appear in each user's home directory on a multi-user machine, but you do not want the disk space consumed for multiple copies.

Unix has two kinds of links: hard links and symbolic links. OS X also brings aliases to the table.

Hard links

As mentioned earlier in the brief overview of the file system, hard links are entries in multiple directories that all refer to the same inode. The file appears in multiple places at once. Use the **ln** command to create a hard link:

```
$ mkdir linktest
$ cd linktest
$ touch spoon
(creates a new file)

$ ln spoon spoon2
(makes a hard link)

$ ls -li
total 0
571668 -rw-r--r-.  2 markd   staff   0 Aug 12 11:52 spoon
571668 -rw-r--r--  2 markd   staff   0 Aug 12 11:52 spoon2
```

The left-hand column shows the inode of the file. As expected, the inodes are the same. Also notice the third column. It says that there are two hard links to this file.

```
$ ln spoon spoon3
$ ls -li
total 0
571668 -rw-r--r--  3 markd   staff   0 Aug 12 11:52 spoon
571668 -rw-r--r--  3 markd   staff   0 Aug 12 11:52 spoon2
571668 -rw-r--r--  3 markd   staff   0 Aug 12 11:52 spoon3
```

Now there are three hard links to the same file.

Hard links cannot cross file system boundaries because they refer to inodes. If you **mv** a hard linked file to another file system, the data will get copied, the original removed, and the link count will go down by one.

Users cannot create hard links to directories. On some file systems, the superuser can make hard links to directories, but in general that is not advisable because hard links can form cycles in the directories, which most software is not designed to handle. Apple's Time Machine does use hard links on its backup volumes, including hard links to directories. An unmodified file that exists in multiple incremental backups will actually exit on disk just once, but will be referred to in multiple places via hard links.

Symbolic links

A symbolic link is a file that contains a path to another file. This path can be relative or absolute. Symbolic links are not included in the reference count of a file and, in fact, do not have to actually point to a real file at all, in which case they become dangling links. Use **ln -s** to create a symbolic link:

```
$ mkdir symlinktest
$ cd symlinktest
$ touch spoon
(makes an empty file)

$ ln -s spoon spoon2
(makes a relative symbolic link)
```

```
$ ls -l
total 8
-rw-r--r--  1 markd  staff  0 Aug 12 12:08 spoon
lrwxr-xr-x  1 markd  staff  5 Aug 12 12:08 spoon2@ -> spoon
```

$ ln -s `pwd`/spoon spoon3
*(use the backtick shell operator to run **pwd**, which then is pasted into the command command, which will give you a full path)*

```
$ ls -l
total 16
-rw-rw-r--  1 markd  staff   0 Aug 12 12:08 spoon
lrwxrwxr-x  1 markd  staff   5 Aug 12 12:08 spoon2 -> spoon
lrwxrwxr-x  1 markd  staff  35 Aug 12 12:08 spoon3 -> /Users/markd/badgers/\
symlinktest/spoon
```

Take a look at the size column. It is the number of characters in the symbolic link. The leading character over in the permissions is a lower case L, signifying that this is a link.

ls -F shows the extra symbols attached to file names:

```
$ ls -F
spoon    spoon2@ spoon3@
```

The at-sign says it is a symbolic link. Additional character suffixes that -F uses are "/" for directories and "*" for executable files. You can alias **ls** to be **ls -F** so that you can see these clues in your directory listings.

Symbolic links are like pointers to files, as shown in Figure 12.5. They were created to work around some of the problems with hard links, such as crossing file systems and making links to directories. You can make a symbolic link to a directory and not cause problems. You can generate loops with symbolic links, but, luckily, function calls that try to resolve them will generate an error.

Figure 12.5   Hard and symbolic links

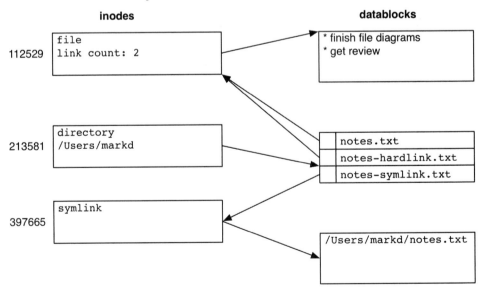

The real power of symbolic links comes when you move things around in the filesystem. Say your webserver log files in `/home/nsadmin/logs/borkware` are filling up your drive. You can copy all the log files to another place, like `/Volumes/BigDisk/logs/borkware`, and then point the first path to the second. No need to change any configuration files, and existing paths to the logs still work. Granted, things can get out of hand and can become unmaintainable if you have too many layers of symbolic link indirection.

Most of the file API you have seen so far will follow symbolic links automatically, like **chmod()**, **chown()**, **open()**, and also **stat()**, which is discussed a bit later.

There are some function calls that let you manipulate the link directly.

```
int lchown (const char *path, uid_t owner, gid_t group);
```

This changes the owner.

```
int readlink (const char *path, char *buf, int bufferLength);
```

This places the contents of the symbolic link path into the buffer. **readlink()** does not append the terminating zero byte. Instead, it returns the number of characters it wrote into the buffer or -1 on error with `errno` set appropriately.

lstat(), described later, will give you metadata for the symbolic link itself rather than the file it points to. **rename()** and **unlink()** also deal with the link directly.

The transparent resolution of links can lead to confusion when dangling links are involved:

```
$ ln -s /no/such/file oopack
$ ls oopack
oopack
(It is there)
$ cat oopack
cat: oopack: No such file or directory
(Actually, it is not there.)

$ ls -l oopack
lrwxr-xr-x  1 markd  staff  13 Aug 12 12:30 oopack@ -> /no/such/file
(oh, it is a symbolic link that points to nowhere)
```

`ls -F` tells you what's happening:

```
$ ls -F oopack
oopack@
```

oopack is now obviously a symbolic link.

Differences between the kinds of links:

- Hard links always point to valid files.

- Symbolic links do not track file moves, but aliases do.

- Symbolic links survive file deletions, aliases do not always.

- Symbolic links can make loops.

Mac OS aliases

Users can create aliases in Finder by explicitly making an alias or performing certain mouse dragging operations. Like symbolic links, aliases are not included in a file's reference count, and they can dangle, pointing nowhere. On HFS+, an alias contains the file's file number (similar to an inode number), so the alias can find the file anywhere on the disk. The path to the file is also stored in case the file is deleted and replaced with a new one.

API for links

```
int link (const char *name1, const char *name2);

int symlink (const char *name1, const char *name2);
```

link() creates a hard link, and symlink() creates a symbolic link with name2 referring to the same file as name1. Zero is returned on success, and -1 is returned on error with errno set appropriately. Use readlink() to get the file name stored in the link.

You will need to use the Carbon API if you want to deal with aliases.

File Metadata

File metadata is data about the file, but it is not the file's data itself. This includes information like the file's size, type, the last access times, and so on.

stat()

Three functions can be used to access metadata that lives in the inode:

```
int stat (const char *path, struct stat *sb);

int lstat (const char *path, struct stat *sb);

int fstat (int fd, struct stat *sb);
```

stat() gets the status, the information about the file at a path, following any intervening symbolic links. lstat() gets information about the symbolic link itself. fstat() gives you metadata about an already open file. As with most Unix file functions, a return value of zero indicates success, a value of -1 indicates an error, and errno is set appropriately.

You do not need read, write, or execute permissions on a file to stat() it, but all directories listed in the path name need to be searchable.

struct stat is the focal point for all of the data returned by these calls. You allocate a struct stat either on the stack or dynamically and pass that to the function.

```
struct stat {
    dev_t     st_dev;                    /* device inode resides on */
    ino_t     st_ino;                    /* inode's number */
    mode_t    st_mode;                   /* inode protection mode */
    nlink_t   st_nlink;                  /* number or hard links to the file */
    uid_t     st_uid;                    /* user-id of owner */
    gid_t     st_gid;                    /* group-id of owner */
    dev_t     st_rdev;                   /* device type, for special file inode */
    struct timespec st_atimespec;        /* time of last access */
```

```
    struct timespec st_mtimespec;   /* time of last data modification */
    struct timespec st_ctimespec;   /* time of last file status change */
    off_t    st_size;               /* file size, in bytes */
    quad_t   st_blocks;             /* blocks allocated for file */
    u_long   st_blksize;            /* optimal file sys I/O ops blocksize */
    u_long   st_flags;              /* user defined flags for file */
    u_long   st_gen;                /* file generation number */
};
```

Here is a breakdown of the more common fields:

st_mode contains the file type and permissions. The lower nine bits have the user, group, and other permissions. You can focus in on those by using the bit mask ACCESSPERMS (0777). You can also bitwise-AND using the macros listed with **chmod()**, such as S_IRWXU and S_IRUSR. There are also bits used to describe the type of file being examined, as shown in Table 12.1.

Table 12.1   File Types

Mask	Convenience Macro	What it is
S_IFIFO	S_ISFIFO()	FIFO, a named pipe, an IPC mechanism
S_IFCHR	S_ISCHR()	character special device like terminals and serial lines
S_IFDIR	S_ISDIR()	directory
S_IFBLK	S_ISBLK()	block special device like disks and tapes
S_IFREG	S_ISREG()	plain old regular file
S_IFLNK	S_ISLNK()	symbolic link
S_IFSOCK	S_ISSOCK()	socket, network communication

The st_uid and st_gid fields tell you the user id of the user that owns the file, as well as the group associated with the file.

st_size has the file size in bytes.

There are three file times associated with each file, access, modification, and metadata change. These file times are of type struct timespec:

```
struct timespec {
    time_t  tv_sec;         // seconds
    long    tv_nsec;        // nanoseconds
};
```

st_atimespec   The last access time. This is the last time the file was opened for reading. You can see this with **ls -lu**. You can also access just the tv_sec field by using st_atime.

st_mtimespec   The last modification time. This is the date displayed by **ls -l**. You can also access just the tv_sec field by using st_mtime.

st_ctimespec   Last change in inode status, like by using **chmod** or **chown**. **ls -lc** shows this time. You can also access just the tv_sec field by using st_ctime.

The shorter-named versions (st_mtime vs st_mtimespec) are of type time_t, which is the number of seconds since the start of the Unix epoch: midnight, Jan 1, 1970. They are conveniences for accessing the tv_sec field of the timespecs. Depending on various circumstances, these could be members of struct stat or #defines that dig into the timespec fields.

The **utimes()** system call can be used to change access and modification times of a file. This is handy if you are writing something like an archive utility and need to preserve access times when you expand an archive.

Example 12.2 is a little program that will print out a whole bunch of stuff from struct stat:

Example 12.2   permtype.m

```
// permtype.m -- Use stat to discover the type and permissions for a file.

// gcc -g -std=c99 -Wall -Wextra -o permtype permtype.m

#import <errno.h>        // for errno
#import <grp.h>          // for group file access routines
#import <pwd.h>          // for passwd file access routines
#import <stdio.h>        // for printf
#import <stdlib.h>       // for EXIT_SUCCESS
#import <string.h>       // for strerror
#import <sys/stat.h>     // for stat() and struct stat
#import <sys/time.h>     // for struct tm, localtime, etc

// Lookup table for mapping permission values to the familiar
// character strings.
static const char *g_perms[]  = {
    "---", "--x", "-w-", "-wx", "r--", "r-x", "rw-", "rwx"
};

// Mapping from the file type bit mask to a human-readable string.
typedef struct FileType {
    unsigned long   mask;
    const char      *type;
} FileType;

static FileType g_filetypes[] = {
    { S_IFREG, "Regular File" },
    { S_IFDIR, "Directory" },
    { S_IFLNK, "Symbolic Link" },
    { S_IFCHR, "Character Special Device" },
    { S_IFBLK, "Block Special Device" },
    { S_IFIFO, "FIFO" },
    { S_IFSOCK, "Socket" },
};

void displayInfo (const char *filename) {
    struct stat statbuf;
    int result = lstat (filename, &statbuf);

    if (result == -1) {
        fprintf (stderr, "error with stat(%s) :  %d (%s)\n",
                filename, errno, strerror(errno));
        return;
    }

    printf ("%s:\n", filename);
```

```
        printf ("  permissions: %s%s%s\n",
                g_perms[(statbuf.st_mode & S_IRWXU) >> 6],
                g_perms[(statbuf.st_mode & S_IRWXG) >> 3],
                g_perms[(statbuf.st_mode & S_IRWXO)]);

        // Get the readable string for the type.
        FileType *scan = g_filetypes;
        FileType *stop = scan + (sizeof(g_filetypes) / sizeof(*g_filetypes));

        while (scan < stop) {
            if ((statbuf.st_mode & S_IFMT) == scan->mask) {
                printf ("  type: %s\n", scan->type);
                break;
            }
            scan++;
        }

        // Any special bits sets?
        if ((statbuf.st_mode & S_ISUID) == S_ISUID) printf ("  set-uid!\n");
        if ((statbuf.st_mode & S_ISGID) == S_ISGID) printf ("  set-group-id!\n");

        // File size.
        printf ("  file is %ld bytes (%.2f K)\n",
                (long)statbuf.st_size, (float) (statbuf.st_size / 1024.0));

        // Owning user / group
        struct passwd *passwd = getpwuid (statbuf.st_uid);
        printf ("  user: %s (%d)\n", passwd->pw_name, statbuf.st_uid);
        struct group *group = getgrgid (statbuf.st_gid);
        printf ("  group: %s (%d)\n", group->gr_name, statbuf.st_gid);

        // Now the dates
        char buffer[1024];
        struct tm *tm;

        tm = localtime (&statbuf.st_atime);
        strftime (buffer, 1024, "%c", tm);
        printf ("  last access: %s\n", buffer);

        tm = localtime (&statbuf.st_mtime);
        strftime (buffer, 1024, "%c", tm);
        printf ("  last modification: %s\n", buffer);

        tm = localtime (&statbuf.st_ctime);
        strftime (buffer, 1024, "%c", tm);
        printf ("  last inode change: %s\n", buffer);

        // double-space output
        printf ("\n");

} // displayInfo


int main (int argc, char *argv[]) {
    if (argc == 1) {
        fprintf (stderr, "usage:  %s /path/to/file ... \n", argv[0]);
        return EXIT_FAILURE;
    }
    for (int i = 1; i < argc; i++) {
        displayInfo (argv[i]);
```

```
    }

    return EXIT_SUCCESS;

} // main
```

A sample run

```
$ ./permtype ./permtype oopack / /dev/klog /usr/bin/passwd nobody-home
(where oopack is a symbolic link)

!.
./permtype ./permtype / /dev/klog /usr/bin/passwd nobody-home
./permtype:
  permissions: rwxr-xr-x
  type: Regular File
  file is 9856 bytes (9.62 K)
  user: markd (501)
  group: staff (20)
  last access: Thu May 26 19:14:23 2011
  last modification: Thu May 26 19:14:18 2011
  last inode change: Thu May 26 19:14:18 2011

/:
  permissions: rwxr-xr-x
  type: Directory
  file is 1292 bytes (1.26 K)
  user: root (0)
  group: admin (80)
  last access: Thu May 26 19:14:18 2011
  last modification: Wed May 25 17:03:21 2011
  last inode change: Wed May 25 17:10:50 2011

/dev/klog:
  permissions: rw-------
  type: Character Special Device
  file is 0 bytes (0.00 K)
  user: root (0)
  group: wheel (0)
  last access: Thu May 26 19:12:02 2011
  last modification: Sun May  1 21:48:14 2011
  last inode change: Sun May  1 21:48:14 2011.

/usr/bin/passwd:
  permissions: r-xr-xr-x
  type: Regular File
  set-uid!
  file is 111968 bytes (109.34 K)
  user: root (0)
  group: wheel (0)
  last access: Sun May  1 21:35:36 2011
  last modification: Wed Mar  9 00:49:27 2011
  last inode change: Sun May  1 21:35:36 2011

error with stat(nobody-home) :  2 (No such file or directory)
```

Now, just to make your life a little more complicated, both Cocoa and Carbon have different kinds of metadata they bring to the table, including things like the HFS+ Creator and Type code for files, and whether the file extension should be hidden.

NSFileManager has a number of constants for use in the attribute dictionary returned by -[NSFileManager fileAttributesAtPath: traverseLink:]. There is some overlap with what you get from struct stat:

- NSFileSize

- NSFileModificationDate

- NSFileOwnerAccountName

- NSFileGroupOwnerAccountName

- NSFileReferenceCount (# of hard links)

- NSFileIdentifier

- NSFilePosixPermissions (the rwx permissions)

- NSFileExtensionHidden

- NSFileHFSCreatorCode

- HSFileHFSTypeCode

- NSFileType (This is a string that says whether it is of type Directory, Regular, Symbolic Link, etc.)

In Carbon, you can use calls like **FSGetCatalogInfo()** to get an FSCatalogInfo structure that has information like AppleShare sharing flags, the creation date, the backup date, Finder information, the logical and physical size of the data and resource fork, as well as a text encoding hint.

getattrlist()

Darwin introduces function, **getattrlist()**, that returns file metadata. In addition to the metadata that **stat()** gives you, **getattrlist()** can give you a whole lot more. You can pick and choose the individual pieces of metadata that you want to look at. If you are only interested in seeing a file's size and last access time, **getattrlist()** can be told to just return those two pieces of metadata and not worry about anything else.

getattrlist() has existed since Mac OS X 10.0, but it was first documented in Mac OS X 10.4. The manpage is full of caveats and a bit of humor, such as "For reasons that are not at all obvious" and "Generally not a useful value." **getattrlist()** is not defined to work for all file system types. You will see the highlights here, and you can find the full description in the **getattrlist()** manpage.

```
int getattrlist (const char *path, struct attrlist *attrList,
                 void *attrBuf, size_t attrBufSize,
                 unsigned long options)
```

path is the file you want the metadata for, and the function will store it into the attrBuf of attrBufSize. The return value from **getattrlist()** is zero on success, -1 on error, with the actual error placed in errno.

One word of warning: if the attribute buffer is too small, **getattrlist()** will truncate the data it places in the buffer. There are some variable-length structures (which you'll see later) that reference data in other places in the buffer, which could end up referencing memory off the end. You need to pre-flight these variable-length structures to make sure they don't reference data that's been cut.

options can be zero or FSOPT_NOFOLLOW to prevent symbolic link resolution if it occurs as the last component of path.

Describing the attributes

A struct attrlist is used to tell **getattrlist()** what metadata you are interested in:

```
struct attrlist {
    u_short       bitmapcount; /* number of bit sets here */
    u_int16_t     padding;     /* for 4-byte alignment */
    attrgroup_t   commonattr;  /* common attributes */
    attrgroup_t   volattr;     /* volume attributes */
    attrgroup_t   dirattr;     /* directory attributes */
    attrgroup_t   fileattr;    /* file attributes */
    attrgroup_t   forkattr;    /* fork attributes */
};
```

The structure starts out with bitmapcount, which is the number of attrgroup_ts that the structure contains. An attrgroup_t is just an unsigned 32-bit integer. The current version of struct attrlist has five entries. Use the constant ATTR_BIT_MAP_COUNT to set that value. After some padding to keep everything on 4-byte alignment, the five bitmaps follow. Set bits in these bitmaps using the bitwise-OR operator to indicate the attributes you are interested in. Be sure to zero out the entire structure before setting any specific attribute flags.

commonattr contains bitmap flags for attributes that relate to all types of file system objects. Here are some common attributes you may be interested in. The typenames mentioned in each attribute are what get placed into your attrBuf:

ATTR_CMN_NAME	The name of the file, represented by an attrreference_t structure. It is a zero-terminated UTF-8 C string. The attrreference_t structure will be described in the section below that talks about parsing the returned attributes.
ATTR_CMN_OBJTYPE	The type of the file. The values are taken from enum vtype that is defined in <sys/vnode.h>. Common values include VREG (regular file), VDIR (directory), and VLNK (symbolic link)
ATTR_CMN_MODTIME	The modification time of the file, represented as a struct timespec. This is equivalent to st_mtimespec in struct stat. You can access other file times by using ATTR_CMN_CRTIME (creation time), ATTR_CMN_CHGTIME (last attribute modification time), and ATTR_CMN_ACCTIME (time of last access).
ATTR_CMN_OWNERID	The owner of the file, represented as a uid_t. You can get the group name with ATTR_CMD_GRPID, which places a gid_t into the attributes buffer.
ATTR_ACCESSMASK	The access permissions of the file represented as a mode_t. This is equivalent to st_mode in struct stat

`volattr` contains bitmap flags for attributes that relate to mounted volumes. The `path` should refer to the volume's mountpoint.

`ATTR_VOL_INFO`	If you want any volume attributes to be returned, you must include this value in the bitmask. This does not result in any attribute data actually being returned.
`ATTR_VOL_SIZE`	The total size of the volume, in bytes, represented by an `off_t`.
`ATTR_VOL_SPACEFREE`	The free space of the volume, in bytes, represented by an `off_t`.
`ATTR_VOL_SPACEAVAIL`	The space, in bytes, on the volume that is available to non-privileged users. Volumes reserve an amount of free space to prevent disk exhaustion errors. You should report this value, and not `ATTR_VOL_SPACEFREE`, to users.
`ATTR_VOL_IOBLOCKSIZE`	The optimal block size to use when reading or writing data. This is an `unsigned long`.
`ATTR_VOL_FILECOUNT`	The number of files currently on the volume. Also an `unsigned long`.
`ATTR_VOL_DIRCOUNT`	The number of directories currently on the volume. An `unsigned long`
`ATTR_VOL_NAME`	An `attrreference_t` structure containing the name of the volume. This is a UTF-8 zero-terminated C string. The data length will not be greater than NAME_MAX + 1.
`ATTR_VOL_CAPABILITIES`	A `vol_capabilities_attr_t` structure that describes the optional features supported by the volume. Consult the **getattrlist()** manpage for the `vol_capabilities_attr_t` and the different volume capabilities supported.
`ATTR_VOL_ATTRIBUTES`	A `vol_attributes_attr_t` structure that describes the attributes supported by the volume. Likewise, consult the manpage for details on using this.

`dirattr` contains bitmap flags for attributes that relate to directories. There are two other flags, but they're documented as either "you should not always rely on this value being accurate" or "Due to a bug, this flag is never set on current systems." So this is the only directory attribute you should use:

`ATTR_DIR_ENTRYCOUNT`	An `unsigned long` with the number of file system objects in the directory, not including things like . and .., termed "synthetic entries."

`fileattr` contains bitmap flags for attributes that relate to regular files. These values are undefined if you get the metadata for something other than a regular file, such as a directory.

`ATTR_FILE_TOTALSIZE`	The total number of bytes of all forks of a file, represented by an `off_t`. This is the logical size of a file. If a text file had 40 characters in it, the logical size would be 40.

`ATTR_FILE_ALLOCSIZE`	The total number of bytes on disk used by all of the file's forks. This is the physical size of a file. If the 40-character text file was living on a volume with a 4K block size, the physical size of the file would be 4K.
`ATTR_FILE_IOBLOCKSIZE`	The optimal block size to use when reading or writing this file's data. This is an `unsigned long`
`ATTR_FILE_DATALENGTH`	The logical size of the data fork for the file. This is an `off_t`. You can use `ATTR_FILE_DATAALLOCSIZE` to get the physical size of the data fork.
`ATTR_FILE_RSRCLENGTH`	The logical size of the resource fork for the file. This is an `off_t`. You can use `ATTR_FILE_RSRCALLOCSIZE` to get the physical size of the resource fork.

The `forkattr` bitmap should be left empty. According to the manpage, "Fork attributes are not properly implemented by any current Mac OS X volume format implementation. We strongly recommend that client programs do not request fork attributes."

Parsing the buffer

The data that is placed into your buffer by **getattrlist()** is placed in the order that the attribute bitmap flags are listed in the manpage (and the order they are listed here). The scalar types, such as `mode_t`, `off_t`, `unsigned long`, are stacked end-to-end, sometimes with padding to align values to four-byte boundaries. Typically, you will define a `struct` that lays out the data types you're expecting back and then pass the address to one of these structs for **getattrlist()** to fill in.

The variable-length attributes, particularly names, are accessed indirectly using an `attrreference_t`. If you are using the `struct`-overlay idiom, you would have an `attrreference_t` in your struct. An `attrreference_t` looks like this:

```
typedef struct attrreference {
    long        attr_dataoffset;
    size_t      attr_length;
} attrreference_t;
```

To get at the actual data, you would add `attr_dataoffset` to the address of the `attrreference_t` in the struct. Say that you are interested in the file name and the modification time. Your overlay struct might look like this:

```
typedef struct PermTypeAttributes {
    unsigned long       length;
    attrreference_t     name;
    struct timespec     modTime;
    char                fileNameSpace[MAXPATHLEN];
} PermTypeAttributes;
```

And then call the function:

```
PermTypeAttributes permAttributes;
int result = getattrlist (filename, &attrList, &permAttributes,
                          sizeof(permAttributes), 0);
```

Then access the name like this:

```
char *filenameFromAttrs =
    ((char *)&permAttributes->name) + permAttributes->name.attr_dataoffset;
```

Example 12.3 is the **permtype** program, but it is implemented using **getattrlist()** rather than **stat()**.

Example 12.3   permtype-getattrlist.m

```
// permtype-getattrlist.m -- use getattrlist() to discover type and
//                           permisisons for a file.

// gcc -g -std=c99 -o permtype-getattrlist permtype-getattrlist.m

#import <errno.h>       // for errno
#import <grp.h>         // for group file access routines
#import <pwd.h>         // for passwd file access routines
#import <stdio.h>       // for printf
#import <stdlib.h>      // for EXIT_SUCCESS
#import <string.h>      // for memset()
#import <sys/attr.h>    // for attribute structures
#import <sys/stat.h>    // for stat() and struct stat
#import <unistd.h>      // for getattrlist()

// Lookup table for mapping permission values to the familiar
// character strings.
static const char *g_perms[]  = {
    "---", "--x", "-w-", "-wx", "r--", "r-x", "rw-", "rwx"
};

// Mapping from the file type bit mask to a human-readable string.
typedef struct FileType {
    unsigned long       mask;
    const char          *type;
} FileType;

static FileType g_types[] = {
    { S_IFREG, "Regular File" },
    { S_IFDIR, "Directory" },
    { S_IFLNK, "Symbolic Link" },
    { S_IFCHR, "Character Special Device" },
    { S_IFBLK, "Block Special Device" },
    { S_IFIFO, "FIFO" },
    { S_IFSOCK, "Socket" },
};

// structure of the data being returned by getattrlist()

typedef struct PermTypeAttributes {
    u_int32_t           length;
    attrreference_t     name;
    struct timespec     modTime;
    struct timespec     changeTime;
    struct timespec     accessTime;
    uid_t               ownerId;
    gid_t               groupId;
#if __LITTLE_ENDIAN__
    mode_t              accessMask;
    short               padding;
```

```
#else
    short             padding;
    mode_t            accessMask;
#endif
    off_t             fileLogicalSize;
    char              fileNameSpace[MAXPATHLEN];
} __attribute__ ((packed)) PermTypeAttributes;

void displayInfo (const char *filename) {
    // Clear out the attribute request structure first, otherwise you'll
    // get undefined results.
    struct attrlist attrList = { 0 };
    attrList.bitmapcount = ATTR_BIT_MAP_COUNT;

    // Get the name, the permissions, and the stat-style times.
    attrList.commonattr = ATTR_CMN_NAME | ATTR_CMN_MODTIME | ATTR_CMN_CHGTIME
        | ATTR_CMN_ACCTIME | ATTR_CMN_OWNERID | ATTR_CMN_GRPID | ATTR_CMN_ACCESSMASK;

    // Also get the file size.
    attrList.fileattr = ATTR_FILE_TOTALSIZE;

    // The returned data cannot be larger than the size of PermTypeAttributes.
    PermTypeAttributes permAttributes;
    int result = getattrlist (filename, &attrList, &permAttributes,
                              sizeof(permAttributes), 0);
    if (result == -1) {
        fprintf (stderr, "error with getattrlist(%s) : %d / %s\n",
                 filename, errno, strerror(errno));
        return;
    }

    // Be a little paranoid about the variable-sized returned data.
    char *nameStart = ((char *) &permAttributes.name)
        + permAttributes.name.attr_dataoffset;
    char *nameEnd = nameStart + permAttributes.name.attr_length;
    char *bufferEnd = permAttributes.fileNameSpace
        + sizeof(permAttributes.fileNameSpace);

    // getattrlist() won't actually clobber past the end of our structure,
    // but blindly following pointers can be painful.
    if (nameEnd > bufferEnd) {
        fprintf (stderr, "Returned filename was truncated\n");
        return;
    }

    // Print the Name, then permissions.
    printf ("%s:\n", nameStart);
    printf ("  permissions: %s%s%s\n",
            g_perms[(permAttributes.accessMask & S_IRWXU) >> 6],
            g_perms[(permAttributes.accessMask & S_IRWXG) >> 3],
            g_perms[(permAttributes.accessMask & S_IRWXO)]);

    // Figure out the type.
    FileType *scan = g_types;
    FileType *stop = scan + (sizeof(g_types) / sizeof(*g_types));

    while (scan < stop) {
        if ((permAttributes.accessMask & S_IFMT) == scan->mask) {
            printf ("  type: %s\n", scan->type);
            break;
```

```
        }
        scan++;
    }

    // Any special bits sets?
    if ((permAttributes.accessMask & S_ISUID) == S_ISUID) printf ("  set-uid!\n");
    if ((permAttributes.accessMask & S_ISGID) == S_ISUID) {
        printf ("  set-group-id!\n");
    }

    // The file size isn't applicable to directories.
    if ((permAttributes.accessMask & S_IFMT) == S_IFREG) {
        printf ("  file is %lld bytes (%lld K)\n",
                permAttributes.fileLogicalSize,
                permAttributes.fileLogicalSize / 1024);
    }

    // Owning user / group.
    struct passwd *passwd = getpwuid (permAttributes.ownerId);
    struct group *group = getgrgid (permAttributes.groupId);

    printf ("  user: %s (%d)\n", passwd->pw_name, permAttributes.ownerId);
    printf ("  group: %s (%d)\n", group->gr_name, permAttributes.groupId);

    // Now the dates.
    char buffer[1024];
    struct tm *tm;

    tm = localtime (&permAttributes.accessTime.tv_sec);
    strftime (buffer, sizeof(buffer), "%c", tm);
    printf ("  last access: %s\n", buffer);

    tm = localtime (&permAttributes.modTime.tv_sec);
    strftime (buffer, sizeof(buffer), "%c", tm);
    printf ("  last modification: %s\n", buffer);

    tm = localtime (&permAttributes.changeTime.tv_sec);
    strftime (buffer, sizeof(buffer), "%c", tm);
    printf ("  last inode change: %s\n", buffer);

    // double-space output
    printf ("\n");

} // displayInfo


int main (int argc, char *argv[]) {
    if (argc == 1) {
        fprintf (stderr, "usage:  %s /path/to/file ... \n", argv[0]);
        return EXIT_FAILURE;
    }
    for (int i = 1; i < argc; i++) {
        displayInfo (argv[i]);
    }

    return EXIT_SUCCESS;

} // main
```

The output from this program is identical to the output from **permtype**.

Metadata in batches

So why talk about **getattrlist()** when there are perfectly functional POSIX calls to do the same work? This function leads up to the somewhat unpronounceable **getdirentriesattr()** function that lets you get file attributes in bulk. You can get metadata for many files with a single call to **getdirentriesattr()**, which in some cases can make your program faster.

```
int getdirentriesattr (int fd, struct attrlist *attrList,
                        void *attrBuf, size_t attrBufSize,
                        uint32_t *count,
                        uint32_t *basePointer,
                        uint32_t *newState,
                        uint32_t options);
```

getdirentriesattr() reads directory entries, like with **readdir()** and **getdirentries()**, and returns their attributes, like with **stat()** and **getattrlist()**. fd is an open file descriptor for the directory you want to iterate through. Just open the directory using **open()**. attrList is the set of attributes you want for each file. This is constructed just like the attribute list for **getattrlist**. attrBuf is the chunk of memory where the attributes should be stored. Pass the length of this buffer in attrBufSize.

count is an in/out parameter. You pass in the number of directory entries you are interested in seeing, and the function will pass back through that parameter the number of entries it actually placed into the buffer. Unlike **getattrlist()**, this function will not silently truncate your data. The basePointer parameter is an out parameter, giving you the offset into the directory, in case you need to **lseek()** at a later time. Usually the value can be ignored, but you still have to pass a valid address here. newState is an out parameter too, which changes value if the directory has been modified since you started iterating through it. Finally, options should have zero passed. There is one option described in the manpage, with the tantalizingly vague statement "This option allowed for specific performance optimizations for specific clients on older systems."

On a successful completion the function returns 0 and returns 1 if the call completed and it has returned the last entry. -1 is returned on errors, so check errno.

The data is arranged in the buffer like it is with **getattrlist()**. Each file's run of attributes starts out with a 4-byte length value. This is the number of bytes of attributes for that file. Add this length to the attribute's starting address to find the next batch. Variable length attributes are stored like **getattrlist()** as well, by using the attr_dataoffset element to find the location in the buffer of the filename data.

Example 12.4 calculates the amount of disk space consumed by a folder. It uses both **stat()** and **getdirentriesattr()**.

Example 12.4   foldersize.m

```
// foldersize.m -- calculate the size of a folder with stat and getdirentriesattr

#import <dirent.h>      // for getdirentries()
#import <errno.h>       // for errno
#import <fcntl.h>       // for O_RDONLY
#import <stdio.h>       // for printf
#import <stdlib.h>      // for EXIT_SUCCESS
#import <string.h>      // for strerror
#import <sys/attr.h>    // for attrreference_t
#import <sys/dirent.h>  // for struct dirent
#import <sys/param.h>   // for MAXPATHLEN
```

```
#import <sys/stat.h>     // for struct statbuf and stat()
#import <sys/types.h>    // for random type definition
#import <sys/vnode.h>    // for VDIR
#import <unistd.h>       // for getdirentriesattr()

// gcc -g -Wall -o foldersize foldersize.m

// show the files and sizes of the files as they are processed
static int g_verbose = 0;

// ---------------------------------------------------
// stat code

// Calculate the directory size via stat().
off_t sizeForFolderStat (char *path) {
    DIR *directory = opendir (path);

    if (directory == NULL) {
        fprintf (stderr, "could not open directory '%s'\n", path);
        fprintf (stderr, "error is %d/%s\n", errno, strerror(errno));
        exit (EXIT_FAILURE);
    }

    off_t size = 0;
    struct dirent *entry;
    while ((entry = readdir(directory)) != NULL) {
        char filename[MAXPATHLEN];

        // don't mess with the metadirectories
        if (strcmp(entry->d_name, ".") == 0
            || strcmp(entry->d_name, "..") == 0) {
            continue;
        }

        // Rather than changing the current working directory each
        // time through the loop, construct the full path relative the
        // given path.  Because the original path is either absolute, or
        // relative to the current working directory, this should
        // always give us a stat-able path
        snprintf (filename, MAXPATHLEN, "%s/%s", path, entry->d_name);

        // Use lstat so we don't multiply-count the sizes of files that
        // are pointed to by symlinks.
        struct stat statbuf;
        int result = lstat (filename, &statbuf);

        if (result != 0) {
            fprintf (stderr, "could not stat '%s': %d/%s\n",
                    entry->d_name, errno, strerror(errno));
            continue;
        }

        // Recurse into subfolders.
        if (S_ISDIR(statbuf.st_mode)) {
            size += sizeForFolderStat (filename);

        } else {
            if (g_verbose) printf ("%lld %s\n", statbuf.st_size, entry->d_name);
            size += statbuf.st_size;
        }
```

```
    }

    closedir (directory);
    return size;

} // sizeForFolderStat


// --------------------------------------------------
// getdirentriesattr code

// The attributes we want to get with each call to getdirentriesattr.
static struct attrlist g_attrlist; // gets zeroed automatically

// The data being returned by each call
typedef struct fileinfo {
    u_int32_t       length;
    attrreference_t name;
    fsobj_type_t    objType;
    off_t           logicalSize;
} fileinfo;

// try to pick up this many entries each time through
#define ENTRIES_COUNT 30

// Don't know how long each file name is, so make a guess so we can
// size the results buffer
#define AVG_NAME_GUESSTIMATE 64

off_t sizeForFolderAttr (char *path) {
    off_t size = 0;
    int fd = open (path, O_RDONLY);

    if (fd == -1) {
        fprintf (stderr, "could not open directory '%s'\n", path);
        fprintf (stderr, "error is %d/%s\n", errno, strerror(errno));
        exit (EXIT_FAILURE);
    }

    // A rough guess on the appropriate buffer size
    char attrbuf[ENTRIES_COUNT * (sizeof(fileinfo) + AVG_NAME_GUESSTIMATE)];

    while (1) {
        u_int32_t count = ENTRIES_COUNT;
        u_int32_t newState = 0;
        u_int32_t base;
        int result = getdirentriesattr (fd, &g_attrlist,
                                        attrbuf, sizeof(attrbuf),
                                        &count, &base, &newState, 0);
        if (result < 0) {
            fprintf (stderr, "error with getdirentriesattr for '%s'. %d/%s\n",
                    path, errno, strerror(errno));
            goto bailout;
        }

        // walk the returned buffer
        fileinfo *scan = (fileinfo *) attrbuf;

        for (; count > 0; count--) {
            if (scan->objType == VDIR) {
```

```
                    char filename[MAXPATHLEN];

                    snprintf (filename, MAXPATHLEN, "%s/%s", path,
                              ((char *) &scan->name)
                              + scan->name.attr_dataoffset);

                    size += sizeForFolderAttr (filename);

                } else {
                    if (g_verbose) {
                        printf ("%lld %s\n", scan->logicalSize,
                                ((char *) &scan->name) + scan->name.attr_dataoffset);
                    }
                    size += scan->logicalSize;
                }

                // Move to the next attribute in the returned set.
                scan = (fileinfo*) (((char *) scan) + scan->length);
            }

            if (result == 1) {
                // We're done.
                break;
            }
        }
    }

bailout:
    close (fd);

    return size;

} // sizeForFolderAttr


int main (int argc, char *argv[]) {
    // sanity check the program arguments first
    if (argc != 3) {
        fprintf (stderr, "usage:  %s {stat|attr} /path/to/directory\n", argv[0]);
        return EXIT_FAILURE;
    }
    off_t size = 0;

    if (strcmp(argv[1], "stat") == 0) {
        size = sizeForFolderStat (argv[2]);

    } else if (strcmp(argv[1], "attr") == 0) {

        // these are the attributes we're wanting.  Set them up
        // globally so we don't have to do a memset + this jazz
        // on every recursion

        g_attrlist.bitmapcount = ATTR_BIT_MAP_COUNT;
        g_attrlist.commonattr = ATTR_CMN_NAME | ATTR_CMN_OBJTYPE;
        g_attrlist.fileattr = ATTR_FILE_DATALENGTH;

        // Using ATTR_FILE_TOTALSIZE would be better so that we get
        // the space consumed by resource forks, but we're using this
        // code to parallel what stat gives us, which doesn't include
        // resource fork size.
```

```
        size = sizeForFolderAttr (argv[2]);

    } else {
        fprintf (stderr, "usage:  %s {stat|attr} /path/to/directory\n", argv[0]);
        return EXIT_FAILURE;
    }

    printf ("size is %lld bytes (%lld K).\n", size, size / 1024);
    return EXIT_SUCCESS;

} // main
```

Run the program by telling it whether you want to run the "stat" or "attr" version of the code, while also giving it a starting directory:

```
% ./foldersize stat /Developer
size is 10659411018 bytes (10409581 K).

% ./foldersize attr /Developer/
size is 10659411018 bytes (10409581 K).
```

Things get interesting when you start timing the program. This timing is done in the C shell because it has a better **time**.

```
% time ./foldersize stat /Developer
size is 10659411018 bytes (10409581 K).
0.249u 3.120s 0:03.37 99.7%      0+0k 0+0io 0pf+0w

% time ./foldersize attr /Developer
size is 10659411018 bytes (10409581 K).
0.038u 0.709s 0:00.75 97.3%      0+0k 0+0io 0pf+0w
```

The **time** command is discussed in Chapter 10: *Performance Tuning*, but the thing to look for here is the time that is shown in bold. It took three seconds to crawl through the Xcode directory with the **stat()** version but about a two-thirds of a second with the **getdirentriesattr()** function. These tests were run multiple times so that the file system metadata cache would be warmed up.

Mac OS X Specific Weirdness

OS X is a hybrid between classic Mac OS and Unix, so there are some peculiarities unique to OS X.

Resource forks

The first weirdness is resource forks, the additional stream that files have which store structured data. At the file system level, forks are really just two files that happen to share a name. Until Mac OS X 10.4, the Unix command-line utilities did not know resource forks were there, so it was possible for the resource fork to get lost or corrupted. **cp** and **tar**, for instance, did not preserve the fork.

In the command-line environment, you cannot really see the resource fork unless you append /..namedfork/rsrc to the name of the file. For example, the outline processor that we used to outline the first edition of this book was the 1990's version of More running in the Classic environment. Here is a look at More in the terminal:

```
$ cd /Applications
$ ls -l MORE
```

```
-rw-r--r--  1 markd  unknown  0 Jun 23 12:18 MORE
```

Hmmm, nothing there. But back in the Old Days, almost nothing was put into an application's data fork. Everything went into the resource fork:

```
$ ls -l MORE/..namedfork/rsrc
-rw-r--r--  1 markd  unknown  607251 Jun 23 12:18 MORE/..namedfork/rsrc
```

Most of the calls you have seen in this chapter do not pay any attention to the resource fork; they just look at the data fork. If you need to support resource fork reading and writing, you will need to use the Carbon libraries. **getattrlist()** and **getdirentriesattr()** will give you metadata about the resource fork.

.DS_Store

If you **ls -a** in directories, you will probably find a file named .DS_Store. This is a cache file the Finder writes that contains file names and icon placement. When mounting network volumes, the Finder will scribble the files into any directory the user visits, which can sometimes lead to friction between the Mac users and the people who run the file servers.

Disk I/O and sleep

A programmer on one of the mailing lists was describing a problem he was having with a program that works like **tail -f**, which monitors the log file and reads any new stuff that is appended. Much to his horror, machines that were running this program would never go to sleep. If a lot of I/O happens (say more than one physical disk I/O every couple of seconds), the OS considers the machine to be busy and will not go to sleep. In this particular case, he was seeking to the end and attempting to read. The suggestion was to use **stat()** instead to see if the file changed size. **stat()** does not cause physical I/O once the inode for a file is cached in memory.

For The More Curious

Differences between HFS+ and UFS

The Apple engineers did a masterful job of integrating HFS+, the Class Mac OS disk format, into the world of Unix. The above discussion about inodes is more accurate for UFS, the Unix file system, also known as the Berkeley Fast File System, but the general concepts apply to both worlds.

In HFS+, file name encoding is in unicode rather than ASCII. File names are also case preserving, but case insensitive. Traditional Unix file systems are case sensitive. The Apple teams originally thought this case preserving / case sensitive difference would cause lots of problems, but it turns out not to be so bad. There are not many examples in the real world where the case of letters in filenames is used to discriminate. Unfortunately, with the **make** command, makefile and Makefile are different beasts. There are some open source projects that have distinct files that differ only in the case of their names. A way around this limitation is to create a UFS partition for these malcontents, or you can use Disk Utility to create a UFS disk image.

The path separator for UFS is /, but in HFS+, it is :. This is addressed by the HFS+ file system implementation converting colons to slashes and vice versa. The file system sees colons, but everything above that is slashes.

Until OS X 10.5, HFS+ lacked support for hard links. Hardlinks are actually implemented by a kernel-level symbolic link visible only to the HFS+ file system. The behavior is very similar to hard links when viewed from above the kernel, but they are relatively inefficient in comparison.

UFS does not support file IDs. File IDs are persistent handles to files like inodes, and they can be used similar to path names in Unix. The nice thing about file IDs is that once the ID is obtained, the file can be renamed or moved anywhere on disk and still be found and opened. Also, in HFS+, access by ID is faster than by path (since it avoids path parsing and traversal). These file IDs are part of how aliases do their thing.

HFS+ also allows for arbitrarily named file attributes. Mac OS X lets you get and set these attributes.

HFS+ filenames are at most 255 characters long, or 512 bytes. Files have a maximum size of 2^{63} bytes.

From running experiments, it does not look like HFS+ supports holes in files. In traditional Unix file systems, if you write a byte, seek 100 megs, then write another byte, your file will only occupy two disk blocks. The intervening zero-filled blocks will not actually be consuming space in the file system. This is a disk space optimization for files that could have large ranges of zeros in them, like core files.

There are some cultural differences regarding file names. Mac OS users use spaces and special characters in their file names, while Unix folks do not. This can lead to really bad situations like an old iTunes installer wiping out entire disks because a script did not consider that a volume name might have a space in it. So if you are doing any file name manipulations, especially in shell scripts, be sure to keep this in mind.

System directories that Unix folks are familiar with (/etc, /usr, /tmp, /var) are hidden at the application level, and some are hidden behind symbolic links so that casual Mac users will not need to worry about them.

The usual Unix software install paradigm (putting library files into */lib, program files into */bin, and documentation into */share) does not work that well with individually administered systems like personal computers. One program can end up scattering junk everywhere, making uninstallation nearly impossible. NeXT bundles, the directories that behave like files, addressed a lot of problems here. The OS X folks liked bundles so much, they followed the same scheme for system-wide libraries. Rather than put stuff into /usr/include and /usr/lib, it goes into framework bundles.

Other random calls

Here are some system calls that did not fit in well anyplace else.

```
int rename (const char *from, const char *to);
```

This causes from to be renamed to to. This is just inode/directory manipulation, so both from and to must live on the same file system. This returns zero on success and -1 / errno on error.

```
int dup (int fd);
```

```
int dup2 (int fd, int newfd);
```

These functions duplicate an existing file descriptor as if you opened the file again. The return value of dup() is a file descriptor that is guaranteed to be the lowest numbered available (or -1 on error). The original file is not closed. A use for dup() is reassigning one of the standard streams. You can close file descriptor zero (standard in), open another file (say a log file), and then dup() that descriptor so that you get fd zero.

dup2() has slightly different semantics. It will create a duplicate file descriptor at a particular file descriptor value. If there is already a file open using that descriptor, it is closed first. This is another way of replacing the standard streams. Since it does a **close()** and **dup()** in one operation, it is atomic.

Note that duplicated file descriptors share the same reference in the per-process file table. So a write to one fd will move the current location of the second fd. If you want a true independent reference, reopen the file.

The **fcntl()** function is the kitchen-sink function for setting various attributes on file descriptors and for performing some operations as well:

```
int fcntl (int fd, int cmd, int arg);
```

fd is the file descriptor to manipulate. This can be an opened file, a socket connection, or any other entity that is referred to by a file descriptor. cmd is the command to apply to the file descriptor, and arg is an argument to the command. Here are some **fcntl()** commands:

F_DUPFD	Duplicate a file descriptor. The new fd is the lowest numbered descriptor that is not open that is greater than or equal to the third argument (as an integer).
F_GETFD / F_SETFD	Get/set per-processor file descriptor flags, such as FD_CLOEXEC, to close the file automatically in child processes. This will prevent your file descriptors from leaking into a subprocess.
F_GETFL / F_SETFL	Get/set kernel status flags: Such as O_RDONLY / O_WRONLY / O_APPEND, etc.
F_GETOWN / F_SETOWN	Get/set async i/o ownership.

Duplicating descriptors low with **dup()** and **dup2()** makes sense when redirecting streams. Why the F_DUPD behavior, then, of duplicating things higher? This actually came in really handy with the AOLserver webserver on older versions of IRIX, the Unix-like system that ran on Silicon Graphics workstations in the 1990s. AOLserver had an embedded Tcl interpreter that used buffered I/O FILEs for certain commands. Unfortunately, the IRIX C library only used a 8-bit value to store the file descriptor in FILEs, so you could have at most 253 of these FILEs. Whenever a non-FILE fd was created, like from a new connection from across the network or opening a file to be returned to the web browser, the fd was duplicated to a value greater than 256 using **fcntl**(F_DUPFD), leaving the lower values free for the Tcl interpreter.

```
int truncate (const char *path, off_t length);
```

```
int ftruncate (int fd, off_t length);
```

These truncate a file, whether by path or an open file descriptor, to be at most the given length. Truncating a file smaller may lose some data. Truncating a file to be larger is not-portable, but is supported on Mac OS X.

```
long pathconf (const char *path, int name);
```

```
long fpathconf (int fd, int name);
```

These provide applications ways to determine the current value of some system limits or options. Here are some possible names:

_PC_LINK_MAX   maximum file link count

_PC_NAME_MAX   maximum number of bytes in a file name

_PC_PATH_MAX   maximum number of bytes in a pathname

_PC_PIPE_BUF   maximum number of bytes that will be written atomically to a pipe

-1 is returned and errno is set if the call fails. If the given variable does not have a limit, -1 is returned and errno is not modified. Otherwise, the current value is returned.

```
int sysctl (int *name, u_int namelen, void *oldp, size_t *oldlenp,
            void *newp, size_t newlen);
```

This retrieves system information and lets processes with appropriate privileges set system information. There are all sorts of information you can get from this, like kernel debug values, machine model, cpu count, native byte order, amount of physical memory, the kernel page size, etc. Check out the manpage for more details.

Other random programs

The **lsof** command shows open files system wide.

chflags program lets you set some attributes on the file. Of particular interest are the [no]schg and [no]uchg flags, which set the system and user immutable flags. When these are set, the files cannot be modified even if their file permissions would allow it. This is handy for hardening a file system against attackers. Many "script-kiddie" system crackers are not prepared for immutable files. This is also the flag that the Finder sets when you select the Locked attribute of a file.

/Developer/Tools/SetFile sets attributes of HFS+ files, which include whether a file is an alias, is a bundle, has a custom icon, is on the desktop, is locked, or is invisible. You can also use it to set the file type and creator.

Access control lists

Mac OS X 10.4 introduced access control lists, commonly abbreviated ACLs. An access control list is a set of permissions in addition to, and sometimes superseding, traditional Unix permissions. This allows you to specify that a particular user has access or is denied access to a particular file with a particular kind of action. Mac OS X's ACLs are based on the Windows NTFS ACLs.

You can use the **chmod** command to grant permissions:

```
$ chmod +a "markd allow read" spoon.txt
```

Use the -le flag to show the extra permissions:

```
$ ls -le spoon.txt
ls -le spoon
-r-------- + 1 oopack  wheel  12 Jun  6 16:58 spoon.txt
 0: user:markd allow read
```

You can specify permissions for all file system objects about who can delete the object, who can read or write attributes or extended attributes, who can read or write security information, and who can **chown** the file.

For files, you can put permissions on who can read, write, append, or execute a file. For directories, you have control over who can list, search, add files to, add subdirectories to, or delete children. The ACL API has over 30 function calls in it, so we will not be discussing it here because the kernel will automatically apply ACLs when you try to open files or perform other file manipulations. Check the acl manpage for details.

Extended attributes

Extended attributes, introduced in Mac OS X 10.4, are name/data pairs associated with file system objects. The name is a zero-terminated UTF-8 string, with the value being any kind of data. You can set an extended attribute with **setxattr()**:

```
int setxattr (const char *path, const char *name, void *value,
              size_t size, uint32_t position, int options);
```

path is the path to the file to set the attribute for. name is the extended attribute to set. The value of the attribute is specified by value and its size. The position is used as an offset into the attribute so you can change parts of an extended attribute in-place. options controls symbolic link following behavior (XATTR_NOFOLLOW) and flags that control creation and replacing behavior: XATTR_CREATE will fail if the named attribute already exists, and XATTR_REPLACE will fail if the named attribute does not exist. If you don't specify either one of these flags, **setxattr()** will allow both creation and replacement. If you already have a file open, you can use **fsetxattr()**, which takes a file descriptor rather than a path name. This function returns zero on success and -1 on failure with errno set appropriately.

You can fetch extended attributes using **getxattr()**:

```
ssize_t getxattr (const char *path, const char *name, void *value,
                  size_t size, uint32_t position, int options);
```

This function retrieves up to size bytes from the attribute named name for the file specified by path. The position is the position within the attribute to start reading from, and size specifies how many bytes to read from the attribute. The only option available is XATTR_NOFOLLOW, which does not follow symbolic links. The function returns the amount of data actually read from the attribute or -1 on error. In the error case, errno is set accordingly. If you already have an open file, you can use **fgetxattr()** to get attributes via an existing file descriptor.

When you are done with an extended attribute, you can remove it with **removexattr()**:

```
int removexattr (const char *path, const char *name, int options);
```

path is the path to the file, name is the name of the attribute to remove, and option can be zero, or XATTR_NOFOLLOW to not follow symbolic links. This function returns zero on success and -1 on failure, with errno set. If you already have an open file, you can use **fremovexattr()**.

To iterate through existing attributes, use **listxattr()**:

```
ssize_t listxattr (const char *path, char *namebuf, size_t size,
                   int options);
```

listxattr() returns a list of names of extended attributes for the file referenced by path and deposits them into the buffer namebuf. If namebuf is NULL, the function returns the size of the list of extended attribute names so you can allocate enough memory. Of course, this is subject to race conditions: somebody else may change the attributes of the file between calling **listxattr()** with a NULL namebuf and the call with the actual buffer. options should either be zero, or XATTR_NOFOLLOW to not follow symbolic links. The size of the name list is returned. If there are no attributes, zero is returned. Otherwise, -1 is returned, and errno is set. As you might have guessed, there is a **flistxattr()** function that takes a file descriptor rather than a path.

NSFileManager - Cocoa and the File System

Cocoa provides a number of classes and categories that make dealing with the file system easier than using the lower-level Unix interfaces. **NSFileManager** encapsulates many file system operations, such as moving and renaming files and creating and resolving symbolic links. **NSString** has categories that make manipulating file paths easier, and starting with Mac OS X 10.6, **NSURL** has become the preferred way of identifying objects in the file system of interest.

Making and Manipulating Paths

Unix identifies objects in the file system with paths. A path is a listing of directories and optionally a filename, collectively known as *path components*, separated by a forward slash. Classic Mac OS, as well as parts of the Carbon layer, use a colon for a path separator. The file extension, such as .txt or .pages, is the path extension. The different pieces are shown in Figure 13.1. The path components are Users, markd, Documents, and Badgers.acorn. The path extension is .acorn.

Figure 13.1   Path components

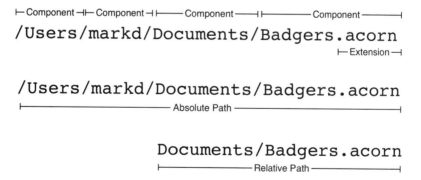

The Unix file system is represented as a single tree of directories that contain files and other objects. Additional file systems are "mounted" in this tree, extending the single file system with the contents of the new file systems. An absolute path starts with a forward slash, signifying that the path originates with the root of the file system. Relative paths do not have a leading path separator and should be interpreted relative to some other directory.

NSString path utilities

The **NSStringPathExtensions** category adds a number of methods to **NSString** for constructing and breaking apart paths. You should choose these methods over hard-coding paths or using other string mechanisms for constructing paths like **-stringByAppendingString:**. Typically you start with a base path, such as the user's home directory or a temporary directory. Then you append path components and path extensions with these methods:

- (NSString *) **stringByAppendingPathComponent:** (NSString *) str;

- (NSString *) **stringByAppendingPathExtension:** (NSString *) str;

To build the path seen in Figure 13.1, you would do something like this:

```
NSString *path = NSHomeDirectory ();
path = [path stringByAppendingPathComponent: @"Documents"];
path = [path stringByAppendingPathComponent: @"Badgers"];
path = [path stringByAppendingPathExtension: @"acorn"];
```

If you already have an array of path components, you can join them together with this:

+ (NSString *) **pathWithComponents:** (NSArray *) components;

If all you are interested in is the last component, which is usually the filename+extension, you can query the string:

- (NSString *) **lastPathComponent**;

- (NSString *) **pathExtension**;

You can ask a path to break itself into components for further processing:

- (NSArray *) **pathComponents**;

You can also modify the path by taking off components. This does not destructively modify the string. Instead, it makes a new one a bit shorter than the original and returns it.

- (NSString *) **stringByDeletingLastPathComponent**;

- (NSString *) **stringByDeletingPathExtension**;

It is common to represent the user's home directory with a tilde (~) allowing a path to be specified relative to the user's $HOME. You can collapse a string by replacing the home directory with ~, as well as expanding it:

- (NSString *) **stringByAbbreviatingWithTildeInPath**;

- (NSString *) **stringByExpandingTildeInPath**;

You can ask a path if it is an absolute path:

- (BOOL) **isAbsolutePath**;

When you need to pass a path to a Unix system call or library function, you should encode the string in a way so that the kernel can handle it. This is known as the "file system representation," which is UTF-8, and is obtainable by this method:

- (__strong const char *) **fileSystemRepresentation**;

The returned memory will automatically be cleaned up.

NSURL path utilities

Starting in OS X 10.6, Apple has added a number of path and file features to **NSURL**, and Apple recommends using **NSURL**s over **NSString**-based paths. **NSURL** performs caching of metadata and other information under the hood to improve overall performance. For instance, there are some operations in Cocoa that happen on paths that end up involving multiple conversions between string paths and Carbon FSRefs, some of which require a disk I/O. The URL-based file system locators remove these inefficiencies.

You can make a file URL with a path or with an array of path components:

```
+ (id) fileURLWithPath: (NSString *) path  isDirectory: (BOOL) isDir;

+ (id) fileURLWithPath: (NSString *) path;

+ (NSURL *) fileURLWithPathComponents: (NSArray *) components;
```

The first form is more efficient if you already know that a path is a directory because it can avoid a disk I/O to make that determination.

There are a number of utility methods that should look familiar:

```
- (NSArray *) pathComponents;

- (NSString *) lastPathComponent;

- (NSString *) pathExtension;

- (NSURL *) URLByAppendingPathComponent: (NSString *) pathComponent;

- (NSURL *) URLByDeletingLastPathComponent;

- (NSURL *) URLByAppendingPathExtension: (NSString *) pathExtension;

- (NSURL *) URLByDeletingPathExtension;
```

These work in an analogous manner to the similarly-named **NSString** methods.

Finding Standard Directories

Frequently, you will construct a path or URL by appending your application's specific path components to another well-known location, such as the user's home directory, or the Application Support directory.

The functions **NSHomeDirectory()** and **NSTemporaryDirectory()** return paths to the home directory and temporary directory, respectively. There are also lookup functions and methods that give you other directories of interest. These share two configuration parameters.

The first is the search *domain*. There are a number of different locations where directories could be. For example, there are a number of "Library" directories: in the user's home, in /Library, in /Network/Library, and /System/Library. When searching for directories, you can bitwise-OR these domain masks:

NSUserDomainMask	The user's home directory. This is the only directory on iOS that you can write to.
NSLocalDomainMask	Local to the current machine. You would put things here that are available to all users on a machine. This would be in /Library.

NSNetworkDomainMask	Publicly available location in the local area network. Usually this is not available, but you may have a system administrator that makes company-wide information and configurations available here. Directories found in this domain would be in /Network.
NSSystemDomainMask	Apple's territory, so hands-off. Apple does not guarantee to preserve any directories in /System/Library during OS update time, even for point-releases, so do not install your own files here.
NSAllDomainsMask	Bitwise-OR of all the above masks.

The second configuration parameter is the *search path directories*. These are not bit flags but enumerations, so you can only search for one particular kind of directory at a time. But you can look for this directory in multiple domains if you wish. This is a sampling of some directories. See the NSPathUtilities.h header file or the documentation for the complete list:

NSApplicationDirectory	Where applications live
NSLibraryDirectory	The library directory, which is the catch-all for random directories of information that is not really user-accessible.
NSUserDirectory	Users' home directories
NSDocumentDirectory	The directory to store documents in
NSAutosavedInformationDirectory	A directory for auto-save documents
NSItemReplacementDirectory	A directory you can write an interim version of a file to. Usually you let **NSDocument** do atomic saves for you, but if you wish to do atomic saves, you would first write the new file to this directory and then replace the original document with this one.
NSApplicationSupportDirectory	A directory in which applications can create subdirectories to store information that may be expensive computationally or impossible to recreate on demand. For instance, a painting program might copy a default set of paint brushes from the potentially read-only application bundle to Application Support so that the user could edit them.
NSCachesDirectory	A place to put discardable cache files
NSDownloadsDirectory	The directory in which Safari (and other applications) places downloaded files from the Internet.
NSMusicDirectory	The user's music directory
NSPicturesDirectory	The user's pictures directory

Path utilities

You can get an array of paths for a particular directory in any number of domains from this function:

```
NSArray *NSSearchPathForDirectoriesInDomains (NSSearchPathDirectory directory,
                                              NSSearchPathDomainMask domainMask,
                                              BOOL expandTilde);
```

You specify a directory you are interested in, such as NSDocumentDirectory, along with a bitwise-OR of the domains you are interested in. Individual returned directories might include tildes. If you pass YES to expandTilde, the tilde will be automatically replaced with the current user's home directory.

The directory returned might not actually exist, so you may need to create it before placing any new files or directories there. Example 13.1 finds all of the application support directories available.

Example 13.1 searchpath.m

```
// searchpath.m -- Show NSSearchPathForDirectoriesInDomains

#import <Foundation/Foundation.h>

// gcc -g -Wall -framework Foundation -o searchpath searchpath.m

int main (void) {
    NSAutoreleasePool *pool = [[NSAutoreleasePool alloc] init];

    NSArray *paths =
        NSSearchPathForDirectoriesInDomains (NSApplicationSupportDirectory,
                                             NSAllDomainsMask, NO);

    for (NSString *path in paths) {
        NSLog (@"a path!  %@", path);
    }

    [pool drain];
    return 0;

} // main
```

And you can see that it found three of them, the user path with a tilde:

```
$ ./searchpath
a path!  ~/Library/Application Support
a path!  /Library/Application Support
a path!  /Network/Library/Application Support
```

URL utilities

You can get an array of URLs in a manner similar to getting an array of paths using this **NSFileManager** method:

```
- (NSArray *) URLsForDirectory: (NSSearchPathDirectory) directory
                     inDomains: (NSSearchPathDomainMask) domainMask;
```

You pass it a directory and a domain mask. There is no tilde equivalent for URLs, so there is no tilde-expansion argument.

One problem with this method (and **NSSearchPathForDirectories**) is that it returns an array of objects. Even if you are only interested in one path or URL, you still need to dig into the array for the path, also making sure the array is not empty lest you generate a run-time exception. Plus, there is no guarantee the directory exists, so you need to create it yourself. The following method addresses these two problems:

```
- (NSURL *) URLForDirectory: (NSSearchPathDirectory) directory
                   inDomain: (NSSearchPathDomainMask) domain
          appropriateForURL: (NSURL *) appropriateURL
                     create: (BOOL) shouldCreate
                      error: (NSError **) error;
```

You give it a single directory and a single domain. You cannot pass NSAllDomainsMask. Pass YES for shouldCreate if the directory should be created with permissions allowing, of course. It returns the URL for the directory, or nil if it was not possible, and returning the proper error in error.

If the directory is NSItemReplacementDirectory, and appropriateURL is non-nil, then the returned URL will vary based on the passed-in URL. In particular, if the URL points to a different machine or file system, the returned URL will be a location on that machine or file system. If the URL is local, the returned URL will be local. Example 13.2 shows **-URLForDirectory:** in action.

Example 13.2   urldirectory.m

```
// urldirectory.m -- Use URLForDirectory:inDomain:etc

#import <Foundation/Foundation.h>

// gcc -g -Wall -framework Foundation -o urldirectory urldirectory.m

int main (int argc, const char *argv[]) {
    NSAutoreleasePool *pool = [[NSAutoreleasePool alloc] init];

    NSURL *appropriateFor = nil;
    if (argc == 2) {
        NSString *path = [NSString stringWithUTF8String: argv[1]];
        appropriateFor = [NSURL fileURLWithPath: path];
    }

    NSFileManager *fm = [[[NSFileManager alloc] init] autorelease];

    NSError *error;
    NSURL *directoryURL =
        [fm URLForDirectory: NSItemReplacementDirectory
            inDomain: NSUserDomainMask
            appropriateForURL: appropriateFor
            create: YES
            error: &error];

    if (directoryURL == nil) {
        NSLog (@"Could not get directory URL. Error %@", error);
    } else {
        NSLog (@"directoryURL is %@", directoryURL);
    }

    [pool drain];
    return 0;
} // main
```

You can supply an argument on the command line to specify the location to pass in the appropriateForURL argument. Here are two sample runs on a machine with two file systems. The first on the main file system.

```
$ ./urldirectory .emacs
directoryURL is file://localhost/private/var/folders/hE/hECLnEMTGRiwaRuPxRjw2E+++TI/
    -Tmp-/TemporaryItems/(A%20Document%20Being%20Saved%20By%20urldirectory)/
```

And the second a drive mounted on /Volumes/Video:

```
$ ./urldirectory /Volumes/Video/AppleTVVideos/Sci-Fi/Zardoz.m4v
directoryURL is file://localhost/Volumes/Video/.TemporaryItems/folders.501/
    TemporaryItems/(A%20Document%20Being%20Saved%20By%20urldirectory)/
```

Notice that the second URL references /Volumes/Video rather than /private/var/folders.

File Metadata

There are a number of functions, system calls, and toolkit APIs for accessing file metadata.
NSFileManager provides a path-based way to acquire metadata, as well as URL-based equivalents. The
URL-based API actually exposes much more file metadata than the path-based one. Unfortunately,
even though the URL-based metadata API is available on iOS, as of iOS 4.3, the methods return nil.
So for iOS, you will need to stay with the path-based metadata API.

Metadata through paths

NSFileManager's **-attributesOfItemAtPath:** returns a dictionary of attributes.

```
- (NSDictionary *) attributesOfItemAtPath: (NSString *) path
                                   error: (NSError **) error;
```

You can access these attributes through an **NSDictionary** category, of which a subset is shown below.
The constant comment following it is the key you would use for dictionary lookup.

```
@interface NSDictionary (NSFileAttributes)
- (unsigned long long) fileSize;                  // NSFileSize
- (NSDate *) fileCreationDate;                    // NSFileCreationDate
- (NSDate *) fileModificationDate;                // NSFileModificationDate
- (NSString *) fileType;                          // NSFileType
- (NSUInteger) filePosixPermissions;              // NSFilePosixPermissions
- (NSNumber *) fileOwnerAccountID;                // NSFileOwnerAccountID
- (NSString *) fileOwnerAccountName;              // NSFileOwnerAccountName
- (NSNumber *) fileGroupOwnerAccountID;           // NSFileGroupOwnerAccountID
- (NSString *) fileGroupOwnerAccountName;         // NSFileGroupOwnerAccountName
- (BOOL) fileExtensionHidden;                     // NSFileExtensionHidden
- (BOOL) fileIsImmutable;                         // NSFileImmutable
- (BOOL) fileIsAppendOnly;                        // NSFileAppendOnly
@end
```

The returned dictionary is not guaranteed to have all of these values. The value of **-fileType** /
NSFileType key is one of these string constants:

```
NSFileTypeDirectory
NSFileTypeRegular
NSFileTypeSymbolicLink
NSFileTypeSocket
NSFileTypeCharacterSpecial
NSFileTypeBlockSpecial
NSFileTypeUnknown
```

You can change metadata values as well:

```
- (BOOL) setAttributes: (NSDictionary *) attributes
         ofItemAtPath: (NSString *) path
                error: (NSError **) error;
```

Give it the path to change and give it a dictionary, populated with keys and values from the above list.

Metadata through URLs

NSFileManager's **-attributesOfItemAtPath:** returns a subset of available metadata for files and file systems. Through the URL API, you can access many more kinds of metadata in a single call. You can also ask for metadata in batches, allowing for more efficient use of system resources. By asking only for what you need, the toolkit doesn't need to fetch attribute values that you will never use. This makes it kind of odd that these URL-based metadata calls are no-ops in iOS, and so the optimizations are not available on that platform.

You can access resource values individually via this **NSURL** method:

```
- (BOOL) getResourceValue: (id *) value
                   forKey: (NSString *) key
                    error: (NSError **) error;
```

Pass a key for the resource value and a pointer to an object of the type you are expecting. Recall that id is a pointer type already, so id* is a pointer to a pointer. The call will fill in your pointer with an object and return YES or NO if the call had problems. On failure, you can check error to see what went wrong. It is possible for this method to return YES and also return nil in value. This can happen if there is no metadata available for it. Figure 13.2 shows all (at the time of writing) available resource keys.

Figure 13.2   NSURL resource keys

NSURLNameKey	NSURLLabelColorKey
NSURLLocalizedNameKey	NSURLLocalizedLabelKey
NSURLIsRegularFileKey	NSURLEffectiveIconKey
NSURLIsDirectoryKey	NSURLCustomIconKey
NSURLIsSymbolicLinkKey	NSURLFileSizeKey
NSURLIsVolumeKey	NSURLFileAllocatedSizeKey
NSURLIsPackageKey	NSURLIsAliasFileKey
NSURLIsSystemImmutableKey	NSURLVolumeLocalizedFormatDescriptionKey
NSURLIsUserImmutableKey	NSURLVolumeTotalCapacityKey
NSURLIsHiddenKey	NSURLVolumeAvailableCapacityKey
NSURLHasHiddenExtensionKey	NSURLVolumeResourceCountKey
NSURLCreationDateKey	NSURLVolumeSupportsPersistentIDsKey
NSURLContentAccessDateKey	NSURLVolumeSupportsSymbolicLinksKey
NSURLContentModificationDateKey	NSURLVolumeSupportsHardLinksKey
NSURLAttributeModificationDateKey	NSURLVolumeSupportsJournalingKey
NSURLLinkCountKey	NSURLVolumeIsJournalingKey
NSURLParentDirectoryURLKey	NSURLVolumeIsTooLoudKey
NSURLVolumeURLKey	NSURLVolumeSupportsSparseFilesKey
NSURLTypeIdentifierKey	NSURLVolumeSupportsZeroRunsKey
NSURLLocalizedTypeDescriptionKey	NSURLVolumeSupportsCaseSensitiveNamesKey
NSURLLabelNumberKey	NSURLVolumeSupportsCasePreservedNamesKey

The types of objects returned are what you would expect from the call. A date resource returns an **NSDate** in the value pointer, a name returns an **NSString**, a color returns an **NSColor**, etc. If your program only uses the Foundation framework and you wish to access resources like colors and images, you will need to link with the AppKit or Cocoa frameworks.

You can get attribute values back in batch as well:

```
- (NSDictionary *) resourceValuesForKeys: (NSArray *) keys  error: (NSError **);
```

Give it an array of keys, and it will return a dictionary of the values. There will not be a corresponding value in the dictionary if there is no value for a key.

You can also change resource values, either individually or in bulk:

```
- (BOOL) setResourceValue: (id) value
                  forKey: (NSString *) key
                   error: (NSError **) error;

- (BOOL) setResourceValues: (NSDictionary *) keyedValues
                     error: (NSError **) error;
```

Using -setResourceValue:error: is straightforward. Try to set the value. It returns NO if the value could not be changed and returns YES otherwise. -setResourceValues:error: lets you supply a dictionary of metadata values to set at one time. It is possible to have multiple failures when setting multiple properties. The userInfo dictionary of the error has an array of keys that were not set.

Finally, you can use NSFileManager to retrieve an array of URLs for each of the mounted volumes currently on the system, as well as pre-fetch metadata about those volumes:

```
- (NSArray *) mountedVolumeURLsIncludingResourceValuesForKeys: (NSArray *) propKeys
               options: (NSVolumeEnumerationOptions) options
```

There are currently two bitmasks for the volume enumeration options:

```
NSVolumeEnumerationSkipHiddenVolumes
NSVolumeEnumerationProduceFileReferenceURLs
```

Pass zero for no special enumerating behavior. Skipping hidden volumes is just that – it will not return any volumes that would otherwise be hidden to the user. If the file reference URLs option is bitwise-OR'd in, the URLs returned are file reference URLs. File reference URLs are discussed later. Example 13.3 shows the accessing metadata for individual objects in the file system, as well as getting all of the mounted volumes.

Example 13.3   urlmeta.m

```
// urlmeta.m -- Get file metadata about a file via URLs

#import <Foundation/Foundation.h>

// gcc -g -Wall -framework Foundation -o urlmeta urlmeta.m

int main (int argc, const char *argv[]) {
    NSAutoreleasePool *pool = [[NSAutoreleasePool alloc] init];

    if (argc != 2) {
        printf ("usage: %s path -- print metadata about file\n", argv[0]);
        printf ("   use / for volume information\n");
        return EXIT_FAILURE;
    }
```

```
    if (strlen(argv[1]) == 1 && argv[1][0] == '/') {
        NSFileManager *fm = [[[NSFileManager alloc] init] autorelease];
        NSArray *volumes = [fm mountedVolumeURLsIncludingResourceValuesForKeys: nil
                                   options: 0];
        NSLog (@"volumes are %@", volumes);

    } else {
        NSArray *keys = [NSArray arrayWithObjects:
                                    NSURLNameKey, NSURLLocalizedNameKey,
                                    NSURLIsDirectoryKey,
                                    NSURLCreationDateKey, nil];

        NSString *path = [NSString stringWithUTF8String: argv[1]];
        NSURL *url = [NSURL fileURLWithPath: path];

        NSError *error;
        NSDictionary *attributes = [url resourceValuesForKeys: keys
                                         error: &error];
        NSLog (@"Attributes for %s", argv[1]);
        NSLog (@"%@", attributes);
    }

    [pool drain];
    return EXIT_SUCCESS;

} // main
```

Here are some sample runs:

```
$ ./urlmeta ./urlmeta
Attributes for ./urlmeta
    NSURLCreationDateKey = "2011-05-29 20:37:13 -0400";
    NSURLIsDirectoryKey = 0;
    NSURLLocalizedNameKey = urlmeta;
    NSURLNameKey = urlmeta;

$ ./urlmeta ~/Library
Attributes for /Users/markd/Library
    NSURLCreationDateKey = "2009-06-18 21:01:21 -0400";
    NSURLIsDirectoryKey = 1;
    NSURLLocalizedNameKey = Library;
    NSURLNameKey = Library;
```

Notice the localized name key. Some directories in the file system are displayed to users with a different name than what is actually in the file system. The Library directory is always called Library in the file system, even if it is presented with a different word in a non-English localization. Set the language of your machine to Italian and re-run the last example:

```
$ ./urlmeta ~/Library
Attributes for /Users/markd/Library
    NSURLCreationDateKey = "2009-06-18 21:01:21 -0400";
    NSURLIsDirectoryKey = 1;
    NSURLLocalizedNameKey = Libreria;
    NSURLNameKey = Library;
```

Now for the volumes. This is a run on a laptop without any extra disks attached:

```
$ ./urlmeta /
volumes are
```

```
    "file://localhost/",
    "file://localhost/home/",
    "file://localhost/net/"
```

And then run on a MacPro with four drives installed in the bays:

```
$ ./urlmeta /
volumes are
    "file://localhost/",
    "file://localhost/Volumes/Video/",
    "file://localhost/Volumes/MediaZ2/",
    "file://localhost/Volumes/DVDImages/",
    "file://localhost/home/",
    "file://localhost/net/"
```

The hard drives are the first four, and the last two are for automounted filesystems.

File Operations

NSFileManager also abstracts out a number of common file operations, such as copying, moving, removing, and linking items. As expected, there are two API families: one using string paths and the other using URLs.

Path operations

You can use the following methods to copy, move, (hard) link, and remove files and directories:

```
- (BOOL) copyItemAtPath: (NSString *) srcPath  toPath: (NSString *) dstPath
              error: (NSError **) error;

- (BOOL) moveItemAtPath: (NSString *) srcPath  toPath: (NSString *) dstPath
              error: (NSError **) error;

- (BOOL) linkItemAtPath: (NSString *) srcPath  toPath: (NSString *) dstPath
              error: (NSError **) error;

- (BOOL) removeItemAtPath: (NSString *) path
              error: (NSError **) error;
```

These methods will potentially invoke delegate methods on your **NSFileManager** instance. If you choose to set a delegate, you should alloc and init your own rather than using the shared **+defaultManager**.

There are two classes of delegate methods. The first asks if a particular file should be copied, moved, linked, or removed:

```
- (BOOL) fileManager: (NSFileManager *) fileManager
shouldCopyItemAtPath: (NSString *) srcPath  toPath: (NSString *) dstPath;

- (BOOL) fileManager: (NSFileManager *) fileManager
shouldMoveItemAtPath: (NSString *) srcPath  toPath: (NSString *) dstPath;

- (BOOL) fileManager: (NSFileManager *) fileManager
shouldLinkItemAtPath: (NSString *) srcPath  toPath: (NSString *) dstPath;
```

```
- (BOOL) fileManager: (NSFileManager *) fileManager
    shouldRemoveItemAtPath: (NSString *) path;
```

If you do not implement any of these, it is assumed that they returned YES for every file. If you return NO for a directory, that directory and all of the directory's children are skipped.

The other delegate methods relate to error handling. Return YES to proceed after an error. Returning NO will stop the operation and return from the original call. Not implementing a delegate method behaves as if it returned NO, that is, it will always give up after the first error.

```
- (BOOL) fileManager: (NSFileManager *) fileManager
     shouldProceedAfterError: (NSError *) error
   copyingItemAtPath: (NSString *) srcPath
            toPath: (NSString *) dstPath;

- (BOOL) fileManager: (NSFileManager *) fileManager
     shouldProceedAfterError: (NSError *) error
   movingItemAtPath: (NSString *) srcPath
            toPath: (NSString *) dstPath;

- (BOOL) fileManager: (NSFileManager *) fileManager
     shouldProceedAfterError: (NSError *) error
   linkingItemAtPath: (NSString *) srcPath
            toPath: (NSString *) dstPath;

- (BOOL) fileManager: (NSFileManager *) fileManager
     shouldProceedAfterError: (NSError *) error
  removingItemAtPath: (NSString *) path;
```

You can also create directories:

```
- (BOOL) createDirectoryAtPath: (NSString *) path
   withIntermediateDirectories: (BOOL) createIntermediates
                    attributes: (NSDictionary *) attributes
                         error: (NSError **) error;
```

This will create a directory at path. If there are any missing directories in the path, they will be created using the given attributes if createIntermediates is YES. The method returns YES or NO depending on its success, with error being filled in if an error happened. If no attributes are provided, directories are created with mode 777, modified by the process' umask. If those permissions are too open for your tastes, then you can provide your own permissions in the attributes dictionary.

URL operations

Even though it may come as a complete surprise, **NSFileManager** can perform file operations using URLs. These are exactly analogous to the path-based operations and invoke the same delegate methods:

```
- (BOOL) copyItemAtURL: (NSURL *) srcURL  toURL: (NSURL *) dstURL
                 error: (NSError **) error;

- (BOOL) moveItemAtURL: (NSURL *) srcURL  toURL: (NSURL *) dstURL
                 error: (NSError **) error;

- (BOOL) linkItemAtURL: (NSURL *) srcURL  toURL: (NSURL *) dstURL
                 error: (NSError **) error;

- (BOOL) removeItemAtURL: (NSURL *) URL
                 error: (NSError **) error;
```

Symbolic links

NSFileManager has API for creating and resolving symbolic links. Ordinarily, symbolic links are transparent to you, but you may need to deal with them directly. This creates a new symbolic link:

```
- (BOOL) createSymbolicLinkAtPath: (NSString *) path
           withDestinationPath: (NSString *) destPath
                         error: (NSError **) error;
```

You can get what a symbolic link points to.

```
- (NSString *) destinationOfSymbolicLinkAtPath: (NSString *) path
                                        error: (NSError **) error;
```

As of Mac OS X 10.6, there are no URL-based calls to create symbolic links or get their values, but you can resolve links. Resolving a link replaces symbolic links in a path with their destinations. This is supported both by paths and URLs:

```
- (NSString *) stringByResolvingSymlinksInPath;
```

```
- (NSURL *) URLByResolvingSymlinksInPath;
```

Directory Enumeration

Processing the contents of a directory is a common operation. There are a number of **NSFileManager** calls, which can process a directory in different ways. Both the path-based and URL-based calls will get you the contents of a directory. The URL-based calls can also prefetch the metadata you want, speeding up the operation.

Enumeration with paths

You can get a flat listing of a directory in an array:

```
- (NSArray *) contentsOfDirectoryAtPath: (NSString *) path
                                 error: (NSError **) error;
```

This returns an array of file names of all the files in the directory. It is flat because it does not recurse into subdirectories. You can get a deep listing that recurses into subdirectories with this call:

```
- (NSArray *) subpathsOfDirectoryAtPath: (NSString *) path
                                 error: (NSError **) error;
```

You can also ask **NSFileManager** for an **NSDictionaryEnumerator** object, which when processed, will walk a directory hierarchy:

```
- (NSDirectoryEnumerator *) enumeratorAtPath: (NSString *) path;
```

Don't forget you can feed this enumerator object to fast enumeration:

```
for (NSString *path in [fileManager enumeratorAtPath: path]) ...
```

NSDirectoryEnumerator provides a number of useful methods:

```
- (NSDictionary *) fileAttributes;
```

This returns an attribute dictionary for this file.

```
- (NSDictionary *) directoryAttributes;
```

This returns an attribute dictionary for the directory being iterated.

- (NSUInteger) **level**;

Available in 10.6. this tells you how deep the iteration has run. The directory that started the iteration is considered to be level zero.

- (void) **skipDescendents**;

This causes the enumerator to skip recursion into the most recently seen subdirectory.

- (void) **skipDescendants**;

This is available in 10.6 only. So says the header file: "This method is spelled correctly."

Enumeration with URLs

The URL-based directory enumeration methods are more complex than the path-based counterparts. For instance:

```
- (NSArray *) contentsOfDirectoryAtURL: (NSURL *) url
            includingPropertiesForKeys: (NSArray *) keys
                               options: (NSDirectoryEnumerationOptions) mask
                                 error: (NSError **) error;
```

This call collects the contents of the directory, prefetches the metadata for the given keys, and returns an array of URLs. Pass nil for keys to prefetch a default set of metadata. Pass an empty array for no prefetching.

The options mask can be composed of these flags:

```
NSDirectoryEnumerationSkipsSubdirectoryDescendants
NSDirectoryEnumerationSkipsPackageDescendants
NSDirectoryEnumerationSkipsHiddenFiles
```

Even though this method takes an enumeration options mask, it does not actually recurse into subdirectories, so you should either pass zero or use the mask to skip hidden files.

To perform a deep iteration, you need to use **-enumeratorAtURL:**

```
- (NSDirectoryEnumerator *) enumeratorAtURL: (NSURL *)  url
                 includingPropertiesForKeys: (NSArray *) keys
                                    options: (NSDirectoryEnumerationOptions) mask
                               errorHandler: (BOOL (^) (NSURL *url, NSError *error) ) handler;
```

Like **-contentsOfDirectoryAtURL**, this will prefetch the metadata indicated by keys. Unlike **-contentsOfDirectoryAtURL**, it honors the options to skip subdirectories and/or package files. The error handler is a block that will get invoked if an error happens. Return YES from the block to continue iteration in the face of errors, and return NO to terminate. One thing that is slightly mind-bending about this method is that, even though iteration is happening in a loop after you acquire the **NSDirectoryEnumerator**, the block you provide could get invoked inside that loop. So code you defined earlier could be called in the iteration loop.

Example 13.4 shows this method being used to walk a directory hierarchy, print out an indented list of files, each file's size, and accumulate a total sum of the bytes of the files.

Example 13.4   urlenumerator.m

```
// urlenumerator.m -- Iterate with -enumeratorAtURL, show a tree listing,
```

```objc
//                      and calculate disk space consumption

// gcc -g -std=c99 -Wall -framework Foundation -o urlenumerator urlenumerator.m

#import <Foundation/Foundation.h>

int main (int argc, const char *argv[]) {
    NSAutoreleasePool *pool = [[NSAutoreleasePool alloc] init];

    // Sanity-check, and make the target URL
    if (argc != 2) {
        printf ("usage: %s path -- enumerate starting from the path\n", argv[0]);
        return EXIT_FAILURE;
    }
    NSString *path = [NSString stringWithUTF8String: argv[1]];
    NSURL *url = [NSURL fileURLWithPath: path];

    // Prefect these values.  The name is always displayed.
    // If the URL is a directory, don't accumulate its size.
    NSArray *keys = [NSArray arrayWithObjects:
                                NSURLLocalizedNameKey,
                                NSURLIsDirectoryKey,
                                NSURLFileSizeKey, nil];

    // Get the enumerator.
    NSFileManager *fm = [[[NSFileManager alloc] init] autorelease];
    NSDirectoryEnumerator *direnum =
        [fm enumeratorAtURL: url
            includingPropertiesForKeys: keys
            options: 0
            errorHandler: ^(NSURL *url, NSError *error) {
                NSLog (@"error for %@ : %@", url, error);
                return YES;
            }];
    // Now actually iterate.  The block will be invoked in this loop if an
    // error happens.

    unsigned long long totalSize = 0;
    for (NSURL *url in direnum) {

        // Get the attributes for the URL.
        NSError *error;
        NSDictionary *attrs = [url resourceValuesForKeys: keys  error: &error];

        if (!attrs) {
            NSLog (@"could not get attributes for %@ : %@", url, error);
            continue;
        }

        // Indent the row.
        for (int i = 0; i < direnum.level - 1; i++) printf ("  ");

        // Display the name
        NSString *name = [attrs objectForKey: NSURLLocalizedNameKey];
        printf ("%s ", [name UTF8String]);

        // Newline and continue if it's a directory.
        NSNumber *isDirectory = [attrs objectForKey: NSURLIsDirectoryKey];
        if ([isDirectory boolValue]) {
            printf ("\n");
```

```
            continue;
        }

        // Otherwise print the size, and accumulate the size sum
        NSNumber *filesize = [attrs objectForKey: NSURLFileSizeKey];
        unsigned long long size = [filesize longLongValue];
        if (size < 1024) printf ("%llu\n", size);
        else             printf ("%lluK\n", size / 1024);

        totalSize +- size;
    }

    printf ("\nTotal Size: %lluM\n", totalSize / 1024 / 1024);

    [pool drain];
    return EXIT_SUCCESS;
} // main
```

And a sample run:

```
$ ./urlenumerator /usr/include
_locale.h 2K
_structs.h 1007
_types.h 2K
_wctype.h 4K
_xlocale.h 1K
aio.h 1K
alloca.h 1K
apache2
  ap_compat.h 1K
  ap_config.h 9K
  ap_config_auto.h 7K
...
xlocale.h 2K
Xplugin.h 20K
zconf.h 9K
zlib.h 64K

Total Size: 28M
```

File References and Bookmarks

One problem with paths and regular file URLs is that they are fragile in the face of changes to the file system. You can create a path or URL that points to a file, and the user could move that file in the Finder behind your back. If you then try to get metadata or open the file, you could fail because the file is no longer living where you think it is living.

File references

A special kind of URL, called a file reference URL, tracks a file by its ID. This means the reference is still good even if the name or location of the file changes in the file system. Usually this is hidden behind classes like **NSDocument**, but it can be useful in other contexts aside from document files.

Get a file reference URL from a regular one by calling **-fileReferenceURL**:

```
- (NSURL *) fileReference;
```

And you can query the URL to see if it is a file reference:

- (BOOL) **isFileReferenceURL**;

The representations of the different kinds of URLs are different: a regular file URL, when **NSLog**ged, looks like

```
file://localhost/Users/markd/track.kml
```

while a file reference URL looks like

```
file:///.file/id=6571367.4306288
```

Because a file reference URL contains a file ID, the URL must actually point to a file. If you have a dangling file URL that points to a non-existent file, **-fileReference** will return nil.

Example 13.5 shows a regular and file reference URL pointing to the same file in /tmp and prints them. The program then renames the file via the **mv** command and prints them again.

Example 13.5   filerefurl.m

```
// filerefurl.m -- Play with file reference urls.

// gcc -g -Wall -framework Foundation -o filerefurl filerefurl.m

#import <Foundation/Foundation.h>

int main (void) {
    NSAutoreleasePool *pool = [[NSAutoreleasePool alloc] init];

    // Create the file.
    system ("touch /tmp/oopack");
    NSURL *url = [NSURL fileURLWithPath: @"/tmp/oopack"];
    NSURL *fileReference = [url fileReferenceURL];

    NSLog (@"url: %@ : %@", url, url.path);
    NSLog (@"ref: %@ : %@", fileReference, fileReference.path);

    NSLog (@"moving the file");
    system ("mv /tmp/oopack /tmp/jo2yfund");

    NSLog (@"url: %@ : %@", url, url.path);
    NSLog (@"ref: %@ : %@", fileReference, fileReference.path);

    [pool drain];
    return EXIT_SUCCESS;

} // main
```

And a sample run:

```
$ ./filerefurl
url: file://localhost/tmp/oopack : /tmp/oopack
ref: file:///.file/id=6571367.7083201 : /private/tmp/oopack
moving the file
url: file://localhost/tmp/oopack : /tmp/oopack
```

```
ref: file:///.file/id=6571367.7083201 : /private/tmp/jo2yfund
```

You can see how the original URL has not changed. It is pointing to /tmp/oopack, which no longer exists. The file reference URL tracks the move and shows you how the path changed.

When it comes time to actually use the path, like to read from it or write to it, you can get the path property and pass that to calls that want a path. A number of Cocoa convenience functions have grown URL-based API over the years and can consume the URL directly, such as **NSData**'s reading and writing to URL:

```
- (BOOL) writeToURL: (NSURL *) url  atomically: (BOOL) atomically;

+ (id) dataWithContentsOfURL: (NSURL *) url;
```

This avoids the race condition you would have if you got the path from the URL and then used that path to read or write the file. It is possible the file has moved between those two calls. Of course, there is not a guarantee as of this writing that Cocoa is not doing the same thing and is subject to the same race condition.

Bookmarks

Even though file reference URLs solve once class of problems, they still have one limitation. The value they use to track files does not necessarily survive reboots. Therefore, you should not store file reference URLs to disk, say as part of your document's object graph, and retrieve them later. If file reference URLs won't work, and regular URLs are fragile in the face of files moving, what can you do? You can use bookmarks, which are Cocoa's equivalent to Carbon's aliases.

Aliases, such as the ones you can create in the Finder, are a kind of sticky symbolic link. You can make an alias to a file, and the system will try its best to follow that file as it moves around from directory to directory and disk to disk. There is Carbon API for creating and resolving aliases, and if you must support OS X prior to 10.6, you will need to use that API, not discussed here. You can find open-source libraries that put a Cocoa wrapper around aliases.

Bookmarks are a serialized version of a file reference URL (along with some extra metadata to help identify the file) that can be saved to disk. If you save the bookmark in a particular way, it can be used as an alias by the Finder and Carbon code.

Create the bookmark data with this **NSURL** method:

```
- (NSData *) bookmarkDataWithOptions: (NSURLBookmarkCreationOptions) options
       includingResourceValuesForKeys: (NSArray *) keys
                        relativeToURL: (NSURL *) relativeURL
                                error: (NSError **) error;
```

The bookmark creation options are bitflags that can be combined:

```
NSURLBookmarkCreationPreferFileIDResolution
NSURLBookmarkCreationMinimalBookmark
NSURLBookmarkCreationSuitableForBookmarkFile
```

PreferFileIDResolution makes the alias created prefer resolving with its embedded file ID. MinimalBookmark will minimize the data but still be resolvable. And SuitableForBookmarkFile is required to create Finder alias files.

You can specify some resource value keys to store values in the bookmark. This means you can query the data without fully resolving the bookmark or alias. The `relativeURL` is the URL the bookmark data will be relative to.

Once you have the **NSData**, you can write it to the file system. You can create a file reference URL from bookmark data by using this **NSURL** class method:

```
+ (id) URLByResolvingBookmarkData: (NSData *) bookmarkData
                        options: (NSURLBookmarkResolutionOptions) options
                  relativeToURL: (NSURL *) relativeURL
              bookmarkDataIsStale: (BOOL *) isStale
                          error: (NSError **) error;
```

The bookmark resolution options can be zero, for default behavior, or a bitwise-OR of these flags:

```
NSURLBookmarkResolutionWithoutUI
NSURLBookmarkResolutionWithoutMounting
```

Sometimes there could be UI involved with resolving an alias. Aliases, and hence bookmarks, could cause a shared disk to be mounted. This can be very convenient for the user, but it could take an arbitrarily long period of time and could fail entirely.

Make a File Browser

In this chapter, you are going to create a simple file browser using **NSFileManager** and **NSTreeController**, as shown in Figure 13.3

Figure 13.3   The file browser

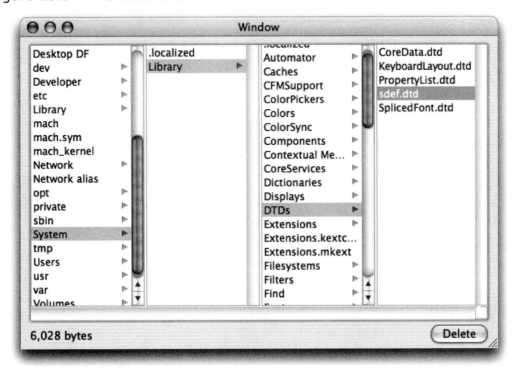

Create a new "Cocoa Application" project called **Remover**. Besides browsing, your app will allow the user to delete files and directories.

To represent the information about one directory entry, which may be a file or a directory, you will create a class called **DirEntry**. You will also be adding an **NSTreeController**, and the **RemoverAppDelegate** has already been created by the Xcode template. The class diagram is shown in Figure 13.4

Figure 13.4   Class diagram for Remover app

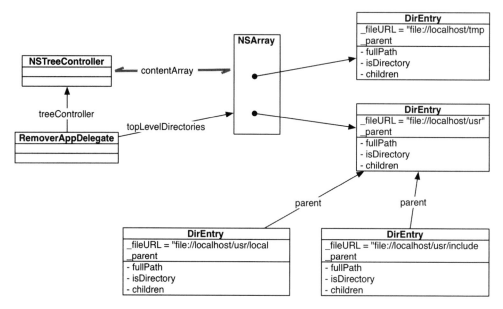

Create the DirEntry class

The file system is essentially a tree; each node of the tree is a directory or a file. You need to create a class to hold onto the information about one node, so create a class called **DirEntry**.

Each instance of **DirEntry** will know its parent and its file URL. If it's a directory, it will know how to create an array containing **DirEntry**s representing its children. So, make DirEntry.h look like this:

Example 13.6   DirEntry.h

```
#import <Foundation/Foundation.h>

@interface DirEntry : NSObject {
    NSURL *_fileURL;
    DirEntry *_parent;
}

+ (NSArray *) entriesAtURL: (NSURL *) url
              withParent: (DirEntry *) parent;
```

```
@property (nonatomic, readonly, retain) NSURL *fileURL;
@property (nonatomic, readonly, assign) DirEntry *parent;
@property (nonatomic, readonly, retain) NSArray *children;
@property (nonatomic, readonly, copy) NSString *fullPath;
@property (nonatomic, readonly, copy) NSString *filename;
@property (nonatomic, readonly, assign) unsigned long long filesize;
@property (nonatomic, readonly, assign) BOOL isDirectory;
@property (nonatomic, readonly, assign) BOOL isLeaf;

@end // DirEntry
```

Now to implement these methods:

Example 13.7   DirEntry.m

```
#import "DirEntry.h"

@interface DirEntry ()
// Let us set and get the parent, but it's not really part of the public API.
@property (nonatomic, assign) DirEntry *parent;
@end // DirEntry

@implementation DirEntry

@synthesize fileURL = _fileURL;
@synthesize parent = _parent;

// The default set of attributes to pre-fetch.
+ (NSArray *) attributeKeys {
    static NSArray *s_keys;
    if (s_keys == nil) {
        s_keys = [[NSArray arrayWithObjects:
                            NSURLNameKey,
                            NSURLFileSizeKey,
                            NSURLIsDirectoryKey,
                            nil] retain];
    }
    return s_keys;
} // attributeKeys

#pragma mark Creation and Initialization

- (id) initWithFileURL: (NSURL *) fileURL
                parent: (DirEntry *) parent {
    if ((self = [super init])) {
        _fileURL = [fileURL retain];
        _parent = parent;  // Don't retain parent, causes retain cycles.
    }
    return self;
} // initWithFilename

+ (NSArray *) entriesAtURL: (NSURL *) url
                withParent: (DirEntry *) parent {
    NSMutableArray *result = [NSMutableArray array];

    // Get URLs for the contents of the given directory.
    NSArray *attributeKeys = [self attributeKeys];
```

```
        NSError *error;
        NSArray *fileURLs =
            [[NSFileManager defaultManager] contentsOfDirectoryAtURL: url
                                      includingPropertiesForKeys: attributeKeys
                                      options: 0
                                      error: &error];
        if (fileURLs == nil)  {
            NSRunAlertPanel(@"Read failed",
                            @"Unable to read \'%@\' with error %@",
                            nil, nil, nil,
                            url, error) ;
            return result;
        }

        // Create DirEntries for each of resulting URLs
        [fileURLs enumerateObjectsUsingBlock:
                    ^(id fileURL, NSUInteger index, BOOL *stop) {
                DirEntry *newEntry =
                    [[DirEntry alloc] initWithFileURL: fileURL
                                      parent: parent];
                [result addObject: newEntry];
                [newEntry release];
            }];

        return [[result copy] autorelease];  // strip off mutability

} // entriesAtURL

- (void) dealloc {
    [_fileURL release];
    [super dealloc];
} // dealloc

#pragma mark File info

- (NSString *) fullPath {
    return [self.fileURL path];
} // fullPath

- (NSString *) filename {
    NSString *filename;
    NSError *error;
    if ([self.fileURL getResourceValue: &filename
            forKey: NSURLNameKey  error: &error]) {
        return filename;
    } else {
        NSRunAlertPanel (@"Attributes failed",
                         @"Unable to get file name for \'%@\' with error %@",
                         nil, nil, nil, self.fileURL, error) ;
        return nil;
    }

} // filename

- (BOOL) isDirectory {
    NSNumber *isDirectory;
    NSError *error;
    if ([self.fileURL getResourceValue: &isDirectory
            forKey: NSURLIsDirectoryKey  error: &error]) {
        return [isDirectory boolValue];
```

```
        } else {
            NSRunAlertPanel (@"Attributes failed",
                            @"Unable to get isDirectory for \'%@\' with error %@",
                            nil, nil, nil, self.fileURL, error) ;
            return NO;
        }

    } // isDirectory

- (unsigned long long) filesize {
        NSNumber *filesize;
        NSError *error;
        if ([self.fileURL getResourceValue: &filesize
                forKey: NSURLFileSizeKey  error: &error]) {
            return [filesize longLongValue];
        } else {
            NSRunAlertPanel (@"Attributes failed",
                            @"Unable to get file size for \'%@\' with error %@",
                            nil, nil, nil, self.fileURL, error) ;
            return 0;
        }
    } // filesize

#pragma mark For use in bindings

- (BOOL) isLeaf {
        return !self.isDirectory;
    } // isLeaf


- (NSArray *) children {
        return [DirEntry entriesAtURL: self.fileURL  withParent: self];
    } // children

@end // DirEntry
```

Edit the nib file adding NSTreeController

The **NSTreeController** is for displaying hierarchical data in an **NSBrowser** or an **NSOutlineView**. Besides setting the contentArray as you would for an **NSArrayController**, you also define a childrenKeyPath and a leafKeyPath.

In our case, the **NSTreeController** will be displaying **DirEntry** objects. Note that the **DirEntry** objects have a **-children** method and an **-isLeaf** method. These will be our childrenKeyPath and our leafKeyPath respectively.

Edit **RemoverAppDelegate** and add an action called **-deleteSelection:** and one outlet of type **NSTreeController** called treeController. Also, add a topLevelDirectories **NSArray**.

```
#import <Cocoa/Cocoa.h>

@interface RemoverAppDelegate : NSObject <NSApplicationDelegate> {
    NSWindow *window;
    NSTreeController *_treeController;
    NSArray *_topLevelDirectories;
}

@property (nonatomic, assign) IBOutlet NSWindow *window;
```

```
@property (nonatomic, assign) IBOutlet NSTreeController *treeController;
@property (nonatomic, readonly, retain) NSArray *topLevelDirectories;

- (IBAction) deleteSelection: (id) sender;

@end // RemoverAppDelegate
```

Open the MainMenu.xib file. To instantiate a tree controller, drag one out the objects library. Make it non-editable and allow the empty selection. Set the children key path to be children and set the leaf key path to be isLeaf. The objects being displayed are **DirEntry** objects. They have a filename attribute and a filesize attribute.

Figure 13.5   Configuring the tree controller's bindings

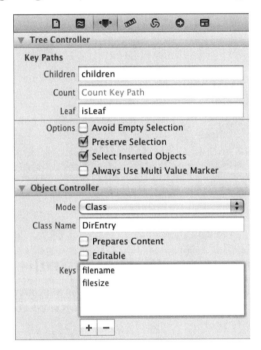

Drop an **NSBrowser** and an **NSButton** on the window. In the inspector, set the **NSBrowser** so that it does not display titles. Make **RemoverAppDelegate** the target of the button and set the action to be **-deleteSelection:**.

Set the autosizing for the **NSBrowser** to grow with the window and for the **NSButton** to remain in place. You might want to change the button's title to "Delete" at this time.

Connect the treeController outlet of **RemoverAppDelegate** to point to the **NSTreeController**.

Bind the contentArray of the tree controller to the topLevelDirectories attribute of the **RemoverAppDelegate**. (Note that you will actually have to type "topLevelDirectories" into the combo box.)

Figure 13.6 Binding the tree controller's contentArray

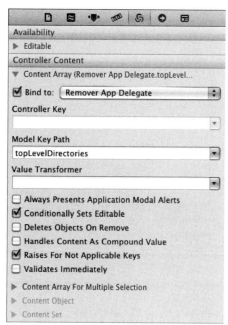

Select the browser and view its bindings. Bind the content to the tree controller's arrangedObjects and bind the contentValues to the tree controller's arrangedObjects' fileName.

Figure 13.7 Binding the browser's arrangedObjects

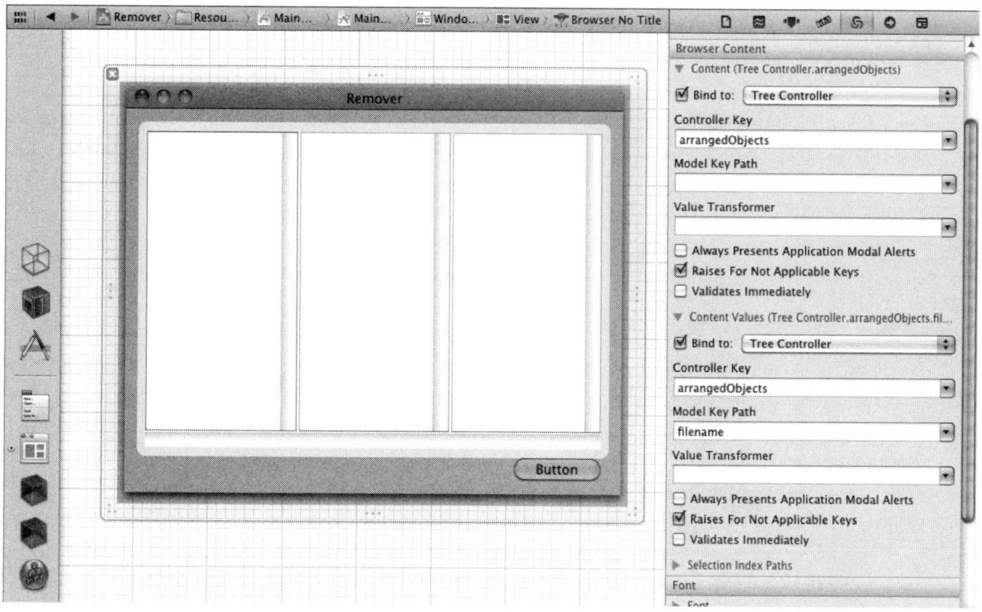

Bind the selectionIndexPaths to the tree controller's selectionIndexPaths.

Figure 13.8   Binding the browser's selection index paths

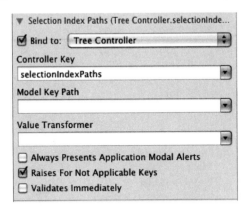

For fun, let's also show the size of the selected file. Drop a Label onto the window. Make sure the label is wide enough to hold a large number and set the autosizing so that the label stays in the bottom-left corner. Next drop a number formatter on top of the label. Select the Mac OS X 10.4+ Custom behavior if it is not already selected.

The size is a number of bytes, so give it a Format (+) of "# bytes." Check the Grouping Separator checkbox and increase the Primary Grouping to 3 and leave the Secondary Grouping at zero. Uncheck Allows Floats because files cannot contain fractional bytes.

Figure 13.9   Configuring the label's number formatter

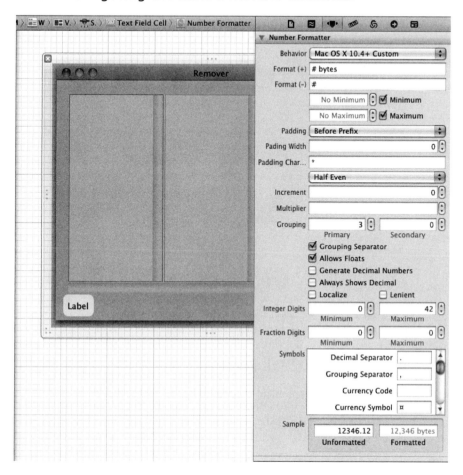

Bind the value of the text field to the tree controller's `selection`'s `fileSize`.

Figure 13.10   Binding the label's contents.

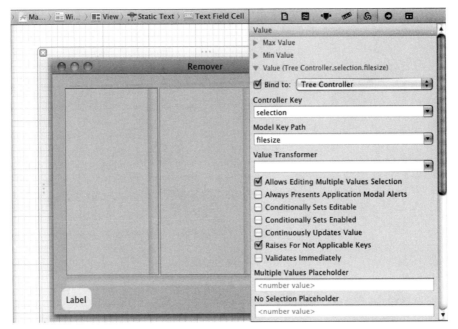

Using NSBrowser and DirEntry

In the RemoverAppDelegate.m file, implement these methods:

Example 13.8   RemoverAppDelegate.m

```
#import "RemoverAppDelegate.h"
#import "DirEntry.h"

@interface RemoverAppDelegate ()
@property (nonatomic, readwrite, retain) NSArray *topLevelDirectories;
@end // RemoveAppDelegate

@implementation RemoverAppDelegate

@synthesize window;
@synthesize topLevelDirectories = _topLevelDirectories;
@synthesize treeController = _treeController;

- (id) init {
    if ((self = [super init])) {
        // Seed the directories to display.
        NSURL *rootURL = [NSURL fileURLWithPath: @"/"  isDirectory: YES];
        _topLevelDirectories =
            [DirEntry entriesAtURL: rootURL  withParent: nil];
    }
    return self;
} // init
```

```
- (void) dealloc {
   [_topLevelDirectories release];
   [super dealloc];
} // dealloc

- (IBAction) deleteSelection: (id) sender {
   NSLog (@"%s to be implemented", __FUNCTION__);
} // deleteSelection

@end // RemoverAppDelegate
```

Build and run the app. You should be able to browse but not delete.

Adding deletion

Replace the **-deleteSelection:** method in **RemoverAppDelegate** to enable deletion:

Example 13.9   -deleteSelection:

```
- (IBAction) deleteSelection: (id) sender {
   // Get the selection
   NSArray *selection = [[[_treeController selectedObjects] retain] autorelease];
   NSUInteger count = [selection count];

   // Bail if there's an empty selection?
   if (count == 0) {
       NSRunAlertPanel (@"Nothing to Delete",
                        @"Select an item to delete and try again.",
                        nil, nil, nil);
       return;
   }

   NSFileManager *fm = [[NSFileManager alloc] init];
   fm.delegate = self;

   [selection enumerateObjectsUsingBlock:
               ^(DirEntry *dirEntry, NSUInteger index, BOOL *stop) {
           NSString *path = dirEntry.fullPath;
           NSString *title =
               [NSString stringWithFormat: @"Delete \"%@\"?", path];

           NSInteger choice = NSRunAlertPanel (title,
                                               @"Deletion cannot be undone.",
                                               @"Delete", @"Cancel",
                                               nil);
           if (choice != NSAlertDefaultReturn) return;

           // Send notifications that trigger KVO to update the browser.
           BOOL didDelete = NO;
           NSError *error;

           [dirEntry.parent willChangeValueForKey: @"children"]; {
               // Actually delete the file or directory
               didDelete = [fm removeItemAtURL: dirEntry.fileURL
                               error: &error];
           } [dirEntry.parent didChangeValueForKey: @"children"];

           // Was the deletion a failure?
```

```
            if (!didDelete) {
                [[NSApplication sharedApplication] presentError: error];
            }
        }];
    [fm release];

} // deleteSelection

// NSFileManager calls this delegate method if something goes wrong.
- (BOOL) fileManager: (NSFileManager *) manager
  shouldProceedAfterError: (NSError *) error
        removingItemAtPath: (NSString *) path {

    NSLog (@"%s: error = %@", __FUNCTION__, error);
    return NO;

} // shouldProceedAfterError
```

Build and test this *carefully*. It will happily delete entire directories.

Figure 13.11   Remover in action

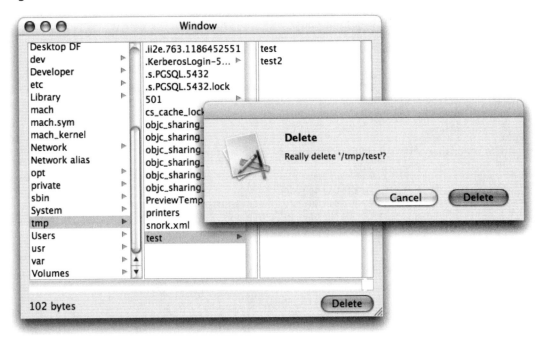

When doing the deletion, you need to tell any KVO observers of the parent **DirEntry** that the children have changed. Because the browser is observing the **DirEntry**s, you need to call the **-willChangeValueForKey:** and **-didChangeValueForKey:** methods. The added scope used here is not necessary, but it makes it very clear what methods are being called between will-change and did-change.

Lastly, you allocate the **NSFileManager** and use it inside of the enumeration block. This makes using the delegate of the file manager easier. Someone else may have set the delegate of the shared file manager, so you would have to save off the delegate beforehand and restore it later – and hope that someone else hasn't changed it in the meantime. If you use your own file manager and set its delegate, **NSFileManager** will let us know when there are problems removing a file.

NSWorkspace

Back in the mists of time, the original NeXT-system UI was called the Workspace. These days it's a combination of the Finder and the Dock. Cocoa's **NSWorkspace** class provides features that were originally available in the NeXT workspace. **NSWorkspace**, actually, is a combination of Finder features as well as being a higher level API on top of Apple's Launch Services. Launch Services is a database of applications, file types, icons, and associated data.

Because the system has one Launch Services database and the user has one Finder, you interact with **NSWorkspace** via a shared instance:

```
+ (NSWorkspace *) sharedWorkspace;
```

You can open files and URLs, and launch applications as if you had double-clicked them in the Finder. **NSWorkspace** will consult with Launch Services to figure out the proper application to run.

```
- (BOOL) openFile: (NSString *) fullPath;
```

Open the file as if it were double-clicked.

```
- (BOOL) openFile: (NSString *) fullPath
  withApplication: (NSString *) appName
    andDeactivate: (BOOL) deactivate;
```

Open the file with the given application. You can specify a path to an application or just the name. Passing YES for deactivate means that the calling application will deactivate itself so that the new application can appear in the foreground.

If you are more into URLs, you can open a file easily:

```
- (BOOL) openURL: (NSURL *) url;
```

-launchApplicationAtURL:options:configuration:error: is a more sophisticated version, but it is more complex and beyond the scope of the current discussion.

You can get a file's icon:

```
- (NSImage *) iconForFile: (NSString *) fullPath;
```

NSWorkspace also has its own notification center:

```
- (NSNotificationCenter *) notificationCenter;
```

You can register handlers for the different notifications it can post. Here is a sampling:

```
NSWorkspaceWillLaunchApplicationNotification
NSWorkspaceDidLaunchApplicationNotification
NSWorkspaceDidTerminateApplicationNotification
NSWorkspaceWillPowerOffNotification
NSWorkspaceDidMountNotification
NSWorkspaceSessionDidBecomeActiveNotification
NSWorkspaceDidPerformFileOperationNotification
```

Exercises

1. Use **NSDirectoryEnumerator** to calculate the true size of the selected directory.

2. Use **NSWorkspace** to find and display an icon for the selected file or directory in an **NSImageView**.

3. If the user double-clicks a file, open it. This also uses **NSWorkspace**.

4. Use **NSWorkspace** to recycle the selected item (move it to the trash) rather than deleting it.

5. Use **DirEntry** in an iPhone app to display the contents of the application's sandbox.

6. Store the user's current location in Remover and restore it on next program launch. Make sure it works after reboots.

7. Remover currently starts up showing the top of the file system. Change Remover so that it starts by showing all mounted volumes at the top level instead.

14

Network Programming With Sockets

The native Mac OS X networking API is Berkeley sockets, variants of which are available on just about every platform available today. The sockets API is simultaneously elegant, needing just a couple of calls to set up network communications of different kinds, and ugly. The data structures involved are awkward because there are few typedefs, so you have to use the struct keyword frequently along with frequent casting.

One of the problems with networking in general, and sockets in particular, is that there is a lot of documentation and a lot of features of varying levels of complexity and obscurity. It is easy to get lost in the details and be unable to get the basics working. In this chapter, we are going to be concerned primarily with basic stream-oriented network communication.

Addresses

Network interfaces, such as ethernet cards or airport cards, are identified by an IP (Internet Protocol) address. An IP address is a numeric value that is used as the source or destination of a network message. A typical network message would be something like, "An interface at IP address 10.0.1.123 is sending 30 bytes of data to another interface at IP 192.168.254.42." There are two major flavors of IP addresses: IPv4 and IPv6, which are ways of saying "Internet Protocol version 4" and "Internet Protocol version 6."

IPv4 are 32-bit addresses, the original addressing mode of the Internet. We have exhausted the 32-bit address space, meaning that there are not enough addresses available to address the current number of computers wanting to connect to the Internet. There are some workarounds, such as Network Address Translation (NAT) and local addressing, that allow multiple machines share the same public IP address, but none is a sustainable solution. The next generation of the Internet Protocol is IPv6, which uses 128-bit addresses. 128 bits can hold 340 undecillion values, where undecillion is ten raised to the 36th power. Hopefully, we will not be running out of IPv6 addresses any time soon.

IP addresses are numeric values. To make them a little easier to read, there are human-readable "presentation" formats. IPv4 addresses are usually represented in "dotted-quad" format, which is the four bytes of the address represented by decimal numbers, separated by periods. 127.0.0.2 is in dotted-quad format, as is 66.227.8.230.

IPv6 addresses are represented by sixteen-bit quantities separated by colons.
FDEC:BA98:7654:3210:FEDC:BA98:7654:3210 could be an IPv6 address, as well as
1080:0000:0000:0000:0008:0800:2000C:417A. You can omit leading zeros in each group to

reduce the amount of clutter, but there has to be at least one digit in every field. The previous address could be written as 1080:0:0:0:8:800:200C:417A. If there are multiple consecutive 16-bit groups of zeros, they can be elided and replaced with ::. The previous address can therefore be written 1080::8:800:200C:417A. To prevent ambiguities, there can only be one :: per address. The last 32 bits can also be written in dotted-quad format, leading to an IPv6 address like 1080::8:800:32.12.65.116.

There are two special IPv6 address formats to help IPv4 and IPv6 interoperate. The first is an IPv4-compatible IPv6 address of the form ::d.d.d.d. This format is leading zeros, followed by a 32-bit IPv4 address in dotted-quad format. It is typically used by hosts and routers to dynamically tunnel IPv6 packets over IPv4 routing.

The other is an IPv4-mapped IPv6 address, which takes the form ::FFFF:d.d.d.d. This address format is leading zeros, followed by 16 bits of ones, followed by a 32-bit IPv4 address. It is how IPv4-only nodes (those that do not support IPv6) are represented to IPv6-aware software. This format allows IPv6 systems to interoperate with IPv4-only systems.

Sockets Address Data Structures

There are a number of data structures used to represent network addresses, along with a number of functions for converting addresses between different formats.

The fundamental data structure in the sockets API is struct sockaddr:

```
struct sockaddr {
    uint8_t     sa_len;
    sa_family_t sa_family;
    char        sa_data[14];
};
```

struct sockaddr acts like an abstract base class in object-oriented languages. It defines two fields that are common amongst all of the different address types. By examining these fields you can see how large the address structure is by looking at sa_len, and you can see what kind of address it is (IPv4, IPv6, local address for Unix sockets, X.25, or other kinds of addresses that have not been invented yet) by looking at the sa_family field. sa_data is there to say that address-specific data follows these two common fields. That data is specified by other structures.

IPv4 address structures

The address structure for IPv4 addresses is struct sockaddr_in, where the _in suffix is short for "Internet":

```
struct sockaddr_in {
    uint8_t        sin_len;
    sa_family_t    sin_family;
    in_port_t      sin_port;
    struct in_addr sin_addr;
    char           sin_zero[8];
};
```

The first two fields match the first two fields of struct sockaddr. Store the constant AF_INET in sin_family for IPv4 addresses. The last element, sin_zero, is padding so that struct sockaddr_in matches the size of struct sockaddr. You must always clear it to zero before passing a sockaddr_in structure to any function.

TCP/IP communication deals with addresses and ports. Every IP address has 65535 ports associated with it. Communication actually happens between address-port pairs. Communicating with the web server at www.bignerdranch.com involves going to address 209.20.82.22 and connecting to port 80. Locally, your web browser will be communicating from a port at your local IP address. The sin_port field indicates which port should be used. The IP address lives in sin_addr.

sin_addr is a struct in_addr, which is one of the annoying parts of the sockets API:

```
struct in_addr {
    in_addr_t s_addr;
};
```

This is a structure with only a single element. The actual address type, in_addr_t, is an unsigned 32-bit integer.

There is one tricky detail: both the port (2 bytes) and the address (4 bytes) need to be in network (big-endian) byte order. The functions that simplify byte swapping to and from the network byte order are described later.

IPv6 address structures

IPv6 addresses have a new address structure, struct sockaddr_in6. The IPv6 addresses are larger, and they have some features that IPv4 doesn't support. struct sockaddr_in6 looks like this:

```
struct sockaddr_in6 {
    uint8_t         sin6_len;
    sa_family_t     sin6_family;
    in_port_t       sin6_port;
    uint32_t        sin6_flowinfo;
    struct in6_addr sin6_addr;
    uint32_t        sin6_scope_id;
};
```

Like struct sockaddr_in, the first field is the length of the structure and the second field is the family, which should be set to AF_INET6. After that comes the port, which is just like the port in IPv4. We will not talk about sin6_flowinfo or sin6_scope_id. These are more advanced IPv6 features that are not necessary to deal with on a daily basis. One interesting thing to notice is that sockaddr_in6 uses more descriptive types than the older sockaddr_in.

sin6_addr is the actual IP address of type struct in6_addr. Like struct in_addr, struct in6_addr is a structure that holds the address:

```
struct in6_addr {
    uint8_t s6_addr[16];
}
```

If you have been following along carefully, you will notice that sockadd_in6 weighs in at 28 bytes, which will not fit into a sockaddr that is 16 bytes large. This makes it awkward to have an array of sockaddrs to hold IPv4 and IPv6 addresses. struct sockaddr_storage was introduced to alleviate this problem:

```
struct sockaddr_storage {
    uint8_t     ss_len;
    sa_family_t ss_family;
    char        __ss_pad1[__SS_PAD1SIZE];
```

```
    int64_t      __ss_align;
    char         __ss_pad2[_SS_PAD2SIZE];
}
```

The only public fields of this structure are those it shares with all socket structures: length and family. The other fields exist purely to pad out the structure and influence its alignment in memory. sockaddr_storage is 128 bytes long, which allows some breathing room for future expansion. This means that you can declare a variable of type sockaddr_storage, cast it to any other socket structure type, and access any field of that structure without violating alignment constraints or worrying about overrunning a chunk of memory.

Network Byte Order

The way bytes are ordered in multi-byte integers can vary from platform to platform. The bytes of the integer value of 0x12345678 could be stored in memory in that order with the most significant byte occurring at a lower address. This is called *big endian* because the big part of the integer (the most significant byte) occurs first. The same value could also be stored in *little-endian* byte order as 0x78563412; here, the least significant byte comes first. The PowerPC stored its integers in big endian byte order, while Intel x86 machines store integers in little endian byte order. The two parties communicating must agree on what order the specific bytes will have when transferring integers between machines over the network. Usually you will use "network byte order," which is defined to be big endian.

Because many Mac developers still support software on both architectures, we have to worry about network byte order, not only with regards to transferring data over a network, but also when writing binary files. It is always a good idea to store your integers in network byte order to prevent surprises later on. There are some useful functions provided that ensure that your data is in network byte order:

uint16_t **htons** (uint16_t hostshort);

uint32_t **htonl** (uint32_t hostlong);

uint16_t **ntohs** (uint16_t netshort);

uint32_t **ntohl** (uint32_t netlong);

The nomenclature uses these conventions: h stands for "host," n for "network," s for "short," and l for "long."

So, **htonl()** is "host to network long," and the converse is **ntohl()**, "network to host long." You do not need to worry about network byte order when sending text data or single bytes.

Short and long are used here from the standpoint of an ILP32 environment, not LP64; the functions are defined using unsigned integral types of a specific number of bits rather than using short and long themselves to avoid any further confusion as to the size of short and long.

Core Foundation provides a number of byte swapping routines as well. There are 15 functions for swapping the bytes of 16, 32, and 64 bit integers. The format of the functions is CFSwapInt + word size + direction of conversion. The word size is 16, 32, or 64. Direction of conversion can be omitted, in which case the bytes are swapped, or it can be one of BigToHost (big endian to the host's native byte order, similar to the ntoh functions), HostToBig (native byte order to big endian, similar to the hton functions), HostToLittle, or LittleToHost. The last two convert between the host's native byte order and little-endian byte order.

Some valid byte swapping functions would then be `CFSwapInt16()`, `CFSwapInt32BigToHost()`, `CFSwapInt64HostToLittle()`, and so on.

Address Conversions

There are two fundamental forms for IP addresses. The first is a human-readable "presentation" form, such as the IPv4 dotted-quad or the IPv6 colon-delimited hex address. The other is a binary format "network" form that can be used by the sockets API to actually send data across the network. The presentation address is what the user interacts with, and the network form is used by the program's code.

IPv4- and IPv6-compatible functions

The **inet_pton()** function converts from an address in presentation format to one in network format, hence the "P to N" in the function name.

```
int inet_pton (int addressFamily, const char *sourceBuffer, void *destinationAddress);
```

This converts from an ASCII representation to a network address. `addressFamily` is the family of the address being passed in and should be either `AF_INET` or `AF_INET6`. `sourceBuffer` is a zero-terminated ASCII string that holds the presentation address. `destinationAddress` should be a `struct in_addr` for an `AF_INET` address or a `struct in6_addr` for an `AF_INET6` address.

inet_pton() returns 1 if the address was valid for the specified address family, 0 if the address was not parsable in the specified address family, or -1 if some system error occurred. Consult `errno` for the specific error.

The **inet_ntop()** converts from a network address to a presentation form.

```
const char *inet_ntop (int addressFamily, const void *sourceAddress,
                       char *destinationBuffer, socklen_t bufferSize);
```

This converts from a network address to an ASCII representation. `addressFamily` is the family of the address and should be either `AF_INET` or `AF_INET6`. The `sourceAddress` parameter is an address in network format, such as a `struct in_addr` or a `struct in6_addr`. The destination buffer is a character buffer that you provide (you cannot pass `NULL` here) which will be filled in with the presentation-format address. The buffer should be at least as large as `INET_ADDRSTRLEN` when using the `AF_INET` address family or at least as large as `INET6_ADDRSTRLEN` when using `AF_INET6`. Using these constants guarantees that the buffer will be large enough to hold the largest possible presentation address.

Upon success, the **inet_ntop()** returns the address of your character buffer. On failure, it returns `NULL`, in which case you should consult `errno` to learn what went wrong.

Example 14.1 shows **inet_pton** and **inet_ntop** in action: an address in ASCII-presentation format is converted into a binary address and back again.

Example 14.1   ptontoa.m

```
// ptontoa.m -- Exercise inet_pton and inet_ntop

// gcc -g -Wall -o ptontoa ptontoa.m

#import <arpa/inet.h>  // for inet_*
```

```
#import <errno.h>        // for errno
#import <netinet/in.h>   // for in_addr and in6_addr
#import <stdio.h>        // for printf()
#import <stdlib.h>       // for EXIT_SUCCESS
#import <string.h>       // for strerror
#import <sys/socket.h>   // for AF_INET[6]
#import <sys/types.h>    // for type definitions, like u_char

// Convert an IPv6 address to a string.
const char *in6ToChar (struct in6_addr *addr) {
    static char s_address[INET6_ADDRSTRLEN];

    uint32_t *base = (uint32_t *)addr->s6_addr;

    snprintf(s_address, sizeof(s_address), "%x%x%x%x",
            ntohl(base[0]), ntohl(base[1]), ntohl(base[2]), ntohl(base[3]));
    return s_address;
} // in6ToChar


int main (void) {
    // --------------------------------------------------
    // IPv4

    // Convert from presentation to numeric, inet_name -> inet_addr
    char inet_name[INET_ADDRSTRLEN];
    strncpy (inet_name, "192.168.254.123", INET_ADDRSTRLEN);
    inet_name[INET_ADDRSTRLEN - 1] = '\0';

    struct in_addr inet_addr;
    int result = inet_pton (AF_INET, inet_name, &inet_addr);

    if (result == 1) {
        printf("address '%s' in binary: %x\n",
                inet_name, ntohl(inet_addr.s_addr));
    } else if (result == 0) {
        printf("*** address '%s' not parsable\n\n", inet_name);
    } else {
        printf("*** inet_pton: error %d: %s\n",
                errno, strerror(errno));
    }

    // Convert from numeric to presentation, inet_addr -> inet_name
    const char *ntop_result = inet_ntop (AF_INET, &inet_addr,
                                    inet_name, sizeof(inet_name));

    if (ntop_result != NULL) {  // ntop_result == inet_name
        printf ("address '%x' presentation: '%s'\n",
                ntohl(inet_addr.s_addr), inet_name);
    } else {
        printf ("*** inet_ntop: error %d: %s\n",
                errno, strerror(errno));
    }

    // --------------------------------------------------
    // IPv6

    // Convert from presentation to numeric,  inet6_name -> inet6_addr
    char inet6_name[INET6_ADDRSTRLEN];
    strncpy (inet6_name, "FE80:0000:0000:0000:0230:65FF:FE06:6523",
```

```
            INET6_ADDRSTRLEN);
    inet6_name[INET6_ADDRSTRLEN - 1] = '\0';

    struct in6_addr inet6_addr;
    result = inet_pton (AF_INET6, inet6_name, &inet6_addr);

    if (result == 1) {
        printf ("address '%s'\n    in binary: %s\n",
                inet6_name, in6ToChar(&inet6_addr));
    } else if (result == 0) {
        printf ("*** address '%s' not parsable\n\n", inet_name);
    } else {
        printf ("*** inet_pton: error %d: %s\n",
                errno, strerror(errno));
    }

    // Convert from numeric to presentation, inet6_addr -> inet6_name
    ntop_result = inet_ntop (AF_INET6, &inet6_addr,
                             inet6_name, sizeof(inet6_name));

    if (ntop_result != NULL) {
        printf("address '%s'\n    presentation: '%s'\n",
               in6ToChar(&inet6_addr), inet6_name);
    } else {
        printf("*** inet_ntop: error %d: %s\n",
               errno, strerror(errno));
    }
    return EXIT_SUCCESS;
}   // main
```

And here is a sample run:

```
$ ./ptontoa
address '192.168.254.123' in binary: c0a8fe7b
address 'c0a8fe7b' presentation: '192.168.254.123'
address 'FE80:0000:0000:0000:0230:65FF:FE06:6523'
    in binary: fe800000023065fffe066523
address 'fe800000023065fffe066523'
    presentation: 'fe80::230:65ff:fe06:6523'
```

inet_ntop() is nice enough to render the IPv6 address in its minimal format, omitting extra zeros.

IPv4-specific functions

The functions described earlier can handle all of your address conversion needs. If you are working on an older platform that does not have those functions or if you are maintaining code that was written before IPv6, you may encounter a couple other address conversion functions.

These functions deal exclusively with 32-bit addresses and the dotted-quad presentation format. **inet_aton** converts from an ASCII to a binary representation, and **inet_ntoa** converts in the opposite direction.

```
int inet_aton (const char *quadString, struct in_addr *address);
```

This converts an ASCII representation of a dotted quad to a numeric address (hence a-to-n). The numeric address is returned by reference. The function returns 1 if the conversion was successful and 0 if the string is invalid.

```
char *inet_ntoa (struct in_addr address);
```

This converts the numeric address to an ASCII representation. The string returned resides in static memory, so it will be clobbered by the next call to **inet_ntoa()**.

Domain Name Lookup

Human beings tend to prefer dealing with hostnames rather than working with raw IP addresses, even if the IP address is in a nice user-friendly presentation format. DNS, short for Domain Name Service, is the mechanism for translating human-readable hostnames, like www.bignerdranch.com, into a corresponding IP address.

You will use struct hostent when looking up hostnames to resolve the address.

```
struct hostent {
    char    *h_name;
    char    **h_aliases;
    int      h_addrtype;
    int      h_length;
    char    **h_addr_list;
    #define h_addr  h_addr_list[0]
};
```

The elements of the structure are:

h_name	Official name of the host.
h_aliases	A NULL-terminated array of alternate names for the host.
h_addrtype	The type of address being returned, AF_INET for Internet addresses.
h_length	The length, in bytes, of the address.
h_addr_list	A NULL-terminated array of network addresses (struct in_addr or struct in6_addr) for the host, in network byte order.
h_addr	The first address in h_addr_list. Here for backward compatibility, or as a convenience if you just want to pick up the first address in the list.

gethostbyname2() looks up a hostname and returns a filled-in hostent, which like inet_ntoa is allocated in static space, so it will get clobbered on the next call. It is also not thread-safe.

```
struct hostent *gethostbyname2 (const char *hostname, int addressFamily);
```

Returns a pointer to a struct hostent that contains the resolved address for hostname, using the specified addressFamily. There is also an older **gethostbyname()** function which takes a hostname argument, but no addressFamily

gethostbyname2() does not return an error in errno. It provides its own variant of errno called h_errno, and you can use **hstrerror()** to get a human-readable message.

Example 14.2 is a program that exercises the address conversion functions.

Example 14.2   resolve.m

```
// resolve.m -- resolve an address using gethostbyname2()

// gcc -std=c99 -g -Wall -o resolve resolve.m

#import <arpa/inet.h>    // for inet_ntop
#import <netdb.h>        // for gethostbyname
#import <netinet/in.h>   // constants and types
#import <stdio.h>        // for fprintf
#import <stdlib.h>       // for EXIT_SUCCESS
#import <sys/socket.h>   // for AF_INET
#import <sys/types.h>    // random types

static void PrintHostEnt (const struct hostent *host) {
    // First the name.
    printf("    official name: %s\n", host->h_name);

    // Then any aliases.
    if (host->h_aliases[0] == NULL) printf ("    no aliases\n");
    else printf ("    has aliases\n");

    for (char **scan = host->h_aliases; *scan != NULL; ++scan) {
        printf ("        %s\n", *scan);
    }

    // The address type.
    const char *addressType = "UNKNOWN";
    if (host->h_addrtype == AF_INET) addressType = "AF_INET";
    else if (host->h_addrtype == AF_INET6) addressType = "AF_INET6";

    printf ("    addrtype: %d (%s)\n", host->h_addrtype, addressType);

    // Walk h_addr_list and print the addresses
    if (host->h_addr == NULL) printf ("    no addresses\n");
    else printf ("    addresses:\n");

    for (char **scan = host->h_addr_list; *scan != NULL; scan++) {
        char addr_name[INET_ADDRSTRLEN];
        if (inet_ntop(host->h_addrtype, *scan, addr_name, sizeof(addr_name))) {
            printf ("        %s\n", addr_name);
        }
    }

} // PrintHostEnt

int main(int argc, char *argv[]) {
    const char *hostname;
    if (argc == 1) hostname = "www.apple.com";
    else           hostname = argv[1];

    struct hostent *hostinfo = gethostbyname2 (hostname, AF_INET);

    if (hostinfo == NULL) {
        fprintf (stderr, "gethostbyname2(%s): *** error %s\n",
                 hostname, hstrerror(h_errno));
        return EXIT_FAILURE;
    }
```

```
        printf ("gethostbyname2: %s\n", hostname);
        PrintHostEnt (hostinfo);

        return EXIT_SUCCESS;

} // main
```

and a sample run:

```
$ ./resolve
gethostbyname2 www.apple.com
    official name: e3191.c.akamaiedge.net
    aliases:
        www.apple.com
        www.apple.com.akadns.net
        www.apple.com.edgekey.net
    addrtype: 2 (AF_INET)
    addresses:
        72.247.109.15
```

That weird official name for www.apple.com that ends with akamaiedge.net is the Akamai service to find the closest host to you when it serves up the page. The first h_aliases entry of www.apple.com has the name that a web browser would display to the user when they go to the site.

And a second run:

```
% ./resolve google.com
gethostbyname2: google.com
    official name: google.com
    no aliases
    addrtype: 2 (AF_INET)
    addresses:
        74.125.93.147
        74.125.93.104
        74.125.93.103
        74.125.93.105
        74.125.93.106
        74.125.93.99
```

Here there are no aliases, but there are multiple addresses that can be used to reach the Google search page.

These name resolution calls are blocking calls and should not be used on the main thread of an iOS program. The DNS timeout is longer than the watchdog timer that kills unresponsive applications. You should either put name lookup into another thread or another process or use the **CFHost** functions described in Chapter 15: *CFRunLoop*

Simple Network Programming

In networking, the terms "client" and "server" describe the party that is waiting for a new connection (the server) and the party that initiates a new connection (the client). Once the communications channel is set up, the client and server are peers that communicate with each other.

Server coding

Here is the set of calls and actions used when writing a server program:

1. Get a **socket()**.

2. Construct an address–port pair that the server will listen on.

3. **bind()** the socket to the address.

4. Tell the socket to start **listen()**ing for new connections.

5. **accept()** new connections from clients.

6. Use **read()** and **write()** to receive and send data over the client connection.

7. **close()** the client connection's socket.

```
int socket (int domain, int type, int protocol);
```

This creates a socket and returns a file descriptor, just like the file descriptors from Chapter 11: *Files, Part 1: I/O and Permissions*. You won't actually read or write through this particular file descriptor for a server. Instead, you'll use it as the focus for other networking calls. The **accept()** call described later returns a file descriptor you can read and write through.

For domain, use AF_INET for an internet socket or AF_INET6 for an IPv6 socket. For type, use SOCK_STREAM for a reliable connection, which means the bytes you send will be received in the same order you sent them and without error.

Apple recommends always making an IPv6 socket to listen on. The OS will automatically "downgrade" it to an IPv4 socket if necessary, so there is no need to listen on two different sockets.

For protocol, just pass zero to have the system use the default protocol.

This returns -1 on error and sets errno appropriately.

Constructing an address

To construct the address, create a struct sockaddr_in6 on the stack and fill out the various fields:

```
struct sockaddr_in6 address = { 0 };
address.sin6_len = sizeof(address);
address.sin6_family = AF_INET6;
address.sin6_port = htons(2342);
address.sin6_addr = in6addr_any;
```

The family for this address is AF_INET6, with AF standing for "address family." in6addr_any is a global value that means that any IP address can be used. You would use INADDR_ANY for IPv4 addresses. This will cause the server program to listen on the network address of your machine. If you have multiple network addresses, it will listen on all of them. You can, of course, provide a particular address to listen on.

The port and address are put into network byte order, and the sin_zero portion of the structure is zeroed out.

bind

bind() brings the address and the socket together. The socket then owns that address-port pair.

```
int bind (int socket, const struct sockaddr *address, int addresslen);
```

This takes a pointer to a `struct sockaddr`, not a `struct sockaddr_in6`, so you need to cast. `addresslen` is the size of your `struct sockaddr_in6`.

bind() will return an error if the address-port pair is already in use. This can be frustrating if your program has crashed, but the previously bound socket still exists in the kernel. The kernel might not release this address-port pair until a timeout of a couple of minutes happens. You can tell the socket to reuse such an abandoned but not yet timed-out address using by calling **setsockopt()** as follows before calling **bind()**:

```
int yes = 1;
result = setsockopt (socket, SOL_SOCKET, SO_REUSEADDR, &yes, sizeof(int));
```

setsockopt() is a generic interface for tweaking different socket parameters. Both **setsockopt()** and **bind()** return -1 on errors and set `errno`.

listen

The `listen()` system call informs the kernel to start accepting connections to the address and port specified in the address passed to **bind()**.

```
int listen (int socket, int backlog);
```

The `backlog` parameter hints at the maximum length of the queue of pending connection requests. Once the queue has filled, all subsequent attempts to connect to the socket garner a "connection refused" error. The system caps the size of the backlog queue to prevent excessive use of system memory.

accept

The **accept()** call will wait for a new incoming connection. When a new connection is made, **accept()** will return with a file descriptor that you can read and write through. This file descriptor is just like any other, so you can use functions like **read()**, **write()**, **send()**, and **readv()**, and you can wrap the descriptor in a standard I/O `FILE` if you so desire. Some file operations, like seeking, will result in errors since you cannot seek with a network connection.

```
int accept (int socket, struct sockaddr *address, socklen_t *addressLength);
```

The `address` parameter will contain the address of the client making the request upon a successful **accept()**. It returns -1 on error and sets `errno` appropriately.

accept() will block until an incoming connection happens or an error happens. The socket can be set into a non-blocking mode to avoid blocking; you will read about that later when we discuss multiplexing connections.

Example 14.3 is a simple server that binds to port 2342 and listens for incoming connections. You can make such a connection using the **telnet** command. When a connection is made, the data from the other program is read and printed. Then it waits for another connection.

Example 14.3   simpleserver.m

```
// simpleserver.m -- listen on a port and print any bytes that come through
//    Run without arguments to bind to an IPv4 address.
```

```
//   Run with any argument to bind to an IPv6 address.

// gcc -std=c99 -g -Wall -o simpleserver simpleserver.m

#import <arpa/inet.h>      // for inet_ntop
#import <errno.h>          // for errno
#import <netinet/in.h>     // for sockaddr_in
#import <netinet6/in6.h>   // sockaddr_in6
#import <stdbool.h>        // true/false
#import <stdio.h>          // for fprintf
#import <stdlib.h>         // for EXIT_SUCCESS
#import <string.h>         // for strerror
#import <sys/socket.h>     // socket(), AF_INET
#import <sys/types.h>      // random types
#import <unistd.h>         // close()

static const in_port_t kPortNumber = 2342;
static const int kAcceptQueueSizeHint = 8;

static void AcceptClientFromSocket (int listenFd);

int main (int argc, char *argv[]) {
    int exitCode = EXIT_FAILURE;

    const bool useIPv6 = (argc > 1);

    // get a socket
    int fd;
    if (useIPv6) fd = socket (AF_INET6, SOCK_STREAM, 0);
    else fd = socket (AF_INET, SOCK_STREAM, 0);

    if (fd == -1) {
        perror ("*** socket");
        goto cleanup;
    }

    // Reuse the address so stale sockets won't kill us.
    int yes = 1;
    int result = setsockopt (fd, SOL_SOCKET, SO_REUSEADDR, &yes, sizeof(yes));
    if (result == -1) {
        perror("*** setsockopt(SO_REUSEADDR)");
        goto cleanup;
    }

    // Bind to an address and port

    // Glom both kinds of addresses into a union to avoid casting.
    union {
        struct sockaddr sa;        // avoids casting
        struct sockaddr_in in;     // IPv4 support
        struct sockaddr_in6 in6;   // IPv6 support
    } address;

    if (useIPv6) {
        address.in6.sin6_len = sizeof (address.in6);
        address.in6.sin6_family = AF_INET6;
        address.in6.sin6_port = htons (kPortNumber);
        address.in6.sin6_flowinfo = 0;
        address.in6.sin6_addr = in6addr_any;
        address.in6.sin6_scope_id = 0;
```

```
    } else {
        address.in.sin_len = sizeof (address.in);
        address.in.sin_family = AF_INET;
        address.in.sin_port = htons (kPortNumber);
        address.in.sin_addr.s_addr = htonl (INADDR_ANY);
        memset (address.in.sin_zero, 0, sizeof (address.in.sin_zero));
    }

    result = bind (fd, &address.sa, address.sa.sa_len);
    if (result == -1) {
        perror("*** bind");
        goto cleanup;
    }

    result = listen (fd, kAcceptQueueSizeHint);
    if (result == -1) {
        perror("*** listen");
        goto cleanup;
    }
    printf ("listening on port %d\n", (int)kPortNumber);

    while (true) AcceptClientFromSocket(fd);
    exitCode = EXIT_SUCCESS;

cleanup:
    close (fd);
    return exitCode;
}

static void AcceptClientFromSocket (int listenFd) {

    struct sockaddr_storage addr;
    socklen_t addr_len = sizeof(addr);

    // Accept and get the remote address
    int clientFd = accept (listenFd, (struct sockaddr *)&addr, &addr_len);

    if (clientFd == -1) {
        perror("*** accept");
        return;
    }

    // Get the port and a pointer to the network address.
    const void *net_addr = NULL;
    in_port_t port = 0;

    if (addr.ss_family == AF_INET) {
        struct sockaddr_in *addr_in = (struct sockaddr_in *)&addr;
        net_addr = &addr_in->sin_addr;
        port = addr_in->sin_port;
    } else {
        struct sockaddr_in6 *addr_in6 = (struct sockaddr_in6 *)&addr;
        net_addr = &addr_in6->sin6_addr;
        port = addr_in6->sin6_port;
    }

    // Convert address to something human readable.
    char buffer[4096];
    const char *name = inet_ntop (addr.ss_family, net_addr, buffer, sizeof(buffer));
    printf ("[%s port %d connected]\n", name ? name : "(unknown)", ntohs(port));
```

```
    // drain the socket
    while (true) {
        ssize_t read_count = read (clientFd, buffer, sizeof(buffer) - 1);

        if (0 == read_count) {
            break;   // end of file
        } else if (read_count == -1) {
            perror ("*** read");
            break;   // error
        } else {
            // Zero-terminate the string and print it out
            buffer[read_count] = '\0';
            printf ("%s", buffer);
        }
    }

    close (clientFd);
    puts("[connection closed]");

} // AcceptClientFromSocket
```

A sample run:

In one terminal window, run **simpleserver**:

```
$ ./simpleserver
```

And in another, run **telnet**:

```
$ telnet localhost 2342
Trying ::1...
telnet: connect to address ::1: Connection refused
Trying fe80::1...
telnet: connect to address fe80::1: Connection refused
Trying 127.0.0.1...
Connected to localhost.
Escape character is '^]'.
Greetings from another terminal!
Farewell!
(press Control-] to get a telnet prompt)
telnet> quit
Connection closed.
$
```

If you have not used **telnet** before, it makes a connection to the address and port indicated. **telnet** will then send any text you enter to the program on the other side, and it will display any returned text (in this case, no text is received).

Notice that we started our **simpleserver** listening on an IPv4 address. When **telnet** tries to connect to localhost on port 2342, you can see from the transcript that it tries and fails to find anything listening to port 2342 on the IPv6 loopback and link-local addresses. It reaches our simple server when it finally tries connecting to port 2342 at 127.0.0.1.

Here is what **simpleserver** prints during that session:

```
$ ./simpleserver
listening on port 2342
[127.0.0.1 port 62820 connected]
```

403

```
Greetings from another terminal!
Farewell!
[connection closed]
```

You can **telnet** again to the server and enter more text. To make the server exit, interrupt it with `Control-C`.

To run the server bound to an IPv6 address, pass any argument:

```
$ ./simpleserver -6
listening on port 2342
```

When you try to connect to `localhost` this time, you'll find the server listening on the IPv6 loopback address:

```
$ telnet localhost 2342
Trying ::1...
Connected to localhost.
Escape character is '^]'.
```

Client Coding

Code on the client is very similar to the server:

1. Figure out the address information of the server.

2. Construct a `struct sockaddr_in` address.

3. Get a **socket()**.

4. **connect()** to the server.

5. Use **read()** and **write()** to send and receive data.

connect

connect() makes the connection to the server. It returns a file descriptor that you read and write with.

```
int connect (int socket, const struct sockaddr *address, socklen_t addresslen);
```

Give it the address to connect to, and it returns zero if the connection succeeds or -1 for an error, with errno set.

Example 14.4 is a client that is a little more convenient than **telnet**. It follows **telnet**'s example in searching for the host address: first it does an IPv6 lookup and tries all addresses listed there; then it tries an IPv4 lookup. In practice, this turns into two nested loops: the outer walks the address families, while the inner walks the addresses listed with that family for the host name.

Example 14.4   simpleclient.m

```
// simpleclient.m -- read from stdin and send to the simpleserver

// gcc -std=c99 -g -Wall -o simpleclient simpleclient.m

#import <arpa/inet.h>   // for inet_ntop
#import <errno.h>       // errno
```

```
#import <netdb.h>        // gethostbyname2(), h_errno, etc.
#import <netinet/in.h>   // sockaddr_in
#import <stdbool.h>      // true/false
#import <stdio.h>        // fprintf()
#import <stdlib.h>       // EXIT_SUCCESS
#import <string.h>       // strerror()
#import <sys/socket.h>   // socket(), AF_INET
#import <sys/types.h>    // random types
#import <unistd.h>       // close()

static const in_port_t kPortNumber = 2342;

static int SocketConnectedToHostNamed (const char *hostname);
static bool GetAddressAtIndex (struct hostent *host, int addressIndex,
                               struct sockaddr_storage *outServerAddress);

int main (int argc, char *argv[]) {
    int exit_code = EXIT_FAILURE;

    // Get the host name.
    if (argc != 2) {
        fprintf (stderr, "Usage: %s hostname\n", argv[0]);
        goto cleanup;
    }

    const char *hostname = argv[1];

    // Get a connected socket.
    int sockfd = SocketConnectedToHostNamed(hostname);
    if (sockfd == -1) {
        fprintf (stderr, "*** Unable to connect to %s port %d.\n",
                 hostname, (int)kPortNumber);
        return EXIT_FAILURE;
    }
    printf ("[connected to %s port %d]\n", hostname, (int)kPortNumber);

    // Echo lines from stdin to sockfd.

    while (true) {
        char buffer[4096];
        const char *bytes = fgets (buffer, sizeof(buffer), stdin);

        // check EOF
        if (bytes == NULL) {
            if (ferror(stdin)) {
                perror("read");
                break;
            } else if (feof(stdin)) {
                fprintf(stderr, "EOF\n");
                break;
            }
        }

        ssize_t write_count = write(sockfd, buffer, strlen(buffer));
        if (write_count == -1) {
            perror("write");
            break;
        }
    }
```

```
        puts("[connection closed]");
        exit_code = EXIT_SUCCESS;

cleanup:
    close(sockfd);
    return exit_code;
}  // main


// Returns -1 on failure, >= 0 on success.
static int SocketConnectedToHostNamed (const char *hostname) {
    int sockfd = -1;

    // For each family call gethostbyname2()
    sa_family_t family[] = { AF_INET6, AF_INET };
    int family_count = sizeof(family) / sizeof(*family);

    for (int i = 0; sockfd == -1 && i < family_count; i++) {
        printf("Looking at %s family:\n",
                family[i] == AF_INET6 ? "AF_INET6" : "AF_INET");

        // Get the host address.
        struct hostent *host = NULL;
        host = gethostbyname2(hostname, family[i]);
        if (host == NULL) {
            herror ("gethostbyname2");
            continue;
        }

        // Try to connect with each address.
        struct sockaddr_storage server_addr;

        for (int addressIndex = 0; sockfd == -1; addressIndex++) {

            // Grab the next address.  Bail out if we've run out.
            if (!GetAddressAtIndex(host, addressIndex, &server_addr)) break;

            char buffer[INET6_ADDRSTRLEN];

            printf("    Trying %s...\n",
                    inet_ntop(host->h_addrtype, host->h_addr_list[addressIndex],
                            buffer, sizeof(buffer)));

            // Get a socket.
            sockfd = socket (server_addr.ss_family, SOCK_STREAM, 0);

            if (sockfd == -1) {
                perror ("        socket");
                continue;
            }

            // Reach out and touch someone.  Clients call connect() instead of
            // bind() + listen().
            int err = connect (sockfd, (struct sockaddr *)&server_addr,
                            server_addr.ss_len);
            if (err == -1) {
                perror ("        connect");
                close (sockfd);
                sockfd = -1;
            }
```

```
            // We successfully connected, so sockfd is not -1.
            // Both loops will exit at this point.
        }
    }
    return sockfd;
} // SocketConnectedToHostNamed

// Index into the hostent and get the addressIndex'th address.
// Returns true if successful, false if we've run out of addresses.
static bool GetAddressAtIndex (struct hostent *host, int addressIndex,
                               struct sockaddr_storage *outServerAddress) {
    // Bad arguments?
    if (outServerAddress == NULL || host == NULL) return false;

    // Out of addresses?
    if (host->h_addr_list[addressIndex] == NULL) return false;

    outServerAddress->ss_family = host->h_addrtype;

    if (outServerAddress->ss_family == AF_INET6) {
        struct sockaddr_in6 *addr = (struct sockaddr_in6 *)outServerAddress;
        addr->sin6_len = sizeof(*addr);
        addr->sin6_port = htons(kPortNumber);
        addr->sin6_flowinfo = 0;
        addr->sin6_addr = *(struct in6_addr *)host->h_addr_list[addressIndex];
        addr->sin6_scope_id = 0;
    } else {
        struct sockaddr_in *addr = (struct sockaddr_in *)outServerAddress;
        addr->sin_len = sizeof(*addr);
        addr->sin_port = htons(kPortNumber);
        addr->sin_addr = *(struct in_addr *)host->h_addr_list[addressIndex];
        memset(&addr->sin_zero, 0, sizeof(addr->sin_zero));
    }
    return true;
} // GetAddressAtIndex
```

Compile this, start the server running in one terminal window, and then run the client in another. This sample run has the server running on a different machine, called "buggun," on the local network,

```
% ./simpleclient biggun.local.
Looking at AF_INET6 family:
    Trying fe80:6::225:ff:fef4:673b...
        connect: Connection refused
Looking at AF_INET family:
    Trying 192.168.254.8...
[connected to biggun.local. port 2342]
Hello there!
I hope the weather is better where you are.
jo2y and monkeybot, sitting in a tree.
(Type Control-D to send EOF to the client.)
EOF
[connection closed]
```

When you send EOF to the client, the **fgets** function returns NULL, and the connection is closed.

On the server side, you will see something like:

```
listening on port 2342
[192.168.254.2 port 55580 connected]
Hello there!
```

```
I hope the weather is better where you are.
jo2y and monkeybot, sitting in a tree.
[connection closed]
```

You can do more than just type text. You can send the contents of a file too:

```
$ ./simpleclient localhost < /usr/share/dict/words
```

This sends about two megs of words across the connection to the server.

More Advanced Issues

Multiplexing connections

A one-connection-at-a-time server like **simpleserver** is OK for some applications, but to truly leverage the power of networking, it is better to have a single server support many connections simultaneously. To do this, you need a way to multiplex multiple input and output streams and only block when there is no work to be done.

The **select()** call is the Berkeley sockets way of doing this multiplexing. You will see in Chapter 16: *kqueue and FSEvents* an alternate way of multiplexing connections, which is superior to **select()** in many ways, but it is not available on many platforms. Grand Central Dispatch also gives you a way to multiplex sockets.

For **select()**, you give it a set of file descriptors. If there is any data to be read, or if there is the ability to write on any of the descriptors, **select()** will tell you so. Otherwise, it will block (with an optional timeout) until network activity is possible.

```
int select (int nfds, fd_set *readfds, fd_set *writefds,
            fd_set *exceptfds, struct timeval *timeout);
```

nfds	One more than the largest file descriptor number.
readfds	A set of file descriptors to see if you can read data from without blocking.
writefds	A set of file descriptors to see if you can write data to without blocking.
exceptfds	A set of file descriptors to see if there are any error conditions.
timeout	How long to wait for activity before breaking out of the select call. Pass NULL for no timeout (wait forever).

The fd_sets are modified by **select()**. You set the file descriptors you are interested in before calling **select()** and then examine the fd_sets to see which ones are interesting afterward.

What are fd_sets? They are an opaque bitvector that can be manipulated with this API:

```
fd_set fdset;
```

FD_ZERO (&fdset);	Clear out the fd_set.
FD_SET (fd, &fdset);	Add a file descriptor to the set.

`FD_CLR (fd, &fdset);`	Remove a file descriptor from the set.
`FD_ISSET (fd, &fdset);`	Test to see if a file descriptor is in the set.

Usually an `fd_set` holds 1024 items. If you try to put more than that into an `fd_set`, you could end up writing over memory after the `fd_set`'s storage. You can alter this by putting a `#define FD_SETSIZE` before including `<sys/types.h>`. The **getdtablesize()** function will return the size of the file descriptor table for a process, but because it is a function call, it is not useful to set to `FD_SETSIZE`.

`struct timeval` is defined like this:

```
struct timeval {
    time_t       tv_sec;        /* seconds */
    suseconds_t tv_usec;        /* and microseconds */
};
```

You can specify the timeout in seconds and microseconds. You are not guaranteed microsecond granularity, though. Specify zero for both values to have **select()** return immediately. You can use this to have **select()** poll rather than block.

The usual way to use **select()** is like this:

```
// Get the memory and clear it out.
fd_set readfds;
FD_ZERO (&readfds);

// Add the listen socket.
FD_SET(myListenSocket, &readfds);
int maxFd = myListenSocket;

// Walk the data structure that has your open sessions.
for (int i = 0; i < whatever; i++) {
    FD_SET (session->fd, &readfds);
    maxFd = MAX (maxFd, session->fd);
}

int result = select (maxFd + 1, &readfds, NULL, NULL, NULL);

if (result == -1) {
    ... handle error
}

// see if our accept socket is there
if (FD_ISSET(myListenSocket, &readfds)) {
    // New connection.  Call accept(), make a new session
}

// Walk the data structure again looking for activity
for (int i = 0; i < whatever; i++) {
    if (FD_ISSET(session->fd, &readfds)) {
        result = read(session->fd, ...);
    }
}
```

Figure 14.1 shows **select()** consuming three file descriptor sets, each filled in with the active connections, and then removing any file descriptors that don't have anything to read or write or that don't have problems.

Figure 14.1   select()

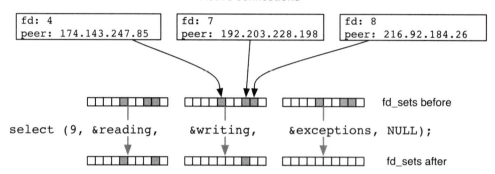

It is important to remember that the first argument to **select()** is *one more* than the largest file descriptor. This is because it is a count of how many values in the FD_SET the kernel needs to test with FD_ISSET(). fd_sets can be copied and kept around. A common technique is to have a master fd_set that has all of the session file descriptors in it. Each time you call **select()**, you pass in a copy instead of the master itself. This saves you from walking your data structures every time before a call to **select()** at the cost of keeping that master set in sync with those data structures. This means clearing fds when sessions close and setting them when sessions open.

When a file descriptor is in the readfds set, it will appear in the set returned by **select()** when it has data available. It will also appear when the connection closes (**read()** will return zero in that case). As seen above, you can also put the listening socket in there to be informed when new connections are ready to be accepted.

One thing you might notice is that **select()** does not tell you how much data is available. If you just do a result = read(session->fd, buffer, bufferSize), the call to **read()** will block until bufferSize bytes have been read or an error occurs. That is not what you want to happen in a busy server program!

To avoid blocking, put the file descriptor into non-blocking mode. This causes **read()** to read however many bytes have arrived on the connection and then return. The return value from **read()** tells you how many bytes were read. To put a file descriptor into non-blocking mode, set the O_NONBLOCK flag using **fcntl()**:

```
result = fcntl (fd, F_SETFL, O_NONBLOCK);
```

As usual, -1 is returned on error and errno set.

There is an alternative multiplexing API you might encounter called **poll()**. It is equivalent to **select()**, and each can be implemented in terms of the other.

Message boundaries

Some networking protocols, like HTTP, are pretty easy to deal with. You can just read everything that comes on the socket and then write out everything you need to. Other networking protocols are harder to deal with due to some of the real world issues regarding network communication and how the kernels on both sides of the connection buffer data.

Consider a little chat program where the client sends the server a message that looks like this:

length   : one byte

message : length bytes of text

Here are some scenarios:

One message is returned from a **read()**.	This is pretty easy. Just look at the first byte for the length, get the subsequent bytes of the message, and send it out to the chat clients.
Multiple complete messages are returned from a **read()**.	Since **read()** does not know where the messages begin and end, you have to walk the read buffer: get a length byte, process subsequent bytes, get another length byte, process those bytes, until you run out.
A message straddles the bytes returned by more than one call to **read()**.	This is where things get complicated. Between calls to **read()**, you need to remember that you only got part of a message. The first part waits around in a buffer until the other parts have arrived.
	Generally, you will keep a buffer large enough to hold two or more complete messages and read into that buffer. When processing messages, you need to know whether you are continuing a partially received message or starting a new one.

Figure 14.2   Worst-case scenario for messages

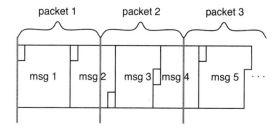

Example 14.5 is the Chatter server side. The more interesting parts are the **select()** loop and **readMessage()**, which handles the various pathological cases of incoming messages.

Example 14.5   chatterserver.m

```
// chatterserver.m -- chat server using standard sockets API

// gcc -g -Wall -std=c99 -o chatterserver chatterserver.m

#import <stdbool.h>      // true/false
#import <stdint.h>       // UINT8_MAX
#import <stdio.h>        // fprintf
#import <stdlib.h>       // EXIT_SUCCESS
```

```
#import <string.h>          // strerror()

#import <errno.h>           // errno
#import <fcntl.h>           // fcntl()
#import <mach/vm_param.h>   // PAGE_SIZE
#import <signal.h>          // sigaction()
#import <sys/uio.h>         // iovec
#import <syslog.h>          // syslog() and friends
#import <unistd.h>          // close()

#import <arpa/inet.h>       // inet_ntop()
#import <netinet/in.h>      // struct sockaddr_in
#import <netinet6/in6.h>    // struct sockaddr_in6
#import <sys/socket.h>      // socket(), AF_INET
#import <sys/types.h>       // random types


// -------------------------------------------------
// Message protocol

// A message is length + data. The length is a single byte.
// The first message sent by a user has a max length of 8 and sets the user's name.

#define MAX(x, y) (((x) > (y)) ? (x) : (y))
#define MAX_MESSAGE_SIZE  (UINT8_MAX)
#define READ_BUFFER_SIZE  (PAGE_SIZE)

// Paranoia check that the read buffer is large enough to hold a full message.
typedef uint8_t READ_BUFFER_SIZE_not_less_than_MAX_MESSAGE_SIZE
    [!(READ_BUFFER_SIZE < MAX_MESSAGE_SIZE) ? 0 : -1];

// There is one of these for each connected user
typedef struct ChatterUser_ {
    int      fd;         // zero fd == no user
    char     name[9];    // 8 character name plus trailing zero byte
    bool     gotName;    // have we gotten the username packet?

    /* incoming data workspace */
    ssize_t  bytesRead;
    char     buffer[READ_BUFFER_SIZE];
} ChatterUser;

#define MAX_USERS 50
static ChatterUser s_Users[MAX_USERS];

static const in_port_t kPortNumber = 2342;
static const int kAcceptQueueSizeHint = 8;

// Returns fd on success, -1 on error.  Based on main() in simpleserver.m
static int StartListening (const bool useIPv6) {
    // get a socket
    int fd;
    if (useIPv6) fd = socket (AF_INET6, SOCK_STREAM, 0);
    else fd = socket (AF_INET, SOCK_STREAM, 0);

    if (fd == -1) {
        perror ("*** socket");
        goto bailout;
    }
```

```
    // Reuse the address so stale sockets won't kill us.
    int yes = 1;
    int result = setsockopt (fd, SOL_SOCKET, SO_REUSEADDR, &yes, sizeof(yes));
    if (result == -1) {
        perror ("*** setsockopt(SO_REUSEADDR)");
        goto bailout;
    }

    // Bind to an address and port

    // Glom both kinds of addresses into a union to avoid casting.
    union {
        struct sockaddr sa;        // avoids casting
        struct sockaddr_in in;     // IPv4 support
        struct sockaddr_in6 in6;   // IPv6 support
    } address;

    if (useIPv6) {
        address.in6.sin6_len = sizeof (address.in6);
        address.in6.sin6_family = AF_INET6;
        address.in6.sin6_port = htons (kPortNumber);
        address.in6.sin6_flowinfo = 0;
        address.in6.sin6_addr = in6addr_any;
        address.in6.sin6_scope_id = 0;
    } else {
        address.in.sin_len = sizeof (address.in);
        address.in.sin_family = AF_INET;
        address.in.sin_port = htons (kPortNumber);
        address.in.sin_addr.s_addr = htonl (INADDR_ANY);
        memset (address.in.sin_zero, 0, sizeof (address.in.sin_zero));
    }

    result = bind (fd, &address.sa, address.sa.sa_len);
    if (result == -1) {
        perror ("*** bind");
        goto bailout;
    }

    result = listen (fd, kAcceptQueueSizeHint);
    if (result == -1) {
        perror ("*** listen");
        goto bailout;
    }
    printf("listening on port %d\n", (int)kPortNumber);
    return fd;

bailout:
    if (fd != -1) {
        close (fd);
        fd = -1;
    }
    return fd;
}  // StartListening

// Called when select() indicates the listening socket is ready to be read,
// which means there is a connection waiting to be accepted.
static void AcceptConnection (int listen_fd) {
    struct sockaddr_storage addr;
    socklen_t addr_len = sizeof(addr);
```

413

```
    int clientFd = accept (listen_fd, (struct sockaddr *)&addr, &addr_len);

    if (clientFd == -1) {
        perror ("*** accept");
        goto bailout;
    }

    // Set to non-blocking
    int err = fcntl (clientFd, F_SETFL, O_NONBLOCK);
    if (err == -1) {
        perror ("*** fcntl(clientFd O_NONBLOCK)");
        goto bailout;
    }

    // Find the next free spot in the users array
    ChatterUser *newUser = NULL;
    for (int i = 0; i < MAX_USERS; i++) {
        if (s_Users[i].fd == 0) {
            newUser = &s_Users[i];
            break;
        }
    }

    if (newUser == NULL) {
        const char gripe[] = "Too many users - try again later.\n";
        write (clientFd, gripe, sizeof(gripe));
        goto bailout;
    }

    // ok, clear out the structure, and get it set up
    memset (newUser, 0, sizeof(ChatterUser));

    newUser->fd = clientFd;
    clientFd = -1; // Don't let function cleanup close the fd.

    // log where the connection is from
    void *net_addr = NULL;

    in_port_t port = 0;
    if (addr.ss_family == AF_INET) {
        struct sockaddr_in6 *sin6 = (struct sockaddr_in6 *)&addr;
        net_addr = &sin6->sin6_addr;
        port = sin6->sin6_port;
    } else {
        struct sockaddr_in *sin = (struct sockaddr_in *)&addr;
        net_addr = &sin->sin_addr;
        port = sin->sin_port;
    }

    // Make it somewhat human readable.
    char buffer[INET6_ADDRSTRLEN];
    const char *name = inet_ntop (addr.ss_family, net_addr,
                                  buffer, sizeof(buffer));

    syslog (LOG_NOTICE, "Accepted connection from %s port %d as fd %d.",
            name, port, clientFd);
bailout:
    if (clientFd != -1) close (clientFd);
    return;
}   // AcceptConnection
```

```
// send a message to all the signed-in users
static void BroadcastMessageFromUser (const char *message, const ChatterUser *user) {
    if (!user->gotName) return;

    static const char separator[] = ": ";

    // All messages are expected to have a terminating newline.
    printf ("Broadcast message: %s%s%s", user->name, separator, message);

    // use scattered writes just for fun. Because We Can.
    const struct iovec iovector[] = {
        { (char *)user->name, strlen(user->name)   },
        { (char *)separator,  sizeof(separator) - 1 }, // omit terminator
        { (char *)message,    strlen(message)       }
    };
    const int iovector_len = sizeof(iovector) / sizeof(*iovector);

    // Scan through the users and send the mesage.
    const ChatterUser *stop = &s_Users[MAX_USERS];
    for (ChatterUser *u = s_Users; u < stop; u++) {
        if (u->fd > 0) {
            ssize_t nwrite = writev (u->fd, iovector, iovector_len);
            if (nwrite == -1) perror ("writev");
            else fprintf(stderr, "\tSent \"%s\" %zd bytes\n", u->name, nwrite);
        }
    }
}   // BroadcastMessageFromUser

// user disconnected.  Do any mop-up
static void DisconnectUser(ChatterUser *user) {
    if (user->fd > 0) {
        close (user->fd);
        user->fd = 0;
        syslog (LOG_NOTICE, "Disconnected user \"%s\" on fd %d\n",
                user->gotName? user->name : "(unknown)", user->fd);

        // broadcast 'user disconnected' message
        if (user->gotName) BroadcastMessageFromUser("has left the channel.\n", user);
    }

    user->gotName = false;
    user->bytesRead = 0;
    user->buffer[0] = 0;

} // DisconnectUser

// the first packet is the user's name.  Get it.
static void ReadUsername(ChatterUser *user) {
    // see if we have read anything yet
    if (user->bytesRead == 0) {
        // Read the length byte.
        const size_t toread = sizeof (user->buffer[0]);
        ssize_t nread = read (user->fd, user->buffer, toread);

        if (nread == toread) {
            // we got our length byte
            user->bytesRead += nread;
            const size_t namelen = (uint8_t)user->buffer[0];
```

```
            if (namelen >= sizeof(user->name)) {
                static const char badNameMessage[]
                    = "Error: Username must be 8 characters or fewer.\n";
                write (user->fd, badNameMessage, sizeof(badNameMessage));
                DisconnectUser (user);
            }

    } else if (nread == 0) {
        // end of file
        DisconnectUser (user);

    } else if (nread == -1) {
        perror("read");
        DisconnectUser (user);

    } else {
        fprintf (stderr,
                "Should not have reached line %d.  nread: %zu toread: %zu\n",
                __LINE__, nread, toread);
    }

} else {
    // ok, try to read just the rest of the username
    const uint8_t namelen = (uint8_t)user->buffer[0];
    const size_t packetlen = sizeof(namelen) + namelen;
    const size_t nleft = packetlen - user->bytesRead;
    ssize_t nread = read (user->fd, user->buffer + user->bytesRead, nleft);

    switch (nread) {
        default:
            user->bytesRead += nread;
            break;

        case 0:  // peer closed the connection
            DisconnectUser (user);
            break;

        case -1:
            perror ("ReadName: read");
            DisconnectUser (user);
            break;
    }

    // Do we have the name?
    if (user->bytesRead > namelen) {
        user->gotName = true;

        // Copy username into the User structure.
        memcpy (user->name, &user->buffer[1], namelen);
        user->name[namelen] = '\0';
        printf ("Received username: %s\n", user->name);

        // no current message, so clear it out
        user->buffer[0] = 0;
        user->bytesRead -= packetlen;

        syslog (LOG_NOTICE, "Username for fd %d is %s.", user->fd, user->name);
        BroadcastMessageFromUser ("has joined the channel.\n", user);
    }
}
```

```
}  // ReadUsername

// Get message data from the given user
static void ReadMessage (ChatterUser *user) {
    // read as much as we can into the buffer
    const size_t toread = sizeof(user->buffer) - user->bytesRead;
    ssize_t nread = read (user->fd, user->buffer + user->bytesRead, toread);

    switch (nread) {
        default:
            user->bytesRead += nread;
            break;
        case 0:
            DisconnectUser (user);
            break;
        case -1:
            perror ("ReadMessage: read");
            return;
    }

    // Send any complete messages. The first byte in the buffer is
    // always the length byte.
    char msgbuf[MAX_MESSAGE_SIZE + 1];

    while (user->bytesRead > 0) {
        const uint8_t msglen = (uint8_t)user->buffer[0];
        // Only a partial message left?
        if (user->bytesRead <= msglen) break;

        // copy message to buffer and null-terminate
        char *msg = &user->buffer[1];
        memcpy (msgbuf, msg, msglen);
        msgbuf[msglen] = '\0';
        BroadcastMessageFromUser (msgbuf, user);

        // Slide the rest of the data over
        const size_t packetlen = sizeof(msglen) + msglen;
        user->bytesRead -= packetlen;
        memmove (user->buffer, msg + msglen, user->bytesRead);
    }

}  // ReadMessage

// we got read activity for a user
static void HandleRead (ChatterUser *user) {
    if (!user->gotName) ReadUsername(user);
    else ReadMessage(user);
}  // HandleRead

int main (int argc, char *argv[]) {
    int exit_status = EXIT_FAILURE;
    const bool useIPv6 = (argc > 1);
    int listenFd = StartListening (useIPv6);

    if (listenFd == -1) {
        fprintf (stderr, "*** Could not open listening socket.\n");
        goto bailout;
    }

    // Block SIGPIPE so a dropped connection won't signal us.
```

```
    struct sigaction act;
    act.sa_handler = SIG_IGN;
    struct sigaction oact;
    int err = sigaction (SIGPIPE, &act, &oact);
    if (err == -1) perror ("sigaction(SIGPIPE, SIG_IGN)");

    // wait for activity
    while (true) {
        fd_set readfds;
        FD_ZERO (&readfds);

        // Add the listen socket
        FD_SET(listenFd, &readfds);
        int max_fd = MAX (max_fd, listenFd);

        // Add the users.
        for (int i = 0; i < MAX_USERS; i++) {
            const int user_fd = s_Users[i].fd;
            if (user_fd <= 0) continue;

            FD_SET (user_fd, &readfds);
            max_fd = MAX (max_fd, user_fd);
        }

        // Wait until something interesting happens.
        int nready = select (max_fd + 1, &readfds, NULL, NULL, NULL);

        if (nready == -1) {
            perror ("select");
            continue;
        }

        // See if a new user is knocking on our door.
        if (FD_ISSET(listenFd, &readfds)) {
            AcceptConnection (listenFd);
        }

        // Handle any new incoming data from the users.
        // Closes appear here too.
        for (int i = 0; i < MAX_USERS; i++) {
            ChatterUser *const user = &s_Users[i];
            if (user->fd >= 0 && FD_ISSET(user->fd, &readfds)) {
                HandleRead (user);
            }
        }
    }
    exit_status = EXIT_SUCCESS;

bailout:
    return exit_status;
}  // main
```

The client program (Example 14.6) also uses **select()** because it needs to be able to read from both the terminal (messages from the user) and the server (messages sent by other users). The protocol from server to client is much simpler: the server just sends the string's characters without any size information.

This compile-time assert is the same general idea as shown in Chapter 5: *Exceptions, Error Handling, and Signals*:

```
typedef uint8_t READ_BUFFER_SIZE_not_less_than_MAX_MESSAGE_SIZE
    [!(READ_BUFFER_SIZE < MAX_MESSAGE_SIZE) ? 0 : -1];
```

The message parsing code assumes that it can process an entire message in the read buffer. If the read buffer is reduced accidentally during program maintenance, **chatterserver** might read or write off the end of a buffer, introducing bugs and security issues. If READ_BUFFER_SIZE is less than MAX_MESSAGE_SIZE, a static array of length negative-one is created, yielding a compiler error:

```
error: size of array 'READ_BUFFER_SIZE_not_less_than_MAX_MESSAGE_SIZE' is negative
```

Example 14.6 is the user-facing portion of the chatter system:

Example 14.6   chatterclient.m

```
// chatterclient.m -- client side of the chatter world

// gcc -g -Wall -std=c99 -o chatterclient chatterclient.m

#import <stdbool.h>         // true/false
#import <stdint.h>          // UINT8_MAX
#import <stdio.h>           // fprintf()
#import <stdlib.h>          // EXIT_SUCCESS
#import <string.h>          // strerror()

#import <errno.h>           // errno
#import <fcntl.h>           // fcntl()
#import <mach/vm_param.h>   // PAGE_SIZE
#import <unistd.h>          // close()

#import <arpa/inet.h>       // inet_ntop()
#import <netdb.h>           // gethostbyname2()
#import <netinet/in.h>      // struct sockaddr_in
#import <netinet6/in6.h>    // struct sockaddr_in6
#import <sys/socket.h>      // socket(), AF_INET
#import <sys/types.h>       // random types

// --------------------------------------------------
// Message protocol

// A message is length + data. The length is a single byte.
// The first message sent by a user has a max length of 8
// and sets the user's name.

#define MAX(x, y) (((x) > (y))? (x) : (y))
#define MAX_MESSAGE_SIZE   (UINT8_MAX)
#define READ_BUFFER_SIZE   (PAGE_SIZE)

static const in_port_t kPortNumber = 2342;

// See simpleclient.m for the definition of these two functions.
static int SocketConnectedToHostNamed (const char *hostname);
static bool GetAddressAtIndex (struct hostent *host, int addressIndex,
                    struct sockaddr_storage *outServerAddress);

// Returns -1 on failure, >= 0 on success.
static int WriteMessage (int fd, const void *buffer, size_t length) {
    if (length > MAX_MESSAGE_SIZE) {
        fprintf (stderr, "*** Truncating message to %d bytes.\n", MAX_MESSAGE_SIZE);
        length = MAX_MESSAGE_SIZE;
```

```
    }

    // Ssend the length byte first
    uint8_t bytesLeft = (uint8_t)length;
    ssize_t nwritten = write (fd, &bytesLeft, sizeof(bytesLeft));

    if (nwritten <= 0) goto bailout;

    // Then, send the string bytes.
    while (bytesLeft > 0) {
        nwritten = write(fd, buffer, bytesLeft);
        if (nwritten <= 0) goto bailout;

        bytesLeft -= nwritten;
        buffer += nwritten;
    }
bailout:
    if (nwritten == -1) perror("write");
    return nwritten;
} // WriteMessage


int main (int argc, char *argv[]) {
    int exit_status = EXIT_FAILURE;

    if (argc != 3) {
        fprintf(stderr, "Usage: chatterclient hostname username\n");
        goto bailout;
    }

    // limit username to 8 characters
    const char *name = argv[2];
    size_t namelen = strlen(name);
    if (namelen > 8) {
        fprintf (stderr, "*** Username must be 8 characters or fewer.\n");
        goto bailout;
    }

    // set stdin to non-blocking
    int err = fcntl(STDIN_FILENO, F_SETFL, O_NONBLOCK);
    if (err == -1) {
        perror ("fcntl(stdin O_NONBLOCK)");
        goto bailout;
    }

    // Get a connected socket.
    const char *hostname = argv[1];
    int serverFd = SocketConnectedToHostNamed (hostname);
    if (serverFd == -1) {
        fprintf (stderr, "*** Unable to connect to %s port %d.\n",
                 hostname, (int)kPortNumber);
        return EXIT_FAILURE;
    }
    printf ("[connected to %s port %d]\n", hostname, (int)kPortNumber);
    // no need to bind() or listen()

    int nwritten = WriteMessage (serverFd, name, namelen);
    if (nwritten == -1) {
        perror("*** Unable to write username");
        goto bailout;
```

```
    }

    // Now set to non-block so we can interleave stdin and messages from the server.
    err = fcntl (serverFd, F_SETFL, O_NONBLOCK);
    if (err == -1) {
        perror ("fcntl(serverFd O_NONBLOCK)");
        goto bailout;
    }

    char incomingBuffer[READ_BUFFER_SIZE];
    char messageBuffer[MAX_MESSAGE_SIZE];

    while (true) {
        fd_set readfds;
        FD_ZERO (&readfds);
        FD_SET (STDIN_FILENO, &readfds);
        FD_SET (serverFd, &readfds);
        int max_fd = MAX (STDIN_FILENO, serverFd);

        int nready = select (max_fd + 1, &readfds, NULL, NULL, NULL);

        if (nready == -1) {
            perror("select");
            continue;
        }

        // Check standard-in.
        if (FD_ISSET(STDIN_FILENO, &readfds)) {
            int nread = read (STDIN_FILENO, messageBuffer, sizeof(messageBuffer));

            if (nread == -1) {
                perror("read(stdin)");
                goto bailout;
            } else if (nread == 0) {
                // closed
                break;
            }

            nwritten = WriteMessage(serverFd, messageBuffer, nread);

            if (nwritten == -1) {
                // WriteMessage logged the error for us.
                goto bailout;
            }
        }

        // Does the server have stuff for us?
        if (FD_ISSET(serverFd, &readfds)) {
            // Read at most 1 less than the buffer size so we can
            // always null-terminate.
            int nread = read (serverFd, incomingBuffer, sizeof(incomingBuffer) - 1);

            if (nread == -1) {
                perror("read(serverFd)");
                goto bailout;

            } else if (nread == 0) {
                fprintf (stderr, "[Server closed connection.]\n");
                break;
```

```
        } else {
            incomingBuffer[nread] = '\0';
            printf ("%s", incomingBuffer);
        }
    }
}

exit_status = EXIT_SUCCESS;

bailout:
    if (serverFd > -1) close(serverFd);
    return (exit_status);

} // main
```

The main thing of interest here is how the string is written by **WriteMessage()**. Just calling **write()** is not sufficient. If the buffer associated with the socket becomes full, **write()** will return a value smaller than what you told it to write. To ensure all bytes are written, you might need to call **write()** repeatedly. This requires tracking where to pick up writing and how many bytes are left to write.

For the More Curious: Datagrams

What we've been talking about in this chapter are "stream sockets." They are a connection-oriented, reliable form of network communication. Berkeley sockets also support "datagram sockets." These are a message-oriented, unreliable form of network communication. They are unreliable in the sense that datagrams may be lost in transit and that the receiver might not get the datagrams in the same order in which they were sent. The data in the payload is checksummed, so it will be correct. Stream sockets use the TCP protocol, and datagram sockets use the UDP protocol.

Figure 14.3   TCP versus UDP

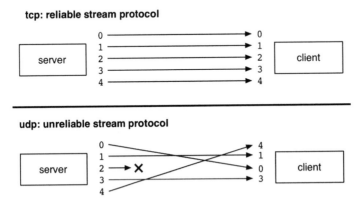

To create a datagram socket you use SOCK_DGRAM rather than SOCK_STREAM for the *type* parameter of **socket()**. For servers, you would still **bind()** your address to the socket, but you do not call **listen()**. Clients do not have to **bind()**; they can just make a socket and then send messages over it.

To send and receive datagrams, you use the **sendto** and **recvfrom** functions:

```
ssize_t sendto (int socket, const void *msg, size_t len, int flags,
                const struct sockaddr *to, socklen_t to_len);
```

Here are its arguments:

socket   The socket to write to

msg, len   The data and its length

flags   Just pass zero

to, tolen   The destination socket address and its size

The return value is the number of bytes sent or -1/errno on error.

```
ssize_t recvfrom (int socket, void *restrict buf, size_t len, int flags,
                  struct sockaddr *restrict from, socklen_t *restrict from_len);
```

Here are its arguments:

socket   The socket to read from

buf, len   Where to deposit the incoming data

flags   Just pass zero (you can pass in MSG_PEEK to peek at incoming data)

from, fromlen The address the message was sent from

The return value is the number of bytes read or -1/errno on an error.

Exercises

1. Change the chatter programs to use datagrams. The messages are small enough to fit into a single datagram. Given the quality of discussion in most chat rooms, a lost packet here or there is probably not too much of an issue. Since the messages fit into packet boundaries and since recvfrom() will not coalesce packets like socket streams, this should simplify a lot of the code.

15

CFRunLoop

Unix networking uses file descriptors for reading and writing. Using file descriptors in server programs is pretty easy with the **select()** and **kevent()** functions. Using sockets in end-user GUI apps presents a problem, though. You cannot call **select()** on the main thread to wait for network activity. This will cause the UI to hang until there is something to be done on the network. Blocking the UI thread would cause your program to become unresponsive, and your process would be killed on iOS devices.

There are some options available to you. You can put your blocking function into a new thread. That thread can then block to its heart's content until there is activity on the network, and then it can inform the UI thread that there is new data available for processing.

Another option is to take advantage of the *run loop*. A run loop is an event loop in a thread that looks for events, such as mouse clicks, key presses, and timer firings (Figure 15.1). The run loop dispatches these events to interested parties and then goes to sleep waiting for more events. **NSRunLoop** from the Foundation framework has a high-level API for watching for activity on mach ports, timers, and distributed object connections. **NSRunLoop** is built on **CFRunLoop**. We will be dealing with **CFRunLoop** here.

Figure 15.1 The run loop

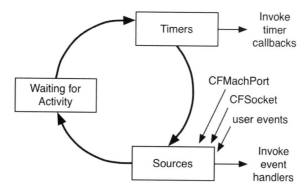

CFRunLoop is provided by the Core Foundation framework, which supplies a number of useful features similar to those found in the Foundation framework. Much of Foundation is implemented on top of Core Foundation, including the various collection classes.

Core Foundation feels like a purely C-based version of Foundation. You use functions to manipulate **CFTypeRef**s, the Core Foundation equivalent of Objective-C's id type. Core Foundation memory management is virtually identical to Foundation memory management; the primary difference is that

Core Foundation has no equivalent to the autorelease pool. Where Cocoa would use the target-action system to specify a callback, Core Foundation uses a C function together with a context pointer.

CFRunLoop is where you can put the socket file descriptors to react to network traffic and not gum up the GUI works. There is one run loop per thread, whether it is created with **NSThread** or the pthread, so in a multithreaded application, you can have multiple run loops, each handling multiple sockets.

Many interfaces that deal with runloops include a "mode" parameter, such as **NSStream**'s **-scheduleInRunLoop:forMode:** or **NSRunLoop**'s **-runMode:beforeDate:**. A runloop mode is just a string, which is analogous to a dictionary lookup key. The runloop keeps collections of runloop sources keyed by the mode. When a runloop is in a particular mode, the runloop ignores any sources that are not in that mode's collection. For instance, you might want to defer network activity while the user is dragging a slider.

CFSocket

CFSocket integrates sockets into the **CFRunLoop** architecture. CFSocketRef is a pointer to an opaque type and is created with **CFSocketCreateWithNative()**:

```
CFSocketRef CFSocketCreateWithNative (CFAllocatorRef allocator,
                                      CFSocketNativeHandle sock,
                                      CFOptionFlags callBackTypes,
                                      CFSocketCallBack callout,
                                      const CFSocketContext *context);
```

There are lots of CF data types here. For CFAllocatorRef, you can pass kCFAllocatorDefault or NULL to get the default memory allocator. This will give you back a chunk of dynamically allocated memory that you should release by calling **CFRelease()**. You must release memory obtained from a Core Foundation function whose name begins with Create or Copy. There are no autorelease pools in Core Foundation.

In a garbage collected environment, the collector doles out the memory, and **CFRetain()** and **CFRelease()** manipulate the collector's reference count for the object, so the object is not freed as soon as its reference count reaches zero. It is instead freed when the collector decides to reclaim its memory. You can thus **CFRelease()** a Core Foundation object immediately after creation to get behavior similar to the autorelease pools ubiquitous in Foundation. When this is the intended behavior, it is better to use the **CFMakeCollectable()** function. **CFMakeCollectable()** has no effect in non-garbage-collected code; in garbage-collected code, in addition to **CFRelease()**ing the object, the function also halts the program if the object was not allocated from the garbage collection zone. It also looks strange reading code to see a Core Foundation object being created and immediately released.

CFSocketNativeHandle is your socket file descriptor, which is just an integer.

CFOptionFlags is one of the CFSocketCallBackType flags:

kCFSocketNoCallBack	No callback function is supplied.
kCFSocketReadCallBack	Call the callback function when data can be read. The callback can get the data by calling **read()**.
kCFSockeWriteCallBack	Call the callback function when there is space in the kernel buffers so that the socket is writable again. This is handy if you are writing large amounts of data to the socket.

kCFSocketAcceptCallBack	Call the callback function when there is a new connection on a listening socket.
kCFSocketDataCallBack	The data will be automatically read and packed into a **CFData** (similar to **NSData**). The callback will be called and be passed this **CFData**.
kCFSocketConnectCallBack	The above constants are mutually exclusive. You can bitwise-OR kCFSocketConnectCallBack if you want your socket to connect to a remote machine in the background.

CFSocketContext is a pointer to a struct that looks like this:

```
typedef struct {
    CFIndex     version;
    void *      info;
    const void *(*retain )(const void *info);
    void        (*release)(const void *info);
    CFStringRef (*copyDescription)(const void *info);
} CFSocketContext;
```

Set everything to zero or NULL for all of these, unless you want to perform some custom memory management. info is a pointer to whatever data you want, such as an Objective-C object pointer if you are using Cocoa. You can see some of the Foundation-flavored behavior with functions to perform retain and release on the context. Passing NULL for the function pointers indicates that the memory management for the item pointed to by info will be handled elsewhere and that info will be valid at least as long as the life of the **CFSocket**.

The CFSocketCallBack is a function of the form

```
void (*CFSocketCallBack)(CFSocketRef s,
                         CFSocketCallBackType type,
                         CFDataRef address,
                         const void *data,
                         void *info);
```

CFDataRef is what you get if you registered a kCFSocketDataCallBack. data can be ignored if you don't need it, but it is used for the kCFSocketAcceptCallBack and kCFSocketConnectCallBack cases. info is the info pointer of the context structure given to **CFSocketCreateWithNative()**.

One memory management note: If your thread is not running AppKit's event loop, which automatically creates and destroys autorelease pools, your callback must create and destroy its own pool to avoid leaking all objects autoreleased by or on behalf of it, such as through an **NSLog()** call.

Here is some code that will register a socket, using self for the *info* pointer (assuming that the code is run from within an Objective-C method):

```
const CFSocketContext context = { 0, self, NULL, NULL, NULL };

CFSocketRef socket = CFSocketCreateWithNative (kCFAllocatorDefault,
                                               server_sockfd,
                                               kCFSocketReadCallBack,
                                               SocketCallBack,
                                               &context);
```

If the returned socket is NULL, something went wrong.

Once you have the CFSocketRef from this call, it is time to create a **CFRunLoopSource** with the socket. A **CFRunLoopSource** wraps the CFSocketRef. A wrapped CFSocketRef can be added to the run loop.

```
CFRunLoopSourceRef CFSocketCreateRunLoopSource (CFAllocatorRef allocator,
                                                CFSocketRef runLoopSocket,
                                                CFIndex order);
```

As you saw earlier, pass kCFAllocatorDefault to use the default allocator. The runLoopSocket parameter is the CFSocketRef you got from **CFSocketCreateWithNative()** earlier. The order parameter can control the order in which multiple callbacks are invoked. If you do not care about the order (which is usually the case), pass zero.

Here it is in action:

```
CFRunLoopSourceRef rls =
    CFSocketCreateRunLoopSource (kCFAllocatorDefault, runLoopSocket, 0);
```

If the return value is NULL, something went wrong.

Finally, add the CFRunLoopSourceRef to a runloop using **CFRunLoopAddSource()**:

```
void CFRunLoopAddSource (CFRunLoopRef rl,
                         CFRunLoopSourceRef source,
                         CFStringRef mode);
```

To get the current run loop, use **CFRunLoopGetCurrent()**. The source parameter is the **CFRunLoopSource** created above. You can pass the constant kCFRunLoopDefaultMode as the mode. On a UI thread, use kCFRunLoopCommonModes so that the socket doesn't get starved during some of the other modes of the UI's runloop, such as when running a modal dialog.

Add the socket to the run loop with

```
CFRunLoopAddSource (CFRunLoopGetCurrent(), rls, kCFRunLoopCommonModes);
```

The run loop takes ownership of the source and so retains it. You have relinquished ownership and so must **CFRelease()** the run loop source to keep the reference count correct.

CFHost

Virtually all network-orientated applications require host name lookup, such as with **gethostbyname2()** described in Chapter 14: *Network Programming With Sockets*. Unfortunately, the standard Unix domain name lookup functions are blocking, which causes the same problems with GUI unresponsiveness and application termination as discussed earlier.

The Core Services framework provides **CFHost** which does runloop-based host name lookup. You can use **CFHost** to look up addresses (mapping hostnames to an IP address) or names (mapping an IP address to a set of hostnames). You look up addresses by creating a **CFHost** and giving it the hostname you are interested in. Then set the "client," which is a callback function and a context block like the socket context described earlier. Then schedule the **CFHost** with a runloop and start resolution:

```
NSString *hostname = [hostnameField stringValue];
CFHostRef host =
    CFHostCreateWithName (kCFAllocatorDefault, (CFStringRef)hostname);
CFHostClientContext context = { .info = self };
Boolean ok = CFHostSetClient (host, nameLookupCallback, &context);
```

```
    // error check
    CFHostScheduleWithRunLoop (host, CFRunLoopGetCurrent(),
                                kCFRunLoopDefaultMode);
    CFStreamError error;
    ok = CFHostStartInfoResolution (host, kCFHostAddresses, &error);
    // error check
```

CFHostStartInfoResolution takes a CFHostInfoType:

kCFHostAddresses   Returns the known addresses for the give hostname. You would create the host ref with **CFHostCreateWithName()**. The callback is passed a **CFArray** of **CFData**s, each wrapping a struct sockaddr.

kCFHostNames   Returns the known hostnames for the given address. You would create the host ref with **CFHostCreateWithAddress()**, which takes a **CFData** wrapping a struct sockaddr. The callback is passed a **CFArray** of **CFStrings**.

kCFHostReachability   The callback is passed a **CFData** wrapping SCNetworkConnectionFlags.

Your callback gets called once the hostname resolution has run.

```
static void nameLookupCallback (CFHostRef host, CFHostInfoType typeInfo,
                                const CFStreamError *error, void *info) {
    NSArray *addresses = (NSArray *) CFHostGetAddressing (host, NULL);

    for (NSData *data in addresses) {
        struct sockaddr *remoteAddress = (struct sockaddr *) data.bytes;
        const char *address;

        if (remoteAddress->sa_family == AF_INET) {
            char buffer[INET_ADDRSTRLEN];

            struct sockaddr_in *ipv4 = (struct sockaddr_in *)remoteAddress;
            address = inet_ntop (AF_INET, &ipv4->sin_addr,
                                buffer, sizeof(buffer));
            // do something with address

        } else if (remoteAddress->sa_family == AF_INET6) {
            char buffer[INET6_ADDRSTRLEN];
            struct sockaddr_in6 *ipv6 = (struct sockaddr_in6 *)remoteAddress;
            address = inet_ntop (AF_INET6, &ipv6->sin6_addr,
                                buffer, sizeof(buffer));
            // do something with address

        } else {
            // complain.
        }
    }

    // Clean up after the CFHost.
    CFHostUnscheduleFromRunLoop (host, CFRunLoopGetCurrent(),
                                kCFRunLoopCommonModes);
    // turn off the callback.
    CFHostSetClient (host, NULL, NULL);
    CFRelease (host);

} // nameLookupCallback
```

GUI Chatter Client

chatterclient from the networking chapter works fine if you like living on the command line. Most Mac users (understandably) want to use GUI programs. CFChatterClient is a GUI version of the chatterclient. It uses **CFRunLoop** and **CFSocket** to communicate across the network without blocking the application runloop.

In Xcode, create a new Cocoa Application project called CFChatterClient. Edit MainMenu.xib and lay out the UI as shown in Figure 15.2.

Figure 15.2   CFChatterClient user interface

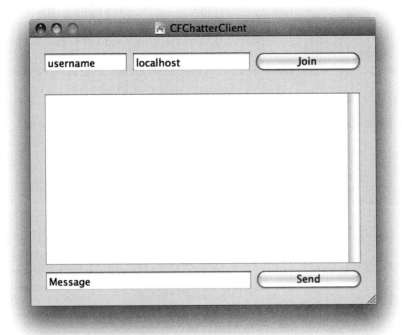

Back in Xcode, edit **CFChatterClientAppDelegate**. Edit the header to look like Example 15.1 and the body like Example 15.2.

Example 15.1   CFChatterClientAppDelegate.h

```
#import <Cocoa/Cocoa.h>

@interface CFChatterClientAppDelegate : NSObject <NSApplicationDelegate> {
    NSWindow *window;

    IBOutlet NSTextField *_usernameField;
    IBOutlet NSTextField *_hostField;
    IBOutlet NSButton    *_joinLeaveButton;

    IBOutlet NSTextView  *_transcript;
    IBOutlet NSTextField *_messageField;
    IBOutlet NSButton    *_sendButton;
```

```
    CFSocketNativeHandle _sockfd;
    CFSocketRef _socketRef;
}
@property (nonatomic, assign) IBOutlet NSWindow *window;
@property (nonatomic, readonly, getter=isConnected) BOOL connected;

- (IBAction) sendMessage: (id) sender;
- (IBAction) join: (id) sender;
- (IBAction) leave: (id) sender;

@end // CFChatterClientAppDelegate
```

Example 15.2   CFChatterClientAppDelegate.m

```
#import "CFChatterClientAppDelegate.h"

#import <errno.h>          // errno
#import <fcntl.h>          // fcntl()
#import <stdbool.h>        // true/false
#import <string.h>         // strerror()
#import <unistd.h>         // close()

#import <arpa/inet.h>      // inet_ntop()
#import <netdb.h>          // gethostbyname2()
#import <netinet/in.h>     // struct sockaddr_in
#import <netinet6/in6.h>   // struct sockaddr_in6
#import <sys/socket.h>     // socket(), AF_INET
#import <sys/types.h>      // random types

#define MAX_MESSAGE_SIZE   (UINT8_MAX)
#define READ_BUFFER_SIZE   (PAGE_SIZE)

static const in_port_t kPortNumber = 2342;
static const int kInvalidSocket = -1;

// See chatterclient.m for the definition of this function.
static int WriteMessage (int fd, const void *buffer, size_t length);

// See simpleclient.m for the definition of these two functions.
static int SocketConnectedToHostNamed (const char *hostname);
static bool GetAddressAtIndex (struct hostent *host, int addressIndex,
                               struct sockaddr_storage *outServerAddress);

// Forward references
@interface CFChatterClientAppDelegate ()

// UI
- (void) updateUI;
- (void) appendMessage: (NSString *) msg;
- (void) runErrorMessage: (NSString *) message  withErrno: (int) err;

// Connection
- (void) connectToHost: (NSString *) hostname  asUser: (NSString *) username;
- (void) closeConnection;

// Socket
- (void) startMonitoringSocket;
```

```
- (void) stopMonitoringSocket;

// Runloop stuffage
static void ReceiveMessage (CFSocketRef, CFSocketCallBackType,
                            CFDataRef, const void *, void *);
- (void) handleMessageData: (NSData *) data;

@end // extension

@implementation CFChatterClientAppDelegate
@synthesize window;

- (id) init {
    if ((self = [super init])) {
        _sockfd = kInvalidSocket;
    }
    return self;
} // init


- (void) awakeFromNib {
    // Prepopulate the username field as a convenience.x
    [_usernameField setStringValue: NSUserName()];
    [self updateUI];
} // awakeFromNib


- (void) dealloc {
    [self closeConnection];
    [super dealloc];
} // dealloc


// Quit the app when the last window closes.
- (BOOL) applicationShouldTerminateAfterLastWindowClosed: (NSApplication *) app {
    return YES;
} // applicationShouldTerminateAfterLastWindowClosed


- (BOOL) isConnected {
    BOOL connected = (_socketRef != NULL);
    return connected;
} // isConnected


- (IBAction) sendMessage: (id) sender {
    if (_sockfd == kInvalidSocket)  return;

    // Add a newline to match command-line client's behavior.
    NSString *messageString =
        [[_messageField stringValue] stringByAppendingString: @"\n"];
    if (messageString.length == 1) {
        // Just the newline - don't send it.  Help prevent channel floods.
        return;
    }

    const char *message = [messageString UTF8String];
    const size_t length = strlen (message);
    int nwritten = WriteMessage (_sockfd, message, length);
```

```
        // Successful send, clear out the message field.
        if (nwritten == length) [_messageField setStringValue: @""];

    } // sendMessage


    // Sent by Join/Leave button when not connected.
    - (IBAction) join: (id) sender {
        NSString *hostname = [_hostField stringValue];
        NSString *username = [_usernameField stringValue];
        [self connectToHost: hostname  asUser: username];

        [self updateUI];

        if ([self isConnected]) {
            NSString *connectMessage =
                [NSString stringWithFormat: @"( * * * connected to %@ as %@ * * * ) \n",
                          hostname, username];
            [self appendMessage: connectMessage];
            [[_messageField window] makeFirstResponder: _messageField];
        }
    } // subscribe


    // Sent by Join/Leave button when connected.
    - (IBAction) leave: (id) sender {
        [self closeConnection];

        [self updateUI];

        NSString *disconnectMessage =
            [NSString stringWithFormat: @"( * * * disconnected from %@ * * *) \n",
                      [_hostField stringValue]];
        [self appendMessage: disconnectMessage];
        [[_hostField window] makeFirstResponder: _hostField];
    } // unsubscribe


    - (void) updateUI {
        const BOOL connected = [self isConnected];

        // Disable username and hostname while connected.
        [_usernameField setEnabled: !connected];
        [_hostField setEnabled: !connected];

        // Join becomes Leave when connected.
        [_joinLeaveButton setTitle: connected ? @"Leave" : @"Join"];
        [_joinLeaveButton setAction: connected ? @selector(leave:) : @selector(join:)];

        // Can only type or send messages while connected.
        [_messageField setEnabled: connected];
        [_sendButton setEnabled: connected];
    } // updateUI


    - (void) appendMessage: (NSString *) msg {
        // Append the message.
        NSRange endOfText = NSMakeRange ([_transcript string].length, 0);
        [_transcript replaceCharactersInRange: endOfText  withString: msg];
```

```
        // Make the end of the message visible.
        endOfText = NSMakeRange ([_transcript string].length, 0);
        [_transcript scrollRangeToVisible: endOfText];
} // appendMessage


- (void) runErrorMessage: (NSString *) message  withErrno: (int) error {
    NSString *errnoString = @"";
    if (error != 0) {
        errnoString = ([NSString stringWithUTF8String: strerror(error)]);
    }

    NSRunAlertPanel (message, errnoString, @"OK", nil, nil);
} // runErrorMessage


- (void) connectToHost: (NSString *) hostname  asUser: (NSString *) username {
    NSString *errorMessage = nil;
    int sysError = noErr;

    if (_sockfd != kInvalidSocket) [self closeConnection];

    // sanity check our nick name before trying to connect
    if (hostname.length < 1) {
        errorMessage = @"Hostname must not be empty.";
        goto bailout;
    }

    if (username.length == 0 || username.length > 8) {
        errorMessage = @"Username must be between 1 and 8 characters long.";
        goto bailout;
    }

    const char *hostnameCStr = [hostname UTF8String];
    _sockfd = SocketConnectedToHostNamed (hostnameCStr);

    // UTF-8 length could be greater than the number of characters.
    const char *name = [username UTF8String];
    NSUInteger namelen = strlen (name);

    int nwritten = WriteMessage (_sockfd, name, namelen);

    if (nwritten == -1) {
        errorMessage = @"Failed to send username.";
        sysError = errno;
        goto bailout;
    }

    // Make the socket non-blocking.
    int err = fcntl (_sockfd, F_SETFL, O_NONBLOCK);
    if (err == -1) {
        errorMessage = @"Could not put socket into nonblocking mode.";
        sysError = errno;
        goto bailout;
    }

    [self startMonitoringSocket];

bailout:
    if (errorMessage != nil) {
```

```
        [self runErrorMessage: errorMessage  withErrno: sysError];
        [self closeConnection];
    }
    return;
} // connectToHost: asUser:


- (void) closeConnection {
    [self stopMonitoringSocket];
    close (_sockfd);
    _sockfd = kInvalidSocket;
} // closeConnection


- (void) startMonitoringSocket {
    CFSocketContext context = { 0, self, NULL, NULL, NULL };
    _socketRef = CFSocketCreateWithNative (kCFAllocatorDefault,
                                           _sockfd,
                                           kCFSocketDataCallBack,
                                           ReceiveMessage,
                                           &context);
    if (_socketRef == NULL) {
        [self runErrorMessage: @"Unable to create CFSocketRef."  withErrno: noErr];
        goto bailout;
    }

    CFRunLoopSourceRef rls =
        CFSocketCreateRunLoopSource(kCFAllocatorDefault, _socketRef, 0);
    if (rls == NULL) {
        [self runErrorMessage: @"Unable to create socket run loop source."
                withErrno: noErr];
        goto bailout;
    }

    CFRunLoopAddSource (CFRunLoopGetCurrent(), rls, kCFRunLoopDefaultMode);
    CFRelease (rls);

bailout:
    return;

} // startMonitoringSocket


- (void) stopMonitoringSocket {
    if (socket != NULL) {
        CFSocketInvalidate (_socketRef);
        CFRelease (_socketRef);
        _socketRef = NULL;
    }
} // stopMonitoringSocket


static void ReceiveMessage (CFSocketRef socket, CFSocketCallBackType type,
                            CFDataRef address, const void *data, void *info) {
    CFChatterClientAppDelegate *self = info;
    [self handleMessageData: (NSData *) data];
} // ReceiveMessage


- (void) handleMessageData: (NSData *) data {
```

```
    // Closed connection?
    if (data.length == 0) {
        [self closeConnection];
        [self runErrorMessage: @"The server closed the connection." withErrno: noErr];
        return;
    }

    // Null-terminate the data.
    NSMutableData *messageData = [NSMutableData dataWithData: data];
    const char NUL = '\0';
    [messageData appendBytes: &NUL length: 1];

    // Get a string to display.
    NSString *message = [NSString stringWithUTF8String: messageData.bytes];
    if (message == nil) {
        [self runErrorMessage: @"Error reading from server."  withErrno: noErr];
        return;
    }

    [self appendMessage: message];
} // handleMessageData:

@end // CFChatterClientAppDelegate
```

Edit the xib file and connect each of the app delegate's outlets to the appropriate view. Then, set each outlet of the app delegate to point to the appropriate view.

Next, rig up the connection management UI. Set the Join button to trigger the **-join:** action. Set the username and hostname text fields to trigger the button's **-performClick:** action.

Finally, set up the chat portion of the UI. The message text field should trigger the Send button's **-performClick:** action. The Send button should trigger the **-sendMessage:** action. Save the xib file and return to Xcode.

Start the chatterserver from the networking chapter, then build and run CFChatterClient. Notice how the joinLeaveButton's label and action are changed from "Join" to "Leave" by **-updateUI** based on whether the client is connected or not.

Runloop Chatter Server

GUI applications aren't the only ones that can benefit from being runloop-driven. Here you will make some changes to **chatterserver** so that it uses a runloop at its core rather than **select()**. You'll perform some surgery to existing functions and add some new ones. There won't be any changes to the fundamental data structures or architecture of **chatterserver**. While the behavior of the server won't change, the changes you do make will set the stage for adding Bonjour support in a later chapter.

Make a copy of chatterserver.m and name it chatterserver-runloop.m. The first thing to change is the signature and the first several lines of **AcceptConnection**. The runloop will call **accept()** for us, so all we need to do is get the remote address using **getpeername()**. The function will return a pointer to the ChatterUser that will be allocated for the new user, so you will need to move the ChatterUser variable to the top of the function. Finally, return the new user at the end.

```
static ChatterUser *AcceptConnection (int acceptedFd) {
    ChatterUser *newUser = NULL;
    struct sockaddr_storage addr;
    socklen_t addr_len = sizeof(addr);
```

```
    int clientFd = acceptedFd;
    int result = getpeername (clientFd, (struct sockaddr *)&addr, &ddr_len);

    if (result == -1) {
        perror ("*** getpeername");
        goto bailout;
    }

    if (clientFd == -1) {
        perror ("*** accept");
    ...
    syslog (LOG_NOTICE, "Accepted connection from %s port %d as fd %d.",
            name, port, clientFd);
bailout:
    if (clientFd != -1) close (clientFd);
    return newUser;
}   // AcceptConnection
```

Next, add a function to register a file descriptor with the runloop, along with two callbacks. **listenCallback** gets a new socket from **accept()** and passes it to **listenCallback**. **userCallback** is called when there's new data to be read. The runloop is told when registering the user callback to *not* read the socket on our behalf. When **userCallback** is called, it gets the pointer to our **User**, and passes it on to **HandleRead** which does the heavy lifting of processing messages from the users.

```
static void RegisterRunLoopSocket (int listenFd, CFSocketCallBack callback,
                                   BOOL listen, ChatterUser *user) {
    CFSocketContext context = { .info = user };

    CFSocketRef socketRef;
    if (listen) {
        socketRef = CFSocketCreateWithNative (kCFAllocatorDefault,
                                              listenFd,
                                              kCFSocketAcceptCallBack,
                                              callback,
                                              &context);
    } else {
        socketRef = CFSocketCreateWithNative (kCFAllocatorDefault,
                                              listenFd,
                                              kCFSocketReadCallBack,
                                              callback,
                                              &context);
    }

    CFRunLoopSourceRef rls =
        CFSocketCreateRunLoopSource (kCFAllocatorDefault, socketRef, 0);

    CFRunLoopAddSource (CFRunLoopGetCurrent(), rls, kCFRunLoopCommonModes);

    CFRelease (rls);
    CFRelease (socketRef);

} // RegisterRunLoopSocket


static void userCallback (CFSocketRef s,
                          CFSocketCallBackType type,
                          CFDataRef address,
                          const void *data,
```

```
                                void *info) {
    HandleRead ((ChatterUser *)info);
} // userCallback


static void listenCallback (CFSocketRef s,
                            CFSocketCallBackType type,
                            CFDataRef address,
                            const void *data,
                            void *info) {
    CFSocketNativeHandle fd = *(CFSocketNativeHandle *) data;
    ChatterUser *user = AcceptConnection (fd);
    RegisterRunLoopSocket (fd, userCallback, NO, user);
} // litenCallback
```

Finally, **main()** comes under the knife. Add an autorelease pool to the top and then register the runloop socket. Cut out the *entire* while loop and replace it with a **-run** call on the current run loop.

```
int main (int argc, char *argv[]) {
    NSAutoreleasePool *pool = [[NSAutoreleasePool alloc] init];

    int exit_status = EXIT_FAILURE;
    const bool useIPv6 = (argc > 2);

    int listenFd = StartListening (useIPv6);

    if (listenFd == -1) {
        fprintf (stderr, "*** Could not open listening socket.\n");
        goto bailout;
    }

    RegisterRunLoopSocket (listenFd, listenCallback, YES, NULL);

    // Block SIGPIPE so a dropped connection won't signal us.
    struct sigaction act;
    act.sa_handler = SIG_IGN;
    struct sigaction oact;
    int err = sigaction (SIGPIPE, &act, &oact);
    if (err == -1) perror ("sigaction(SIGPIPE, SIG_IGN)");

    // Axe everything here.  Really!

    [[NSRunLoop currentRunLoop] run];

    exit_status = EXIT_SUCCESS;

bailout:
    [pool drain];
    return exit_status;
} // main
```

You should be able compile and run your server. You should be able to connect to this server both from the command-line client as well as the GUI client.

The System Configuration Framework

The user is free to change aspects of their system configuration at any time, such as changing their network location from "Office" to "Home." Changing the network location could change a number of lower-level settings, such as which IP addresses the machine has available and which DNS servers to use. There are also system parameters that change dynamically, such as the battery level in laptops. In some situations, your application needs to be able to react to these changes. For example, if you have a network socket listening on a particular IP address (as opposed to listening on all of them), you'll need to listen on the new IP if the user changes it.

In Mac OS X 10.1, Apple introduced the system configuration framework, which provides an architecture for storing configuration and run-time information. Currently, it only supports network configuration and the battery monitor, but in the future more information could be supported.

Architecture

At the heart of the system configuration framework is `configd`, the system configuration daemon. `configd` holds the dynamic store, which is an online database of configuration information consisting of key-value pairs. These pairs are arranged in a hierarchy, like nested dictionaries, and are addressed by paths similar to the URLs used to identify Web pages. There are two major spaces, one for "setup" information (preferences set by configuration applications) and one for "state" information (the actual current system state). The keys look like `State:/Network/Service/ServiceUUID/IPv4` for the current IP state and `Setup:/Network/Service/ServiceUUID/PPP` for PPP configuration, where `ServiceUUID` is a 128-bit unique ID.

Much of the persistent configuration information is stored in property lists under the `/Library/Preferences/SystemConfiguration/` directory. `configd` reads these files and places their contents into the dynamic store. There are also configuration agents, which are bundles that `configd` loads that provide configuration and notification services. Currently, there are agents to monitor the preferences, to monitor the kernel, and to track the state of all network interfaces, as well as a PPP controller.

Basic API

The system configuration framework source code is included in Darwin if you are interested in poking around and seeing how things work. The API lives at the Core Foundation level, so it has a lot in common with the rest of the Core Foundation API. The examples here that query the dynamic store will be primarily Foundation-based and take advantage of the toll-free bridging between many equivalent Core Foundation and Foundation data structures. Toll-free bridging lets you manipulate a CF*Ref reference as its equivalent NS* object and vice-versa. Some common toll-free-bridged types are **CFStringRef** and **NSString**, **CFArrayRef** and **NSArray**, and **CFDataRef** and **NSData**. Take care not to assume that all such pairs of types are toll-free bridged. For example, the pairs **CFBundleRef** / **NSBundle** and **CFRunLoopRef** / **NSRunLoop** aren't toll-free bridged. When in doubt, check the documentation.

To query the dynamic store, perform these steps:

1. Connect to `configd`'s dynamic store with **SCDynamicStoreCreate()**.

2. Construct some access keys, either by explicitly constructing the paths or by supplying a regular expression to **SCDynamicStoreCopyKeyList()**.

3. Iterate over the keys and call **SCDynamicStoreCopyValue()** to fetch each one's value. The system configuration could change in the course of your iteration; if this is a concern, use **SCDynamicStoreCopyMultiple()** to atomically fetch the requested values at once. This will provide a consistent snapshot of the keys' values.

4. If you want to be notified when a particular value changes, use
   SCDynamicStoreSetNotificationKeys() to tell the system which keys you are interested in.

Here are the calls in more detail.

```
SCDynamicStoreRef SCDynamicStoreCreate (CFAllocatorRef allocator,
                                        CFStringRef name,
                                        SCDynamicStoreCallBack callback,
                                        SCDynamicStoreContext *context);
```

SCDynamicStoreCreate() creates a new session to talk to configd. The parameters are:

allocator   The allocator used to allocate memory for the local object and for any storage it may
             need. Use kCFAllocatorDefault to use the default memory allocator.

name   A string (which can be cast from an **NSString** pointer) that names the calling process.

callback   A callback function that will get called when values change for the keys given to
             SCDynamicStoreSetNotificationKeys().

context   A structure just like CFSocketContext, where you give the version, a pointer, and some
             function pointers to retain and release functions. From an Objective-C method, you can
             gain access to the calling object from the callback using a context like this:

```
                SCDynamicStoreContext context = {
                    0, self, NULL, NULL, NULL
                };
```

```
CFArrayRef SCDynamicStoreCopyKeyList (SCDynamicStoreRef store,
                                      CFStringRef pattern);
```

SCDynamicStoreCopyKeyList() returns an array of string keys that match a given regular expression.

store   The dynamic store reference that **SCDynamicStoreCreate()** returned.

pattern   A regular expression (not the simple shell globs used elsewhere) that matches the
             keys you're looking for. For instance, CFSTR(".*") will match everything, and
             CFSTR("State:/Network/Service/[^/]+/IPv4") will match the IPv4 network services
             of all service IDs.

```
CFPropertyListRef SCDynamicStoreCopyValue (SCDynamicStoreRef store,
                                           CFStringRef key);
```

SCDynamicStoreCopyValue() returns either a string or a dictionary with the value requested.

store   The dynamic store reference from **SCDynamicStoreCreate()**.

key   The key representing the data you want, either specified explicitly or taken from
             SCDynamicStoreCopyKeyList().

440

```
CFDictionaryRef SCDynamicStoreCopyMultiple (SCDynamicStoreRef store,
                                            CFArrayRef keys,
                                            CFArrayRef patterns);
```

SCDynamicStoreCopyMultiple() is like **SCDynamicStoreCopyValue()** but returns the values for a set of keys. It returns a dictionary containing the values.

store   The dynamic store reference from **SCDynamicStoreCreate()**.

keys   The set of keys that indicate the values to return.

patterns   Regular expression patterns to match keys in the dynamic store.

```
Boolean SCDynamicStoreSetNotificationKeys (SCDynamicStoreRef store,
                                           CFArrayRef keys,
                                           CFArrayRef patterns);
```

SCDynamicStoreSetNotificationKeys() tells the dynamic store which keys and patterns of keys are interesting. When the values change, the callback function specified with **SCDynamicStoreCreate()** is called.

store   The dynamic store connection.

keys   The keys of interest.

patterns   Regular expression indicating more keys of interest.

The callback function should look like this:

```
void StoreCallback (SCDynamicStoreRef store, CFArrayRef changedKeys,
                    void *info);
```

store   The dynamic store the callback has been associated with.

changedKeys   An array of keys that have new values.

info   The pointer specified in the second field of the context passed to
               SCDynamicStoreCreate().

System Configuration framework provides convenience functions to simplify retrieving common values from the store. **SCDynamicStoreCopyLocalHostName()** gets the current host name. **SCDynamicStoreKeyCreateHostNames()** returns the key needed to register using **SCDynamicStoreSetNotificationkeys()** to receive notification of changes to the HostNames entity, which includes the local host name.

Seeing all values

Example 15.3 is a Foundation tool that will show all of the keys and values in configd's dynamic store:

Example 15.3   scf-dump.m

```
// scf-dump.m -- Dumps the current state of the System Configuration dynamic store.
```

```
// gcc -g -Wall -framework Foundation -framework SystemConfiguration
//     -o scf-dump scf-dump.m

#import <Foundation/Foundation.h>
#import <SystemConfiguration/SystemConfiguration.h>

int main (void)  {
    CFArrayRef patterns = NULL;
    CFDictionaryRef snapshot = NULL;
    SCDynamicStoreRef store = NULL;

    NSAutoreleasePool *pool = [[NSAutoreleasePool alloc] init];

    // Connect to configd.
    SCDynamicStoreContext context = {
        0, NULL, NULL, NULL, NULL
    };

    store = SCDynamicStoreCreate (kCFAllocatorDefault, CFSTR("com.amosx.scf-dump"),
                                  NULL, // callback
                                  &context);
    if (store == NULL) {
        NSLog (@"*** Unable to connect to dynamic store.");
        goto bailout;
    }

    // Copy all keys and values.
    // SCDynamicStoreCopyMultiple() lets you simultaneously request values for
    // both specific keys and all keys matching a list of patterns.

    // Build the patterns array.
    // Use const void * instead of CFStringRef to avoid cast in CFArrayCreate().
    const void *matchAllRegex = CFSTR(".*");
    patterns = CFArrayCreate (kCFAllocatorDefault, &matchAllRegex, 1,
                              &kCFTypeArrayCallBacks);
    if (patterns == NULL) {
        NSLog (@"*** Unable to create key pattern array.");
        goto bailout;
    }

    // Perform the copy.
    snapshot = SCDynamicStoreCopyMultiple (store, NULL, patterns);

    if (snapshot == NULL) {
        NSLog(@"*** Unable to copy keys and values from dynamic store.");
        goto bailout;
    }

    // Use toll-free bridging to get a description.
    NSString *desc = [(id)snapshot descriptionInStringsFileFormat];

    // |desc| already ends in a newline, so use fputs() instead of puts()
    // to avoid appending another.
    fputs ([desc UTF8String], stdout);

bailout:
    if (patterns) CFRelease (patterns);
    if (snapshot) CFRelease (snapshot);
    if (store) CFRelease (store);
```

```
        [pool drain];
        return EXIT_SUCCESS;

}  // main
```

and part of a sample run:

```
$ ./scf-dump
"State:/Network/Interface/en0/IPv6" = {
    Addresses =      (
        "fe80::21e:c2ff:fe14:5ebb"
    );
    Flags =    (
        0
    );
    PrefixLength =      (
        64
    );
};
"Setup:/Network/Service/B4F97D77-FD6B-4EB7-8348-CAF6CB02986C/IPv6" = {
    ConfigMethod = Automatic;
};
"Setup:/Network/Service/CDCA0E23-7546-416D-99A3-3E0C44A055EE/IPv4" = {
    ConfigMethod = DHCP;
};
...
```

Creating SCFMonitor

Now let's use the System Configuration framework to create the SCFMonitor application shown in Figure 15.3. This application displays the current host name, the person logged in on the console, and all local IP addresses. Notifications are registered to keep the values up to date, although the console user won't change without a logout. The System Configuration framework does not provide any notification or information about users logged in via the network.

Figure 15.3 SCFMonitor window

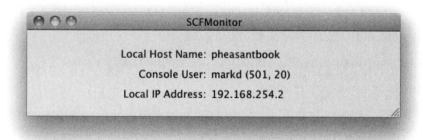

In Xcode, create a new Cocoa Application project called SCFMonitor. Add the System Configuration framework. Then edit the MainMenu.xib file and layout the UI as shown in Figure 15.4 using six static text labels.

Figure 15.4 SCFMonitor static text labels

Figure 15.5 shows the SCFMonitor object diagram. There are three **NSTextField** outlets in the class: hostnameField, consoleUserField, and localIPField.

Figure 15.5 SCFMonitor object diagram

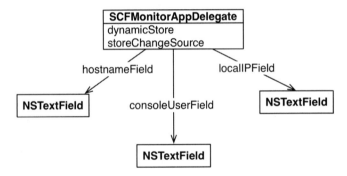

Edit the app delegate:

Example 15.4 SCFMonitorAppDelegate.h

```
#import <Cocoa/Cocoa.h>
#import <SystemConfiguration/SystemConfiguration.h>

@interface SCFMonitorAppDelegate : NSObject <NSApplicationDelegate> {
    NSTextField *_hostnameField;
    NSTextField *_consoleUserField;
    NSTextField *_localIPField;

    SCDynamicStoreRef _dynamicStore;
    CFRunLoopSourceRef _storeChangeSource;
}

@property (assign) IBOutlet NSTextField *hostnameField;
@property (assign) IBOutlet NSTextField *consoleUserField;
@property (assign) IBOutlet NSTextField *localIPField;

@end // SCFMonitorAppDelegate
```

Set each outlet of the **SCFMonitorAppDelegate** to point to the appropriate text field. Save the xib file and then add the app delegate:

Example 15.5 SCFMonitorAppDelegate.m

```
#import "SCFMonitorAppDelegate.h"

// Useful regular expressions.  See re_format(7) for details.
// Match any service's IP address.
// "[^/]+" means "match at least one non-slash character."
#define ANY_NETWORK_SERVICE "State:/Network/Service/[^/]+"

// "[[:digit:]]" means match one digit.
#define kIPPattern ANY_NETWORK_SERVICE "/IPv[[:digit:]]"

static void StoreDidChange(SCDynamicStoreRef, CFArrayRef, void *);

@interface SCFMonitorAppDelegate ()

// Declare private accessors.  These dudes always hit the dynamic store for values.
@property(readonly) NSString *hostname;
@property(readonly) NSString *consoleUser;
@property(readonly) NSString *localIPs;

// Forward references
- (SCDynamicStoreRef) newDynamicStore;
- (void) setNotificationKeys;
- (void) unsetNotificationKeys;
- (void) updateUI;

@end // extension


@implementation SCFMonitorAppDelegate

@synthesize hostnameField = _hostnameField;
@synthesize consoleUserField = _consoleUserField;
@synthesize localIPField = _localIPField;

- (id) init {
    if ((self = [super init])) {
        _dynamicStore = [self newDynamicStore];
        [self setNotificationKeys];
    }
    return self;
} // init


- (void) awakeFromNib {
    [self updateUI];
} // awakeFromNib

- (BOOL) applicationShouldTerminateAfterLastWindowClosed: (NSApplication *) app {
    return YES;
} // applicationShouldTerminateAfterLastWindowClosed

- (void) dealloc {
    [self unsetNotificationKeys];
    CFRelease(_dynamicStore) , _dynamicStore = NULL;
```

```
    [super dealloc];
} // dealloc


// This value changes if the user changes the Computer Name in the
// Sharing preference pane.
- (NSString *) hostname {
    if (_dynamicStore == NULL) return nil;

    CFStringRef hostname = SCDynamicStoreCopyLocalHostName (_dynamicStore);
    return [(id)hostname autorelease];
} // hostname


// This value changes if this user logs in as a different user.
// Somewhat difficult to catch at runtime.
- (NSString *) consoleUser {
    if (_dynamicStore == NULL) return nil;

    uid_t uid = 0;
    gid_t gid = 0;
    CFStringRef name = SCDynamicStoreCopyConsoleUser(_dynamicStore, &uid, &gid);

    // Build a string like "name (uid, gid) ".
    NSString *desc = [NSString stringWithFormat: @"%@ (%lu, %lu) ",
                                name, (unsigned long) uid, (unsigned long) gid];
    if (name != NULL) CFRelease (name);
    return desc;
} // consoleUser


// This value can change easily, especially if a new network is joined.
- (NSString *) localIPs {
    if (_dynamicStore == NULL) return nil;

    static NSString *const kIPErrorMsg = @"<error retrieving addresses>";

    // Use SCDynamicStoreCopyMultiple() to get a consistent snapshot.
    const void *pattern = CFSTR (kIPPattern);
    CFArrayRef patterns =
        CFArrayCreate (kCFAllocatorDefault, &pattern, 1, &kCFTypeArrayCallBacks);

    if (patterns == NULL) {
        NSLog (@"%s: *** Unable to create IP pattern array.");
        return kIPErrorMsg;
    }

    NSDictionary *results =
        [(id)SCDynamicStoreCopyMultiple (_dynamicStore, NULL,
                                         patterns) autorelease];
    CFRelease(patterns);

    if (results == nil) {
        NSLog (@"%s: *** Unable to copy IP addresses.");
        return kIPErrorMsg;
    }

    // Accumulate the addresses.
    NSString *const separator = @", ";
    NSMutableArray *addressStrings = [NSMutableArray array];
```

```
        for (NSString *key in results) {

            // Each result dictionary has a key "Addresses" whose value
            // is an array of IP addresses as strings.
            NSDictionary *value = [results objectForKey: key];

            // The same key is actually used for both IPv4 and IPv6 addresses.
            NSArray *addresses = [value objectForKey: (id) kSCPropNetIPv4Addresses];
            NSString *addressString = [addresses componentsJoinedByString: separator];
            [addressStrings addObject: addressString];
        }

        NSString *localIPs = [addressStrings componentsJoinedByString: separator];
        return localIPs;
    } // localIPs


    - (void) updateUI {
        [self.hostnameField setStringValue: self.hostname];
        [self.consoleUserField setStringValue: self.consoleUser];
        [self.localIPField setStringValue: self.localIPs];
    } // updateUI


    static void StoreDidChange(SCDynamicStoreRef store, CFArrayRef changedKeys,
                    void *selfContext) {
        NSLog (@"%s: <SCDynamicStoreRef: %p> changed %@", __func__, store, changedKeys);
        SCFMonitorAppDelegate *self = (SCFMonitorAppDelegate *) selfContext;
        [self updateUI];
    } // StoreDidChange


    - (SCDynamicStoreRef) newDynamicStore {
        SCDynamicStoreContext selfContext = { 0, self, NULL, NULL, NULL };

        CFStringRef name = CFBundleGetIdentifier(CFBundleGetMainBundle());
        SCDynamicStoreRef store = SCDynamicStoreCreate (kCFAllocatorDefault, name,
                                              StoreDidChange, &selfContext);
        if (store == NULL) NSLog (@"%s: *** Failed to create SCDynamicStoreRef.");

        return store;
    } // newDynamicStore


    - (void) setNotificationKeys {
        // Build the key list.
        NSString *hostNameKey =
            [(id)SCDynamicStoreKeyCreateHostNames(kCFAllocatorDefault) autorelease];
        NSString *consoleUserKey =
            [(id)SCDynamicStoreKeyCreateConsoleUser(kCFAllocatorDefault) autorelease];
        CFArrayRef keys =
            (CFArrayRef)[NSArray arrayWithObjects: hostNameKey, consoleUserKey, nil];

        // Build the pattern list.
        CFArrayRef patterns =
            (CFArrayRef) [NSArray arrayWithObject: (id) CFSTR(kIPPattern) ];

        // Register for notifications.
        Boolean success =
```

```
        SCDynamicStoreSetNotificationKeys (_dynamicStore, keys, patterns);
    if (!success) {
        NSLog(@"%s: *** Failed to set notification keys.", __func__);
        return;
    }

    // Add the store to the run loop.
    _storeChangeSource = SCDynamicStoreCreateRunLoopSource (kCFAllocatorDefault,
                                                          _dynamicStore, 0);
    if (_storeChangeSource -- NULL) {
        NSLog(@"%s: *** Failed to create dynamic store run loop source.", __func__);
        [self unsetNotificationKeys];
        return;
    }

    CFRunLoopRef rl = CFRunLoopGetCurrent ();
    CFRunLoopAddSource (rl, _storeChangeSource, kCFRunLoopCommonModes);

    // Orinarily we'd release _storeChangeSource, but we will invalidate it
    // when unsetting the notification keys.

} // setNotificationKeys


- (void) unsetNotificationKeys {
    if (_storeChangeSource != NULL) {
        CFRunLoopSourceInvalidate (_storeChangeSource);
    }

    Boolean success = SCDynamicStoreSetNotificationKeys (_dynamicStore, NULL, NULL);
    if (!success) {
        NSLog(@"%s: SCDynamicStoreSetNotificationKeys to NULL failed.", __func__);
    }
} // unsetNotificationKeys

@end // SCFMonitorAppDelegatex
```

Build and run it. If you have two IP addresses, they should both show up in the window. If you have an Airport card and built-in ethernet, they can each have their own address. You will likely need to plug in an ethernet cable to have an IP address assigned to the corresponding interface.

If you change an address, you can see it disappear from the window for a couple of seconds and then reappear as the network interface is taken down and brought back up to effect the change. You can change the hostname by editing the Computer Name in the Sharing preference pane.

For the More Curious: Run Loop Observers

You can hook more stuff into the run loop, such as an observer. A run loop observer has its callback function invoked at a number of well defined places, shown Figure 15.6. These are the observation points:

- When the run loop is entered

- Before timers are fired

- After timers are fired

- Before sources (like the **CFSocket**) are checked

- Before the run loop waits for activity (blocking until it can do something)

- After it wakes up

- When the run loop exits

Figure 15.6   Run loop observation points

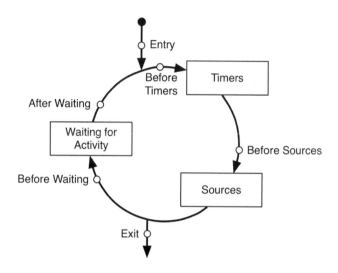

Here is a function that will register an observer:

```
void addRunLoopObserver () {
    CFRunLoopRef rl;
    CFRunLoopObserverRef observer;

    rl = CFRunLoopGetCurrent ();

    observer = CFRunLoopObserverCreate (kCFAllocatorDefault,
                                        kCFRunLoopAllActivities, // activites
                                        1, // repeats
                                        0, // order
                                        observerCallback,
                                        NULL); // context
    CFRunLoopAddObserver (rl, observer, kCFRunLoopDefaultMode);

    CFRelease (observer);

} // addRunLoopObserver
```

This works in a very similar way to the CFSocketRef, except here you do not have to create an independent run loop source. You can't use an observer for anything useful outside of a run loop, so the designers removed that step.

Here is an observer function that will print out what action is being observed:

```
typedef struct observerActivity {
    int         activity;
    const char *name;
} observerActivity;

observerActivity g_activities[] = {
    { kCFRunLoopEntry,         "Run Loop Entry" },
    { kCFRunLoopBeforeTimers,  "Before Timers" },
    { kCFRunLoopBeforeSources, "Before Sources" },
    { kCFRunLoopBeforeWaiting, "Before Waiting" },
    { kCFRunLoopAfterWaiting,  "After Waiting" },
    { kCFRunLoopExit,          "Exit" }
};

void observerCallback (CFRunLoopObserverRef observer,
                       CFRunLoopActivity activity,
                       void *info) {
    observerActivity *scan, *stop;

    scan = g_activities;
    stop = scan + (sizeof(g_activities) / sizeof(*g_activities));

    while (scan < stop) {

        if (scan->activity == activity) {
            NSLog (@"%s", scan->name);
            break;
        }
        scan++;
    }

} // observerCallback
```

Exercises

1. Add **NSHost** to CFChatterClient.

2. Add the observer callback to your CFChatterClient.

3. If you run **scf-dump** on a laptop, you'll probably see something like this:

```
key is State:/IOKit/PowerSources/InternalBattery-0
    Max Capacity : 962
    Current Capacity : 962
    Name : InternalBattery-0
    Is Present : 1
    Is Charging : 0
    Time to Full Charge : 0
    Transport Type : Internal
    Time to Empty : 0
    Power Source State : AC Power
```

Extend the SCFMonitor application to monitor battery information and display it, over time, in a tableview.

16

kqueue and FSEvents

Several of the technologies you have seen so far date back to Unix's earlier days. Some of the APIs are awkward and difficult to use correctly, such as signal handling, and some are awkward and do not scale well, such as **select()** and **poll()**.

In 2000, the FreeBSD project created Kernel Queues, abbreviated as "kqueues," to address the shortcomings in the older APIs. Apple adopted kqueues in Mac OS X 10.3 and extended them in 10.6. kqueues are a unified notification mechanism used by the kernel that can inform your program about interesting events.

Inside the kernel are a number of filters, as shown in Figure 16.1. As the kernel does its work, it tells the filters what's going on. There is a filter for process handling, another for the network stack, another one associated with the file system, and so on. Each of the filters has a set of interesting events that it watches for, such as data appears on a socket, a program has **fork()**ed, a signal has been sent, or a directory has had a file added to it.

Figure 16.1   Kernel filters adding new events to a kqueue

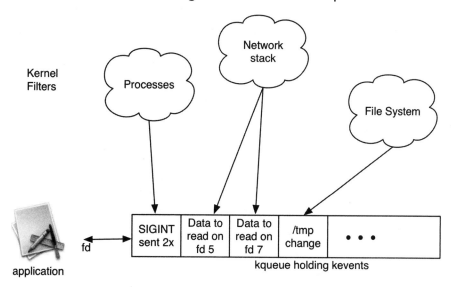

Your program registers its interest with the kernel about what entities it is interested in, like which file descriptors or signal numbers, and what specific events associated with those entities it wants to know about, such as "I want to know about new data to be read on the socket, but I do not care if I can write to it or not." Events are put into a queue as they occur, and the program can pick them up at its leisure.

kqueue()

First, you ask the kernel to create a new queue for you by using **kqueue()** function:

```
int kqueue ();
```

kqueue() returns a file descriptor that represents the queue. Your application can have any number of active kqueues, and it is perfectly OK for a library or framework to make kqueues for its own use. When you are done with a kqueue, **close()** it like any other file descriptor. **kqueue()** returns -1 if an error occurred and sets errno appropriately.

The thread-safety of kqueues is not documented, so do not use the same kqueue in multiple threads simultaneously. It is safe, though, to manipulate an object such as a file in a different thread than the one that has kqueue watching it for changes. These operations, such as removing the events for a file that has been closed, happen atomically.

Even though **kqueue()** returns a file descriptor, you do not use it with **read()** or **write()**. Instead, you interact with the file descriptor via the **kevent()** function described below. Because the kqueue is represented by a file descriptor, you can put it into a **select()** or **poll()** call, into another kqueue, as well as into a runloop to see if there are any pending notifications. if there are any pending notifications, the file descriptor will behave as if there were bytes to be read from it, such as waking up **select()** or causing a runloop notification.

Events

You interact with kqueues using kevents, which describe which entities and filters you are interested in. struct kevent works on all Mac OS X systems starting with 10.3:

```
struct kevent {
    uintptr_t    ident;      /* identifier for this event */
    int16_t      filter;     /* filter for event */
    uint16_t     flags;      /* general flags */
    uint32_t     fflags;     /* filter-specific flags */
    intptr_t     data;       /* filter-specific data */
    void         *udata;     /* opaque user data identifier */
};
```

This structure is used both for communication from your program to the kernel and vice versa. When registering interest in an event you fill in the fields of the structure. When responding to an event you look at the fields to see what event happened and to find any associated data about the event.

Snow Leopard introduced 64-bit versions of the structures and calls for kevents. struct kevent64_s is available on Mac OS X 10.6 and iOS:

```
struct kevent64_s {
    uint64_t     ident;      /* identifier for this event */
    int16_t      filter;     /* filter for event */
    uint16_t     flags;      /* general flags */
    uint32_t     fflags;     /* filter-specific flags */
```

```
    int64_t      data;      /* filter-specific data */
    uint64_t     udata;     /* opaque user data identifier */
    uint64_t     ext[2];    /* filter-specific extensions */
};
```

The main difference, aside from the larger pointer sizes, is that struct kevent64_s has two additional 64-bit values that are used to pass filter-specific information.

Here are the fields the two structures have in common plus the two additional 64-bit values:

ident   The identifier for the event. You can only have one particular pairing of filter and identifier with a given kqueue. What the identifier actually is varies based on the filter. A file descriptor is used for most of the filters, which is nice because a file descriptor can unambiguously identify a file in the file system. Sockets are represented by file descriptors. The signal filter uses the signal number here, such as SIGINT or SIGHUP.

filter   A constant that is defined for each of the filters supplied by the kernel. Some of the available filters include EVFILT_READ (data is available to be read on a file descriptor), EVFILT_WRITE (you can write to a file descriptor without blocking), EVFILT_VNODE (monitor changes to files and directories), EVFILT_PROC (trace process activity), EVFILT_SIGNAL (receive signals in a synchronous manner), and EVFILT_MACHPORT for Mach ports.

flags   A bitmask that tells kqueue what to do with the event as it is being registered. Valid flags include EV_ADD (add the event to the kqueue), EV_ENABLE (start issuing notifications about the event), EV_DISABLE (stop issuing notifications about the event), EV_DELETE (remove the event from the kqueue), EV_ONESHOT (notify about the event only once, then delete it from the kqueue), and EV_CLEAR (reset the state of the event). flags is also set on an event notification.

fflags   "Filter Flags" is a bitmask that contains arguments for a specific filter. The vnode filter has flags that indicate interest in specific file operations, such as the file getting deleted, the contents changing, the size increasing, and so on. Some filters do not have any extra flags.

data   An integer containing any filter-specific data. For example, data would have the number of bytes pending in the kernel's read buffer for an EVFILT_READ notification. data would have the number of bytes you can write before blocking for an EVFILT_WRITE notification.

udata   "user data" is a pointer that you can use for any purpose. It's like a rock you can hide data under. You can use it to store a pointer to a string, data structure, or object that you want to associate with the event. You can also store a function pointer here that you can use for a flexible event notification mechanism. The kernel passes this value back to you for each event so you can use it for your own purposes.

ext   Filter-specific extensions. These are two 64-bit values that filters can use for the cases where a set of flags is not sufficient. The Mach port filter uses ext[0] to return a pointer to the message when retrieving an event. Other filters pass ext[0] through untouched. ext[1] is not used by any filters, so its value is also passed through untouched, like a second udata field.

The **EV_SET** macro is provided for quick initialization of the structure:

```
EV_SET (&key, ident, filter, flags, fflags, data, udata);
```

You give the address to your struct kevent as the first argument, and then the subsequent arguments to the macro match the same-named entry in the kevent structure. There's also a 64-bit version:

```
EV_SET64 (&kev, ident, filter, flags, fflags, data, udata, ext[0], ext[1]);
```

Registering and Handling Events

kevent() registers your interest in specific filters and events with a kqueue, and it is also the function used to block on a kqueue waiting for event notifications. The signature of kevent() is a bit long because it lets you do both operations at the same time.

```
int kevent (int kqueue,
            const struct kevent *changeList, int numChanges,
                  struct kevent *eventList,  int numEvents,
            const struct timespec *timeout);
```

The first argument to kevent() is the kqueue you want to manipulate. changeList holds the set of new events for the kqueue to monitor, as well as any changes to events the kqueue is already monitoring. If changeList is non-NULL and numChanges is greater than zero, then the events in changeList will be applied to the kqueue saying "tell me about anything that happens about these."

eventList holds the events that kevent() is reporting. If eventList is non-NULL and numChanges is greater than zero, the event list gets filled in by kevent() with any pending events.

timeout is a struct timespec; its two fields specify how long you want to wait in seconds and nanoseconds.

```
struct timespec {
    time_t  tv_sec;    /* seconds */
    long    tv_nsec;   /* nanoseconds */
};
```

The system will do its best to honor your timeout as accurately as possible, but the granularity of the system clock can be much coarser than one nanosecond.

kevent() will wait indefinitely if the timeout parameter to kevent() is NULL unless eventList is also NULL, in which case you are only registering new events and not asking if any new events occurred. In this case, kevent() will return immediately. If you are waiting for events, kevent() will block until an event happens. If you want to poll the kqueue to see if there is anything there, give it a timeout of {0, 0}.

kevent() returns the number of events it has written to eventList. It can return zero if there were no events prior to the timeout expiring. If an error happened while processing changeList, kevent() tries to place an event with the EV_ERROR bit set in the flags field and the errno in the data field. Otherwise, kevent() returns -1, and errno will be set.

Here is how you would create a kqueue, register an event, and then block waiting for the event:

```
int kq = kqueue ();

if (kq == -1) {
    fprintf (stderr, "could not kqueue.  Error is %d/%s\n",
             errno, strerror(errno));
```

```
        // exit or goto an error handler
}

struct kevent event;
EV_SET (&event,       // event structure
        SIGINT,        // identifier
        EVFILT_SIGNAL, // filter
        EV_ADD | EV_ENABLE, // action flags
        0,             // filter flags
        0,             // filter data
        NULL);         // user data

// register the event
if (kevent(kq, &event, 1, NULL, 0, NULL) == -1) {
    fprintf (stderr, "could not kevent signal.  Error is %d/%s\n",
             errno, strerror(errno));
    // exit or goto an error handler
}

...

// block here until an event arrives
if (kevent(kq, NULL, 0, &event, 1, NULL) == -1) {
    fprintf (stderr, "could not kevent.  Error is %d/%s\n",
             errno, strerror(errno));
    // exit or goto an error handler
}

// look at change and handle the event

// close the kqueue when finished with it
close (kq);
```

Here we are re-using event. **kevent()** copies out the data it needs, so you do not have hang onto the struct kevent you used to register the event. You just fill out the structure and hand it to the kernel via **kevent()**.

The EV_ADD and EV_ENABLE flags are necessary to have the event added to the kqueue and to have event notification enabled. You can pass EV_CLEAR to say that you are not interested in any previous events that may be been recorded. The state of a kernel resource, such as data in a read buffer for a network socket, can also trigger an event. Using EV_CLEAR will suppress an event notification in this case.

You use **kevent64** to register and receive events using struct kevent64_s:

```
int kevent64 (int kqueue,
              const struct kevent64_s *changeList, int numChanges,
                  struct kevent64_s *eventlist, int numEvents,
                  unsigned int flags,
                  const struct timespec *timeout);
```

It is nearly the same as **kevent()**, but takes 64-bit kevent structures and also takes a flags argument, the use of which is currently undocumented, so just pass in zero.

kqueues for Signal Handling

Unix signals, due to their asynchronous nature, are difficult to handle correctly. Race conditions are possible, plus you have to be aware of functions you can or can't call at signal interrupt time. Most of the time, you really do not *have* to handle a signal the instant it is delivered. You can handle it later at a more convenient time. That is why a common signal handling technique is to set a global variable and then check it later.

You can use kqueues and **kevent()** to handle signals, saving you from the headaches caused by the signal handling API. The filter for signals is also one of the simplest of the kqueue filters.

kqueue event handling can be used in tandem with the classic signal handling API. Calls like **signal()** and **sigaction()** have priority over events registered with a kqueue, so if someone has installed a signal handler or left the handler as SIG_DFL, it will get called, and your kqueue event will not. Therefore, you will need to remove any default signal handlers by calling

```
signal (signum, SIG_IGN);
```

To handle a signal, place the signal number of interest into the ident portion of the struct kevent. Set filter to EVFILT_SIGNAL. When **kevent()** reports a signal-related event, the data member of the kevent structure will have a count of the number of times the signal has occurred since the last time it appeared on **kevent()**. This is a huge improvement over the traditional signal API where you never know exactly how many times a signal has happened due to signal coalescing.

Example 16.1 is a command-line tool that registers a number of signals with a kqueue and then blocks on **kevent()** waiting for signals to happen. When they do, the name of the signal is printed out along with the number of times that signal has happened since the last time it was seen in **kevent()**. A timeout of 5 seconds is used to show a heartbeat for the program – to show that it actually is alive and stays alive while signals get handled. A SIGINT signal will cause the program to exit cleanly.

Example 16.1   sigwatcher.m

```
// sigwatcher.m -- watch for signals happening

// gcc -g -Wall -o sigwatcher sigwatcher.m

#import <errno.h>        // for errno
#import <stdio.h>        // for fprintf()
#import <stdlib.h>       // for EXIT_SUCCESS
#import <string.h>       // for strerror()
#import <sys/event.h>    // for kqueue() etc.
#import <sys/signal.h>   // for SIGINT, etc
#import <sys/time.h>     // for struct timespec
#import <unistd.h>       // for getpid()

int main (int argc, const char *argv[]) {
    // Program success/failure result.
    int result = EXIT_FAILURE;

    // Register signal events with this queue.
    int kq = kqueue ();
    if (kq == -1) {
        fprintf (stderr, "could not kqueue.  Error is %d/%s\n",
                errno, strerror(errno));
    }

    // The list of events we're interested in, mostly just pulled
    // at random from <sys/signal.h>.
    int signals[] = { SIGHUP, SIGINT, SIGQUIT, SIGILL, SIGTRAP, SIGABRT,
```

```
                        SIGBUS, SIGSEGV, SIGPIPE, SIGTERM, SIGCHLD, SIGWINCH };
    int *scan = signals;
    int *stop = scan + sizeof(signals) / sizeof(*signals);

    // Register each event with the kqueue.
    while (scan < stop) {
        struct kevent event;
        EV_SET (&event, *scan,
                EVFILT_SIGNAL,
                EV_ADD | EV_ENABLE,
                0, 0, NULL);

        // kqueue event handling happens after legacy API, so make
        // sure it the signal doesn't get eaten.
        signal (*scan, SIG_IGN);

        // Register the signal event.  kevent() will return immediately.
        if (kevent(kq, &event, 1, NULL, 0, NULL) == -1) {
            fprintf (stderr, "could not kevent signal.  Error is %d/%s\n",
                    errno, strerror(errno));
            goto done;
        }
        scan++;
    }

    printf ("I am pid %d\n", getpid());

    // Now block and display any signals received.
    while (1) {
        struct timespec timeout = { 5, 0 };
        struct kevent event;
        int status = kevent (kq, NULL, 0, &event, 1, &timeout);

        if (status == 0) {
            // Timeout.
            printf ("lub dub...\n");

        } else if (status > 0) {
            // We got signal!
            printf ("we got signal: %d (%s), delivered: %d\n",
                    (int)event.ident, strsignal((int)event.ident),
                    (int)event.data);

            if (event.ident == SIGINT) {
                result = EXIT_SUCCESS;
                goto done;
            }

        } else {
            fprintf (stderr, "cound not kevent.  Error is %d/%s\n",
                    errno, strerror(errno));
            goto done;
        }
    }
done:
    close (kq);
    return result;

} // main
```

And here is a sample run. One terminal window is running the program, and another terminal window has the kill commands used to send signals to **sigwatcher**.

```
$ ./sigwatcher
I am pid 15341
lub dub...
we got signal: 11 (Segmentation fault), delivered: 1
we got signal: 11 (Segmentation fault), delivered: 1
lub dub...
we got signal: 11 (Segmentation fault), delivered: 3
lub dub...
lub dub...
we got signal: 2 (Interrupt), delivered: 1
```

And these commands were issued in the other terminal:

```
$ kill -s SEGV 15341
$ kill -s SEGV 15341
$ kill -s SEGV 15341 ; kill -s SEGV 15341 ; kill -s SEGV 15341
$ kill -s INT 15341
```

kqueues for Socket Monitoring

Like the signal handling API, the API for monitoring sockets and other file descriptors can be awkward and inefficient. **select()** is the function used most often on Mac OS X to determine the liveness of a socket (is it still connected?) and to see if there is any activity on a socket (can I read from it without blocking?)

The problem with **select()**, and its functionally equivalent counterpart **poll()**, is that it is a stateless call. Every time you call **select()** or **poll()** you have to tell the kernel what file descriptors you are interested in. The kernel then copies this list of descriptors into its own memory space, does whatever work it does to test for liveness and activity, and then copies stuff back to the program's address space to let the program know what is going on.

The main problem with this is scalability. If you are dealing with hundreds or thousands of file descriptors, you have to ask the kernel about *all* of them *every* time even if only a small percentage actually have anything interesting going on. High volume server applications can often find themselves spending a lot of CPU time on maintenance of the FD_SETs for **select()**.

The other problem with the **select()** technique is convenience. When **select()** tells you a file descriptor has data to be read, you have to loop over the returned FD_SET looking for the file descriptors of interest. Then you have to attempt a **read()** to see if the connection is still open. If the connection is still open, you do not know how much data is available to read. You have to guess how much to read, usually using a hard-coded argument, and looping if there is more than that amount.

Both of these problems are solved when using kqueues for monitoring your sockets. You register all of your sockets of interest with **kevent()**, and then subsequent **kevent()** calls will tell you exactly which sockets have activity. Included in the event is how much data is there to be read. You can then slurp this data up with a single **read()**, rather than issuing multiple reads and stitching together the data.

For read operations on a socket (or file, or pipe), use the EVFILT_READ filter. It takes a file descriptor as the struct kevent identifier. You can use **listen()** sockets and sockets that have already been **accept()**ed. When **kevent()** returns, the data field of the event has the amount of data in the kernel buffers waiting to be read.

This behavior is called a "level-triggered" event because the event is triggered based on the level of data in the buffer. You will be notified by the EVFILT_READ filter if there is any data to be read from the socket. This allows you to read a convenient number of bytes from the socket, say the size of a message, and leave the rest of the data there. The next time **kevent()** is called, you will be told about the rest of the unread data.

Other filters are said to use "edge-triggered" events, whereby you get notifications when the entity of interest changes state. This is used more often with the EVFILT_VNODE filter, which is described below.

Getting back to EVFILT_READ, the filter also sets the EV_EOF flag in the flags field if a socket has been shut down, with any errno value in the event's fflags field. It is possible for EV_EOF to be set in the event flags and there still be data pending in the socket buffer.

The EVFILT_WRITE filter works in a similar manner. When a write event is received for a file descriptor, the data field of the event structure will contain the amount of space remaining in the write buffer, which is how much you can write before blocking. This filter will also set EV_EOF when the reader disconnects.

kqueues for File System Monitoring

Usually when you hear kqueue being discussed on the Internet, it is regarding monitoring the file system. You can use EVFILT_VNODE to watch a file or a directory for changes and then react to those changes. You might want to watch a directory for changes and then pick up any files that have been placed in that directory, leading to "drop-box" functionality for the user. You could also implement an efficient **tail -f** feature by waiting for a file to have data written to it.

The filter used is EVFILT_VNODE. A vnode, short for virtual node, is a kernel data structure that contains information about a file or folder, with a unique vnode allocated in the kernel for each active file or folder. vnodes are part of VFS, a virtual file system in the kernel, which provides an abstraction around specific file system implementations. There are a number of events you can monitor on a vnode, represented by bit flags you can bitwise-OR together in the filter flags of the event structure. When you receive a notification, you can bitwise-AND the filter flags to see what event(s) happened.

Here are some of the different events relating to EVFILT_VNODE:

NOTE_DELETE   The **unlink()** function was called on the file.

NOTE_WRITE   The contents of the file have been changed due to a **write()** operation.

NOTE_EXTEND   The file's size increased.

NOTE_ATTRIB   The file has had its attributes changed.

NOTE_LINK   The (hard) link count to the file has changed. This is not triggered if a new symbolic link is made to the file.

NOTE_RENAME   The file has been renamed.

NOTE_REVOKE   Access to the file was revoked via the **revoke()** system call, or the underlying file system has been unmounted.

dirwatcher is a command-line tool that takes a set of directories as program arguments, as in Example 16.2. Each of those directories is opened, and the resulting file descriptor is placed in a kqueue using the NOTE_WRITE filter flag. When a directory changes, such as a file being added or removed, **kevent()** will return reporting which directory has changed. The program then prints out the name of the directory that has changed.

Because **dirwatcher** puts a pointer to the directory's name into the event's user data pointer field, mapping the change event to the directory name is simple. The program also catches SIGINT to do a clean shutdown. Many kinds of events can be mixed and matched in the same kqueue. You can use the user data field of the event structure to determine what kind of event it is, which is what **dirwatcher** does, or you can look at the filter field to see which filter generated the event.

Example 16.2   dirwatcher.m

```
// dirwatcher.m -- watch directories for changes

// gcc -std=c99 -g -Wall -o dirwatcher dirwatcher.m

#import <errno.h>        // for errno
#import <fcntl.h>        // for O_RDONLY
#import <stdio.h>        // for fprintf()
#import <stdlib.h>       // for EXIT_SUCCESS
#import <string.h>       // for strerror()
#import <sys/event.h>    // for kqueue() etc.
#import <unistd.h>       // for close()

int main (int argc, const char *argv[]) {

    // Program success/failure result
    int result = EXIT_FAILURE;

    // Make sure there's at least one directory to monitor
    if (argc == 1) {
        fprintf (stderr, "%s directoryname [...]\n", argv[0]);
        fprintf (stderr, "   watches directoryname for changes\n");
        goto done;
    }

    // The queue to register the dir-watching events with
    int kq = kqueue ();

    if (kq == -1) {
        fprintf (stderr, "could not kqueue.  Error is %d/%s\n",
                errno, strerror(errno));
    }

    // Walk the set of directories provided by the user and monitor them
    for (int i = 1; i < argc; i++) {
        // The vnode monitor requires a file descriptor, so
        // open the directory to get one.
        const char *dirname = argv[i];
        int dirfd = open (dirname, O_RDONLY);

        if (dirfd == -1) {
            fprintf (stderr, "could not open(%s). Error is %d/%s\n",
                    dirname, errno, strerror(errno));
            continue;
```

```
    }

    // Fill out the event structure.  Store the name of the
    // directory in the user data
    struct kevent direvent;
    EV_SET (&direvent,
            dirfd,              // identifier
            EVFILT_VNODE,       // filter
            EV_ADD | EV_CLEAR | EV_ENABLE,  // action flags
            NOTE_WRITE,         // filter flags
            0,                  // filter data
            (void *)dirname); // user data

    // register the event
    if (kevent(kq, &direvent, 1, NULL, 0, NULL) == -1) {
        fprintf (stderr, "could not kevent.  Error is %d/%s\n",
                 errno, strerror(errno));
        goto done;
    }
}

// Register interest in SIGINT with the queue.  The user data
// is NULL, which is how we'll differentiate between
// a directory-modification event and a SIGINT-received event.

struct kevent sigevent;
EV_SET (&sigevent,
        SIGINT,
        EVFILT_SIGNAL,
        EV_ADD | EV_ENABLE,
        0, 0, NULL);

// kqueue event handling happens after the legacy API, so make
// sure it doesn't eat the signal before the kqueue can see it.
signal (SIGINT, SIG_IGN);

// Register the signal event.
if (kevent(kq, &sigevent, 1, NULL, 0, NULL) == -1) {
    fprintf (stderr, "could not kevent signal.  Error is %d/%s\n",
             errno, strerror(errno));
    goto done;
}

while (1) {
    // camp on kevent() until something interesting happens
    struct kevent change;
    if (kevent(kq, NULL, 0, &change, 1, NULL) == -1) {
        fprintf (stderr, "cound not kevent.  Error is %d/%s\n",
                 errno, strerror(errno));
        goto done;
    }

    // The signal event has NULL in the user data.  Check for that first.
    if (change.udata == NULL) {
        result = EXIT_SUCCESS;
        printf ("that's all folks...\n");
        goto done;

    } else {
        // udata is non-null, so it's the name of the directory
```

```
                // that changed
                printf ("%s\n", (char*)change.udata);
        }
    }

done:
    close (kq);
    return result;

} // main
```

Here is a sample run that watches the user's home directory and /tmp:

```
$ ./dirwatcher ~ /tmp
/tmp
/Users/markd
/Users/markd
/tmp
^C
that's all folks...
```

Files were created and deleted in each directory using **touch** and **rm** in another terminal window. These triggered the output in **dirwatcher**. **dirwatcher** will also notice changes that are made with the Finder. Finally Control-C, which generates a SIGINT, is used to shut down the program.

kqueues and Runloops

You can use kqueues in your Cocoa and Carbon applications to monitor OS events of interest by making a thread that sits on **kevent()**, or you can use the runloop.

You can create a thread that contains the **kevent()** call. If given no timeout, **kevent()** will block the thread until something interesting happens. That thread, after it wakes up, can notify the application's main thread about what happened or do whatever work is appropriate.

It is safe, though, to manipulate a file descriptor in one thread while another thread is monitoring it with a kqueue. If the file is closed, the kernel atomically removes any pending events associated with this file descriptor in the process. However, there is one gotcha. If a file descriptor gets recycled (by being closed and then a new file opened with the same file descriptor number) while an event is currently being serviced on the old file, then there may be confusion about what file is actually being referenced. This is known as a "recycle race." You can use the udata field in the event structure to disambiguate things if this is a problem for you. (Thanks to Jim Magee for pointing this out.)

Another technique is to put the file descriptor into the main thread's runloop. A kqueue is referenced by a file descriptor, and its behavior is such that **select()**, **poll()**, and **kevent()** can be used to see if there is an event notification waiting on a particular queue. You can wrap the kqueue file descriptor in a **CFSocket** just like you did with CFChatterClient and add it to the runloop. This is safe to do so long as you do not try to directly read or write using the kqueue file descriptor.

Figure 16.2 shows CocoaDirWatcher, a Cocoa application that watches three directories: /tmp, the user's home directory, and the user's preferences directory. When any of these directories change, the name of the directory is sent to the console via **NSLog()**, and the directory is also added to the **NSTextView** in the window.

Figure 16.2   CocoaDirWatcher in action

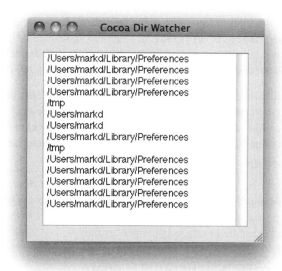

Create the CocoaDirWatcher project in Xcode. Edit CocoaDirWatcherAppDelegate.h to look like Example 16.3

Example 16.3   CocoaDirWatcherAppDelegate.h

```
#import <Cocoa/Cocoa.h>

@interface CocoaDirWatcherAppDelegate : NSObject <NSApplicationDelegate> {
    NSWindow *_window; // from template

    // Directory changed messages are appended here.
    IBOutlet NSTextView *_logView;

    // File descriptor for the directory-watching kqueue.
    int _kqfd;

    // The socket placed into the runloop
    CFSocketRef _runLoopSocket;
}

@property (assign) IBOutlet NSWindow *window;
@property (assign) IBOutlet NSTextView *logView;

@end // CocoaDirWatcherAppDelegate
```

Open MainMenu.xib. Add an **NSTextView** to the window and connect the logView outlet. Tweak the window's layout to look nice.

Example 16.4 shows CocoaDirWatcherAppDelegate.m, which uses some code taken from CFChatterClient. When **CocoaDirWatcherAppDelegate**'s **-applicationDidFinishLaunching:** method is called, it creates a new kqueue and starts a watch on the three directories. An **NSString** with the directory name is put into the user data field of the kevent structure. That is how we'll know what to add to the logview when a directory changes.

After adding the events we are interested in to the kqueue, the kqueue's file descriptor is added to the current runloop with the **addFileDescriptorMonitor:** method. This method puts the file descriptor into a **CFSocket**, sticks that into a **CFSocketRunLoopSource**, and then adds that to the runloop. self, the pointer to the **CocoaDirWatcherAppDelegate** object, is used for the context of the **CFSocket**.

The callback function is called when an event is placed in the kqueue by the kernel. The callback then finds the pointer to the **CocoaDirWatcherAppDelegate** object that had been placed in the callback's context pointer. The kqueue file descriptor is read from the **CocoaDirWatcherAppDelegate** and used in a call to **kevent()**. A new event is pulled off of the kqueue. This event has the name of the directory in the user data pointer. Finally, that directory name is put into the logview.

Previous editions of this book had the **socketCallBack()** access the file descriptor directly from the **CocoaDirWatcherAppDelegate** structure using the arrow (->) operator. This technique is no longer required, now that private @properties will let you create an API to the guts of a class without requiring that they go into the public interface in the header file.

Example 16.4   CocoaDirWatcherAppDelegate.m

```
#import "CocoaDirWatcherAppDelegate.h"

#import <sys/event.h>   // for kqueue() and kevent()
#import <errno.h>       // for errno
#import <strings.h>     // for strerror()


@interface CocoaDirWatcherAppDelegate ()
// Add a property for the kqueue file descriptor.  This will let the runloop callback
// function to get the fd.
@property (assign) int kqfd;
@end // extension

@implementation CocoaDirWatcherAppDelegate

@synthesize window = _window;
@synthesize logView = _logView;
@synthesize kqfd = _kqfd;

// Inform the user that something interesting happened to path
- (void) logActivity: (NSString *) path {
    // log it to the console
    NSLog (@"activity on %@", path);

    // Add it to the text view.
    [self.logView.textStorage.mutableString appendString: path];
    [self.logView.textStorage.mutableString appendString: @"\n"];

    // Scroll to the end
    NSRange endPoint = NSMakeRange ([[self.logView string] length], 0);
    [self.logView scrollRangeToVisible: endPoint];

} // logActivity
```

```objc
// Some activity has happened on the kqueue file descriptor.
// Call kevent() to pick up the new event waiting for us
void socketCallBack (CFSocketRef socketref, CFSocketCallBackType type,
                     CFDataRef address, const void *data, void *info) {
    CocoaDirWatcherAppDelegate *me = (CocoaDirWatcherAppDelegate *) info;

    struct kevent event;
    if (kevent(me.kqfd, NULL, 0, &event, 1, NULL) == -1) {
        NSLog (@"could not pick up event.  Error is %d/%s",
               errno, strerror(errno));
    } else {
        [me logActivity: (NSString *)event.udata];
    }

} // socketCallBack


// Add the given directory to the kqueue for watching
- (void) watchDirectory: (NSString *) dirname {
    int dirfd = open ([dirname fileSystemRepresentation], O_RDONLY);

    if (dirfd == -1) {
        NSLog (@"could not open %@.  Error is %d/%s",
               dirname, errno, strerror(errno));
        return;
    }

    struct kevent direvent;
    EV_SET (&direvent,
            dirfd,
            EVFILT_VNODE,
            EV_ADD | EV_CLEAR | EV_ENABLE,
            NOTE_WRITE,
            0, [dirname copy]);

    // Register event.
    if (kevent(self.kqfd, &direvent, 1, NULL, 0, NULL) == -1) {
        NSLog (@"could not kevent watching %@.  Error is %d/%s",
               dirname, errno, strerror(errno));
    }

} // watchDirectory


// Add the file descriptor to the runloop.  When activity happens,
// such as new data on a socket or a new event in a kqueue(),
// call the socketCallBack function.
- (void) addFileDescriptorMonitor: (int) fd {
    CFSocketContext context = { 0, self, NULL, NULL, NULL };

    _runLoopSocket = CFSocketCreateWithNative (kCFAllocatorDefault,
                                               fd,
                                               kCFSocketReadCallBack,
                                               socketCallBack,
                                               &context);
    if (_runLoopSocket == NULL) {
        NSLog (@"could not CFSocketCreateWithNative");
        goto bailout;
    }
```

```
        CFRunLoopSourceRef rls = CFSocketCreateRunLoopSource (kCFAllocatorDefault,
                                                              _runLoopSocket, 0);

        if (rls == NULL) {
            NSLog (@"could not create a run loop source");
            goto bailout;
        }

        CFRunLoopAddSource (CFRunLoopGetCurrent(), rls, kCFRunLoopDefaultMode);
        CFRelease (rls);

bailout:
        return;

} // addFileDescriptorMonitor


- (void) applicationDidFinishLaunching: (NSNotification *) notification {
        self.kqfd = kqueue ();

        if (self.kqfd == -1) {
            NSLog (@"could not create kqueue.  Error is %d/%s",
                    errno, strerror(errno));
            [[NSApplication sharedApplication] terminate: self];
        }

        [self watchDirectory: @"/tmp"];
        [self watchDirectory: NSHomeDirectory()];
        [self watchDirectory: [@"~/Library/Preferences" stringByExpandingTildeInPath]];

        [self addFileDescriptorMonitor: self.kqfd];

} // applicationDidFinishLaunching

@end // CocoaDirWatcherAppDelegate
```

Compile and run the program. Make some changes to the watched directories and see the program react. Opening and closing GUI applications can also cause activity in the ~/Library/Preferences directory.

fsevents

kqueue is a wonderful tool if you want to monitor individual things, like detecting single file changes or modifications to a single folder. However, kqueue doesn't scale well (API-wise) if you need to monitor a hierarchy of directories. To see changes to a directory hierarchy, you have to open each of the directories and subdirectories and add them to a kqueue. You also need to open any new subdirectories that are created and add them to your kqueue. Open file descriptors are a scarce resource, so you could run out of them before you run out of directories to monitor. OS X 10.5 introduced FSEvents, file system events, which will notify you if something changes in the file system as a whole, or in a particular directory hierarchy. FSEvents is a good alternative to kqueue for these kinds of operations.

Tiger (OS X 10.4) has an undocumented way of watching file system events that happen in real time, through the device /dev/fsevents. Spotlight uses this to keep up to date on changes to files and directories as they happen. The problem with /dev/fsevents, aside from it being undocumented, is that it has a limited buffer to store changes before they are read. Userland programs are not responsive enough to really keep up with the stream of events. If the file system event buffer overflows, events get dropped, and Spotlight may end up having to recrawl and reindex your drive. Not a good situation to get into. Later versions of Mac OS X still have /dev/fsevents, with the same limitations, but they have an API wrapped around the device.

fseventsd

Rather than having multiple programs listening to /dev/fsevents, OS X introduces a daemon, **fseventsd**, that reads from the device, as shown in Figure 16.3. **fseventsd** coalesces the change stream into fewer events and then notifies other programs that have registered an interest in particular directories. Apple provides an API that talks to **fseventsd** under the hood and feeds you file system changes via a callback function whenever an interesting event happens.

Figure 16.3   fseventsd notifying a file system change

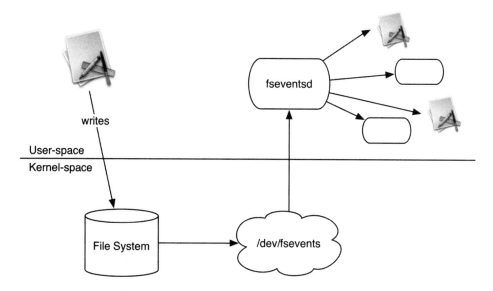

You will not be able to get events in absolutely real time because of this intermediary daemon. This is fine for most applications, although Spotlight needs to see everything, as do things like virus checkers, so those applications would not use the FSEvents API. Time Machine, though, does not need to know about changes immediately, so it uses FSEvents to do its work when it is time to do a backup. Because of the non-real time nature of the events, you can provide a latency to FSEvents, saying "I want to be notified of events, but it's ok if it is 10 seconds stale."

Watching Directories

One way **fseventsd** reduces the amount of data it, and other applications, have to slog through is by only reporting file system changes on a per-directory basis. If the user adds a file to ~/blah/, modifies a file in there, and deletes another file, you'll only get one "hey, ~/blah/ changed" notification. It is up to you to decide what to do in that case. In order to figure out which file changed, you will need to have a cached copy of the contents of the directories and then compare. If you are implementing something like drop boxes, where putting a file in a directory causes some action to happen, you can just scan the directory for new files.

You can choose which directory hierarchies to watch, and you can choose whether to watch them on a particular device or across the whole system. You will get notifications of any newly mounted drives and disk images if you watch the entire system, as well as notifications when these file systems go away. If you watch individual devices, you will not get these mount and unmount notifications.

Application bundles, as well as bundled files like Aperture vaults or Final Cut Pro documents, also count as directory hierarchies. You can use FSEvents to watch a document directory and notice when new graphic assets are dragged in, for instance.

Events

FSEvents are identified by a 64-bit event ID. These event IDs have no relationship with any particular date and time; they are just guaranteed monotonically increasing values. They are not necessarily continuous values because you might not see the activity of another user for security reasons. Also, when you mount a drive, its event database might have a higher eventID value than the current system maximum, so the system will increase its current event ID value to account for this new device.

Each disk has as an event database on it, which can be discarded if the disk is modified by an older version of OS X. If the disk is modified by another operating system, you will not know about what changes were made to it. Alas, FSEvents is not a perfect solution to all problems.

You can save event IDs for use later. If you do this, you will want to look at events on a per-device basis rather than across the whole machine. Each drive gets a unique identifier in the form of a UUID, which is a 128-bit universally unique identifier value guaranteed to be unique across time and space. You can use this UUID to make sure you are looking at the drive you think you are looking at, since it is possible for the user to mount a different drive with the same name as the one you were watching beforehand. Your program might get confused if it sees a strange stream of event IDs or an unexpected directory hierarchy. If you are just watching a drop box or an application bundle, then per-host event streams are fine to use.

Even though 64 bits can hold impossibly huge values (increasing a 64 bit value 1000 times a second will take over 500 million years to roll over), it is possible for the event IDs to wrap around on a system. Your FSEvents callback function will be passed a special notification flag when this happens. Perhaps this will become a Y500,000K problem.

History

FSEvents keeps a history of these directory changes and stores them in a database of sorts at the top of each device in a directory named .fseventsd. If you want to prevent the accumulation of this change history, say for security reasons or general paranoia, create an empty file called no_log in this directory.

Because each device keeps a history of changes, an application can be notified of events that have happened since the last time the program was run. Only directory changes are kept, so this database is fairly small. You can ask FSEvents "Hey, what happened since this last event I saw?" or "Hey, what happened since last Tuesday?" Your application can even crash and then pick up from the last event ID that it remembers seeing.

If you save events, be careful if you are monitoring the directory where the event ID is being stored, such as ~/Library/Preferences if you're saving it in the user's defaults. Saving the preference will trigger a notification, which will cause you to save the new id, which will trigger a notification, over and over again.

Also, even if you save off an event ID and a UUID, you may still get events earlier than the last one stored. The user may have restored a volume from a backup, the IDs may have wrapped, or even may have been manually purged by the user or an administrator.

There are still possibilities for buffer overruns in /dev/fsevents, and in **fseventd**, so you may be notified that you need to recrawl a particular directory hierarchy.

Visibility

FSEvents checks the permissions of directories before telling you about changes. This way you won't be able to see another user's directory names if they have sufficiently locked-down permissions. So if you have a directory named PinkWearsPants, and you know that Pink will be offended if you accuse him of wearing pants, then you should keep this directory in one with strict directory permissions that Pink would not be able to see into. Processes running as root will of course be able to see all events.

FSEvents API

The FSEvents notification mechanism is a runloop source, sitting around waiting for stuff to happen. A C callback function is called when a message from **fseventsd** shows up. The **FSEventsStreamRef** type is what you use to reference a particular event stream.

Creating the stream

Before you can start receiving events, you need to create the event stream with one of these two functions:

```
FSEventStreamRef FSEventStreamCreate (CFAllocatorRef allocator,
                                      FSEventStreamCallback callback,
                                      FSEventStreamContext *context,
                                      CFArrayRef pathsToWatch,
                                      FSEventStreamEventId sinceWhen,
                                      CFTimeInterval latency,
                                      FSEventStreamCreateFlags flags);
```

or

```
FSEventStreamRef
FSEventStreamCreateRelativeToDevice (CFAllocatorRef allocator,
                                     FSEventStreamCallback callback,
                                     FSEventStreamContext *context,
                                     dev_t deviceToWatch,
                                     CFArrayRef pathsToWatchRelativeToDevice,
                                     FSEventStreamEventId sinceWhen,
                                     CFTimeInterval latency,
                                     FSEventStreamCreateFlags flags);
```

There are a lot of common parameters between these two functions. CFAllocator is the typical Core Foundation allocator. Most often you pass NULL or kCFAllocatorDefault. callback is a pointer to the callback function to call when new events are available. context is the typical Core Foundation 5-element context pointer that you saw earlier in Chapter 15: *CFRunLoop*.

Each function takes a **CFArray** of **CFStrings** of paths to watch. You can use an **NSArray** of **NSString**s because they are toll-free bridged. **FSEventStreamCreateRelativeToDevice** takes relative paths to the root of the device, and **FSEventStreamCreate** takes absolute paths from the top of the file system.

sinceWhen is an eventID. Pass kFSEventStreamEventIdSinceNow to start seeing new events, or pass an eventID that you have stored previously. If you pass an eventID, FSEvents will start feeding you historic events until you have caught up with the current event, and then it will start feeding you new events. The callback function is given a set of flags, one of which tells you when FSEvents has stopped feeding you history and is now giving you new events.

The latency parameter is the number of seconds that will pass between new events. A longer latency will result in a less responsive user interface, but it also reduces the number of events you will get, which can ultimately lead to more efficient processing. A user might unpack a 10,000 file **tar**ball or **zip** archive in their home directory. With a low latency, you will get a lot of events because of the home directory being modified. With a high latency the entire tarball might be extracted between events, so you will only get one home directory notification event.

FSEventStreamCreateRelativeToDevice takes an additional argument, a dev_t for a device to watch. This dev_t is easy to obtain using **stat()**:

```
NSString *pathOnDevice = "/Volumens/Vikki";
struct stat statbuf;
int result = stat([path fileSystemRepresentation], &statbuf);
if (result == -1) // handle error
dev_t deviceToWatch = statbuf.st_dev;
```

If you have a stream and want to see what device it is watching, use this call:

dev_t **FSEventStreamGetDeviceBeingWatched** (ConstFSEventStreamRef streamRef);

This returns the device the stream is watching. If the stream is not watching a device, it returns zero.

The flags parameter can be one of these values or a bitwise-OR of flags you want to combine:

```
kFSEventStreamCreateFlagNone
kFSEventStreamCreateFlagUseCFTypes
kFSEventStreamCreateFlagNoDefer
kFSEventStreamCreateFlagWatchRoot
```

kFSEventStreamCreateFlagUseCFTypes tells FSEvents that your callback function will be given a **CFArray** containing **CFStrings** of the paths have been modified. A C array of UTF-8 C strings is passed otherwise.

kFSEventStreamCreateFlagNoDefer controls what happens when the latency timer expires. **fseventsd** waits for the latency period before notifying your application if this flag is not set, leading to a possible double length of time before you get notifications. By setting this flag, you tell **fseventsd** to deliver any pending events as soon as the latency timer expires. You will want to set this flag if you have an interactive program to improve responsiveness. Background programs should leave this flag clear.

Setting kFSEventStreamCreateFlagWatchRoot requests notifications of changes along the paths you are watching. If you watch /Users/markd/blah/ for notifications with this flag set, you will receive a notification if the blah directory is moved or if the markd directory is moved or deleted, on up to the root of the path.

The stream objects have retain / release semantics. Use **FSEventStreamRetain** to increment the reference count and **FSEventStreamRelease** to decrement it.

Hook up to the runloop

You need to schedule your stream with a runloop and runloop mode:

```
void FSEventStreamScheduleWithRunLoop (FSEventStreamRef streamRef,
                                       CFRunLoopRef runLoop,
                                       CFStringRef runLoopMode);
```

You can get the **CFRunLoop** from an **NSRunLoop** by using **-getCFRunLoop**.

Then tell FSEvents to start feeding you events:

```
Boolean FSEventStreamStart (FSEventStreamRef streamRef);
```

FSEventStreamStart() returns True if it succeeds, False if it fails. If it fails, you won't be getting any events from **fseventsd**.

Your callback will be called for new events while the run loop runs. Tell FSEvents to stop sending events once you are done. You can re-start the stream if you wish, and the event stream will pick up where it left off.

```
void FSEventStreamStop (FSEventStreamRef streamRef);
```

And then unschedule it from the runloop with these calls:

```
void FSEventStreamUnscheduleFromRunLoop (FSEventStreamRef streamRef,
                                         CFRunLoopRef runLoop,
                                         CFStringRef runLoopMode);
```

And then invalidate the stream. This unschedules it from any runloops it has been scheduled in.

```
void FSEventStreamInvalidate (FSEventStreamRef streamRef)l
```

Finally, release it when done.

The FSEvents callback

The callback function should have this signature:

```
void callbackFunction (ConstFSEventStreamRef streamRef,
                       void *context,
                       size_t numEvents,
                       void *eventPaths,
                       const FSEventStreamEventFlags eventFlags[],
                       const FSEventStreamEventId eventIds[]);
```

streamRef is the event stream created earlier. context is the pointer you supplied as the callback info when the stream was created. numEvents tells you how many events to process in this call.

If you set kFSEventStreamCreateFlagUseCFTypes during stream creation, eventPaths will be a pointer to a **CFArray** containing numEvents **CFString**s. If you did not set this flag, eventPaths is a C array of numEvents UTF-8 C strings.

eventFlags and eventIds contain numEvents elements, too, which parallel the eventPaths array. eventIds contains the 64-bit event id for each path. eventFlags is the bitwise-OR of zero or more of these flags:

```
kFSEventStreamEventFlagMustScanSubDirs
kFSEventStreamEventFlagUserDropped
kFSEventStreamEventFlagKernelDropped
```

Sometimes events are dropped because they happen too fast, in which case the MustScanSubDirs flag will be set. You then need to scan the directory and any of its subdirectories to see wh̶a̶t̶ ̶h̶a̶v̶e changed. The UserDropped or KernelDropped flag will be set depend̶i̶ ̶ ̶e̶n̶ed. This is mainly informational. There is not a lot you can do about drop̶ ̶ ̶ ̶ ̶in debugging. You just need to look at the MustScanSubDirs flag.

```
kFSEventStreamEventFlagEventIdsWrapped
```

The end of time has been reached, and the 64-bit event ID has wrapped event ID, say to know when to ignore historic event notifications, you w̶ ̶ ̶ ̶ ̶d̶ value.

```
kFSEventStreamEventFlagHistoryDone
```

When you specify a sinceWhen value at stream creation, FSEvents will feed you any events that happened since then and now. An event is sent with this flag set to mark the end of the historical events. Any events received from now on will be new. Ignore the path if you get this flag.

```
kFSEventStreamEventFlagRootChanged
```

This is another special event, which is sent when one of the parent directories of a watched path change. When this flag is set, the event ID is zero, and the path is the watched path that changed. This path might not exist because it or something earlier in the path may have been renamed or removed. You will only get this event if you include kFSEventStreamCreateFlagWatchRoot when you created the stream.

```
kFSEventStreamEventFlagMount
kFSEventStreamEventFlagUnmount
```

This is another special event sent when a volume is mounted or unmounted on a directory (or subdirectory) that you are watching. The path passed to the callback is the volume mount point. You will not receive this event if you create an event stream relative to a device, only if you are watching events system-wide. These notifications are mainly informational. If you're wanting to monitor disk mounts and unmounts, or wish to exert some kind of control over them, you will want to use the disk arbitration framework.

Miscellaneous calls

You can find out the current event ID, either system-wide or for a specific stream.

FSEventStreamEventId **FSEventsGetCurrentEventId** (void);

FSEventStreamEventId **FSEventStreamGetLatestEventId** (ConstFSEventStreamRef streamRef);

The event ID returned is the current system-wide event ID or the most recent one the stream has seen at the time of the call. Due to the asynchronous nature of all of this stuff, this value can change after you make this call and potentially use the event ID elsewhere.

You can ask for the last event ID for a given device before a given time:

```
FSEventStreamEventId
FSEventsGetLastEventIdForDeviceBeforeTime (dev_t dev, CFAbsoluteTime time);
```

This is a conservative value. That is, the returned event ID can be used as the sinceWhen parameter for an **FSEventStreamCreateRelativeToDevice** call. You will not miss any unseen events, but you might see some older events. Be aware time can be slippery. The system clock can change due to daylight savings time changes, or even if the user's laptop travels to a different time zone.

CFAbsoluteTime is the number of seconds since January 1, 2001. To get a CFAbsoluteTime from an **NSDate**, you can pass the **NSDate** to **CFDateGetAbsoluteTime**. If you have a posix timestamp, which is 1970-based, subtract kCFAbsoluteTimeIntervalSince1970 from it.

When you are creating a stream relative to a device and you are using a stored event ID, you should check to make sure that the device you are using is the one you think you're using. **FSEventsCopyUUIDForDevice** will give you a unique identifier for a given device. You can store this with your event ID and compare the device identifier the next time you create an event stream.

```
CFUUIDRef FSEventsCopyUUIDForDevice (dev_t dev);
```

This function returns a pointer to a UUID with copy semantics, so you are responsible for **CFRelease()**ing it when you are done. You will get NULL back if there is no UUID available, say for a read-only device, or if there are no historical events available. In that case, do not supply a sinceWhen value other than kFSEventStreamEventIdSinceNow when creating the stream.

You can extract the UUID's bytes from the CFUUID object, or you can convert between string representations of the UUID and a CFUUID object by using these calls:

```
CFUUIDRef CFUUIDCreateFromString (CFAllocatorRef alloc, CFStringRef uuidStr);
```

```
CFStringRef CFUUIDCreateString (CFAllocatorRef alloc, CFUUIDRef uuid);
```

These calls create objects, so you are responsible for **CFRelease()**ing them. If you are going to be saving UUIDs, it is easiest to convert it to a string, store that string, and then convert it back to a CFUUID when needed. You can compare UUID equality easily by testing for string equality.

Example

Example 16.5 shows a program that displays all of the historical events for the boot drive that have happened since it was last run. After that, it displays new events as they occur. To keep things simple, it exits after seeing 20 new events. It saves the device UUID and last event ID to the user defaults when it quits.

Example 16.5   fsevents.m

```
// fsevents.m -- Watch file system events.

// gcc -std=c99 -g -Wall -framework Foundation -framework CoreServices
//      -o fsevents fsevents.m

#import <Foundation/Foundation.h>

#import <CoreServices/CoreServices.h>  // FSEvents()
#import <sys/stat.h>                    // stat()
```

```
// Dump out all historic events before exiting after seeing N new events.
#define MAX_CALLBACKS 20
static BOOL g_newEvents = YES;

// String constants so typos won't cause debugging headaches.
#define LAST_EVENT_KEY @"fseventsSampleLastEvent"
#define DEVICE_UUID_KEY @"fseventsSampleDeviceUUID"


// Lookup table for displaying human-readabile translations of flags
typedef struct FlagMap {
    int bitflag;
    const char *description;
} FlagMap;

static FlagMap flagmap[] = {
    { kFSEventStreamEventFlagMustScanSubDirs, "must scan subdirs"     },
    { kFSEventStreamEventFlagUserDropped,     "user dropped events"   },
    { kFSEventStreamEventFlagKernelDropped,   "kernel dropped events" },
    { kFSEventStreamEventFlagEventIdsWrapped, "event ids wrapped"     },
    { kFSEventStreamEventFlagHistoryDone,     "history playback done" },
    { kFSEventStreamEventFlagRootChanged,     "root changed"          },
    { kFSEventStreamEventFlagMount,           "mounted"               },
    { kFSEventStreamEventFlagUnmount,         "unmounted"             }
};


static void callbackFunction (ConstFSEventStreamRef stream,
                              void *clientCallBackInfo,
                              size_t numEvents,
                              void *eventPaths,
                              const FSEventStreamEventFlags eventFlags[],
                              const FSEventStreamEventId eventIds[]) {
    printf ("----------------\n");
    printf ("event count: %lu\n", numEvents);

    // Keep track of the eventIds so we can save it off when we're
    // done looking at events.
    FSEventStreamEventId currentEvent = 0;

    for (int i = 0; i < numEvents; i++) {
        // Add an extra blank line for breathing room.
        printf ("\n");

        // Dump out the arguments.
        printf ("path[%d] : %s : id %llu\n",
                i, ((char **)eventPaths)[i], eventIds[i]);

        FSEventStreamEventFlags flags = eventFlags[i];
        printf ("  flags: %x\n", (int)flags);

        if (flags == kFSEventStreamEventFlagNone) {
            printf ("    something happened\n");
        }

        // Display all of the set flags.
        FlagMap *scan = flagmap;
        FlagMap *stop = scan + sizeof(flagmap) / sizeof(*flagmap);
        while (scan < stop) {
```

```
            if (flags & scan->bitflag) {
                printf ("    %s\n", scan->description);
            }
            scan++;
        }

        if (flags & kFSEventStreamEventFlagHistoryDone) {
            // We can stop printing historic events.
            g_newEvents = YES;

            // Don't drop into new event case.
            if (i == numEvents - 1) goto done;
        }

        // Remember what our last event was.
        currentEvent = eventIds[i];
    }

    // Don't count history events against our callback count.
    if (!g_newEvents) goto done;

    static int s_callbackCount;
    s_callbackCount++;

    printf ("%d left\n", MAX_CALLBACKS - s_callbackCount);

    if (s_callbackCount >= MAX_CALLBACKS) {
        NSUserDefaults *defs = [NSUserDefaults standardUserDefaults];

        // Save the last event ID seen into user defaults.
        NSNumber *eventIdNumber = [NSNumber numberWithUnsignedLongLong: currentEvent];
        [defs setObject: eventIdNumber  forKey: LAST_EVENT_KEY];

        // Save the device UUID.
        dev_t device = FSEventStreamGetDeviceBeingWatched (stream);

        if (device != 0) {
            CFUUIDRef devUUID = FSEventsCopyUUIDForDevice (device);

            if (devUUID != NULL) {
                CFStringRef stringForm =
                    CFUUIDCreateString(kCFAllocatorDefault, devUUID);
                [defs setObject: (id)stringForm  forKey: DEVICE_UUID_KEY];
            }
            CFRelease (devUUID);
        }
        // Make sure it reaches the disk.
        [defs synchronize];

        printf ("all done\n");
        exit (EXIT_SUCCESS);
    }
done:
    return;

} // callbackFunction


int main (void) {
```

```
NSAutoreleasePool *pool = [[NSAutoreleasePool alloc] init];

// Watch the whole device.
NSString *path = @"/";

// Get the device ID.
struct stat statbuf;
int result = stat([path fileSystemRepresentation], &statbuf);
if (result == -1) {
    printf ("error with stat.  %d\n", errno);
    return EXIT_FAILURE;
}
dev_t device = statbuf.st_dev;

// Find the last event we saw.
FSEventStreamEventId lastEvent = kFSEventStreamEventIdSinceNow;
NSUserDefaults *defs = [NSUserDefaults standardUserDefaults];
NSNumber *lastEventNumber = [defs objectForKey: LAST_EVENT_KEY];

if (lastEventNumber != nil) {
    // Make sure it's the right device by making sure the UUIDs match.
    NSString *uuidString = [defs stringForKey: DEVICE_UUID_KEY];
    CFUUIDRef devUUID = FSEventsCopyUUIDForDevice (device);
    CFStringRef devString = CFUUIDCreateString (kCFAllocatorDefault, devUUID);

    if ([uuidString isEqualToString: (id)devString]) {
        // We have a good point to pick up from.
        lastEvent = [lastEventNumber unsignedLongLongValue];
        printf ("Picking up where we left off:  %llu\n",
                lastEvent);
        // We should be getting some history then.
        g_newEvents = NO;
    } else {
        printf ("uuid mismatch: %s vs %s\n",
                [uuidString UTF8String], [(id)devString UTF8String]);
    }
}

CFAbsoluteTime latency = 3.0; // latency in seconds
NSArray *paths = [NSArray arrayWithObject: path];

FSEventStreamRef stream =
    FSEventStreamCreateRelativeToDevice (kCFAllocatorDefault,
                                         callbackFunction,
                                         NULL, // context
                                         device,
                                         (CFArrayRef)paths, // relative to device
                                         lastEvent,
                                         latency,
                                         kFSEventStreamCreateFlagNone);

if (stream == NULL) {
    printf ("could not create stream\n");
    return EXIT_FAILURE;
}

NSRunLoop *loop = [NSRunLoop currentRunLoop];
FSEventStreamScheduleWithRunLoop (stream, [loop getCFRunLoop],
                                  kCFRunLoopDefaultMode);
BOOL success = FSEventStreamStart (stream);
```

```
    if (!success) {
        printf ("could not start FSEvent stream\n");
        return EXIT_FAILURE;
    }

    [loop run];

    // This isn't actually reached, but you would clean up the
    // stream like this.
    FSEventStreamStop (stream);
    FSEventStreamUnscheduleFromRunLoop (stream, [loop getCFRunLoop],
                                        kCFRunLoopDefaultMode);
    FSEventStreamInvalidate (stream);
    FSEventStreamRelease (stream);

    [pool drain];

    return EXIT_SUCCESS;

} // main
```

And some sample runs. Here is the first run, watching new events.

```
$ ./fsevents
-----------------
event count: 1

path[0] : Users/markd/Library/Preferences/ : id 8319636
   flags: 0
     something happened
19 left
-----------------
event count: 2

path[0] : Users/markd/.emacs.d/auto-save-list/ : id 8319642
   flags: 0
     something happened

path[1] : Users/markd/Writing/core-osx/kqueue-chap/Projects/ : id 8319654
   flags: 0
     something happened
18 left
-----------------
...
```

You can see that the first callback saw a change in my preferences directory. The second callback had two events: one for an editor autosave list and the other editing this chapter's source file.

Next, the system has had a chance to do stuff without **fsevents** running.

```
$ ./fsevents
Picking up where we left off!   8320630
-----------------
event count: 1

path[0] : Users/markd/Library/Preferences/ : id 8320646
   flags: 0
     something happened
-----------------
```

```
event count: 1

path[0] : Users/markd/Library/Caches/Metadata/Safari/History/ : id 8320710
  flags: 0
    something happened
-----------------
event count: 1

path[0] : Users/markd/Documents/iPhone.vpdoc/pages/d/ : id 8320803
  flags: 0
    something happened
-----------------
```

Here you can see that while **fsevents** was not running, the preferences directory was updated, a web page was visited, and a VoodooPad document was edited.

You can see the current settings with the **defaults** command.

```
$ defaults read fsevents
{
    fseventsSampleDeviceUUID = "0138CB9E-EBBF-424B-8B39-AF5284E936BC";
    fseventsSampleLastEvent = 8321353;
}
```

And you can use **defaults** to remove the settings to run the program from a beginning state again.

```
$ defaults delete fsevents
```

Exercises

1. Add kqueue support to `fsevents.m` so that it will keep on showing all new events until the program is interrupted by a Control-C (SIGINT). Save off the event stream information and device UUID when that happens.

2. Modify `fsevents.m` to watch the entire system. Watch what happens if you mount a file system and modify things on that file system. You can create read/write disk images with Disk Utility.

3. Modify `fsevents.m` to watch more than one directory. Also watch what happens when you move a directory being watched. Find out where the directory got moved to by opening the root of the directory hierarchy with **open()** and then use **fcntl()** with F_GETPATH to see where it is living in the file system.

17

Bonjour

Bonjour, which is Apple's implementation of the Zeroconf standard, is a very compelling idea. It extends the idea of DNS so that things on the network can declare their intentions. For example, when a Zeroconf-compliant device is plugged into a network, it can declare "I am grouse.local, and my IP address is 168.254.32.1!" If another device already has that IP address, it can complain. The new device will then change its address. Thus, a network device can get an IP address without a DHCP server. This capability is known as *link local addressing*.

However, the beauty of Zeroconf does not end at devices and IP addresses. It also allows services to declare their name, type, address, and port number. Thus, the local network is informed of new devices and services as they are added. Furthermore, it adds the ability for the services to be browsed. That is, if you are looking for a type of service, you can ask for all the information about all the individual servers on a particular network.

The DNS standard actually already had a mechanism by which a service could be advertised – the SRV record. For example, to find all the ftp servers in the `bignerdranch.com` domain, your ftp client would ask for the SRV record for `_ftp._tcp.bignerdranch.com`. There are two reasons why you have probably never heard of the SRV record:

1. No one uses it.

2. Only a DNS server can advertise the service.

To make it possible for many, many machines to advertise services on a network, Multicast DNS was created. Essentially, every machine is running a Multicast DNS server. This daemon is `/usr/sbin/mDNSResponder`.

Thus, Zeroconf is a clever marriage of link local addressing and multicast DNS. Zeroconf is the name of the standard, and Bonjour is Apple's implementation of that standard. There are three different APIs for dealing with Bonjour:

1. The mach-level API called DNSServiceDiscovery is what all the other APIs are based upon.

2. The C API in the CoreServices framework uses DNSServiceDiscovery but integrates more easily with the rest of Core Foundation.

3. The Objective-C classes **NSNetService** and **NSNetServiceBrowser** are part of the Foundation framework.

In this chapter, we will use the Objective-C API to let our chatter server declare its availability and let our chatter client browse for servers.

Publishing an NSNetService

In a server, you advertise the availability of your service by creating an instance of **NSNetService** and publishing it. You give the server a name, you tell it what service it provides, what port it runs on, and the name of the network it is part of (the domain). The important methods are:

```
- (id) initWithDomain: (NSString *) domain
                 type: (NSString *) type
                 name: (NSString *) name
                 port: (int) port
```

This is the initializer that you use when creating a service to be published. You may pass in @"" as the domain, and the host's default domain will be used. The type is a string of the form "service_type.protocol". As a convention, host names are not prepended with an underscore, whereas service and protocols are. The protocol is usually either _tcp or _udp. (For our example, the type will be @"_chatter._tcp.".) You can use any Unicode string as the name. The only tricky bit is that your name may conflict with another. The port is the port number upon which the server is waiting.

```
- (void) publish
```

This method advertises the service on the network. It returns immediately, and the delegate is informed later if it was a failure.

The delegate can implement:

```
- (void) netService: (NSNetService *) sender
    didNotPublish: (NSDictionary *) errorDict
```

Notifies the delegate that the service offered by sender could not be published. You can use the dictionary keys NSNetServicesErrorCode and NSNetServicesErrorDomain to determine the cause of the error. A common error is that the name of your server was already claimed by another server in the same domain.

Make chatterserver Zeroconf-compliant

Copy chatterserver-runloop.m to chatterserver-bonjour.m and edit it. To make chatterserver Bonjour-aware, you will need to accept a command-line parameter with the service name, along with creating and configuring the **NSNetService** object. **NSNetService** can take a delegate, and it uses the delegate to report errors. So far, nothing in **chatterserver** is Objective-C object-oriented goodness, so you will need a small class just to be a delegate. Place this right after the wall of header file #includes:

```
@interface NetServiceDelegate : NSObject <NSNetServiceDelegate>
@end

@implementation NetServiceDelegate

- (void) netService: (NSNetService *) sender
    didNotPublish: (NSDictionary *) errorDict {

    NSLog (@"failed to publish net service: %@", errorDict);

} // didNotPublish
```

```
@end // NetServiceDelegate
```

Now edit main to do the rest of the stuff:

```
int main (int argc, char *argv[]) {
    NSAutoreleasePool *pool = [[NSAutoreleasePool alloc] init];

    if (argc == 1) {
        fprintf (stderr, "usage: %s <servicename> [ipv6]\n", argv[0]);
        return EXIT_FAILURE;
    }

    int listenFd = StartListening (useIPv6);

    if (listenFd == -1) {
        fprintf (stderr, "*** Could not open listening socket.\n");
        goto bailout;
    }

    RegisterRunLoopSocket (listenFd, listenCallback, YES, NULL);

    NSString *serviceName = [NSString stringWithUTF8String: argv[1]];
    NSNetService *netService =
        [[NSNetService alloc] initWithDomain: @""
                              type: @"_chatter._tcp."
                              name: serviceName
                              port: kPortNumber];
    NetServiceDelegate *delegate
        = [[[NetServiceDelegate alloc] init] autorelease];
    netService.delegate = delegate;
    [netService publish];

        ...
```

Et voilà, the trick, she is done! A Bonjour-aware server. Build and run it. It must be run with at least one argument – the name of the service. You can run it with two arguments to put the server into IPv6 mode.

Browsing Net Services

When a client needs to find a service, it multicasts a message onto the network. The published servers respond. Notice, however, that with busy servers on a busy or slow network, this might take some time. So a browser is told to start a search, and then, as responses come in, the delegate is informed.

NSNetServiceBrowser has the following method:

```
- (void)searchForServicesOfType:(NSString *)type
                       inDomain:(NSString *)domainString
```

This method kicks off the search for services of the given type in the given domain. Once again, @"" can be supplied as the domain.

The delegate gets sent these messages:

```
- (void)netServiceBrowser:(NSNetServiceBrowser *)aNetServiceBrowser
          didFindService:(NSNetService *)aNetService
             moreComing:(BOOL)moreComing
```

This method gets called as net services are discovered. If there are several to be processed, the moreComing flag will be YES. Thus, you will know to wait before updating your user interface.

```
- (void)netServiceBrowser:(NSNetServiceBrowser *)aNetServiceBrowser
         didRemoveService:(NSNetService *)aNetService
               moreComing:(BOOL)moreComing
```

This method gets sent if a server disappears.

Make ChatterClient browse for servers

Open the CFChatterClient project. First, we are going to replace the hostname text field with a combo box. Open CFChatterClientAppDelegate.h. Change the type of the _hostname pointer and add a mutable array for the discovered services, as well as a net service browser.

```
#import <Cocoa/Cocoa.h>

@interface CFChatterClientAppDelegate : NSObject <NSApplicationDelegate> {
    NSWindow *window;

    IBOutlet NSTextField *_usernameField;
    IBOutlet NSButton    *_joinLeaveButton;

    IBOutlet NSTextView  *_transcript;
    IBOutlet NSTextField *_messageField;
    IBOutlet NSButton    *_sendButton;

    CFSocketNativeHandle  _sockfd;
    CFSocketRef _socketRef;

    NSNetServiceBrowser *_browser;
    NSMutableArray      *_services;
    IBOutlet NSComboBox *_hostField;
}
@property (nonatomic, assign) IBOutlet NSWindow *window;
@property (nonatomic, readonly, getter=isConnected) BOOL connected;

- (IBAction) sendMessage: (id) sender;
- (IBAction) join: (id) sender;
- (IBAction) leave: (id) sender;

@end // CFChatterClientAppDelegate
```

Save CFChatterClientAppDelegate.h and open MainMenu.xib. Remove the host name field and add a combo box in its place. Point its datasource to the app delegate, and point the app delegate to the combo box as well. Inspect the combo box and check the box that says "Uses data source."

Update the -awakeFromNib method in CFChatterClientAppDelegate.m, create a browser, and start the search:

```
- (void) awakeFromNib {
    // Prepopulate the username field as a convenience.x
    [_usernameField setStringValue: NSUserName()];
    [self updateUI];

    _browser = [[NSNetServiceBrowser alloc] init];
    _services = [[NSMutableArray alloc] init];
```

```
    _browser.delegate = self;
    [_browser searchForServicesOfType: @"_chatter._tcp."
              inDomain: @"local."];
    NSLog (@"Begun browsing: %@", _browser);
} // awakeFromNib
```

Before using a discovered net service, you will want to resolve it – that is, look up an address for it. This is another method that returns immediately but actually waits in the background for success.

If the net service has not resolved, when you ask it for its array of addresses (yes, there might be more than one), it will return an empty array.

Add these browser delegate methods to CFChatterClientAppDelegate.m:

```
- (void)netServiceBrowser: (NSNetServiceBrowser *) aNetServiceBrowser
        didFindService: (NSNetService *) aNetService
           moreComing: (BOOL) moreComing
{
    NSLog (@"Adding new service: %@", aNetService);
    [_services addObject: aNetService];
    if (!moreComing) {
        [_hostField reloadData];
    }
} // didFindService

- (void)netServiceBrowser: (NSNetServiceBrowser *) aNetServiceBrowser
        didRemoveService: (NSNetService *) aNetService
           moreComing: (BOOL) moreComing
{
    NSLog (@"Removing service");
    for (NSNetService *service in [_services objectEnumerator]) {
        if ([[service name] isEqual: [aNetService name]] &&
            [[service type] isEqual: [aNetService type]] &&
            [[service domain] isEqual: [aNetService domain]]) {

            [_services removeObject: service];
            break;
        }
    }
    if (!moreComing) {
        [_hostField reloadData];
    }
} // didRemoveService
```

Add methods for the combo box data source:

```
- (int) numberOfItemsInComboBox: (NSComboBox *) aComboBox {
    return [_services count];
} // numberOfItemsInComboBox

- (id) comboBox: (NSComboBox *) aComboBox  objectValueForItemAtIndex: (int) index {
    NSNetService *item;
    item = [_services objectAtIndex:index];
    return [item name];
} // objectValueForItemAtIndex

- (unsigned int) comboBox: (NSComboBox *) aComboBox
                indexOfItemWithStringValue:(NSString *) string {
    unsigned int max = [_services count];
```

```
    for (unsigned int i = 0; i < max; i++) {
        NSNetService *item = [_services objectAtIndex: i];
        if ([string isEqual:[item name]]) {
            return i;
        }
    }
    return 0;
} // indexOfItemWithStringValue
```

In **-join:**, kick off a resolution of the net service and then connect when the address is resolved.

```
- (IBAction) join: (id) sender {
    if ([self isConnected]) {
        [_messageField setStringValue: @"unsubscribe first!"];
    } else {
        NSNetService *currentService =
            [_services objectAtIndex: [_hostField indexOfSelectedItem]];
        currentService.delegate = self;
        [currentService resolveWithTimeout: 30];
    }

} // join

- (void) netServiceDidResolveAddress: (NSNetService *) currentService {
    NSArray *addresses = [currentService addresses];

    // Take the first address.
    NSData *address = [addresses objectAtIndex: 0];

    NSString *username = [_usernameField stringValue];
    [self connectToAddress: address  asUser: username];

    [self updateUI];

    if ([self isConnected]) {
        NSString *hostname = @"TOOO";
        NSString *connectMessage =
            [NSString stringWithFormat: @"( * * * connected to %@ as %@ * * * ) \n",
                hostname, username];
        [self appendMessage: connectMessage];
        [[_messageField window] makeFirstResponder: _messageField];
    }

} // netServiceDidResolveAddress

- (void) netService: (NSNetService *) sender
        didNotResolve: (NSDictionary *) errorDict {

    NSString *errorString = [NSString stringWithFormat: @"Unable to resolve %@",
                                [sender name]];
    [_messageField setStringValue: errorString];
} // didNotResolve
```

We're not connecting to a hostname anymore, but we have gotten an Internet address encoded as an **NSData**. Change **-connectToHost:asUser:** to **-connectToData:asUser:**, such that the method signature takes the **NSData**, and removing the unnecessary hostname check.

```
- (void) connectToAddress: (NSData *) address asUser: (NSString *) username {
    NSString *errorMessage = nil;
```

```
    int sysError = noErr;

    if (_sockfd != kInvalidSocket) [self closeConnection];

    // sanity-check our nickname before trying to connect
    if (username.length == 0 || username.length > 8) {
        errorMessage = @"Username must be between 1 and 8 characters long.";
        goto bailout;
    }

    _sockfd = SocketConnectedToAddress (address);
    if (_sockfd == -1) {
        errorMessage = @"Could not connect.";
        sysError = errno;
        goto bailout;
    }

    // UTF-8 length could be greater than the number of characters.
    const char *name = [username UTF8String];
    ...
```

And finally, add the new **SocketConnectedToAddress** function. It works like
SocketConnectedToHostNamed, but instead of looking up a host by name, it takes the address data
given to us by Bonjour. You'll want to put a forward reference at the top of the file, and then implement
the function:

```
static int SocketConnectedToAddress (NSData *data) {
    struct sockaddr_storage server_addr;
    [data getBytes: &server_addr length: data.length];

    // Get a socket.
    int sockfd = socket (server_addr.ss_family, SOCK_STREAM, 0);

    if (sockfd == -1) {
        perror ("        socket");
        goto bailout;
    }

    int err = connect (sockfd, (struct sockaddr *) &server_addr,
                       server_addr.ss_len);
    if (err == -1) {
        perror ("        connect");
        close (sockfd);
        sockfd = -1;
    }

bailout:
    return sockfd;

} // SocketConnectedToAddress
```

That's it – build and run it. If your server is running, its name should appear in the combo box. If you
have several servers running, you should be able to choose among them.

For the More Curious: TXT Records

Besides the standard information for a service (host, port, name), the DNS record used to publish the
services has a TXT record. This is a place where you can put any sort of data that clients might want

to know about. For example, your chatter server might want to advertise the number of users already connected. It could use the TXT record to do this. **NSNetService** has a method that would be used on the server side:

```
- (BOOL) setTXTRecordData: (NSData *) data;
```

On the client side, you would ask the **NSNetService** for the data using:

```
- (NSData *)TXTRecordData;
```

Of course, the server might change the TXT record. (For example, if more people subscribe, your **chatterd** server would want to change the advertised number of subscribers.) On the client, you would become a delegate of the **NSNetService**. When the TXT record is changed, you will be sent:

```
- (void)netService:(NSNetService *)sender
       didUpdateTXTRecordData:(NSData *)data;
```

Exercises

1. Using the TXT record, have the **chatterd** server advertise the number of subscribers. On the client, display the number of subscribers for each server in the server list pop-up.

18

Multiprocessing

All modern operating systems are *multiprocessing*, meaning that multiple independent programs are running simultaneously and sharing the system's resources. The OS time-slices among the runnable programs, dividing the available CPU time among runnable processes, that is, those processes that are not blocked waiting for some event such as I/O completion.

Process Scheduling

The scheduler is the part of the OS that figures out which process should get the CPU next. It often uses information such as process priority, how much CPU time a process has previously gotten, and whether it has just completed an I/O operation in making this decision.

Each process has an associated *niceness* that influences its priority. Niceness is specified by an integer in the range from -20 through +20. By default, processes have a niceness of 0. The higher the niceness number, the lower the process' priority: nicer processes are less demanding about how much CPU time they get.

You can start a process with a specific niceness number using the **nice** command. You can change the niceness of an already running process using the **renice** command. You can "nice down" ("down" in terms of priority; you are in fact increasing the niceness number) your own programs, but you cannot "nice up" a program unless you have superuser privileges.

You can think of the scheduler as having a list of processes with their individual priorities, as shown in Figure 18.1. Those processes that are not blocked are put into a run queue in order of their priority. When it is time to run a new process, the scheduler pulls a process off the front of the queue, lets it run until it blocks for some reason or its time slice expires, and then sticks it back in the queue.

Figure 18.1   The scheduler

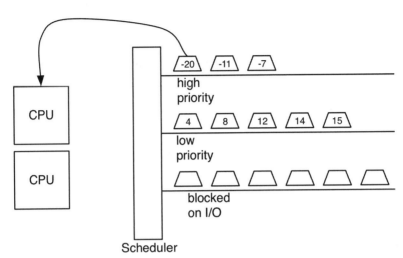

You can examine the average length of the run queue with the **uptime** command:

```
18:28  up 31 days, 20:40, 3 users, load averages: 0.29 0.29 0.27
```

The three load averages at the end of the output represent the number of runnable processes (the depth of the run queue) over the last 1, 5, and 15 minutes. Here, you can see that the average system load over the last minute is about half what it was over the preceding five and fifteen minutes. A general rule of thumb is that a healthy machine, CPU-wise, has a load average at or less than twice the number of processors.

Mac OS X's load average just reports the depth of the run queue. It does not include the time blocked in disk I/O, which some Unix-like OSs (including Linux) report.

Convenience Functions

Starting new processes can be a powerful tool in your programming arsenal. Unix comes with a lot of little command-line utilities that perform useful functions. Sometimes it makes more sense to take advantage of these utilities rather than reimplementing their behavior. For example, you may have a Perl script that strips tags from HTML. If your application has a need for that kind of tag-stripping feature, it can be easier to start the Perl script and feed it your HTML rather than playing around with regular expression code in Objective-C.

The easiest way to start another program is to use the **system()** function. This will start a program, wait until it finishes, and then return the result code. **system()** actually passes control to a new shell, /bin/sh, so you can use shell features like redirection.

```
int system (const char *string);
```

The return value from **system()** is the result value returned from the program. Otherwise, you get -1, and errno is set if there was an error before starting the shell. A return value of 127 means the shell failed for some reason, probably due to bad syntax in the command string. **system()** invokes the shell with the -c argument, passing in the command line as the next argument after the -c. You can do the same from your shell if you get this error and want to experiment with your command line from the Terminal.

If you want to actually read or write to the program you start, use **popen()** to start the program and open a pipe to it. **pclose()** closes the connection:

```
FILE *popen (const char *command, const char *type);

int pclose (FILE *stream);
```

Like **system()**, **popen()** invokes a shell to run the command. Example 18.1 is a little program that **popen()**s the **cal** program to get a current calendar. Just for fun, the output from **cal** gets run through **rev** to reverse the lines, which shows that pipelines work in **popen()**. The program does the equivalent of a head -9 by only reading the first nine lines.

Example 18.1   pcal.m

```
// pcal.m -- display a calendar using popen

// gcc -std=c99 -g -Wall -Wextra -o pcal pcal.m

#import <stdio.h>   // perror(), popen(), printf()
#import <stdlib.h>  // EXIT_SUCCESS

#define BUFFER_SIZE (4096)
static const int kLinesToPrint = 9;

int main (void) {
    int result = EXIT_FAILURE;

    // Reverse the lines just for fun.
    FILE *pipeline = popen("cal 2011 | rev", "r");
    if (!pipeline) {
        perror("popen");
        return result;
    }

    char buffer[BUFFER_SIZE];
    for (int i = 0; i < kLinesToPrint; i++) {
        char *line = fgets (buffer, sizeof(buffer), pipeline);

        if (line != NULL) {
            printf("%s", buffer);

        } else if (feof(pipeline)) {
            // All done
            break;

        } else if (ferror(pipeline)) {
            perror ("fgets");
            goto bailout;

        } else {
            // Shouldn't happen.
            fputs ("fgets returned NULL without EOF or error\n", stderr);
```

```
                goto bailout;
        }
    }
    result = EXIT_SUCCESS;

bailout:
    pclose (pipeline);
    return result;
}  // main
```

Here is a sample run of pcal:

```
$ ./pcal
                       1102

          hcraM                   yraurbeF                  yraunaJ
S  F  hT W   uT M  S    S  F  hT W   uT M  S    S  F  hT W   uT M  S
5  4  3  2   1          5  4  3  2   1          1
21 11 01 9   8  7  6    21 11 01 9   8  7  6    8  7  6  5   4  3  2
91 81 71 61  51 41 31   91 81 71 61  51 41 31   51 41 31 21  11 01 9
62 52 42 32  22 12 02   62 52 42 32  22 12 02   22 12 02 91  81 71 61
      13 03  92 82 72         82 72  92 82            72 62  52 42 32
```

The manpage for **popen()** points out that it uses a bidirectional pipe, so you can specify a mode of read and write (r+) instead of just one (r) or the other (w). Unfortunately, using the returned stream both for reading and writing is unlikely to work in practice, as it requires the cooperation of the **popen()**ed process. Use of a bidirectional stream can easily run afoul of the buffering done under the hood by the stream I/O functions. It also raises the specter of deadlock: your process could block writing data to the child process while it blocks writing already-processed data back. Neither process will ever get a chance to drain those full buffers and unblock the other. Your best bet if you need both to read and write to the child process is to either redirect its output to a file and handle that afterwards or, if you must interleave reads and writes, create the child process yourself and use two pipes, one for reading and one for writing.

fork

To create a new process in Unix, you must first make a copy of an existing process. That copy can continue to execute the code of the original process, or it can begin executing another program. The **fork()** system call performs the process copying:

```
pid_t fork (void);
```

fork() makes a copy of the running process, and it is one of the few functions that can return twice. In the original process, called the *parent* process, **fork()** returns the process ID of the new process. In the new process, called the *child* process, **fork()** returns zero. When an error occurs, there is no child process, and **fork()** returns -1 in the parent and sets errno.

As a copy of the parent process, the child inherits the parent process' memory, open files, real and effective user and group IDs, current working directory, signal mask, file mode creation mask (umask), environment, resource limits, and any attached shared memory segments. This copying behavior can be seen in Figure 18.2:

Figure 18.2   Fork

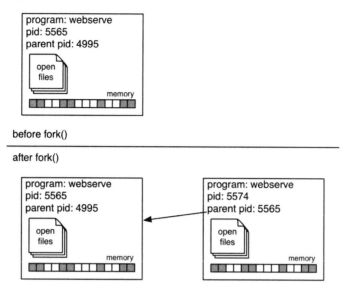

Figure 18.3   Copy on write

Copying that much data sounds time consuming, but Mac OS X takes shortcuts. Rather than duplicate the parent's memory space immediately, it shares the original copy between both parent and child and delays copying until necessary using a technique called *copy on write*, also called COW (see Figure 18.3). All the physical pages that relate to the parent process are marked read-only. When a process tries to write to a page of the "duplicated" memory, the page is first copied for its private use, and each copy becomes the separate, read- and writeable property of one process. The modifying process gets to make its changes, the other process is none the wiser, and no more copying than strictly necessary occurs. This greatly reduces the amount of work the OS does on a **fork()**.

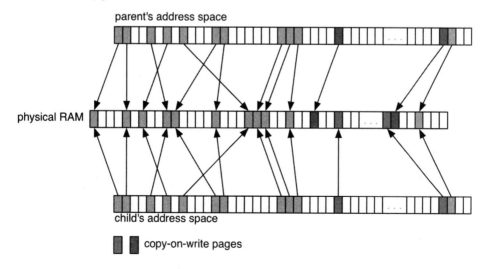

The convenience functions in the previous section – **system()** and **popen()** – call **fork()** under the hood, but, for most purposes, they use more resources than a careful use of **fork()** would, particularly in their invocation of a shell to run the new processes.

Example 18.2 shows a minimal program that forks a child:

Example 18.2   fork.m

```
// fork.m -- show simple use of fork()

// gcc -std=c99 -g -Wall -Wextra -o fork fork.m

#import <unistd.h>      // fork(), pid_t, sleep()
#import <stdlib.h>      // EXIT_SUCCESS, EXIT_FAILURE
#import <stdio.h>       // printf()

int main(void) {
    fputs ("Hello there!", stdout);   // no newline

    pid_t child = fork();

    switch (child) {
        case -1:
            perror ("fork");
            exit (EXIT_FAILURE);

        case 0:
            printf ("\nChild: My parent is %lu.\n", (unsigned long)getppid());
            _exit (EXIT_SUCCESS);

        default:
            printf ("\nParent: My child is %lu.\n", (unsigned long)child);

            // Delay a bit to improve the odds that the child will log before
            // the parent exits.
            sleep (2);
            exit (EXIT_SUCCESS);
    }

    // not reached
    return EXIT_FAILURE;
} // main
```

and a sample run:

```
$ ./fork
Hello there!
Parent: My child is 78733.
Hello there!
Child: My parent is 78732.
```

As with just about everything in Unix-land, there are some gotchas that can catch the unwary. The first involves race conditions between the parent and the child: you are not guaranteed which will run first. You cannot depend on some code being run after the **fork()** in the parent before the child gets scheduled.

The other gotcha relates to how open files are shared between the two processes. Both the parent and child share the same file table entry in the kernel, as shown in Figure 18.4. This means that all of the attributes of the open files are shared, such as the current offset. This is commonly the desired behavior – when you want both child and parent to print to the same standard out, each process will increment the offset in the file when they print, so they'll avoid writing over each other. However, it can also be confusing when your file offsets move from underneath you and you were not expecting them to.

Related to the file table issue is the state of the buffers for buffered I/O. The buffered I/O buffers in the parent's address space get duplicated across the fork (Figure 18.4). If there is data in the buffer before the fork, both the child and the parent could print out the buffered data twice (as you can see in Example 18.2), which is likely not what you want.

Figure 18.4   Files after fork

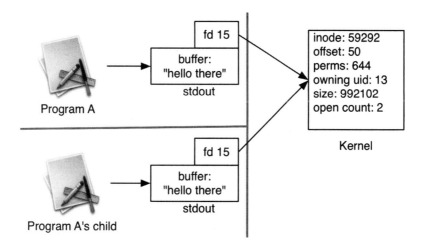

Notice the use of **_exit()** in Example 18.2. It behaves like **exit()**, closing file descriptors and generally cleaning up, but it does not flush the file stream buffers, so you do not have to worry about **_exit()** flushing a buffer for you that has duplicate data. In the example, the newlines in the subsequent **printf()**s flushed the buffer for us.

Notice too that the parent sleeps a bit before exiting. This improves the odds of its still being the child's parent when the child logs its message. If the parent exits before the child writes its message, the child's parent will be process 1. You can see this behavior by deleting the **sleep()** line, recompiling, and rerunning the program. As the output depends on a race condition, it might take a few runs.

Parent and Child Lifetimes

Due to the nature of **fork()**, every process has exactly one parent process, while a parent can have multiple child processes. Unix enforces the rule that, while any process might or might not have children, every process always has a parent process. If a child process' parent exits before the child does, then the child process is adopted by process 1. Under most Unixes, this is the **init** process; under Mac OS X, it is the versatile **launchd**.

When a child process exits, that is not the end of it. After a process terminates, the operating system keeps some information associated with it alive, such as its exit code and system resource usage statistics. Only after this information has been delivered to the child's parent is the process finally allowed to die. Requesting this postmortem information is called *reaping* the child process. You reap the process using one of the **wait()** system calls.

```
pid_t wait (int *status);

pid_t waitpid (pid_t wpid, int *status, int options);

pid_t wait3 (int *status, int options, struct rusage *rusage);

pid_t wait4 (pid_t wpid, int *status, int options, struct rusage *rusage);
```

Calling any one of the wait functions will collect the result code from the child. **wait()** will block until there is a child waiting to be reaped. If multiple child processes are waiting, the **wait()** will return an arbitrary one. If you want to wait for a specific child process, use **waitpid()**. The options that **waitpid()**, **wait3()**, and **wait4()** use are:

WNOHANG   Do not block waiting for a child. Return immediately if there are no exited children.

WUNTRACED   Report job-control actions on children (like being stopped or backgrounded).

wait3() is like **wait()**, and **wait4()** is like **waitpid()**. The one waits on an arbitrary child, while the other waits on a specific one. **wait3()** and **wait4()** also fill in a structure describing the resources consumed by the child. You can find the full struct rusage in /usr/include/sys/resource.h. The more interesting elements of this structure are:

```
struct rusage {
    struct timeval ru_utime;    /* user time used */
    struct timeval ru_stime;    /* system time used */
    long           ru_maxrss;   /* max resident set size */
}
```

These tell you how much CPU time was consumed by the child and the high water mark of its memory usage.

The return value from the child, along with several other useful bits of information, is encoded in the status result returned by all **wait()** functions. Use these macros to pull out the items you are interested in:

WIFEXITED()   Returns true if the process terminated normally via a call to **exit()** or **_exit()**.

WEXITSTATUS()   If WIFEXITED(status) is true, returns the low-order byte of the argument the child passed to **exit()** or **_exit()**. The return value from **main()** is used as the argument to **exit()**.

WIFSIGNALED()   Returns true if the process terminated due to receipt of a signal.

WTERMSIG   If WIFSIGNALED(status) is true, returns the number of the signal that caused the termination of the process.

WCOREDUMP   If WIFSIGNALED(status) is true, returns true if the termination of the process was accompanied by the creation of a core dump.

WIFSTOPPED   Returns true if the process has not terminated, but was just stopped, such as by job control in a shell (for example, Control-Z will suspend a process).

WSTOPSIG   If `WIFSTOPPED(status)` is true, returns the number of the signal that caused the process to stop.

Example 18.3 shows these macros in action:

Example 18.3   status.m

```
// status.m -- play with various child exiting status values

// gcc -g -Wall -o status status.m

#import <errno.h>            // for errno
#import <stdio.h>            // for printf
#import <stdlib.h>           // for EXIT_SUCCESS
#import <string.h>           // for strerror
#import <sys/resource.h>     // for rlimit
#import <sys/time.h>         // for ru_utime and ru_stime in rlimit
#import <sys/types.h>        // for pid_t
#import <sys/wait.h>         // for wait()
#import <unistd.h>           // for fork


void printStatus (int status) {
    if (WIFEXITED(status)) {
        printf ("program exited normally.  Return value is %d",
                WEXITSTATUS(status));

    } else if (WIFSIGNALED(status)) {
        printf ("program exited on signal %d", WTERMSIG(status));
        if (WCOREDUMP(status)) {
            printf (" (core dumped)");
        }

    } else {
        printf ("other exit value");
    }

    printf ("\n");

} // printStatus


int main (int argc, char *argv[]) {
    int status;

    // normal exit
    if (fork() == 0) {
        _exit (23);
    }

    wait (&status);
    printStatus (status);

    // die by a signal (SIGABRT)
    if (fork() == 0) {
        abort ();
    }

    wait (&status);
```

```
    printStatus (status);

    // die by crashing
    if (fork() == 0) {
        int *blah = (int *)0xFeedFace;  // a bad address
        *blah = 12;
    }

    wait (&status);
    printStatus (status);

    // drop core
    if (fork() == 0) {
        struct rlimit rl;

        rl.rlim_cur = RLIM_INFINITY;
        rl.rlim_max = RLIM_INFINITY;

        if (setrlimit (RLIMIT_CORE, &rl) == -1) {
            fprintf (stderr, "error in setrlimit for RLIMIT__COR: %d (%s)\n",
                    errno, strerror(errno));
        }
        abort ();
    }

    wait (&status);
    printStatus (status);

    return EXIT_SUCCESS;

} // main
```

A sample run looks like this:

```
$ ./status
program exited normally.  Return value is 23
program exited on signal 6
program exited on signal 11
program exited on signal 6 (core dumped)
```

In between the child process' **_exit()** and the parent's **wait()**, the kernel needs to store the child's status and resource information somewhere. It disposes of most of the child's resources (memory, files, etc.) immediately but preserves its process table entry, which includes the information provided to the parent by **wait()**. The process is dead, but its process table entry lives on: such an undead child process is known as a *zombie*, not to be confused with the Objective-C NSZombieEnabled memory debugging feature. Zombies show up in parentheses in the output of the **ps** command:

```
$ ps
  PID TTY           TIME CMD
  237 ttys000    0:03.60 -bash
79855 ttys000    0:00.00 ./spawn_zombie
79856 ttys000    0:00.00 (zombie)
```

The occasional zombie is nothing to worry about. When its parent exits, it will be reparented to process 1, which will reap it. Only en masse do zombies become dangerous: if a program continually creates zombies and does not exit, it can fill up the process table and render the machine useless. More likely is that it runs up against the per-user process limit, rendering the account of the process' user id useless but not affecting other users.

How do you know when to call **wait()**? When a child exits, the system sends a SIGCHLD signal to the parent. This signal is ignored by default, but you can set a handler and use it to set a flag indicating that a child process needs waiting on. Note that the parent cannot count on receiving one SIGCHLD for each child process that exits, as several might exit while the parent is waiting in the kernel's run queue.

You will likely want to continue to ignore SIGCHILD and instead **wait()** periodically, such as during idle processing. Alternatively, you can use a kqueue (see Chapter 16: *kqueue and FSEvents*) to monitor for process termination and SIGCHLD signals.

You can see the parent process ID by passing the ppid keyword to the -o option of **ps** (more stuff added to make the output more useful):

```
$ ps -axo user,pid,ppid,vsz,tt,state,start,time,command
USER     PID  PPID   VSZ   TT  STAT  STARTED     TIME  COMMAND
root       1     0  1308   ??  Ss    20Sep02  0:00.00  /sbin/launchd
root      51     1 15912   ??  Ss    20Sep02  0:02.45  kextd
root      73     1  1292   ??  Ss    20Sep02  0:20.98  update
...
root     429   397 14048   p2  Ss    21Sep02  0:00.84  login -pf markd
markd    430   429  5872   p2  S     21Sep02  0:00.05  -tcsh (tcsh)
markd    431   430 15840   p2  S+    21Sep02  2:34.63  emacs
markd    432   431  9952  std  Ss    21Sep02  0:01.10  -bin/tcsh -i (tcsh)
root    2894   432  5192  std  R+    11:18AM  0:00.00  ps -axo user pid pp
...
```

Here you can see some daemon processes with /sbin/launchd as the parent. There is also the login process (the parent pid 397 is Terminal.app), as well as some other programs like the shell and **emacs**.

exec

Most often after a fork, you just want to run some other program. The **exec()** family of functions replaces the current running process with a new one. You will typically hear of **fork()** and **exec()** spoken of together, since they are rarely used apart from each other.

There are several variants of **exec()** depending on how you specify the file to run, how you specify the program arguments, and how you specify the environment variables for the new program.

Table 18.1   exec() Variants

	Finding the Executable	**Program Arguments**	**Environment**
execl	given path	NULL-terminated argument list	environment inherited
execlp	PATH search	NULL-terminated argument list	environment inherited
execle	given path	list of arguments	explicit environment (NULL-terminated string array)
execv	given path	NULL-terminated string array	environment inherited
execvp	PATH search	NULL-terminated array of strings	environment inherited
execvP	search using specified path	NULL-terminated array of strings	environment inherited
execve	given path	NULL-terminated string array	explicit environment (NULL-terminated string array)

How to decipher the names:

p   If the given file name contains a slash, it is treated as a path to use. Otherwise, the call uses the PATH environment variable to do shell-style program lookup.

P   As p, but the provided path string, such as "/sbin:/bin:/usr/sbin:/usr/bin", is used instead of the PATH environment variable.

v   Program arguments are an array ("vectore") of strings.

l   Program arguments are a list of separate (varargs) arguments in the **exec()** command.

e   Environment variables are an array of strings of the form "VARIABLE=value".

No e   Environment variables are inherited using the environ variable.

If you do not use an e version of **exec()**, the global variable environ will be used to construct the environment for the new process. The **execve()** function is the actual system call that all the other functions are based on.

You are expected to pass the executable name or path as the first argument. The argument list, argument vector, and environment vector must be terminated by a NULL pointer:

```
char *envp[] = {"PATH=/usr/bin", "EDITOR=/usr/bin/vim", NULL};
char *argv[] = {"/usr/bin/true", NULL};
```

A number of attributes are inherited across the **exec()** call, including:

- open files

- process ID, parent process ID, process group ID

- access groups, controlling terminal, resource usages

- current working directory

- umask, signal mask

Pipes

Open files are inherited across an **exec()** unless you explicitly tell the file descriptors to "close on exec." This behavior forms the basis of building pipelines between programs. A process calls **pipe()** to create a communications channel before **fork()**ing:

```
int pipe (int fildes[2]);
```

pipe() fills the fildes array with two file descriptors that are connected in such a way that data written to fildes[1] can be read from fildes[0]. If you wanted to **fork()** and **exec()** a command and read that command's output, you would do something like this, as illustrated in Figure 18.5:

1. Create the pipe

2. **fork()**

3. The child uses **dup2()** to move `filedes[1]` to standard out.

4. The child **exec()**s a program.

5. The parent reads the program's output from `filedes[0]`. After the child exits, its file descriptors are closed, and reads from `filedes[0]` will return end of file once any buffered data is drained from the pipe.

6. Finally, the parent **wait()**s on the child.

Figure 18.5   Pipe and fork

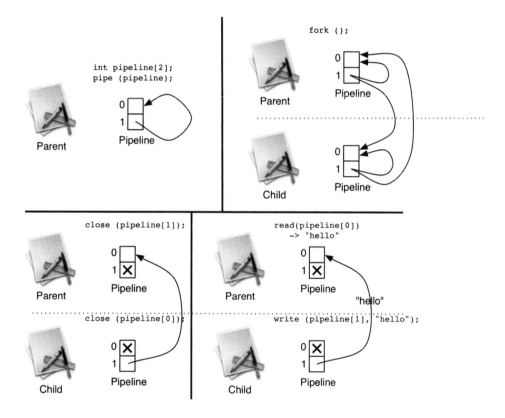

You can chain the input and output of multiple programs together using multiple pipes.

Example 18.4 is a program that builds a pipeline equivalent to

```
$ grep -i mail /usr/share/dict/words | tr '[:lower:]' '[:upper:]'
```

That is, get words from `/usr/share/dict/words` that contain "mail" and translate them to uppercase.

Example 18.4   pipeline.m

```
// pipeline.m -- manually create a pipeline to run the command
```

```
//                  grep -i mail /usr/share/dict/words | tr '[:lower:]' '[:upper:]'

// gcc -g -Wall -o pipeline pipeline.m

#import <sys/types.h>    // for pid_t
#import <sys/wait.h>     // for waitpid
#import <unistd.h>       // for fork
#import <stdlib.h>       // for EXIT_SUCCESS, pipe, exec
#import <stdio.h>        // for printf
#import <errno.h>        // for errno
#import <string.h>       // for strerror

#define BUFSIZE 4096

int main (int argc, char *argv[]) {
    int status = EXIT_FAILURE;

    int pipeline1[2];    // write on 1, read on zero
    int result = pipe (pipeline1);

    if (result == -1) {
        fprintf (stderr, "could not open pipe 1\n");
        goto bailout;
    }

    // start the grep

    pid_t grep_pid = 0;
    if ((grep_pid = fork())) {
        // parent

        if ((grep_pid == -1)) {
            fprintf (stderr, "fork failed.  Error is %d/%s\n",
                    errno, strerror(errno));
            goto bailout;
        }
        close (pipeline1[1]); // we're not planning on writing

    } else {
        // child

        char *arguments[] = { "grep", "-i", "mail", "/usr/share/dict/words", NULL };

        close (pipeline1[0]); // we're not planning on reading

        // set the standard out to be the write-side of the pipeline1

        result = dup2 (pipeline1[1], STDOUT_FILENO);
        if (result == -1) {
            fprintf (stderr, "dup2 failed.  Error is %d/%s\n",
                    errno, strerror(errno));
            goto bailout;
        }
        // The file is open on STDOUT_FILENO, so we don't need this fd anymore.
        close (pipeline1[1]);

        // exec the child
        result = execvp ("grep", arguments);
        if (result == -1) {
            fprintf (stderr, "could not exec grep.  Error is %d/%s\n",
```

```
                    errno, strerror(errno));
        goto bailout;
    }
}

// start the tr

int pipeline2[2];
result = pipe (pipeline2);
if (result == -1) {
    fprintf (stderr, "could not open pipe\n");
    goto bailout;
}

pid_t tr_pid = 0;
if ((tr_pid = fork())) {
    // parent

    if ((tr_pid == -1)) {
        fprintf (stderr, "fork failed.  Error is %d/%s\n",
                errno, strerror(errno));
        goto bailout;
    }
    close (pipeline2[1]); // we're not planning on writing

} else {
    // child

    close (pipeline2[0]); // we're not planning on reading

    // set the standard out to be the write-side of the pipeline2

    result = dup2 (pipeline1[0], STDIN_FILENO);
    if (result == -1) {
        fprintf (stderr, "dup2 failed.  Error is %d/%s\n",
                errno, strerror(errno));
        goto bailout;
    }
    close (pipeline1[1]);

    result = dup2 (pipeline2[1], STDOUT_FILENO);
    if (result == -1) {
        fprintf (stderr, "dup2 failed.  Error is %d/%s\n",
                errno, strerror(errno));
        goto bailout;
    }
    close (pipeline2[1]);

    // exec the child

    result = execlp ("tr", "tr", "[:lower:]", "[:upper:]", NULL);
    if (result == -1) {
        fprintf (stderr, "could not exec tr.  Error is %d/%s\n",
                errno, strerror(errno));
        goto bailout;
    }
}


// this is only in the parent.  read the results
```

```
    FILE *blarg;
    char buffer[BUFSIZE];

    blarg = fdopen (pipeline2[0], "r");

    while (fgets(buffer, BUFSIZE, blarg)) {
        printf ("%s", buffer);
    }

    // and wait
    int childStatus;
    waitpid (grep_pid, &childStatus, 0);
    waitpid (tr_pid, &childStatus, 0);

    // whew!  All done.

    status = EXIT_SUCCESS;

bailout:

    return (status);

} // main
```

A sample run:

```
$ ./pipeline
AIRMAIL
AUMAIL
BEMAIL
BLACKMAIL
BLACKMAILER
CAMAIL
...
UNMAIL
UNMAILABLE
UNMAILABLENESS
UNMAILED
```

fork() Gotchas

While Unix file descriptors are inherited across **fork()**, most Mach ports are not. Cocoa relies on Mach ports for much of its private interprocess communication, including communication with the window server. Expect problems if you try to use Cocoa after a **fork()**.

When you are using threads (which Cocoa and Core Foundation programs use implicitly), only the thread that calls **fork()** is running in the child. Unfortunately, all of the other thread stuff (mutexes and other data structures) still exists, and data structures that are protected by mutexes are potentially still in an indeterminate state, which can lead to total mayhem.

If you are using threads (or if a framework or library is using them on your behalf), the only safe functions to call after a **fork()** are the **exec()** functions and any of the async-signal-safe functions (the ones you can call in a signal handler). Under Mac OS X 10.6 and later, if you are using run loops, they are spinning up the Grand Central Dispatch workqueue threads on your behalf. The Foundation URL loading system uses threads, as do certain services in Core Foundation. Many other Apple frameworks use threads under the hood, as well.

If you attempt to use various Core Foundation functions from the child before **exec()**ing, the framework will scold you roundly via the aptly named function __THE_PROCESS_HAS_FORKED_AND_ YOU_CANNOT_USE_THIS_ COREFOUNDATION_FUNCTIONALITY ___YOU_MUST_EXEC__. When you fork, it will also helpfully update the Crash Reporter information to include whether it was a single- or multi-threaded process that forked.

In short: if you are using multiprocessing as an alternative to multithreading by **fork()**ing to continue your current program, you should look into using multithreading or some other, more modern approach to concurrency. And, unless you are writing such a single-threaded, BSD-style program and not touching any Apple frameworks or Mach functions, you should only **fork()** in order to **exec()**.

Summary

Mac OS X is a multiprocessing operating system. Independent processes are given slices of CPU time, giving the illusion that all of the programs on the system are running concurrently.

Sometimes your programs need to create new processes to do their work. You can use one of the convenience functions like **system()** or **popen()** to run pipelines in a shell. You can also use **fork()** and **exec()** directly to create a new child process and execute a new program in that processes. You can use **pipe()** to establish a communications channel between related processes.

Exercises

1. In pipeline.m, if the parent does not close tr_pipe[WRITE], the program will hang in the loop that reads results from the children. Why does it behave like that?

19

Using NSTask

In this section, you will learn:

- how to create new processes using **NSTask**,

- how to send data to the new process' standard in and read data from its standard out and standard error using **NSPipe** and **NSFileHandle**, and

- how **NSProcessInfo** supplies the program with information about itself.

NSProcessInfo

Your application can access its own process information using the **NSProcessInfo** object. Here are some of the commonly used methods on **NSProcessInfo**:

+ (NSProcessInfo *)**processInfo**

You will use this class method to get hold of the shared instance of **NSProcessInfo** for the current process.

- (NSDictionary *)**environment**

Returns a dictionary containing all the environment variables as keys and their values.

- (NSString *)**hostName**

The name of the computer upon which the program is running.

- (NSString *)**processName**

The name of the program. This is used by the user defaults system.

- (NSString *)**globallyUniqueString**

This method uses the host name, process ID, and a timestamp to create a string that will be unique for the network. It uses a counter to ensure that each time this method is invoked it will create a different string.

NSTask

The **NSTask** object is used to create and control new processes. When the process ends, the object will post an NSTaskDidTerminateNotification notification. Before creating (or *launching*) the new process, you will set the attributes of the new process with these methods:

- (void)**setLaunchPath:** (NSString *)path

Sets the path to the code that will be executed when the process is created.

- (void)**setArguments:** (NSArray *)arguments

Takes an array of strings that will be the arguments to the program.

- (void)**setEnvironment:** (NSDictionary *)dict

You can use this to set the environment variables. If unset, the environment variables of the parent process will be used.

- (void)**setCurrentDirectoryPath:** (NSString *)path

Every process has a directory from which all relative paths are resolved. This is known as the current directory. If unset, the current directory of the parent process is used.

- (void)**setStandardInput:** (id)input

You can provide an object (either an **NSPipe** or an **NSFileHandle**) to act as a conduit to the new process' standard input.

- (void)**setStandardOutput:** (id)output

You can provide an object (either an **NSPipe** or an **NSFileHandle**) to act as a conduit from the new process' standard output.

- (void)**setStandardError:** (id)error

You can provide an object (either an **NSPipe** or an **NSFileHandle**) to act as a conduit from the new process' standard error.

There are also methods you'll use once the new process is running. Here are the most commonly used:

- (void)**launch**	Creates the new process.
- (void)**terminate**	Kills the new process by sending it a SIGTERM signal.
- (int)**processIdentifier**	Returns the new process' process ID.
- (BOOL)**isRunning**	Returns YES if the new process is running.

NSFileHandle

When reading a file, Cocoa programmers often read in an entire file and pack it into an **NSData** or **NSString** before parsing it. When writing a file, Cocoa programmers usually create a complete **NSData** or **NSString** which is then written to the file system. Sometimes you want more control over reading from and writing to files. For example, you might read a file just until you find what you want and then close it. For more control over reading and writing from files, you use an **NSFileHandle** object.

An **NSFileHandle** is used for reading and writing files. Some of the reading methods are blocking (that is, the application stops and waits for the data to become available), and others are non-blocking. We'll discuss the non-blocking methods later in the chapter. Here are some commonly used methods for reading, writing, and seeking:

```
- (NSData *) readDataToEndOfFile
- (NSData *) readDataOfLength: (unsigned int) length
```

These methods read data from the file handle.

```
- (void) writeData: (NSData *) data;
```

is a method for writing data to a file handle.

```
- (unsigned long long) offsetInFile
- (void) seekToFileOffset: (unsigned long long) offset
```

are methods for finding and changing your current location in a file.

```
- (void)closeFile
```

closes the file.

NSPipe

The class **NSPipe** has two instances of **NSFileHandle** – one for input and the other for output.

```
- (NSFileHandle *) fileHandleForReading
```

```
- (NSFileHandle *) fileHandleForWriting
```

Creating an App that Creates a New Process

Unix systems have a program called **sort** that reads data from standard input, sorts it, and outputs it to standard output. You are going to write a program that invokes **sort** as a new process, writes data to its input, and reads data from its output. The user will type in an **NSTextView**, click a button to trigger the sort, and read the result in another **NSTextView**. It will look like Figure 19.1:

Figure 19.1   SortThem application running

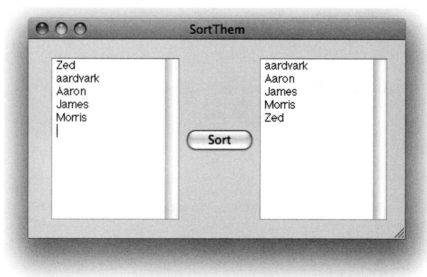

For the record, this is not how we would do a sort in a real application. The **NSArray** class has a couple of elegant ways to do sorting. This is just a simple example of using other processes.

Figure 19.2 is an object diagram of the nib file:

Figure 19.2   SortThem nib file

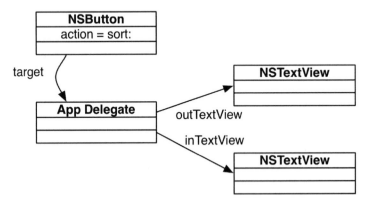

Create a new project of type Cocoa Application and name it SortThem. Edit SortThemAppDelegate.h and set up the outlets and action:

Example 19.1   SortThemAppDelegate.h

```
#import <Cocoa/Cocoa.h>

@interface SortThemAppDelegate : NSObject <NSApplicationDelegate> {
    NSWindow *_window;
    NSTextView *_inText;
    NSTextView *_outText;
}

@property (assign) IBOutlet NSWindow *window;
@property (assign) IBOutlet NSTextView *inText;
@property (assign) IBOutlet NSTextView *outText;

- (IBAction) sort: (id) sender;

@end // SortThemAppDelegate
```

Edit MainMenu.xib. Drop two **NSTextView** objects and an **NSButton** on the window. Make the text view on the right non-editable:

Figure 19.3   Laying out the SortThem window

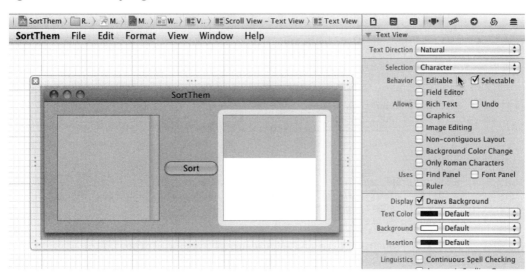

Before creating the code, take a look at the object diagram shown in Figure 19.4.

Figure 19.4   SortThem object diagram

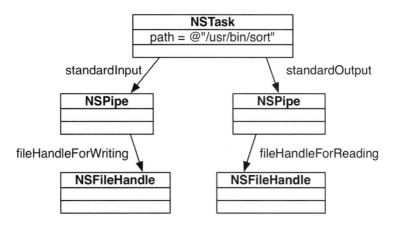

In Xcode, add a **-sort:** method in SortThemAppDelegate.m:

Example 19.2   SortThemAppDelegate.m

```
#import "SortThemAppDelegate.h"

@implementation SortThemAppDelegate
```

```
@synthesize window = _window;
@synthesize inText = _inText;
@synthesize outText = _outText;

- (IBAction) sort: (id) sender {
    NSTask *task = [[NSTask alloc] init];
    NSPipe *inPipe = [[NSPipe alloc] init];
    NSPipe *outPipe = [[NSPipe alloc] init];

    [task setLaunchPath: @"/usr/bin/sort"];
    [task setStandardOutput: outPipe];
    [task setStandardInput: inPipe];
    [task setArguments: [NSArray arrayWithObject: @"-f"]];

    [task launch];

    NSFileHandle *writingHandle = [inPipe fileHandleForWriting];
    NSData *outData = [[self.inText string] dataUsingEncoding: NSUTF8StringEncoding];
    [writingHandle writeData: outData];
    [writingHandle closeFile];

    NSData *inData = [[outPipe fileHandleForReading] readDataToEndOfFile];
    NSString *string = [[NSString alloc] initWithData: inData
                                        encoding: NSUTF8StringEncoding];
    [self.outText setString: string];
    [string release];

    [task release];
    [inPipe release];
    [outPipe release];
} // sort

@end // SortThemAppDelegate
```

Build and run your application.

Non-blocking reads

If a process takes a long time to return output, you don't want your application to stop while waiting for output from the program. To avoid this case, you create a file handle that does non-blocking reading. In particular, you set up the file handle so that it posts a notification when there is data to be processed.

In this section, you are going to create a task which runs **traceroute**. **traceroute** sends out packets to discover the routers between your machine and another host. The responses from the routers sometimes take a while to get back. You will read the data in the background and append it to the text view.

The notification created will be an NSFileHandleReadCompletionNotification. To start the file handle waiting for the data, you will send it the message **-readInBackgroundAndNotify**. Each time you receive this notification, you will read the data using the **-availableData** method of **NSFileHandle**. You will also need to call **-readInBackgroundAndNotify** again to restart the wait for data.

The running application is shown in Figure 19.5.

Figure 19.5   TraceRoute application running

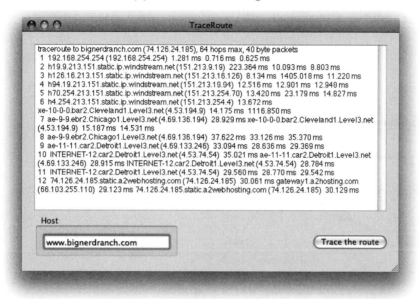

Create the header and edit the xib file

Create a new project of type Cocoa Application. Name it TraceRoute. Edit `TraceRouteAppDelegate.h` to add references to the moving pieces:

Example 19.3

```objc
#import <Cocoa/Cocoa.h>

@interface TraceRouteAppDelegate : NSObject <NSApplicationDelegate> {
    NSWindow *_window;
    NSButton *_button;
    NSTextField *_hostField;
    NSTextView *_textView;
    NSPipe *_pipe;
    NSTask *_task;
}

@property (assign) IBOutlet NSWindow *window;
@property (assign) IBOutlet NSButton *button;
@property (assign) IBOutlet NSTextField *hostField;
@property (assign) IBOutlet NSTextView *textView;

- (void) dataReady: (NSNotification *) notification;
- (void) taskTerminated: (NSNotification *) notification;
- (void) appendData: (NSData *) ddata;
- (void) cleanup;

- (IBAction) startStop: (id) sender;

@end // TraceRouteAppDelegatex
```

Edit MainMenu.xib. Drag in an **NSTextView**, **NSTextField**, and an **NSButton**. Hook up the connections from the app delegate to the objects in the window, and also connect the button's action to **startStop:**.

Here are the moving pieces for when the **NSTask** is running:

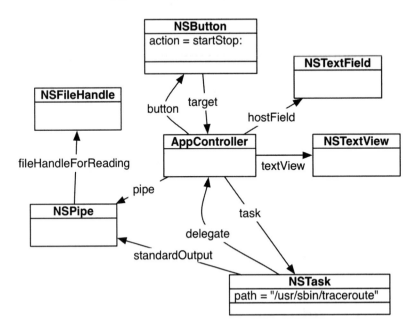

Edit the code

Edit TraceRouteAppDelegate.m and make it look like this:

Example 19.4   TraceRouteAppDelegate.m

```
#import "TraceRouteAppDelegate.h"
#import <dispatch/dispatch.h>

@implementation TraceRouteAppDelegate

@synthesize window = _window;
@synthesize button = _button;
@synthesize hostField = _hostField;
@synthesize textView = _textView;

// Append the data to the string in the text view

- (void) appendData: (NSData *) data {
    NSRange endRange = NSMakeRange (self.textView.string.length, 0);
    NSString *string = [[NSString alloc] initWithData: data
                                    encoding: NSUTF8StringEncoding];
    [self.textView replaceCharactersInRange: endRange  withString: string];
    [string release];
} // appendData


- (void) cleanup  {
```

```
    // Release the old task
    [_task release];
    _task = nil;

    // Release the pipe
    [_pipe release];
    _pipe = nil;

    // Change the title on the button
    [self.button setTitle: @"Trace the route"];

    // No longer an observer
    [[NSNotificationCenter defaultCenter] removeObserver: self];
} // cleanup


- (void) taskTerminated: (NSNotification *) notification {
    NSData *leftInPipe;

    // Flush data still in pipe.
    leftInPipe = [[_pipe fileHandleForReading] readDataToEndOfFile];

    if (leftInPipe) [self appendData: leftInPipe];
    [self cleanup];
} // taskTerminated


- (IBAction) startStop: (id) sender {
    // Is the task already running?
    if ([_task isRunning])  {
        // Stop it and tidy up
        [_task terminate];
        [self cleanup];

    } else {
        // Create a task and pipe
        _task = [[NSTask alloc] init];
        _pipe = [[NSPipe alloc] init];

        // Set the attributes of the task
        [_task setLaunchPath: @"/usr/sbin/traceroute"];
        [_task setArguments: [NSArray arrayWithObject: self.hostField.stringValue]];
        [_task setStandardOutput: _pipe];
        [_task setStandardError: _pipe];

        // Register for notifications
        [[NSNotificationCenter defaultCenter]
            addObserver: self
            selector: @selector(dataReady:)
            name: NSFileHandleReadCompletionNotification
            object: [_pipe fileHandleForReading]];

        [[NSNotificationCenter defaultCenter]
            addObserver:  self
            selector: @selector(taskTerminated:)
            name: NSTaskDidTerminateNotification
            object: _task];

        // Launch the task
        [_task launch];
```

```
        [self.button setTitle: @"Terminate"];
        [self.textView setString: @""];

        // Get the pipe reading in the background
        [[_pipe fileHandleForReading] readInBackgroundAndNotify];
    }
}


- (void) dataReady: (NSNotification *) notification {
    NSData *data =
        [[notification userInfo]  valueForKey: NSFileHandleNotificationDataItem];
    if (data != nil) [self appendData: data];

    // Must restart reading in background after each notification
    [[_pipe fileHandleForReading] readInBackgroundAndNotify];

} // dataReady

@end // TraceRouteAppDelegate
```

Build and run the application.

Exercises

1. The **traceroute** command still runs if you quit TraceRoute before the route tracing finishes. This is OK, since you might want to kick off longer-running commands that will finish their processing at a later time. How would you clean up the task on application exit? Fix TraceRoute to tidy up things when it finishes.

20

Multithreading

Multithreading is another method for achieving concurrency in your application. While multiprocessing uses multiple independent processes with their own address spaces and resources, threads are multiple execution streams that all run within a single application, with a single address space, all sharing the available resources.

Multithreading, like multiprocessing, can take advantage of multiple CPUs. You can also use it to simplify some kinds of programming. Each thread can go on its merry way, computing values and calling functions that block, while other threads can run independently and are unaffected. One very common use of threads is handling requests in a network server (like a web server). A new connection is **accept()**ed and a thread is created to handle the request. This thread can then use **read()** to get the request and **write()** to send data back. It can also open files and perform loops, so there is no need to multiplex the I/O using **select()**, and there is no need to go through contortions to do computations piecemeal.

Posix Threads

Mac OS X uses the Posix thread API, more commonly known as "pthreads," for its native threading model. Unfortunately, pthreads have a different convention for reporting error conditions than the rest of the Unix API. While it returns zero on success like you would expect, it returns the error code on error, rather than returning -1 and setting errno.

Creating threads

pthread_create() is used to create a new thread:

```
int pthread_create (pthread_t *threadID, const pthread_attr_t *attr,
                    void *(*startRoutine)(void *), void *arg);
```

This function returns zero on success and an error value on failure. These are the arguments it takes:

threadID   A pointer to a pthread_t. The thread ID for the new thread will be written here.

attr   A set of attributes. Pass NULL to use the default attributes. Specific attributes are not discussed; they tend to confuse discussions about the basics of threaded programming.

startRoutine A pointer to a function with a signature of

```
void *someFunction (void *someArg);
```

This is where execution in the thread will start. The thread will terminate when this function returns. The someArg parameter is the value of the arg parameter passed to **pthread_create()**. The return value is some pointer to return status. You can pass whatever data structure you want for these two values.

arg   The argument given to the startRoutine.

The system allocates a private stack, similar to the main function call stack, for a thread when it gets created, as shown in Figure 20.1. The thread uses this stack for function call housekeeping and local variable storage.

Figure 20.1   Thread stacks

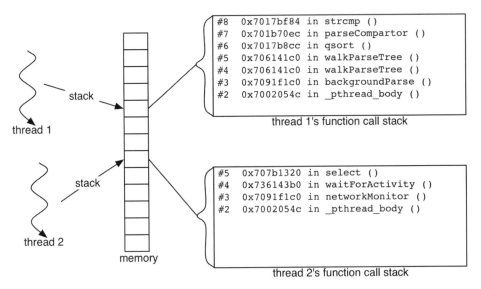

```
#8   0x7017bf84 in strcmp ()
#7   0x701b70ec in parseCompartor ()
#6   0x7017b8cc in qsort ()
#5   0x706141c0 in walkParseTree ()
#4   0x706141c0 in walkParseTree ()
#3   0x7091f1c0 in backgroundParse ()
#2   0x7002054c in _pthread_body ()
```
thread 1's function call stack

```
#5   0x707b1320 in select ()
#4   0x736143b0 in waitForActivity ()
#3   0x7091f1c0 in networkMonitor ()
#2   0x7002054c in _pthread_body ()
```
thread 2's function call stack

Threads are like processes because they have a return value that could be of interest to whoever created the thread. Using a mechanism similar to **waitpid()** for processes you can use **pthread_join()** to rendezvous with a particular thread:

```
int pthread_join (pthread_t threadID, void **valuePtr);
```

pthread_join() will block until the indicated thread exits. The return value will be written into the valuePtr.

To determine your own threadID, use **pthread_self()**;

Sometimes you want to detach a thread so that you do not have to **pthread_join()** it. The thread will run to completion, exit, and be deleted. To do that, use **pthread_detach()**:

```
int pthread_detach (pthread_t threadID);
```

516

Detached threads are sometimes called "daemon threads" because they run independently of their parents like daemons.

A common idiom is for a thread function to call

```
pthread_detach (pthread_self());
```

to turn itself into a daemon thread.

Example 20.1 is a little program that spins off a couple of threads that all count from zero to some value. Some are detached, and some aren't and should be waited on:

Example 20.1   basics.m

```
// basics.m -- basic thread creation

// gcc -g -Wall -std=c99 -Wall -o basics basics.m

#import <pthread.h>      // for pthread_* calls
#import <stdio.h>        // for printf
#import <stdlib.h>       // for exit
#import <string.h>       // for strerror()
#import <unistd.h>       // for usleep()

#define THREAD_COUNT 6

// information to tell the thread how to behave

typedef struct ThreadInfo {
    pthread_t   threadID;
    int         index;
    int         numberToCountTo;
    int         detachYourself;
    int         sleepTime;      // in microseconds (1/100,000,000)
} ThreadInfo;


void *threadFunction (void *argument) {
    ThreadInfo *info = (ThreadInfo *) argument;

    printf ("thread %d, counting to %d, detaching %s\n",
            info->index, info->numberToCountTo,
            (info->detachYourself) ? "yes" : "no");

    if (info->detachYourself) {
        int result = pthread_detach (pthread_self());
        if (result != 0) {
            fprintf (stderr, "could not detach thread %d. Error: %d/%s\n",
                    info->index, result, strerror(result));
        }
    }

    // now to do the actual "work" of the thread

    for (int i = 0; i < info->numberToCountTo; i++) {
        printf ("  thread %d counting %d\n", info->index, i);
        usleep (info->sleepTime);
    }
```

```
    printf ("thread %d done\n", info->index);

    return (NULL);

} // threadFunction


int main (void) {
    ThreadInfo threads[THREAD_COUNT];
    int result;

    // initialize the ThreadInfos:
    for (int i = 0; i < THREAD_COUNT; i++) {
        threads[i].index = i;
        threads[i].numberToCountTo = (i + 1) * 2;
        threads[i].detachYourself = (i % 2); // detach odd threads
        threads[i].sleepTime = 500000 + 200000 * i;
        // (make subseuqent threads wait longer between counts)
    }

    // create the threads
    for (int i = 0; i < THREAD_COUNT; i++) {
        result = pthread_create (&threads[i].threadID, NULL,
                                 threadFunction, &threads[i]);
        if (result != 0) {
            fprintf (stderr,
                    "could not pthread_create thread %d.  Error: %d/%s\n",
                    i, result, strerror(result));
            exit (EXIT_FAILURE);
        }
    }

    // now rendezvous with all the non-detached threads
    for (int i = 0; i < THREAD_COUNT; i++) {
        void *retVal;
        if (!threads[i].detachYourself) {
            result = pthread_join (threads[i].threadID, &retVal);
            if (result != 0) {
                fprintf (stderr, "error joining thread %d.  Error: %d/%s\n",
                        i, result, strerror(result));
            }
            printf ("joined with thread %d\n", i);
        }
    }

    return EXIT_SUCCESS;

} // main
```

The sample run is much more interesting in real life. Here is a part of it:

```
$ ./basics
thread 0, counting to 2, detaching no
   thread 0 counting 0
thread 1, counting to 4, detaching yes
   thread 1 counting 0
thread 2, counting to 6, detaching no
   thread 2 counting 0
...
   thread 2 counting 1
```

```
thread 0 done
joined with thread 0
  thread 3 counting 1
  thread 4 counting 1
...
  thread 4 counting 9
  thread 5 counting 8
thread 4 done
joined with thread 4
```

There are a couple of things of interest. The first is there is no predefined order in which the threads will run. They are at the mercy of the OS scheduler. The second is that the main thread (where **main()** runs) is special. In all other threads, return is equivalent to **pthread_exit()**. When **main()** returns, however, it is equivalent to **exit()**, which terminates the process. If **main()** instead calls **pthread_exit()**, the application will not terminate until all threads have exited. This is why thread five sometimes does not finish its work by the time the program exits.

Synchronization

Remember the discussion about race conditions and concurrency when talking about signals? Threads have the same kinds of problems. There is something mentioned above that bears repeating: there is no predefined order in which the threads will run; they are at the mercy of the OS scheduler.

This can cause a lot of problems and introduces a lot of complexity to make sure that this (possibly) random order of execution will not corrupt data.

For example, in basics.m above, an array of ThreadInfo structures was first initialized with all of the information every thread would need, and after that, each thread received a pointer to its own array element.

```
ThreadInfo info;

for (i = 0; i < THREAD_COUNT; i++) {
    info->index = i;
    info->numberToCountTo = (i + 1) * 2;
    ...
    result = pthread_create (&threads[i].threadID, NULL,
                             threadFunction, &info);
}
```

Then **threadFunction** would copy the data it wanted.

There are three cases to consider:

1. **threadFunction** *starts executing immediately.* The thread copies the data out of its argument pointer and goes on its merry way. Things work OK in this mode.

2. **threadFunction** *starts executing a little later, like at the top of the loop.* The thread gets created when the i loop variable is 2. The loop then goes to index 3 and creates a thread and now is about to do loop number 4. The "2 thread" finally gets scheduled and starts executing, looks at the memory for its control information, and uses the same configuration information intended for thread four.

3. **threadFunction** *starts executing a little later, in the middle of the loop.* This is the worst-case scenario: corrupted data. If the "2 thread" wakes up while index and numberToCountTo have been

updated for i = 4, but detachYourself and sleepTime still have i = 3's values, it will get half the data of the "3 thread" and half from the "4 thread" info.

Along the same lines, unprotected manipulations to data structures in a threaded environment can lead to corruption. Imagine a linked list that is in the middle of the pointer manipulations for adding a new node. This thread gets preempted by another thread that tries to add something of its own to that list. In the best case, you will crash because a pointer being modified is pointing to a bad address. The worst case is that one or the other insertions gets lost and you have slightly corrupted data, an error that will only manifest itself later, far away from the race condition that caused it.

Getting synchronization right is hard to do, and problems can be very hard to debug. There is a fine line between safe data access and efficient data access, and this is the primary reason threaded programming is much harder than people think it is.

To help address these problems, the pthread API provides some synchronization mechanisms, specifically mutexes (mutual exclusion locks) and condition variables.

Mutexes

Mutexes are used to serialize access to critical sections of code, meaning that when mutexes are used properly, only one thread of execution can be executing that section of code, as shown in Figure 20.2. All other threads wanting to run there will be blocked until the original thread finishes. After that, an arbitrary thread will be picked to run that piece of code.

Figure 20.2   A mutex

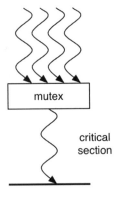

The use of a mutex over a section of code eliminates any concurrency that code may have, which is the general motivation for using threads in the first place, so you want the duration of a mutex lock to be as short as possible. Be aware that although mutexes control access to *code*, you are just using that to control access to *data*.

The datatype for a mutex is pthread_mutex_t. You can declare them as local variables, global variables, or **malloc()** memory for them. There are two ways to initialize a mutex. The first way is to use a static initializer, which is handy for a singleton mutex that you want to stick outside of a function:

```
static pthread_mutex_t myMutex = PTHREAD_MUTEX_INITIALIZER;
```

The other is to get a chunk of memory the size of pthread_mutex_t and use **pthread_mutex_init()** on that memory:

```
int pthread_mutex_init (pthread_mutex_t *mutex,
                        const pthread_mutexattr_t *attr);
```

Like with **pthread_create()**, specific attributes aren't discussed.

You would use **pthread_mutex_init()** when you have a mutex per data structure (like you create a new tree, and create a mutex just for that tree).

When you are done with a mutex you initialized with **pthread_mutex_init()**, use **pthread_mutex_destroy()** to release its resources:

```
int pthread_mutex_destroy (pthread_mutex_t *mutex);
```

To acquire a mutex use **pthread_mutex_lock()**:

```
int pthread_mutex_lock (pthread_mutex_t *mutex);
```

If the mutex is unavailable, this call will block until it becomes free. When execution resumes after this call (with a zero return value), you know you have sole possession of the mutex.

To release a mutex, use **pthread_mutex_unlock()**:

```
int pthread_mutex_unlock (pthread_mutex_t *mutex);
```

If you do not want to block when acquiring a mutex, use **pthread_mutex_trylock()**:

```
int pthread_mutex_trylock (pthread_mutex_t *mutex);
```

If this returns with zero, you have locked the mutex. If it returns EBUSY, the mutex is locked by another party, and you need to try again.

Example 20.2 shows mutexes in action.

Example 20.2   mutex.m

```
// copy basic.m to mutex.m first, then change threadFunction to this:


pthread_mutex_t g_mutex = PTHREAD_MUTEX_INITIALIZER;

void *threadFunction (void *argument) {
    ThreadInfo *info = (ThreadInfo *) argument;

    printf ("thread %d, counting to %d, detaching %s\n",
            info->index, info->numberToCountTo,
            (info->detachYourself) ? "yes" : "no");

    if (info->detachYourself) {
        int result = pthread_detach (pthread_self());
        if (result != 0) {
            fprintf (stderr, "could not detach thread %d. Error: %d/%s\n",
                     info->index, result, strerror(result));
        }
```

```
    }

    // now to do the actual "work" of the thread

    pthread_mutex_lock (&g_mutex);

    for (int i = 0; i < info->numberToCountTo; i++) {
        printf ("  thread %d counting %d\n", info->index, i);
        usleep (info->sleepTime);
    }

    pthread_mutex_unlock (&g_mutex);

    printf ("thread %d done\n", info->index);

    return NULL;

} // threadFunction
```

Now see that execution has been serialized:

```
$ ./mutex
  thread 0 counting 1
thread 0 done
  thread 1 counting 0
joined with thread 0
  thread 1 counting 1
  thread 1 counting 2
  thread 1 counting 3
thread 1 done
...
```

Also notice how much slower the entire program runs now that the critical section (the counting loop) is serialized.

Deadlocks

If you are dealing with multiple mutexes for a single operation (such as locking two data structures before manipulating them together) and you are not careful about acquiring the mutexes in the same order every time you use them, you could be open to a deadlock situation.

Suppose thread one has

```
    pthread_mutex_lock (mutexA);
    pthread_mutex_lock (mutexB);
```

and thread two has

```
    pthread_mutex_lock (mutexB);
    pthread_mutex_lock (mutexA);
```

Figure 20.3 shows an execution path like this:

- Thread one locks A. It gets pre-empted.

- Thread two locks B. It gets pre-empted.

- Thread one attempts to lock B. It blocks.

- Thread two attempts to lock A. It blocks.

Figure 20.3   Deadlock

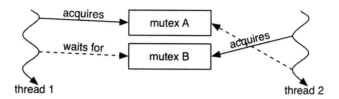

Both threads are now deadlocked, each waiting on the other to release its resource, and there is no way to break it. Each thread instead should do something like:

```
while (1) {
    pthread_mutex_lock (mutexA);
    if (pthread_mutex_trylock(mutexB) == EBUSY) {
        pthread_mutex_unlock (mutexA);
    }
}
```

That is, lock the first mutex and try locking the second. If it is locked, someone else has it, so release the first lock and try all over again, just in case someone has mutexB held and is waiting for mutexA.

Condition variables

Mutexes are great for what they do – protecting critical regions of code. Sometimes, though, you have situations where you want to wait until some condition is true before locking your mutex, like checking if a queue has an item in it before you process a request. If you use mutexes for this, you will end up writing loops to test the condition and then release the mutex. In other words, this is a polling operation, which is wasteful of CPU time.

Condition variables (pthread_cond_t) address this problem. Condition variables let interested parties block on the variable. The blocking will stop via a signal from another thread. *Signal* is an unfortunate choice of words, because this signaling has *no* relation to the Unix signals that were discussed earlier.

Like the mutex, you can initialize conditional variables statically with PTHREAD_COND_INITIALIZER, or you can use

```
int pthread_cond_init (pthread_cond_t *cond,
                       const pthread_condattr_t *attr);
```

Similarly, if you initialize a condition variable, destroy it with

```
int pthread_cond_destroy (pthread_cond_t *cond);
```

A mutex and a condition variable are associated. To use a condition variable, you lock the associated mutex, then while the condition you are interested in is false, call **pthread_cond_wait()**:

```
int pthread_cond_wait (pthread_cond_t *cond, pthread_mutex_t *mutex);
```

The mutex is automatically unlocked, and the call blocks. When another thread calls **pthread_cond_signal()**:

```
int pthread_cond_signal (pthread_cond_t *cond);
```

a single thread that is currently blocked on **pthread_cond_wait()** will wake up (use **pthread_cond_broadcast()** to wake up all blocked threads). Be aware that **pthread_cond_wait()** can spuriously return. You should always check the value of your condition before moving on.

OK, so what is this "value of your condition"? Consider Figure 20.4, the request queue for a web server:

Figure 20.4   Server request queue

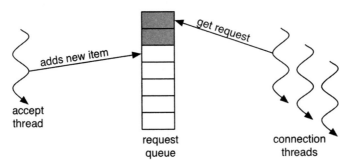

A single thread blocks on the **accept()** call waiting for new connections. When a new connection comes in, it gets put at the end of the request queue. At the same time, connection threads are hanging around, pulling the topmost entry off of the queue and processing them. This is a version of the classic "producer/consumer" problem that just about every concurrent programming book talks about.

For both the "accept" and "connection" threads, there are two states they can be in with respect to the queue. Accept thread accepts a new connection:

The queue has free space to put a new request	1. Put request on queue
	2. Signal a connection thread to wake up
The queue is full:	1. block on a condition variable until there is space in the queue
	2. when it wakes up, put the request in the queue In pseudo code:

```
pthread_mutex_lock (queueLock);
while (queue is full) {
    pthread_cond_wait (g_queueCond, queueLock);
}
put item on the queue;
pthread_mutex_unlock (queueLock);
```

```
signal a connection thread
go back to accept()
```

The **pthread_cond_wait()** will only happen when the queue is full, and you hang around in that loop until there is free space in the queue. The while loop is to protect against spurious returns.

Connection thread:

The queue has a request on it:

1. get the request from the queue

2. if the queue had been completely full, signal the accept() thread that there is now space available, in case it is blocked waiting or free space in the queue

The queue is empty:

1. block on a condition variable until there is space in the queue

2. when it wakes up, get the request from the queue
Likewise in pseudo code:

```
pthread_mutex_lock (queueLock);
while (queue is empty) {
    pthread_cond_wait (g_queueCond, queueLock);
}
get item from the queue;
pthread_mutex_unlock (queueLock);
signal the accept thread
process the request.
```

If you do not want to block indefinitely, you can specify a timeout for waiting on a condition variable by using **pthread_cond_timedwait()**:

```
int pthread_cond_timedwait (pthread_cond_t *cond,
                            pthread_mutex_t *mutex,
                            const struct timespec *abstime);
```

The timeout is specified by filling out this structure:

```
struct timespec {
    time_t  tv_sec;     // seconds
    long    tv_nsec;    // nanoseconds
};
```

pthread_timed_condwait() differs from similar calls like **select()** in that the timeout is an absolute time, not a relative time. This makes it easier to handle the case of spurious wake-ups because you do not have to recalculate the wait interval each time.

Example 20.3 is a simple webserver which has a request queue that uses condition variables.

Example 20.3   webserve-thread.m

```
// webserve-thread.m -- a very simple web server using threads to
//                      handle requests
```

```
// gcc -g -std=c99 -Wall -o webserve-thread webserve-thread.m

#import <arpa/inet.h>          // for inet_ntoa
#import <arpa/inet.h>          // for inet_ntoa and friends
#import <assert.h>             // for assert
#import <errno.h>              // for errno
#import <netinet/in.h>         // for sockaddr_in
#import <pthread.h>            // for pthread_*
#import <stdio.h>              // for printf
#import <stdlib.h>             // for EXIT_SUCCESS, pipe, exec
#import <string.h>             // for strerror
#import <sys/param.h>          // for MIN/MAX
#import <sys/resource.h>       // for struct rusage
#import <sys/socket.h>         // for socket(), AF_INET
#import <sys/time.h>           // for struct timeval
#import <sys/types.h>          // for pid_t, amongst others
#import <sys/wait.h>           // for wait3
#import <unistd.h>             // for fork
#import <unistd.h>             // for close

#define PORT_NUMBER 8080       // set to 80 to listen on the HTTP port
#define MAX_THREADS 5          // maximum number of connection threads


// ----- queue for handling requests

#define QUEUE_DEPTH 10

typedef struct Request {
    int                fd; // file descriptor of the incoming request
    struct sockaddr_in  address;
} Request;

static Request g_requestQueue[QUEUE_DEPTH];
static int g_queueEnd = -1; // 0 is the head.  end == -1 for empty queue

static pthread_mutex_t g_queueMutex = PTHREAD_MUTEX_INITIALIZER;
static pthread_cond_t g_queueCond = PTHREAD_COND_INITIALIZER;

void dumpQueue (void) {
    printf ("%d items in queue:\n", g_queueEnd + 1);

    for (int i = 0; i <= g_queueEnd; i++) {
        printf ("%d:  fd is %d\n", i, g_requestQueue[i].fd);
    }
} // dumpQueue


void getRequest (int *fd, struct sockaddr_in *address) {
    int doSignal = 0;

    printf ("before getRequest\n");
    dumpQueue ();

    pthread_mutex_lock (&g_queueMutex);
    while (g_queueEnd == -1) { // queue is empty
        pthread_cond_wait (&g_queueCond, &g_queueMutex);
    }

    printf ("after wakeup\n");
```

```
    dumpQueue ();

    // copy the request to the caller
    *fd = g_requestQueue[0].fd;
    memcpy (address, &g_requestQueue[0].address, sizeof(struct sockaddr_in));

    if (g_queueEnd == QUEUE_DEPTH - 1) {
        // going from full to not quite so full
        doSignal = 1;
    }

    // shift up the queue
    if (g_queueEnd > 0) {
        memmove (g_requestQueue, g_requestQueue + 1,
                 sizeof(Request) * g_queueEnd);
    }
    g_queueEnd--;

    pthread_mutex_unlock (&g_queueMutex);

    if (doSignal) {
        pthread_cond_signal (&g_queueCond);
    }

} // getRequest


void queueRequest (int fd, struct sockaddr_in *address) {
    pthread_mutex_lock (&g_queueMutex);

    assert (g_queueEnd <= QUEUE_DEPTH);

    printf ("before queue\n");
    while (g_queueEnd == QUEUE_DEPTH - 1) { // queue is full
        pthread_cond_wait (&g_queueCond, &g_queueMutex);
    }
    printf ("after queue\n");

    assert (g_queueEnd < QUEUE_DEPTH - 1);

    g_queueEnd++;
    g_requestQueue[g_queueEnd].fd = fd;
    memcpy (&g_requestQueue[g_queueEnd].address, address,
            sizeof(struct sockaddr_in));

    pthread_mutex_unlock (&g_queueMutex);
    pthread_cond_signal (&g_queueCond);

    printf ("enqueued another one\n");
    dumpQueue ();

} // queueRequest


// HTTP request handling

// these are some of the common HTTP response codes

#define HTTP_OK        200
#define HTTP_NOT_FOUND 404
```

```
#define HTTP_ERROR        500


// return a string to the browser

#define returnString(httpResult, string, channel) \
        returnBuffer((httpResult), (string), (strlen(string)), (channel))

// return a character buffer (not necessarily zero-terminated) to the browser

void returnBuffer (int httpResult, const char *content,
                   int contentLength, FILE *commChannel) {
    fprintf (commChannel, "HTTP/1.0 %d blah\n", httpResult);
    fprintf (commChannel, "Content-Type: text/html\n");
    fprintf (commChannel, "Content-Length: %d\n", contentLength);
    fprintf (commChannel, "\n");
    fwrite (content, contentLength, 1, commChannel );
} // returnBuffer


// stream back to the browser numbers being counted, with a pause between
// them.  The user should see the numbers appear every couple of seconds

void returnNumbers (int number, FILE *commChannel) {
    int min, max, i;
    min = MIN (number, 1);
    max = MAX (number, 1);

    fprintf (commChannel, "HTTP/1.0 %d OK\n", HTTP_OK);
    fprintf (commChannel, "Content-Type: text/html; charset=ISO-8859-1\n");
    fprintf (commChannel, "\n"); // no content length since this is dynamic

    // Send 4K of dummy data so that browsers will start showing the incremental
    // text.
    char buffer[4 * 1024];
    memset (buffer, ' ', sizeof(buffer));
    fwrite (buffer, 1, sizeof(buffer), commChannel);

    fprintf (commChannel, "<h2>The numbers from %d to %d</h2>\n", min, max);

    for (i = min; i <= max; i++) {
        sleep (2);
        fprintf (commChannel, "%d\n", i);
        fflush (commChannel);
    }

    fprintf (commChannel, "<hr>Done\n");

} // returnNumbers


// Return a file from the file system, relative to where the webserver
// is running.  Note that this doesn't look for any nasty characters
// like '..', so this function is a pretty big security hole.

void returnFile (const char *filename, FILE *commChannel) {
    const char *mimetype = NULL;

    // try to guess the mime type.  IE assumes all non-graphic files are HTML
    if (strstr(filename, ".m") != NULL) {
```

```
        mimetype = "text/plain";
    } else if (strstr(filename, ".h") != NULL) {
        mimetype = "text/plain";
    } else if (strstr(filename, ".txt") != NULL) {
        mimetype = "text/plain";
    } else if (strstr(filename, ".tgz") != NULL) {
        mimetype = "application/x-compressed";
    } else if (strstr(filename, ".html") != NULL) {
        mimetype = "text/html";
    } else if (strstr(filename, ".html") != NULL) {
        mimetype = "text/html";
    } else if (strstr(filename, ".xyz") != NULL) {
        mimetype = "audio/mpeg";
    }

    FILE *file = fopen (filename, "r");

    if (file == NULL) {
        returnString (HTTP_NOT_FOUND, "could not find your file.  Sorry\n.",
                      commChannel);
    } else {
        char *buffer[8 * 1024];
        int result;
        fprintf (commChannel, "HTTP/1.0 %d OK\n", HTTP_OK);
        if (mimetype != NULL) {
            fprintf (commChannel, "Content-Type: %s\n", mimetype);
        }
        fprintf (commChannel, "\n");
        while ((result = fread (buffer, 1, sizeof(buffer), file)) > 0) {
            fwrite (buffer, 1, result, commChannel);
        }
    }

} // returnFile


// using the method and the request (the path part of the url), generate the data
// for the user and send it back.

void handleRequest (const char *method, const char *originalRequest,
                    FILE *commChannel) {
    char *request = strdup (originalRequest); // we'll use strsep to split this

    if (strcmp(method, "GET") != 0) {
        returnString (HTTP_ERROR, "only GETs are supported", commChannel);
        goto bailout;
    }

    char *nextString = request;
    char *chunk;
    chunk = strsep (&nextString, "/");  // urls start with slashes, so chunk is ""
    chunk = strsep (&nextString, "/");  // the leading part of the url

    if (strcmp(chunk, "numbers") == 0) {
        // url of the form /numbers/5 to print numbers from 1 to 5
        chunk = strsep (&nextString, "/");
        if (chunk == NULL) {
            returnString (HTTP_ERROR, "Form is /numbers/23 - Sorry\n.",
                          commChannel);
        } else {
```

```
                int number = atoi(chunk);
                returnNumbers (number, commChannel);
        }

    } else if (strcmp(chunk, "file") == 0) {
        chunk = strsep (&nextString, ""); // get the rest of the string
        returnFile (chunk, commChannel);

    } else {
        returnString (HTTP_NOT_FOUND, "could not handle your request.  Sorry\n.",
                        commChannel);
    }

bailout:
    fprintf (stderr, "child %ld handled request '%s'\n",
            (long)pthread_self(), originalRequest);

    free (request);

} // handleRequest


// read the request from the browser, pull apart the elements of the
// request, and then dispatch it.

void dispatchRequest (int fd, struct sockaddr_in *address) {
#define LINEBUFFER_SIZE 8192
    char linebuffer[LINEBUFFER_SIZE];
    FILE *commChannel;

    commChannel = fdopen (fd, "r+");
    if (commChannel == NULL) {
        fprintf (stderr, "could not open commChannel.  Error is %d/%s\n",
                errno, strerror(errno));
    }

    // this is pretty lame in that it only reads the first line and
    // assumes that's the request, subsequently ignoring any headers
    // that might be sent.

    if (fgets(linebuffer, LINEBUFFER_SIZE, commChannel) != NULL) {
        // ok, now figure out what they wanted
        char *requestElements[3], *nextString, *chunk;
        int i = 0;
        nextString = linebuffer;
        while ((chunk = strsep (&nextString, " "))) {
            requestElements[i] = chunk;
            i++;
        }
        if (i != 3) {
            returnString (HTTP_ERROR, "malformed request", commChannel);
            goto bailout;
        }

        handleRequest (requestElements[0], requestElements[1], commChannel);

    } else {
        fprintf (stderr, "read an empty request.  exiting\n");
    }
```

```
bailout:
    fclose (commChannel);

} // dispatchRequest


// Sit blocking on accept until a new connection comes in.  Queue the
// connection (which should eventually wake up a connection thread to
// handle it

void acceptRequest (int listenSocket) {
    struct sockaddr_in address;
    socklen_t addressLength = sizeof(address);

    printf ("before accept\n");
    int result = accept (listenSocket, (struct sockaddr *)&address,
                    &addressLength);
    printf ("after accept\n");

    if (result == -1) {
        fprintf (stderr, "accept failed.  error: %d/%s\n",
                errno, strerror(errno));
        goto bailout;
    }
    int fd = result;

    queueRequest (fd, &address);

bailout:
    return;

} // acceptRequest


// ----- network stuff

// start listening on our server port

int startListening () {
    int fd = -1, success = 0;

    int result = socket (AF_INET, SOCK_STREAM, 0);
    if (result == -1) {
        fprintf (stderr, "could not make a scoket.  error: %d / %s\n",
                errno, strerror(errno));
        goto bailout;
    }

    fd = result;

    int yes = 1;
    result = setsockopt (fd, SOL_SOCKET, SO_REUSEADDR, &yes, sizeof(int));
    if (result == -1) {
        fprintf (stderr, "could not setsockopt to reuse address. %d / %s\n",
                errno, strerror(errno));
        goto bailout;
    }

    // bind to an address and port
    struct sockaddr_in address;
```

```
    address.sin_len = sizeof (struct sockaddr_in);
    address.sin_family = AF_INET;
    address.sin_port = htons (PORT_NUMBER);
    address.sin_addr.s_addr = htonl (INADDR_ANY);
    memset (address.sin_zero, 0, sizeof(address.sin_zero));

    result = bind (fd, (struct sockaddr *)&address, sizeof(address));
    if (result == -1) {
        fprintf (stderr, "could not bind socket.  error: %d / %s\n",
                errno, strerror(errno));
        goto bailout;
    }

    result = listen (fd, 8);

    if (result == -1) {
        fprintf (stderr, "listen failed.  error: %d /  %s\n",
                errno, strerror(errno));
        goto bailout;
    }

    success = 1;

bailout:
    if (!success) {
        close (fd);
        fd = -1;
    }
    return fd;

} // startListening


// ----- thread functions

// there's just one of these. It's the producer of new requests
void *acceptThread (void *argument) {
    int listenSocket = *((int *)argument);

    while (1) {
        acceptRequest (listenSocket);
    }

} // acceptThread


// There's N of these to handle requests.
void *requestThread (void *argument) {
    // Spin out on our own.
    int result = pthread_detach (pthread_self());

    if (result != 0) {
        fprintf (stderr, "could not detach connection thread.  error %d/%s\n",
                result, strerror(result));
        return NULL;
    }

    while (1) {
        int fd;
        struct sockaddr_in address;
```

```
        getRequest (&fd, &address); // This will block until a request is queued
        dispatchRequest (fd, &address);
    }

} // requestThread


// ----- get things started in main

int main (void) {
    pthread_t acceptThreadID;
    int status = EXIT_FAILURE;

    int listenSocket = startListening ();

    if (listenSocket == -1) {
        fprintf (stderr, "startListening failed\n");
        goto bailout;
    }

    // Block SIGPIPE so we don't croak if we try writing to a closed connection
    if (signal (SIGPIPE, SIG_IGN) == SIG_ERR) {
        fprintf (stderr, "could not ignore SIGPIPE.  error is %d/%s\n",
                errno, strerror(errno));
        goto bailout;
    }

    // Start the accept thread
    int result = pthread_create (&acceptThreadID, NULL, acceptThread, &listenSocket);
    if (result != 0) {
        // pthread_* doesn't use errno :-|
        fprintf (stderr, "could not create accept thread.  error is %d/%s\n",
                result, strerror(result));
        goto bailout;
    }

    // Start the connection threads
    for (int i = 0; i < MAX_THREADS; i++) {
        pthread_t connThreadID;
        result = pthread_create (&connThreadID, NULL, requestThread, NULL);
        if (result != 0) {
            fprintf (stderr, "could not create connection thread.  "
                    "error is %d/%s\n", result, strerror(result));
            goto bailout;
        }
    }

    pthread_join (acceptThreadID, NULL);

    status = EXIT_SUCCESS;
  bailout:
    return status;

} // main
```

Compile and run the program. You can use **telnet** to communicate with the server, or you can fire up a web browser and use URLs like http://localhost:8080/file/webserve-thread.m to return a file or http://localhost:8080/numbers/37 to see the numbers. Safari does some aggressive caching of data before displaying, so you may not see the individual numbers being displayed until they are all generated. Other browsers, like FireFox or Camino, will show the numbers as they are generated.

Cocoa and Threading

You can use multiple threads in a Cocoa program. As usual, Cocoa brings a nice set of clean APIs that provide the threading features. All of the caveats above regarding race conditions and performance apply when using Cocoa, as well as some additional gotchas.

NSThread

NSThread is the class that abstracts threads. To create a new thread, use the class method

```
+ (void)detachNewThreadSelector: (SEL) aSelector
                      toTarget: (id) aTarget
                    withObject: (id) anArgument;
```

aSelector is a selector that describes a method aTarget can receive. aSelector's signature is

```
- (void) aSelector: (id) anArgument;
```

anArgument is what gets passed to this method. This call works just like **pthread_create()** in that the thread starts executing with the first instruction of aSelector and the thread terminates when the method exits. This is a daemon thread, so there is no need to do any kind of waiting for it to finish.

When the first **NSThread** object is created, the **NSThread** class posts an NSWillBecomeMultiThreadedNotification. Afterward, calls to [NSThread isMultiThreaded] will return YES. You can use this call and the notification to decide whether you need to use synchronization for your data structures. If you are single threaded, using synchronization will just slow you down for zero benefit. **pthread_create()** does not post this notification nor does it cause **-isMultiThreaded** to return YES, so be aware of this if you mix pthreads and **NSThread**.

When you create an **NSThread**, you also get an **NSRunLoop** that you can use for event handling and Distributed Objects operations. If you are going to be using any Cocoa calls in the thread, you should create an **NSAutoreleasePool**. **NSApplication**'s **+detachDrawingThread:toTarget:withObject:** method is a convenience for making a new thread and setting up an autorelease pool. And you are not constrained to only doing drawing in that thread.

The **NSLock** class behaves very much like a pthread_mutex_t. You can lock and unlock it, try the lock, and have a lock timeout. Likewise, **NSConditionLock** fills the role of pthread_cond_t. The Cocoa condition lock API hides the loop that you had to use when using **pthread_cond_wait()**. Instead, it is a little state machine that keeps track of what state it is in (all programmer definable), and you can tell it to wait until a particular state occurs, as well as tell it what state to move to.

Prior to OS X 10.2, child threads could not draw into Cocoa views. Jaguar added this ability. You need to call **-(BOOL)lockFocusIfCanDraw** before doing your drawing. You also have to explicitly flush the window before the window server will show the updated contents:

```
if ([drawView lockFocusIfCanDraw]) {
    // set colors, use NSBezierPath and NSString drawing functions
    [[drawView window] flushWindow];
    [drawView unlockFocus];
}
```

Cocoa and thread safety

Parts of the Foundation and AppKit frameworks are thread safe, and some are not. In general, immutable objects are thread safe and can be used by multiple threads. Mutable objects are not thread safe and should not be used by multiple threads. You have to be careful about how you create an object before making assumptions about the mutability of an object – for instance, consider a method that takes an **NSString**. **NSString**s are generally immutable. Given inheritance though, a caller can legally create an **NSMutableString** and give it to a method that takes an **NSString**. In the same way, immutable containers are safe to share amongst threads, but mutable containers are not.

User interface objects are not thread safe and should only be used on the main thread. In general, you should assume that an object is not thread safe unless it is explicitly documented as such.

Objective-C @synchronized blocks

When you tell the compiler to use native Objective-C exceptions, whether with the checkbox in Xcode or by giving the compiler the -fobjc-exceptions flag, you also get to use the Objective-C thread synchronization operator.

The @synchronized() directive locks a section of code that operates on a particular object. Only a single thread can manipulate that object in this chunk of code at a time. Other threads using the same object will be blocked until the @synchronized block is exited.

@synchronized() takes a single argument, which can be any Objective-C object. You can use an object that is stored in an instance variable, you can use self, or you can even use a class object. If you are using @synchronized(self) inside of a class method, you will be @synchronized with the class object. @synchronized(someObject) acts like a recursive mutex, so a thread can use the same object in different blocks that are synchronized with the same object. Exceptions thrown from within a @synchronized() block will automatically release the lock.

For the More Curious: Thread Local Storage

Sometimes it is very handy to have storage that is private to a thread. In the basics.m program above, you could stash the contents of the ThreadInfo stack into thread local storage instead of on the function call stack. Thread local storage behaves like global variables but are private to the thread. errno is stored in thread local storage so that every thread has its own errno.

To use thread local storage, initialize a pthread_key_t using **pthread_key_create()**:

```
int pthread_key_create (pthread_key_t *key, void (*destructor)(void *));
```

This creates an abstract key. Usually you name a variable with a descriptive name or associate this key with a descriptive string in a dictionary, as shown in Figure 20.5. The destructor function is called when the thread exits, so that dynamic memory (or other resources) can be cleaned up.

Set a thread-local value by using **pthread_setspecific()**:

```
int pthread_setspecific (pthread_key_t key, const void *value);
```

and get the value by using **pthread_getspecific()**:

```
void *pthread_getspecific (pthread_key_t key);
```

Figure 20.5   Thread local storage

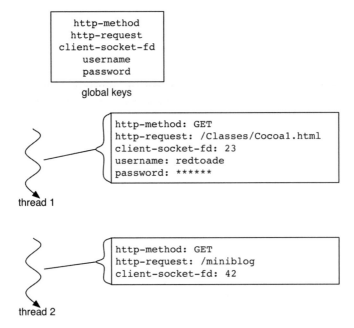

If you are using **NSThread**, you can use

- (NSMutableDictionary *) **threadDictionary**

To put stuff into thread local storage, just store stuff in the dictionary. This is an **NSThread** instance method, so you need to find your current **NSThread** object by using [NSThread currentThread].

For the More Curious: Read/Write Locks

Both Cocoa and pthreads provide read/write locks. These allow a data structure to be read by a number of readers simultaneously but only allow one thread write access at a time.

pthread_rwlock_t works just like pthread_mutex_t but with a couple of extra calls. Here are the details:

pthread_rwlock_init (pthread_rwlock_t *lock,
                    const pthread_rwlockattr_t *attr);

OS X does not define PTHREAD_RWLOCK_INITIALIZER, so you cannot create them statically.

int **pthread_rwlock_destroy** (pthread_rwlock_t *lock);

Rather than use **lock()**, you specify which kind of locking you want:

- int **pthread_rwlock_rdlock** (pthread_rwlock_t *rwlock);

- int **pthread_rwlock_tryrdlock** (pthread_rwlock_t *rwlock);

- int **pthread_rwlock_wrlock** (pthread_rwlock_t *rwlock);

- int **pthread_rwlock_trywrlock** (pthread_rwlock_t *rwlock);

And unlock by using

int **pthread_rwlock_unlock** (pthread_rwlock_t *rwlock);

In general, using read/write locks can be a bad idea because it doubles the number of actual lock operations. Read/write locks can be implemented with a mutex and two condition variables. Unless you have some really expensive data structures, the overhead of the read/write lock operations will be more than the operation you are protecting. Given that caveat, there are some times when they are quite useful, especially when there are a lot of readers, not many modifications, and accessing the data structure is time consuming.

Exercises

1. Use conditions to implement the producer-consumer problem. One thread should generate integers in the Fibonacci sequence; another should print those numbers. Use **sleep()** and ifdefs to vary the rate at which the two threads work, so that, depending on defined constants, either the producer or consumer ends up having to wait for the other thread.

2. Tweak basics.m to use Thread Local Storage to store the index, number to count to, and the sleep time.

3. Make nodepool.m from Chapter 7: *Memory* thread safe so that multiple threads can allocate stuff out of the same pool.

21

Operations

As you saw in Chapter 10: *Performance Tuning*, multiple processors in a single computer are a fact of life today. CPU manufacturers cannot scale processor speed as they have in the past, so they are putting their transistors into more CPU cores. Getting the best performance out of today's systems requires parallel programming, which usually means using threads. Threaded programming is difficult and error prone, making it harder and more expensive to take full advantage of the processing power of today's systems

Mac OS X 10.5 introduced some classes that simplify some kinds of parallel programming. The **NSOperation** class represents a unit of parallelizable work, and the **NSOperationQueue** class takes **NSOperation**s and executes them. Even though "queue" implies first-in, first-out execution of operations, **NSOperationQueue** is more flexible because you can specify dependencies between operations. One operation can wait until other operations are done. You can also specify operation priorities, allowing one kind of operation to always take precedence over other kinds of operations.

In Mac OS X 10.5, there are two main kinds of operations, concurrent and non-concurrent. *Non-concurrent operations* cause an **NSOperationQueue** to run the operation in its own thread, while multiple *concurrent operations* can be active in a single thread.

This nomenclature is a bit backwards from the point of view of someone creating a new operation, but it makes sense from the point of view of the **NSOperationQueue**. The queue runs **NSOperation**s. If an operation wants a thread all to itself, it cannot run concurrently with any **NSOperation** on that same thread; hence, it is a non-concurrent operation. Similarly, if an operation is fine with having multiple operations running at the same time (perhaps they all are doing asynchronous I/O), then they are run concurrently all on the same thread.

In Mac OS X 10.6, all operations are non-concurrent. In fact, the concurrency flag is ignored by **NSOperationQueue**. Every operation will be started in its own thread. This can be a surprising gotcha if you have concurrent operations that you wrote under Leopard being compiled into a 10.6-and-beyond application. iOS 4 has the Mac OS X 10.6 behavior.

Aside from the concurrent and non-concurrent distinction, there are, for lack of a better term, simple-lifetime and complex-lifetime operations. Simple-lifetime operations override **-main**, do their work, and then fall out the bottom of the method. Once **-main** returns, the operation queue assumes that your operation has completed and will schedule the next one to run. For Mac OS X 10.5, all non-concurrent operations (each getting its own thread) are simple operations.

Complex-lifetime operations let you control the entire lifetime of the operation. Instead of overriding **-main** you override **-start**. You can exit from **-start**, but the operation will still be considered to be running. Operations have a KVO component, and with complex-lifetime operations you are responsible for maintaining the KVO contracts. Details of implementing complex-lifetime operations will be discussed later in this chapter. For Mac OS X 10.5, all concurrent operations (multiple operations sharing a thread) are complex-lifetime.

Simple-Lifetime Operations

If you have synchronous work to do, like a large computation, you will want to use a simple-lifetime operation. This is what you get by default when you subclass **NSOperation** and override **-main**.

```
- (void) main;
```

Do your work, and when you are done, just return from the method. That is enough to tell the **NSOperationQueue** that ran the operation that the operation has completed its work.

Operations can be cancelled at any time, so you should poll **-isCancelled** when convenient:

```
- (BOOL) isCancelled;
```

The **NSOperation** form of cancellation differs from the cancellation provided by the pthread API. pthread cancellation will terminate a thread, and is a tricky game to play because the thread may be in the middle of manipulating some global data structure, like in **malloc()**, when it is cancelled. **NSOperation** does not use thread cancellation, instead it relies on the operation to notice whether it has been cancelled and do any tear down of its environment. You should also check **-isCancelled** first thing when your **-main** method is run. **NSOperationQueue** will always run its operations, even if they have been cancelled.

You can add and remove dependencies between operations:

```
- (void) addDependency: (NSOperation *) op;
- (void) removeDependency: (NSOperation *) op;
```

Circular dependencies are not supported and are not detected. **NSOperationQueue** is the entity that actually honors the dependencies, so there is nothing preventing you from manually running an **NSOperation** before its dependencies run. If you want to see all the dependencies a particular operation has, you can look at its dependencies array:

```
- (NSArray *) dependencies;
```

You can set and get the relative priority of an operation by manipulating its queue priority:

```
- (NSOperationQueuePriority) queuePriority;
- (void) setQueuePriority: (NSOperationQueuePriority) p;
```

where NSOperationQueuePriority is one of:

```
enum {
    NSOperationQueuePriorityVeryLow,
    NSOperationQueuePriorityLow,
    NSOperationQueuePriorityNormal,
    NSOperationQueuePriorityHigh,
    NSOperationQueuePriorityVeryHigh
};
```

Changing an operation's priority does not impact the operating system scheduler, so setting a Very High priority will not cause your operation to be allocated more CPU time. This value is only used by an **NSOperationQueue** to decide which operation to run next.

NSOperationQueue

NSOperationQueue is a class that accepts **NSOperation** instances and runs them. On Mac OS X 10.5, the queue will run the operation in the current thread if the operation says that it is a concurrent operation. If the operation is non-concurrent, or you are on 10.6, the queue will create and manage threads automatically.

Add an operation to an **NSOperationQueue** with **-addOperation:**

```
- (void) addOperation: (NSOperation *) op;
```

-operations returns the current set of operations that are currently running or that are waiting:

```
- (NSArray *) operations;
```

By default, an **NSOperationQueue** will choose the number of concurrent threads it manages based on the number of processors, as well as vague "other factors" mentioned in Apple's documentation. You can manually tweak and query the concurrency factor with these calls:

```
- (NSInteger) maxConcurrentOperationCount;
- (void) setMaxConcurrentOperationCount: (NSInteger) count;
```

If you decide to abandon the work a queue is doing, you can tell it to cancel all of the operations:

```
- (void) cancelAllOperations;
```

You can wait synchronously for all operations to complete:

```
- (void) waitUntilAllOperationsAreFinished;
```

Threading issues

Because non-concurrent operations run on their own thread, you need to be aware of the thread safety issues of any API that you are using in your operation. For example, you cannot safely set an **NSTextField**'s value from another thread because user interface manipulations must be done on the main thread.

One subtle point to remember is that the current thread is used when posting an **NSNotification** or when handing a KVO observer notification. If you plan on using an **NSNotification** or KVO to notify other objects that an operation has completed, you need to be aware that the other object's notification methods will run in the same thread that ran the operation and not the main thread, which unfortunately is often not what you want to happen. You can use one of the **-performSelectorOnMainThread:** family of methods to trigger a notification on the main thread.

MandelOpper

The Mandelbrot set is a favorite graphical pastime amongst many programmers. It is a fractal geometry construct that can generate really cool images. Generating the Mandelbrot set is a computationally intensive process, which lends itself to parallel processing. The MandelOpper application will calculate a Mandelbrot set and display it in a window, using instances of a simple-lifetime **NSOperation** class to do the actual calculation (Figure 21.1).

Figure 21.1 MandelOpper screen being filled in

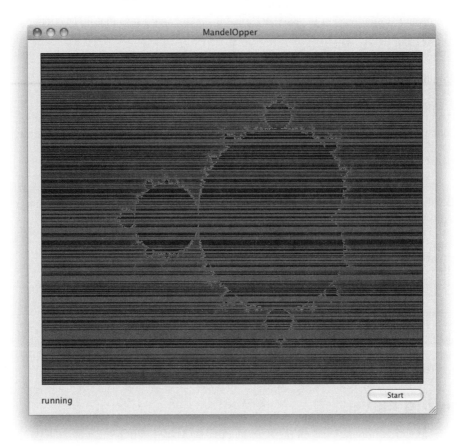

Figure 21.2 shows the general class layout. **MandelOpperAppDelegate** is your typical Cocoa application controller, coordinating the user interface and initiating the Mandelbrot calculations. The **Bitmap** class holds a bucket of bytes that the **CalcOperation** operations will write their pixel colors into. Each **CalcOperation** will calculate one row of pixels. The **BitmapView** displays the contents of a **Bitmap**.

Figure 21.2 MandelOpper classes

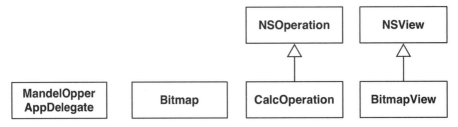

Bitmap

Bitmap wraps an array of bytes, gives callers the starting address for a particular row of pixels, and generates an image representation suitable for drawing. The pixels are 4-byte values, in the form RGBA, one byte for the red, green, blue, and alpha (transparency) components.

Create a new Cocoa Application in Xcode and name it MandelOpper. Create new source files for Bitmap.h and Bitmap.m. Here is Bitmap.h:

```
// Bitmap.h -- Wrap a bucket of 4-byte pixels, with ready access to
//             the base address of individual scanlines and easy image rep
//             creation.

#import <Cocoa/Cocoa.h>

// The buffer is composed of a linear array of 32-bit elements, ordered RGBA.

@interface Bitmap : NSObject {
    NSUInteger _width;      // number of pixels per line.
    NSUInteger _height;     // number of lines.
    unsigned char *_buffer; // A bucket of bytes.
}

@property (readonly) NSUInteger width;
@property (readonly) NSUInteger height;

// Make a new bitmap with the given width and height.
- (id) initWithWidth: (NSUInteger) width
              height: (NSUInteger) height;

// Returns an image representation suitable for drawing.
- (NSBitmapImageRep *) imageRep;

// Get the location in memory for a particular scanline in the bitmap.
// You can safely travel width * 4 bytes along its path without a lock.
- (unsigned char *) baseAddressForLine: (NSUInteger) line;

@end // Bitmap
```

Now edit Bitmap.m and add the initializer, basic accessors, and cleanup methods. The bitmap's memory is initialized to 0x55, giving all the pixels a semi-transparent gray color.

```
#import "Bitmap.h"

@implementation Bitmap

@synthesize width = _width;
@synthesize height = _height;

- (id) initWithWidth: (NSUInteger) width
              height: (NSUInteger) height {

    if (self = [super init]) {
        _width = width;
        _height = height;

        // Get a chunk of memory, then fill it with gray.
        _buffer = malloc (_width * _height * 4);
```

```
        // Fill with a semitransparent gray color.
        memset (_buffer, 0x55, _width * _height * 4);
    }

    return self;

} // initWithWidth

- (void) dealloc {
    free (_buffer);
    [super dealloc];

} // dealloc
```

Next is **-baseAddressForLine:**, which returns the address in memory where a particular row of pixels live. This is just basic pointer math, assuming four bytes per pixel. **CalcOperation** will use this base address to know where it should start placing pixel values.

```
// Perform some pointer math to give the caller the starting address for
// a particular scanline.

- (unsigned char *) baseAddressForLine: (NSUInteger) line {
    unsigned char *addr = _buffer + (line * self.width * 4);
    return addr;

} // baseAddressForLine
```

And finally, **-imageRep** wraps the pixel buffer in an **NSBitmapImageRep** for drawing. It is also the last method for the class.

```
- (NSBitmapImageRep *) imageRep {
    NSBitmapImageRep *rep;
    rep = [[NSBitmapImageRep alloc]
            initWithBitmapDataPlanes: &_buffer
            pixelsWide: self.width
            pixelsHigh: self.height
            bitsPerSample: 8
            samplesPerPixel: 4
            hasAlpha: YES
            isPlanar: NO
            colorSpaceName: NSDeviceRGBColorSpace
            bytesPerRow: self.width * 4
            bitsPerPixel: 32];

    return [rep autorelease];

} // imageRep

@end // Bitmap
```

BitmapView

The pixels have a place to live. Now they need a place where they can show themselves off. Make a new **NSView** subclass called **BitmapView**. Edit BitmapView.h with the class interface, which just hangs onto the bitmap and gives callers a way to set the bitmap to use for drawing:

```
// BitmapView.h -- View that displays a Bitmap, which usually contains a
//                 Mandelbrot set.
```

```
#import <Cocoa/Cocoa.h>

@class Bitmap;

@interface BitmapView : NSView {
    Bitmap *_bitmap; // Contains the bits to draw
}

// The bitmap to use for drawing.
@property (retain) Bitmap *bitmap;

// Cause a redraw from another thread becaue passing a scalar through
// to -performSelectorOnMainThread is awkward.  The prefix is to avoid
// any future name collision, because "setNeedsDisplay" is a very
// obvious name, and Apple may add their own setNeedsDisplay that
// takes no parameters.
- (void) bnr_setNeedsDisplay;

@end // BitmapView
```

Edit BitmapView.m to include the requisite headers and then implement **dealloc** and **setBitmap**:

```
#import "BitmapView.h"
#import "Bitmap.h"

@implementation BitmapView
@synthesize bitmap = _bitmap;

// Time to use a new bitmap.
- (void) setBitmap: (Bitmap *) bitmap {
    [_bitmap autorelease];
    _bitmap = [bitmap retain];

    [self setNeedsDisplay: YES];

} // setBitmap

// Clean up our mess.
- (void) dealloc {
    [_bitmap release];
    [super dealloc];
} // dealloc
```

The view will need to redraw itself after any calculation operation has completed. Usually you do this by calling [view setNeedsDisplay: YES]. Unfortunately **-setNeedsDisplay:** is not thread safe. Ordinarily you would use one of the **-performSelectorOnMainThread:** methods to do this, but **-performSelectorOnMainThread:** only lets you pass an object parameter, not a BOOL. Cocoa does not do "autoboxing," which automatically wraps primitive C types in an object type, so wrapping a BOOL in an **NSValue** will not work either. To work around this, add a method that takes no arguments which just does a **setNeedsDisplay:YES** so that it can be called easily via another thread:

```
- (void) bnr_setNeedsDisplay {
    [self setNeedsDisplay: YES];
} // bnr_setNeedsDisplay
```

The prefix on the call is to future-proof this code. **setNeedsDisplay**, taking no arguments, is an obvious name. Apple already has a method named this in the iOS UIKit, but not in desktop AppKit. It is entirely possible that Apple will add **setNeedsDisplay** in a future version of Mac OS X. By prefixing this method, we make it obvious it's one of our methods rather than one of Apple's. Ordinarily, you do not need to worry about this, but being paranoid in this particular case is prudent.

And then add **-drawRect:**, which fills in the view's bounds and frames it with a black rectangle and also draws the contents of the bitmap:

```
- (void) drawRect: (NSRect) rect {
    // Go ahead and just draw everything every time.
    NSRect bounds = [self bounds];

    // Fill in the area with a nice (?) purplish color prior to drawing the bitmap
    [[NSColor purpleColor] set];
    NSRectFill (bounds);

    // Get the calculated bits and draw them.
    NSBitmapImageRep *rep = [self.bitmap imageRep];
    [rep drawAtPoint: NSZeroPoint];

    // And finally put a nice thin border around the view.
    [[NSColor blackColor] set];
    NSFrameRect (bounds);

} // drawRect
```

CalcOperation

Now for the calculation portion of our program. The **CalcOperation** class is a subclass of **NSOperation**, and will be a simple-lifetime, non-concurrent operation which calculates a row of pixels. Recall that in 10.5, non-concurrent operations will run in their own threads. This operation will need a few of pieces of information: what bitmap to use, what line in that bitmap to deposit its pixel calculations into, the **BitmapView** that is showing the bitmap so that it can get redrawn, and the bounds of the area of the Mandelbrot set to calculate. Since each **CalcOperation** is responsible for filling in a row, it needs to know the vertical location within the Mandelbrot set, as well as the start and end points in the horizontal direction that denote the bounds of the portion of the Mandelbrot set being calculated.

Make a new class called **CalcOperation**. Edit the header file and add instance variables to store the different bits of state that it needs and an initializer to make a new operation.

```
// CalcOperation.h -- Operation to calculate a single line of the Mandelbrot Set
//

#import <Cocoa/Cocoa.h>

@class Bitmap, BitmapView;

@interface CalcOperation : NSOperation {
    Bitmap *_bitmap;    // The bitmap that holds the pixel's memory.
    NSUInteger _line;   // The scanline of the bitmap we're responsible for
    BitmapView *_view;  // Whom to tell to redraw when we're done calculating.

    // The region of the Mandelbrot set to calculate.
    double _xStart;
    double _xEnd;
    double _y;
}

- (id) initWithBitmap: (Bitmap *) bitmap
          bitmapView: (BitmapView *) view
```

```
    calculateLine: (NSUInteger) line
          xStart: (double) xStart
            xEnd: (double) xEnd
               y: (double) y;
```

@end // CalcOperation

Edit CalcOperation.m and add the functions that actually calculate the Mandelbrot set, as well as the initializer and -dealloc.

```
#import "CalcOperation.h"

#import "Bitmap.h"
#import <complex.h>

// This determines how fine the Mandelbrot set calculations are.
#define LOOP 500
#define LIMIT 256


@implementation CalcOperation

// This determines what colors go with which values.
// I've set it up for a pleasing blue-cast scheme.

void gradient (int value, unsigned char *buffer) {
    unsigned char *ptr = buffer;
    value = value * 4;
    if (value > 255) value = 255;

    *ptr++ = value / 3;   // Red
    *ptr++ = value / 2;   // Green
    *ptr++ = value;       // Blue
    *ptr++ = 0xFF;        // Alpha
} // gradient


// buffer is a pointer to the four bytes that will hold
// the resulting color

void mandelbrot (double x, double y, unsigned char *buffer) {
    int i;
    complex z,c;

    c = x + (y * 1.0i);
    z = 0;

    for (i = 0; i < LOOP; i++) {
        z = (z * z) + c;
        if (cabs(z) > LIMIT) {
            gradient (i, buffer);
            return;
        }
    }
    gradient (0, buffer);
} // mandelbrot


- (id) initWithBitmap: (Bitmap *) bitmap
          bitmapView: (BitmapView *) view
```

```
        calculateLine: (NSUInteger) line
                xStart: (double) xStart
                  xEnd: (double) xEnd
                     y: (double) y {

    if ((self = [super init])) {
        _bitmap = [bitmap retain];
        _line = line;
        _xStart = xStart;
        _xEnd = xEnd;
        _y = y;
    }

    return self;

} // initWithBitmap


- (void) dealloc {
    [_bitmap release];
    [_view release];

    [super dealloc];

} // dealloc
```

And finally, the real interesting work of the program. Since **CalcOperation** is a simple-lifetime operation, you just need to override **-main**. If an operation is cancelled while it is still in its queue, the operation will still be run, so it is necessary to check **-isCancelled** first thing in the method so you do not do unnecessary work. And to make the display look cool, **-main** will sleep for a little bit so that the lines will filter in slow enough to see them.

```
- (void) main {

    // Make sure we weren't cancelled before starting.
    if ([self isCancelled]) {
        NSLog(@"Cancelling");
        return;
    }

    // Putting in a pause makes the scan lines fill in slower, giving
    // a groovier look to things.  Take this out for maximum performance.
    int usec = random() % 1000;
    usec *= 3000;
    usleep (usec);
```

Recall that **NSOperationQueue**, if left to its own devices, will choose the number of concurrent threads it manages based on the number of processors, as well as vague "other factors" mentioned in Apple's documentation. One of those hidden other factors is that if the **NSOperation** blocks, then the operation queue may create another thread and assign it an operation to run. In this case, when the **usleep()** function is called to sleep the current thread for a specified number of microseconds, **NSOperationQueue** notices the operation has entered kernel-space and will schedule another **CalcOperation**. I have witnessed over sixty threads being created by MandelOpper. Performing I/O (e.g. **NSLog**, network communications, file I/O) or even entering an @synchronized block is enough for **NSOperationQueue** to think it needs to create more threads. If this turns out to be a problem for you, you can determine the number of processors in your system and pass that value to **-setMaxConcurrentOperationCount:** See the exercises for more information.

Next, set up some of the state that is necessary for the pixel calculations: the address in the bitmap to put the pixel values, how far in the Mandelbrot set to advance horizontally for each pixel, and a "you are here" variable that gets scooted after we calculate a pixel's values.

```
// This is where we start filling in memory.
unsigned char *scanline = [_bitmap baseAddressForLine: _line];

// How far in the Mandelbrot set to advance for each pixel.
double xDelta = (_xEnd - _xStart) / _bitmap.width;

// Start here.
double x = _xStart;
```

Now loop over every pixel in the row and calculate the pixel values. Since Mandelbrot calculations could take a fair amount of time, check occasionally if we have been cancelled. If so, bail out because there is no need to do any more work.

```
for (int i = 0; i < _bitmap.width; i++) {

    // Figure out where in memory to put the next pixel.
    unsigned char *pixel = (scanline + i * 4);

    // Scoot over and draw.
    x += xDelta;
    mandelbrot (x, _y, pixel);

    // Check every now and then for a cancellation.
    if (i % 50 == 0) {
        if ([self isCancelled]) {
            NSLog(@"cancelling!");
            return;
        }
    }
}
```

If you have successfully completed a scan line, tell the **BitmapView** to draw itself again, using the no-argument **-bnr_setNeedsDisplay** added to BitmapView. This also ends CalcOperation.m.

```
    // We're done!  Tell the view to update itself when convenient.
    [_view performSelectorOnMainThread: @selector(bnr_setNeedsDisplay)
            withObject: nil
            waitUntilDone: NO];
} // main

@end // CalcOperation
```

MandelOpperAppDelegate

Now that all of the worker classes have been written, it is time to hook everything together. Edit MandelOpperAppDelegate.h and add the interface for the class, including two IBOutlets for a **BitmapView** and a text field for a status line, which says whether the program is idling or calculating. There is also an IBAction for starting the calculations. There is an **NSOperationQueue** which will hold all of the **CalcOperation**s created, one for each row in the bitmap, as well as the region of the Mandelbrot set that is being displayed.

```
#import <Cocoa/Cocoa.h>

@class Bitmap, BitmapView;

@interface MandelOpperAppDelegate : NSObject {
    Bitmap *_bitmap;                      // Where the Mandelbrot set image lives
    IBOutlet BitmapView *_bitmapView;  // Where it gets displayed

    IBOutlet NSTextField *_statusLine; // Tell the user what we're doing

    NSOperationQueue *_queue;          // Holds the calculation operations

    NSRect _region;                    // The region of the set being displayed.
}

@property (assign) IBOutlet BitmapView *bitmapView;
@property (assign) IBOutlet NSTextField *statusLine;

// Start calculating the set and display the results.
- (IBAction) start: (id) sender;

@end // MandelOpperAppDelegate
```

Open MainMenu.xib and drop a CustomView on the window. Make it the **BitmapView** class and add a text field. Set up the resizing connections so that the view will expand and the text field will stay at the bottom. Hook up the outlets to the **BitmapView** and the text field and hook up the button action, too, as shown in Figure 21.3.

Figure 21.3   MandelOpper window

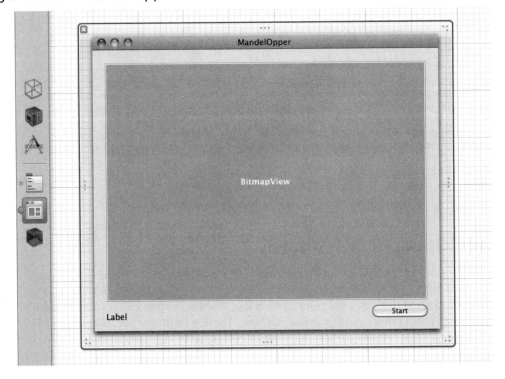

Now edit MandelOpperAppDelegate.m. First off, add a method to update the status line. Also, override **-awakeFromNib** to set the status to "idle" and set the region to a rectangle that snuggles up to the Mandelbrot set, along with a **-dealloc** to release the objects that will eventually get created.

```objc
#import "MandelOpperAppDelegate.h"

#import "Bitmap.h"
#import "BitmapView.h"
#import "CalcOperation.h"

// Adopt the protocol here so we don't have to pollute our header with it.
@interface MandelOpperAppDelegate () <BitmapViewDelegate>
@end // extension


@implementation MandelOpperAppDelegate
@synthesize bitmapView = _bitmapView;
@synthesize statusLine = _statusLine;

// Change the message in a text field in the window.
- (void) updateStatus: (NSString *) message {
    [self.statusLine setStringValue: message];
} // updateStatus


- (void) awakeFromNib {
    // Awaiting instructions, O Master
    [self updateStatus: @"idle"];

    // This gives us a nice view of the entire Mandelbrot set
    _region = NSMakeRect (-2.0, -1.2, 3.0, 2.4);
} // awakeFromNib


// Clean up our mess.
- (void) dealloc {
    [_bitmap release];
    [_queue release];

    [super dealloc];
} // dealloc
```

NSBlockOperation

You will be creating a bunch of **CalcOperations** for calculating individual rows of the Mandelbrot set. But how do you know when you are done? Operations of the same priority that are not blocking on a dependency can be run in any arbitrary order. Even if they were started in a predictable order, they may not all complete in a predictable order. One way to determine when all the calculations are done is to have a special "I'm done!" operation that is dependent on all of the calculation operations which would tell the app delegate that all the work has been finished. It would be annoying to have to create a special operation subclass just for this task, so you will use an **NSBlockOperation**, which you initialize with a block. When the **NSBlockOperation** runs, it runs its block.

You are not guaranteed which thread the all-done operation will be run from, and you should not do anything UI-related from anything other than the main thread, so the block uses

-performSelectorOnMainThread to set the status line. Do not enter this code yet; it will appear partway through the **-start** method:

```
...
NSBlockOperation *allDone = [NSBlockOperation blockOperationWithBlock: ^{
        // Most likely we are *not* the main thread when this block runs,
        // and we need to be on the main thread to update the status line
        // text field.

        [self performSelectorOnMainThread: @selector(updateStatus:)
                withObject: @"done!"
                waitUntilDone: NO];
    }];
...
```

So, now let's create the operation queue, make the calc operations, and add them to the operation queue. The **-start:** method is hooked up to a button, so that's a good place to start things. If there are calculations currently running, cancel them and dispose of any previous operations. Update the status line to "running," and make an **NSOperationQueue** to hold our new operations:

```
- (IBAction) start: (id) sender {
    // Stop any in-flight calculations.
    [_queue cancelAllOperations];
    [_queue release];

    // Inform the user what's going on.
    [self updateStatus: @"running"];

    // This is the queue that will run all of our operations.
    _queue = [[NSOperationQueue alloc] init];
```

Next, make the "all done" **NSBlockOperation**. You have to make this first so that you will have it available when you create the **CalcOperation**s so you can hook up the dependencies.

```
    // Make a new operation to tell us we've finished calculating.
    // Every other action will become a dependency of this one, making
    // it wait until all of the calculations are done.
    NSBlockOperation *allDone = [NSBlockOperation blockOperationWithBlock: ^{
            // Most likely we are *not* the main thread when this block runs,
            // and we need to be on the main thread to update the status line
            // text field.

            [self performSelectorOnMainThread: @selector(updateStatus:)
                    withObject: @"done!"
                    waitUntilDone: NO];
        }];
```

You will need a **Bitmap** to draw in, so create one. Associate that **Bitmap** with the **BitmapView** and also set up the various values used in creating the **CalcOperation**s.

```
    // Construct a bitmap the size of the frame (using one point == one pixel)
    NSRect frame = self.bitmapView.frame;
    NSUInteger height = frame.size.height;
    NSUInteger width = frame.size.width;

    [_bitmap release];
    _bitmap = [[Bitmap alloc] initWithWidth: width  height: height];

    // Tell the bitmap view to use this new bitmap.
```

```
    [self.bitmapView setBitmap: _bitmap];

    // This is the change in Y covered by one line of the bitmap
    double deltaY = _region.size.height / height;

    // The starting point for the y coordinates given to each
    // calculation operation.
    double y = NSMaxY (_region);
```

Now create a **CalcOperation** for each row and add the new **CalcOperation** as a dependency for the **allDone** operation.

```
    // Create a new CalcOperation for each line of the bitmap.
    for (int i = 0; i < frame.size.height; i++) {
        CalcOperation *op;
        op = [[CalcOperation alloc]
                initWithBitmap: _bitmap
                bitmapView: self.bitmapView
                calculateLine: i
                xStart: NSMinX(_region)
                xEnd: NSMaxX(_region)
                y: y];

        // Set the dependency for the allDone operation, and put in the
        // queue.  The operation may start running immediately.
        [allDone addDependency: op];
        [_queue addOperation: op];

        y -= deltaY;
    }
```

The **CalcOperation**s will start running as soon as they are added to the queue, so they can start doing real work while we are still adding other operations to the queue.

Finally add the **allDone** operation to the queue. The order that operations are added to the queue is important: if we added the all-done operation first, the queue would keep checking to see if all of the **allDone** operation's dependencies have completed. It would be possible for us to add the **allDone** operation, add a couple of calculation operations, and then have the calculations complete on other processors before adding the rest of the operations to the queue. The queue would then fire the **allDone** operation, this loop would then add more operations, and mayhem would ensue.

```
    // Finaly add the all-done operation.  We could not have done this
    // first, because the queue may have drained before we added all of
    // the CalcOperations
    [_queue addOperation: allDone];

} // start
```

This wraps up the app delegate class and this exercise. Compile and run your application.

Complex-Lifetime Operations

MandelOpper used simple-lifetime operations, meaning that **-main** started, ran to completion, and exited. In Mac OS X 10.5, it is a non-concurrent operation and gets its own thread.

You may have operations that do work that is asynchronous in nature, such as accessing the network or waiting for data to arrive from a radiation detector. These operations could wait in **-main**, or they could be implemented as complex-lifetime operations that have more control over their lifetime.

In Mac OS X 10.5, you can create concurrent operations by overriding **-isConcurrent** and returning YES. This tells **NSOperationQueue** to start the operation in the current thread. In 10.6, the operation will be started in its own thread. The Cocoa documentation makes vague and scary sounding references to "setting up the execution environment" in relation to concurrent operations. This just means that you need to do whatever setup is necessary for your operation to do its work. If you wanted to run your concurrent operation in your own thread, you would need to create this thread yourself (in Mac OS X 10.5). If you were doing a network operation, you would decide what server you want to talk to and make the connection.

When writing a complex-lifetime operation, you need to override four methods, compared to just overriding **-main** for a non-concurrent / simple-lifetime operation:

```
- (void) start;
- (BOOL) isConcurrent; // 10.5 only
- (BOOL) isExecuting;
- (BOOL) isFinished;
```

-start is where you "set up your execution environment" and start your work. This is where you would build your network connection or initiate asynchronous I/O. It is important not to [super start]! The default **-start** does extra work and calls **-main**, which defeats the purpose of making our own **-start** method.

KVO properties

Override **-isExecuting** and **-isFinished** so that they return YES if your operation is currently executing or if it has finished executing. These should be KVO compliant. That is, when your execution state transitions from "not executing" to "executing", or when you transition to a "finished" state, you should make sure that KVO notifications for the isFinished and isExecuting key occur.

There are actually a number of properties you can observe with KVO on **NSOperation**. All are read-only, except for **queuePriority**:

isCancelled is YES if the operation has been cancelled, NO if it is still free to execute.

isConcurrent is YES if the operation sets up its own execution environment, NO if **NSOperationQueue** should create a thread for it.

isExecuting is YES if the operation is currently running. The value starts off at NO, changes to YES when the operation runs, and then changes back to NO when the operation stops running.

isFinished is YES when the operation has finished.

isReady is YES if the operation can be run. **NSOperation** looks at its dependencies to decide if it is ready.

dependencies is an **NSArray** of all of the operations this operation is dependent on.

queuePriority is one of the NSOperationQueuePriority* constants. This is a mutable property.

Be aware of the KVC/KVO work that is performed under the hood when you are determining the granularity of your operations. If you have very fine-grained operations, you may spend more processor time in KVO overhead than actually doing real work.

ImageSnarfer

The next exercise is ImageSnarfer, which loads a batch of images from a website, controlled by a text file containing URLs, and displays them in a view. The **NSOperation** subclass will be a complex-lifetime operation.

Figure 21.4   ImageSnarfer screen

The **SnarfOperation** class uses **NSURLConnection** to download an image asynchronously. This exercise uses Objective-C 2.0 features and KVO notifications.

There are two other classes involved: **ImageCanvas**, which draws an array of images (fed by SnarfOperations), and **AppController**, which reads a text file of URLs and creates operations. All of these classes are shown in Figure 21.5.

Figure 21.5   ImageSnarfer classes

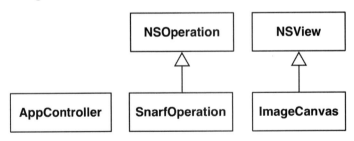

ImageCanvas

Create a new Cocoa Application project called ImageSnarfer. Turn on Objective-C Garbage Collection (-fobjc-gc-only). Create a new **NSView** subclass called **ImageCanvas**. The canvas has an array of images and also an array of NSPoints (wrapped in **NSValues**) that hold the randomized locations in the window to draw each image. For example, index zero in the origins array is the point to draw the image at index zero in the images array. There is also a method to add a new image to the canvas. Edit ImageCanvas.h and add the class definition:

```
#import <Cocoa/Cocoa.h>

@interface ImageCanvas : NSView {
    NSMutableArray *_images;  // array of NSImages
    NSMutableArray *_origins; // array of NSPoint values
}

// Add an image to the canvas.  The canvas will choose a random location
// to draw the image.
- (void) addImage: (NSImage *) image;

@end // ImageCanvas
```

Now edit ImageCanvas.m. The **-initWithFrame:** method creates the arrays. The **-addImage:** method puts an image on the list of images and chooses a random point where to draw the image.

```
#import "ImageCanvas.h"

@implementation ImageCanvas

- (id) initWithFrame: (NSRect) frame {
    if (self = [super initWithFrame: frame]) {
        // Create the place to store the images and their display locations.
        _images = [NSMutableArray array];
        _origins = [NSMutableArray array];
    }

    return self;

} // initWithFrame


// Add an image to the view's list of images to display.
```

```
- (void) addImage: (NSImage *) image {
    // Bail out if we're given an obviously bad image.
    if (image == nil) return;

    // Add it to the list.
    [_images addObject: image];

    // In parallel to the images list, store an origin NSPoint wrapped
    // in an NSValue.  Pick a random location in the view so that the
    // entire image is visible in the view.
    NSRect bounds = [self bounds];
    int maxX = bounds.size.width - [image size].width;
    int maxY = bounds.size.height - [image size].height;

    NSPoint origin = NSMakePoint (random() % maxX, random() % maxY);

    // Wrap the point in an NSValue and add to the list of origins.
    NSValue *value = [NSValue valueWithPoint: origin];
    [_origins addObject: value];

    // New stuff to see, so cause a redraw sometime in the future.
    [self setNeedsDisplay: YES];

} // addImage
```

The final method for the **ImageCanvas** is draws the images. One point of interest is the array is being enumerated by a block. The block is passed the index of the currently enumerated item, which makes looking up the corresponding image origin very easy.

```
// Display all of the images.
- (void) drawRect: (NSRect) rect {

    // Redraw everything every time.
    NSRect bounds = [self bounds];

    // Make a nice white background.
    [[NSColor whiteColor] set];
    NSRectFill (bounds);

    // We'll be putting a black rectangle around each image, so go ahead
    // and make black the current drawing color.
    [[NSColor blackColor] set];

    // Walk the images
    [_images enumerateObjectsUsingBlock: ^(id object, NSUInteger index, BOOL *stop) {
        // Get the image to draw, and where it lives
        NSValue *pointValue = [_origins objectAtIndex: index];
        NSPoint origin = [pointValue pointValue];

        NSImage *image = (NSImage *)object;

        // Draw the image.
        [image drawAtPoint: origin
                  fromRect: NSZeroRect // the entire image
                 operation: NSCompositeCopy
                  fraction: 1.0];

        // Give it a nice little border.
        NSRect imageBounds = { origin, image.size };
```

```
            NSFrameRect (imageBounds);
    }];

    NSFrameRect (bounds);

} // drawRect
```

SnarfOperation

SnarfOperation is our **NSOperation** subclass that loads an image from the Internet using **NSURLConnection**. **NSURLConnection** uses an **NSURLRequest** to specify what URL to fetch, along with other request information, like HTTP headers and cookies. **NSURLConnection** informs a delegate with callbacks, which you will see shortly. Because **NSURLConnection** works asynchronously, we can use it as the workhorse for our concurrent **NSOperation** subclass.

Create a new class called **SnarfOperation** and add this interface to SnarfOperation.h. There is storage for the isExecuting and isFinished properties and a BOOL for noting whether the image loading was successful or had an error. There are also instance variables for the various bits of overhead needed for the data download.

```
#import <Cocoa/Cocoa.h>

// In 10.5, this would be a concurrent operation, meaning that we
// won't get a thread automatically from Cocoa.  For 10.6, this is a
// complex-lifetime operation, meaning we will be controlling the
// object lifetime and handling the KVO foobage.
// All SnarfOperations operation will perform their url loading on the main thread.

@interface SnarfOperation : NSOperation {
    BOOL _isExecuting;          // YES if we're loading an image
    BOOL _isFinished;           // YES if the image loaded (or theres an error)
    BOOL _wasSuccessful;        // YES if life is groovy

    NSURL *_url;                // Where to load the image from
    NSImage *_image;            // The completed image.

    NSURLConnection *_connection;  // Our conduit to the internet
    NSMutableData *_imageData;     // Data accumulates here as it comes in.
}

// Generate the appropriate interfaces.

@property (readonly) BOOL isExecuting;
@property (readonly) BOOL isFinished;
@property (readonly) BOOL wasSuccessful;
@property (readonly) NSURL *url;
@property (readonly) NSImage *image;

// Make a new operation what URL to download images from.
- (id) initWithURL: (NSURL *) url;

@end // SnarfOperation
```

Start off SnarfOperation.m with a redeclaration of the Objective-C 2.0 properties so that they can be modified in this source file and then generate the accessors:

```
#import "SnarfOperation.h"

// Republish our read-only properties so we they are mutable for us.

@interface SnarfOperation ()

@property (readwrite) BOOL isExecuting;
@property (readwrite) BOOL isFinished;
@property (readwrite) BOOL wasSuccessful;
@property (assign, readwrite) NSImage *image;

@end // SnarfOperation


@implementation SnarfOperation

// Generate the accessors.
@synthesize isExecuting = _isExecuting;
@synthesize isFinished = _isFinished;
@synthesize wasSuccessful = _wasSuccessful;

@synthesize url = _url;
@synthesize image = _image;
```

NSOperation is KVO compliant for its isExecuting and isFinished properties. We can change the values of these properties and have KVO notifications happen for us automatically, except that **NSOperation** disables it for these two properties. Add this class method to allow the automatic KVO machinery to work again for these properties.

```
// NSOperation disengages the KVO machinery for the "finished" and
// "executing" properties.  Re-engage the automatic machinery to do
// automagic KVO notifications when we change the values.

+ (BOOL) automaticallyNotifiesObserversForKey: (NSString *) key {
    // We're lazy, so let Cocoa do all the KVO grooviness for these
    // attributes.
    if ([key isEqualToString: @"isFinished"]
        || [key isEqualToString:@"isExecuting"]) {
        return YES;

    } else {
        // Otherwise do whatever NSOperation does.
        return [super automaticallyNotifiesObserversForKey: key];
    }

} // automaticallyNotifiesObserversForKey
```

-initWithURL: just hangs on to the URL. It does not actually begin the download until told to later.

```
- (id) initWithURL: (NSURL *) u {
    if ((self = [super init])) {
        _url = u;
    }

    return self;

} // initWithURL
```

Since this a complex-lifetime operation, don't override **-main** but instead override **-start**, which is where we set up our execution environment. In our case, "setting up the execution environment" just entails starting the **NSURLConnection**:

```
- (void) start {
    // Avoid unnecessary work.
    if (self.isCancelled) return;

    // In 10.6, all NSOperations are run on a thread.  NSURLConnection is
    // runloop based, and the thread that we are initially kick off the connect
    // with might disappear, courtesy of GCD, before we finish the loading
    // operation.
    // So we force the run of ourselves on the main thread, which we know will
    // stick around, and glom on to its runloop to run NSURLConnection.

    if (![NSThread isMainThread]) {
        [self performSelectorOnMainThread: @selector(start)
              withObject: nil
              waitUntilDone: NO];
        return;
    }

    // Since we've started, we're executing.
    self.isExecuting = YES;

    // Build a request to fetch the image.  The default URLs in the
    // sample are at borkware.com, and this will let us know how much
    // traffic is being generated by this sample.
    // Cookies are also turned off to reduce load on the server.
    NSMutableURLRequest *request = [NSMutableURLRequest requestWithURL: self.url];
    [request setValue: @"ImageSnarfer"  forHTTPHeaderField: @"User-Agent"];
    [request setHTTPShouldHandleCookies: NO];
    [request setCachePolicy: NSURLRequestReloadIgnoringLocalCacheData];

    // _imageData holds the data that comes down from the internet.
    _imageData = [NSMutableData data];

    _connection = [[NSURLConnection alloc] initWithRequest: request
                                            delegate: self];
    [_connection start];

} // start
```

The **-done** method is a utility method used elsewhere in the class. It releases the reference to the **NSURLConnection** so that it will get collected and sets the executing and finished attributes. KVO notifications will happen automatically because the values are changing through a property assignment.

```
- (void) done {
    _connection = nil;

    self.isExecuting = NO;
    self.isFinished = YES;

} // done
```

One user of **-done** is **-cancel**, which is called when the operation is cancelled. We may have a connection currently in use, so tell the connection to cancel itself. Also throw away any data that may have accumulated.

```
- (void) cancel {
    [_connection cancel];

    _imageData = nil;

    [self done];
    [super cancel];

} // cancel
```

-isExecuting and **-isFinished** need to be overridden when making a concurrent operation. Luckily, the implementations of these were created automatically for us by the isExecuting and isFinished properties.

-image builds an NSImage and returns it to the caller.

```
- (NSImage *) image {
    if (self.wasSuccessful && _image == nil) {
        // Use the property so that someone interested in the image via
        // KVO will get a notification.
        self.image = [[NSImage alloc] initWithData: _imageData];
        _imageData = nil; // Don't need to hang on to it anymore
    }

    return _image;

} // image
```

NSURLConnection delegate methods

The rest of **SnarfOperation**'s implementation is four delegate methods that are called during the URL loading process:

-connection:didReceiveResponse: is called when the connection is made to the web server and a response has been received. This may be called multiple times, like in the face of HTTP redirects, so forget about any data that may have been previously downloaded.

```
- (void) connection: (NSURLConnection *) c
 didReceiveResponse: (NSURLResponse *) response {

    // This can be called multple times (like for redirection),
    // so toss any accumulated data.

    [_imageData setLength: 0];

} // didReceiveResponse
```

-connection:didReceiveData: will be called zero or more times with data received from the web server.

```
- (void) connection: (NSURLConnection *) c
     didReceiveData: (NSData *) data {

    [_imageData appendData: data];

} // didReceiveData
```

-connection:didFailWithError: will be called if there was a failure, such as an inability to connect with the web server, or if the family dog pulled out the network cable part way through. You should release the accumulated data, make a note that the operation failed, and then tell observers that the operation is done.

```
- (void) connection: (NSURLConnection *) c
  didFailWithError: (NSError *) error {

    _imageData = nil;

    self.wasSuccessful = NO;
    [self done];

} // didFailWithError
```

Finally, **-connectionDidFinishLoading** is called when all the data has been successfully read from the web server. Make a note that the operation was a success.

```
- (void) connectionDidFinishLoading: (NSURLConnection *) c {

    self.wasSuccessful = YES;
    [self done];

} // connectionDidFinishLoading

@end // SnarfOperation
```

ImageSnarferAppDelegate

The last class for ImageSnarfer is the **ImageSnarferAppDelegate**, created for you in the Xcode template. Here is the header:

```
#import <Cocoa/Cocoa.h>

@class ImageCanvas;

@interface ImageSnarferAppDelegate : NSObject {
    NSOperationQueue    *_runQueue;    // Holds the image loading operations
    ImageCanvas *_imageCanvas;         // Where to draw the images
    int _concurrentExecution;          // The number of operations currently in-flight.
}

@property (assign) IBOutlet ImageCanvas *imageCanvas;

// Start loading the images.
- (IBAction) start: (id) sender;

@end // ImageSnarferAppDelegate
```

There are three instance variables: the **NSOperationQueue** that will hold a lot of **SnarfOperation**s, an **ImageCanvas** to draw loaded images, and a count of the number of operations that are currently running. This count will be updated by observing the operations and seeing when they start and stop.

In ImageSnarferAppDelegate.m, start out with some local property definitions so that getters and setters will be generated. The user interface will access them via bindings.

```
#import "ImageSnarferAppDelegate.h"

#import "SnarfOperation.h"
#import "ImageCanvas.h"
```

```
// Tell Objective-C that these are properties.  These are not in
// the header because users of this class shouldn't be poking at these.

@interface ImageSnarferAppDelegate ()
@property NSOperationQueue *runQueue;
@property int concurrentExecution;
@end // extension


@implementation ImageSnarferAppDelegate

@synthesize runQueue = _runQueue;
@synthesize imageCanvas = _imageCanvas;
@synthesize concurrentExecution = _concurrentExecution;
```

The URLs to fetch are http:// URLs in a text file in the application's bundle, one to a line. The
-contents method reads the file, puts the URL strings into an array, and randomizes it.

```
- (NSArray *) contents {
    // Get the path to the contents file.
    NSBundle *bundle = [NSBundle mainBundle];
    NSString *contentsPath = [bundle pathForResource: @"contents"  ofType: @"txt"];

    // Read the file and turn it into an array of strings split
    // on newlines.
    NSString *contentsString =
        [NSString stringWithContentsOfFile: contentsPath
                    encoding: NSUTF8StringEncoding  error: NULL];

    NSArray *rawContents = [contentsString componentsSeparatedByString: @"\n"];
    NSMutableArray *mutableContents = [rawContents mutableCopy];

    // Eat a stray newline at the end which would cause an empty
    // string.
    NSUInteger count = [mutableContents count];
    if (count == 0) goto bailout;

    if ([[mutableContents objectAtIndex: count - 1] length] == 0) {
        [mutableContents removeLastObject];
        count--;
    }

    // Shuffle the array.
    srandom (time(NULL));

    // Shuffle the image addresses.
    for (NSUInteger i = count - 1; i != 0; i--) {
        NSUInteger newIndex = random() % i;
        [mutableContents exchangeObjectAtIndex: i  withObjectAtIndex: newIndex];
    }

bailout:
    return mutableContents;

} // contents
```

-start: is an action hooked up to a button which initiates the downloading process. First are some
preliminaries, such as canceling any previous runs and making an **NSOperationQueue**. The queue is
manually set to have a concurrency of four to be nice to the web server. The number of requests to put

into the queue is capped at 50, also to be nice to the web server. You can get a pleasing display with 50 images vs. using every URL in the contents file.

```
- (IBAction) start: (id) sender {
    // Stop any work that's in-progress.
    [self.runQueue cancelAllOperations];

    // Make a new queue to put our operations.
    self.runQueue = [[NSOperationQueue alloc] init];

    // Since we're funneling everything into one thread, we
    // don't really care about the number of processers.  But it's good
    // to throttle ourselves so we're not too mean to the server.
    [self.runQueue setMaxConcurrentOperationCount: 4];

    // Get the set of URLs to load
    NSArray *contents = [self contents];

    // Also be nice to the server.  50 should be enough to demonstrate
    // concurrency and still give a pleasing display, vs always loading
    // 290 images every run.
    int max = MIN ([contents count], 50);
```

Then convert the URL strings to **NSURL**s and make a **SnarfOperation** for each one. Add KVO observers for isFinished (so you know the operation is done) and isExecuting (when it starts and stop executing, so you can keep the concurrency count accurate). Finally the operation is added to the run queue:

```
    // Walk the array and make download operations.
    for (NSInteger i = 0; i < max; i++) {
        // Turn the string into an URL
        NSString *urlString = [contents objectAtIndex: i];
        NSURL *url = [NSURL URLWithString: urlString];

        // Make a new operation to download that URL
        SnarfOperation *op = [[SnarfOperation alloc] initWithURL: url];

        // Watch for the finished state of this operation.
        [op addObserver: self
            forKeyPath: @"isFinished"
            options: 0  // It just changes state once, so don't
                        // worry about what's in the notification
            context: NULL];

        // Watch for when this operation starts executing, so we can update
        // the user interface.
        [op addObserver: self
            forKeyPath: @"isExecuting"
            options: NSKeyValueObservingOptionNew
            context: NULL];

        // Schedule the operation for running.
        [self.runQueue addOperation: op];
    }
} // start
```

The last method is the KVO observation method. Put the image onto the **ImageCanvas** and unhook the app delegate from the KVO machinery when isFinished floats by. When isExecuting floats by, update the concurrentExecution instance variable.

```
- (void) observeValueForKeyPath: (NSString *) keyPath
                       ofObject: (id) object
                         change: (NSDictionary *) change
                        context: (void *) context {

    if ([keyPath isEqualToString: @"isFinished"]) {
        // If it's done, it has downloaded the image.  Get the image
        // from the operation and put it on the display list.
        SnarfOperation *op = (SnarfOperation *) object;
        NSImage *image = op.image;
        [_imageCanvas addImage: image];

        // Unhook the observation.
        [op removeObserver: self  forKeyPath: @"isFinished"];
        [op removeObserver: self  forKeyPath: @"isExecuting"];

    } else if ([keyPath isEqualToString: @"isExecuting"]) {
        SnarfOperation *op = (SnarfOperation *) object;

        // Update concurrentExecution to reflect to the number of
        // operations currently running.  A status line text field is
        // bound to concurrentExecution.
        if (op.isExecuting) self.concurrentExecution++;
        else self.concurrentExecution--;

    } else {
        // The notification is uninteresting to us, let someone else
        // handle it.
        [super observeValueForKeyPath: keyPath
                ofObject: object
                change: change
                context: context];
    }
} // observeValueForKeyPath
```

Mop-up

That's it for the code. Add a text file to the project called contents.txt and add some image URLs to it, like:

```
http://borkware.com/corebook/snarferImages/BRK_5592.jpg
http://borkware.com/corebook/snarferImages/BRK_7853.jpg
http://borkware.com/corebook/snarferImages/RCK_1722.jpg
```

You can fetch a file of over 250 image URLs from http://borkware.com/corebook/snarferImages/ contents.txt. Make sure that the file is included in the Copy Bundle Resources phase of the ImageSnarfer target.

Finally, open MainMenu.xib and add an **ImageCanvas** to the window, along with two text fields and a Start button. Adjust the resizing behavior to your liking.

Figure 21.6   ImageSnarfer window

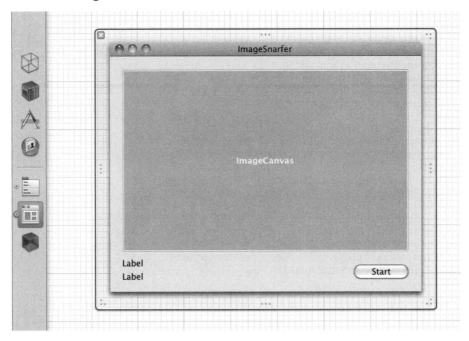

Hook up the **ImageSnarferAppDelegate**'s imageCanvas outlet to point to the **ImageCanvas**, and hook up the Start button action to the **ImageSnarferAppDelegate**'s **-start:** method.

Set up bindings for the two Labels. Each are "Value With Pattern" bindings:

```
Top label:
      Bind to:  App Controller
      Model Key Path: runQueue.operations.@count
      Display Pattern: Goodies in the queue: %{value1}@

Bottom label:
      Bind to:  App Controller
      Model Key Path: concurrentExecution
      Display Pattern: Concurrency: %{value1}@
```

Now you should be able to compile and run your program and have it display some images.

Exercises

1. Add the ability for the user to click and drag out a region of the Mandelbrot set to zoom in on.

2. Existing images do not move if you resize the ImageSnarfer window. They either get clipped or the window gets a large expanse of white space, which looks strange. Make the window resize prettier, according your own definition of pretty.

3. The **SnarfOperation**s stop loading when the window is resized or when a menu is being displayed. Why? (Hint: run loops.) Make the images continue loading even when the window is being resized.

4. **NSOperationQueue** can create new threads for non-concurrent operations if one of the currently running operations enters the kernel. You can work around this by explicitly calling **-setMaxConcurrentOperationCount:** on your **NSOperationQueue**. Try changing the queue in MandelOpper to only use the number of processors on your machine. Here is a function to give you the number of processors on your system:

```
#import <string.h>      // for strerror
#import <sys/sysctl.h> // for sysctlbyname()
#import <sys/types.h>
#import <errno.h>        // for errno
...
int processorCount () {
    int processorCount = 1;

    int count;
    size_t size = sizeof (count);

    int result = sysctlbyname ("hw.cacheconfig", &count, &size,
                               NULL, 0);  // new value, not used
    if (result == -1) {
        printf ("sysctlbyname returned error: %d/%s\n", errno, strerror(errno));
    } else {
        processorCount = count;
    }

    return processorCount;

} // processorCount
```

Are there any drawbacks to this technique?

22

Grand Central Dispatch

As mentioned in Chapter 10: *Performance Tuning*, we have reached the end of free performance as the transistors of new processors are being put into more and more cores rather than drastically speeding up existing cores.

Multi-threaded programming can be hard. You have race conditions, which can be fixed by locking, but it can be difficult to get the proper granularity of locking to prevent all of your threads from serializing on one code path. Finding the right locking granularity is hard. Make your locks too big, and they force serialization. Make them too small, and you drown in locking and unlocking overhead. Parallel algorithms also are more difficult to understand than serial algorithms, or at least they are not as familiar as serial algorithms.

Figure 22.1 shows a typical scenario. There are multiple threads wanting to do work with some sensitive data structure. By using locks, the critical sections are serialized. Threads block while waiting for the locks to become available so that they can work with the sensitive data structure.

Figure 22.1   The traditional locking model

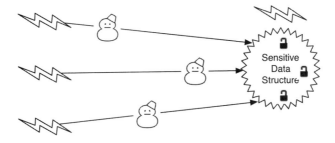

Mac OS X 10.6 and iOS 4 introduced Grand Central Dispatch (GCD), which is fundamentally a queueing mechanism. It provides a way of taking chunks of work, usually expressed as blocks, and serializing them. But does this undo all the work you have done with threads to take advantage of multiple cores? In isolation, yes.

Figure 22.2   Working with a serial queue

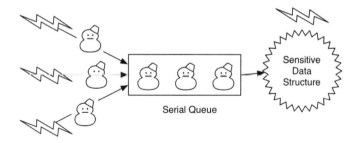

Serial Queue

Figure 22.2 shows GCD's view of the world. You have a serial queue. The queue controls access to the sensitive data structure. All work manipulating that data structure happens on only one thread, so you do not need to deal with locking. Individual threads can perform work on this data structure by putting work blocks onto the queue.

If the work is fire-and-forget, the thread can go off and do more work while the sensitive queue gets drained. If the thread needs to wait for the work to be done, it can wait until the work completes and then continue. In this case, performance really is not worse than waiting for a contentious lock. In fact, the performance characteristics become more deterministic. Once you have some work in a queue (which drains in FIFO order), your work will be handled. With a highly contentious lock, your thread might become starved for attention, or at least CPU time.

But, if you add more queues, you have more opportunities for parallelism.

Figure 22.3   Multiple serial queues

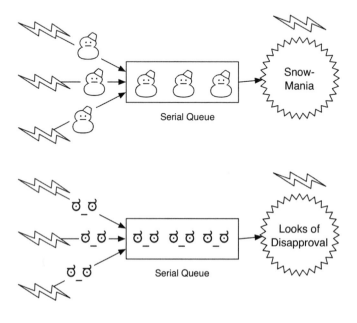

Figure 22.3 shows two different sensitive data structures protected by a queue and threads putting units of work onto the queues. Each of the sensitive data structures has serialized access, but no locks. By having a number of these queue-faced data structures, you can have good parallelism application-wide.

Apple has called this architecture "islands of serialization in a sea of concurrency."

A program can optimize its use of multiple processors so that it always takes advantage of the cores available on the user's machine. As time goes forward, more and more applications will be doing that. If the user decides to run two programs crunching on large data sets, and if each naively assumes it has free reign of the user's processors, there could be a lot of contention as both programs fight for CPU time.

Individual programs do not have the system-wide gestalt of resource consumption. Scaling to the degree of concurrency to best utilize the available computing resources on a machine requires an awareness of hardware that can't be baked into an existing framework. GCD cooperates with the kernel, so it knows system-wide who is vying for computing resources and can properly schedule tasks for maximum throughput.

In short, GCD's promise is if you give it work, it will make sure it runs as soon as reasonably possible.

Grand Central Dispatch is the marketing name for libdispatch, which is included in the OS X C library, and all of its public functions and types are prefixed with `dispatch_`. You get GCD's data types and functions with every program, and you don't need to pull in any extra libraries or frameworks. All you need to start using GCD is to include the `<dispatch/dispatch.h>` header file and use its functions. No special compiler or linker flags are required.

GCD integrates with the Foundation and Core Foundation runloop architecture. Running the main thread's runloop drains GCD's main queue. If you aren't using a runloop, you will have to call `dispatch_main()` on your main thread to drain the main queue.

If you are running on an OS that predates GCD support, you can use **NSOperationQueue** to provide some of the behaviors of GCD. You will not get the system-wide coordinating view like you do with GCD, of course.

GCD Terminology

GCD *tasks* are the things that need to be done, like rendering a web page or displaying a new message that comes from a social network. A task is a discrete goal your application wants to accomplish. Tasks can depend on other tasks, and they can be broken down into subtasks. Tasks are ultimately broken up into work items.

Work items are the individual chunklets of work that need to be done. For a web page, this would be work like parsing the request, hitting a database, running a template engine, merging the results, and so on.

Tasks are built from work items. Work items get put onto queues. Dispatching happens when work items run. When a work item gets to the front of a queue, it gets assigned to a thread so the work can actually happen.

GCD operates at a level of abstraction above threads. Threads become an implementation detail.

Queues

Dispatch queues are GCD's fundamental structure. A queue is a list of work items. A queue, by definition, is drained in a FIFO manner – first in, first out order. GCD maintains a thread pool where it actually runs the work items that are pulled from queues. Work items can be submitted as a block or a function pointer/context pair. Each serial queue is backed by a global queue.

There are two kinds of queues, serial queues and global queues. Serial queues dispatch their work items and complete them in FIFO order. Serial queues will not have two different work items executing simultaneously. This is what serializes access to sensitive data structures. The main queue, the queue for doing work on the main thread, is a serial queue.

A global queue issues work in FIFO order, but it does not have any guarantees on the order in which work completes. The actual work blocks are run from a thread pool maintained by GCD and are balanced system-wide by the OS kernel. There are three global queues of different priority: high, default, and low. The global queues have effectively unlimited "width," that is, the number of work items they can have running simultaneously. Serial queues have a width of one.

It is important to remember that the three global queues are the only ones that run concurrently. Serial queues dispatch *and complete* in FIFO order, whereas global queues just dispatch in FIFO order.

Every serial queue needs a target queue. The target queue is where the work ultimately gets scheduled to run. You can have serial queues target other serial queues. So long as the chain of queues eventually reaches a global queue, work will get done, as shown in Figure 22.4

Figure 22.4   Dispatch queue architecture

A global queue dispatches queued work items to its thread pool.
A serial queue runs at most one queued work item at a time on its target queue.

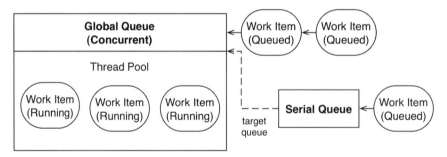

A serial queue's priority is determined by the priority of its target queue. By targeting a serial queue to the default priority global queue, its work items end up scheduled on the default priority queue's work queue. Retargeting the serial queue to the high priority global queue will cause any enqueued work items not already scheduled by the default priority global queue to run on the high priority global queue.

Serial queues are very lightweight data structures, being measured in bytes rather than dozens of kilobytes. Feel free to create as many special purpose queues as makes sense for your design, without worrying about having to manage an expensive data structure, such as threads, which are pretty heavyweight.

That being said, unless there is a reason to run work items serially, such as ensuring only a single thread manipulates a resource at a time, you should directly enqueue work items to one of the global queues.

Object-Oriented Design

Grand Central Dispatch is an object-oriented library, even though it is implemented purely in C. The fundamental GCD types are pointers to opaque data structures, but there is an inheritance model involved. The base class for dispatch objects is `dispatch_object_t`. You never directly create one of these; instead, you create concrete objects such as queues, sources, or groups. There are a couple of types, such as `dispatch_once_t` and `dispatch_time_t`. These are not objects but semi-opaque scalar types, as shown in Figure 22.5

Figure 22.5   Dispatch classes and functions

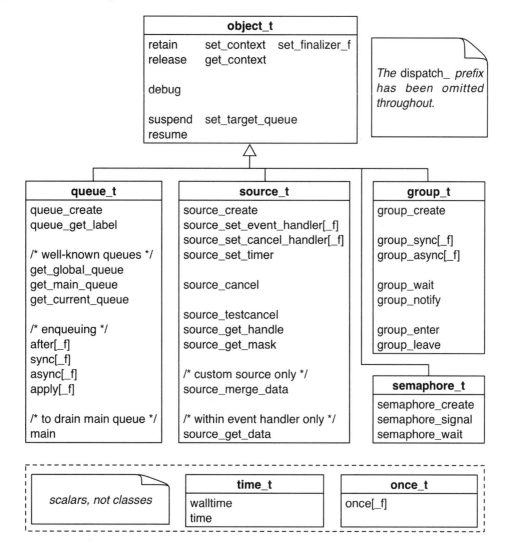

573

Dispatch API

Queues

Before you can schedule work on a queue, you need to get ahold of a queue to do the work on. You can get the main queue with

```
dispatch_queue_t dispatch_get_main_queue (void);
```

You can schedule activity on the main thread by using this queue. This is a serial queue, so work will issue and complete in FIFO order.

```
dispatch_queue_t dispatch_get_global_queue (long priority,
                                            unsigned long flags);
```

This gives you one of the global concurrent queues, whose priority is one of the DISPATCH_QUEUE_PRIORITY_LOW, DEFAULT, or HIGH priority constants. Pass 0UL for flags; it is ignored now and is an expansion point for the future. The priority refers to which queue gets its blocks scheduled. The default queue's blocks only get run on threads if the high priority queue is empty. Similarly, low priority queues will only issue its blocks to threads if no blocks are pending in the high or default priority queues.

You can get the current queue with:

```
dispatch_queue_t dispatch_get_current_queue (void);
```

"Current queue" is the queue that issued the currently running piece of work. If you are not in the middle of a piece of work, this will return the main queue, if you are on the main thread, or the default priority global queue otherwise. The actual queue this returns may be surprising, having unexpected properties, such as serial vs concurrent. Apple recommends only using **dispatch_get_current_queue()** for identity tests ("Am I really running on the main queue?") or for debugging.

Create your own queues with

```
dispatch_queue_t dispatch_queue_create (const char *label,
                                        dispatch_queue_attr_t attr);
```

label can be anything, but Apple recommends using the reverse-DNS naming scheme. e.g. something like com.bignerdranch.BigGroovy.FacebookQueue. The label is optional but because it appears in Instruments, the debugger, and in crash reports, it can be a very useful piece of information. Pass NULL for attr. It is unused in OS X 10.6 and iOS 4, but can be used as an expansion point for the future. The queue returned from this call is a serial queue.

Set a queue's target queue with this function:

```
void dispatch_set_target_queue (dispatch_object_t object,
                                dispatch_queue_t target);
```

Work items issued from the queue will be placed into this queue for ultimate scheduling. You can set the target queue for arbitrary GCD objects. For non-queue objects, this will tell the object where to run its context pointer finalization function.

Dispatching

Now you have a queue. What do you do with it? You dispatch work to it. **dispatch_async()** will throw a chunk of work on the queue and then return. The work will eventually find its way to a global queue where it is run on a thread. Because this work happens asynchronously, it is possible that the work started running before **dispatch_async()** returns. It is also possible, if it is a short piece of work, that it started *and* completed before **dispatch_async()** returns.

There are two flavors of many calls in GCD: one that takes a block and another that takes a function:

```
void dispatch_async (dispatch_queue_t queue, void (^block)(void));

void dispatch_async_f (dispatch_queue_t queue, void *context,
                       void (*function)(void *));
```

The function-taking variants follow the same convention of having _f appended to the name, taking a context pointer, and a function pointer. It is just an implementation detail, but much of GCD has the _f functions as the fundamental implementation with the block versions being wrappers on top of it. Only the block versions will be discussed here. The function versions work the same way.

You can choose to block your thread's execution until the work item has completed execution by calling **dispatch_sync()**:

```
    void dispatch_sync (dispatch_queue_t queue, void (^block)(void));
```

Be careful that you do not make recursive calls to **dispatch_sync()**. This can create a deadlock situation where the inner synchronous dispatch has to wait for the outer one to complete, but the outer **dispatch_sync()** can't complete until the inner one has finished.

A runloop on the main thread will cause GCD to start processing blocks for the main queue. If you do not have a runloop handy, or are running at a lower level than Core Foundation, you can use **dispatch_main()**:

```
void dispatch_main (void);
```

This function never returns. It will loop forever, handling work items added to the main queue.

dispatch_after(), described later, lets you schedule a block for execution sometime in the future.

Memory management

Grand Central Dispatch is near the bottom of the OS X food chain, living in the system library. You do not get fancy things like garbage collection, so there is API for managing object life cycles. GCD uses reference counting, like in Cocoa. Express your long-term interest in an object by retaining it:

```
void dispatch_retain (dispatch_object_t object);
```

Because GCD objects have an inheritance relationship with dispatch_object_t, you use this function to retain a dispatch_queue_t or a dispatch_source_t. Objects received from calls like **dispatch_queue_create()** are already retained for you. When you are done with an object, release it.

```
void dispatch_release (dispatch_object_t object);
```

Over-releasing an object will crash your program, so be sure to check the crash log after a crash. The library tries to supply useful application-specific information in the crash report, such as:

```
BUG IN CLIENT OF LIBDISPATCH:
Over-release of an object
```

Queues and dispatch sources also have context pointers, where you can put a pointer to your own data. You can set and retrieve the context pointer using these functions:

```
void dispatch_set_context (dispatch_object_t object, void *context);
```

```
void *dispatch_get_context (dispatch_object_t object);
```

It is not easy to figure out exactly when an object is finally destroyed so that you can clean up your context pointer. You can specify a finalizer function that is invoked asynchronously when the object is destroyed:

```
void dispatch_set_finalizer_f (dispatch_object_t object,
                               dispatch_function_t finalizer);
```

A `dispatch_function_t` is a function that takes a void pointer parameter, which would be your context pointer, and returns nothing:

```
typedef void (*dispatch_function_t) (void *);
```

Oddly enough, there is no block version of the finalizer.

The queue and dispatch source objects can be suspended and resumed. These objects have a "suspend count" that when non-zero, causes a queue to stop issuing work items or a dispatch source from dispatching event handling blocks. The suspended state is checked before a block is executed, say by taking a block off of a queue or by triggering a dispatch source. Currently executing blocks or functions will not be preempted, so suspension only controls if something starts executing or not.

```
void dispatch_suspend (dispatch_object_t object);
```

```
void dispatch_resume (dispatch_object_t object);
```

It is important to always balance your suspends with resumes; otherwise, things like finalizer functions or cancellation handlers will not be called. Over-resuming an object will crash your program, and releasing a suspended object is undefined.

WordCounter

Figure 22.6 shows a program that counts the number of words in a text field as well as the number of unique words. Text fields are updated with the values.

Figure 22.6   WordCounter screenshot

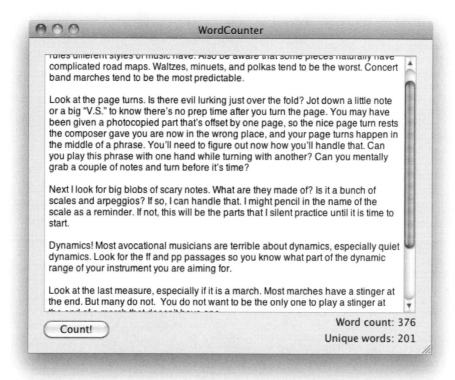

The code for this application is straightforward. In Xcode, make a new Cocoa Application (not document-based) called WordCounter. Add the objects seen in Figure 22.6: an **NSTextView**, a count button, a progress indicator, and two labels for the different counts. Configure your object layout appropriately. Update your **AppDelegate** class to point to the UI items, as well as the **-count:** action method:

```
#import <Cocoa/Cocoa.h>

@interface WordCounterAppDelegate : NSObject <NSApplicationDelegate> {
    NSWindow *_window;

    NSTextView *_wordsView;
    NSTextField *_countLabel;
    NSTextField *_uniqueLabel;
    NSButton *_countButton;
    NSProgressIndicator *_spinner;
}
@property (assign) IBOutlet NSWindow *window;
@property (assign) IBOutlet NSTextView *wordsView;
@property (assign) IBOutlet NSTextField *countLabel;
@property (assign) IBOutlet NSTextField *uniqueLabel;
@property (assign) IBOutlet NSButton *countButton;
@property (assign) IBOutlet NSProgressIndicator *spinner;
```

```
- (IBAction) count: (id) sender;
@end // WordCounterAppDelegate
```

Make the connections in Interface Builder. AppDelegate.m has the code that actually Does Stuff, with the beginning of the file is standard boilerplate:

```
#import "WordCounterAppDelegate.h"

@implementation WordCounterAppDelegate
@synthesize window = _window;
@synthesize wordsView = _wordsView;
@synthesize countLabel = _countLabel;
@synthesize uniqueLabel = _uniqueLabel;
@synthesize countButton = _countButton;
@synthesize spinner = _spinner;
```

The method that does the work actually wants to return two values: the count of words and an **NSCountedSet** that has the word frequencies. You cannot really return two values at the same time. One approach is returning one of the values via the ordinary method return and returning the other value as an out parameter. You can also make a struct that contains the two return values:

```
typedef struct {
    NSUInteger count;
    NSCountedSet *frequencies;
} CountAndSet;
```

-countWords does the heavy lifting:

```
- (CountAndSet) countWords: (NSString *) string {
    NSScanner *scanner = [NSScanner scannerWithString: string];
    NSCharacterSet *whiteSpace = [NSCharacterSet whitespaceAndNewlineCharacterSet];

    NSUInteger count = 0;
    NSCountedSet *wordSet = [NSCountedSet set];

    NSString *word;
    while ([scanner scanUpToCharactersFromSet: whiteSpace  intoString: &word]) {
        [wordSet addObject: [word lowercaseString]];
        count++;
    }

    CountAndSet result = { count, wordSet };

    sleep (2); // Machines these days are too dang fast!

    return result;

} // countWords
```

There is a **sleep()** in there just to slow things down a bit to make a point later on. Then call **countWords** in the button handler:

```
- (IBAction) count: (id) sender {
    CountAndSet result = [self countWords: self.wordsView.string];

    NSString *labelString =
        [NSString stringWithFormat: @"Word count: %u", result.count];
    [self.countLabel setStringValue: labelString];
```

```
    labelString =
        [NSString stringWithFormat: @"Unique words: %u", result.frequencies.count];
    [self.uniqueLabel setStringValue: labelString];

} // count
```

This method gets the count and the word frequency set out of the returned structure and populates the labels. You can go ahead and build and run the app. It works! But because **-countWords:** takes a couple of seconds, you get the Spinning Pizza of Death showing that the UI has locked up. On a desktop system, a locked up app is annoying but not a big deal. You can go work on something else and come back. It is a big deal on a mobile device. If your app's user interface is locked up, the user cannot do anything but stare. If you stay locked up too long, say longer than fifteen or thirty seconds, the iOS watchdog will kill your program.

WordCounter cheats by putting in a two-second sleep, simulating a lot of processing work being done. Machines these days are too fast to bog down with simple code like this. A MacBookPro took less than a quarter second to count all of /usr/share/dict/words, which is 235,000 words long. But the point still stands that it is possible to block the main thread by doing work.

The solution is to not do all the heavy lifting at the same time on the main thread. There are a couple of approaches you could use. You could slice the work apart and do it in the main thread in an asynchronous manner. Count a thousand words, then return to the RunLoop, count a thousand more words, then return to the RunLoop. You could also spin off a pthread or an **NSThread** to do the work.

The downside of these approaches is that it's a lot of work. You will end up rewriting your code in the first case, and in the thread cases, you will need to have a way to rendezvous with the main thread and get the results, not to mention setting up thread functions or methods that get run on an actual thread.

Grand Central Dispatch makes "throw this piece of work onto a background thread for awhile. Ok, throw this other piece of work on to the main thread to clean up" kinds of work very easy. A common "GCD is Cool!" demo is to put a **dispatch_async()** onto a background thread into **-countWords:** for the counting, and a **dispatch_async()** onto the main thread to update the labels. Real life is a little more complicated, but not much more. And certainly easier than manually spinning off another thread.

One thing you'll need to do is prevent the user from interacting with the window's controls. You don't want the user to click "Count!" while the counting is happening. You also don't want the user to change the text. The count would then be different from the text in the text field. Also, it would be nice to put up a spinning progress indicator so the user knows something is happening. Two helper methods do this work:

```
- (void) disableEverything {
    // NSTextView doesn't have an enabled binding, so we'll just do it all here.
    [self.wordsView setEditable: NO];
    [self.countButton setEnabled: NO];
    [self.spinner setHidden: NO];
    [self.spinner startAnimation: self];
} // disableEverything


- (void) enableEverything {
    [self.wordsView setEditable: YES];
    [self.countButton setEnabled: YES];
    [self.spinner stopAnimation: self];
    [self.spinner setHidden: YES];
} // enableEverything
```

Now, before GCDing things, add in the enabling and disabling of stuff:

```
- (IBAction) count: (id) sender {

    [self disableEverything];

    CountAndSet result = [self countWords: self.wordsView.string];

    // The set is autoreleased, but we want it to survive until the
    // next block runs, at some unspecified point in the future.
    [result.frequencies retain];

    NSString *labelString =
        [NSString stringWithFormat: @"Word count: %u", result.count];
    [self.countLabel setStringValue: labelString];

    labelString =
        [NSString stringWithFormat: @"Unique words: %u",
                    result.frequencies.count];

    [self.uniqueLabel setStringValue: labelString];

    [self enableEverything];
    [result.frequencies release];

} // count
```

There is one bit of memory management subtlety. The plan is to put the word calculations onto a background thread. That thread has its own autorelease pool, and the **NSCountedSet** created is put into the pool. The pool can be, and most likely will be, drained before we get around to running the UI code on the main thread. That is why `result.frequencies` is retained. You can run the app now, and it should behave the way it did before.

Now to figure out what needs to be run in the background and what needs to be run on the main thread. The UI manipulation code needs to be run on the main thread. **-countWords:** and retaining the word frequency set need to happen on the background thread. Knowing that, you can write the final GCD-enhanced version:

```
- (IBAction) count: (id) sender {
    [self disableEverything];
    dispatch_async (dispatch_get_global_queue (DISPATCH_QUEUE_PRIORITY_DEFAULT, 0), ^{
            CountAndSet result = [self countWords: self.wordsView.string];

            // The set is autoreleased, but we want it to survive until the
            // next block runs, at some unspecified point in the future.
            [result.frequencies retain];

            dispatch_async (dispatch_get_main_queue(), ^{
                    NSString *labelString =
                        [NSString stringWithFormat: @"Word count: %u", result.count];
                    [self.countLabel setStringValue: labelString];

                    labelString =
                        [NSString stringWithFormat: @"Unique words: %u",
                                    result.frequencies.count];

                    [self.uniqueLabel setStringValue: labelString];
                    [self enableEverything];
```

```
        [result.frequencies release];

    });
});
} // count
```

Here is how this method runs: first, **-disableEverything** is called. The IBAction is handled on the main thread, so we are on the main thread for this method. The UI is disabled. Then, the rest of the method is a block that gets thrown on the default priority global queue. The method then exits and control returns to the runloop.

At some point in time in the future, the block will be taken off the front of the global queue and run. The first thing it does is call **-countWords:**. That will happily do the work it needs to do. Then the frequencies set is retained. The retain happens on the same thread where **-countWords:** was called.

Next, another block is put onto the main queue, and this block exits because there is no more work to do. At some unspecified point in time in the future, the main queue block starts running. It updates the UI and releases the frequencies set.

This is a common coding pattern when using GCD. You have nested dispatch_async blocks. The "outer" block is put on a queue, some work is done, then it is peeled away like an onion, and an inner block is put on another queue. Then that block runs, is peeled away, and an even more nested block is run.

Notice that the main queue block referenced result, the return from **-countWords:**. This is simply the block capturing the variables in the outer scope. The frequency set was not automatically retained by the block because it was living inside of a struct. If we had an **NSCountedSet** variable in the outer scope, the main queue block would have retained it, and the explicit retain here would not have been necessary.

Iteration

Even something as simple as a for-loop iterating over data performing work can be enhanced by GCD. The classic way of iterating through an array and performing an operation on each element is through a for loop.

```
enum {
    kNumberCount = 200000
};

static int numbers[kNumberCount];
static int results[kNumberCount];

for (int i = 0; i < kNumberCount; i++) {
    results[i] = Work (numbers, i);
}
```

You could walk through the array doing work that is not really interrelated and then sift through the work to make the final conclusion, like a map/reduce operation.

You can parallelize these by using **dispatch_apply()**. The call itself is synchronous, so you know all the work has been completed when the function returns, but the call fans out over as many CPUs as it deems optimal to do the work.

```
dispatch_queue_t queue =
```

```
    dispatch_get_global_queue (DISPATCH_QUEUE_PRIORITY_DEFAULT, 0);

dispatch_apply (kNumberCount, queue, ^(size_t index) {
        results[index] = Work (numbers, index);
    });
```

This is similar to **NSArray**'s **-enumerateObjectsWithOptions:usingBlock:** and giving it the NSEnumerationConcurrent option. Be sure you use a global queue for your **dispatch_apply()**. Using a scrial queue will serialize all your work, defeating any attempt to parallelize this operation.

There is a certain amount of overhead for each operation that is put on the queue and subsequently executed. If the work you are doing inside of the block is very fast, you may want to do more work inside of each parallel operation:

```
enum {
    kNumberCount = 200000,
    kStride = 1000
};
dispatch_apply (kNumberCount / kStride, queue, ^(size_t index) {
        size_t jindex = index * kStride;
        size_t jStop = MIN(jindex + kStride, kNumberCount);
        while (jindex < jStop) {
            results[jindex] = Work (numbers, jindex);
        }
    });
```

This would do 1000 iterations inside of each dispatched operation. You would determine the optimal stride by experimentation.

You should also make sure that your array processing works correctly when run in parallel. Iterations depending on the results of subsequent iterations usually cannot be easily parallelized. One quick check you can make is to iterate through your array backwards. If the result is correct, then there is a good chance your iteration can be parallelized.

Safe Global Initialization

Sometimes you need to perform one-time initialization and have the work performed exactly one time, no matter how many threads are wanting that initialization to happen. This is often used for lazy initialization or for creating the One True Object when using singletons. There is a technique called Double-Checked Locking to do this, but it is very hard to get right. You can use **pthread_once()** to serialize a one-time initialization. You can also use **dispatch_once()**.

```
void dispatch_once (dispatch_once_t *predicate, void (^block)(void));

static dispatch_once_t initializationPredicate;
static blah *stuffToInitialize

dispatch_once (&initializationPredicate, ^{
    stuffToInitialzie = goop ();
});
...
```

A dispatch_once_t is used as the guard variable and **dispatch_once()** will execute its block exactly once, no matter the number of threads and cores wanting the initialization to happen.

If possible, prefer the dispatch* family of functions to similar pthread functions. The dispatch functions will have the best performance possible.

Time, Time, Time

When dealing with real-world code, you frequently need to interact with time, whether having calls time out after awhile or scheduling things to happen at specific times. GCD calls these times "temporal milestones," and they are represented by a dispatch_time_t. This type is a "semi-opaque" integer; it has an integer value, but its contents are subject to change. Time can be expressed relative to another time or relative to two distinguished moments in time – now and forever:

```
static const dispatch_time_t DISPATCH_TIME_NOW = 0;
static const dispatch_time_t DISPATCH_TIME_FOREVER = ~0ull;
```

Use DISPATCH_TIME_FOREVER for an infinite timeout.

There are two different kinds of time used in GCD. The "host clock," also known a the system clock, is based on a counter in the OS. The counter increases so long as the machine is running. Sleeping the machine freezes the host clock. If you set a timeout for one hour in the future and then sleep the machine for thirty minutes, the operation will actually timeout one hour and thirty minutes into the future.

The other clock is the "wall clock," which represents a moment in time that could be reported by a clock and calendar sitting on your desk. Wall clock time continues in motion if the machine is slept and could move forward or backwards arbitrarily. The user might travel to a different time zone, or daylight savings time could kick in. So, if you set a timeout for an hour in the future using wall clock time and you sleep the machine for thirty minutes, the timeout will happen thirty minutes later, barring time zone changes.

dispatch_time() returns a milestone value relative to an existing milestone, after adding the given number of nanoseconds

```
dispatch_time_t dispatch_time (dispatch_time_t base,
                               int64_t nanoseconds);
```

If the base time is a wall clock time, the return time will be a wall clock time too. DISPATCH_TIME_NOW counts as using a host clock time.

Use dispatch_walltime() to create a milestone relative to a fixed point in time using the wall clock.

```
dispatch_time_t dispatch_walltime (struct timespec *base,
                                   int64_t nanoseconds);
```

You can pass a struct timespec for a particular point in time, which is the number of seconds and nanoseconds since the Unix epoch of 1970, or you can pass NULL to use the current time.

Overflow returns DISPATCH_TIME_FOREVER, while underflow causes the smallest representable value to be returned.

A milestone for twenty three seconds in the future would be created with:

```
dispatch_time_t  milestone = dispatch_time (DISPATCH_TIME_NOW,
                                            23ull * NSEC_PER_SEC);
```

The ull modifier for the constant keeps the math from being truncated to 32 bits. NSEC_PER_SEC is a handy constant for multiplying seconds by a billion. There are other constants for easily working with time at different granularities: USEC_PER_SEC for microseconds and NSEC_PER_USEC for converting between microseconds and nanoseconds.

You can set a timeout for an absolute time by putting the time into a `struct tm`, and then converting it `struct timespec` with **mktime()**:

```
struct tm tm = {0};
strptime ("2016-09-13 13:13", "%Y-%m-%d %H:%M", &tm);

struct timespec ts = {};
ts.tv_sec = mktime (&tm);

dispatch_time_t timeout = dispatch_walltime (&ts, 0);
```

You can use a `dispatch_time_t` in calls to **dispatch_after()**:

```
void dispatch_after (dispatch_time_t when, dispatch_queue_t queue,
                     void (^block)(void));
```

This function enqueues a work item to be run after a given time. Passing `DISPATCH_TIME_NOW` to **dispatch_after()** has the same effect as calling **dispatch_async()**.

Dispatch Groups

Sometimes you want to fan some work out to a number of different queues and then wait until everything completes. For instance, rendering a page in a server might involve hitting a database, running the text through a rendering engine, and appending any insightful and relevant comments that have been left on the page.

A dispatch group is a collection of blocks that have been dispatched onto queues asynchronously. To create a group to track the collection of blocks, you use

```
dispatch_group_t dispatch_group_create (void);
```

Rather than dispatching directly onto other queues, you would use **dispatch_group_async()** to put the block onto a queue, but you also add the work item to the work group.

```
void dispatch_group_async (dispatch_group_t group,
                           dispatch_queue_t queue,
                           void (^block)(void));
```

In this case, the block is added to the group, and then **dispatch_async()**'d to the given queue. There are two ways to get notified when all of the blocks in the group have completed. You can specify a block to run with **dispatch_group_notify()**.

```
void dispatch_group_notify (dispatch_group_t group,
                            dispatch_queue_t queue,
                            void (^block)(void));
```

group, after it has finished with the last block that has been scheduled with it, will **dispatch_async()** the notification block onto queue.

You can also block until the group has drained by using **dispatch_group_wait()**, giving it a timeout.

```
long dispatch_group_wait (dispatch_group_t group,
                          dispatch_time_t timeout);
```

The function returns zero if the group drained before `timeout` and returns a non-zero value if the timeout expires. Give a timeout of `DISPATCH_TIME_FOREVER` for an infinite timeout.

You can manually control the count of work items currently in a group by using **dispatch_group_enter** and **_leave**:

```
void dispatch_group_enter (dispatch_group_t group);

void dispatch_group_leave (dispatch_group_t group);
```

Entering a dispatch group increments its count by one, and leaving decrements it. The group won't notify or break out of a wait until its count goes to zero.

Example 22.1 shows dispatch groups in action.

Example 22.1   group.m

```
#import <Foundation/Foundation.h>
#import <dispatch/dispatch.h>
#import <stdio.h>
#import <unistd.h>

// gcc -g -Wall -framework Foundation -o group group.m

int main (void) {
    NSAutoreleasePool *pool = [[NSAutoreleasePool alloc] init];

    dispatch_group_t group = dispatch_group_create ();

    // Fan out the work
    dispatch_group_async (group, dispatch_get_global_queue(0, 0),
                          ^{ printf ("I seem to be a verb\n"); });
    dispatch_group_async (group,
                          dispatch_get_main_queue(),
                          ^{ printf ("main queue groovy!\n"); });
    dispatch_group_async (group,
                          dispatch_get_global_queue(DISPATCH_QUEUE_PRIORITY_LOW, 0),
                          ^{ sleep (5);  printf ("background groovy!\n"); });

    dispatch_group_notify (group, dispatch_get_global_queue(0, 0),
                                  ^{ printf ("all done!\n"); });

    dispatch_async (dispatch_get_global_queue(0, 0), ^{
            printf ("Starting to wait\n");
            long result = dispatch_group_wait (group, DISPATCH_TIME_FOREVER);
            printf ("Wait returned with result %ld!\n", result);
            dispatch_release (group);
        });

    sleep (10);

    printf ("starting runloop\n");
    [[NSRunLoop currentRunLoop] runUntilDate:
        [NSDate dateWithTimeIntervalSinceNow: 10]];
    printf ("out of runloop\n");

    [pool drain];

    return 0;
} // main
```

A dispatch group is created, and three blocks are dispatched – two to global queues and one to the main queue. A notification handler is added, as well as a work item to wait on the dispatch group. The waiting is done on a global queue (hence, a background thread) so that the main thread will be free to run the block dispatched to the main queue.

Finally, a runloop is spun for ten seconds to drain any work items on the main queue. When run, **group** produces this output:

```
% ./group
I seem to be a verb
Starting to wait
background groovy!   // 5 seconds later
starting runloop     // 5 seconds later
main queue groovy!
Wait returned with result 0!
all done!
out of runloop
```

There are some things of interest to notice. The first work item ("I seem to be a verb") completes before the wait happens. The third work item ("background groovy!") has most likely started, but it has not completed yet. You can see the background groovy item completing before the main thread has finished sleeping. Also notice that the work item dispatched to the main queue does not get run until the runloop starts.

An implementation of **dispatch_group_async()** shows how you would use **dispatch_group_enter()** and **_leave**.

```
void groovy_dispatch_group_async (
    dispatch_group_t group,
    dispatch_queue_t queue,
    dispatch_block_t work)
{
    dispatch_retain(group);
    dispatch_group_enter(group);

    dispatch_async(queue, ^{
        work();

        dispatch_group_leave(group);
        dispatch_release(group);
    });
}
```

Here's the interesting takeaway from this: the group is retained before being entered and is not released until after it has been left. This prevents the group from becoming empty between the calls and getting destroyed. The group is entered before dispatching the work item and left after the actual work of the item has been completed.

Also, be aware that your application will crash if it disposes of a dispatch group while it still contains work items. Over-leaving the group, that is calling **dispatch_group_leave()** when there are no work items in the group, will also cause a crash.

Dispatch Sources

Dispatch sources represent streams of events. When an event associated with a dispatch source occurs, an event handler (such as a block) is scheduled on a designated queue. You make a new dispatch source with **dispatch_source_create()**:

```
dispatch_source_t dispatch_source_create (dispatch_source_type_t type,
                                           uintptr_t handle,
                                           unsigned long mask,
                                           dispatch_queue_t queue);
```

type is one of these constants:

```
DISPATCH_SOURCE_TYPE_DATA_ADD
DISPATCH_SOURCE_TYPE_DATA_OR
DISPATCH_SOURCE_TYPE_MACH_SEND
DISPATCH_SOURCE_TYPE_MACH_RECV
DISPATCH_SOURCE_TYPE_PROC
DISPATCH_SOURCE_TYPE_READ
DISPATCH_SOURCE_TYPE_SIGNAL
DISPATCH_SOURCE_TYPE_TIMER
DISPATCH_SOURCE_TYPE_VNODE
DISPATCH_SOURCE_TYPE_WRITE
```

These constants should look familiar, seeing some of the common culprits you have seen with **kqueue()**: signals, sockets, files, processes and presses. There are also less common things like mach messages.

You can also create your own custom sources to handle other kinds of events within GCD. Dispatch sources are like using **kqueue()** but without having to create your own kernel queue or poll for new events. Your block gets scheduled automatically onto a queue when a new event happens.

The expected values of the handle and mask arguments depend on the dispatch source type you are creating. For example, the signal source type would use the signal number as the handle.

queue is the queue where the event handling block is enqueued when something interesting happens on the dispatch source.

The handler block is set with **dispatch_source_set_event_handler()**:

```
void dispatch_source_set_event_handler (dispatch_source_t source,
                                         void (^block)(void));
```

Dispatch sources are created in a suspended state. They will do nothing until you make it active by calling **dispatch_resume()** on it. This lets you do all your configuration of the source without worrying about it firing underneath you. When you are done with a dispatch source, you need to **dispatch_source_cancel()** it:

```
void dispatch_source_cancel (dispatch_source_t source);
```

You can set a handler block that is enqueued when the dispatch source is cancelled:

```
void dispatch_source_set_cancel_handler (dispatch_source_t source,
                                          void (^block)(void));
```

Some source types, like those that monitor mach ports and file descriptors, require a cancellation handler where you close the file descriptor. If you close the descriptor before the cancellation handler runs, it might result in a race condition where the file descriptor is re-used for another file and then the dispatch source has a block executed, which could read or write with this different file.

Cancellation does not interrupt any currently executing handler block. You can test for cancellation inside of your handler by calling **dispatch_source_testcancel()**:

```
long dispatch_source_testcancel (dispatch_source_t source);
```

This returns a non-zero value if the source has been cancelled.

You also need to set a handler for your dispatch source. The handler is a block which will be dispatched onto the queue that you specified in the **dispatch_source_create()**.

```
void dispatch_source_set_event_handler (dispatch_source_t source,
                                         void (^block)(void));
```

Inside of the handler, you can query the source. For instance, you can get the handle and mask parameters used to create the handler:

```
uintptr_t dispatch_source_get_handle (dispatch_source_t source);
```

```
unsigned long dispatch_source_get_mask (dispatch_source_t source);
```

You can also get at the pending "data" that is peculiar to each handler with **dispatch_source_get_data()**, such as the number of bytes available to read on a file descriptor or the number of times a signal has fired.

```
unsigned long dispatch_source_get_data (dispatch_source_t source);
```

Figure 22.7 shows the different sources and their moving parts.

Figure 22.7   Dispatch source types

TIMER
handle: none
mask: none
data: times fired since last run

READ
handle: file descriptor
mask: none
data: bytes available

SIGNAL
handle: SIG number
mask: none
data: times received since last run

WRITE
handle: file descriptor
mask: none
data: bytes available

PROC
handle: pid_t
mask: events to watch for (bit-or of DISPATCH_PROC_EXIT, FORK, EXEC, REAP, SIGNAL)
data: mask of events occurred since last run

VNODE
handle: file descriptor
mask: events to watch for (bit-or of DISPATCH_VNODE_DELETE, WRITE, EXTEND, ATTRIB, LINK, RENAME, REVOKE)
data: mask of events occurred since last run

MACH_SEND
handle: mach port (send or send-once)
mask: DISPATCH_MACH_SEND_DEAD
data: mask of events occurred since last run

DATA_ADD
handle: none
mask: none
data: sum of data merged since last run

MACH_RECV
handle: mach port (receive)
mask: none
data: none (but a message is waiting)

DATA_OR
handle: none
mask: none
data: logical-or of data merged since last run

Signal sources

As if we did not have enough signal handling API already, GCD adds its own. That being said, this is probably the easiest way to handle signals on OS X and iOS. The source type is

DISPATCH_SOURCE_SIGNAL, the handle is the signal number, and the mask is unused so leave it at zero. This code will print on the main queue when a SIGUSR1 is delivered to the application:

```
dispatch_source_t source = dispatch_source_create
    (DISPATCH_SOURCE_TYPE_SIGNAL,
     SIGUSR1,
     0,
     dispatch_get_main_queue ());

dispatch_source_set_event_handler (source, ^{
        printf("signal with data %ld\n",
               dispatch_source_get_data(source));
    });

signal (SIGUSR1, SIG_IGN);
dispatch_resume (source);
```

This is a very compact way to handle signals, even compared to kqueue. Notice that this does not supersede existing signal-handling mechanics. You could still kqueue this signal. And do not forget to SIG_IGN the signal so that the default signal handing behavior does not kill your process. Also notice that you have to **dispatch_resume()** the handler for it to start working.

File read source

Much like kqueue's EVFILT_READ, DISPATCH_SOURCE_TYPE_READ will monitor file descriptors and tell you when they can be read from. The handle is the file descriptor, and the mask is not used, so pass zero. The data returned by **dispatch_source_get_data()** is an "estimated" number of bytes that can be read from the descriptor. This is a minimum read buffer size, but the system does not guarantee that it will actually read this number of bytes. Apple recommends using non-blocking I/O and handling any truncated reads or error conditions that might occur. This differs from kqueue, which tells you how many bytes you can read before blocking.

This code will read from standard-in and print the characters as they come in.

```
fcntl (STDIN_FILENO, F_SETFL, O_NONBLOCK);

dispatch_source_t reader = dispatch_source_create
    (DISPATCH_SOURCE_TYPE_READ,
     STDIN_FILENO,
     0,
     dispatch_get_global_queue (DISPATCH_QUEUE_PRIORITY_DEFAULT, 0));

dispatch_source_set_event_handler (reader, ^{
        unsigned long bytesAvailable = dispatch_source_get_data (reader);

        printf ("source_data: %lu\n", bytesAvailable);
        char buffer[1024];

        ssize_t amountRead = read (STDIN_FILENO, buffer, sizeof(buffer - 1));

        if (amountRead == 0) {
            dispatch_source_cancel (reader);
            return;
        }
        if (amountRead == -1) {
            printf ("error reading: %d/%s\n", errno, strerror(errno));
        }
```

```
        buffer[amountRead] = '\000';
        printf ("actually read %ld: |%s|\n", amountRead, buffer);
    });

    dispatch_source_set_cancel_handler (reader, ^{
        printf ("cancel handler!\n");
        close (dispatch_source_get_handle(reader));
        dispatch_release (reader);
    });

    dispatch_resume (reader);
```

Notice that the standard-in file descriptor is set to a non-blocking mode. The event handler block is eventually run on a background thread when there is data to be read. Here it just reads in the maximal amount it can into its buffer, relying on the non-blocking I/O to only read the number of bytes available if it is less than the buffer size. Once the end of file happens, the source cancels itself, causing the cancellation handler to be run, which closes the file descriptor and releases the dispatch source.

File write source

The file write source works like kqueue's EVFILT_WRITE. These sources monitor file descriptors for buffer space for writing. The dispatch source handle is the file descriptor, and the mask is unused and should be zero.

Using write sources is a bit more difficult than using kqueue, because the source does not tell you how much data you can write before blocking. File descriptors for DISPATCH_SOURCE_TYPE_WRITE dispatch sources should be configured for non-blocking I/O, and you should handle any truncated writes or errors that might happen.

Timer sources

A timer source is one that submits the event handler block to the queue periodically, using the interval given to **dispatch_source_set_timer()**:

```
void dispatch_source_set_timer (dispatch_source_t source,
                                dispatch_time_t start,
                                uint64_t interval, uint64_t leeway);
```

The system tries its best to submit the event handler block to the queue on time, but the time the block actually runs might be later.

start is the initial fire time for the timer. Use DISPATCH_TIME_NOW to have the timer start now. interval is in nanoseconds and tells the timer source the period of the timer. leeway is a hint to the system that it can defer the timer's scheduling in order to help overall system performance. This value is also in nanoseconds. Of course, there will be some latency for all timers even if you use a zero leeway, because OS X is not a real-time system.

The timer will repeat forever until the program exits or **dispatch_source_cancel()** is called. If you want a one-shot timer, have the timer's event handler cancel the timer.

The handle and mask arguments when creating the dispatch source are unused and should be set to zero. The data returned by **dispatch_source_get_data()** is the number of times the timer has fired since the last invocation of the event handler block.

This code will print "timer" to standard out every two seconds. The timer will not actually start until the dispatch source is resumed:

```
dispatch_source_t timer = dispatch_source_create
    (DISPATCH_SOURCE_TYPE_TIMER, 0, 0,
     dispatch_get_global_queue (DISPATCH_QUEUE_PRIORITY_LOW, 0));

dispatch_source_set_event_handler(timer, ^{ printf("timer\n"); });

dispatch_source_set_timer (timer, DISPATCH_TIME_NOW,
                           2ull * NSEC_PER_SEC,
                           1000000);
dispatch_resume (timer);
```

Custom sources

Custom sources are created by specifying a source type of DISPATCH_SOURCE_TYPE_DATA_ADD or _OR and configuring them like you would any other source. Trigger them with **dispatch_source_merge_data()**:

```
void dispatch_source_merge_data (dispatch_source_t source,
                                 unsigned long data);
```

The data is an unsigned long, which is merged into the data that has been accumulated since the last time the event handler was run, either by adding/summing or or-ing the supplied value, per the type of the source. Only if the merged data is non-zero will the source be triggered. So if you wish to ensure the source is triggered, you must ensure the supplied data is non-zero. The data buffer is zeroed out for each invocation of the data source's event handler.

If the data being merged in is irrelevant to you and you simply want the source to be triggered, do not worry about the type or the data, just create a custom source, rig up the handlers, and trigger it with a non-zero value.

Under the Hood

Dispatch sources are actually dispatch queues with some extra frobs. This explains their having a target queue property and a meaningful suspend count property.

Every source except timers and custom sources ends up being expressed as a kevent added to a single kqueue. This kqueue is owned and managed by a manager GCD queue. If you attempt to track a file descriptor that kqueue does not support, GCD will fall back and use **select()**.

The manager queue itself is responsible for handling timers and custom sources. These use pseudo-kevent in order to fit in with the kevent-centric design of the manager queue.

Dispatch timers are kept in two lists corresponding to the type of timer (walltime or clocktime). The lists are sorted in ascending order by the next fire time and terminated by a sentinel timer with a fire time of DISPATCH_TIME_NOW.

Semaphores

GCD provides semaphores – objects that threads can wait on and signal with (where signal is not a Unix signal). There are two kinds of semaphores: binary semaphores and counting semaphores.

A binary semaphore is a single flag. The flag starts out "signaled." Waiting on it claims the flag. Any further attempts to wait on it require blocking until it is signaled again.

A counting semaphore is often initialized with the count of some resource and then used to allocate that resource. Waiting on the semaphore claims a unit, and signaling releases that claim. Only when the units have run out (the semaphore's count being zero) does waiting on the semaphore actually block, requiring waiting for a unit to become available. Waiting can block, but signaling is always non-blocking.

A dispatch semaphore is a counting semaphore. What makes it special is that it takes care to be as fast as possible in its implementation. It only calls down to the kernel when a thread has to block or be woken. The kernel is not involved if there is no contention in the semaphore operation.

Unlike Unix semaphores, dispatch semaphores only work within a single process, so they can't be used for any form of interprocess communication.

Create a dispatch with **dispatch_semaphore_create()**. Get rid of it by releasing it.

```
dispatch_semaphore_t dispatch_semaphore_create (long count);
```

count initializes the semaphore's count. Pass a count of zero to make a binary semaphore. You can wait on a semaphore up until a specific time with **dispatch_semaphore_wait()**:

```
long dispatch_semaphore_wait (dispatch_semaphore_t semaphore,
                              dispatch_time_t timeout);
```

The return value will be zero on success, non-zero if the wait timed out. Signal a semaphore with this function:

```
long dispatch_semaphore_signal (dispatch_semaphore_t semaphore);
```

It returns a non-zero value if a thread was woken up due to the signal, and zero otherwise.

Under the hood, dispatch groups are just dispatch semaphores created with a very large value. A work item is marked as entering by waiting on the semaphore. A work item is marked as leaving by signaling it. Unfortunately, this abstraction leaks in a bad way if you over-leave a group. The program will crash without any handy application-specific information, with the reported reason being something like EXC_ARITHMETIC (SIGFPE) with the backtrace showing the crash in **dispatch_semaphore_signal()**.

GCD or NSOperation?

You have now seen two different ways of architecting your code to support task-oriented parallelism, **NSOperation** and Grand Central Dispatch.

With GCD, the code for a particular operation tends to be concentrated in one place. You have a block that does work and then puts blocks onto other queues to do other work – the whole "layers of an onion" thing. GCD is very fast. There is little baggage associated with it. There is no reliance on KVO. GCD calls tend to be more ad-hoc and disposable, "I'll just put this here to run this on the main queue" kinds of things. Plus, it is easier to copy and paste and create similar blocks doing the same work.

NSOperation tends to have the code more spread around. The code implementing an operation is usually in its own class with its own set of source files. Operations live at a higher level of abstraction, too. **NSOperation** is available pre-Snow Leopard, in case you are supporting older operating systems. **NSOperation** allows dependencies between operations. Constructing similar things in GCD can become complicated as you build up dispatch groups and control things with counted semaphores. Operations are easier to cancel. You need to invent your own cancellation mechanism in GCD. Finally, because operations are frequently expressed as classes, they are more concrete, reusable objects.

If you need to do work in the background, you should seriously consider using GCD or **NSOperation**s for partitioning the work. The farther away from raw threads you can get, the happier you will be.

For the More Curious: Synchronizing Tasks

Synchronization enforces a temporal ordering among events. If you were using threads directly, you would use mutexes, semaphores, and condition variables (see Chapter 20: *Multithreading*) to express the desired synchronization.

Grand Central Dispatch allows for a simpler approach. To serialize access to a resource, use a serial queue associated with the resource rather than a mutex.

To wait for an asynchronous event, use a dispatch source rather than a condition variable.

To wait for a task to complete, simply dispatch the follow-up task from the end of that task. If a task depends on several tasks that can execute concurrently, target them all to a concurrent queue and use a dispatch group to asynchronously follow up on the completion of the group of tasks that were blocking the one task.

If you must drop down to basics, prefer using GCD's semaphores and dispatch predicates to the Posix threads equivalents, except where portability is a concern.

If you have access to **NSOperation**, prefer that to Grand Central Dispatch; it is layered on top of GCD, but it simplifies expressing interdependencies between tasks. As a higher-level API, it is also less likely to change (or at least likely to change more slowly) as the system evolves.

For the More Curious: The dispatch_debug() Function

Dispatch objects provide one more function we have yet to discuss. The **dispatch_debug** function logs debugging information about any dispatch object:

```
void dispatch_debug (dispatch_object_t object,
                     const char *message, ...);
```

In the released version of the library, **dispatch_debug()** logs to the system log rather than to the console.

The logged information is intended to assist developers of the libdispatch library and is only marginally useful to users of Grand Central Dispatch. For example, here is the output generated for several different kinds of dispatch objects:

```
com.bignerdranch.dispatch_debug:
    com.apple.root.default-priority[0x7fff71001af0] = {
        refcnt = 0xffffffff, suspend_cnt = 0x1, parent = 0x0
    }: global queue example
com.bignerdranch.dispatch_debug:
    com.bignerdranch.exampleq[0x100100200] = {
        refcnt = 0x2, suspend_cnt = 0x0, parent = 0x7fff71001b98
    }: serial queue example
```

```
com.bignerdranch.dispatch_debug:
    semaphore[0x1001002b0] = {
        refcnt = 0x1, suspend_cnt = 0x0, port = 0x0,
        value = 9223372036854775807, orig = 9223372036854775807
    }: group example
com.bignerdranch.dispatch_debug:
    semaphore[0x100100320] = {
        refcnt = 0x1, suspend_cnt = 0x0, port = 0x0,
        value = 0, orig = 0
    }: semaphore example
com.bignerdranch.dispatch_debug:
    kevent-source[0x100100390] = {
        refcnt = 0x2, suspend_cnt = 0x0,
        target = com.apple.root.default-priority[0x7fff71001af0],
        pending_data = 0x0, pending_data_mask = 0x18,
        filter = EVFILT_VNODE
    }: vnode source example
com.bignerdranch.dispatch_debug:
    kevent-source[0x1001004c0] = {
        refcnt = 0x2, suspend_cnt = 0x2,
        target = com.bignerdranch.exampleq[0x100100200],
        pending_data = 0x1, pending_data_mask = 0xffffffff,
        filter = DISPATCH_EVFILT_CUSTOM_OR
    }: data-or source example
```

Notice that the data-or source is suspended (as indicated by a suspend_cnt of 2 or more) and has pending data. The pending data mask for the vnode source indicates that it will be triggered by the LINK and ATTRIB events; the debug output does not include the handle, so it is impossible to tell which file descriptor is being monitored.

The reference count it reports is the internal reference count, not the external reference count. It provides no information whatsoever about how many times you'd have to call **dispatch_release()** to dispose of the object. Dispatch objects have no equivalent to the Objective-C **-retainCount** method.

The suspend count reported is that manipulated by the library. The number of times you'd have to call **dispatch_resume()** on the object is half the reported suspend count. This means that only a reported suspend count greater than 1 indicates a suspended object. The first bit of the suspend count does not in fact indicate suspension, but it is used by the library as a lock bit.

Exercises

1. Rewrite WordCounter's **-countWords:** method to return its value in a way other than a struct. How does that affect the memory management that was done in the main queue block? Is the rewritten version cleaner and easier to understand than the original version?

2. Do more word analysis calculations in WordCounter. Display the word frequencies in a tableview. Hit the network and download definitions of words. Or hit the network and download images from Google Image Search and display them in a tableview.

3. What happens if a serial queue is made to target itself?

4. What happens if you create a "target queue cycle" between two or more serial queues? Start by creating two serial queues and setting each to target the other. Enqueue a work item on one of the queues and then sleep.

5. Write and test the function **dispatch_time_add**:

```
dispatch_time_t dispatch_time_add (dispatch_time_t time,
                                   int seconds);
```

dispatch_time() and NSEC_PER_SEC.)

6. Write and test the function **dispatch_groups_async**:

```
void dispatch_groups_async (dispatch_group_t groups[],
                            const size_t group_count,
                            dispatch_queue_t queue,
                            dispatch_block_t work)
```

This should enqueue and asynchronously run a single work block. This block should be entered into all of the provided groups before it is dispatched to the queue and should be made to leave all of the groups after its work is complete.

7. Use a timer source to implement **sleep_ns()**:

```
void sleep_ns (uint64_t nanos)
```

This function should block execution of the current thread for the provided number of nanoseconds. (You might find a dispatch group or semaphore helpful.)

8. Put the nodepool from Chapter 7: *Memory* behind a queue-based interface. Compare the performance to the thread-safe nodepool from the exercises in Chapter 20: *Multithreading*.

23

Accessing the Keychain

A *keychain* is a file that holds passwords and certificates as well as information about those passwords and certificates. For the purposes of this chapter, "password" is used interchangeably with "password or certificate." Each user can have several keychains, but most people only have one: `~/Library/Keychains/login.keychain`. There is a set of functions and data structures in the Security framework that allow you to read and write passwords and their associated data. A password and its associated data is known as a keychain item.

Users can inspect their keychains using the application Keychain Access, as shown in Figure 23.1:

Figure 23.1   The Keychain Access application

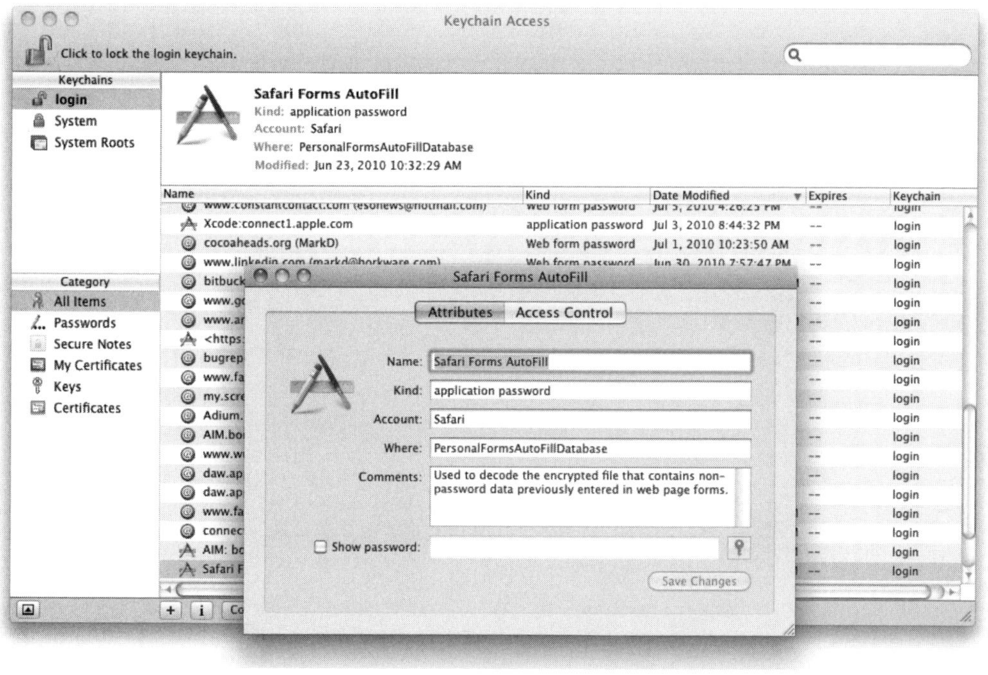

Some data inside the keychain is encrypted and can only be accessed if the keychain is unlocked. The user unlocks a keychain by typing a password into a keychain panel, as shown in Figure 23.2

Figure 23.2   Unlocking the keychain

Using the Keychain Access application, users can control access to individual keychain items, as shown in Figure 23.3

Figure 23.3   Keychain access control

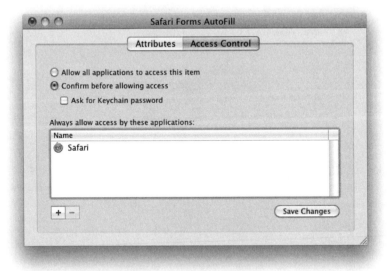

Items and Attribute Lists

Keychains can hold a number of different types of items. Internet passwords are associated with a particular user on a server domain and protocol. AppleShare passwords are used for remote access credentials to AppleShare servers. Certificate items hold certificates, not passwords. Private and Public keys, such as those used in the iOS development portal, are also kept in the keychain.

Password items have the user's password as its data item, as well as a collection of attributes. The attributes are identified by a four-byte code. There are a few dozen of these codes. Refer to /System/ Library/Frameworks/Security.framework/Headers/SecKeychainItem.h Here are a few examples of four-byte codes:

kSecCreationDateItemAttr
('cdat') Identifies the creation date attribute. You use this tag to set or get a value of type UInt32 that indicates the date the item was created.

kSecDescriptionItemAttr
('desc') Identifies the description attribute. You use this tag to set or get a value of type string that represents a user-visible string describing this particular kind of item (for example, "disk image password").

kSecLabelItemAttr
('labl') Identifies the label attribute. You use this tag to set or get a value of type string that represents a user-editable string containing the label for this item.

kSecCustomIconItemAttr
('cusi') Identifies the custom icon attribute. You use this tag to set or get a value of type Boolean that indicates whether the item has an application-specific icon. To do this, you must also set the attribute value identified by the tag kSecTypeItemAttr to a file type, for which there is a corresponding icon in the desktop database, and set the attribute value identified by the tag kSecCreatorItemAttr to an appropriate application creator type. If a custom icon corresponding to the item's type and creator can be found in the desktop database, it will be displayed by Keychain Access. Otherwise, default icons are used.

kSecAccountItemAttr
('acct') Identifies the account attribute. You use this tag to set or get a string that represents the user account. It also applies to generic and AppleShare passwords.

kSecSecurityDomainItemAttr
('sdmn') Identifies the security domain attribute. You use this tag to set or get a value that represents the Internet security domain. This is unique to Internet password attributes.

kSecServerItemAttr
('srvr') Identifies the server attribute. You use this tag to set or get a value of type string that represents the Internet server name or IP address. This is unique to Internet password attributes.

Use a SecKeychainAttributeList to read and write these attributes:

```
struct SecKeychainAttributeList {
    UInt32 count;
    SecKeychainAttribute *attr;
};
```

count is the number of attributes in the list. And attr is a pointer to the first one.

```
struct SecKeychainAttribute  {
    SecKeychainAttrType tag;
    UInt32 length;
    void *data;
};
```

The tag is the four-byte code listed above. The length is the number of bytes in the data buffer. Usually, the data buffer is just a string.

Figure 23.4 shows a keychain attribute list with three attributes. The first attribute is the account name, with a value of "aaron", the second is description of the item, and the last is when the keychain item was created.

Figure 23.4   Keychain attribute list

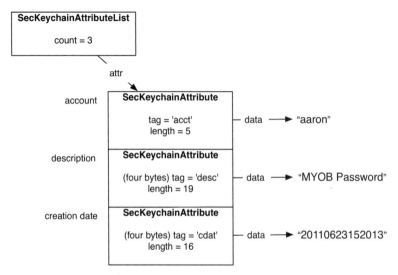

Searching for Items

Attribute lists are used in three ways:

1. to specify a search for items.

2. to read data from an item.

3. to set the data for an item.

For example, to create a search for all generic passwords that have *bignerdranch* as the account name, you would create an attribute list and invoke **SecKeychainSearchCreateFromAttributes()**.

```
OSStatus SecKeychainSearchCreateFromAttributes (CFTypeRef  keychainOrArray,
                                    SecItemClass  itemClass,
                         const SecKeychainAttributeList *attrList,
                                SecKeychainSearchRef *searchRef);
```

Most of the functions in the Security framework deal well with NULLs. They do what you would hope. For example, if you pass NULL as the first argument, the search will check all the user's normal keychains. Usually, this is what you want. For the second argument, you will pass one of the following:

- `kSecInternetPasswordItemClass`

- `kSecGenericPasswordItemClass`

- `kSecAppleSharePasswordItemClass`

- `kSecCertificateItemClass`

If you pass NULL as the attribute list, all items of that class will be returned. The final argument is a pointer to a search-specifying structure.

Example 23.1 is a search that counts the number of Internet passwords on your keychain for the account specified on the command line. We will use just SecKeychainItemRef here and fill in the details in the next section:

Example 23.1   dumpem.m

```
// dumpem.m -- look into the keychain

// gcc -std=c99 -g -Wall -framework Security -framework Foundation -o dumpem dumpem.m

#import <Security/Security.h>
#import <Foundation/Foundation.h>

#import <stdlib.h>      // for EXIT_SUCCESS
#import <stdio.h>       // for printf() and friends
#import <string.h>      // for strncpy

int main (int argc, char *argv[]) {
    NSAutoreleasePool *pool = [[NSAutoreleasePool alloc] init];
    if (argc != 2) {
        printf ("usage: %s account-name\n", argv[0]);
        return EXIT_FAILURE;
    }

    // Build an attribute list with just one attribute.
    SecKeychainAttribute attribute;
    attribute.tag = kSecAccountItemAttr;
    attribute.length = strlen(argv[1]);
    attribute.data = argv[1];

    // Make a list to point to this new attribute.
    SecKeychainAttributeList list;
    list.count = 1;
    list.attr = &attribute;

    // Create a search handle with the attribute list.
    SecKeychainSearchRef search;
```

```
OSErr result = SecKeychainSearchCreateFromAttributes
    (NULL, kSecInternetPasswordItemClass, &list, &search);

if (result != noErr) {
    printf ("result %d from "
            "SecKeychainSearchCreateFromAttributes\n",
            result);
}

// Iterate over the search results
int count = 0;
SecKeychainItemRef item;
while (SecKeychainSearchCopyNext (search, &item) != errSecItemNotFound) {
    CFRelease (item);
    count++;
}

printf ("%d items found\n", count);
CFRelease (search);
[pool drain];

return EXIT_SUCCESS;

} // main
```

Before building and running the program, launch **Keychain Access**, which lives in /Applications/ Utilities/. Look around and find an item with an account property that you can display. Then run **dumpem**.

```
$ ./dumpem borkware
3 items found
```

Reading Data From an Item

Of course, once you have fetched the item, you can do all sorts of nifty things with it. For example, if you wanted to read the password, the account name, the description, and the modification date from an item, you would create an attribute list containing those attributes and call **SecKeychainItemCopyContent()**:

```
OSStatus SecKeychainItemCopyContent (SecKeychainItemRef  itemRef,
                                     SecItemClass *itemClass,
                             SecKeychainAttributeList *attrList,
                                         UInt32 *length,
                                         void **outData);
```

Note that here the attrList is specifying what data you want and is also acting as a receptacle. Add these functions to dumpem.m:

```
// Given a carbon-style four character code, make a C string that can
// be given to printf.
const char *fourByteCodeString (UInt32 code) {
    // Splat the bytes of the four character code into a character array.
    typedef union theCheat {
        UInt32 code;
        char string[4];
    } theCheat;
```

```
        // C string that gets returned.
        static char string[5];

        // Byte-swap, otherwise string will be backwards on little endian systems.
        ((theCheat*)string)->code = ntohl(code);
        string[4] = '\0';
        return (string);

} // fourByteCodeString


// Display each attribute in the list.
void showList (SecKeychainAttributeList list) {
    for (int i = 0; i < list.count; i++) {
        SecKeychainAttribute attr = list.attr[i];

        char buffer[1024];
        if (attr.length < sizeof(buffer)) {
            // make a copy of the data so we can stick on
            // a trailing zero byte
            strncpy (buffer, attr.data, attr.length);
            buffer[attr.length] = '\0';

            printf ("\t%d: '%s' = \"%s\"\n",
                    i, fourByteCodeString(attr.tag), buffer);
        } else {
            printf ("attribute %s is more than 1K\n",
                    fourByteCodeString(attr.tag));
        }
    }

} // showList

// Display a keychain item's info.
void dumpItem (SecKeychainItemRef item, bool displayPassword) {
    // Build the attributes we're interested in examining.
    SecKeychainAttribute attributes[3];
    attributes[0].tag = kSecAccountItemAttr;
    attributes[1].tag = kSecDescriptionItemAttr;
    attributes[2].tag = kSecModDateItemAttr;

    SecKeychainAttributeList list;
    list.count = 3;
    list.attr = attributes;

    // Get the item's information, including the password.
    UInt32 length = 0;
    char *password = NULL;
    OSErr result;
    if (displayPassword) {
        result = SecKeychainItemCopyContent (item, NULL, &list, &length,
                                             (void **)&password);
    } else {
        result = SecKeychainItemCopyContent (item, NULL, &list, NULL, NULL);
    }

    if (result != noErr) {
        printf ("dumpItem: error result of %d\n", result);
        return;
    }
```

```
    if (password != NULL) {
        // Copy the password into a buffer and attach a trailing zero
        // byte so we can print it out with printf.
        char *passwordBuffer = malloc(length + 1);
        strncpy (passwordBuffer, password, length);

        passwordBuffer[length] = '\0';
        printf ("Password = %s\n", passwordBuffer);
        free (passwordBuffer);
    }

    showList (list);
    SecKeychainItemFreeContent (&list, password);

} // dumpItem
```

When you call **SecKeychainItemCopyContent()**, if the keychain requires authentication, it will automatically bring up an authentication panel. If you only read publicly available data, no authentication panel will appear. The code above will probably trigger the panel for each item. If you use a different call that does not fetch the password, the panel will not appear at all.

```
    SecKeychainItemCopyContent(item, NULL, &list, NULL, NULL);
```

The displayPassword argument to **dumpItem()** controls which call to use.

Add a call to **dumpItem()** in **main()**:

```
    while (SecKeychainSearchCopyNext (search, &item) == noErr) {
        dumpItem (item, true);
        CFRelease (item);
        i++;
    }
```

This is what the final version looks like:

```
$ ./dumpem borkware
Password = ab4d0b03
        0: 'acct' = "borkware"
        1: 'desc' = ""
        2: 'mdat' = "20100623202907Z"
Password = dsch-4acgs
        0: 'acct' = "borkware"
        1: 'desc' = "Web form password"
        2: 'mdat' = "20100623210725Z"
Password = grumblecake
        0: 'acct' = "borkware"
        1: 'desc' = "Web form password"
        2: 'mdat' = "20100713173203Z"
3 items found
```

Build and run the program. Note that if you choose Always Allow, the program will have access to the keychain item until you log out. However, if you recompile the program, you will have to re-authenticate. The Security framework keeps checksums of the applications that have access.

Editing the Keychain

With the item, you can also make changes using an attribute list:

```
OSStatus SecKeychainItemModifyContent (SecKeychainItemRef  itemRef,
                          const SecKeychainAttributeList *attrList,
                                          UInt32  newPasswordLength,
                                   const void *newPassword)
```

The new attribute values would go into the `attrList`. A new password would go into `newPassword`.

To delete an item:

```
OSStatus SecKeychainItemDelete (SecKeychainItemRef itemRef)
```

Note that you would still have to call **CFRelease()** on the item to prevent a memory leak.

Getting Specific Keychains

As an argument to many of the keychain functions, you can specify a particular keychain. Usually, you will simply use the user's default keychain. For all of these functions, if you just supply NULL as the keychain, it will use the default keychain. However, if you want to explicitly get the default keychain you use:

```
OSStatus SecKeychainCopyDefault (SecKeychainRef *keychain)
```

If you wanted to specify a different keychain (remember that a keychain is just a file), you could use:

```
OSStatus SecKeychainOpen (const char *pathName,
                      SecKeychainRef *keychain)
```

When you are done with a keychain, make sure that you call **CFRelease()** to free it.

Keychain Access

Each keychain item defines how it may be accessed. The information about access privileges is kept in a `SecAccessRef` structure. To get the access structure for a particular keychain item, you use the following function:

```
OSStatus SecKeychainItemCopyAccess (SecKeychainItemRef  item,
                          SecAccessRef *access);
```

To change the access on a keychain item, you edit the `SecAccessRef` and write it to the keychain item using:

```
OSStatus SecKeychainItemSetAccess (SecKeychainItemRef item,
                          SecAccessRef access);
```

What, then, is a `SecAccessRef`? You can get a list of access control lists (ACLs) from it. Each access list has a list of trusted applications that are allowed to access the keychain item. Some applications can access the keychain item only after the user types in the keychain password.

Figure 23.5 shows the different types involved in keychain access. The single-headed arrows indicate a to-one relationship. A `SecKeychainItem` has a single `SecAccess`. The double-headed arrows indicate a to-many relationship. A `SecKeychain` can contain multiple `SecKeychainItems`.

Figure 23.5   Keychain data structures

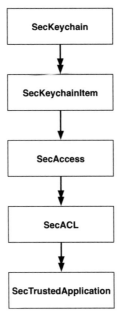

As an example of reading the ACLs for a keychain item, add the following code to **main()** in
dumpem.m:

```
while (SecKeychainSearchCopyNext (search, &item) != errSecItemNotFound) {
        errSecItemNotFound) {
    dumpItem (item, true);
    // Get the SecAccess
    SecAccessRef access;
    SecKeychainItemCopyAccess (item, &access);
    showAccess (access);
    CFRelease (access);

    CFRelease (item);
    count++;
}
```

Add the following function:

```
void showAccess (SecAccessRef accessRef) {
    CFArrayRef aclList;
    SecAccessCopyACLList(accessRef, &aclList);

    int count = CFArrayGetCount(aclList);
    printf ("%d lists\n", count);

    for (int i = 0; i < count; i++) {
        SecACLRef acl = (SecACLRef) CFArrayGetValueAtIndex(aclList, i);

        CFArrayRef applicationList;
        CFStringRef description;
        CSSM_ACL_KEYCHAIN_PROMPT_SELECTOR promptSelector;
        SecACLCopySimpleContents (acl, &applicationList, &description,
```

```
                                &promptSelector);
        if (promptSelector.flags
            & CSSM_ACL_KEYCHAIN_PROMPT_REQUIRE_PASSPHRASE) {
            printf ("\t%d: ACL %s - Requires passphrase\n", i,
                    [(NSString *)description UTF8String]);
        } else {
            printf ("\t%d: ACL %s - Does not require passphrase\n", i,
                    [(NSString *)description UTF8String]);
        }
        CFRelease(description);

        if (applicationList == NULL) {
            printf ("\t\tNo application list %d\n", i);
            continue;
        }

        int appCount = CFArrayGetCount(applicationList);
        printf ("\t\t%d applications in list %d\n", appCount, i);

        for (int j = 0; j < appCount; j++) {
            SecTrustedApplicationRef application;
            CFDataRef appData;
            application = (SecTrustedApplicationRef)
                CFArrayGetValueAtIndex(applicationList, j);
            SecTrustedApplicationCopyData(application, &appData);
            printf ("\t\t%s\n", CFDataGetBytePtr(appData));
            CFRelease(appData);
        }
        CFRelease(applicationList);
    }
} // showAccess
```

And here is the access info for one of the keychain items:

```
$ ./dumpem borkware
...
Password = dsch-4acgs
    0: 'acct' = "borkware"
    1: 'desc' = "Web form password"
    2: 'mdat' = "20100713173203Z"
3 lists
    0: ACL twitter.com (borkware) - Does not require passphrase
        No application list 0
    1: ACL twitter.com (borkware) - Does not require passphrase
        3 applications in list 1
            /Users/markd/Writing/core-osx/keychain-chap/Projects/dumpem
            /Local/Apps/Google Chrome.app
            /Applications/Safari.app
    2: ACL twitter.com (borkware) - Does not require passphrase
        0 applications in list 2
...
```

Here you can see this is a web form, and Safari, Chrome, and **dumpem** have been given access to it.

The keychain access API is not 100% complete. You can do everything an application needs to do on a day-to-day basis. The keychain API is implemented using the CSSM, Common Security Services Manager, which is the programming interface to the CDSA, the Common Data Security Architecture. Here we needed to dip into the CSSM to see if the keychain item requires a prompt. When this bit is set, the system will ask for the user's password before trusting the application with the keychain item.

Making a New Keychain Item

To create a new keychain item, you use this function:

```
OSStatus SecKeychainItemCreateFromContent (SecItemClass    itemClass,
                               SecKeychainAttributeList *attrList,
                                           UInt32  passwdLength,
                                     const void *password,
                               SecKeychainRef  keychainRef,
                                 SecAccessRef  initialAccess,
                           SecKeychainItemRef *itemRef);
```

where the itemClass is kSecInternetPasswordItemClass, kSecGenericPasswordItemClass, kSecAppleSharePasswordItemClass, or kSecCertificateItemClass. If you supply NULL as the keychainRef, the item will be added to the default keychain. itemRef will be set to point to the newly created item. To use the default access, just supply NULL as the initialAccess.

As an example, here is a short program that will insert a new item into your default keychain.

Example 23.2   add_item.m

```
// additem.m -- add a new item to the keychain

// gcc -g -Wall -framework Security -o additem additem.m

#import <Security/Security.h>

#include <stdio.h> // for printf()

int main (int argc, char *argv[]) {
    SecKeychainAttribute attributes[2];
    attributes[0].tag = kSecAccountItemAttr;
    attributes[0].data = "fooz";
    attributes[0].length = 4;

    attributes[1].tag = kSecDescriptionItemAttr;
    attributes[1].data = "I seem to be a verb";
    attributes[1].length = 19;

    SecKeychainAttributeList list;
    list.count = 2;
    list.attr = attributes;

    SecKeychainItemRef item;
    OSStatus status = SecKeychainItemCreateFromContent
        (kSecGenericPasswordItemClass, &list,
         5, "budda", NULL, NULL, &item);

    if (status != 0) {
        printf ("Error creating new item: %d\n", (int)status);
    }
    return EXIT_SUCCESS;

} // main
```

After running this program, look at the keychain item in Keychain Access, as shown in Figure 23.6

Figure 23.6   Looking at the new keychain item

Also, note what "default access" is, as shown in Figure 23.7.

Figure 23.7   Keychain item default access

Convenience Functions

That's the whole story on keychains. There are some convenience functions that make common activities possible, but they simply use the functions that we have talked about already.

These functions allow you to create a new item without creating an attribute list:

```
OSStatus SecKeychainAddInternetPassword (SecKeychainRef keychain,
                        UInt32          serverNameLength,
                        const char  *serverName,
                        UInt32          securityDomainLength,
                        const char  *securityDomain,
                        UInt32          accountNameLength,
                        const char  *accountName,
                        UInt32          pathLength,
                        const char  *path,
                        UInt16          port,
                        SecProtocolType         protocol,
                        SecAuthenticationType authenticationType,
                        UInt32          passwordLength,
                        const void  *passwordData,
                        SecKeychainItemRef     *itemRef)

OSStatus SecKeychainAddGenericPassword (SecKeychainRef keychain,
                        UInt32          serviceNameLength,
                        const char  *serviceName,
                        UInt32          accountNameLength,
                        const char  *accountName,
                        UInt32          passwordLength,
                        const void  *passwordData,
                        SecKeychainItemRef *itemRef)
```

Note that neither of these can be used to change a password in an existing item. If you try this, the function will complain that the item already exists.

These methods allow you to find items without creating an attribute list:

```
OSStatus SecKeychainFindInternetPassword (CFTypeRef keychainOrArray,
                        UInt32          serverNameLength,
                        const char  *serverName,
                        UInt32          securityDomainLength,
                        const char  *securityDomain,
                        UInt32          accountNameLength,
                        const char  *accountName,
                        UInt32          pathLength,
                        const char  *path,
                        UInt16          port,
                        SecProtocolType protocol,
                        SecAuthenticationType authenticationType,
                        UInt32      *passwordLength,
                        void        **passwordData,
                        SecKeychainItemRef *itemRef)

OSStatus SecKeychainFindGenericPassword (CFTypeRef keychainOrArray,
                        UInt32          serviceNameLength,
                        const char  *serviceName,
                        UInt32          accountNameLength,
                        const char  *accountName,
                        UInt32      *passwordLength,
```

```
        void       **passwordData,
        SecKeychainItemRef *itemRef)
```

Notice that the protocol and authentication types are not strings. Here are the constants for the commonly used protocols:

- kSecProtocolTypeFTP
- kSecProtocolTypeFTPAccount
- kSecProtocolTypeHTTP
- kSecProtocolTypeIRC
- kSecProtocolTypeNNTP
- kSecProtocolTypePOP3
- kSecProtocolTypeSMTP

- kSecProtocolTypeSOCKS
- kSecProtocolTypeIMAP
- kSecProtocolTypeLDAP
- kSecProtocolTypeAppleTalk
- kSecProtocolTypeAFP
- kSecProtocolTypeTelnet
- kSecProtocolTypeSSH

There are several types of authentication, but you will almost certainly use kSecAuthenticationTypeDefault.

If you are writing a daemon or something else that should not be interrupting the user, you can prevent the authentication panel from appearing:

```
SecKeychainSetUserInteractionAllowed (NO);
```

Code Signing

You probably noticed that the keychain redisplays its authorization dialog when you run a newer version of **dumpem** was run. This can be annoying for the user every time they upgrade your software.

Starting in Mac OS X 10.5, Apple introduced *code signing*, which is a way to digitally sign application code and resources. When the user OKs a keychain authorization dialog, the system sees if the application was signed. If it is, this fact is noted. If a newer version of the application accesses the keychain, the system sees if the app is signed by the same entity that signed the prior version. If so, the system knows that both applications came from the same place and allows the keychain access to happen without interruption. Keychain is not the only system service that uses code signing to identify applications. The system firewall does, as well as parental controls.

Signing is a way to verify the integrity of something, like an application. A digital certificate, along with a privately generated key, is used to sign the code. The certificate contains a public key associated with the private key and is included in the signed application, along with a hash of the application's contents. The system looks at the certificate, calculates the application's hash, and uses the public key to verify that this set of bits matches the set of bits created by the application's author. Your application's identity is safe so long as your private key is kept secret.

Certificates can also include a chain of trust, a set of identities of *Certificate Authorities* like VeriSign. This chain of trust can be verified by the system. If your certificate is trusted by another entity, which is trusted by yet another entity, the system can use that to determine if it should trust the identity of the signer.

You can generate a self-signed certificate using the Keychain Access utility, and it can be used to sign your applications. So long as the private key is kept private, an attacker cannot masquerade a malicious application as the one that you have signed. Self-signed certificates cannot be used to verify the identity of the signer. All the system knows is BigShow 2.0 was signed by the same certificate as BigShow 1.0. The system firewall does not trust self-signed certificates, so if your application requires holes in the firewall, the user will have to re-authenticate on each app upgrade.

If you purchase a signing certificate from a signing authority, the identity of the owner of the certificate can be trusted, again as long as the private key is kept secret. If the firewall can verify the identity of the application's signature, then it will behave like Keychain Access and not disturb the user when the software is upgraded.

In MacOS, code signing is optional, although in the future Apple may require it to access OS services. Everything is code signed in iOS. To run anything on a device, you need to purchase a signing certificate from Apple.

To generate a self-signed certificate, use the certificate assistant in Keychain Access to create a new self-signed keychain, as shown in Figure 23.8.

Figure 23.8   Creating a self-signed certificate

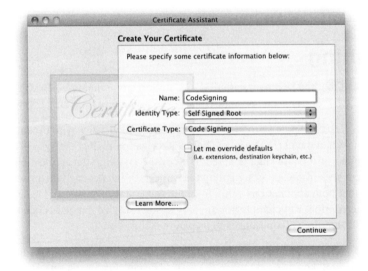

Once the certificate has been created, Keychain Access displays detailed information. Figure 23.9 shows that the certificate is untrusted.

Figure 23.9 The self-signed certificate is untrusted.

Now that you have a certificate, you can sign your program using the **codesign** tool, giving it the name of the certificate:

```
$ codesign -s "CodeSigning" dumpem
```

codesign will look in your keychain for the named certificate. It will look for substrings if it cannot find a complete match. You can use **codesign** to verify your program was codesigned:

```
$ codesign -d dumpem
Executable=/Users/markd/Writing/core-osx/keychain-chap/Projects/dumpem
```

You can ask for more verbose output, too:

```
% codesign -dv dumpem
Executable=/Users/markd/Writing/core-osx/keychain-chap/Projects/dumpem
Identifier=dumpem
Format=Mach-O thin (x86_64)
CodeDirectory v=20100 size=175 flags=0x0(none) hashes=4+2 location=embedded
Signature size=1346
Signed Time=Aug 10, 2010 12:46:39 PM
Info.plist=not bound
Sealed Resources=none
Internal requirements count=1 size=104
```

Freshly compiled programs are not signed. If you rebuild **dumpem** and try to verify it, **codesign** will tell you it is unsigned:

```
$ codesign -dv dumpem
dumpem: code object is not signed
```

You can also sign application bundles:

```
$ codesign -s "CodeSigning" BigShow.app
```

This signs the contents of the bundle, such as resources, the `Info.plist`, and executable code. If any part of the bundle is modified, the signing will become invalid. You cannot sign text files, such as shell scripts individually, but you can include them as part of a signed bundle. Be sure to sign as the last stage of your build. You will invalidate your signing if you **strip** your application after the signing phase.

Xcode will sign your programs as part of its regular build process if you put the name of the signing certificate into the Code Signing Identity build setting.

You will want to use different signing certificates for development and release builds of your application. A signed application, especially one signed with a trusted certificate, says to end-users that this application is a tested representative of this company or individual and should be trusted with your keychain or firewall.

Exercises

1. Write an app that saves a username and password to the default keychain.

2. Write an app that can read and change the saved password.

3. Extend **chatterd** to require a password. Add password solicitation to a Chatter client, and store the password into the keychain

4. Code-Sign your Chatter client so that upgrades do not trigger the keychain dialog.

Index

Symbols

! (bitwise operator), 23
##__VA_ARGS__, 20
#define, 2, 44
   contraindications, 3
#else, 4
#endif, 4
#if, 4
#ifdef, 4
#ifndef, 4
#import, 10
#include, 8
#pragma, 239
#pragma once, 10
%zu format specifier, 19
& (bitwise operator), 22
*_FILENO constants, 286
-- (argument terminator), 92, 95
-arch compiler flag, 56
-D compiler flag, 3
-DNDEBUG, 129
-F linker flag, 140
-fast compiler flag, 51
-fastcp compiler flag, 51
-fastf compiler flag, 51
-flat_namespace, 135
-fobjc-exceptions, 535
-fobjc-gc, 183
-fobjc-gc-only, 183
-O compiler flag, 48, 49
-Wconversion compiler flag, 54
-Wformat, 15
-Wno-protocol compiler flag, 52
-Wno-unused, 45
-Wundeclared-selector compiler flag, 52
. (dot operator), 38
.DS_Store, 351
.fseventsd, 468
.gdbinit, 212
/dev/fsevents, 466
64-bit computing
   description, 53
   interoperability limitations, 53
   and Objective-C runtime, 37, 56, 120

programming model, 53-56
: (return value), 92
<< (bitwise operator), 23
>> (bitwise operator), 23
? (return value), 92
@catch, 117
@finally, 117
@optional directive, 29
@required directive, 29
@synchronized, 535
@throw, 117
@try, 117
^ (bitwise operator), 23
_exit(), 493
_longjmp(), 111
_setjmp(), 111
__APPLE_CC__, 6
__APPLE__, 6
__attribute((packed)), 50
__attribute__((format_arg)), 16
__attribute__((sentinel)), 15
__BIG_ENDIAN__, 6
__block, 65, 74
__cplusplus, 6
__DATE__, 6
__FILE__, 6
__FUNCTION__, 6
__func__, 6
__GNUC__, 50
__i386__, 56, 58
__LINE__, 6
__LITTLE_ENDIAN__, 6
__LP64__, 6, 58
__MACH__, 6
__OBJC__, 6
__ppc64__, 56, 58
__ppc__, 56, 58
__PRETTY_FUNCTION__, 7
__strong, 187
__TIME__, 6
__VA_ARGS__, 20
__x86_64__, 56, 58
| (bitwise operator), 22
| (pipeline character), 83
~ expansion, 358

SOFTWARE

TRAINING

CONSULTING

Achieve Nerdvana

ABOUT US

BiG
NERD
ranch

THE BIG NERD STORY

Big Nerd Ranch exists to broaden the minds of our students and the businesses of our clients. Whether we are training talented individuals or developing a company's mobile strategy, our core philosophy is integral to everything we do.

The brainchild of CEO Aaron Hillegass, Big Nerd Ranch has hosted more than 2,000 students at the Ranch since its inception in 2001. Over the past ten years, we have had the opportunity to work with some of the biggest companies in the world such as Apple, Samsung, Nokia, Google, AOL, Los Alamos National Laboratory and Adobe, helping them realize their programming goals. Our team of software engineers are among the brightest in the business and it shows in our work. We have developed dozens of innovative and flexible solutions for our clients.

The Story Behind the Hat

Back in 2001, Big Nerd Ranch founder, Aaron Hillegass, showed up at WWDC (World Wide Developers Conference) to promote the Big Nerd Ranch brand. Without the money to buy an expensive booth, Aaron donned a ten-gallon cowboy hat to draw attention while passing out Big Nerd literature to prospective students and clients. A week later, we landed our first big client and the cowboy hat has been synonymous with the Big Nerd brand ever since. Already easily recognizable at 6'5, Aaron can be spotted wearing his cowboy hat at speaking engagements and conferences all over the world.

The New Ranch – Opening 2012

In the continuing effort to perfect the student experience, Big Nerd Ranch is building its own facility. Located just 20 minutes from the Atlanta airport, the new Ranch will be a monastic learning center that encompasses Aaron Hillegass' vision for technical education featuring a state-of-the-art classroom, fine dining and exercise facilities.

TRAINING

BiG
nerD
ranch

ACHIEVE NERDVANA

Since 2001, Big Nerd Ranch has offered intensive computer programming courses taught by our expert instructors in a retreat environment. It is at our Ranch where we think our students flourish. Classes, accommodations and dining all take place within the same building, freeing you to learn, code and discuss with your programming peers and instructors. At Big Nerd Ranch, we take care of the details; your only job is to learn.

Our Teachers

Our teachers are leaders in their respective fields. They offer deep understanding of the technologies they teach, as well as a broad spectrum of development experience, allowing them to address the concerns you encounter as a developer. Big Nerd Ranch instructors provide the necessary combination of knowledge and outstanding teaching experience, enabling our students to leave the Ranch with a vastly improved set of skills.

The Big Nerd Way

We have developed "The Big Nerd Ranch Way". This methodology guides the development and presentation of our classes. The style is casual but focused, with brief lectures followed by hands-on exercises designed to give you immediate, relevant understanding of each piece of the technology you are learning.

Your Stay At The Ranch

One fee covers tuition, meals, lodging and transportation to and from the airport. At the Big Nerd Ranch, we remove the distractions inherent in standard corporate training by offering classes in quiet, comfortable settings in Atlanta, Georgia and Frankfurt, Germany.

Available Classes

Advanced Mac OS X
Android
Beginning Cocoa
Beginning iOS (iPhone/iPad)
Beginning Ruby on Rails
Cocoa Commuter Class in Spanish
Cocoa I
Cocoa II
Commuter iOS Class
Django
iOS (iPhone/iPad)
OpenGL
Python Mastery
Ruby on Rails I
Ruby on Rails II

Interested in a class?

Register online at www.bignerdranch.com or call 404.478.9005 for more information.
Full class schedule, pricing and availability also online.

ON-SITE TRAINING

OUR NERDS, YOUR LOCATION

Through our on-site training program you can affordably and conveniently have our renowned classes come to you. Our expert instructors will help your team advance through nerd-based instructional support that is fresh, engaging and allows for unencumbered hands-on learning.

Clients around the globe have praised our on-site instruction for some of the following reasons:

Flexibility
- Classes can be booked when the timing is right for your team.
- We can tailor our existing syllabi to ensure our training meets your organization's unique needs.
- Post-class mentorship is available to support your team as they work on especially challenging projects.

Affordability
- No need for planes, trains and automobiles for all of your staff; our Nerds come to you.
- Train up to 22 students at a significant discount over open-enrollment training.

Nerd Know-how
- Our instructors are highly practiced in both teaching and programming. They move beyond theory by bringing their real-life experiences to your team.
- On-site training includes post-class access to our Nerds, our extensive Alumni Network, and our Big Nerd Ranch Forums. Learning support doesn't end just because your class does.

For your on-site training, we provide an instructor, all Big Nerd Ranch copyrighted class materials, gifts, certificates of completion and access to our extensive Alumni Network. You'll provide the classroom set up, computers and related devices for all students, a projector and a screen.

Ready to book an on-site training course?
For a free Big Nerd Ranch on-site proposal, please contact us at 404.478.9005.

CONSULTING

BiG
neRD
RancH

ACHIEVE NERDVANA
IN-HOUSE & ON-SITE

When you contract with Big Nerd Ranch, we'll work directly with you to turn your needs into a full-fledged desktop and/or mobile solution. Our developers and designers have consistently created some of the iPhone App Store's most intriguing applications.

Management Philosophy

Big Nerd Ranch holistically manages every client relationship. Our goal is to communicate and educate our clients from project initiation to completion, while ultimately helping them gain a competitive advantage in their niche marketplace.

Project Strategy

We take a detail-oriented approach to all of our project estimations. We'll work with you to define a strategy, specify product offerings and then build them into software that stands alone.

Our Process

Our consulting process is broken down into three distinct phases: Requirements, Execution and Monitoring/Controlling. Bring your business case to us and we'll develop a plan for a user interface and database design. From there, we'll develop a quote and begin the design and implementation process. Our Nerds will perform many tests, including debugging and performance tuning, ensuring the app does what you want it to do. Finally, we'll beta test your app and get it ready for submission and deployment in the iTunes store and/or the Android Market. Once your app is finished, the Nerds will work with you on subsequent version updates and can even help with the marketing of your app.

Testimonials

"tops has worked closely with Big Nerd Ranch for over eight years. Consistently they have delivered high-quality code for our projects; clean and poetic. Thanks to their contributions, we have become a leader in our field."

Dr. Mark Sanchez
President/Founder
tops Software
topsortho.com

"From the simplest GUI design gig to jobs that plumb the darkest corners of the OS, Big Nerd Ranch should be the first contact in your virtual Rolodex under Mac/iPhone consulting. It's no exaggeration to say that Aaron Hillegass literally wrote the book on Cocoa programming, and you couldn't possibly do better than to bring his and his team's expertise to bear on your application. I've yet to work with a consulting firm that is as competent and communicative as Big Nerd Ranch. Simply put, these guys deliver."

Glenn Zelniker
CEO
Z-Systems Audio Engineering
www.z-sys.com

"We turned to Big Nerd Ranch to develop the Teavana concept into an iPhone app. More than just a developer, they partnered with us to make the app better than we could have imagined alone. The final app was bug-free and functioned exactly as expected. I would definitely recommend Big Nerd Ranch and can't speak highly enough about their work."

Jay Allen
VP of Ecommerce
Teavana Corporation
www.teavana.com

We'd love to talk to you about your project.
Contact our consulting team today for a free consultation at consult@bignerdranch.com
or visit www.bignerdranch.com/consulting for more information.

SOFTWARE

FINELY-CRAFTED APPLICATIONS

Big Nerd Ranch is a leading developer of downloadable mobile and desktop Mac applications. Several of our most intriguing iPhone and desktop apps are available for purchase in the iTunes store.

Mobile Applications

Smartphones have started to take over the mobile phone market. Since the inception of the iPhone, we have created dozens of apps for our clients and now have a roster of our own applications including games, utilities, music and educational apps. As an ever-evolving frontier of technology, Big Nerd Ranch is committed to staying ahead of the curve.

Mobile Apps

The world has gone mobile. If your company doesn't have a mobile application, you are behind the curve. As of early 2011, the iTunes app store has grown to nearly 400,000 apps and the Android market has climbed to more than 250,000 applications. Google has unveiled its Android platform with an app store of its own and dozens of smartphone manufacturers have announced Android-powered devices. RIM has launched App World, Palm has its Palm Store, Nokia launched Ovi (its online store) and Microsoft has unveiled Windows Marketplace.

While still leading the way, the iOS market has put up some staggering statistics:

- *Total iOS app store downloads: 10.3 billion*
- *iPhone apps are being downloaded at a rate of 30 million per day.*
- *As of early 2011, when the app store hit 10 billion downloads, it did so in half the time (31 months versus 67 months) that it took for songs in the iTunes store to hit the same mark.*
- *The average number of apps downloaded for iPhone/iPad/iPod touch is currently at more than 60.*